DIPLOMATIC RELATIONS BETWEEN THE UNITED STATES AND THE KINGDOM OF THE TWO SICILIES

INSTRUCTIONS AND DESPATCHES
1816—1861

Edited with Introduction and Notes

BY

HOWARD R. MARRARO

IN TWO VOLUMES

Vol. I: 1816—1850

S. F. VANNI (RAGUSA)

Publishers & Booksellers

30 WEST 12TH STREET, NEW YORK

Prepared under the auspices of the Columbia University Council for Research in the Social Sciences and the Casa Italiana of Columbia University

UNITED STATES MINISTERS TO THE KINGDOM OF THE TWO SICILIES

INSTRUCTIONS AND DESPATCHES
1816-1850

226484

TABLE OF CONTENTS

PREFACE

In the preparation of this series of documentary publications on Italo-American diplomatic and consular relations, the editor deemed as first in importance, an annotated edition of the hitherto unpublished official correspondence between the State Department of the United States Government and its chargés d'affaires and ministers to the Kingdom of the Two Sicilies from the appointment of William Pinkney in 1816 to the year 1861 when the United States Legation at Naples was closed following the annexation of the Kingdom of the Two Sicilies to the newly constituted Kingdom of Italy. These volumes also contain the unpublished official communications between the Neapolitan Legation in Washington, D. C., and the State Department, and whatever notes and other correspondence were exchanged between our chargés and the Neapolitan Ministers of Foreign Affairs and other officials of that Kingdom.

During this period, the Kingdom of the Two Sicilies was one of a group of small sovereign states of the Italian peninsula toward which the United States, a nation passing through its own first half century of independent existence, felt constrained, after the settlement of the spoliation claims, to direct particular efforts to negotiate treaties of amity, commerce, navigation, and extradition. This policy, as directed toward these states of the Italian peninsula, was part of a broad foreign policy resulting in the negotiation of similar treaties with all the larger European countries. The young American nation was rapidly developing its manufactures, and by these treaties sought to ensure the peaceful plying of the high seas for American and other vessels, so that commerce with these nations could be expanded and made reciprocal in all its facilitating regulations as to port duties, warehouse fees, police procedures, etc.

The growth of American imports and exports during these years before the American Civil War strongly underscored the wisdom of this broad foreign policy. Tourists also flocked to these countries, and problems arising in connection with many commercial, diplomatic, and personal matters increasingly oc-

1

cupied the attention of United States chargés d'affaires, ministers, and consuls. The changing political and commercial situation called for a gradual alteration in the type of man chosen for these posts. Numerous less momentous matters also required attention. Only by a study of the full documentation of the period, for each country, and by comparing one country with the others, can a clear concept of the whole of that United States foreign policy be grasped. It is to facilitate that study — at this time for the Kingdom of the Two Sicilies, from 1816 to 1861 — that these United States official documents are now being published in full.

Certainly this country, and the world for that matter, could profit by a better understanding of Italo-American relations throughout the years. The treaties that the chargés d'affaires struggled to evolve were being made at that time throughout the world. The policies therein were worked out in the State Department and in Congress with the utmost diligence, and were further complicated by a great mass of peripheral circumstances within the countries treated with, as well as within our own, by the progress of debates in Congress. This second half century of our national life is a part well nigh forgotten by the citizenry of today; as also by the more — and worse — harassed minds of disturbed Europe.

These documents also reveal the earliest efforts of the United States to establish, for its own needs it is true, the beginning of certain practices based on the law of nations, and, in the historical perspective, to establish what might now be called 'enlightened self-interest,' that is, to assume and enforce through treaties with all nations, a leadership which will show that a nation can serve its own interests, and at the same time those of humanity, and thereby establish fair relations between men of all nations. The more this editor works among the documents of that period, the more he sees how many of the policies, foreign and domestic, then established still live in our democracy's ideals, if not in our daily practice.

In other respects, too, the history of our relations with the Kingdom of the Two Sicilies is highly significant. The matter of the indemnity claims alone arrested the attention of three federal administrations and held the interest of the American people for a period of twenty years. Besides, from the point of view of Italian history, the documents are important since they have not been accessible even to Italian historians, including Benedetto

2

Croce, who have written on the Kingdom of the Two Sicilies. The almost complete destruction of the *Archivio di Stato* of Naples by the Germans, immediately before they evacuated the city in the last war, adds immeasurably to the significance of these documents. In fact, in a letter to the editor, signor Croce heartily endorsed this project, adding that "these documents cannot but prove to be very useful, especially since the destruction caused by a cruel and barbarous war has resulted in the burning of all of the most essential documents on the history of the old Kingdom of Naples stored in its large State Archives."

Indeed, these documents present a picture of the social, political and economic conditions in the Neapolitan Kingdom during a very important period of Italian history. When it is remembered that our diplomatic representatives were for the most part men of intelligence, shrewd observers of men and events, and endowed with keen judgment, their despatches assume special significance. Since England, France, Spain, and Austria played a significant rôle in the development of Italian political history during the nineteenth century, the observations of American ministers on what they saw and heard will give the reader a more intimate knowledge of the part that these nations played in the unfolding of the events that culminated in the political unification and independence of the Italian people. At one point in these relations, for example, the Neapolitan officials would not negotiate a treaty of commerce with the United States until after similar treaties had been negotiated with other European governments.

Much more than the mere achievement of the treaties themselves and the enforcement of their provisions was done on both sides, officially, to promote amity, especially in the then rapidly developing fields of science, literature, and art. Noted citizens and officials of both countries eagerly followed the published works issuing from the other and notable exchanges of most valuable publications were effected from time to time and committed eventually to the newly established Smithsonian Institution and the Library of Congress in this country and to equally prominent institutions under royal patronage in Naples.

It has been possible, through the most diligent search, to unearth the whole fascinating history of that interchange and to descry its importance. To the delight of the Librarian of the Smithsonian Institution of today, the research assistant of this editor found the actual volumes, which, to everyone's great surprise, bear not a line to indicate that they ever were a royal gift. The editor has emphatically commented upon the importance of these publications because of the difficulty most researchers in the United States experience in trying to identify and locate these works which are now so nearly forgotten in modern scholarship. The fact that the Government in those early years did most of its subsidizing of publications through indirect means, e.g., the purchase of entire editions of such works as those listed in these despatches, causes few persons today to realize that actually these were works of constant use by all government department officials, as well as in all our legations abroad. As a background for understanding what went to make up the mental attitudes of our diplomats, consuls, and other officials abroad, as well as, to a great extent, the official minds at home, prior to the Civil War, these publications even today need to be brought back to the attention of scholars.

The fact that these volumes, both those sent by the United States and those sent by Naples, were published over the half century these despatches cover, and the fact that there were changes in government practice in both countries, explains why the volumes were not only published in different ways, but differently labelled as to cover titles, and then were shipped in both directions by changing routes, through changing official auspices. These circumstances so confuse the trail, that no library has ever been able to straighten them out adequately in cataloguing or shelving them. It is strange that the series of gift volumes sent by the King of the Two Sicilies were not kept intact, but were scattered into several Library of Congress letteral classifications. The Librarian of the Smithsonian Institution, who received the Royal volumes, later went to Boston as a Librarian and the Boston Public Library showed notable interest in acquiring these Neapolitan works. The Harvard University Library also has some of these volumes, perhaps more than even the *Union Catalogue* lists, for it is far from complete, especially on some of the older works. The whole story of these interchanges became clear only after careful investigation. These exchanges involved a definite United States foreign policy of intellectual comity which began not with the Wilkes volumes, but earlier with the authorization by Congress to expend money to "interchange government publications" with other governments, for mutual information and the promotion of understanding of this new American democracy by the kingdoms of Europe. The part the Smithsonian In-

4

stitution played in developing these interchanges was contemporaneously recognized as part of its intended function; but the process, even during the years these despatches cover, saw so many changes in the focus and expansion of United States government departments, that taking these interchanges separately one gets but a small part of their significance and less still of a realization of how seriously Congress, the United States Government, and the presidents in turn considered the details of careful building up of the objectives and the *modus operandi* of such interchanges.

A similar "rara avis" turned up when the editor tried to make sense out of badly written money symbols in one of the despatches. In the end there was discovered, tucked away in the Treasury Records, a first edition (1811) of Patrick Kelly's volume on foreign exchange, *Universal Cambist and Commercial Instructor,* a British printed work, so rare, that apparently no library in this country has one! Evidently it is also lacking in the British Museum and in the Library of Congress. Some modern clerk in the Treasury Department thought the work "interesting" and ordered it rebound many years after the title page and the author's name had disappeared from it. After diligent search, the editor's staff was finally able to identify the work as the first edition, discovering also much information about the author, and the later editions of his work, all of which are in the Library of Congress; some of them, too, were once in the custody of the United States Treasury and of the United States Mint at Philadelphia and only a rare few of them are found in the libraries in this country. The author and his works have been related to the British world of commerce and to our commercial accounting practices, and to the whole field of foreign exchange, along with the work of Tait who carried on after Kelly's death, as also to the work done in the United States by Patterson of the United States Mint, and by such men as Blount, whose work in the field was published at the end of the period of these despatches. Among men who handle this kind of material constantly and know what is of most practical worth, this phase of the research is highly appreciated.

Another important result of the study of these despatches is to be found in the lists of the inventories of books existing in the Legation library in Naples. These inventories are of very real significance as affecting the concepts — economic, political and social — of that period, for they went not only to the King-

5

dom of the Two Sicilies, but to all American representatives abroad, and indubitably were more widely read, and more generally used for reference by foreigners who called upon our diplomats than were many of the more numerous publications of the debates of Congress, the journals, etc. To anyone who uses these old volumes constantly, it is a bit startling to discover how few even today are aware of the existence of these volumes, let alone to know the history of their creation, or the contemporary fame they enjoyed. In the hope of rendering a service to the readers of these despatches, the editor has tried to give some clear statement regarding these volumes, at least in the form of short annotations regarding each one.

Another interesting sidelight of the research was the location of the Persico statues, the two full-length figures (Mars and Ceres), which today stand partly within individual huge niches, back against the building proper (the Capitol) and are a bit dwarfed in impressiveness by the more prominently placed groups of statuary added later, outside the columns, on a section of the grand stairway. But Persico's are very fine, and definitely in the old classical tradition. These statues stand so far behind the tall columns that in most photographs, taken at a distance for the sake of including so extended a triple winged façade and so elevated a height, they are almost indiscernible. Great vision was present in the man who could fit those statues not only to the Capitol as it was in the day they were installed, but so conceive them that they lose nothing now by the great expansion of the original designs for the building. The same is true of the several pediments he executed so skillfully for the Capitol. It enables the reader to understand that 'willful' embarcation described in one of the despatches!

In the light of what this research project has yielded, it is surprising that this phase of American diplomatic history should have been ignored for so long by students and especially by scholars. Except for the Papal States, there has been no comprehensive study of the conditions and circumstances or of the personalities and motivations surrounding the treaties of commerce and friendship that were enacted, nor of how the changing events in these nations during the Risorgimento affected the progress of these negotiations with the United States. However, several official United States Government publications, dealing with the spoliation claims against the Government of the Two Sicilies, contain extracts from the official correspondence of United States ministers to Naples. The following are some of these publications: United States President. *Message from the President of the United States Transmitting in conformity to a resolution of the House of Representatives of the 30th of January last, sundry papers, in relation to the claim of the merchants of the United States, for their property seized and confiscated under the authority of the King of Naples.* Read, and ordered to lie upon the table: March 2, 1818 (House Document No. 130); United States President. *Message from the President of the United States Transmitting a copy of a convention between the United States and the King of the Two Sicilies.* January 24, 1833, referred to the Committee on Foreign Affairs. (22nd Congress, 2nd session, v.2, Ex. Doc. No. 60. House; United States President. *Message from the President of the United States to the Two Houses of Congress at the Commencement of the First Session of the Twenty-third Congress. Dec. 3, 1833.* (23rd Cong., 1st sess., v. 1, n. 1); United States President. *Message from the President of the United States Transmitting copies of a convention between the United States and the King of the Two Sicilies, respecting depredations inflicted upon American commerce.* (23rd Cong., 1st sess., 1833-1834. Ex. Doc. No. 414. House); United States Senate. *Documents relating to the convention with Sicily.* February 9, 1833. 22nd Cong., 2d sess. (Senate Doc. 70).

Besides these Government publications, several Americans have published articles and books on the subject of our relations with other sovereign states in the peninsula. The late Mr. Nelson H. Gay gave the initial impetus to these studies on Italo-American relations. His "Relazioni fra l'Italia e gli Stati Uniti" published in *Atti Congresso per la Storia del Risorgimento Italiano,* Milan, 1906, I, 134-136; his "Le relazioni fra l'Italia e gli Stati Uniti (1847-1871)" Rome, 1907, reprinted from *Nuova Antologia,* Rome, 1907, ser. 5, CXXVII, 657-671; and his "Garibaldi's Sicilian campaign as reported by an American diplomat," in *American Historical Review,* New York, Jan. 1922, are among the earliest contributions on the subject. Mr. Gay also reprinted the story, with documents, of the Perkins diplomatic incident in Perugia, "Uno screzio diplomatico fra il governo pontificio e il governo americano e la condotta degli svizzeri a Perugia il 20 giugno 1859," (Perugia, 1907), from *Archivio Storico del Risorgimento Umbro,* anno III, 1907, pp. 113-201.

Much more extensive and comprehensive has been the research

conducted by Dr. Leo F. Stock on various aspects of American official relations with the Vatican. Besides many articles in American scholarly magazines, he has edited two volumes which are of outstanding importance: *United States Ministers to the Papal States: Instructions and Despatches 1848-1868.* Catholic University Press (Washington, D. C.) 1933. American Catholic Historical Association Document Volume 1; *Consular relations between the United States and the Papal States: Instructions and Despatches.* American Catholic Historical Association. Washington, D. C., 1945, Documents, Volume II. Our official relations with the Vatican have also been studied by Sister Loretta Clare Feiertag, in her *American Public Opinion concerning the Diplomatic Relations between the United States and the Papal States 1847-1867.* (Washington, 1933).

Several other studies have been published on our relations with the Two Sicilies. The doctoral dissertation of the Reverend Paul Christopher Perrotta on *The Claims of the United States against the Kingdom of Naples. A dissertation . . . to . . . the Catholic University of America.* Washington, D. C., 1926, is a comprehensive study on our early relations with the Kingdom of the Two Sicilies. L. Sears published an article on "The Neapolitan mission of Enos Thompson Throop 1838-1842" in *Quarterly Journal of the New York State Historical Association,* Oct. 1928, IX, no. 4.

This editor wishes to refer, with all due modesty, to his own interest in Italo-American relations. His *American Opinion on the Unification of Italy 1846-1861* (New York, 1932), deals also with the diplomatic relations between the United States and the various states of the Italian peninsula for the period covered. He has also published a series of articles on various aspects and personalities identified with Italo-American relations. These articles include: "William H. Polk's mission to Naples, 1845-1847," *Tennessee Historical Quarterly,* Nashville, Tenn., Sept. 1945, IV, 222-231; "John Rowan's mission to the Two Sicilies (1848-1850)," *The Register of the Kentucky Historical Society,* Frankfort, Ky., July 1945, XLIII, 263-271; "Edward Joy Morris' mission to Naples (1850-1853)," *Pennsylvania History,* Phila., Pa., Oct. 1945, XII, 270-292; "An American diplomat views the dawn of liberalism in Piedmont (1843-1848)," *Journal of Central European Affairs,* Boulder, Col., July 1946, VI, 167-186; "Nathaniel Niles' missions at the Court of Turin (1838, 1848-1850)," *Vermont Quarterly,* Montpellier,

Vt., Jan. 1947, XV, 14-32; "Ambrose Baber at the Court of Sardinia (1841-43)," *The Georgia Historical Quarterly,* Savannah, Ga., June 1946, XXX, 105-117; "William Burnet Kinney's mission to the Kingdom of Sardinia *(1850-1853)", Proceedings of the New Jersey Historical Society,* Newark, N. J., Oct. 1946, LXIV, 187-215; "American opinion and documents on Garibaldi's march on Rome, 1862," *Journal of Central European Affairs,* Boulder, Col., July 1947, VII, 143-161; "Unpublished American documents on Garibaldi's march on Rome in 1867," *The Journal of Modern History,* Chicago, June 1944, XVI, 116-123; "Unpublished American documents on the Roman Republic of 1849," *The Catholic Historical Review,* Washington, D. C., January 1943, XXVIII, 459-490; "The closing of the American diplomatic mission to the Vatican and efforts to revive it, 1868-1870," *The Catholic Historical Review,* Washington, D. C., January 1948, XXXIII, 423-447; "Unpublished American documents on Italy's occupation of Rome," *The Journal of Modern History,* Chicago, Ill., March 1941, XIII, 48-64; "American documents on Italy's annexation of Venetia (1866)," *Journal of Central European Affairs,* Boulder, Col., January 1946, V. 354-377.

The documents herein published are careful transcripts of the originals or record copies now preserved in the United States National Archives in Washington, D. C., and include only such documents of Italian origin as may have been sent to the State Department of the United States as enclosures in despatches from American representatives in the Kingdom, or may possibly have been transmitted directly to the State Department, during periods when we had no American chargés in Naples, in which case the route of transmission was through the Neapolitan consul general or minister in the United States. Documents from the National Archives have been supplemented to a considerable extent by text or footnote references to documents in the *Archivio di Stato* of Naples. These, in turn, have been, to some extent, supplemented, for purposes of background and contemporary historical setting, by materials dealing with contemporary negotiations and conditions in the other states of the Italian peninsula. These materials have, in part, been drawn personally by the author and more recently by assistants in Italy, from the *Archivi di Stato* in Naples, Rome, Turin, and Florence. To a considerable extent, therefore, the work also includes references to materials, seen in these Italian archives, found to duplicate the record copies. These record copies are printed in full in these text sections and are based entirely on records in the United States National Archives, Washington, D. C.

Mr. Pinkney's despatches on his Neapolitan mission are filed with the Despatches from the United States Ministers to Russia, volume 6. The originals of the Instructions from James Monroe to Pinkney are filed under Record Group No. 59, General Records of the Department of State. Instructions, United States Ministers, volume 8 (Nov. 2, 1815-Dec. 7, 1819). Mr. Pinkney's credences are filed under Record Group No. 59, General Records of the Department of State, Credences, Volume 1 (Oct. 9, 1789-Nov. 16, 1824). The despatches from John J. Appleton, and copies of credences, concerning his mission to Naples are in the records of the Department of State, Diplomatic Despatches, Naples-Sweden, volume 5 (February 8, 1825-August 15, 1830). The State Department Instructions to Appleton are found in volume 10 (July 15, 1823-December 30, 1825), Instructions, United States Ministers.

The letters, with their enclosures, addressed to the State Department, by William H. Polk, Alexander Hammett, John Rowan, Thomas W. Chinn, Edward Joy Morris, Robert Dale Owen, are found in a volume which is part of a body of records in the National Archives described as Record Group No. 59, General Records of the Department of State. The volume itself is volume 2 of a series which is cited as Diplomatic Despatches, Italy. This volume also contains letters from Arthur L. Payton and Daniel Draper, Boston merchants, and from their attorneys, Howland and Pope (Boston, November 30, 1850-April 14, 1852), relating to claims against the Government of the Kingdom of the Two Sicilies.

The volume containing letters, with their enclosures, addressed to the Department of State by Joseph R. Chandler, Minister Resident from the United States to the Kingdom of the Two Sicilies, consisting of unnumbered letters dated at Philadelphia (June 21 and 29, 1858; April 18 and May 22, 1861), Naples (October 29, 1858; May 24, 1860), and Paris (January 7, 1861); and despatches 1-73 (Naples, September 21, 1858-November 1860) forms a part of the body of records in the National Archives described as Record Group No. 59, General Records of the Department of State. The volume itself is volume 3, of a series that may be cited as Diplomatic Despatches, Italy.

The record copies of communications addressed by the Department of State to diplomatic representatives of the United States in the Kingdom of the Two Sicilies, May 18, 1838-May 27, 1861, are in a volume numbered 14 of the series with respect to the Kingdom of the Two Sicilies. Separately filed Instructions to representatives in the Kingdom are confined to this volume, which extends to the year (1861) in which the Kingdom was absorbed into the Kingdom of Italy.

Among the records of the Department of State in the National Archives are several series of volumes that contain further documents pertaining to the early relations between the United States and the Italian states and the later Kingdom of Italy. A single volume, numbered 3 by the Department of State and evidently regarded formerly as a continuation of the two volumes described above, actually contains a separate, though parallel, series of notes addressed to the Department by ministers and other representatives from the Kingdom of Sardinia to the United States from October 1, 1838 to March 1861. Other series containing pertinent documents are the notes from the Department of State to foreign ministers and consuls in "Notes to Foreign Legations" (File Microcopy 38), the notes to the Department from foreign consuls in the United States, the despatches to the Department from American ministers to the Italian states and from American consuls in Italian ports, and the instructions from the Department of State to American ministers and consuls abroad (File Microcopy 28).

The notes, with their enclosures, addressed to the Department of State between July 19, 1826, and May 6, 1848, by ministers and other representatives from the Kingdom of the Two Sicilies to the United States, are in the first of what may be considered a series of two, of which the second (labelled "Sicilian Legation") contains notes addressed to the Department of State between October 19, 1848 and December 15, 1860. These two volumes are parts of a body of records in the National Archives, Washington, D. C., that constitute Record Group 59, General Records of the Department of State. These volumes are among the records of the Department of State in the United States National Archives.

The editorial policy adopted in publishing these documents requires a brief explanation. The arrangement is, of course, chronological under the successive ministers. Enclosures, printed in smaller type, irrespective of dates, follow the despatch in which they were enclosed. In general, the original spelling, capi-

11

talization, punctuation, abbreviations, and paragraphing have been retained. Occasionally, a comma or a period was inserted to clarify the meaning. Old symbols and contractions for "and" and "th" (after dates) have also been retained. Names of vessels, newspapers, printed books and pamphlets, and foreign words and phrases have been rendered in italics. Omissions are indicated by the usual dots; the customary square brackets have been employed to enclose additions made to the original by the editor. The salutation in a letter has uniformly been retained, but the formal conclusion and the signature have in most instances been omitted.

No attempt has been made to cite in footnote references all bibliographical titles bearing upon the subject. Since these footnotes are used merely to explain the text and not to give extended accounts of political happenings in Italy, it seemed sufficient in each instance to list but one or two authorities from the enormous bibliography on the Risorgimento movement.

The editor wishes to thank the Council for Research in the Social Sciences of Columbia University for the grants-in-aid which enabled him to collect, transcribe, and annotate the documents herein published. To the Publication Committee of the Council the editor wishes to express his appreciation for the financial assistance which has made possible the publication of these volumes. To Professor Dino Bigongiari, Da Ponte Professor of Italian, Columbia University, to the late Professor Harry Morgan Ayres, formerly Director of the Casa Italiana of Columbia University, Professor John A. Krout, formerly the Acting Director of the Casa Italiana, and to Benedetto Croce, the Italian philosopher and critic, the editor is especially grateful for the support and encouragement given him at various stages in the preparation of the manuscript. He is also especially grateful to Professor Basil Rauch, the Executive Officer of the History Department of Barnard College, Professor Harold C. Syrett, of the History Department of Columbia University, who with Professor Dino Bigongiari constituted an Advisory Committee of the Council. These three colleagues read the manuscript and made appropriate recommendations to the Council.

The list of persons who have helped the editor, in the various phases of the project, is quite long, but this work could not have progressed with ease without the assistance of the following: Professor Ernesto Portieri, University of Naples; Dr. Sergio Camerani, *Archivio di Stato,* Florence, Italy; Dr. Solon J.

Buck, Archivist of the United States; P. M. Hamer, Records Control Officer of the National Archives, Washington, D. C.; Mr. W. Neil Franklin, Chief, General Reference Division, the National Archives; Roscoe R. Hill, Chief, Division of State Department Archives, of the National Archives; Almon R. Wright, Head, Executive and Foreign Affairs Branch, The National Archives, and also Acting Director, General Records Office, The National Archives, Washington, D. C., and Dr. Leo F. Stock, Division of Historical Research of the Carnegie Institution of Washington, D. C.

In the identification of many less prominent names and events connected with local history, the editor received help from the following persons: John B. Hefferman, Director, Naval Records and Library, United States Navy Department; Edward F. Witsell, Major General, The Adjutant General, The United States War Department; Leslie W. Dunlap, Acting Chief, General Reference and Bibliography Division, The Library of Congress, Washington, D. C.; D. A. Bigby, The Under-Secretary of State, the Foreign Office, London; The Under-Secretary of State of the War Office, London; the Director of the *Service des Archives, Ministère des Affaires Étrangères,* Paris; the Director of the *Hauptarchiv für Behördenakten,* Berlin; the Chief of the Administrative Department, *Ministerio das Relações Exteriores*, Rio de Janeiro, Brazil; Count Lemenhaupt, Counsellor of Legation, Kungl. *Utrikes Departementet,* Stockholm, Sweden; the Hon. José Xara Brasil Rodrigues, *Ministerio dos Negocios Estrangeiros,* Lisbon, Portugal; Dr. Leopold Figl, Chancellor and Minister of Foreign Affairs, Vienna, Austria; Dr. Atilio Garcia Mellid, *Director del Departamento de Cultura, Ministerio de Relaciones Exteriores y Culto,* Buenos Aires, Argentina; R. N. Williams, 2nd, Director of the Historical Society of Pennsylvania, Philadelphia, Pa.; Robert S. Hardy, Acting Associate Director, Near East College Association, Inc., New York City; Margaret C. Norton, Archivist, Illinois State Library, Springfield, Illinois; Stanley C. Arthur, Executive Director, Louisiana State Museum, New Orleans, La.

For their unselfish and untiring assistance in the preparation of the footnotes, the editor is particularly grateful to Mrs. Laura S. Young who worked largely in the library of Columbia University and at the New York Public Library; Miss Estella T. Weeks, whose considerable familiarity with the routines and records at the National Archives, Washington, D .C., was placed at the disposal of this project; and Dr. Yole Mazzoleni, the *Archivio di Stato* of Naples, Italy, who confined herself to research from Italian sources. To Mrs. Natalia Summers, until recently of the Division of General Records of the State Department, who gave of her time and interest unstintingly in this project, the editor is under a special debt of gratitude. Mrs. Summers proved a never-failing joy and blessing as a collaborator, far in excess in the generosity of her time, and great wealth of factual information than my research assistant in Washington had any right to claim of her.

Finally, I wish to thank Miss Catherine Hall, Miss Shirley Rae Meyer, Miss Carolyn Pickering, Miss Edna Falk, Mr. Evan Farber, Miss Jean Hudson, Mrs. James McNelis, and Miss Armenie Onigian, the last two of the Casa Italiana secretarial staff, for transcribing the documents from the microfilms and for secretarial assistance. To Miss Gioconda Savini, Secretary of the Casa Italiana, and to my colleague, Mr. Gino Bigongiari, who gave valuable assistance in proof reading the galleys and page proofs, the editor is under a special debt of gratitude.

HOWARD R. MARRARO

Columbia University
July 1950.

14

INTRODUCTION

Italy's declaration of war against the United States in December 1941, unhappily brought to a sudden and abrupt end more than a hundred years of cordial relations existing between the Italian and American peoples. Indeed up to the outbreak of the Second World War there had been few diplomatic incidents of any consequence in the relations between the United States and Italy, the sole exception being the controversy which arose over the lynching of Italian subjects in the eighteen nineties in New Orleans and other cities of the South and West.[1] When the first New Orleans incident occurred in 1890, except for the ordinary routine business, the diplomatic relations between the two countries were suspended for several months, and there was even much idle talk of war. However, as soon as the United States Congress voted an indemnity to be paid to the families of the victims, the relations were promptly restored. Except for this incident — it may be worth repeating — the relations between the Italian and American peoples have always been marked by mutual esteem and admiration and by unbounded sympathy for and a desire to help whenever war, death, and destruction attended the other.

---

[1] These incidents must be explained by the fact that in those years there were in the United States and particularly in Louisiana condemned criminals who had escaped from Italian jails and who had organized the "Black Hand" by which they terrorized many persons. Americans were furious at the "Black Hand," but unfortunately in the fury of the popular uprisings they made no attempt to distinguish between the millions of law-abiding citizens of Italy and the members of the "Black Hand." The New Orleans controversy received wide attention in Italy. Among the more significant documents and studies on the subject, see: Augusto Pierantoni, *I fatti di Nuova Orleans e il diritto internazionale.* Rome Pallotta, 1891, 120 p. 8°.; P. Nocito, "La legge di Lynch e il conflitto italo-americano." *Nuova Antologia,* Florence, 1891, XXXIII, 337-362, 551-583; Alberico Pincitore, *Sulla maniera di risolvere il conflitto italo-americano.* Conferenza. Palermo, Tip. Giornale di Sicilia, 1891 19 p. 8°; Francesco Auriti, *Questioni giuridiche nella vertenza fra l'Italia e la federazione americana pei fatti di Nuova Orleans.* Rome, Loescher, 1893, 16 p. 8°; Domenico Zanichelli, *La questione fra l'Italia e gli Stati Uniti.* Florence, M. Ricci 1891. 8°; Italy, Ministero degli Affari Esteri. *Documenti diplomatici presentati al Parlamento italiano dal Presidente del consiglio, Ministro degli Affari Esteri (di Rudini). Incidente di Nuova Orleans Seduta del 30 aprile 1891. Seduta del 4 maggio 1892.* Rome, Camera dei Deputati, 1891-1892, 2 vols. 29 cm. The following study in English is a satisfactory resumé of the incident: John E. Coxe, "New Orleans Mafia incident," *Louisiana Historical Quarterly,* 1937, XX, 1067-1110.

It should be noted that the promptness with which the two governments had always sought to understand and appreciate the other's points of view and policies was an important factor in strengthening the bonds of friendship between the two peoples.

The political division of Italy by the Congress of Vienna into several minor independent states[2] made it necessary for the United States up to 1870, when Italy finally achieved her political unity, to maintain diplomatic and consular relations with most of these sovereign nations in the peninsula: the Kingdom of the Two Sicilies, the Kingdom of Sardinia, the Papal States, the Grand Duchy of Tuscany, the Duchy of Parma, and the Kingdom of Lombardo-Venetia. As these states gradually became a part of the united Kingdom of Italy, the United States Government withdrew its diplomatic officers from the defunct states, extending, at the same time, the power and jurisdiction of the minister accredited to the Government of Victor Emmanuel II.

In 1870, after Rome became the capital of united Italy, and the Pope was deprived of his temporal powers, the United States Government had the following diplomatic and consular officers accredited to Italy: a legation in Rome; a consulate general in Rome; twelve consulates in Ancona, Brindisi, Carrara, Florence, Genoa, Leghorn, Messina, Naples, Palermo, Spezia, Taranto, and Venice; thirteen consular agencies in Cagliari, Milan, Turin, Catania, Gioja, Syracuse, Castellamare, Pozzuoli, Girgenti Licata, Marsala, Trapani, and Civitavecchia. On its part the Italian Government maintained a legation in Washington; a consulate general in New York; a consulate in San Francisco; seven vice-consulates in Philadelphia, New Orleans, Louisville, Memphis, Richmond, Mobile, and Vicksburgh; and five consular agencies in Boston, Baltimore, Saint Louis, Cincinnati, and Chicago.

The earliest official American contacts with Italy were established through the appointment of American consuls in the peninsula. Official records of the State Department show that by the beginning of the nineteenth century there were four American consuls in the peninsula: Leghorn (1793),[3] Naples (1796), Rome (1797), and Genoa (1799). It was not until after the downfall of Napoleon that the United States Government found it necessary to send diplomatic representatives to the several Italian states, usually for the purpose of improving the com-

---

2 These comprised: the Kingdom of Sardinia, the Kingdom of Lombardo-Venetia, the Grand Duchy of Tuscany, the Duchy of Parma, Piacenza and Guastalla, the Duchy of Modena, the States of the Church, and the Kingdom of the Two Sicilies.
3 The dates indicate the year in which the consuls were appointed.

merce between the United States and the Italian states as follows: to the Kingdom of the Two Sicilies in 1816; to the Kingdom of Sardinia in 1840; and to the States of the Church in 1848. In this the young American Republic was following its expanding foreign policy exemplified already by similar treaties achieved with the major nations of Europe.

The first United States treaty with any of the sovereign states in the Italian peninsula was the treaty of indemnity of October 14, 1832 with the Kingdom of the Two Sicilies. With the same kingdom we negotiated a treaty of commerce and navigation in 1845; a convention defining the rights of neutrals at sea in 1855; and another treaty of commerce, navigation, extradition, etc. in 1855. With the Kingdom of Sardinia we negotiated a treaty of commerce and navigation in 1838. After the Constitution of the Kingdom of Italy in 1861, the United States negotiated a treaty of friendship, commerce, and extradition in 1868, another treaty defining the rights of consuls in 1868, additional articles on consuls and extradition in 1869, and a treaty of commerce and navigation in 1871. The rapidly changing political scene in the States of the Church made it impossible for the American ministers to negotiate any treaty with the Government of Pius IX.

Although the full texts of these treaties have been published,[4] there is no comprehensive study of the conditions and circumstances under which they were enacted, the discussions that accompanied and followed the establishment of official diplomatic relations between the United States and the various Italian states, the course of these relations during Italy's struggle for unification and independence and during the American Civil War, and the gradual suspension of these relations with those states of the peninsula as they became incorporated into the Kingdom of Italy. The only exception to this statement is our relations with the Papal States. Since the creation of the City of the Vatican in 1929 as a sovereign state, several American scholars have published important studies bearing on America's diplomatic and consular relations with the Vatican. Otherwise, little or nothing is known on the subject. It is the purpose of this introduction to trace briefly these relations as they existed before the outbreak of the recent conflict.

---

[4] See Hunter Miller, *Treaties and other International Acts of the United States of America*. United States Government Printing Office, Washington, D. C., 1931-1942, 7 volumes; William M. Malloy, *Treaties, conventions, international acts, protocols and agreements between the United States of America and other powers 1776-1909*. Washington, D. C., Government Printing Office, 1910, 2 volumes.

On May 20, 1796,[5] consular relations were established with what was then known as the Kingdom of Naples by the appointment of John S. M. Matthiew as consul of the United States at the city of Naples, capital of the country.[6]

Joseph Barnes was appointed consul of the United States for the island of Sicily on February 10, 1802. On March 20, 1805, Abraham Gibbs and John Broadbent were appointed by President Jefferson, during the recess of the Senate, as consuls at the Sicilian cities of Palermo and Messina, respectively. The appointments were confirmed by the Senate on January 3, 1806, and new commissions were issued to Gibbs and Broadbent on January 17, 1806.[7]

The history of the relations between the United States and the Kingdom of the Two Sicilies is so important that it arrested the attention of three federal administrations and held the interest of the American people for more than two decades. In his *Thirty Year's View*,[8] Senator Thomas H. Benton (Missouri), a keen and shrewd observer of his times, wrote "that the indemnity obtained from Naples . . . may be looked upon as the most remarkable of Jackson's diplomatic successes." The controversy goes back to the years 1809 to 1812 when the Great Napoleon appointed his brother-in-law, Prince Joachim Murat, to the throne of the Two Sicilies. To carry out Napoleon's wishes, Murat promulgated decrees which permitted him to seize and confiscate American ships that ventured into Neapolitan waters. These arbitrary acts brought about the first diplomatic contact of the American people with an Italian state,[9] for at the close of our second war with Great Britain, the United States Government demanded reparation and indemnity for the losses American merchants had sustained.

---

5 Date his appointment as consul was confirmed by the United States Senate.

6 Personnel records of State Department. This as well as other information in this introduction credited to "Personnel records of the Department of States," is based on a typewritten memorandum prepared in the Division of Research and Publication of the Department of State, which was sent to the author by Dr. E. Wilder Spaulding, the Chief of that Division.

7 *Journal of the Executive Proceedings of the Senate*, III, pp. 7 and 13; and Personal Records of the Department of State.

8 New York, 1854, I, 604.

9 It is true that Ralph Izard in 1777 was appointed by Congress commissioner to Tuscany, but since he never reached his post, his cannot be regarded as the first diplomatic intercourse. Nor can the fruitless mission of Philip Mazzei to the Grand Duke of Tuscany from 1779 to 1783 be considered, strictly speaking, a diplomatic mission. See also notes 33, 34, p. 37.

In the meantime, however, Murat had been dethroned and the former Bourbon dynasty was restored with Ferdinand I (formerly Ferdinand IV) whom the Congress of Vienna recognized as King of the Kingdom of the Two Sicilies. At the request of those merchants who had suffered losses, on February 28, 1816, William Pinkney, of Maryland, a leading diplomatist of his day, was nominated by President Madison as Minister to Russia, "with a special mission to the King of the Two Sicilies." (Executive Journal III, 32). The nomination of Pinkney as Minister to Russia was confirmed on March 7, but in respect to the special mission to the King of the Two Sicilies it was rejected (*ibid*, 35). On April 17 Pinkney was again nominated by the following presidential message (*ibid*, 45, April 20):

"It being presumed that further information may have changed the views of the Senate relative to the importance and expediency of a mission to Naples, for the purpose of negotiating indemnities to our citizens of spoliations committed by the Neapolitan government, I nominate William Pinkney, Envoy Extraordinary and Minister Plenipotentiary to Russia, to be Minister Plenipotentiary to Naples, especially charged with that trust."

"The nomination of Pinkney was duly confirmed by the Senate on April 23, 1816, by a vote of eighteen to fifteen (*ibid.*, 46); and he was commissioned on the same day."

In an instruction of May 11, 1816, Secretary of State Monroe wrote to Pinkney on the subject of his mission as follows: "The President desires . . . that you will use every effort in your power to terminate the business with Naples as soon as it may be possible, and that you will proceed thence, immediately afterwards, to St. Petersburg."

On August 29, 1816, after his arrival at Naples, Pinkney wrote to Secretary Monroe that his reception by the Neapolitan Government was "extremely friendly, and in the highest degree respectful to the Government of the United States." However, in the discussions that ensued, the Neapolitan Government took the position that Murat had been an usurper and that the legitimate ruler of Naples could not be held responsible for the acts committed by an intruder. In keenness and ability Pinkney was an able match for King Ferdinand and his ministers, but he was not allowed sufficient time to carry out the negotiations. The Marquis di Circello, Secretary of State and Minister of Foreign Affairs, avoided an answer to Pinkney's note until after he had been forced to proceed to Russia. Finally, he addressed a note on

October 1, 1816 to the Marquis di Circello, requesting the "usual passports" and stating that he wished to "set out at the end of this week." In this manner Pinkney's mission failed and compensation was not then secured.

Serious domestic and international problems left the indemnity question in abeyance during Monroe's two terms, but in 1825 the issue was reopened following the accession of Francis I as King of Naples, and the election of John Quincy Adams as President of the United States. In an Instruction of May 12, 1825 John James Appleton, Secretary of the Legation in Madrid, was informed of his appointment as "Special Agent of the United States, at Naples." In the Instruction, Secretary of State Clay reviewed previous efforts of the United States to settle the claims against the Government of Naples and stated that, although Appleton was being sent to Naples without a formal commission, such a commission, as chargé d'affaires, would be sent to him if he were able to observe that there was "a reasonable hope of obtaining an acknowledgment of the obligation of Naples to pay the claims, and a provision for their payment, at even a distant day." Appleton's efforts proved fruitless, for the Neapolitan Government assumed the same position it had taken in 1816. On June 8, 1826 Secretary Clay instructed Appleton that he had been appointed Chargé d'Affaires of the United States at Stockholm, Sweden, and that "since a reasonable hope" was "no longer to be indulged" of Appleton's obtaining a settlement of the claims the President had decided to "postpone to a more propitious moment, the further prosecution of them." Thus, again, the United States Government saw fit to delay insistence upon its claims.

Meanwhile, the New England merchants continued to send memorials to Congress, insisting on a settlement. Finally, President Jackson in his third annual message to Congress, December 6, 1831, pledged himself to secure indemnity for the wrongs committed against American merchants by Naples and other countries of Europe.[10]

Late in 1831 President Jackson sent John Nelson, of Maryland, to Naples with explicit orders to obtain a settlement of the dispute by March of the following year or to ask for his passports. When March came and the dispute remained unsettled, Nelson advised the application of stern measures against the Neapolitan

---

[10] American merchants also had outstanding claims for spoliations against France, Holland, Denmark, and Spain.

Government. Jackson astounded him by advising him to allow Naples additional time to reply.

A definite agreement was reached by October, 1832, when Nelson returned to the United States with the text of the first convention entered into between the United States and the Kingdom of the Two Sicilies. According to the terms of this treaty, which was signed by John Nelson and the Prince of Cassaro, His Majesty the King of the Kingdom of the Two Sicilies obliged himself to pay the sum of 2,115,000 Neapolitan ducats with interest as indemnity for the destruction of vessels and cargoes. Of the total amount the sum of 7,675 ducats was to be applied to reimburse the United States Government for the expense incurred by it in the transportation of American seamen from the Kingdom of Naples in 1810, and the residue was to be distributed among the claimants in such a manner and according to such rules as the United States Government might prescribe. It was generally believed that the sum covered the principal of all the just and well-founded claims. In a letter dated Naples, October 8, 1832, addressed to the Secretary of State, Mr. Nelson pointed out that the negotiation had been a very arduous one; but if the result proved satisfactory to the Government of the United States, "I shall find in its approbation a full remuneration for the toils and vexations to which I have been exposed during its progress."

The payments of the indemnity proceeded in accordance with the terms of the Convention of October 14, 1832, and were made in each year up to 1842, when the ninth instalment was paid. Although an agreement had been signed on December 26, 1835, by the two governments providing for the reception in one payment of the balance of the indemnity remaining under the original convention, it was not approved by the Government of the Two Sicilies. Meanwhile, the United States Government had appointed an American commission of three to examine all claims and to determine the distribution of the indemnity. The total awards of the commission amounted to $1,925,034.68.

The satisfactory conclusion of the indemnity claims led American Government officials to believe that the time was now ripe to negotiate a treaty of general commerce between the two countries. Acting on this assumption, on January 30, 1833, President Jackson empowered August Davezac of Louisiana, who was then chargé d'affaires at The Hague, to proceed to Naples to negotiate such a treaty. However, Davezac was not successful in his efforts, so he took leave and returned to The Hague about February 19, 1834.

Two other fruitless attempts followed. On February 6, 1838, President Van Buren appointed Enos T. Throop of New York as chargé d'affaires. Although Mr. Throop remained at his post for about four years, no treaty of commerce was executed during his stay at the Neapolitan court. No more successful was William Boulware, of Virginia, who, on September 13, 1841, was commissioned by President Harrison, as chargé d'affaires at Naples. Boulware remained at Naples to June 19, 1845, but he too failed in his efforts to negotiate a treaty of commerce.

It was not until the administration of President Polk that a treaty of commerce and navigation was finally concluded between the United States and the Government of the Two Sicilies. On March 13, 1845, the President appointed William H. Polk, of Tennessee, chargé d'affaires. On July 24, 1845, Mr .Polk was received by His Excellency the Prince of Scilla, charged with the Portfolio of Foreign Affairs. Although their conversation was chiefly of a general character, the Prince of Scilla took occasion to mention, without any remark on Polk's part calculated to elicit it, that he had very recently succeeded in negotiating treaties with England and France, but supposed that his labors were not closed, as the United States would also "probably insist" on making a treaty. To this observation, Mr. Polk replied that the United States had for a number of years urged the necessity and represented the advantages which would result to the commerce of both countries by the adoption of liberal commercial regulations, adding that since the treaties with England and France were concluded, there was now no obstacle to prevent the adoption of a similar treaty between Naples and the United States. In reply the Prince of Scilla distinctly expressed a willingness and disposition to enter into a treaty regulation with the United States.

In his despatch No. 1, dated Naples July 26, 1845, to the Hon. James Buchanan, the Secretary of State, in which he gave an account of his first interview with the Neapolitan Foreign Minister, Mr. Polk pointed out that the Prince of Scilla was reputed to be a very feeble man and was not usually trusted by the government with the exclusive control of the country's foreign affairs. For this reason Mr. Polk feared that the Prince of Scilla's avowal of a willingness and disposition to make a treaty did not correctly reflect the views of the government. But the

Prince of Scilla's declaration when taken with the general tone of the despatches and correspondence of Mr. Polk's immediate predecessor which looked to the ratification of treaties with England and France as removing the main difficulty which had heretofore prevented the settlement of treaty regulations with the United States, inclined Mr. Polk to believe that every disposition was felt by the Neapolitan Government to enter into negotiations for a treaty. Trusting that the Prince of Scilla truly reflected the inclination of his government, Mr. Polk was determined not to lose any time or spare any exertion to frame such a treaty as would remove the restrictions then existing, and place American commerce on a fair field of competition with that of England and France. However, Mr. Polk feared that he was going to encounter some difficulty in obtaining a fair reduction of the duties then imposed on American cotton, tobacco, and other products imported into Sicily, and on American cotton and other products imported into Naples. Since the tobacco trade at Naples was a government monopoly from which an annual revenue of close to a million dollars was derived, Mr. Polk could not entertain any reasonable hope of effecting any change in the regulations then in force. In the ports of Sicily no influence operated to forbid a reduction, but from what he was able to learn from the American Consul, Mr. Alexander Hammett, who, from his long residence in Italy, was somewhat familiar with the views of the Neapolitan Government, Mr. Polk was induced to expect that the Neapolitan Government would demand and insist upon, in consideration of such reduction as would justify the importation of American cotton and other products into Naples and American cotton, tobacco, and other products into Sicily, a corresponding diminution of the duties then levied in the United States on their wines, oils, sewing silks, etc. Mr. Polk made this suggestion merely to solicit Mr. Buchanan's attention to a difficulty which he thought was likely to arise.

On November 28, 1845, Tulio Ruffo di Calabria, in the name of King Ferdinand II,[11] appointed Don Giustino Fortunato, Don Michele Gravina Prince of Comitini, and Don Antonio Spinelli to conclude a treaty with the United States. After protracted discussions which continued for several days, the treaty was finally concluded and signed on December 1, 1845, by Mr. Polk on behalf of the United States and by the three representatives appointed to act for the King of the Two Sicilies. The treaty

---

[11] He came to the throne on Nov. 8, 1830.

contained thirteen articles dealing with freedom, commerce, and navigation; discrimination in duties, drawbacks; discrimination in tonnage, harbor, etc.; coasting trade; discrimination in purchase imports; right of travel, etc.; privileges of citizens; consuls; shipwrecks; asylum for vessels; difference of duty; duration; and ratification.

On December 1, 1845, the same day that the treaty was signed in Naples, Mr. Polk transmitted a copy of the treaty to Secretary of State Buchanan for ratification by the President and Senate. In his depatch No. 3, dated Naples, December 1, 1845, Mr. Polk pointed out that throughout the negotiation he had endeavored, and hoped successfully, to confine himself to the instructions furnished him by the Department of State, adding that he had made every effort to secure a treaty of general and perfect reciprocity, embracing the produce of the soil and industry of every nation entering the ports of the Two Sicilies, under the American flag, but without success. He explained, however, that the recent treaties the Government of the Two Sicilies had concluded with England, France, and Russia restricted their commercial intercourse to the direct trade between the countries, and it could not be reasonably expected that the Neapolitan Government would change its settled policy, and extend to the United States greater privileges than it accorded to other countries.

In another despatch, No. 4, dated Naples, May 5, 1846, to Mr. Buchanan, Mr. Polk expressed the hope that the treaty, if approved by the Senate, would arrive in Naples before the expiration of the six months, for he entertained "indefinite fear" that the King might possibly be disposed to take advantage of any circumstance which would relieve him from direct obligation to refuse his sanction to the treaty. Mr. Polk explained that his fear was not founded on any information received or even rumor in circulation, but from the well-known character of His Majesty who was governed frequently on questions of the gravest importance, by impulse, or the wayward disposition of the moment.

The ratification of the treaty was advised by the United States Senate on April 11, 1846; it was then ratified by the President on April 14, 1846. The ratifications were exchanged on June 1, 1846; and the treaty was finally proclaimed on July 24, 1846.

Several months after the proclamation of the treaty, the Government of the Two Sicilies appointed Chevalier Rocco

Martuscelli,[12] as first chargé d'affaires at Washington. When Mr. Polk left Naples on May 1, 1847, to return to the United States, Secretary of State Buchanan empowered Mr. Hammett, our Consul at Naples, to act as chargé d'affaires *ad interim*.

During the political revolutions that swept through the Two Sicilies in 1848, the American people quite naturally sympathized with the Italians in their struggle against despotism and tyranny. The savage bombardment of Palermo in January 1848 by the Neapolitan fleet aroused the indignation of the foreign consuls accredited to that city. In fact, in January 1848, all the consuls residing in Palermo, with the exception of the Austrian consul, signed a protest[13] against the useless and wanton destruction of life and property in the Sicilian capital. The protest, which also bore the signature of Mr. John M. Marston[14] as Consul General of the United States of America, was sent to the Duke of S. Pietro de Majo, Lieutenant General of Sicily, stationed at Palermo.

In the United States the sympathy of the people for the Sicilians was so strong, and there were such persistent reports that their independence would be recognized by the United States Government,[15] that Secretary of State Buchanan on July 27, 1848, was impelled to inform Chevalier Martuscelli, in reply to several of his communications to the Department of State, that though the President had observed with deep interest the progress of

[12] The first representative of the Two Sicilies in the United States was Count Ferdinando Lucchesi, whose exequatur as Consul General at Washington, D. C., was signed by President John Quincy Adams on May 30, 1826. [*Exequaturs*, volume 2 (manuscript in The U. S. National Archives), p. 46]. The representatives of the Two Sicilies in the United States continued to be consular officers until 1846. On December 7, of that year, Chevalier Rocco Martuscelli, who had been Consul General at New York, presented his credentials as Chargé d'Affaires of the Two Sicilies. [Notation on letter of credence in *Ceremonial Letters, Sicilies* (manuscript volume in The U. S. National Archives), p. 114]. From then until 1861 the Government of the Two Sicilies was almost continuously represented in the United States by a chargé d'affaires. The last of these representatives was Giuseppe Anfora dei Duchi di Liccignano, Consul General, who acted as Chargé d'Affaires *ad interim* from September 24, 1860 to December 15, 1861. [*Register*, 1874, part II, 124.]

[13] The text of the protest appeared also in the supplement No. 26 of January 31, 1848, of the *Concordia*, a liberal newspaper of Turin.

[14] John M. Marston, of Massachusetts, was appointed consul of the United States at Palermo on Sept. 18, 1837. He was removed from his post, as will be seen below, in July, 1850.

[15] In the issue of July 28, 1848, the *Libertà Italiana*, a liberal newspaper published in Naples, reported the widespread rumor that the United States had offered its Mediterranean Naval Squadron, during the war of independence, to King Charles Albert, authorizing him to unfold the flag of the Kingdom of Italy. It was said, according to the newspaper, that a despatch on the subject had been sent to Turin by the commander of the *Princeton* which had arrived at Naples two days previously.

events in Italy, yet, acting in accordance with the long established policy of the United States, this Government had carefully abstained from taking part in "the intestine struggles" which agitated that country. The Secretary restated America's policy in regard to all foreign nations as being one of peace, friendship, and neutrality, leaving to each to choose that form of government which it deemed best adapted to promote the happiness and prosperity of its people. In accordance with its policy of neutrality, Mr. Buchanan added, the American Government had not recognized the independence of Sicily, nor had it taken the subject into consideration.

To avoid any misunderstanding on the subject, Secretary Buchanan reaffirmed the position of the United States Government in a letter dated August 31, 1848, to John Rowan, American Minister to Naples, in which he referred the chargé to his despatch to Mr. Richard Rush, the American Minister at Paris, dated March 31, 1848, containing an exposition of the policy of the Government in regard to the recognition of foreign governments, and to America's non-interference in the domestic concerns of foreign nations.

In his despatch No. 1, dated Naples, July 1, 1848, to Secretary of State Buchanan, Mr. Rowan gave an account of the ceremony held in connection with the presentation of his credentials to the Court at which the usual expressions of esteem and friendship were exchanged. Mr. Rowan informed the Secretary of State that after repeated delays, the representative Chamber had opened on that same day. However, the King, who was apprehensive for his personal safety, had not appeared in person, but was represented by a delegate. Conditions were very much unsettled, according to Mr. Rowan. Sicily was *de facto* a separate state, except for the citadel of Messina; and the Calabrians, he added, were in a state of anarchy and confusion. It was expected, however, that the insurgents in Calabria would be ultimately put down, and that Sicily would be able to maintain her independence.

In the meantime, however, John M. Marston, the United States Consul at Palermo, on July 11, 1848, had notified the State Department in Washington that he had recognized the new Sicilian Government. The State Department supposed that this act of recognition was a mere nullity in itself, and that it would soon have been forgotten. But from a later communication dated August 28, 1848, and the copy of a note of August 14, 1848, addressed to Mr. Marston by the Marquis of Torrearsa, both of which were transmitted to the State Department, it appeared that the new Sicilian Government viewed the subject in a different light. Therefore, Secretary of State Buchanan in his instruction to Mr. Marston, dated October 21, 1848, admitted that the Government of the United States had, from its origin, always recognized *de facto* governments as soon as they had clearly manifested their ability to maintain their independence, and that it did not go behind the existing government to involve itself in the question of legitimacy. However, Mr. Buchanan warned the consul that this act of high sovereign power certainly could not, without instructions, be performed by a consul, whose functions were purely commercial; and he ought never, under any conceivable circumstances, to assume such a serious responsibility.

"The President," continued Mr. Buchanan, "has no desire to delay the recognition of the independence of the Sicilian Government on the part of the United States a single moment beyond the time when this acknowledgment can be made in conformity with our uniform practice, since the origin of the Government. On the contrary, we can never be indifferent spectators to the progress of liberty throughout the world; and we acknowledge, in the fullest manner, the rights of all nations to create and reform their political institutions according to their own will and pleasure."[16]

The revolution was eventually put down, and despotism ruled again in the Kingdom of the Two Sicilies. The American people viewed with scorn the persecution and suffering to which liberty-loving Neapolitans and Sicilians were subjected by the arbitrary rule that followed the failure of the revolutionary outbreaks of 1848. Americans were horrified to learn that the islands in the Bay of Naples, as well as the prisons and galley-hulks in the Kingdom — as a result of a system of military terror — were filled with political prisoners, and that new arrests, without pretext or provocation, were being made daily on suspicion for participating in the revolution of 1848. Returning American visitors and newspaper correspondents told of hundreds of men of refined, intellectual tastes and of high position who were laboring in the galleys side by side with the most infamous and abandoned criminals. Encouraged by the example set by William E. Gladstone,[17] the English statesman, a number of distinguished

---

16 James Buchanan, *Works,* VIII, 234-236.

17 Mr. Gladstone had been so profoundly impressed by the pitiable plight of the political prisoners of Naples that, on his return to England, he published two letters which he addressed to Lord Aberdeen, the head of the British Government, in which, among other things, he declared that "the conduct of the Bourbon Government was a permanent outrage to religion, civilization, humanity, and public

Americans visiting Italy in 1851, among them Professor Benjamin Silliman, of New Haven, and Mr. John Van Schaick Lansing Pruyn, a famous lawyer of Albany, New York, addressed a communication to the State Department at Washington, in which they stated that they had discovered in Naples acts of such barbarous tyranny that they could not "live and let such things be." The State Department, of course, sympathized with the Neapolitans, but following its old settled policy of non-interference in the domestic affairs of other countries, it replied that it could not do anything to bring about an improvement in the situation.[18]

Officially the two governments continued to show mutual marked respect and a desire for the prosperity and happiness of their respective subjects. In fact, when on April 4, 1850 Edward Joy Morris was received by Giustino Fortunato, the Minister of Foreign Affairs, in order that the new chargé might present his letter of credence as American chargé d'affaires, he [Mr. Morris] was welcomed in the most cordial and courteous manner. In accordance with the customary diplomatic language between two friendly countries, Mr. Morris assured the Foreign Minister of "the President's earnest desire to maintain the existing relations of friendship between the two countries, and also manifesting the interest taken by the American Republic in the prosperity of the Kingdom of the Two Sicilies."

In 1850, on the occasion of the celebration of the Fourth of July, in Naples, the salutes of the Frigate *St. Lawrence* were responded to not only by the French and Spanish navies, but also by the Neapolitan battery on the Molo head. Mr. Morris regarded this complimentary salvo as a marked act of courtesy, especially as no salute was fired from the shore in connection with the celebration that had been held to commemorate the anniversary of the proclamation of the French Republic in the month of February of the same year, although it was celebrated by the French squadron in the Bay of Naples. Another instance of friendly feelings toward the United States occurred on January 12, 1852, His Majesty's birthday. On this occasion the King went out of his way, in the presence of the largest court circle of the year, to address to Mr. Morris "the most earnest complimentary remarks to the people and government of the North American Republic."

decency." See: W. E. Gladstone, *Two letters to the Earl of Aberdeen on the state of persecutions of the Neapolitan Government.* 1st American from the 5th London edition. New York: J. S. Nichols, 1851.

[18] Crittenden to Pruyn, Oct. 8, 1851. Original MS in files of United States State Department.

One may well doubt the sincerity of these diplomatic courtesies, when it is remembered that Mr. Morris, realizing the disturbed state of the political conditions of the Kingdom, deemed it prudent to address a note to Commodore Charles W. Morgan, the Commander of the American Mediterranean Squadron, urging him to remain in the Mediterranean to protect American interests.

Furthermore, the American people continued to show their dislike of the Neapolitan Government. Their indignation became strong especially when it was learned that the government authorities were subjecting American travellers to no end of annoyances. In fact, these annoyances became so frequent that Mr. Morris was compelled to send an official protest to the Minister of Foreign Affairs. As a result of Mr. Morris' efforts, a change was effected in the Neapolitan quarantine system, which the authorities had been accustomed to abuse for political purposes. Thereafter, however, American citizens were no longer detained on board steamers upon their arrival at Naples at the caprice of a dishonest police.

On August 25, 1853, Mr. Morris presented his letter of recall through Mr. Hammett, the United States Consul, because he himself was physically incapable, in consequence of a most violent attack of fever and existing prostration therefrom. In retiring from the mission which he had had the honor to occupy for nearly four years, Mr. Morris, acting on instructions from the Department of State, expressed to Mr. Carafa, the Minister of Foreign Affairs, the most friendly sentiments entertained by the "President for the Government of the Two Sicilies and of his desire to preserve and improve the relations of harmony so happily subsisting between the two countries." Mr. Morris tendered Mr. Carafa his most grateful appreciation of the personal courtesies with which he had been honored and of the just and honorable spirit he had always manifested in the official relations he had had the honor to hold with him.

However, as soon as Mr. Morris resigned his commission in 1853, the Neapolitan Government renewed its insults to America. The case of Mr. James Carbone, a Sicilian by birth, but a naturalized citizen of the United States, was a case in point. Mr. Carbone went to visit his native island in 1853; upon landing, he was immediately seized and imprisoned on the accusation of being there for the purpose of concerting with those inimical to the government. Upon representation made by the United States Consul, the police explained that Mr. Carbone had not been allowed to land at Messina, because he had taken part in political disturbances at a former period. The Consul proved that Mr. Carbone was in America at the time indicated, and that the charge consequently was fictitious. The Consul, moreover, offered to be a guarantee for Mr. Carbone while he transacted his necessary mercantile business at Messina, but without effect. Even the requests of the American chargé d'affaires, Mr. Robert Dale Owen, for the man's liberation, proved ineffectual; his communications to the Government remained unanswered. But the opportune arrival of the United States steam frigate *Saranac* in the Bay of Naples put an entirely new face upon the matter. Mr. Carbone was then released.

But no sooner was this case settled, than the United States was again the subject of another attack. On or about February 6, 1854, the arms of the American nation, exhibited at the United States Vice Consulate in Girgenti, Sicily, were maliciously defaced by some unidentified Sicilians. In spite of all the representations made to the Girgentian authorities on the part of Mr. Gotthiel, the United States Vice Consul at that place, no effort was made to repair this wrong. Mr. Julius C. Kretschmar, the American Consul at Palermo, took the matter in hand with Prince Satriano, Lieutenant General of His Sicilian Majesty. The correspondence between the American Consul and Prince Satriano, which was published in American newspapers, showed that with the exception of the punishment of the offenders, whom His Excellency stated the strictest search on the part of the police had failed to discover, the fullest reparation was made for the outrage.[19]

In spite of these annoyances and of the general disapproval in which the Neapolitan Government was held in America because of its treatment of political prisoners and of foreigners, the suggestion was made in 1854, that the United States send a full mission to Naples.[20] It was pointed out that more than three

---

19 New York *Herald,* Apr. 22, 1854.

20 The question of raising the rank of the United States minister at Naples was first brought up by President Fillmore in June 1850 during the ceremony at which Mr. Martuscelli, already the Chargé of the Two Sicilies, presented his credentials accrediting him as the representative of the Duke of Parma in this country. According to Mr. Martuscelli, at the end of the formal ceremonies, President Fillmore invited the chargé d'affaires to sit next to him. In the course of a friendly conversation on Italy and its various states, the President stated that since the Kingdom of the Two Sicilies was larger and more important than the other states in the peninsula, it should be represented in this country in a manner more commensurate to its dignity and importance. This it could do by establishing a full mission in the United States. The President added that, at his suggestion, certain members of his cabinet had discussed the matter informally with the Senate, but on account of party opposition these discussions had been discontinued. Not knowing what the position of his government was on this subject, Mr. Martuscelli

hundred American ships visited the Two Sicilies every year, and that hundreds of American travelers were to be counted all over Italy. Such facts created a great amount of work and imposed many duties, all of which fell on the chargé d'affaires personally, even to the signing of passports! All the great powers, excepting the United States, had full ministers at Naples; America, on the contrary, sent a chargé d'affaires, with no assistants whatever, not even an attaché. And yet America sent full ministers to Brazil and Chile, which were considered less important than Naples, both from commercial and social points of view. The suggestion was favorably acted upon, and Mr. Owen's title was changed on June 29, 1854, from chargé d'affaires to minister resident.[21]

Immediately upon receipt of the official advice from the Secretary of State Marcy, on August 13, 1854, Mr. Owen informed Commendatore Luigi Carafa dei duchi di Traetto, the Minister of Foreign Affairs, that he had received on that same day a despatch from the Secretary of State of the United States, informing him that the rank of mission at this court had been raised, and that the President of the United States had accredited him as Minister Resident of the United States of America near His Majesty. Mr. Owen asked Commendatore Carafa for an appointment in order to present his new credentials. The presentation ceremony took place on September 20, 1854.

It is of interest to note that the Government of the Two Sicilies did not reciprocate by increasing the rank of its representatives in Washington. In fact, during the absence of Chevalier Martuscelli from his post, the Neapolitan Government appointed J. C. Vertu, who was vice-consul, chargé d'affaires *ad interim*, a position that Mr. Vertu held from February 21, to November 1, 1853. After the death of Chevalier Martuscelli on November 8, 1853, there was no representative from the Neapolitan Government in Washington until the arrival of Baron Winspeare with the rank of chargé d'affaires. The exact date of Baron Winspeare's arrival in Washington is not known; however, the first

---

merely thanked the President for his good sentiments of friendship and for the preference he showed toward the Kingdom of the Two Sicilies, assuring him, at the same time, that his own government reciprocated these sentiments. In bringing these facts to the attention of his foreign minister, Mr. Martuscelli concluded that in the United States the title "minister" had such "a magic power" that very often a minister was willingly granted many concessions which were difficult to obtain by one who held a lower rank. [Martuscelli to Foreign Minister Fortunato, despatch No. 30, New York, June 25, 1850. MS *Archivio di Stato,* Naples.]

21 State Department *Register,* 1874, II, 104.

communication from him was received by the State Department about July 10, 1855.

During the year he held the post of chargé d'affaires, Baron Winspeare continued the negotiations or brought to conclusion two important conventions: the first relative to the rights of neutrals at sea, proclaimed July 16, 1855, and the second of amity, commerce, navigation and extradition, proclaimed December 10, 1856. The first convention, signed by Robert Dale Owen and Luigi Carafa, consisting of four articles, deals with such topics as free ships, free goods; application of principle of article I; accession by other nations; ratification. This convention was superseded by the treaty of 1871 between the United States and the Government of Italy.

The second convention — that of amity, commerce, navigation and extradition — was by far the more important of the two. As the time for the renewal of the treaty of commerce and navigation of December 1, 1845 drew near, Baron Winspeare wrote a despatch[22] to Mr. Carafa in which the chargé outlined certain suggestions which he thought would prove useful to the Neapolitan Minister of Foreign Affairs in the negotiations attending the renewal of the treaty. In the belief that one of the reasons why the Neapolitan merchant marine made infrequent trips to the United States was the want of direct exchanges of the products of the two countries, and the uncertainty of Neapolitan ships having a return cargo for Europe, Baron Winspeare advised Mr. Carafa to try to remedy this condition in the new treaty. Another matter to which Baron Winspeare referred was the clause concerning the arrest and delivery of deserting seamen, which, as stipulated in the 1845 treaty, it was impossible to enforce, so far as Naples was concerned. The Neapolitan chargé d'affaires expressed the hope that he [Carafa] would prevail upon the State Department to ask Congress to assign the power of arrest to the Federal Marshal and not to the municipal authorities of the various states.

The Convention of amity, commerce, navigation and extradition as finally proclaimed on December 10, 1856, consisted of twenty-six articles, embodying the following topics: amity, blockade, contraband, right of travel, exemptions from military service, reciprocal privileges of citizens, property rights, commerce and navigation, character of vessels, discrimination in duties, drawbacks, discrimination in purchase of imports, application of

---

[22] Despatch Winspeare to Carafa, New York, Nov. 12, 1855. MS *Archivio di Stato*, Naples.

foregoing articles, fisheries, discrimination based on nationality of vessels, most favored nation, asylum for vessels, shipwrecks, consuls, settlement of disputes, deserters, extradition of criminals, crimes, how surrender was to be made, political offenses, duration, ratification. This convention, signed by Robert Dale Owen on behalf of the United States Government, and by Luigi Carafa, Principe di Comitini, and Giuseppe Mario Arpino on behalf of the Government of the Two Sicilies, also became obsolete by the consolidation of the Two Sicilies with the Kingdom of Italy in 1861.

It is of interest to note that the amendment advised by the Senate, which was ultimately incorporated in the Convention, permitted citizens of the Kingdom of the Two Sicilies in the United States to remain here free from the despotic sway of their tyrant king.

The commerce between the two countries steadily increased during this period. Achille Ferrer, Consul General of the Two Sicilies in New York, on May 11, 1857,[23] sent to the Foreign Minister in Naples, a report (No. 126), showing the increase in the commerce between the Kingdom of Naples and the United States. He produced statistics for the preceding six years which he obtained from the registers of the commercial house of Chamberlain and Robinson for the entire United States. The statistics showed that for the first quarter of 1856-57 the importations into the United States of the four principal products of the Kingdom of the Two Sicilies exceeded the total importations for the year 1850. The exact figures were:

Importations into the United States from the Kingdom of the Two Sicilies

Year	Cases of oranges	Cases of lemons	Bags of sumach	Cantars[24] of sulphur
1850-51	348,531	119,480	31,109	60,105
1851-52	242,103	164,600	47,987	108,749
1852-53	293,138	151,376	68,479	114,858
1853-54	215,899	155,409	70,089	125,106
1854-55	397,567	229,734	44,944	87,004
1855-56	346,556	209,213	65,906	113,028
1856-57[25]	374,699	212,018	37,639	69,606

Despite the improvement in the commercial relations between the two countries, it cannot be said that the relations between

---

23 MS *Archivio di Stato,* Naples.
24 Equivalent to 150 pounds.
25 First quarter only.

the two governments were cordial during that period, and the suspicious attitude which prevailed in the Two Sicilies is proven by the fact that the Neapolitan consuls in other parts of Italy were deprived of the right to visé or issue passports to the United States. During the Garibaldian expedition to Sicily in 1860, the sympathies of the American people were overwhelmingly in favor of the Italian patriot who was claimed everywhere in the United States as "the Washington of Italy." Interpreting the sentiments of the American people, the sympathies of Mr. Chandler, then American minister at Naples, were decidedly in favor of the revolution.

The only unpleasant incident during the campaign for the liberation of Sicily was attributed to Mr. H. H. Barstow, the American Consul at Palermo, who used his influence, in a marked manner, in favor of the despotic King. It was even suspected that Mr. Barstow had pocketed a few hundred pounds of Neapolitan gold. A letter from the Palermo correspondent of the New York Herald,[26] dated April 26, 1860, described the conduct of the American consul during this period. The correspondent said that Mr. Barstow had neither decision, resolution, nor an appreciation of the dignity and rights of the United States, which, as its representative in a foreign country, it was his duty to assert and maintain. Mr. Barstow was in fact recalled in August 1861; he was replaced by Luigi Monti, Professor of Italian at Harvard University.

In the United States, Mr. Pasquale Massone, the Neapolitan chargé, was subjected to all kinds of abuses and ill-treatment from Italian and other residents. On one occasion he was forced to seek the protection of the police to prevent a projected demonstration against him. To avoid disorder, and at the suggestion of the police, Mr. Massone left Washington for several days, seeking refuge in Philadelphia.[27]

After the liberation of the Kingdom of the Two Sicilies by the Garibaldian forces, Mr. Chandler on November 17, 1860, notified Mr. John M. Daniel, then United States Minister at the Court of Turin, that in consequence of the political changes in the south of Italy, he had closed the mission submitted to his care. He added that he had sealed the archives of the legation and placed them in the hands of Mr. Hammett, the Consul in that city. Upon the receipt of this letter, Mr. Daniel forwarded a

26 New York *Herald,* May 24, 31, 1860.
27 Massone to Carafa, No. 83, Washington, June 13, 1860. MS *Archivio di Stato,* Naples.

copy to Secretary of State Cass, adding that Mr. Chandler was awaiting the final instructions of the Department at Paris.

Meanwhile, Duke Giuseppe Anfora, the Neapolitan Consul in New York, on November 26, 1860, informed the Minister of Foreign Affairs of Naples, that whereas the "glorious government of Victor Emmanuel II founded on universal suffrage, had legally established itself in the Kingdom," he had deemed it his duty to give his support to the new government, thereby recognizing the existent new order. At the same time Duke Anfora informed his former chief that he had addressed a communication to the royal chargé d'affaires of Sardinia and that he had forwarded to him his oath of allegiance and other legal documents. The Duke made it clear that during the recent political disturbances in the Two Sicilies, the consulate under his charge had functioned without any interruption in the conduct of its affairs, but that from the date of his letter the affairs of the consulate would be placed under the direction of the chargé d'affaires of Sardinia on whom he would depend until the proper authorities should decide otherwise.

In this manner the official diplomatic relations between the United States and the Two Sicilies were terminated. In 1865. the books and archives belonging to the United States Legation at Naples were transferred, upon instructions from the State Department, to the United States Consul General at Florence.[28] In recent years, they were deposited with the National Archives in Washington, D. C.

THE DUCHY OF PARMA

With the duchies of central Italy, the United States did not formally maintain diplomatic relations. However, in June 1850, the Duke of Parma, with the consent of the Government of the Two Sicilies, appointed Mr. Martuscelli, who was the chargé d'affaires of the Two Sicilies at Washington, as his representative in this country. Accordingly, toward the end of June 1850, Mr. Martuscelli went to Washington to present his new credentials.

Upon his return from Washington, Mr. Martuscelli addressed a despatch dated New York, June 25, 1850,[29] to Chevalier

28 T. Bigelow Lawrence (Florence) to Hugh Darley, United States Acting Vice Consul at Naples, dated Sept. 26, 1865. MS archives American consulate, Florence. (Records now in U. S. National Archives).
29 MS *Archivio di Stato*, Naples.

Fornacchia in charge of the foreign office of Parma, in which he gave a brief account of the ceremony held in connection with the presentation of his credentials as representative of the Duke of Parma in this country. Mr. Martuscelli expressed the hope that he would be able to initiate matters which would result to the advantage of both countries. He also hoped to avoid misunderstandings during difficult times, especially, he said, "with a government where often party spirit not only dictated the law, but led it from the path which under favorable circumstances it would willingly pursue."

The following is the text of the address Mr. Martuscelli delivered to the President of the United States during the official ceremonies:

"The relations of amity and commerce which are daily increasing between the different states of Italy and America have induced H. R. H. the Duke of Parma, with my august Sovereign's consent, to honor me with the pleasing mission to establish and to cultivate similar relations of amity with the United States and directly to attend to the interests of his subjects. In this determination you will easily perceive, Sir, the esteem in which H. R. H. holds your character and his regard towards the United States. I will endeavor Mr. President to merit in this new capacity the same kindness which I have for many years experienced from this government as chargé d'affaires of His Sicilian Majesty."

To this the President replied:

Sir:

I am gratified to receive the friendly assurances which you have conveyed on the part of H. R. H. the Duke of Parma, and the manifestation of his desire to cultivate the relations of amity with the United States. Those sentiments are cordially reciprocated by this government and it is a cause of special satisfaction that H. R. H. has selected to represent his government and to attend to the interest of his subjects in this country a gentleman so long and so favorably known as chargé d'affaires of the King of the Two Sicilies.[30]

After the death of Mr. Martuscelli in 1853, it appears that the interests of the Duchy of Parma in the United States were represented by the Minister Resident from Spain. On June 20, 1853, Secretary of State William L. Marcy addressed a note to Don Angel Calderón de la Barca, Minister Resident from Spain, stating that the President would receive him on the following day for the ceremony of presentation of his credentials as Envoy

---

[30] Enclosed with Mr. Martuscelli's despatch of June 25, 1850. MS *Archivio di Stato,* Naples.

Extraordinary and Minister Plenipotentiary of the Duke of Parma.[31]

On January 24, 1853, President Franklin Pierce signed the exequatur of Don Giovacchino Marco di Sastrustegui as Consul of Parma for the State of California, resident at San Francisco. It appears that the ministers of Spain represented Parma in the United States up to the incorporation of that Duchy in Piedmont-Sardinia in 1859.[32]

No record has been found of American representation in Parma.

GRAND DUCHY OF TUSCANY

While no diplomatic relations were ever established between the United States Government and the Government of the Grand Duchy of Tuscany, several efforts were made, during and for many years after the American Revolution, to effect these relations. On May 7, 1777, the Continental Congress elected Ralph Izard,[33] who was at the moment in Paris, as Commissioner to the Court of the Grand Duke of Tuscany and was commissioned as such by that body on July 1, 1777.[34] The choice had been a fortunate one, for Izard was one of the very few Americans who in those days had ever visited Italy. In 1774 his passion for music and painting had caused him unofficially to visit the country. Endowed with a keen political mind, Izard thought that the small Italian states bordering on the Mediterranean would willingly lend money to the American colonies in their war against England, for the defeat of England would enable the Italians to free themselves more readily from the English supremacy in the Mediterranean.

To an unidentified friend at Aix-la-Chapelle, Izard wrote a letter dated Paris, September 26, 1777, in which he mentioned the honor he had received from Congress by appointing him one of

31 *Notes to Spain,* (manuscript volume in U. S. National Archives), VI, 329.
32 *Notes to Spain,* volume 7, pp. 24, 78, and 103. See J. A. R. Marriott, *The Makers of Modern Italy.* (Oxford, The Clarendon Press, 1931, p. 110).
33 Ralph Izard (1741-1804), revolutionary patriot, diplomat, senator, was born near Charleston, S. C. See Jared Sparks (editor), *The diplomatic correspondence of the American Revolution. Being the letters of Ralph Izard.* (Boston, 1829). *Correspondence of Mr. Ralph Izard of South Carolina from the year 1774-1804; with a short memoir.* Vol. I. (New York, 1844). (Volume 2 was never published). *Register of the Department of State,* 1937, p. 336. F. Wharton, *The revolutionary correspondence of the United States.* 1889, (6 vols.). Vol. I, par. 97a, p. 178-179.
34 Ralph Izard did not visit Tuscany (officially) and was recalled June 8, 1779. United States Department of State, *Register,* 1874, II, 57.

their commissioners in that part of the world, adding: "I shall go to Florence, as soon as I understand that anybody from America . . . in a public character . . . will be admitted there . . . which at present . . . will certainly not be the case."[35]

To Henry Laurens,[36] Mr. Izard wrote a letter from Paris, dated October 6, 1777, in which he stated:

I flatter myself, I may be of more service here — than I could be in America. A very advantageous connexion may unquestionably be formed, between us — and the commercial parts of Italy. It is very much their interest to promote the success of our cause.

The King of Naples — and the Pope — I know are both exceedingly alarmed, in time of war — whenever an English Squadron is in the Mediterranean — one for his Capital — and the other for Civita Vecchia. They would, therefore, wish this formidable Naval Power to be a little humbled — and possibly — if they could be persuaded to think that lending a few Sequins would contribute to such an event — a Loan might be negotiated.

I have written to the Committee of Foreign Affairs, on this subject — and if the proposition meets with your approbation — and that of your Colleagues, from Charlestown — I hope it will have your support . . .[37]

To Robert Morris, Chairman of the Committee for Foreign Affairs, Mr. Izard also wrote a letter from Paris, dated October 6, 1777, in which he stated that the powers of Europe seemed to be waiting for the determination of the Court of Versailles, respecting the acknowledgment of the independence of America. With reference to Italy, Mr. Izard added:

It is very much the interest of most of the powers of Italy — that the strength of the British Navy should be lessened. Some of their Ports — particularly those of Naples, and Civitta [sic] Vecchia — have been frequently insulted — and all of them are liable to be so — by a Nation, not remarkable for its moderation.

I think therefore — that they must be disposed to afford assistance to the States of America — privately — either by subsidy, or loan. Congress will be pleased to honor me with their Instructions on this point; and in the mean time, I shall endeavour to procure every information on the subject in my power. Should the proposition be approved of — they will furnish me with proper powers. If I should be so fortunate as to

---

[35] Ralph Izard, *Correspondence* etc., 346-347.
[36] Henry Laurens, (1724-92). American patriot, born in Charleston, S. C. In 1780 he was sent to Holland to negotiate a loan, but was captured en route by a British vessel; and, in 1780-81, was imprisoned in the Tower, London, where he was treated with considerable severity. Subsequently he was one of the American peace commissioners in Paris, and signed the preliminary treaty (November, 1782).
[37] Ralph Izard, *Correspondence* etc., 350-351.

succeed in procuring money — I should be glad to know how it should be disposed of — whether in the purchase of such articles, as are wanted, or remitted in specie . . .[38]

On February 4, 1778, Mr. Izard was authorized to proceed to Tuscany in order to contract with the Grand Duke a loan of one million dollars. Mr. Izard's appointment was fruitless, for despite the Grand Duke's secret sympathies on behalf of the American Colonies, Leopold did not dare to act in any way that might have displeased England. This fact explains not only why the Grand Duke never recognized the right of the Colonies to secede, but also his refusal to receive Mr. Izard, who, having been fore-warned by Mr. Niccoli, the chargé d'affaires of the Grand Duke in Paris, determined not to proceed to Florence at all. For this reason, on June 8, 1779, Congress terminated Mr. Izard's mission.[39] However, during the negotiations, Mr. Izard kept up a regular correspondence with Mr. Niccoli, as a result of which he was in a position to transmit useful information to the American Congress.

Even before the official termination of Mr. Izard's mission, the Government of Virginia took the necessary steps to renew the efforts of Americans to establish official relations with Tuscany. In January 1779 Philip Mazzei was commissioned by Governor Patrick Henry and the Virginia Council to proceed to his native Tuscany in order to obtain a loan of gold and silver, not exceeding £900,000, and to purchase goods in Italy for the use of the state troops. Although Mazzei remained abroad more than four years, his mission was rendered fruitless as a result of numerous unexpected and what proved to be insurmountable obstacles over which he had no control.[40]

Soon after the close of the Revolution, another effort was made to open diplomatic relations with Tuscany. On September 30, 1784, from Passy, near Paris, John Adams, Benjamin Franklin, and Thomas Jefferson, acting as ministers plenipotentiary, addressed a communication to Francesco Favi, the chargé d'affaires

38 Ralph Izard, *Correspondence*, etc., 354-55.
39 Instructions to Commissioner to Tuscany. Commission Foreign Affairs. Phila., July 1, 1777. *Secret Journals of Congress.* v. 2, p. 52-54; Giuseppe Prezzolini, *Come gli Americani scoprirono l'Italia:1750-1850.* (Milan, 1933), 34, 38-39.
40 For a full account of Mazzei's mission, see: Howard R. Marraro (editor) *Philip Mazzei: Virginia's agent in Europe, The story of his mission as related in his own dispatches and other documents.* (N. Y. 1935), 106 pp.; Howard R. Marraro, "Mazzei's correspondence with the Grand Duke of Tuscany during his American mission." *William and Mary College Quarterly Historical Magazine*, Williamsburg, Va., July 1942, XXII, 361-380. In his *Memoirs* (Columbia University Press, 1942), Mazzei refers extensively to his mission in Europe on behalf of his adopted country.

of the Grand Duke of Tuscany in Paris, in which they informed the Italian that they had been empowered by Congress "to confer, treat, and negotiate with the ambassador, minister or commissioner of the Most Serene Grand Duke of Tuscany," of and concerning a treaty of amity and commerce, "to make and receive propositions for such treaty and to conclude and sign the same transmitting it to the said United States in Congress assembled for their final ratification."[41]

Mr. Favi transmitted the original letter of the American commissioners to the Secretary of State of Tuscany. In an accompanying despatch, dated Paris, October 11, 1784,[42] Mr. Favi pointed out that the American ministers had first sent a similar invitation to the Austrian ambassador in Paris, that the court of Vienna had accepted their propositions, and that negotiations for a treaty of commerce between Austria and the United States were to be held in Bruxelles.[43]

On October 29, 1784,[44] Mr. Favi was notified by his government that His Royal Highness was favorable to the proposed convention and that he [Mr. Favi] was to obtain from the American ministers an exact outline of the plan so that it could be submitted to the consideration of His Royal Highness. Meanwhile, the Tuscan Government asked the fiscal auditor Pierallini to submit his observations and recommendations on the subject.[45] In accordance with a report submitted by Pierallini on November 26, 1784,[46] Mr. Favi was instructed to notify the American ministers that Tuscany could not grant the United States in the free port of Leghorn any more than it accorded to all other friendly nations provided, moreover, that the same privileges were granted to Tuscany in the ports of the United States.

In December 1784, the three American commissioners sent to

---

41 MS *Archivio di Stato,* Florence.

42 MS *Archivio di Stato,* Florence.

43 In May 1777, William Lee, of Virginia, was appointed a commissioner to the courts of Vienna and Berlin. He was not received by the emperor, the court of Vienna positively refusing to have anything to do with the revolted colonies; nor does it appear that he was allowed to hold an official station at Berlin. The first treaty with Prussia was that of 1785 negotiated on the part of America by Messrs. Franklin, Jefferson, and Adams, and on the part of Prussia by M. de Thulemeyer. Theodore Lyman, *The diplomacy of the United States. Being an account of the foreign relations of the country from the first treaty with France, in 1778, to the treaty of Ghent in 1814, with Great Britain.* (Boston, 1826), 379 pp. The negotiations with Austria also failed, for the first treaty of commerce and navigation between the United States and Austria-Hungary was not concluded until August 27, 1829. See, Miller, *op. cit.,* III, 507-522.

44 MS *Archivio di Stato,* Florence .

45 MS Letter to His Royal Highness from Count Vincenzo degli Alberti and Riguccio Galluzzi, dated Florence Nov. 20, 1784. MS *Archivio di Stato,* Florence.

46 MS *Archivio di Stato,* Florence.

Mr. Favi a plan of the proposed treaty of amity and commerce which they were ready to sign if it met with the approbation of the court of Tuscany. Expressing the hope that the treaty was founded on those principles of equal right which "are the surest guardians of every treaty, and calculated to promote the interests of humanity in general," the three commissioners expressed their readiness to examine any amendments which the Tuscany Government saw fit to propose and they concurred "cheerfully in accommodating it more perfectly to the true interests of commerce and happiness of the two nations, well knowing that we cannot better gratify the wishes of our Constituents & the respect which they entertain for His Royal Highness than by opening a liberal & friendly intercourse between His Subjects and them."[47]

In transmitting the proposed plan to the Secretary of State of Tuscany, Mr. Favi, in a letter dated December 27, 1784, stated that having forewarned the American commissioners that Tuscany could not grant to the citizens of the United States more than what it accorded in the port of Leghorn to other friendly nations, they had replied that they did not desire for more and that Tuscany would receive the same privileges in the ports of the United States.[48]

On January 17, 1785, the Secretary of State of Tuscany submitted the proposed treaty to the attention and consideration of Count Federico Barbolani di Montanto, the Governor of Leghorn.[49]

At this point the negotiations were interrupted for reasons that are unknown, as a result of which the treaty was never concluded.

The next important step in the relations between the United States and the Grand Duchy of Tuscany was the establishment in 1794 of an American consulate to protect what was described as the "considerable" commercial interests of the United States in that area. Philip Felicchi,[50] an Italian by birth, was appointed consul at Leghorn on December 10, 1794.[51] He was superseded, in February 1798, by Thomas Appleton, of Massachusetts, who held the post to his death in 1840. At various times during the Napoleonic era in Italy from 1800 to 1815, Tuscany was under different sovereignties and controls, including its status as the puppet kingdom of Etruria under the Duke of Parma; as a for-

---

[47] MS *Archivio di Stato*, Florence.
[48] MS *Archivio di Stato*, Florence.
[49] MS *Archivio Cittadino*, Leghorn. *Lettere Civili anno 1785 Filza No. 30.*
[50] The name is also spelled Filiechy.
[51] Personnel records of the U. S. Department of State.

mally annexed part of the French Empire; and as a grand duchy under French control. During the subjugation of Italy by the Napoleonic forces, Mr. Appleton frequently sent despatches to the Secretary of State in Washington in which he gave precise and detailed accounts of the political and military situation in the peninsula and its effects on the commerce of the United States. In his despatches Mr. Appleton displayed a keen judgment, showing that he was an accurate observer of the events that transpired before him.

Although Philip Mazzei never held any official post during the years of his retirement in Pisa, Italy, still in his letters to Jefferson he frequently gave accounts of important incidents affecting Commodore Rogers and other American officers in Italy, advising him to make changes in the consular and diplomatic appointments in the Mediterranean area for the good of the service.[52]

After the fall of Napoleon and the restoration of the Grand Duke to his throne in Tuscany, President James Madison, on November 20, 1815, offered the Grand Duke his congratulations "on his safe return and the assurances of his high esteem."[53]

A few years later, on May 15, 1819, an American consular agency was established in Florence. The first officer of whom there is any record is James Ombrosi who acted as vice consular agent under the jurisdiction of the American consulate at Leghorn from 1819 to 1824, when his duties ceased owing to the refusal of the Government of Tuscany to allow the exercise of consular acts in Florence. However, on May 17, 1825, this difficulty was apparently overcome, for an instruction of that date from the Department of State was addressed to Mr. Ombrosi as "Consul of the United States at Florence."[54]

In 1834 the Government of Tuscany again refused to acknowledge Mr. James Ombrosi as consul of the United States at Florence. Therefore, in a letter dated Washington, March 15, 1834,[55] Louis McLane in informing Mr. Ombrosi that the President had thought proper to revoke his commission, requested him to forward that instrument to consul Thomas Appleton, who,

---

[52] See Howard R. Marraro (editor), Unpublished Mazzei Letters to Jefferson. *The William and Mary Quarterly*, Williamsburg, Va., Oct. 1944, I, 374-396.
[53] MS *Archivio di Stato*, Florence. (*Carteggio di S. A. I. e R. cogli Stati Uniti d'America, No. 2198*).
[54] MS Archives American consulate, Florence.
[55] Letter from Louis McLane to Ombrosi, Wash., D. C., March 15, 1834. MS Archives American consulate, Florence.

at the same time, was instructed to receive and to transmit it to the Department of State in Washington. As to any papers, books, or other property belonging to the consulate, Mr. Ombrosi was instructed to hold them subject to the directions of Mr. Appleton, who, in turn, would receive instructions from the Government on the subject.

It is not known when or under what circumstances Mr. Ombrosi was again re-instated as a consular officer. The fact is that the last instruction to him from John M. Clayton, Secretary of State, dated May 24, 1849,[56] Mr. Ombrosi was addressed as "Acting United States Consul, Florence." An instruction dated April 12, 1838,[57] is interesting in that it informed Mr. Ombrosi that his commission had been revoked by the President four years previously, although it does not appear that the Consul allowed this fact to interfere with his consular functions.

The reason for the termination of Mr. Ombrosi's connection with the consulate is unknown. Under date of June 16, 1849, however, the State Department addressed an instruction to Edward Gamage as "consul of the United States at Florence and Leghorn." This combination of the two consulates apparently continued until the appointment of Francis Lance as commercial agent at Florence on September 2, 1852.[58]

It is interesting to note that in notifying Mr. Amasa Hewins of his appointment as "Commercial agent of the United States at Florence," Mr. W. L. Marcy, the Secretary of State, in a letter dated Washington, August 16, 1854,[59] informed him that the Tuscan Government recognized only diplomatic agents at the capital, and that the Department of State had received no intimation of its disposition to change this system by admitting consuls or commercial agents. Mr. Marcy pointed out that the duties of a commercial agent were similar to those of a consul, and the same instructions were given to each, yet he did not, like the latter, bear a commission from the Government which was given only under the seal of the United States. Mr. Marcy explained that a commercial agent was a mere executive agent, sent abroad for the promotion and advantage of American commercial interests, selected by the Department, corresponding with, instructed and controlled by it, and bearing an authority from

---

[56] MS Archives American consulate, Florence.
[57] MS Archives American consulate, Florence.
[58] MS Archives American consulate, Florence.
[59] MS Archives American consulate, Florence.

the President under the seal of the Department. His recognition by the local authorities, where he resided, although always important as affording facilities in the performance of his duties, was not necessary to it. In some instances these agencies were conferred upon persons who were directed to keep secret the trust confided to them; these appointments did not necessarily carry with them a recognition on the part of the government of existing authority at the places to which they were made. "The proper course for you to observe as commercial agent," concluded Mr. Marcy, "will be under the laws of your country to confine your official duties to such as relate solely to it and its citizens, and in this field to act in the capacity conferred by your certificate of appointment."

In a letter dated Bordeaux, February 5, 1855,[60] Giuseppe Provenzal, Tuscan consul at that city, notified His Excellency the Duke of Casigliano, the Minister of Foreign Affairs in Florence, that Mr. L. Knowles Bowen, an intimate friend of the United States and, at the time, United States consul in Bordeaux, with whom he was tied by bonds of close friendship, had begged him to ask the Foreign Minister whether he thought it advisable to negotiate a treaty of commerce and navigation between the Government of Tuscany and the United States Government, on the same basis as that which had been concluded between the United States and Sardinia in 1839 or between the United States and the Kingdom of the Two Sicilies in 1845. If the Tuscan Foreign Minister was favorable to this suggestion, Mr. Provenzal begged the honor to have the negotiations entrusted to him. Mr. Provenzal suggested the inclusion in the proposed treaty of a clause that would not only make it illegal for captains of American war ships to receive deserters on board these ships, but that would also oblige them to surrender these deserters to the proper authorities at once. Mr. Provenzal pointed out that the improvements made in the new port of Leghorn would undoubtedly stimulate the maritime movement in that port and would result to the advantage of the commerce of the Grand Duchy. He added that treaties with foreign countries were indispensable to the maritime and commercial prosperity of Tuscany. A notation on the margin of Mr. Provenzal's letter indicated the nature of the reply he received from the Minister of Foreign Affairs. Mr. Provenzal was instructed that

---

[60] MS *Archivio di Stato*, Florence, *Filza Estera 2554*,

the Tuscan Government usually did not reply to similar over-tures except when they were made through regular diplomatic channels.

On October 22, 1858,[61] General E. J. Mallett notified H. E. Ottavio Lenzoni, Minister of Foreign Affairs, of his arrival in Florence under appointment from the Secretary of State to reside in that city, for the purpose of performing such consular duties as were limited by his appointment and doing such consular acts as did not conflict with the laws and usage of the Tuscan Gov-ernment. In a reply dated Florence, October 23, 1858,[62] H. E. Lenzoni notified General Mallett that these same Tuscan laws and customs were opposed, and had been invariably opposed, to the residing in Florence of consular agents, the capital being exclusively intended for the residence of diplomatic agents. In consequence, H. E. Lenzoni was obliged to decline *the official* intercourse which General Mallett had proposed, although he considered himself always honored by any private and personal intercourse "which I may have the opportunity of holding with you."

Fearing that Minister Lenzoni had misinterpreted his letter of October 22, 1858, General Mallett wrote to him again on Octo-ber 25, 1858.[63] In this letter General Mallett stated that he was fully aware that it was not the usage of the Tuscan minister to grant an exequatur to consuls, except in some peculiar emergency. Since no such emergency existed in the case in question, General Mallett wished to assure the Foreign Minister that nothing was more remote than even to intimate that diplomatic recognition was asked or expected by him. "I cannot but think, however," continued General Mallet, "it is a *non sequitur* that because an exequatur cannot be consistently conceded to a consul, that he should be interdicted in the discharge of such consular acts as are purely commercial; and which are confined to the citizens and the institutions of his own country." General Mallett pointed out that an examination of the archives of his office revealed that an officer of similar grade with himself had performed such consular acts (as were purely commercial) in Florence, up to the period of his death, which had occurred about two years previously. Assuming that a like courtesy could be extended to him, in a like capacity, General Mallett solicited an audience

---

[61] MS Archives American consulate, Florence.
[62] MS Archives American consulate, Florence.
[63] MS Archives American consulate, Florence.

with H. E. Lenzoni, "not to request or obtain any diplomatic immunity," but to present himself in person, as he felt both constrained and inclined to do "in respect for an officer of your distinguished merit and position."

In accordance with General Mallett's request, H. E. Lenzoni granted the American consul a personal interview. Accordingly, on October 27, 1858, General Mallett presented himself to the Foreign Minister with the following hitherto unpublished letter:

Florence, October 27, 1858.[64]

H. E. Chev. Grande Croix Octave Lenzoni
Minister of Foreign Affairs

In accordance with your permission I now present myself in person to his Excellency the Minister of Foreign Affairs.

As I am not invested with diplomatic powers, I do not feel entitled (in such capacity) to address myself to your Government and, therefore, I the more highly appreciate the personal privilege you have so courteosuly extended; and in that capacity I beg Your Excellency to receive this communication, and to give it that consideration which the subject matter merits.

As I feel myself amenable to your laws, it will be my steady aim to act in strict conformity therewith; and neither to assume or ask any right or privilege at variance with your institutions.

Your Government may consistently adhere to withhold an exequatur to any diplomat of lower grade than a chargé d'affaires, or minister resident, and the United States Government may not deem that its political relations or commercial intercourse demands a permanent minister here; yet, in my opinion, it should not disturb their friendly intercourse in other international courtesies.

I know this to be the position of the United States with several governments in Europe; but nevertheless it has been found mutually beneficial to open every possible channel for the freedom of commerce and to grant every consistent facility for an interchange of national commodities.

It is my desire to make myself fully acquainted with all the products of your country — agricultural, mechanical, as well as the fine arts — and particularly the classification and value of exports to the United States, and if it is not overstepping my privilege to ask, I will esteem it a personal favour to be informed how such statistics can be procured. Such knowledge will be most welcome to my Government, whether communicated in an official or personal capacity; and reliable information may [result] in mutual benefits.

If as indicated in your note of the 22nd inst., it is irreconcilable for you to take positive cognizance of my official acts, allow me to assume the negative, and enquire if I would be interdicted in the following acts: 1) to open an office as United States Commercial Agent and to

---

[64] MS Archives American consulate, Florence.

give a newspaper advertisement thereof or publish a card? 2) to administer an oath, or take an affidavit to be used in the United States? 3) to administer on the estate of Americans who should die here intestate? 4) to visa an American passport? 5) to certify to invoices of goods, wares and merchandise exported to the United States?

There would seem to be a necessity for the last, based on the requisition of our revenue system, and in order that you may see the force of it I enclose you a circular from the Secretary of the Treasury and ask your notice to that part marked by me in parenthesis (See Consular regulations, page 79, Sec. 173). An adherence to such a course (apart from the requisition) would obviously contribute both to the convenience and economy of the shippers, who are mostly your own subjects, because, when a case of goods is prepared for shipment, to break the fastenings carries damage and delay, and this must be done after it reaches Leghorn, or the owner must accompany it, and thus consume time and money which a verification here would save.

(Signed) E. J. Mallett.

Meanwhile, General Mallett had requested the State Department to include the cost of a flag and a coat of arms in his account with this Department. In a reply dated Washington, November 13, 1858,[65] John Appleton, Assistant Secretary of State, informed General Mallett that since the Government of the Grand Duke had repeatedly declined to recognize a consular officer at Florence, and since he himself was without any official recognition by the Tuscan Government, the State Department did not consider it expedient, under all the circumstances, to affix the consular arms to his place of residence or needlessly display from it the national flag. Therefore, their cost was not allowed.

Even before the receipt of Mr. Appleton's letter, General Mallett in the following unpublished despatch No. 9, dated Florence, November 27, 1858, gave Secretary of State Lewis Cass a detailed account of the result of the personal interview he had had with the Tuscan Foreign Minister.

Despatch No. 9   Florence, November 27, 1858.[66]

Honorable Lewis Cass,
Secretary of State,
Washington, D. C.

Dear Sir:

I proceed in connection with my despatch No. 5 of the 11th inst.
The Minister of State is about 55 years of age, a man of uncommonly

---

[65] MS Archives American consulate, Florence.
[66] MS Archives American consulate, Florence.

fine personal appearance, most agreeably courteous, of excellent colloquial powers, and I should judge of high intellectual cultivation.

He declined to recognize me officially; but read the letter I handed to him, and went into an explanation, during which he evinced the highest consideration for our Government.

It seems that England, France, and Austria have full ministers here, and Prussia, Sardinia, Saxony, Naples, and Rome have ministers resident.

An exequatur is granted only to diplomats of the above ranks. Hence, even a consul general would not be recognized unless specially invested by his Government with *diplomatic* powers. Recognition requires executive action, and is tantamount to an exequatur, and would place a consul general or a consul on a court equality with ministers which is irreconcilable to European etiquette or usage.

On reference to my Despatch No. 5, you will perceive I made no request or effort for an exequatur and I think the explanation was made to allay any apprehensions I might have that the court usage applied to me, as coming from a Republican Government.

In our interview, no allusion was made to any other obstacle. The Minister merely said: if the President found it agreeable to invest diplomatic powers in his appointment for Florence, he would receive a courteous welcome here.

I, however, did hear (unofficially) that there was a little feeling in this connection.

Our Government has a Minister resident at Turin, Naples and Rome, embracing all the Italian States but this; which is the very smallest, and the weaker the power, the more sensitive on such considerations.

In reply to the first query (see despatch No. 5) he said objection would be made to the last paragraph: because no such publications were allowed without a government permit — that permission required executive action, and carried with it a *tacit recognition*. To the second he said there was no objection; to the third he said, no objection; unless at the request of some real or pretended party at interest whom on petition the public administrator would supersede me; to the fourth, he applied the same objections as to the first.

To the fifth no objection, but the refusal to allow me to advertise, works a double objection. First, because the shippers cannot know of my presence, and second, not being constrained by their own commercial laws, they will evade our requisition if they can; and I learn from the United States Consul at Leghorn that it is the constant practice there to carry out sometimes as many as 50 invoices in one vessel, and never ask his verification.

This is not only at variance with our Revenue laws (See Sec. 179 of Consular Regulations, page 79) but it opens a wide channel for frauds on arrival at our ports of entry for the appraisers cannot be fully posted; and if they were, could often be deceived.

It will perhaps be better to make this matter the subject of a separate despatch.

(Signed) E. J. Mallett

United States Consular Agent

In his despatch No. 10, dated Florence, December 4, 1858, addressed to the Secretary of State, General Mallett invited the Department of State to consider anew the subject of establishing diplomatic relations with Tuscany. The text of the hitherto unpublished despatch follows:

Despatch No. 10   Florence, December 4, 1858.[67]

Hon. Secretary of State
Washington, D. C.

Dear Sir:

I do not find in the archives of this office any treaty of commerce, or otherwise in relation to the Tuscan Government. I find nothing to guide me in relation to our commercial intercourse with this Government, and nothing in relation to any other Government of a later date than the year 1853. The limited powers of my appointment leaves me remediless as touching the violation of our Revenue system under the Treaty Circular No. 9, September 20, 1853: General Instructions.

If our Government does not view the political and commercial intercourses with Tuscany sufficient to send a Minister resident, with plenary powers, it might ultimate in much mutual benefit to confer special diplomatic powers for purposes specially indicated.

It could be mutually agreed that both governments would extend aid and protection to their respective officers, by which their several laws and edicts could be enforced commercially. Such a remedy could not be applied to the violation reported in Despatch No. 9, dated Nov. 27, 1858, to which I now refer.

There is another very important international concession requiring diplomatic powers to acquire it "the mutual right to arrest and surrender such fugitives from justice as have been conceded by other powers."

For lack of such treaty agreement several of our citizens (and some within my own knowledge) have fled to this country, living luxuriously on the fruits of frauds, remitted secretly to Europe, prior to their own departure.

I believe with some, if not all the Italian States (except Tuscany) we have such treaty agreement.

Hence, this country affords an asylum for men to dwell in palaces; who are more worthy tenants of a prison at home.

As near as I can learn, the number of Americans who annually visit this great school house of ancient and modern art and science for longer or shorter periods reaches nearly 2,000 and the amount of money expended by Americans annually in Rome, Naples and Tuscany exceeds $1,000,000, more than 1/3 of which is spent in Tuscany on works of art.

It would seem that such numbers of our citizens, and such amount of their property, should have some protection within reach, if needed.

Being without a constitution, this Government is arbitrary, and by a

---

[67] MS Archives American consulate, Florence.

Royal edict the laws of today can be changed tomorrow, even the matter of costume can be restricted: and for the innocent violation of it our citizens would be subjected to the penalty, or to imprisonment until the case could be reported and acted on by the Department of State in Washington.

I know an American citizen now residing in this city who while visiting a neighbouring city was arrested and imprisoned for wearing a hat, the shape of which he was told was forbidden. Had he been alone, it would have detained him a long [while], but his companion applied to the American Minister Resident and obtained his release in four hours.

But if such occur here, we have no Minister to interpose, nor any channel, through which I can communicate *officially* with this Government; because, as the Minister of State informed me by letter (which I sent you) that "diplomatic agents only were recognized." As stated in a former despatch, commercial or monetary statistics are not made general by publication; and a reliable knowledge of them can only be procured by special personal favour, or by official intercourse. You will thus perceive, that my official disability precludes me from obtaining much valuable information. The extensive culture of the grape, olive, fig, and the culture and manufacture of silk, are all subjects of deep interest to a country like ours, possessing climates and soil congenial to all those products.

On a review of all the points embraced in this despatch, I cannot but think that the appointment of a diplomatic officer here would result beneficially in a national point of view.

I think it at least worthy the experiment, in a limited commission touching the main objects herein noticed, and then if the occasion merited, continue a permanent diplomat here.

If on reference to the files in your Department, recommending me for a foreign appointment, and the personal knowledge which the president, yourself, and Mr. Secretary Appleton have of my ability, and think proper to confide in me, I will execute the trust with my best skill and fidelity.

(Signed) E. J. Mallett,

United States Consular Agent.

In acknowledging receipt of this communication, John Appleton, the Assistant Secretary of State, notified General Mallett that the entire subject of diplomatic relations with Tuscany had been heretofore considered by the Department, and that the expediency of making provision for it had been presented to the consideration of the appropriate committee of Congress. However, Mr. Appleton explained that the Department did not at the moment feel warranted in renewing its recommendation.[68]

The reply of the State Department was undoubtedly prompted

---

68 MS letter Appleton to Mallett, dated Feb. 14, 1859. Archives American consulate, Florence.

by the political situation in Italy. A war between the Kingdom of Sardinia and Austria for the liberation of Lombardo-Venetia seemed imminent. Even then it appeared that the war would cause uprisings in the duchies of central Italy which would result in their liberation and ultimate annexation to the Kingdom of Italy which was emerging. In this connection it is of interest to note that Pasquale Massone, the chargé d'affaires of the Two Sicilies at Washington, informed Foreign Minister Carafa at Naples, that in conformance with their democratic institutions, Americans desired the triumph of the national will in the Italian duchies in order to introduce the principles of popular sovereignty in the public law of Europe. "This is what is being said and thought," concluded Mr. Massone, "in this land of liberty; the near future will prove the righteousness or the incompatibility of these wishes."[69]

An unpleasant incident involving the American consul at Leghorn occurred during the political disturbances of this period in Tuscany. It would seem that after the departure of the Grand Duke from Tuscany, Mr. J. A. Binda, the United States Consul at Leghorn, a warm friend of the rule of Duke Leopold, so incensed the Provisional Government of Tuscany by his advocacy of the restoration of the Hapsburg-Lorraine dynasty that it withdrew his exequatur and disqualified him for the exercise of the duties of his office. The consul's hostility to Baron Bettino Ricasoli, the Chief of the Provisional Government, was manifested at a dinner given by Prince Poniatowski, on which occasion Mr. Binda proposed a toast to the speedy return to power of the old régime. The consul was accused of being an active member of a party regarded with great aversion at that time — the *codini* — composed of a class of persons better known in America as "fogies" or reactionaries. It was pointed out that the great respectability of Mr. Binda, the fact of his being an Italian, and his extensive acquaintance with persons of position in Tuscany, perhaps gave more significance to his opinions and rendered his active partisanship of more consequence to the Government than would have been the case if he had been of foreign birth.[70] For these reasons, Mr. Binda's exequatur was withdrawn.

Tuscany was formally annexed to the Kingdom of Italy in

---

[69] Despatch No. 42, dated Washington, September 24, 1859 from Massone to Carafa. MS *Archivio di Stato*, Naples.
[70] New York *Herald*, Oct. 29, 1859; Philadelphia *Press,* Nov. 2, 1859.

March, 1860.[71] Immediately thereafter Mr. Bertinatti, the Sardinian Minister in Washington, sent an official communication to the United States Government informing it of the annexation of Emilia and Tuscany to Sardinia. In acknowledging the receipt of this communication, Secretary of State Cass hastened to offer his congratulations, adding: "You have taken the wisest measure you could have adopted in accepting the annexation of Emilia and Tuscany; I shall cause to be registered the despatch you have just communicated to me on behalf of your government." In informing Prime Minister Cavour of these facts,[72] Bertinatti added that the statement by Mr. Cass was nothing but the expression of the feeling of all Americans concerning the recent events in Italy. Mr. Buchanan, whom he had met a few days before, told Mr. Bertinatti: "You are today a great power," assuring him, at the same time, that he intended to pass the Burlingame Bill as soon as it passed the House.[73]

The Catholic party in America was doing everything possible to oppose the Burlingame resolution, according to Mr. Bertinatti in his despatch No. 56, dated Washington, June 10, 1860. Especially in the Senate had the Catholic party tried to prevent its passage and, at the same time, keep the federal government from recognizing the accomplished facts in central Italy. "Most of them," continued Mr. Bertinatti, "are Irish fanatics, and this is why Senator Cass has delayed so long to reply." An amendment to the Burlingame Bill, proposed by Mr. Mason, Chairman of the Senate Foreign Affairs Committee, was partly the effect of these intrigues, Mr. Bertinatti explained. Mr. Bertinatti assured Prime Minister Cavour that he had done all he could — in a dignified manner — to oppose and neutralize these influences which, he said, originated in the Vatican, England, and Bremen. "It is necessary to add," continued Mr. Bertinatti, "that, during this interval, the United States Government had received disconcerting news on the conditions of Italy. It had received

---

[71] In its issue of July 14, 1859, *La Nazione,* a daily political newspaper of Florence, under the dateline "United States" stated that recent news from America permitted one to foresee the disposition of the Government of the United States to recognize the Tuscan Government by sending a representative to Tuscany both as an attestation of its sympathy for the cause of Italy as well as to assure an efficient protection of America's commercial interests in that region.

[72] MS *Archivio di Stato,* Turin. Despatch No. LVI, Washington, June 10, 1860, Bertinatti to Cavour.

[73] Mr. Anson Burlingame, Republican, of Massachusetts, introduced a bill in the House of Representatives, on April 20, 1860, which was approved by both the House and Senate in June 1860, raising the American mission to Sardinia to a first class one. (H. R. Marraro, *American opinion,* etc. 300-303).

advanced notice of the insurrection in Sicily; it was rumored that Sardinia was working in an under-handed manner to encourage the Sicilians to revolt. It was added that the cabinet presided over with firmness and moderation by Your Excellency was on the verge of being undermined. I countered these rumors with the most formal denials, pointing out both their absurdity and the political loyalty of our country."[74]

With the pretext of congratulating him on his appointment as Minister at St. Petersburg, Mr. Bertinatti called on Mr. Appleton. During the course of the conversation, Mr. Bertinatti observed that the request made by the United States Government to the Government of Sardinia for the issuance of an exequatur for Mr. Mallett at Florence, implied the recognition of the annexation of Tuscany to Sardinia, and that therefore there was no real reason why Congress should oppose the raising of the American mission at Turin.

Following the constitution of the Kingdom of Italy in 1860, in accordance with instructions received from the State Department, Edward J. Mallett, in July of that year, asked the governor of the region, Ricasoli, to be recognized as the Consul General in Florence.[75] In 1860 the former agency was raised to the grade of Consulate General, and it so remained during the period (1865-1870) when Florence was the Italian capital. According to the official records there were in 1864 eleven consulates and nine consular agencies under the jurisdiction of the Consulate General at Florence.

In 1870, after Rome became the capital of Italy the Florence office was reduced to the grade of consulate, which it retained to the outbreak of the Second World War. For many years it had under it only a single consular agency at Cagliari, Sardinia, which appears to have been established on or about March 10, 1863. It remained under the jurisdiction of the Florence consulate until about 1888. In the same year the agency at Bologna was included in the Florence consular district. The Bologna agency was not closed until June 17, 1910.

---

[74] Despatch No. 56, Washington, June 10, 1860, Bertinatti to Cavour. MS *Archivio di Stato*, Turin.

[75] MS *Protocollo No 4 degli Affari del Ministero delle Relazioni Estere spedito dal Governatorato Ricasoli nel mese di luglio 1860. Archivio di Stato*, Florence, Mr. Mallett was severely rebuked by Wm. Henry Trescot, the Assistant Secretary of State, in an instruction dated Washington, September 17, 1860, for entering into official correspondence with Baron Ricasoli. General Mallett was told to refer all such matters to Mr. Daniel, the American minister at Turin. MS Archives American consulate, Florence.

The first representative of Tuscany in the United States was John F. Mansony, whose exequatur as consul for the states of New Hampshire, Massachusetts, Rhode Island, Vermont, and Connecticut (with residence at Boston) was signed by President James Monroe on November 6, 1817.[76] The Grand Duchy of Tuscany continued to be represented in the United States by consular officers. The last representative of Tuscany in the United States was G. B. Tagliaferri, whose exequatur as Consul at New York was signed by President Franklin Pierce on November 1, 1854.[77]

GENOA

On October 25, 1791, the exequatur of Joseph Ravara as Consul General of the Doge and Governors of the Republic of Genoa (for a time called the Ligurian Republic) at Philadelphia was signed by President George Washington.[78]

On February 27, 1797, Francis Childs was appointed Consul of the United States at the city of Genoa. There is evidence in the State Department's records that Childs did not go to his post. On July 10, 1797 Frederick H. Wollaston was appointed as the American Consul at Genoa. With the exception of Thomas H. Storm, who was appointed commercial agent on March 31, 1808, the United States continued to appoint a consular representative at the city of Genoa during the period of Genoa's incorporation in the French Empire (from 1805 to 1814) and its brief restoration of sovereignty in 1814, and after its incorporation in Piedmont-Sardinia in 1815.[79]

VENICE

The United States never entered into diplomatic relations with Venice, neither before it came under Austrian rule nor during 1848-49 when, for a brief period, it enjoyed the status of a Republic under the presidency of Daniele Manin. However, an

---

[76] *Exequaturs,* (Manuscript volume in the United States National Archives), I, 223, 516 and volume containing Index to Exequaturs, 660.

[77] *Exequaturs,* V, 147.

[78] *Exequaturs,* I, 8.

[79] Personnel records of the Department of State; Despatches from Genoa, vol. I (manuscript volume in The United States National Archives). No record has been found of any despatches from Childs and the first despatch from Wollaston in the volume containing despatches from Genoa is dated March 2, 1799.

interesting manifestation of Italo-American friendship occurred shortly after March 22, 1848, when the city of Venice proclaimed a republic and established a provisional government.

On that day, one of the first acts of the citizens of the new republic was to march in a great body to the American consulate,[80] where, assembled beneath the windows, they shouted, "Long live the United States; long live our sister republic." The American Consul, William A. Sparks, appeared during the celebration held in Piazza San Marco, bearing in one hand the flag of the United States and in the other the Italian tricolor with the winged lion. While the National Guard stood at attention, and amid the cries of vivas of the crowd, General Giuseppe Giurati and Consul Sparks greeted each other in a fraternal embrace.[81] Mr. Sparks thanked the people for their good will toward the government he had the honor to represent among them, and expressed a hope that, by their dignified and tranquil demeanor, they might give proof to the world that they were capable of governing themselves, and that they comprehended the full significance of the important step they had taken. He assured them in advance, that when the intelligence had traversed the Atlantic, that "the ancient queen of the Adriatic" had thrown off the yoke of the stranger, and had again proclaimed herself a republic, there would be a simultaneous outburst of joy from one extremity of the Union to the other. He wished them prosperity and happiness, and trusted they would never dement their capability of enjoying the blessings of free and enlightened institutions.

Later, Mr. Sparks presented himself before the provisional government, as the representative of a republic, to offer them his felicitations upon the new order of things. Too far distant, he said, to wait for instructions, he took the first opportunity to tender his congratulations, convinced that his government would give its entire approbation to the step he had taken. In the name of his country he wished the new government "grandeur and prosperity," and welcomed the Venetian Republic back again as a sister. The President of the new Republic, Daniele Manin, responded, assuring the American Consul of the great satisfaction it had given the provisional government to receive so promptly the spontaneous good wishes of an American republican.

---

80 An American consulate had been established at Venice in 1830.
81 *Gazzetta di Venezia*, Venice, March 24, 1848.

On March 28, 1848, the Provisional Government of the Republic of Venice sent the following address to the Republic of America:

TO THE UNITED STATES OF AMERICA[82]

By his spontaneous congratulations, the Consul (W. A. Sparks, Esq., of South Carolina) of your Republic hastened to salute the day of our regeneration, and we have received them as one of the most happy of auguries. The citizens of one Italian Republic first discovered the land to which the citizen of another Italian Republic gave his name, as if to stamp it with the seal of greatness. The ocean divides us, but we are not divided by the bonds of sympathy; and liberty, like the electric current traversing the seas, will bring us your examples, and maintain the communion of thought and feeling, which is far more precious than that of interest. We have much to learn from you; and, though your elders in civilization, we blush not to acknowledge it. We have no other ambition, and have to live in the enjoyment of peace and liberty to recover the heritage of our ancestors, and to contribute, in some degree, by our efforts, also to the infinite development of the human mind.

By the Provisional Government of the Republic of Venice

Manin, President
Tommaseo, Minister of Foreign Affairs
Zennari, Secretary

Venice, March 28, 1848.

STATES OF THE CHURCH[83]

The first official contact between the United States and the States of the Church dates back to December 15, 1784, when the papal nuncio at Paris informed the American commissioners that his government had opened the ports of Civita Vecchia on the Mediterranean and Ancona on the Adriatic, to the ships of the young republic of America. Thirteen years later, on June 26,

---

[82] The French version of the address was published in *Gazzetta di Venezia: foglio ufficiale della Repubblica Veneta*, Venice, April 4, 1848.

[83] Since 1929, when the State of the Vatican became a sovereign state, many studies have been published, particularly by Catholic scholars, which give a fairly complete picture of the more important phases of the relations between the two countries. Aside from the rather fragmentary study, based upon documents found in Italy, by H. Nelson Gay in which he gave an incomplete account of the Roman mission in his article, "Le relazioni fra l'Italia e gli Stati Uniti" (Rome, 1907), reprinted from *Nuova Antologia*, CCXX (1907), pp. 657-671; and his complete version with documents of the Perkins incident in Perugia, "Uno screzio diplomatico fra il governo pontificio e il governo americano e la condotta degli Svizzeri a Perugia il 20 giugno 1859" (Perugia, 1907), from *L'Archivio Storico del Risorgimento Umbro,* anno III, 1907, p. 113-201, the official documents which are now deposited in the National Archives in Washington, D. C., were not utilized until 1922, when Dr. Leo Francis Stock used them in connection with a

1797, John Baptiste Sartori,[84] a native of Rome, was appointed the first United States consul in the Papal States.[85] Until diplomatic relations were established in 1848, the papal government granted unusual privileges and favors to the American consuls in Rome; in fact, they were received at all formal functions on the same footing with full diplomatic representatives of other nations.

Following the enlightened policy and liberal reforms of

paper he read the following December before the American Catholic Historical Association, under the title "The United States at the Court of Pius IX" (*Catholic Historical Review*, n. s., III, 102-122, April 1923). Since then Dr. Stock has published other studies relating to our relations with the Papal States, e.g., Leo Stock, "American consuls to the Papal States, 1797-1870." *Catholic Historical Review*, XV, 233-251, Oct. 1929; "Catholic participation in the diplomacy of the Southern Confederacy." *Catholic Historical Review*, XVI, 1-18 April 1930; "An American consul joins the Papal Zouaves," *Catholic World*, CXXXII, 146-150, Nov. 1930. In 1933 The American Catholic Historical Association published a monumental work containing a collection of the official documents illustrating the diplomatic relations between the United and Papal States, edited with introduction and notes by Dr. Stock. Leo Francis Stock, *United States Ministers to the Papal States: instructions and desptaches 1848-1868*. Washington, D. C. 1933, 456 pp. (American Catholic Historical Association Documents: Volume I.) In 1945, the same Association published *Consular Relations between the United States and the Papal States,* also under the editorship of Dr. Stock.

Among other studies dealing with our relations with the Holy See, attention should be called to Sister Loretta Clare Feiertag's dissertation, prepared at the Catholic University of America, on *American Public Opinion concerning the Diplomatic Relations between the United States and the Papal States* (Washington, D. C., 1933).

This writer's *American Opinion on the Unification of Italy, 1846-1861* (New York, 1932), very naturally and frequently cuts across the diplomatic relations between the United States and the Vatican for the period covered by this work. In recent issues of the the *Catholic Historical Review* the writer has published other studies on the same subject, e.g., H. R. Marraro, "Unpublished American documents on the Roman Republic of 1849." *The Catholic Historical Review,* Jan. 1943, XXVIII, 459-490. "American travellers in Rome, 1848-50." *The Catholic Historical Review*, Jan. 1944, XXIX, 470-509.

Among other American students who have studied this phase of American diplomacy mention should be made of the article entitled "American notes in Vatican diplomacy" *United States Catholic Historical Society, Historical Records and Studies,* XX, 7-27, 1931, by the Rev. Dr. Joseph F. Thorning to which he appended a group of documents relating to the closing of the American mission. The Rev. Dr. Joseph T. Durkin has published a paper on "The early years of Italian unification as seen by an American diplomat, 1861-70," *The Catholic Historical Review*, Washington, D. C., Oct. 1944, XXX, 271-289, based almost entirely on some unpublished despatches of Minister Marsh to the Secretary of State deposited in the National Archives, Washington, D. C.

[84] The name Baptiste is sometimes spelled "Baptist," the name "Sartori" sometimes "Satori." The Italian spelling of the name is Giovanni Battista Sartori.

[85] The other American consuls at Rome to 1870 were Felix Cicognani, George W. Greene, Nicholas Browne, William C. Sanders, Daniel Le Roy, Horatio de V. Glentworth, William Dean Howells (who, although accepting the appointment, never served), W. J. Stillman, Edwin C. Cushman, and David M. Armstrong, who remained as the first consul to the Kingdom of Italy. Three other American consulates were established in papal territory: Ancona (1840), Ravenna (1844), Carrara (1852). For instructions to and despatches from these consuls, see Stock, *Consular relations,* etc.

Pius IX, soon after his accession to the throne of St. Peter in June 1846, numerous demonstrations of sympathy were held in many parts of the United States hailing the new Pope as a great liberator and a true friend of freedom. Such was the enthusiasm he aroused in this country that suggestions were made at several of these gatherings to establish diplomatic relations with the Holy See.[86]

These suggestions took concrete form especially when it was reported and believed that the Pope was about to send Monsignor Ferrari, Apostolic Nuncio Extraordinary, to Washington, to institute diplomatic relations with the United States Government. Americans who were in Rome at that time expressed the hope that Mr. Polk would in return send to the Holy See some distinguished, prudent, liberal, and high-minded man to represent the New World at that court.

In connection with this suggestion, Mr. Nicholas Browne, United States Consul at Rome, informed Mr. Buchanan, Secretary of State, in a letter dated June 1, 1847, that on several occasions persons holding high official stations in the papal government, including the Cardinal Secretary of State Gizzi, had expressed a desire to him that diplomatic relations might be established between the United States and the States of the Church, on a footing similar to those which existed between the Papal States and other countries where the Roman Catholic religion was not the prevailing faith. He also stated in this letter that on the occasion of his first presentation to Pope Pius IX, when alone with the Pontiff, His Holiness took the opportunity to express the same wish. His replies, Mr. Browne said, were in every case general and cautious, as he considered it no part of his business to make any statement from which the papal court might draw the slightest conclusion favorable or unfavorable to their wishes.[87]

Encouraged by these official overtures and wide demonstrations of sympathy for Pope Pius IX, President James K. Polk in his annual message to Congress of December 7, 1847, recommended the opening of diplomatic relations with the Papal States. "The interesting political events now in progress in these States," said the President, "as well as a just regard to our

---

[86] The most imposing of these demonstrations was held in New York City. See, *Proceedings of the public demonstration of sympathy with Pope Pius IX and with Italy in the city of New York on Monday, November 29, 1847.* (Prepared under the auspices of the Committee on Arrangements.). New York: Wm. Van Norden, 1847.

[87] The original of this letter is among the Buchanan Papers, Historical Society of Pennsylvania. See Buchanan, *op. cit.*, VIII, 42.

commercial interests, have, in my opinion, rendered such a measure highly expedient."[88]

The Committee on Foreign Affairs of the House of Representatives was shortly afterwards instructed 'to inquire and report to this House on the expediency of abolishing the present missions of chargés des affaires, to Sardinia and Naples, and substituting therefore, together with the mission lately recommended by the President to the States of the Church, a full mission by minister plenipotentiary or ambassador to Italy, with secretaries of legation to reside at Rome, Turin, and Naples,[89] Mr. Henry W. Hilliard, of Alabama, a member of the Committee on Foreign Affairs, reported on January 12, 1848, that it was not believed, by the Committee, to be expedient to abolish the separate missions to Sardinia and Naples, with a view of substituting in their place a single mission, so arranged as to embrace both courts, although the committee "heartily" concurred in the suggestion of sending a minister to the Papal States.

No immediate action was taken on the report of the Committee. The question was discussed again on March 4, by Henry W. Hilliard in a speech delivered in the House of Representatives. The speech of Congressman Hilliard brought about a spirited debate which took place in the House on March 8, and in which Whigs, Democrats, and representatives of the American Party took part. Two weeks later, on March 20 and 21, the question of the United States mission to Rome was also the subject of a debate in the United States Senate. The Deficiency Bill finally passed the Senate with some amendments and was then sent back to the House for concurrence. The section relating to the mission to Rome was not amended, and a chargé d'affaires was decided upon.[90]

---

[88] For President Polk's recommendation for opening diplomatic relations with the Papal States, see his message of December 7, 1847; James D. Richardson, *A compilation of the messages and papers of the Presidents 1788-1897*. Washington, 1897), IV 551.

[89] United States. 30th Cong., 1st session, House of Representatives No. 80. Washington.

[90] For the prolonged and bitter debate in both houses of Congress upon this recommendation see the *Congressional Globe*, XVII (13th Cong., 1st sess.), pp 57, 418, 430, 439-445, 476-477, 509, 514, 520-521; Appendix, pp. 403-410, 437-445. In the House of Representatives where the opposition was led by the Native Americanist, Lewis C. Levin, of Pennsylvania, the proposal was sustained by a vote of 137 to 15; in the Senate, where Dix of New York, Foote of Miss., and Hannegan of Ind., upheld the proposal against objections made by Senators Badger of N. C., Benton of Mo., and Hale of N. H., the vote was 36 to 7 in favor of establishing the diplomatic relations. For additional information regarding the discussion in this country on the establishment of diplomatic relations with the Papal States, see the section entitled "The question of diplomatic relations with

There were many eager candidates for this post. Finally, on April 7, 1848, Jacob L. Martin, former Chief Clerk of the State Department, was commissioned as chargé d'affaires of the United States near the Papal States.[91]

James Buchanan, Secretary of State, in a letter of April 5, 1848, notifying Dr. Martin of his appointment, emphasized that there was one consideration which he ought always to keep in mind in his intercourse with the papal authorities, namely, that most if not all of the governments which had diplomatic representatives at Rome were connected with the Pope as head of the Catholic Church. In this respect (wrote Mr. Buchanan) the Government of the United States occupies an entirely different position. ". . . Your efforts, therefore, will be devoted exclusively to the cultivation of the most friendly civil relations with the papal government, and to the extension of the commerce beween the two countries. You will carefully avoid even the appearance of interfering in ecclesiastical questions, whether these relate to the United States or any other portion of the world. It might be proper, should you deem it advisable, to make these views known, on some suitable occasion, to the papal government, so that there may be no mistake or misunderstanding on the subject."[92] The direct relations of the United States with the Papal States could be of a commercial character only, emphasized Mr. Buchanan. The spirit of reform which was then abroad in Italy would doubtless, he said, lead to removal or reduction of those ancient restrictions upon trade which were opposed to the genius of the age and the true interests of the people. It was known that a more liberal commercial policy had begun to pervade Italy. Among the proposed reforms of Pius IX was the formation of a commercial league of the nature of the German *Zollverein*, with which it was hoped that commercial treaties would be concluded. "On this subject," read the letter, "you are instructed to report to the Department the fullest and most accurate information which you can obtain. We desire all possible information relative to the best mode of increasing America's commerce, not only with the Papal States, but with the other independent states of Northern Italy. The President desires to conclude commercial treaties with the Papal States separately,

---

the Papal States" in Marraro's *American opinion,* etc. pp. 17 ff. Also Sister Feiertag's *American public opinion* etc. pp. 5 ff.

[91] *Register of the Department of State,* 1874, 101.

[92] Moore's *Digest,* I, 130.

or with the proposed commercial league of which they may form a part, and awaits the necessary information to confer upon the chargé full instructions and powers for this purpose."

The Pope, on receiving the envoy from the United States, expressed his pleasure in entering into a treaty with so "great a nation, especially with one in which the Church has nothing to fear from the Government, nor the Government from the Church."[93]

The sudden death of Dr. Martin shortly after his arrival in Rome was much lamented there .The Pope spoke with apparently deep feeling on the loss, and expressed a hope that another man as good might soon be sent to fill the vacancy.[94]

The United States mission to Rome remained vacant for several months. But early in January 1849, after protracted and spirited debates in Congress, Lewis Cass Jr., was appointed successor to Dr. Martin; but by this time revolutionary forces had gained the upper hand in Rome, and the Pope had been forced to flee from the city. Some American statesmen argued, therefore, that the Papal States had ceased to exist and that it was, in consequence, unnecessary and inexpedient to send a representative of the United States Government to Rome. Mr. Cass, however, went to Rome, but, with instructions from the Secretary of State, not to deliver his credentials to either the Minister of Foreign Affairs of Pope Pius IX, or to the revolutionary government, until he should receive further instructions from the State Department. As it was, when the papal government was restored in Rome late in 1849, Mr .Cass presented his credentials as chargé d'affaires of the United States.[95]

The tyranny of the reinstated papal government after 1850 called forth much indignation in America. Antipapal feeling steadily increased on this side of the Atlantic, stimulated by the Pontiff's interference with Protestant worship in Europe and by the fear that he was seeking to gain influence in American political affairs, as well as by his reactionary rule in the Roman States. Debates took place in the United States Congress as to whether

---

[93] See Martin's Despatch No. 2, Rome Aug. 20, 1848, to Buchanan in Stock, op. cit., 8-15.

[94] On Dr. Martin's sojourn in Rome as American minister, see: Howard R. Marraro, "American travellers in Rome, 1848-50." The Catholic Historical Review, Washington, D. C., January 1944, XXIX, pp. 470-509.

[95] Concerning the part played by America's diplomatic and consular representatives in the Papal States during these turbulent years, see: Howard R. Marraro, "Unpublished American documents on the Roman Republic of 1849." The Catholic Historical Review, Washington, D. C., Jan. 1943, XXVIII, 459-490.

or not the papal claims to temporal sovereignty implied the right of the Pontiff to interfere in the civil and political affairs of the countries of the world and to absolve citizens from allegiance to the government under which they lived.[96]

In 1853 anti-papal feeling in certain sections of this country became pronounced as a result of the visit of Archbishop Gaetano Bedini. Before the prelate's departure for the United States, Cardinal Antonelli, the Papal Secretary of State, had requested Mr. Cass to apprise, in advance, his government of the intended visit of Mgr. Bedini, in order to secure for him a cordial welcome, the more especially as he was the bearer of a letter from His Holiness, in which Pius IX requested President Pierce to extend his protection to the Catholics of the United States. Mgr. Bedini was cordially received by the government officials and treated with great consideration. However, shortly after his arrival criticism of Bedini's visit began to be voiced in the public press. The attacks against the papal Nuncio became bitter when Father Alessandro Gavazzi,[97] an apostate priest, and a political exile from Italy then in America, in a lecture decried Bedini as having commanded the degradation and execution at Bologna of Ugo Bassi, who was described as "a holy priest, and a pure-minded patriot, who had been chaplain in the legion of the 'great' Garibaldi." Mgr. Bedini was defended by the Catholic press, but within one month of his arrival and until after his departure, he suffered severe insults in various parts of the United States, particularly in Pittsburgh, Pa., Cincinnati, Carthage, and Cleveland, Ohio, Covington, Kentucky, New Orleans, La., Baltimore, Md., and New York City. These disturbances gave rise to a discussion in the United States Senate on January 23, 1854.[98] With one exception, all the speakers concurred in condemning the insults. The demonstrations continued, however, even after the Nuncio's sudden and secret departure from the United States.

The American Government was chagrined by these demonstra-

---

[96] *Appendix to the Congressional Globe,* 33rd Cong., 2nd Sess., 1854-1855, 50-51.

[97] Alessandro Gavazzi, *A biography of Father Gavazzi with corrections by himself.* New York, DeWitt & Davenport, 1853.

[98] United States President. Message from the President of the United States communicating a copy of the correspondence with the Government of the Papal States relative to the mission of Archbishop Gaetano Bedini to the United States. (33d Cong., 1st sess., 1853-54. Ex. Doc. 23, Senate). 4 pp. See H. R. Marraro, *American opinion* etc. 138-145. For texts of letters of the Pope to the President and from Cardinal Antonelli to the Secretary of State, see Marraro, *ibid.,* 317-318.

tions against a representative of the Holy See. To correct any misunderstanding on the subject, Secretary of State Marcy, instructed Mr. Cass to assure Cardinal Antonelli of the friendly reception given to Mgr. Bedini by the President, "and his regret that any part of the people should have forgotten in moments of excitement what was due to a distinguished functionary charged with a friendly mission from a foreign power with which this country has hitherto maintained, and is still desirous of maintaining amicable relations." Mr. Cass replied that the annoyance to which Mgr. Bedini was subjected excited considerable indignation among his friends and the displeasure of the Papal Government. To the minister's communication, containing Marcy's expression of regret, Antonelli replied that "although he had learned with pain of the occurrences which had taken place," he was "nevertheless well persuaded that the American Government would disapprove and condemn them."[99]

This explanation of the unfortunate incident seemed to have satisfied the Papal Government. In fact, that same year it was pleased to learn that Mr. Cass had just been elevated to the rank of minister. Mr. Cass remained in Rome to July 1858, when he was succeeded by John P. Stockton.

Less than a year after Stockton's arrival in Rome, another diplomatic difficulty arose between the two governments. Among the principal persons who suffered harm by the famous siege of Perugia by the papal troops in June 1859, was the American Edwin N. Perkins, "a highly respected citizen of Boston," who lived with his family at the Hotel de France. The owner of the hotel, a waiter, and a stableboy were killed "under their eyes." The Perkins, after having been obliged to hide for fourteen hours in a secret recess of the house, were miraculously saved by the friendly aid of a subordinate officer. In the claim for damages which was made to Cardinal Antonelli, Mr. Stockton denounced in no uncertain terms the action of the "brutal and savage soldiers," adding that "similar outrages seldom occur among civilized nations." While denying the main facts of the case, Cardinal Antonelli maintained that Perugia had been taken by siege and that the troops had the right to declare it in a state of siege. The American minister countered with the statement that "no Christian government could sanction this point of view." These were undoubtedly strong accusations against the temporal government of the Vicar of Christ. Anxious not to prolong the

---

99 Stock, *United States ministers to the Papal States,* etc., xxvi.

discussion further, the Papal Government promptly satisfied the financial claim to indemnify the Perkins family for the loss it had sustained.[100]

A few months later, on the night of March 18, 1860, the political situation provoked another incident which threatened to disturb the cordial relations of the two governments. During a band concert in Piazza Colonna in Rome, a disorder occurred during which Mr. Glentworth, the American Consul, and two other American citizens were assaulted. Mr. Glentworth owed his own safety to the intervention of a French officer. For these outrages the excuses of the Papal Government were asked, and a full apology was made.

On April 2, 1861, Mr. Stockton asked to be recalled, and Rufus King was appointed to succeed him. But Mr. King did not accept this commission, for he became brigadier-general in the Union army. Alexander Randall, of Wisconsin, was appointed to fill the post at Rome. Soon realizing that he was not fitted for the post, Mr. Randall, in August 1862, was succeeded by Richard Blatchford. When the latter resigned in October 1863, Mr. King received the appointment for the second time.[101]

Another unpleasant diplomatic incident between the two governments occurred toward the close of 1867 when Garibaldi made an attempt to occupy Rome. On this occasion, Mr. Cushman, the American Consul, accompanied the pontifical troops for four days and witnessed the battle which resulted in the capture of Garibaldi's garrison at Nerola. Cushman was reprimanded by the State Department for his participation in the affair.[102]

Meanwhile, the political situation in Rome became so confused that Secretary of State Seward directed Rufus King to remain with the Papal Government "in the same political relations hereafter as heretofore, so long as you receive no countervailing instruction . . ." In the event of a change in government, diplo-

---

[100] See Henry N. Gay, *Uno screzio diplomatico* etc.; H. R. Marraro, *American opinion*, etc., p. 263-264; United States President. Message of the President of the United States communicating, in compliance with the resolution of the Senate, papers in relation to an alleged outrage on an American family at Perugia, in the Pontifical States. (36th Cong., 1st sess., 1859-60. Ex. Doc. 4). 12 pp.

[101] Stock, *op. cit.*, xxix, xxx.

[102] See Howard R. Marraro, "Unpublished American documents on Garibaldi's march on Rome in 1867." *The Journal of Modern History*, Chicago, Ill., June 1944, XVI, 116-123. For the discussion in the United States Senate on the incident, see United States Senate: Message of the President of the United States (Andrew Johnson) communicating, in compliance with a resolution of the Senate of the 17th of February, ultimo, information in relation to the alleged interference of our consul at Rome in the late difficulties in Italy. U. S. Senate Documents, 40th Session, 2nd session; Executive Document No. 37, March 4, 1868.

matic functions were to be suspended. If the Papal Government removed to some other place, Mr. King was instructed not to follow it, but was told to take up his residence in Rome or in some adjacent country and await further instructions.[103]

The United States continued to be represented by a minister accredited to the Holy See until 1867. In that year the American mission to Rome came to an official end, but through no fault or action of the Papal Government. The pretext offered by Congress for refusing to continue the appropriation for the mission was the erroneous charge that the American Protestant Church had been ordered outside the walls of Rome. The reports of Mr. Rufus King to the State Department show that this was not so. Mr. King explained that to guard against the possibility of removing the Church outside of Rome, he had the arms of the Legation placed over the building in which services were held. The American minister insisted that this arrangement was satisfactory to the papal authorities who permitted it in order to show the good feeling of the government towards the United States. He emphatically denied the statements that had been made in Congress, and maintained that only in the event of the closing of the Legation would the American Church be forced to leave the city, in which case the cause of removal must be laid to Congress and not to the Holy See.[104]

There is no doubt, as the debates in Congress abundantly prove, that several motives influenced the action of Congress in failing to support the mission. Religious feeling certainly played its part. The domestic political situation which had led to open quarrel between the President and Congress also contributed to the opposition of the latter to the mission. Finally, as Mr. King

---

[103] Stock, *op. cit.*, xxxii.

[104] For a full account of the subject, see: Protestant Church at Rome: Message from the President of the United States in answer to a resolution of the House of 24th instant, relative to the removal of the Protestant Church at the American Embassy from the city of Rome by order of the government. United States House of Representatives: 39th Congress: 2nd session: Executive Document, No. 57; Protestant Church at Rome: Message from the President of the United States in answer to a resolution of the House of January 24th, last, relative to the removal of the American Protestant Church from the city of Rome (transmitting a report from the Secretary of State, concerning the removal of American Protestant Church). United States House of Representatives: 39th Congress; 2nd Session, Ex. Doc. 115; March 2, 1867. 3 p.; Protestant Church at Rome: Message from the President of the United States communicating additional information in answer to a resolution of the House of the 24th of January last, relative to the removal of the American Protestant Church from the city of Rome. United States House of Representatives: 40th Congress; 1st session; Ex. Doc. No. 60. These should be read along with Mr. King's despatches of the period published in Stock, *op. cit.*, 409 ff.

intimated, there was much sympathy for the aspirations of the Italians for a united Italy. In closing diplomatic relations with what remained of the Papal States the way was cleared for the early recognition of the government of Victor Emmanuel II.[105] Mr. King's judgment is supported by a heretofore unpublished despatch dated Washington, July 20, 1868, from the Italian chargé, Cerruti, to Menabrea, the Foreign Minister:

It is not at all correct to state that the United States are severing their diplomatic relations with the Holy See. The truth is merely that Mr. Rufus King is not returning to Rome any more because Congress did not approve this year the appropriation for that Legation. The motion for this economy measure was made by Senator Sumner who, in truth, had spoken to me about it last winter when he informed me confidentially that he was proposing it as an economy measure simply to render the discontinuance of the mission more acceptable, but that he intended to do everything possible to have the Legation abolished, and this, he added, because of his sympathy for Italy.[106]

It may be noted in passing that for the Vatican the breaking off of diplomatic relations with the United States was somewhat simpler than it was for Washington, since in spite of the appointment of an American minister to Rome, Pope Pius IX had never sent a diplomatic representative to Washington. Be that as it may, it is a source of great regret that American statesmen were not more candid in closing the mission. From a legal point of view, the action of Congress, as Seward himself acknowledged, left the mission "still existing, but without compensation." But no official communication was ever sent to the Papal Government, informing it of the action taken by Congress. Mr. King protested that he could not tell the Holy Father that the United States was withdrawing its representative for the alleged but erroneous reason that the Pope had refused to permit Protestant worship within the walls of Rome. Even the official letter of recall was not sent to Mr. King, so that he was unable to take formal leave of the papal authorities. It certainly was not a courteous exit nor a dignified ending of this chapter of American diplomacy. Small wonder Mr. King was given to understand that the Holy Father felt hurt "by the hasty and apparently groundless action of Congress," and thought it "an unkind and ungenerous return for the good will" he had always manifested towards the American Government and its people. [107]

[105] Stock, op. cit., xxxviii-xxxix
[106] MS Archives of Ministry of Foreign Affairs, Rome.
[107] Stock, op. cit., xxxix. See Howard R. Marraro, "Our diplomatic relations with the Vatican." The Catholic World, New York, Nov. 1946, CLXIV, 131-139.

After the occupation of Rome by the Italian troops in 1870, several attempts were made to involve the United States in the struggle between the papal church and the Kingdom of Italy, but Mr. Hamilton Fish, who was Secretary of State under President Grant, succeeded in preserving a strict neutrality, and, after the abolition of the civil authority of the pope, the United States Government had no relations with the Vatican.

However, shortly after the creation of the State of the Vatican in 1929, rumors became increasingly more persistent in America concerning the re-establishment of diplomatic relations between the United States and the Holy See. Statements that the administration in Washington was studying the question were so frequently repeated after President Hoover had in July of that year received Archbishop Fumasoni-Biondi, Apostolic Delegate to the United States, that the latter was forced to deny any diplomatic purpose of his visit, while high administration official circles denied any intention of recognizing the Vatican or of sending a representative there. The same rumors were revived in 1936 when Pope Pius XII, then Papal Secretary of State, suddenly decided to visit the United States. It was then generally believed that the object of his visit was to discuss plans for the re-opening of diplomatic relations between the two countries. The fact that throughout his administration, President Roosevelt consistently manifested a friendly and sympathetic attitude toward the Vatican caused wide discussion of the subject in the public press, especially when, on December 23, 1939, Mr. Roosevelt announced that he had appointed Myron C. Taylor as his Personal Representative to the Pope with the rank of Ambassador, but without portfolio.[108] There were numerous favorable responses to the President's appointment in many government and religious quarters. However, these were tempered in some instances by expressions of hope that Mr. Roosevelt was not aiming to restore formal diplomatic relations with the Vatican. Until recently Mr. Taylor continued as President Truman's Personal Representative. During the extensive absences of Mr. Taylor from Vatican City, Harold H. Tittman, Jr. (American Foreign Service Officer designated as Assistant to the Personal Representative) was chargé d'affaires *ad interim*.

The first representative of the Papal States in the United States was Count Ferdinando Lucchesi, who was mentioned above as

---

[108] *Department of State Bulletin,* Dec. 23, 1939, 711.

being the first representative of the Two Sicilies in the United States and whose exequatur as Consul General of the Papal States at Washington, D .C., was signed by President John Quincy Adams on May 30, 1826.[109] Consular officers from the Papal States were stationed in various parts of the United States down to at least 1876. No papal representative has since had official diplomatic relations with this country.[110]

KINGDOM OF PIEDMONT-SARDINIA[111]

(Also known as Piedmont or Sardinia)

The first official contact between the United States Government and the Kingdom of Piedmont-Sardinia goes back to January 28, 1818, when Victor Adolphus Sasserno was appointed Consul of the United States at Nice.[112] It is not known how long Sasserno held the office. There were only two other American consular officers in Piedmont-Sardinia prior to the establishment of formal diplomatic relations with that country. They were R. Campbell, who on December 23, 1822, was nominated Consul of the United States for Genoa, a post he held to April 24, 1834, and C. Barnet, of New Jersey, who was then nominated United States Consul in that city to supersede Mr. Campbell who was a foreigner.[113]

The first representative of Piedmont-Sardinia to the United States was Gaspare Deabbate, whose exequatur as Consul General at Philadelphia was signed by President James Monroe on May 18, 1820. Consular officers continued to be the sole official representatives of Piedmont-Sardinia in this country until after the establishment of formal diplomatic relations.[114]

Negotiations for the opening of diplomatic relations between the Kingdom of Piedmont and the United States were started in

109 *Exequaturs*, II, 45.

110 Since 1895, the Holy See has been regularly represented in Washington by an Apostolic Delegate, who is understood to be charged with religious and ecclesiastical duties in connection with relations between the Holy See and the Roman Catholic Church in this country. The Apostolic Delegate does not, however, have diplomatic status and is not accredited to the United States Government.

111 The Kingdom of Sardinia, as established by the Congress of Vienna under Victor Emmanuel I of the House of Savoy, comprised Piedmont (with| Savoy and Nice), the island of Sardinia, and the extinct Republic of Genoa.

112 Personnel records of the Department of State.

113 Curiously enough, Barnet held the post to September 1837, when Campbell was again nominated consul of the United States for Genoa, a post he now held to July 1840.

114 *Exequaturs*, I, 286 and 518; and volume containing index to exequaturs, 68.

1838, when Count de Sambuy, envoy extraordinary and minister plenipotentiary of His Majesty the King of Sardinia at Vienna, in a private conversation with Mr. Nathaniel Niles, of Vermont, who, on June 7, 1837, early in the Van Buren administration, had been appointed special agent of the United States to Austria to procure a modification of the duties and restrictions on the importation of American tobacco, discussed the mutual advantages which both countries would derive from the removal of existing barriers in the way of an exchange of each other's products and from the establishment of permanent diplomatic relations between them. Both representatives were of the opinion that an extensive market for American tobacco and the products of America, and fisheries could be found if steps were taken to develop commerce between the two countries.[115] Hitherto the commercial relations between the two countries had been governed by domestic regulations which, however, were founded upon a mutual agreement between the two governments.[116]

Mr. Niles submitted a brief account of this interview to the Honorable John Forsyth, the Secretary of State, in a letter dated February 18, 1838, pointing out that Sardinia formed "by far the most enlightened, active, and wealthy population of any of the independent states of Italy," and that it was "making considerable advances in manufacturing industry." As proof of this fact, Mr. Niles indicated that Sardinia had some very large establishments for the manufacture of silk and cotton, particularly plain silks, which were sent to the United States through Lyons and Havre, *in transitu*, to the amount of many millions of francs. "The eagerness with which both the King and his minister seized upon the idea of opening diplomatic relations with the expressed view to encourage a commerce with us," concluded Mr. Niles, "affords a reasonable ground to believe that the absolute authority with which the Sardinian Government is clothed, will be directed to the accomplishment of the object, whenever diplomatic relations may be established between the two countries."[117]

[115] United States Senate — *Message of the President of the United States transmitting in compliance with a resolution of the Senate, copies of correspondence touching the origins, progress, and conclusion of the late convention between the United States and the Kingdom of Sardinia.* 29th Congress, 1st Session, Senate Document, 118. Read September 13, 1841. 3-4. On Mr. Nelson's two missions to Piedmont, see: Howard R. Marraro, "Nathaniel Niles' missions at the Court of Turin (1838; 1848-50)." *Vermont Quarterly,* Montpelier, Vt., Jan. 1947, XV, 14-32.

[116] Eighth annual message of Monroe, Dec. 7, 1824, Richardson, *Messages and Papers,* II, 251.

[117] United States Senate, *Message from the President,* etc., 4.

Following the receipt of this communication, Mr. Niles on May 2, 1838, was ordered by President Martin Van Buren to go to Sardinia "and endeavor to conclude a commercial arrangement, securing upon the most advantageous terms the admission of American tobacco into the ports of that country, and if practicable, to extend it so as to embrace the general trade between the two nations."[118] It was anticipated that in the event of a successful negotiation, a diplomatic officer would be accredited to the Sardinian court; in case of the failure of the negotiations, matters would continue as in the past.[119] Arriving in Sardinia, Mr. Niles interviewed Count Solar de la Marguerite, First Secretary of State for Foreign Affairs, and was "very cordially received" as a diplomatic agent of the United States by King Charles Albert who avowed "the greatest interest" in the government, institutions and prosperity of our country. The King at once expressed his desire to enter into treaty relations with the United States, and "by every other means to cultivate and enlarge the commerce between his states and those of the American union."[120]

A treaty of commerce and navigation consisting of twenty articles was finally concluded and signed at Genoa on November 26, 1838,[121] by the two agents — Nathaniel Niles and Count Solar de la Marguerite. The treaty dealt with numerous phases of commerce and navigation: commerce and navigation, vessels in ports, duties on imports, discrimination in duties, coasting trade, purchase of articles of commerce, most favored nation, most favored nation as to vessels, shipwrecks, asylum for vessels, blockade ports, free passage from Genoa through Sardinia, consuls, Sardinian as consul, privileges of consuls, disposal of property, duration and ratification.

The spirit which animated the two contracting parties is found in the first article which stipulated that "there shall be between the territories of the contracting parties a reciprocal liberty of

---

[118] Letter from Mr. Forsyth to Mr. Niles, Wash., May 2, 1838. United States Senate, *Message from the President*, etc., 8. MS National Archives, Washington, D. C.

[119] MS Inst. Italy, I, 3-4; serial 473, Doc. 118, 8. United States Senate, *Message from the President*, etc. 8. MS National Archives, Washington, D. C.

[120] Letter from Mr. Niles to Mr. Forsyth, Turin, Sept. 26, 1838. United States Senate, *Message of the President*, etc., 8-11. MS National Archives Washington, D. C.

[121] For the text of the treaty of commerce and navigation concluded Nov. 26, 1838, see Miller, *op. cit.*, IV, 145-170. This treaty was superseded by the treaty of 1871 with Italy (see Malloy, *op. cit.*, 969), Sardinia having become merged with that Kingdom.

commerce and navigation," and that "the inhabitants of their respective states shall mutually have liberty to enter the ports and commercial places of the territories of each party, wherever foreign commerce is permitted. They shall be at liberty to sojourn or reside in all parts whatsoever of said territories in order to attend to their affairs, and they shall enjoy to that effect the same security and protection as the natives of the country wherein they reside, on condition of their submitting to the laws and ordinances there prevailing."[122]

The effects of the treaty of November 26, 1838, were important and far-reaching. Mr. Niles in a letter to the Honorable John Forsyth, dated Turin, May 14, 1839, stated: "No measure that the King can possibly adopt would tend so much to render him popular and powerful in the north of Italy as making Sardinia virtually a free port by the admission of the products of our fisheries, our woods, and cotton to consumption throughout his dominions free of all duty. This policy would greatly develop the elements of his maritime power, which, in the next general war that may occur on the continent, is destined powerfully to aid in the territorial aggrandizement of this Kingdom."[123]

In another interview with King Albert in July 1839, Mr. Niles was struck with the liberal principles advanced by the King who felt highly gratified at the unqualified approbation of the advantage of a convention which would admit to consumption in Sardinia and the United States certain products of each, free of all duty. The King also understood the advantages to himself of admitting free of duty United States cottons, and some other bulky articles of transatlantic produce, as affording at once a proper encouragement to manufacture, and as a means of employing and enlarging his navigation, as well as of placing his neighbors in upper Italy in such easy business relations with Genoa as to secure their friendly dispositions, and to his subjects the benefit of carrying on their foreign commerce.[124]

In his message to the two Houses of Congress at the commencement of the first session of the twenty-sixth Congress, December 24, 1839, President Van Buren laid before them the

---

122 United States Executive Document No. 2: Documents accompanying the message of the President of the United States to the two Houses of Congress, at the commencement of the first session of the 29th Congress (1839), I, (1839-40). This document also contains the text of this treaty.
123 Mr. Niles to Hon. Forsyth, Turin, May 14, 1839. United States Senate, *Message from the President*, etc. 23-25. MS National Archives, Washington, D. C.
124 Mr. Niles to the Hon. Forsyth, Paris, July 29, 1839. *Ibid.*, 25-26. MS National Archives, Washington, D. C.

treaties of commerce negotiated with the kings of Sardinia and of the Netherlands, the ratifications of which had been exchanged since the adjournment of Congress. "The liberal principles of these treaties," remarked President Van Buren, "will recommend them to their approbation." "That with Sardinia," he added, "is the first treaty of commerce formed by that Kingdom, and it will, I trust, answer the expectations of the present sovereign by aiding the development of the resources of his country, and stimulating the enterprise of his people."[125]

While the negotiations necessary to effect the treaty of commerce were still in progress, the King of Sardinia appreciating the views of the President of the United States in appointing Mr. Niles as diplomatic agent,[126] and being desirous on his own part to establish political relations between his subjects and this country, appointed Count August Avogadro de Collobiano,[127] his chargé d'affaires near the United States.[128]

Even before the final conclusion of the treaty of commerce, the Sardinian Government showed its desire to develop and strengthen the friendly relations with the United States. Early in October 1838, the authorities at Genoa gave up quarantines on arrivals from America provided with clean bills of health. Commenting on this measure, in a letter to the Honorable Mr. Forsyth, Mr. Niles remarked that the "effects of this measure must be great on American commerce, and insure Genoa the advantage of becoming the centre of Italian commerce, or to force other cities to follow her examples."[129]

On its part, the United States Government also showed its desire to cultivate the friendship of Sardinia, although an American chargé was not promptly sent to Turin. President Van Buren said that it was his intention to express his appreciation of the cordial spirit of the Sardinian Government in making with the United States its first commercial treaty, by the immediate

---

[125] Message from the President of the United States to the two Houses of Congress at the commencement of the first session of twenty-sixth Congress, Dec. 24, 1839.

[126] Nathaniel Niles, of Vermont, had been appointed special agent on May 3, 1838, concerning general trade and the admission of tobacco.

[127] Count Augusto Avogadro de Collobiano, presented credential as chargé d'affaires on Feb. 7, 1839. Last communication to him from the State Department Aug. 8, 1842. See the *Register*, 1874, 122.

[128] Solar de la Marguerite to Mr. Niles, Turin, Sept. 29, 1838. United States Senate, *Message from the President*, etc., p. 13. MS National Archives, Washington, D. C. MS Inst. Italy, I, 13.

[129] Mr. N. Niles to Mr. Forsyth, Turin, Oct. 8, 1838. United States Senate, *Message from the President*, 13. MS National Archives, Washington, D. C.

appointment of a diplomatic officer to reside at the Sardinian Court. The failure of the Senate to consent promptly to ratification postponed the request of the President for the necessary appropriation. Therefore, it was decided to send Abraham Van Buren as a special agent to Turin to explain that at the following session of Congress the President would request the appropriation.[130] Van Buren failed to carry out his instructions and the explanations were made instead to the Sardinian chargé at Washington.[131]

Finally, in May 1840, Mr. H. Gold Rogers,[132] was appointed chargé d'affaires to Sardinia and the relations were now placed on a regular footing.[133] In a letter dated June 6, 1840, the Secretary of State informed him of the stipulations of the treaty of November 26, 1838, adding that it was "the sincere desire of the President that a mutual spirit of fairness and confidence should characterize this first establishment of diplomatic relations between the two countries; and that their governments should unite in efforts to draw from the circumstances the highest attainable amount of benefits to their respective citizens. Nothing will contribute more to this result than a candid interchange of views, a fair exposition of the principles by which each part is actuated, and a prompt and liberal performance of mutual obligations."[134]

The treaty of commerce, as intended, helped to stimulate commerce. Mr. Crokat, acting consul at Genoa, in his report dated January 10, 1841, to Mr. Forsyth on the American vessels entered at that port and cleared during the previous six months, stated that the arrivals of American vessels continued, as in the beginning of the year, to be unusually numerous, "which may perhaps in some measure be attributed to the late treaty of commerce, but I should be inclined to refer it to other causes growing out of the channels which commerce in general has taken." Five cargoes of tobacco were received from Richmond, and as this branch of trade appeared to be assuming a certain importance, it became necessary, according to Mr. Crokat, "that

---

[130] Forsyth to Van Buren, April 18, 1839, MS Inst. Italy, I, 1-2.
[131] Van Buren to Forsyth, Nov. 29, 1839, MS Desp. Sardinia (Italy); Forsyth to Van Buren, *loc. cit.*
[132] H. Gold Rogers of Pennsylvania. Commissioned chargé d'affaires, June 30, 1840. Left Nov. 22, 1841.
[133] Sen. Ex. Jol., V, 284; Forsyth to Rogers, June 6, 1840, Serial 473, Doc. 118, 26.
[134] Mr. Forsyth to Mr. Rogers, Washington, D. C. June 6, 1840. Untied States Senate, *Message from the President,* etc., 28. MS National Archives, Washington, D. C.

some determination be come to respecting the transit duty which continues to be levied by the government here."[135]

In spite of the improvement in the commercial relations between the two countries, an attempt was made in the United States Senate on June 15, 1844,[136] to strike out "Sardinia" and "Belgium" from the appropriations that were being made for the salaries of the chargés d'affaires to thirteen countries. Mr. Archer, Chairman of the Committee on Foreign Relations, called upon the Chairman of the Committee on Finance, Mr. Evans, for information as to this proposition. The latter explained that the Finance Committee understood the gentleman in charge of the mission to Sardinia had asked and obtained a leave to resign during the first half of 1844, though his salary was provided for till December in an amendment already adopted.[137] Mr. Evans added that it was probable that the mission to Sardinia might be dispensed with; but if found necessary to continue it, the salary for the next half year could be provided for during the following session. The subject was debated at great length. Messrs. Evans, Crittenden, and Berrien contending that the treaty having been satisfactorily concluded, it was now only necessary to keep a consul at Sardinia, a mission of higher grade being wholly useless; and Messrs. Archer, Merrick, and Choate, maintaining that the population of Sardinia being five millions, and America's indirect trade with that country having grown up to $1,600,000 yearly, America's interest required the continuance of the mission then established, particularly, as the United States had requested of Sardinia a reciprocity of ministers, and that court kept one of equal grade at Washington. Mr. Woodbury suggested that a minister to Sardinia was required not only because of the commerce that existed, but because debatable points were likely to arise on the construction of the new treaty. A consul was a mere merchant, and not a lawyer or a statesman, and therefore unqualified to grapple with such questions, argued

---

[135] Mr. Crokat to Mr. Forsyth, Genoa, Jan. 10, 1841. United States Senate, *Message from the President,* etc., 45. MS National Archives, Washington, D. C.

[136] United States Senate — Civil and diplomatic appropriation bill. *Congressional Globe,* June 15, 1844, XIII, 673.

[137] The person referred to was Ambrose Baber, of Georgia, who was commissioned chargé d'affaires Aug. 16, 1841. He left Dec. 15, 1843. An interesting biographical sketch of Baber was published by R. B. Flanders, "Ambrose Baber," in *The Georgia Historical Quarterly,* Savannah, Ga., Sept. 1938, XXII, 209-248. See also, Howard R. Marraro, "Ambrose Baber at the Court of Sardinia (1841-1843)." *The Georgia Historical Quarterly,* Savannah, Ga., June 1946, XXX, 105-117. His successor, Robert Wickliffe, Jr., of Kentucky, was commissioned chargé d'affaires Sept. 22, 1843. He wrote to minister of foreign affairs from Aix-la-Chapelle, enclosing letter of recall, about May 6, 1848.

Mr. Woodbury, adding that even a higher minister than a chargé would not, for a time, be amiss for this place and for the rest of Italy. He observed that there were no more open questions in Austria or Russia, in Sweden or Denmark, in Holland or Belgium, Venezuela or New Granada, Peru or Chile, than there were in Sardinia; and if this mission was to be discontinued on that account, so should these be. "But in truth," said Mr. Woodbury, "under a growing commerce, a resort of our large squadron, and a new treaty with Sardinia, difficult questions were more likely to arise, than at most of the old missions." At the conclusion of his speech the yeas and nays were demanded, and resulted yeas 15, nays 28, so the word "Sardinia" was not stricken out.[138]

Mr. Woodbury's reference to "a resort for our Mediterranean naval squadron" was prophetic, for in June 1848, the United States Government requested and obtained the permission of the Sardinian Government to establish a naval depot at Spezia on the Ligurian coast. The initial privilege was granted for a period of three years, with provision for annual renewals thereafter. The cordial relations that were established between the American naval officers stationed at the depot and the Piedmontese Government authorities made it possible for the United States to occupy the naval depot until 1868 when the Italian Government found it necessary to use Spezia for its own expanding navy, since the facilities at Genoa had become inadequate for its purpose.[139]

Meanwhile, the adoption of the liberal constitution granted by Charles Albert in 1848 to his subjects facilitated the aim of the official representatives of Sardinia in the United States to promote the commercial relations of the two countries. During the five years — from 1848 to 1853 — that Chevalier L. Mossi held the post of chargé d'affaires in Washington, he took great pains to increase the existing trade between the two countries. He examined particularly into the feasibility of shipping American coal for the use of the railway to Turin, and some cargoes were accordingly dispatched as an experiment. He also favored the plan of a line of steamers between Genoa and New York. Though the plan failed the contract and advantages remained open to American enterprise for several years.[140]

---

[138] *Congressional Globe,* June 15, 1844, XIII, 673.

[139] H. R. Marraro, "Spezia: an American naval base, 1848-68." *Military Affairs,* Washington, D. C., Winter 1943, VII, no. 4, 202-208.

[140] New York *Herald,* May 11, 1856. This subject is treated in H. R. Marraro, "Italians in New York in the eighteen fifties." *New York History,* Cooperstown, N. Y., April 1949, XXX, 181-203; July 1949, XXX, 276-303.

It is noteworthy that within ten years of the date in which the liberal constitution was granted to the Sardinians, commerce between that country and the United States increased from three hundred thousand to three million dollars annually.[141]

During the administration of President Franklin Pierce one or two incidents occurred which threatened the peaceful relations between the two countries. In May 1853, President Pierce appointed E. Felix Foresti,[142] an avowed Mazzinian, American consul at Genoa. Secretary of State William L. Marcy, not anticipating any difficulties in the appointment, sent Foresti's commission to the Legation of the United States at Turin, with instructions to apply to the Sardinian Government for the usual exequatur.[143] In the meantime, however, the news of this appointment had reached Mr. I. Valerio,[144] the Sardinian chargé d'affaires at Washington, who immediately communicated the information to General Giuseppe Dabormida,[145] the Sardinian Minister of Foreign Affairs at Turin. In a confidential despatch, dated New York, June 28, 1853, Mr. Valerio accused Foresti of being an avowed agent of Mazzini in the United States, and of having recently shown "great hostility toward the Government of His Majesty." With his antecedents, Mr. Valerio feared "that, in coming to Genoa, Mr. Foresti could abuse his position and create embarrassments to the Government of the King; in my opinion, therefore, the exequatur should be declined."

Mr. John M. Daniel who, in the meantime, had reached Turin as American chargé, was instructed to assure the Minister of Foreign Affairs of Sardinia that the President had duly considered the objections which had been urged against Mr. Foresti, but he did not find them to be of such character as to induce him to cancel his appointment.

In transmitting to Secretary of State Marcy a report of his interviews with General Dabormida, and a copy of the despatch

---

[141] New York *Herald,* May 17, 1856.

[142] Howard R. Marraro, 'Eleuterio Felice Foresti." *Columbia University Quarterly*, New York, 1933, 34-64.

[143] John M. Daniel, of Virginia, was commissioned chargé d'affaires July 23, 1853. Commissioned minister resident June 29, 1854. Presented credentials as such about Sept. 4, 1854. Presented letter of recall, through private secretary, March 2, 1861.

[144] I. Valerio, chargé d'affaires ad interim, from Apr. 6 to July 20, 1853 and from Apr. 12 to June 28, 1855.

[145] Giuseppe Dabormida (1799-1869). In 1848 he was Sardinian minister of war and navy; in 1849 minister plenipotentiary to conclude peace with Austria. From 1852 to 1855 and from 1859 to 1860, minister of foreign affairs. In 1852 he was appointed a senator.

dated November 21 1853, he had received from General Dabor-mida, Mr. Daniel concluded as follows:

Taking a general view of the whole, I am inclined to think the authori-ties are perfectly sincere in the regret which they express at finding themselves at issues with the United States. We are popular in this country. The sympathy and respect of the United States are regarded as one of the supports of this little liberal Kingdom in the midst of hostile despotisms. I do not believe either the people or the Government would willingly disoblige the United States. But the unwillingness of the Government to receive Mr. Foresti became so well known at the first announcement of the appointment, that they really would be in a rather awkward position if, after all, they should have yielded; and this at last I believe they would have done but for the same publicity.

But with a stubbornness which would amaze any modern statesman, Mr. Marcy upon the receipt of the above despatch replied to Mr. Daniel on December 19, 1853, as follows: "When the Sardinian Minister of Foreign Affairs becomes aware that there has been a strange misapprehension of the true import of these declarations it will be awkward for that Government to take any other objection. Presuming that there is entire good faith in this matter, I do not expect that there will be any objec-tion to receiving Mr. Foresti after erroneous impressions shall have been removed."

At this point the Marquis A. Taliacarne[146] arrived to take over the office of Sardinian chargé d'affaires in the United States. This was in December 1853, but in view of the publicity which the subject had received in the American press, the Marquis Taliacarne deemed it advisable to postpone the official request for his own exequatur.

Meanwhile, Sardinia remained firm in the position she had assumed from the very beginning, and definitely informed the American Government through her representative that she would not accept Foresti as American consul at Genoa. When this became known Mr. Marcy, at an interview with the Marquis Taliacarne, on February 10, 1854, informed the Sardinian that the President had learned of the refusal of the exequatur to Mr. Foresti with deep regret, and that since Sardinia did not wish to receive Mr. Foresti as consul of the United States at Genoa, and since the reasons for refusing him were not justi-fiable, he did not think that the President would appoint some one else in his place, and he regretted that the friendly relations which had happily existed between the two countries would

146 Marquis A. Taliacarne, chargé d'affaires. Presented credentials Dec. 19, 1853. Last note to him from State Department Jan. 23, 1855.

suffer some coolness, as a result of an incident which was of so little importance. Fortunately, however, President Pierce soon saw the right of the Sardinian Government to refuse the exequatur to Mr. Foresti, and on June 21, 1854, the Chief Executive nominated Mr. A. Herbemont, of South Carolina, consul of the United States at Genoa, where he remained to 1858.[147]

Another unfortunate incident which undermined the relations between the United States and Sardinia involved Mr. Daniel, our chargé. In a letter to the Richmond (Va.) *Examiner*, he denounced the Sardinian Court as little better than a collection of *lazzaroni*, charging that even the nobility "stank of onions and garlic," and that the whole country was surcharged with the "effluvia of those vulgar vegetables." William L. Marcy, Secretary of State, in a letter to President Pierce, frankly admitted that there was "some danger to be apprehended from the impulsive character of the young gentleman, Daniel, at Turin, and his radical democratic proclivities." As a means of forestalling the unpleasant consequences which might otherwise have resulted from this letter, the Secretary of State suggested the advisability of having Mr. Mason, Chairman of the Foreign Relations Committee of the Senate, address a familiar note to this "ardent Virginian," recommending a proper apology to the Court of Turin and the nobility of Sardinia, or such "an explanation of his violent animadversions upon onions and garlic as might preserve the entente cordiale with King Emmanuel." Mr. Daniel's letter in fact excited great annoyance at Turin, and the American chargé was not only expelled from a club at Turin, but was even threatened with a duel.[148]

With the exception of these incidents, Sardinia maintained friendly relations with the United States, and her representatives were highly respected in diplomatic and fashionable circles at Washington. In fact, during the second war of Italian independence, 1859, the American people gave many evidences of their sincere interest in the ultimate victory of the Sardinian forces. That the Sardinian Government appreciated these expressions of sympathy from America is indicated in a letter from Count Cavour dated Turin, July 9, 1859, addressed to Professor V. Botta, President of the Italian Committee. Count Cavour

---

[147] Mr. Foresti was again appointed United States consul for Genoa in May 1858, and since, in the meantime, he had become sympathetic to the rule of Victor Emmanuel II, there was no difficulty in obtaining the exequatur from the Sardinian Government. But he enjoyed the honor only a few months, for he died at his post in the fall of that year.

[148] New York *Herald*, Nov. 22, 1854.

wrote: "The country of Washington was ever among the first to give us effectual and practical proofs of its benevolence. . . . I beg of you to thank publicly, in my name, the Italians who have contributed to the promotion of the subscription, as well as those American citizens who have so generously seconded your efforts."[149] Similarly, during the American Civil War, the Italian Government and people gave their undivided moral and material support to those forces that worked for the preservation of the American Union. In acknowledging this aid, President Lincoln on one occasion declared that "at no state in this unhappy fraternal war . . . has the King or the people of Italy faltered in addressing to us the language of respect, confidence and friendship."[150]

KINGDOM OF ITALY

At the successful conclusion of the Italian war of liberation in 1859-60, the Turin Parliament on March 4, 1861, adopted the necessary measures for the proclamation of Victor Emmanuel as King of Italy. The action taken by Parliament was communicated on March 19, 1861 by Prime Minister Cavour to Giuseppe Bertinatti,[151] the Italian minister in Washington. Immediately upon receipt of the despatch, Mr. Bertinatti officially communicated the vote of Parliament to Mr. William H. Seward, the Secretary of State. In his reply to Mr. Bertinatti (printed here for the first time from the original dated April 13, 1861, now in the archives of the Ministry of Foreign Affairs, Rome), Mr. Seward said:

The undersigned, Secretary of State of the United States, has the honor to acknowledge the receipt of the Chevalier Bertinatti's note of the 11th instant, communicating a copy of Count Cavour's despatch to him of the 19th ultimo, announcing that His Majesty Victor Emmanuel II, in virtue of the law voted by the National Parliament, has assumed the title of King of Italy.

The undersigned cannot doubt that the extended authority of His

---

149 New York *Herald,* Sept. 24, 1859.

150 H. R. Marraro, Italy and Lincoln. *The Abraham Lincoln Quarterly,* Springfield, Ill., March 1944, III, 3-16.

151 Chevalier Joseph Bertinatti, chargé d'affaires. Presented credentials Oct. 2, 1855. On April 11, 1861, he announced the assumption by Victor Emmanuel of the title of King of Italy, which occurred on Mar. 17, preceding. Presented letter of credence as Envoy Extraordinary and Minister Plenipotentiary, June 30, 1864. Left the United States on leave June 8, 1866.

Majesty, so entirely in accordance with the wishes of the Italian people, will be exercised with the moderation and wisdom for which he has ever been conspicuous; and he trusts that His Majesty's reign may be prosperous and happy to himself and acceptable to his subjects.

The undersigned has the honor, in conclusion, to announce to the Chevalier Bertinatti that Mr. Marsh, the newly appointed Envoy Extraordinary and Minister Plenipotentiary of the United States to Sardinia, has been accredited to His Majesty Victor Emmanuel II as King of Italy . . .

(Signed) William H. Seward

The United States had officially recognized the new organization of the Kingdom of Italy as early as April 1860. Following the recognition of the Kingdom of Italy by England, France, and Switzerland, the United States House of Representatives adopted a resolution introduced by Mr. Anson Burlingame, Republican, of Massachusetts, on April 20, 1860, instructing the Committee on Foreign Affairs to inquire into the expediency of raising the Sardinian mission to a first class one, adding that commercial considerations also made it advisable to take this step. Encouraged by the favorable reaction to his resolution, Mr. Burlingame, upon authorization of the Committee on Foreign Affairs, on May 7, 1860, reported a bill according Sardinia a first class mission. Specifically the bill provided that after June 30, 1860, the Kingdom of Sardinia be ranked in schedule A of the consular and diplomatic bill, approved August 18, 1856, with Russia, Austria, Brazil, and China; that the President, by and with the advice and consent of the Senate, appoint a representative to the Kingdom of Sardinia of the grade of Envoy Extraordinary and Minister Plenipotentiary, who would receive for his services an annual compensation of $12,000; that the president appoint a secretary of legation, who would receive for his services an annual compensation of $1,800; and that all acts and parts of acts fixing the rank and compensation of the representative of the United States and secretary of Legation at Sardinia be repealed, in so far as the same were inconsistent with this act.[152]

The first full diplomatic representative of the United States to Italy was George P. Marsh, who was commissioned Envoy Extraordinary and Minister Plenipotentiary on March 20, 1861, and who presented his credentials as such on June 23, 1861.[153]

---

[152] *Congressional Globe*, 36th Cong., 1st Sess., 1859-1860, pt. 3, 1944; New York *Herald*, Apr. 26, May 8, 1860.

[153] *Register*, 1874, II, 82; *Register*, 1937, 345; and *Papers Relating to Foreign Affairs*, 1861, 104.

The United States continued to appoint a diplomatic representative of the rank of minister to Italy until October 20, 1893; when James J. Van Alen was appointed Ambassador Extraordinary and Plenipotentiary.[154] Van Alen declined the appointment, however, and did not go to the post at Rome.[155] On December 20, 1893, Wayne MacVeagh was appointed Ambassador Extraordinary and Plenipotentiary to Italy, and he presented his credentials as such on March 11, 1894.[156]

The first diplomatic representative of Italy to the United States was Chevalier Joseph Bertinatti, who had been Minister Resident of Piedmont-Sardinia to the United States and who, as was noted above, announced the assumption by King Victor Emmanuel II of the title of King of Italy. Bertinatti presented his credentials as Envoy Extraordinary and Minister Plenipotentiary on July 30, 1864.[157] Italy continued to be represented in the United States by a representative of the rank of minister until June 24, 1893, when Baron de Fava presented his credentials as Ambassador Extraordinary and Plenipotentiary of Italy to the United States.[158] The last ambassador of Italy to the United States before the outbreak of war in 1941 between the two countries was Don Ascanio dei principi Colonna, who presented his credentials on March 22, 1939.[159]

After the constitution of the Kingdom of Italy in 1861, two imporant conventions were concluded between the United States and Italy. The first was a consular convention, concluded on February 8, 1868,[160] comprising eighteen articles dealing with: consuls, exequaturs, exemptions, consuls as witnesses, arms and flag, archives, death or absence of consuls, vice-consuls, infrac-

---

[154] Personnel records of the Department of State. A section of the act of Congress of March 1, 1893, making appropriations for the diplomatic and consular services for the fiscal year ending June 30, 1894, provided that "Whenever the President shall be advised that any foreign government is represented, or is about to be represented, in the United States by an ambassador, envoy extraordinary, minister plenipotentiary, minister resident, special envoy, or chargé d'affaires, he is authorized, in his discretion, to direct that the representative of the United States to such government shall bear the same designation." (See *Statutes at Large*, volume 27, p. 497). As noted below, Italy conferred the title of ambassador upon its representative at Washington on June of 1893, and the United States responded by accrediting its representative at Rome with the same title. (See Richardson's *Messages and Papers*, IX, 442).

[155] *Register*, 1937, 345: and despatch of March 12, 1894, from MacVeagh at Rome in Despatches from Italy, volume 28. Records of the United States State Department now in the United States National Archives.

[156] *Register*, 1894, 115.

[157] *Ibid.*, 116.

[158] Register for the years 1875 to 1893.

[159] *Diplomatic List*, December 1941, 19.

[160] For the text of this convention, see Malloy, *op. cit.*, 961.

81

tion of treaties, powers of consuls, merchant vessels, settlement of disputes, deserters, damages at sea, salvage, disposition of property, duration, and ratification. This treaty which was signed by William H. Seward and Marcello Cerruti,[161] was superseded by the Convention of 1878 upon the exchange of ratifications on September 17, 1878.

The other convention of the same year, also signed by William H. Seward and Marcello Cerruti, was the extradition convention, concluded on March 23, 1868.[162] Comprising eight articles, this convention besides providing for the delivery of the accused, defined extraditable crimes and political offenses. It also dealt with such topics as persons under arrest, procedure, expenses, duration, and ratification.

The United States Government and people watched with intense interest the final stages that led to the unification of Italy with the occupation of Rome by the Italian troops in 1870 and the declaration of Rome as the capital of united Italy. Except for the Catholics, the event was hailed by Americans everywhere as a significant accomplishment in that the Italian people had at long last achieved their just aspirations.[163]

Soon after the accomplishment of Italian unity, a new treaty of commerce was concluded between the two countries on February 26, 1871.[164] The twenty-six articles of this treaty, signed by George P. Marsh and Visconti-Venosta, comprised:—1. freedom of commerce and navigation, 2. liberty to trade and travel, 3. rights of person and property, exemptions, 4. embargo, 5. no shipping discriminations, 6. no discriminations of imports and exports, 7. shipping privilege, 8. exemptions from shipping dues, etc., 9. shipwrecks, 10. completing crews, 11. piratical captures, 12. exemptions in war, 13. blockade, 14. regulation of blockades,

---

161 Chevalier Marcello Cerruti, envoy extraordinary and minister plenipotentiary. Presented credentials Aug. 30, 1867. Successor presented May 13, 1870. As a matter of fact Count Luigi Collobiano, the secretary of the Legation, acted as chargé d'affaires ad interim from July 2, 1869 to May 13, 1870, when Count Luigi Corti presented his credentials as envoy extraordinary and minister plenipotentiary. Corti left on Oct. 7, 1873, leaving the legation in charge of Count Zannini who acted as chargé *ad interim*.

162 For text, see Malloy, *op. cit.*, 966.

163 U.S. Congress: Italian occupation of Rome: Resolution calling for correspondence on reference to the occupation of Rome by King of Italy: by Mr. James Brooks of New York. *Congressional Globe,* March 31, 1871; p. 364 (42nd Congress: 1st session: v. 98.); United States House of Representatives: 42nd Congress, 1st session: Executive Documents, No. 18. Occupation of Rome by the King of Italy: Message from the President of the United States in answer to a resolution of the House of the 31st ultimo, relative to the occupation of Rome by the King of Italy.

164 For text of this treaty, see Malloy, *op. cit.*, 969.

15. contraband articles, 16. rights of neutrals; free ships; free goods; 17. proof of nationality of vessels, 18. right of search, 19. vessels under convoy, 20. conduct of commanders of war vessels; 21. protection in case of war, 22. disposal of property, 23. legal rights, 24. most favored nation privileges, 25. duration, 26. ratification.

Seven years later, a new consular convention between the two countries was concluded on May 8, 1878.[165] Signed by William Maxwell Evarts and A. Blanc, this convention included eighteen articles, as follows: 1. consular recognition, 2. exequaturs, 3. exemptions, 4. status in legal proceedings, 5. arms and flags, 6. archives, 7. vacancies, 8. vice-consuls and agents, 9. dealings with officials, 10. general powers, 11. shipping disputes, 12. disputes between passengers and officers of vessels, 13. deserters from ships, 14. damages at sea, 15. shipwrecks, 16. death of citizens, 17. most favored nation privileges, 18. duration; ratification.

On February 24, 1881, a convention supplemental to the consular convention of 1878 was concluded.[166] Signed by William Maxwell Evarts and Paolo Beccadelli Bologna, Prince of Camporeale, the 1881 document provided for shipping disputes, being a substitute for article 11 of the earlier convention.

On June 11, 1884 a convention additional to the extradition[167] convention of 1868 was concluded and signed by Frederick T. Frelinghuysen and Baron Fava. The main provision of the new convention was the addition of kidnapping to the extraditable crimes, and provided also for the preliminary detention of the criminals.

One minor incident affecting the relations between the two countries occurred in 1885 when the Italian Government refused to accept Mr. A. M. Keiley, of Virginia, who had been appointed American minister to Italy on the ground that the remarks he had made at Richmond, Va., in 1871 in protest against the abolition of the temporal power of the Pope rendered him a *persona non grata*. The difficulty, however, was soon forgotten, as the United States did not insist on the appointment.

With the rapid increase of Italian immigration into the United States after 1890 several questions were raised that affected both the domestic policy and Italo-American relations, including such

---

165 For text, see Malloy, *op. cit.*, 977.
166 For text, see Malloy, *op. cit.*, 983.
167 For the text of the June 11, 1884 convention, see Malloy, *op. cit.*, 985.

problems as expatriation and naturalization, new immigrant laws designed to prevent the admission of criminals and paupers, the *padrone* system and the protection of Italian emigrants against it, and the inspection of emigrants at Naples by American consular officers. Besides the difficulty arising out of the lynching episodes in New Orleans, and other cities, referred to in another part of this introduction, other minor incidents occurred which interfered with the relations between the two countries. These were: the closing of the Italian emigration bureau at Ellis Island in 1898 and 1899, and reflections of the American Industrial Commission upon the integrity of Italian officials.

Since 1900, friendly relations have been accompanied by the negotiation of several important treaties. Under the provision of the Dingley Tariff Act, a new commercial treaty was concluded on February 8, 1900.[168] Signed by John A. Kasson and Baron Fava, it consisted of three articles, as follows: 1, concessions by the United States; 2, concessions by Italy; 3, approval and duration.

An arbitration convention, signed at Washington, D. C., on March 28, 1908[169] by Elihu Root and Mayor des Planches, provided that any differences that arose as a result of the legal interpretation of treaties existing between Italy and the United States would be referred to the Permanent Court of Arbitration at The Hague.

In the Italian-Turkish War of 1911 and 1912, the United States demonstrated only a remote interest.

A treaty of commerce and navigation, amendatory of article III of the treaty of 1871, and providing for right of action by aliens in cases of injury or death caused by negligence or fault, was signed and ratified at Washington in February 1913. A treaty providing for reciprocal military service for citizens of the two countries was ratified in the latter part of 1918.

In 1924, there was signed a convention for the prevention of smuggling of intoxicating liquors.[170]

In 1925, the Italian war debt to the United States was fixed at $2,042,000,000 (including interest), payable in 62 years.

In 1928 there was signed at Washington, D. C. a treaty of arbitration dated April 19, 1928.[171]

---

[168] For the text of the treaty, see Malloy, *op. cit.*, 987.
[169] For the text of the treaty, *Ibid.*, 992.
[170] United States — Senate. *Treaties, conventions, international acts etc. betwen the United States of America and other powers 1923-37.* United States Gov't Pr. Office, 1938, IV, 4381-4383 [Doc. No. 134].
[171] *Ibid.*, 4383-4385.

The last Ambassador of the United States to Italy before the outbreak of World War II was William Phillips, who was appointed on August 4, 1936, and who presented his credentials on November 4, 1936.[172]

Information relating to various aspects of the diplomatic relations of the United States with Italy during the decade preceding 1941 may be found in Publication No. 1983 of the Department of State entitled *Peace and War: United States Foreign Policy, 1931-1941*. (Attention is particularly invited to pages 72 to 75 of that publication, which deals with American efforts to keep Italy out of the European war.)

The following paragraph regarding the suspension of consular relations between the United States and Italy is quoted from Green H. Hackworth's *Digest of International Law* (7 volumes thus far, Washington, Government Printing Office, 1940-), volume IV, page 682:

"On June 19, 1941, the American Ambassador at Rome was in receipt of a note from the Italian Foreign Office stating that that Government had come to the conclusion that activities of the United States Consulates in Italy —

have gone and go in many instances far beyond the functions which are attributed and permitted to consular offices and are assuming a character especially in the field of information that is wholly illicit and in any case incompatible with the duties which are incumbent upon consuls towards the country in which they perform their function.

It was requested that American consuls and consulate employees be withdrawn from Italian territory. The Department, on June 20, 1941, instructed the Ambassador to inform the Italian Foreign Office that the United States rejected the allegations that American consular officers had been guilty of improper acts. At the same time it addressed a note to the Italian Ambassador in Washington, stating that in its opinion "it is obvious that the continuing functioning of Italian consular establishments in territory of the United States would serve no desirable purpose"; and it was requested that "all agencies in the United States connected with the Italian Government be closed and

---

[172] *Register*, 1937, 345; and telegram no. 443 of November 4, 1936, 5 p.m., from Phillips at Rome, Department of State file no. 123. P54/313. Mr. Phillips had departed from his post on October 6, 1941, leaving George Wadsworth, Counselor of the Embassy, as Chargé d'Affaires *ad interim*; Mr. Wadsworth was still in charge of the Embassy at the time Italy declared war in December 1941 (See telegram no. 1554 of October 6, 1941 from Phillips at Rome, Department of State file no. 123P54/474.)

personnel withdrawn with the exception of duly accredited representation in Washington."[173]

The Italian Foreign Minister, Count Ciano, sent for George Wadsworth, American chargé d'affaires at Rome, on December 11, 1941, 2:30 p.m. (8:30 a.m. Washington time), and when Mr. Wadsworth arrived at his office, Count Ciano informed him that as of that date Italy considered itself at war with the United States. On the same day, President Roosevelt requested the Congress of the United States "to recognize a state of war" between the United States and Italy. At 3:06 p.m. on December 11, President Roosevelt approved a joint resolution of the Congress which stated, in part, that "the state of war between the United States and the Government of Italy which has thus been thrust upon the United States is hereby formally declared."[174]

An announcement which was issued by Allied Headquarters in North Africa at noon on September 8, 1943, and which was read over the radio by General Eisenhower beginning at noon on September 8, 1943 read in part as follows: "Some weeks ago the Italian Government made an approach to the British and American Governments with a view to concluding an armistice. . . . The Armistice was signed . . . on September third, but it was agreed . . . that the Armistice should come into force at a moment most favorable for the Allies. . . . That moment has now arrived. . . ."[175]

On October 13, 1943, it was announced by the White House that Marshal Badoglio of the Italian Government had communicated to General Eisenhower a message which stated that the King of Italy had declared war on Germany and that the declaration would be handed to the German Ambassador at Madrid on October 13, 1943.[176] A joint statement, issued by the President of the United States, the Prime Minister of Great Britain, and the Premier of the Union of Soviet Socialist Republics, concerning the declaration of war by Italy, stated that the American, British, and Soviet Governments accepted, "the active cooperation of the Italian nation and armed forces as a co-belligerent in the war against Germany." The statement added that:

---

[173] Information to the establishment, severance, etc. Typewritten report prepared by the State Department and sent to the editor, 8-9.
[174] *Department of State Bulletin,* December 13, 1941, 475-476 and 482.
[175] Information relating to the establishment, etc. 9.
[176] *Department of State Bulletin,* Oct. 16, 1943, 253.

"The relationship of co-belligerency between the Government and the United Nations governments cannot of itself affect the terms recently signed, which retain their full force and can only be adjusted by agreement between the allied governments in the light of the assistance which the Italian Government may be able to afford the United Nations' cause."[177]

The American Consulate at Palermo, Sicily, which had been closed in 1941, was re-opened on February 11, 1944.[178]

On January 8, 1945, Alexander Kirk presented his credentials to Prince Humbert, Lieutenant General of the Kingdom, as Ambassador of the United States at Rome, in an elaborate and formal ceremony which took place in the throne room of the Quirinal. Mr. Kirk was thus the first allied Ambassador to present his credentials to the Head of the Italian State since the armistice of 1943. Although no official speeches were made, Prince Humbert requested that the ceremony be formal. In this manner he wished to show his appreciation of the action of the United States in becoming the first Allied Nation to send to Rome a diplomatic representative with the rank of ambassador. During the ceremony, however, Prince Humbert and Ambassador Kirk drew away from the official group and conversed for twenty-five minutes. After the conversation, Mr. Kirk presented to Prince Humbert eight members of the personnel of the American Embassy.[179]

On March 8, 1945, in accepting from Alberto Tarchiani his letters of credence as the first Italian Ambassador since the declaration of war, President Roosevelt gave words of encouragement to Italy and her people. "The friendship between our two peoples," Mr. Roosevelt said to the Italian Ambassador in the ceremony at the White House, "has passed the bitter test of hostilities between us. With good-will and understanding, the friendship can find more solid basis than ever before. I know that this is the sincere desire of the people and Government of the United States." The American people, Mr. Roosevelt told Ambassador Tarchiani, "admire the courage of patriotic Italians in the struggle against the enemy, and they watch sympathetically every sign that the Italians — aware of their individual responsibilities at home and abroad — are resolved to build a genuine democracy which will be proof against oppression from within

---

[177] *Ibid.*, 254.
[178] *Department of State Bulletin*, February 19, 1944, 195.
[179] *Progresso Italo-Americano*, New York, Jan. 9, 1945.

and guarantee of Italy's value to the world. . . . In the difficult process of her rehabilitation, Italy has one great and indestructible resource: the quality of her people. The American people know how valuable that quality can be, for the generous life streams flowing from Europe have brought much of it to the formation of their own country. Above and beyond such moral and material assistance as we and our allies can give, it is the development of this great human resource — the hard-working, intelligent mass of the Italian people — which alone can reconstruct Italy on firm foundations," the President concluded

In reply, Ambassador Tarchiani extended on behalf of the Italian nation "most hearty wishes for a complete victory over the enemy and for the ever greater fortunes of the American nation in the new era that awaits the world." The "earnest aspiration" of the "new Italy," he said, "is to be an active and constructive element in the community of the United Nations."[180]

[180] New York *Times*, March 9, 1945, 10. On the relations between the United States and Italy from 1936 to 1946, see: *United States and Italy 1936-1946: documentary record*. Department of State: Publication 2669, European Series 17. United States Government Printing Office, Washington, D. C., 1946, 236 pp., maps. Concerning the new treaty of friendship between the two countries, see: United States, Congress. Senate. Committee on Foreign Relations. *Proposed treaty of friendship, commerce, and navigation between the United States and the Italian Republic*. Hearing before a subcommittee of the Committe on Foreign Relations, United States Senate, Eightieth Congress, second session . . . Apr. 30, 1948. Washington, U. S. Govt. Print. Off., 1948, iii, 37p.

UNITED STATES MINISTERS TO THE KINGDOM OF THE TWO SICILIES

Instructions and Despatches

WILLIAM PINKNEY[1]
(Apr. 23, 1816 - Feb. 27, 1817)

JAMES MADISON TO WM. PINKNEY

Greeting:

Reposing especial Trust and Confidence in your Integrity, Prudence and Ability, I have nominated, and by and with the advice and consent of the Senate, appointed you the said William Pinkney, Minister Plenipotentiary of the United States of America to the Court of His Majesty the King of the two Sicilies; authorizing you hereby to do and perform all such matters and things as to the said place or office do appertain, or as may be duly given you in charge hereafter; and the said Office to Hold and exercise during the pleasure of the President of the United States for the time being.

In Testimony whereof, I have caused the Seal of the United States to be hereunto affixed. Given under my hand at the City of Washington the twenty third day of April in the year of our Lord 1816; and of the Independence of the United States of America the Fortieth.

JAMES MADISON

I. S.   By the President,

JA⁸ MONROE SECʸ OF STATE[2]

---

[1] William Pinkney (1764-1822). Lawyer, statesman, diplomat, was born at Annapolis, Maryland. He resigned his seat in Congress in April 1816, to accept an appointment as minister to Russia with a special mission to Naples en route. Specifically, Mr. Pinkney was commissioned minister plenipotentiary to Naples, April 23, 1816, to obtain indemnity for losses sustained by American citizens by the seizure and confiscation of their property by the Neapolitan Government. For biographies on Pinkney see: Rev. William Pinkney, *The life of William Pinkney,* by his nephew. New York, D. Appleton & Co., 1853, 407 pp.; Henry Wheaton, *Some account of the life, writings, and speeches of William Pinkney.* Philadelphia, Carey & Lea, 1826, 616 pp.; Henry Wheaton, "Life of William Pinkney" in *Lives of William Pinkney, William Ellery, and Cotton Mather.* New York, Harper & Bros., 1844, 1-84; *Dictionary American Biography.* 1934, XIV, 626-629; Horace Henry Hagan, *Eight Great American Lawyers.* Oklahoma City, Harlow Publishing Company, 1923, 293 pp. On his diplomatic career, see: *American State Papers: Foreign Relations,* 1823-24, III, IV; Hunter Miller (editor), *Treaties and other International acts of the United States of America* (Washington, D. C., 1931), III, 717.

[2] James Monroe. (1758-1831). Virginian statesman, diplomat and fifth President of the United States. Minister to France 1794-96; Special envoy to Madrid 1804, to Great Britain 1805; Secretary of State 1811-1817; President of the United States, 1817-1825. *Dictionary American Biography,* 1934, XIII, 87.

JAMES MADISON, PRESIDENT OF THE UNITED STATES OF AMERICA, TO HIS MAJESTY THE KING OF THE TWO SICILIES[3]

Great and Good Friend,

In order to confirm between your Majesty and the United States of America perfect harmony and a good correspondence and to remove all grounds of dissatisfaction by a friendly discussion, I have appointed with the advice and consent of the Senate of the United States William Pinkney, of the State of Maryland, to be Special Minister to your Majesty on subjects of high importance to both Nations. From the knowledge I have of the fidelity, probity and good conduct of this Minister, I have entire confidence that he will render himself acceptable to your Majesty in this charge. I therefore beseech your Majesty to give full credence to whatever he shall say on the part of the U. States, and most of all when he shall assure you of our friendship and wishes for your prosperity. And I pray God to have your Majesty in his safe and holy keeping.

Written at the City of Washington the 26ᵗʰ. day of April in the year of our Lord 1816.

Your Good Friend

JAMES MADISON

By the President

JAS MONROE SECY OF STATE

JAMES MONROE TO WM. PINKNEY

DEPARTMENT OF STATE, May 11, 1816.

Sir

Being appointed with [sic] the President, with the advice and consent of the Senate, Envoy Extraordinary and Minister Plenipotentiary to the Emperor of Russia, and in a similar trust, to the King of Naples, the duties of the latter mission which is special, will engage your attention, in the first instance. The Washington, a Ship of the Line, is ordered into the Chesapeake, to receive on board, and to convey you and your family to Naples. You will be furnished with the usual Commission and Letter of Credence to the King.

---

3 The originals of this communication and of the foregoing are in The National Archives, Washington, D. C. See *Record Group No 59, General Records of the Department of State. Credences*, I, (Oct. 9, 1789-Nov. 16, 1824). The original of the following communication (Monroe to Pinkney, May 11, 1816) is in The National Archives, *Record Group No. 59, General Records of the Department of State. Instructions, United States Ministers*, VIII, 53-56. (Nov. 2, 1815-Dec. 7, 1819).

A principal object of your mission to Naples, is, to obtain indemnity, for the losses which our citizens sustained by the illegal seizure and confiscation of their property by the Neapolitan government. You will be furnished with such evidence in support of the claim, as is in possession of this Department, and as notice has been given to the Collectors in the principal cities of your appointment and its object, that it might be communicated to the parties interested, it is expected that you will receive much further light on the subject directly from them.

The President does not entertain a doubt of the right, of the United States, to a full idemnity for these losses. They were inflicted by the then government of the country without the slightest cause. The commerce of the United States was invited into the Neapolitan ports, by special Decrees, with the promise of protection and encouragement, on the faith of which, many ships having entered, with valuable cargoes, the whole amount was seized, by the Government itself, and converted to public use. For this very extraordinary and unlawful act, no plea has been urged, that we have heard of, except that of necessity, which is no argument against indemnity. The injury being inflicted by a government in full possession of the sovereignty of the country, exercising all its powers, recognized by the Nation, and by Foreign Powers by Treaties and other formal acts, of the highest authority, it is not perceived, on what ground, an indemnity can be refused. No principle is better established, than that the nation is responsible, for the acts of its government, and that a change in the authority does not affect the obligation. In the disordered state of that country for several years past, it has been thought useless, to press this claim, but now that affairs appear to be better settled, it would be improper, longer, to delay it. The President indulges a strong hope that reparation will now be made. In the discharge of this trust, in the manner of the negotiation, and in the provision for the debt, should such be made you will manifest a spirit of conciliation towards the government of Naples. Any reasonable accommodation, as to the time and mode of payment, which may be desired, will be cheerfully allowed.

As you will be well acquainted with the nature of these claims, and the right of the United States to an indemnity; with the principles on which it is founded, and the arguments and facts which support it; it is unnecessary for me, to enter further, into the subject. The President has full confidence that nothing will be wanting on your part, to secure success to the mission. Satisfied that you will discharge its duties with equal ability and discretion it is thought improper, by too much precision, to impose any restraint on your judgment, either as to the manner, or the argument, to be used, in the negotiation.

Other objects will claim your attention in this mission. It is important to place the commerce of the two Nations, on a footing of reciprocal advantage. You are acquainted with the laws of the United States, regulating their commerce with other Powers, by which, that of Naples, enjoys the advantage, of nations, the most favored, with whom there is no Treaty. By explaining these Laws to the Government of Naples, you may be able to promote, corresponding regulations, in favor of our trade, there. It is desirable to form a Treaty of Commerce for the enlargement and protection of this trade, and altho' the nature of your mission, and the duties you will have to perform elsewhere, forbid, such a delay at Naples, as would be required, for that purpose, it may be in your power, to acquire information, as to the importance of the object, and the practicability of attaining it, which may be very useful. You will therefore make this an object of your attention, and communicate the result of your enquiries, to this Department.

The relations between the United States and the Powers bordering on the Mediterranean are becoming dayly [sic] more interesting. Our trade, with the dominions, of the Powers of Europe, in that quarter, is already important, and it is extending to those of Turkey, in Europe and Asia, and of Russia, on the Black-Sea. For the protection of this trade, against the Barbary Powers, the United States have been compelled, to send a strong naval force, into the Mediterranean, which, it is probable, from present appearances, they will find it, equally necessary, to maintain there, for some time. A liberty to resort to the ports of the King of Naples, with a security for amicable treatment in them, is very desireable [sic]. The favorable influence which our Squadron, while in the Mediterranean, will have on the trade of the Italian States, in regard to the Barbary Powers, will be, a sufficient inducement, it is presumed, to any of them, to offer this asylum to our ships of war, with hospitality and kindness. You will endeavour to obtain the sanction, of the Neapolitan Government, to this accommodation, without, however, pledging any protection in return, on the part of our squadron, to the commerce of Naples. A letter to the Minister, with his answer, to this effect, will be sufficient.

You will have a favorable opportunity at Naples to acquire much information, of the state and prospect of our commerce, with the Italian States and the Levant, and of the disposition of the several powers, including Turkey to encourage it. All the information which you can acquire on this subject will be useful.

Your mission to Naples being special, its object limited, and being likewise anticipated by the Neapolitan government, it is expected, that it may be concluded, in a few interviews. It is very important that the United States should be represented at S^t. Petersburg, by a Minister of the highest grade, employed by them, without any delay, which can be avoided. The President desires therefore, that you will use every effort in your power, to terminate the business with Naples, as soon as it may be possible, and that you will proceed thence, immediately afterwards, to S^t. Petersburg.

THE MARQUIS DI CIRCELLO[4] TO WM. PINKNEY

Naples le 16 Juillet 1816 (Copy)

Le Marquis de Circello s'empresse d'accuser la reception des deux lettres que Monsieur Pinkney lui a fait l'honneur de Lui adresser jointes à son billet du 14 du courant. En le priant de vouloir bien en agréer ses remercimens distingués, le Marquis de Circello desire bien vivement de voir terminer au plutôt la quarantaine indispensable qu'on a dû imposer au Vaisseau le

---

4 Tommaso Di Somma, Marquis of Circello (1737-1826). A member of a noble family, he assumed the title of Marquis of Circello (in the province of Benevento), although he was the second child. One of the most outstanding men in the Kingdom, he was envoy extraordinary of the Neapolitan Court at Copenhagen in 1776-1777; in 1805, he was Neapolitan Minister of Foreign Affairs; he was head of the Provisional Government after March 1821; he was minister of foreign affairs from June 4, 1815 to June 10, 1822. For the distinguished services he rendered to his country, he was awarded the Cross of the Royal Order of S. Gennaro and later the Great Cross of S. Ferdinando and of Merit. For good accounts on the history of the Kingdom of Naples, during this period, see: Benedetto Croce, *Storia del regno di Napoli*. Bari, Laterza, 1925; Nicola Vivenzio, *Dell'Istoria del regno di Napoli e suo governo dalla decadenza dell'Impero Romano fino al presente Re Ferdinando IV*. Naples, 1847; Francesco Carta, *Storia del Reame delle Due Sicilie*, Naples, 1848; Edouard Deriault, *Etudes Napoléoniennes: Napoléon en Italie, 1800-1812*. 1906; Antonio Scialoia, *I bilanci del regno di Napoli*. Turin, 1847; Carlo Tivaroni, *Storia critica del risorgimento italiano 1735-1870*. Naples, 1888-1897, 9 volumes.

Washington, pour avoir le plaisir de faire la connaissance personelle de Monsieur Pinkney.

Il saisit, en attendant, cette occasion pour lui offrir les assurances de sa consideration très distinguée.

WM. PINKNEY TO THE MARQUIS DI CIRCELLO

Naples Hotel Della Gran Bretagna, July 27th, 1816 (Copy)

The Undersigned has the honour to seize the earliest occasion after his landing in Naples to inform his Excellency the Marquis di Circello that he is charged by the President of the United States of America with credentials as Envoy extraordinary to the Court of his Majesty the King of the two Sicilies, and that he will have the honour to wait on his Excellency, with his letters of Credence, at such time as he may think proper to appoint. He takes this opportunity to offer to his Excellency the Marquis di Circello the assurances of his distinguished Consideration.

THE MARQUIS DI CIRCELLO TO WM. PINKNEY

Naples 29th July 1816

The Undersigned Secretary of State, Minister for foreign affairs of His Majesty the King of the Two Sicilies, at the same time that he with eagerness presents his sincere congratulations to His Excellency Mr. Pinkney on his happy arrival in this Capital, hastens to inform him in reply to his esteemed note of the 27th. inst. that, if it be not inconvenient to his Excellency, the undersigned will see him Wednesday next the 31st. of this month between one and two o'clock P. M. He profits in the mean time of this occasion to present to His Excellency Mr. Pinkney the sentiments of his most distinguished Consideration. —

THE MARQUIS DI CIRCELLO TO WM. PINKNEY

Naples 5th of August [1816].

The undersigned Secretary of State, Minister for Foreign Affairs, has received the esteemed note of the 3^{d}. instant in which His Excellency Mr. Pinkney has signified his Desire of being presented to His Majesty the King of the two Sicilies and he will lose no time in taking the orders of his Sovereign thereupon, and will apprize His Excellency Mr. Pinkney of the Day on which His Majesty may be disposed to receive him.

In the meantime, the Undersigned avails himself of this occasion to renew to His Excellency Mr. Pinkney the protestations of his most distinguished consideration.

THE MARQUIS DI CIRCELLO TO WM. PINKNEY

Naples 7 August 1816 Translation[5]

The Undersigned Secretary of State, Minister for foreign affairs hastens to inform his Excellency Mr. Pinkney that His Majesty the King of the two Sicilies will receive him tomorrow the 8th Instant at half past eleven o'clock in the forenoon at the royal Villa of Capodimonte.

The undersigned renews on this occasion to his Excellency the assurances of his most distinguished Consideration.

P. S. The Marquis di Circello has the honour to inform his Excellency that tomorrow at the hour indicated he will be at Capodimonte where he will meet Mr. Pinkney for the purpose of presenting him to his Majesty.

THE MARQUIS DI CIRCELLO TO WM. PINKNEY

Naples 15 Aug. 1816 (Copy)

The Marquis di Circello hastens to inform H. E. M. Pinkney that on Monday evening the 19th instant there will be an attendance at Court, on account of its being the birthday of his royal Highness the hereditary Prince of the two Sicilies on which occasion H. E. may bring with him Mrs. Pinkney, the gentlemen attached to his mission, and the Commander and such other officers of the American Squadron as he may judge it convenient to introduce to His Majesty the King.

The Marquis di Circello will have the pleasure to be near His Majesty and in the meantime profits of this occasion to renew &c.

---

5 Written on the margin: (*Copies of Notes*)

WM. PINKNEY TO JAMES MONROE

Naples 24. August 1816. *Private*

My dear Sir,

I had hoped to have sent you by the Vessel on board of which this Letter will be put a public Dispatch, enclosing a Copy of my Note, on the subject of Murat's Spoliations, to the Marquis di Circello, the Minister for foreign affairs at this Court. — Unluckily, however, I am not able to send in my Note today on account of some alterations in it which make it necessary that it should again be copied. — You shall have it, however, by the next opportunity. —

We have been very kindly & respectfully received by this Government. — I have seen the Marquis di Circello several times and the King twice; but I cannot yet say positively what will be done on the Spoliation Concern.[6] — My public Dispatch will explain the reason of this particularly. The account of it is, however, that I found it worse than idle to attempt to persist in a Conversation Discussion of this matter with the Marquis di Circello, and that it came after some time to be arranged between us that it sh^d. be in writing. — My note has been delayed by various Causes, but principally by the necessity of making enquiries here as to facts. — It will be sent in Tomorrow, or early on Monday morning, and will be answered as I am assured without Delay. — The Subject is extremely delicate & difficult, but I venture to hope that my note will not be disapproved by The President.

My stay here will now be very short. A Note which I have this moment received from the Marquis di Circello states that he is much indisposed — so that I ought not to regret that my Note cannot be sent in today. — The President may be assured that I shall omit nothing, consistent with Discretion, by which I can have a Chance of securing Success to my Mission, and that I shall hasten my Departure for S^t. Petersburgh as much as possible. I have the Honour to be, my dear Sir, Your sincere & most obedient Servant

---

[6] A comprehensive study of the subject of these early claims is that made by the Rev. Paul Christopher Perrotta, *The claims of the United States against the Kingdom of Naples*. A dissertation. Washington, D. C., The Belvedere Press, 1926, 121 pp.

P. S. Please to tell Mr. Richard Forrest[7] that I have sent him some antient copper coins, found in Pompei & Herculaneum, by this opportunity, to the Care of Robert Oliver[8] of Baltimore.

THE MARQUIS DI CIRCELLO TO WM. PINKNEY

Naples, 24th August 1816.

The Marquis di Circello has not been able on account of Indisposition to take the King's Orders upon the proposition of the Commodore of the American Squadron communicated in Mr. Pinkney's note of the 22[d]. Instant — but he has been occupied in the meantime in procuring the information necessary to put His Majesty in a situation to decide upon the subject.

He will hasten to communicate the Result to Mr. P. as soon as he will be in a Situation to see the King — and in the meantime &c.

WM. PINKNEY TO THE MARQUIS DI CIRCELLO

Naples August 24, 1816 (Copy)

The Undersigned, Envoy Extraordinary of the United States of America, has already had the honour to mention to His Excellency the Marquis di Circello, Secretary of State and Minister for foreign affairs of His Majesty the King of the two Sicilies, the principal Objects of his Mission; and he now invites His Excellency's attention to a more detailed and formal exposition of one of those Objects. —

The Undersigned is sure that the Appeal, which he is about to make to the well-known Justice of His Sicilian Majesty, in the name and by the orders of his Government, will receive a deliberate and candid Consideration; and that, if it shall appear, as he trusts it will, to be recommended by those principles which

---

[7] Richard Forrest. Agent for the State Dept. in the chartering of the Ship *Alleghany* to be used to carry supplies from U. S. to Algiers, in 1812. (21st Cong. 1st Session House Report 100. See Forrest's signature and title, page 24 of the Report.)

[8] Robert Oliver. An Irishman who came from Belfast to Baltimore at the close of the Revolutionary War. During the war between France and England, his activity and enterprise enabled his house to make a very large fortune, principally by licences from the Spanish Government by which he carried on a profitable trade with Vera Cruz. (*Maryland Historical Magazine*, XVII, 235, note 8). In the claims of the United States against the Kingdom of Naples, Robert and John Oliver are listed as having suffered the heaviest monetary loss. (Perrotta, *op. cit.*; also American State Papers, *Foreign Relations*, VI, 482, 494-496.)

97

it is the interest as well as the duty of all Governments to observe and maintain, the Claim involved in it will be admitted, effectually and promptly.

The Undersigned did but obey the Instructions of The President of the United States when he assured His Excellency The Marquis di Circello, at their first interview, that his Mission was suggested by such Sentiments toward His Sicilian Majesty as could not fail to be approved by Him. — Those sentiments are apparent in the desire which The President has manifested, through the Undersigned, that the commercial relations between the territories of His Majesty and those of The United States should be cherished by reciprocal arrangements, sought in the spirit of enlightened friendship, and with a sincere view to such equal advantages as it is fit for Nations to derive from one another. — The representations which the Undersigned is commanded to make upon the Subject of the Present Note will be seen by His Majesty in the same light. — They show the firm reliance of The President upon the disposition of the Court of Naples impartially to discuss and ascertain, and faithfully to discharge its Obligations towards foreign States and their Citizens; a reliance which the Undersigned partakes with his Government, and under the influence of which he proceeds to state the Nature and Grounds of the reclamation in question.

It cannot but be known to His Excellency The Marquis di Circello that, on the 1st of July 1809, the Minister for foreign affairs[9] of the then Government of Naples addressed to Frederick Degan Esquire,[10] then Consul, of The United States, an official

---

9 Mastrillo Marzio. Marquis and later Duke of Gallo (1753c-1833). Diplomat. Neapolitan minister at Turin in 1782, and at Vienna in 1786. He represented Ferdinand IV in the peace preliminaries with France (1796); on behalf of Austria, he stipulated with Bonaparte the preliminaries of the Peace of Leoben; he signed the treaty of Campoformio (1797). In 1798 he was minister of foreign affairs and of the navy, and as such he tried to avoid the conflict between France and the Bourbons. He was again minister of foreign affairs under Joseph Bonaparte (June 3, 1806) and under Murat (1808) who bestowed upon him the title of duke. After the fall of the Napoleonic empire, the Duke of Gallo served the Bourbons, who, at first, would not have anything to do with him. In July 1820, he was a member of the Provisional Board (Giunta Provvisoria) of the government; he was again interim minister of foreign affairs from Dec. 10, 1820 to March 23, 1821. In this capacity he accompanied the Neapolitan King to Laibach, but was forced to wait at Gorizia until the King called him to inform him of the decisions taken by the powers. After the Restoration, he was removed from office and withdrew to private life. "Memorie del Duca di Gallo." Edited by B. Maresca in *Archivio Storico per le Provincie Napoletane*, 1888, XIII, 205-441. See also "Correspondence inédite de Marie Caroline avec le Marquis de Gallo." Edited by M. H. Weil and Di Somma Circello. Paris, 1911. 2 vols. See also *hic opus*, Nelson Chapter, p. 257, note 47.

10 Frederic Degan of Naples, commissioned Consul for the U. S. at Naples Mar. 20, 1805; again, Jan. 17, 1806. (Dates from the State Department Of-

Letter, containing an invitation to all American vessels, having on board the usual certificates of origin and other regular Papers, to come direct to Naples with their Cargoes, and that the same Minister caused that invitation to be published in every possible mode, in order that it might come to the knowledge of those whom it concerned.[11] — It will not be questioned, that the promise of security necessarily implied in this measure had every title, in the actual Circumstances of Europe, to the Confidence of distant and peaceful Merchants. — The Merchants of America, as was to have been expected, *did* confide. — Upon the credit and under the protection of that Promise they sent to Naples many valuable Vessels and Cargoes, navigated and documented with scrupulous regularity, and in no respect obnoxious to molestation; but scarcely had they reached the destination to which they had been allured when they were seized, without distinction, as prize or as otherwise forfeited to the Neapolitan Government, upon pretexts the most frivolous and idle. — These arbitrary seizures were followed, with a rapacious haste, by summary decrees, confiscating in the name and for the use of the same Government the whole of the property which had thus been brought within its grasp, and these decrees, which wanted even the decent affectation of Justice, were immediately carried into execution against all the remonstrances of those whom they oppressed, to enrich the treasury of the State.—

The Undersigned persuades himself that it is not in a note addressed to the Marquis di Circello that it is necessary to enlarge upon the singularly atrocious character of this procedure, for which no apology can be devised, and for which none that is intelligible has hitherto been attempted. — It was, indeed, an undisguised abuse of power, of which nothing could well enhance the deformity but those studied deception that preceded and prepared it; a deception which, by a sort of Treason against Society, converted a proffer of hospitality into a snare, and that

ficial List of Consuls). In his letter of July 1, 1809, to Frederic Degan, Gallo, then Secretary of Foreign Affairs at Naples, stated that it was "the intention of His Majesty, as a general measure, freely to admit American vessels coming directly into his ports, provided they had regular papers and had not by paying duty to Great Britain, or by submitting to be searched by British cruisers, brought themselves within the decrees of December 21, 1806, and January 9, 1808." Degan ceased to be consul in September 1809, when Alexander Hammett succeeded him. The following is the list of consuls in Italy in 1810: Thomas Appleton at Leghorn; Alexander Hammett, Naples; Thomas H. Storm, Genoa; John Broadbent, Messina; Abraham Gibbs, Palermo; and Richard O'Brien, Sardinia. (See Perrotta, *op. cit.,* 15, citing *Annals of Congress, Eleventh Congress, first and second sessions, 1999*).
11 See above, note 9.

salutary Confidence, without which Nations and Men must cease to have intercourse, into an Engine of Plunder.—

The Right of the innocent victims of this unequalled act of fraud and rapine to demand retribution cannot be doubted. — The only question is, from whom are they entitled to demand it? — Those who at that Moment ruled in Naples, and who were in fact and in the view of the World The Government of Naples, have passed away before retribution could be obtained, although not before it was required; and, if the right to retribution regards only the persons of those rulers as private and ordinary wrongdoers, the American Merchant, whom they deluded and despoiled in the garb and with the instruments and for the purposes of Sovereignty, must despair forever of Redress.

The Undersigned presumes that such is not the view which the present Government will feel itself justified in taking of this interesting Subject; He trusts that it will, on the contrary, perceive that the Claim, which the injured Merchant was authorized to prefer against the Government of this Country before the recent change, and which, but for that Change, must sooner or later have been successful, is now a valid Claim against the Government of the same Country, notwithstanding that Change. — At least, the Undersigned is not at present aware of any Considerations which, applied to the facts that characterize this Case, can lead to a different conclusion; and certainly it would be matter for sincere regret that any Considerations should be thought sufficient to make the return of His Sicilian Majesty to his former Power fatal to the rights of friendly Strangers to whom no fault can be ascribed. —

The general principle that a civil society may contract Obligations through its actual Government, whatever that may be, and that it is not absolved from them by reason simply of a Change of Government or of Rulers, is universally received as incontrovertible. — It is admitted, not merely by Writers on public Law as a speculative truth, but by States and Statesmen as a practical rule; and, accordingly, history is full of examples to prove that the undisturbed possessor of sovereign power in any society, whether a rightful possessor or not with reference to other Claimants of that power, may not only be the lawful Object of allegiance, but by many of his Acts, in his quality of Sovereign de facto, may bind the Society, and those who come after him as rulers, although their title be adversary to or even better than his own. — The Marquis di Circello does not need to be informed

that the earlier annals of England in particular abound in instruc
tion upon this head.

With regard to just and beneficial contracts, entered into by
such a Sovereign with the merchants of foreign Nations, or
(which is the same thing) with regard to the detention and confiscation of their property, for public Uses and by his authority,
in direct violation of a pledge of safety, upon the faith of which
that property arrived within the reach of confiscation, this continuing responsibility stands upon the plainest foundations of
natural equity. —

It will not be pretended that a merchant [is] called upon to
investigate, as he prosecutes his Traffick [sic], the title of every
Sovereign, with whose ports, and under the guaranty of whose
plighted word, he trades. — He is rarely competent, there are
few in any station who are competent, to an investigation so full
of delicacy, so perplexed with facts and principles of a peculiar
character far removed from the common concerns of life. — His
predicament would be to the last degree calamitous if in an
honest search after commercial profit he might not take Governments as he finds them, and consequently rely at all times upon
the visible exclusion of acknowledged possession of supreme
Authority. If he sees all the usual indications of established rule,
all the distinguishing concomitants of real undisputed Power, it
cannot be that he is at his peril to discuss mysterious theories
above his capacity or foreign to his pursuits, and moreover to
connect the results of those speculations with events of which
his knowledge is either imperfect or erroneous. If he sees the
obedience of the People and the acquiescence of neighbouring
Princes it is impossible that it can be his duty to examine, before
he ships his Merchandize whether it be fit that these should
acquiesce or those obey. — If, in short, he finds nothing to interfere with or qualify the dominion which the Head of the
Society exercises, over it and the Domain which it occupies, it is
the dictate of reason, sanctioned by all Experience, that he is
bound to look no farther. —

It can be of no importance to him that, notwithstanding all
those appearances announcing lawful Rule, the mere right to
fill the Throne is claimed by, or even resides in, another than the
actual occupant. — The latent right (supposing it to exist) dis-
joined from and controverted by the fact, is to him nothing while
it continues to be latent. It is only the Sovereign in possession that
it is in his power to know. It is with him only that he can enter into

engagements. — It is through him only that he can deal with the Society. — And if it be true that the Sovereign in possession is incapable, on account of a conflict of title between him and another who barely claims but makes no effort to assert his claim, of pledging the public faith of the Society and of the Monarch of foreign traders for commercial and other objects, we are driven to the monstrous conclusion that the Society is, in effect and indefinitely, cut off from all communication with the rest of the world. — It has, and can have, no organ by which it can become accountable to or make any contract with foreigners, by which needful supplies may be invited into its harbours, by which famine may be averted, or redundant productions be made to find a market in the wants of strangers. — It is, in a word, an outcast from the bosom of the great community of nations at the very moment too when its existence in the form which it has assumed may everywhere be admitted. — And, even if the dormant claim to the Throne should, at last, by a fortunate coincidence of circumstances, become triumphant and unite itself to the possession, this harsh and palsying[12] [sic] theory has no assurance to give, either to the Society or to those who may incline to deal with it, that its moral capacity is restored, that it is an outcast no longer, and that it may now through the protecting will of its new Sovereign do what it could not do before. It contains of course, no adequate & certain provision against even the perpetuity of the dilemma which it creates. — If, therefore, a civil Society is not competent, by rulers in entire possession of the Sovereignty, to enter into all such promises to the members of other Societies as necessity or convenience may require, and to remain answerable for the breach of them, into whatsoever shape the society may ultimately be cast or into whatsoever hands the government may ultimately fall; if a Sovereign,[13] entirely in possession, is not able, for that reason alone, to incur a just responsibility in his political or corporate character, to the citizens of other countries, and to transmit that responsibility, even to those who succeed him by displacing him, it will be difficult to show that the moral capacity of a civil society is any thing but a name, or the responsibility of Sovereigns any thing but a

---

12 Writer may have meant to say "paralysing," but both in the original manuscript and in the printed version House Document No. 130 (see note 20, p. 109) the word used is as given here "palsying" which is perhaps not so strong an expression.

13 On April 17, 1808 Napoleon issued the Bayonne Decree, ordering the seizure of all American vessels in the ports of France.

shadow. — And here the undersigned will take the liberty to suggest that it is scarcely for the interest of sovereigns to inculcate as a maxim, that their lost Dominions can only be recovered at the expense of the unoffending citizens of States in amity, or, which is equivalent to it, to make that recovery the practical consummation of intermediate injustice, by utterly extinguishing the hope of indemnity and even the title to demand it.

The undersigned will now, for the sake of perspicuity and precision, recall to the recollection of His Excellency the Marquis di Circello the situation of the Government of Murat at the epoch of the confiscations in question.[14] Whatever might be the origin or foundation of that Government, it had for some time been *established*. — It had obtained such obedience as in such times was customary, and had manifested itself not only by active internal exertions of legislative and executive Power, but by important external transactions with old and indisputably regular governments. It had been (as long afterwards it continued to be) recognized by the greatest Potentates as one of the European family of States and had interchanged with those ambassadors and other public ministers and consuls. And Great Britain, by an order in Council of the 26th of April 1809, which modified the system of constructive blockade promulgated by the orders of November 1807[15] had excepted the Neapolitan Territories with other portions of Italy, from the operation of that system, that Neutrals might no longer be prevented from trading with them.

Such was the state of things when American vessels were tempted into Naples by a reliance upon the passport of its Government, to which perfidy had lost more than ordinary solemnity, upon a declaration, as explicit as it was formal and notorious, that they might come without fear and might depart in peace. — It was under those circumstances that, instead of being permitted to retire with their lawful gains, both they and their Cargoes were seized & appropriated in the manner already related. — The undersigned may consequently assume that, if ever there was a claim to compensation for broken faith, which survived the political power of those whose iniquity produced it

---

14 For a detailed account of Murat's reign, see Maurice Henri Weil, *Joachin Murat, Roi de Naples*. Paris, 1910. 5 vols.

15 This British Order in Council of November 1, 1807, issued by George Canning, interdicted neutral trade with the entire coast of Europe from Trieste to Copenhagen, unless the vessels first entered a British port and paid a duty: on their homeward way, they were to call again to make another payment. (Perrotta, *op. cit.*, 10).

and devolved in full force upon their successors, the present claim is of that description.

As to the Demand itself, as it existed against the Government of Murat, the Marquis di Circello will undoubtedly be the first to concede, not only that it is above reproach, but that it rests upon grounds in which the civilized world has a deep and lasting interest. — And with regard to the liability of the present government as standing in the place of the former, it may be taken as a corollary from that concession; at least until it has been shown that it is the natural fate of obligations, so high and sacred, contracted by a Government in the full and tranquil enjoyment of power, to perish with the first revolution either in form or rulers through which it may happen to pass; or (to state the same proposition in different terms) that it is the natural operation of a political revolution in a State to strip unfortunate traders, who have been betrayed and plundered by the former Sovereign, of all that his rapacity could not reach — the right of reclamation.

The wrong which the Government of Murat inflicted upon American Citizens wanted nothing that might give to it atrocity or effect as a robbery introduced by treachery; but, however pernicious or execrable, it was still reparable. It left in the sufferers and their nation a Right, which was not likely to be forgotten or abandoned, of seeking and obtaining ample redress, not from *Murat* simply (who individually was lost in the Sovereign) but from the Government of the Country whose power he abused. By what course of argument can it be proved that this incontestable right, from which that Government could never have escaped, has been destroyed by the reaccesion of His Sicilian Majesty, after a long interval, to the Sovereignty of the same Territories?

That such a Result cannot in any degree be inferred from the misconduct of the American claimants is certain; for no misconduct is imputable to them. — They were warranted, in every view of the public law of Europe, in holding commercial communication with Naples in the predicament in which they found it, and in trusting to the direct and authentic assurances which the government of the place affected to throw over them as a shield against every danger. Their shipments were strictly within the terms of those assurances; and nothing was done, by the shippers or their agents, by which the benefit of them might be lost or impaired. —

From what other source can such result be drawn? Will it be said that the proceeds of those confiscations were not applied to public purposes during the Sovereignty of Murat, or that they produced no public advantages with reference to which the present government ought to be liable? The answer to such a suggestion is, that, let the fact be as it may, it can have no influence upon the subject. It is enough that the confiscations themselves, and the promise of safety which they violated, were acts of State, proceeding from him who was, then and for several successive years, the Sovereign. The derivative liability of the present government reposes, not upon the good, either public or private, which may have been the fruit of such a revolting exhibition of Power emancipated from all the restraints of principles, but upon the general foundations which the undersigned has already had the honour to expose.

To follow the proceeds of those spoliations into the public treasury, and thence to all the uses to which they were finally made subservient, can be no part of the Duty of the American Claimant. — It is a task which he has no means of performing and which if performed by others could neither strengthen his case nor enfeeble it. And it may confidently be insisted, not only that he has no concern with the particular application of those proceeds, but that, even if he had, he would be authorized to rely upon the presumption that they were applied as public money to public ends, or left in the public coffers. — It must be remembered, moreover, that, whatever may have been the destiny of those unhallowed spoils, they cannot well have failed to be instrumental in meliorating the condition of the Country. — They afforded extraordinary pecuniary means, which, as far as they extended, must have saved it from an augmentation of its burthens [sic], by relieving the ordinary revenue, made that revenue adequate to various improvements either of use or beauty which otherwise it could not have accomplished. — The Territories, therefore, under the sway of Murat must be supposed to have returned to His Sicilian Majesty less exhausted, more embellished, and more prosperous, than if the property of American Citizens had not in the meantime been sacrificed to cupidity & cunning. It must further be remembered, that a part of that property was notoriously devoted to the public service. — Some of the vessels, seized by the orders of Murat, were, on account of their excellent construction, converted into vessels of war and as such commissioned by the Government; and the undersigned is informed that they are now in the possession of the officers of His Sicilian Majesty, and used and claimed as belonging to him.

The undersigned, having thus briefly explained to the Marquis di Circello the nature of the claim, which the Government of the United States, has commanded him to submit to the reflection of the government of His Sicilian Majesty forbears at present to multiply arguments in support of it. He feels assured that the equitable disposition of His Majesty renders superfluous the further illustrations of which it is susceptible.

The undersigned has the Honour to renew to His Excellency the Marquis Circello the assurances of his distinguished consideration.[16]

---

[16] When it became known that Mr. Pinkney had submitted this 1816 memorandum to the Neapolitan Government, speculation became rife as to the answer that the Neapolitan Government would make, especially since it was known that Mr. Pinkney had gone to Naples accompanied by the Mediterranean Squadron. The *British Annual Register* (London, 1817, LVIII, 132) reported that the presence of the Squadron had "the appearance of intimidation, excited great alarm in Naples, almost all of the ships of the royal navy having been disarmed ٫ . . the Marquis di Circello, Minister of Foreign Affairs, delivered a note to each of the foreign ministers relative to the American claims, and couriers were sent to engage the protection of different courts." *Niles Weekly Register* (Baltimore, 1816, XI, 138-140) gave circulation to rumors already voiced by London newspapers, citing "the Neapolitan Government had manned batteries with heavy calibre cannon, and that 12,000 Austrian troops in Neapolitan service were placed on guard in the Castle and at the principal forts," and that Naples "counted on the arrival of an English fleet to cool the ardor of American seamen." (Paraphrased from account in the *London Star* (*Niles*, 1816, XI, 138-139). Further, *Niles* quoted from the *London Times* of September 6, 1816, a somewhat different rumor:—this "contradicts the report of the American Squadron intending to bombard Naples," and adds, "whatever are the claims of the Americans, they have been brought forward in a more decent way. On the 8th of August, Mr. Pinkney presented his letters of credentials to the King of the Two Sicilies. He has been sent to Naples on a special mission, and he is to proceed to St. Petersburg, when that is accomplished. It is pretended, already, that he is to propose a cession of territory, in case the Neapolitan Government shall not discover the disposition, or the means of satisfying the demand of the Americans in money. The Lipari Isles have been mentioned, but it is not probable that the court of Naples will consent to such an arrangement!!!" (Note: The triple exclamation points are within the quote mark in *Niles'* quotation from the *Times*. See *Niles Weekly Register*, 1816, XI, 139). On page 140 of the same issue, *Niles* gives still further rumor in a despatch from Naples:—"August 18. The American Squadron remains in our road. It is said they are desirous to enlist the colonists that are here. By a regulation of the Squadron, the indiscriminate visit [sic] of all persons thereunto is prohibited. 24th. As to the American claims, the first demand of four millions was at first referred by the government to the Congress at Vienna. But it appears that at the time, its intervention was not accepted. The urgent demands of Mr. Pinkney gave rise to a thousand rumors. Some say that the government has promised to pay, others that they have definitely consented to the cession of a port in the Mediterranean. But it has not been determined, as has been pretended, to cede Syracuse. The Lipari Isles are likewise spoken of, situated in the North West extremity of Sicily, called in the classical ages the Œonian islands; but they have no port fit for accommodating the wants of the Americans."

106

W. R. KING[17] TO JAMES MONROE

Naples August 24th 1816

Dear Sir

Enabled by the sailing of a vessel direct for Baltimore I take the liberty of writing a few lines to you, principally with a view of making an enquiry on a subject which when I had the pleasure of seeing you last I believed I perfectly understood, but which subsequent events have induced me to doubt. — Did I not correctly understand from the conversation I had the pleasure to hold with you previous to my departure from the U. States, that my ordinary expences would be defrayed by the Government, untill [sic] I reached St. Petersburg, and that Mr. Pinkney would be authorised to draw for those expences? Pardon me Sir for stating it in the form of an interrogatory; I wish to be informed as Mr. Pinkney entertains a different opinion, and in consequence I have been compelled to dispose of Bills on my purse in America at a great loss, to enable me to defray the expences of this long Jorney [sic], which I had failed to provide under the impression that it had been arranged by you with Mr. Pinkney—I will esteem it a particular favour if you will have the goodness to give me the information asked for at St. Petersburg. As Mr. Pinkney will write you relative to the subjects of his mission, I will not trouble you with any speculative opinions of mine, but simply observe that from all I can collect both from interviews with the Marquis di Circello, who is the minister for foreign affairs and from other sources, there is little prospect of success; our stay here will I trust be short — Naples with all its beauties has failed greatly to interest me — Present to Mrs. Monroe my sincere respects, and accept the assurances of my high consideration —

WM. PINKNEY TO JAMES MONROE

Naples. August. 29th 1816[18]

Sir

The Washington cast anchor in the Bay of Naples on the 13th of last month, and was immediately ordered into Quarantine because she had touched at Gibraltar. — Although I was aware

---

[17] William R. King of Alabama, was commissioned secretary of legation to Russia, on April 23, 1816. He was superseded by Charles Pinkney, of Maryland, who was commissioned November 30, 1818. *Register of the Department of State,* corrected to March 1, 1874. Part II. Historical Register. Washington, Government Printing Office, 1874, 94 p.

[18] This despatch marked "private," was not received at the State Department until January 4, [1817].

that the appearance of the Plague in Calabria and elsewhere had excited such alarm in the Mediterranean as that a public Ship, conveying one of the Princesses of the Neapolitan royal Family, had been subjected to Quarantine at Naples, and another public Ship, conveying the present Duchess of Berri from Naples to the South of France, had been subjected to Quarantine at Marseilles, I thought it advisable to make known without Delay to the Minister for foreign affairs (the Marquis of Circello) by an informal Note my public character, and at the same time to invite him to use his authority to shorten our Quarantine as far as might be found consistent with Prudence. A copy of his reply to that Communication (and to another informal Note, in which I transmitted two Letters received for him by the Legation from the Neapolitan Consul at Gibraltar) is enclosed.— This reply was accompanied by some verbal explanations through a Gentleman at Naples; and the result of the whole was that, however it might be regretted by the Government, a Quarantine of thirteen or fourteen Days was indispensable.

In the Course of the 26th, our quarantine being at an End, I came on Shore. — The necessary orders were given by the proper Department for the landing, without Inspection, of the Baggage of all who were attached to the Legation; and every Disposition was shown to treat the Mission with the utmost Civility.[19]

On Saturday the 27th I prepared an official Note to the Marquis di Circello, announcing my Quality of Envoy Extraordinary to The King; but, as I wished that it should be delivered by the American Consul with a view to an Enquiry as to some matters of Ceremony, it did not come to the Hands of the Marquis until the Morning of Monday the 29th; — His answer, appointing Wednesday the 31.st for our Interview, was sent immediately. You will find enclosed a Copy of each of these Notes.

My reception on the 31.st was extremely friendly, and in the highest Degree respectful to the Government of The United States.—The regular purpose of my Visit was to show my credentials, furnish a Copy, and arrange the customary audience. — I did not therefore suppose that it presented a suitable opportunity for introducing a very detailed Explanation of the objects of my Mission; but, in Conformity with a desire expressed by the Mar-

---

[19] Records in the United States National Archives indicate that at about this time Mr. Pinkney attended several important social functions. On August 25th, 1816, Mr. and Mrs. Pinkney attended a royal ball held at His Majesty's Casino at Chiatamone. The following day, the Minister Plenipotentiary of Sardinia informed Mr. and Mrs. Pinkney that the Duke and Duchess of Genovese would receive them on August 27th at 11 A. M.

quis himself, I stated them to him as fully as was necessary to enable him to communicate them to The King. — With regard to my audience (for which I was not yet prepared with the Dress which Usage requires) he referred it to myself to request it by a Note whenever it should be convenient to me.

Although the Marquis di Circello was (as you know) for several years the Minister of this Court in London, he does not speak a word of English, and does not understand it when it is spoken by others. — Our Conversation was therefore in French, which he speaks much better than I do. — Amidst a good deal of well managed Discourse on his part which rather related to me than to my Mission, he made several observations which had a bearing upon my principal Errand. — He[20] spoke of the poverty of their public Treasury in Terms somewhat more strong than I expected, of the unprincipled manner in which Mons[r]. Murat (as he styled him) appropriated to his own use whatever of value he could lay his Hands upon and, in particular, the Vessels and merchandize belonging to our Citizens, of the prodigality with which he dried up all the usual Resources of the Country and dissipated moreover all the Means which Rapacity afforded. — He drew no very precise Conclusion from those & similar remarks, although I took such notice of them as their Tendency prescribed; but upon the whole it was evident that the Claim which I was charged to make in behalf of our Merchants was not likely to be very readily admitted, and that I should only waste my Time by talking over its merits from day to day with a Minister[21] who could of himself decide nothing, and whose

---

[20] This text follows, in its capitalization of the pronouns, 'He' and 'I', the printed, rather than the manuscript (original) version, in order to bring out more clearly the sense of the conversation. For this and 17 other despatches in this Pinkney series (of which we include 43 to and from Pinkney), see *Message of the President . . . transmitting Sundry Papers, in relation to the claims of the Merchants of the United States for their property seized and confiscated under the authority of the King of Naples. 15th Cong. 1st Session.* March 2, 1818. Read and ordered to lie on the Table. Washington, Printed by F. De Krafft, 1818. 35 pp. Being bound as House Document No. 130. (For list of the 18 documents printed in House Document No. 130, see Appendix herein. The date of the *Message* of President Monroe was Feb. 28, 1818; the documents transmitted were dated from May 11, 1816 to Feb. 21, 1817.)

[21] Luigi Medici (de'). Prince of Ottaviano and Duke of Sarno (1759-1830). Chevalier and statesman. Involved in the Jacobin plots, he was arrested on Feb. 27, 1795. He was President of the Royal Finances (July 1803) and Director of the State Secretaryships (April 1804). He conceived the idea of a Discount Bank which he wanted to unite to the regular banks. He believed that money was mere merchandise and permitted its unrestricted exportation. In 1806, he followed the Bourbons in Sicily. He got into difficulties with the Sicilian Parliament as a result of which William Cavendish Bentinck (1774-1839), the English agent in Sicily, who had instituted a liberal government, forced the King to exile him. In 1814

Report, of my Statements & Arguments, to those who must make or greatly* influence the final Decision, would not be the most advantageous Channel by which they might be communicated. — In Consequence, before the interview was closed, I determined to propos[e] the Claim as soon as possible in an official Note, and in the meantime to forbear to urge it in conversation, with any other view than to obtain from the Marquis di Circello such intimations as might be useful to me in the preparation of my Paper.—

On the 3.ᵈ of the present month, I wrote to the Marquis, as I had promised, respecting my Audience, which took place on Wednesday the 8th, at a palace of the King at Capodimonti on the Edge of Naples. — In the short speech which on this occasion I made to the King in French (for he too appears not to understand English) I confined myself to the customary general Expressions. — His Reply was very courteous, and his whole Deportment and Conversation were then (and have been since) of the same complexion. After my audience I presented Mr. King, the Secretary of Legation, together with my Son Charles, and the three other American Gentlemen who are with me; and they were received with great politeness.

On Sunday the 11ᵗʰ I had another Interview with the Marquis di Circello, to which Mr. King accompanied me. — The main Object of it was to ascertain, according to my Instructions, the Inclinations of this Government as to commercial arrangements. — In reply to the suggestions, by which I thought it proper to lead to a Conversation on that Subject, the Marquis observed that he could not at that moment say anything definite upon it; that if I would mention to him specifically, then or at some future Interview, my own Ideas of the Nature & Conditions

---

de' Medici participated in the Congress of Vienna. After June 5, 1822, he was minister of finance, and after Aug. 16, 1823, he became interim president of the Council of Ministers and minister of foreign affairs. In 1827, he succeeded in forcing the Austrians to leave the Kingdom, but he was disgusted with Metternich and to prove that he was powerful, he used severe measures to quell the uprising in Cilento in 1828. On de' Medici, consult: Luigi Blanch, "Luigi de' Medici come uomo di stato e amministratore." Edited by Cortese. *Archivio Storico Napoletano,* Naples, 1925, 101-197; A. Simioni, *Le origini del risorgimento politico dell'Italia meridionale.* Messina, Principato, 1921, I, 414 ff; II, 188 ff; L. Arezio, "Ferdinando I di fronte ai triumviri del quinquennio." *Nuova Antologia,* Rome, March 1, 16, 1931; Piero Pieri, *Il regno di Napoli dal 1789 al 1806.* Naples, 1928; Nino Cortese, *Saggio di bibliografia collettiana.* Bari, Laterza, 1917, 77-79; Walter Maturi, *Il concordato del 1818 tra la Santa Sede e il regno delle due Sicilie.* Florence, Sansoni, 1929; Ruggero Moscati, "La questione greca e il governo napoletano." *Rassegna Storica del Risorgimento,* Rome, 1933, 21-49.

* The Minister of Finance (The Chevalier di Medici) is understood to be the ablest man in the Government. [This footnote is in the original despatch. Editor.]

of such a Treaty as the Government of the United States would probably desire, he would willingly receive the Statement as informal and consult the King upon it; that he ought however in Candour to inform me that in the present unsettled Situation of Europe he did not believe it would be agreeable to the King to conclude a commercial Convention with any Power; that he thought it not improbable that hereafter and by Degrees, they might be so circumstanced as to find it practicable to make such a Convention with the United States; and that at any rate it would give him pleasure to receive from me any thing which looked to that Event. — I closed the Conversation on this Head by telling the Marquis that I should perhaps take another opportunity for further Explanation with regard to it.

I then adverted to the "principal object of my Mission," and intimated that I should very soon send him a Note upon it. — To my Surprize he professed not to understand to what I alluded as the *principal object of my Mission*; but, when I mentioned the Spoliations by Murat, he seemed suddenly to remember that I had at least talked to him of them before, and immediately, without giving me Time to proceed, remarked that he would relate to me frankly all that the present Government had been able to discover respecting them. — He said that Murat's conduct in that affair appeared to be so bad that nothing could be worse and that it amounted to a downright Robbery; that it appeared that the proceeds of the Sales had been ordered by Murat into the public Treasury, but that in a few months he took them out again, and they knew not what he had done with them. — To all this I thought it sufficient to answer that, whatever might have become of these proceeds, I hoped the King would cause our merchants to be indemnified for the Loss of them; but that I had no Desire at this interview to do more than inform the Marquis di Circello that I believed it would be as well to present the whole of that Subject to him without Delay in a note to which I flattered myself I should have such a Reply in writing as would be satisfactory to my Government. — Without either admitting or denying the responsibility of his Government, he said that such a Course would be acceptable to him and proper in itself, and that his answer should not be unnecessarily postponed. — His Manner, while this Topick [sic] was under Notice, was kind and even good humoured, although he could not and perhaps did not wish to disguise that it was by no means a pleasant one. —

Before I left him I mentioned to him (informally) a wish,

111

which had been suggested to me by Commodore Chauncey, that, if he should think fit to frequent a Port in Sicily with our Squadron, this Government would allow him to have a Depot there for its Use, as had formerly been done. — The Marquis replied that certainly the Squadron would have a perfectly hospitable reception in all the Ports of His Majesty, but that he doubted about the Depot. His Impression was that it had never been granted to any Nation, but he would enquire & let me know. He has since written to me to say that Indisposition has prevented him from attending fully to this Matter, and that the Moment he is able he will take the King's orders upon it,* and apprize me of them.

On the 24ᵗʰ. Instant, yesterday morning, I sent in my Note[22] upon Murat's Confiscations. The necessity of making some previous Enquiries here, upon matters connected with them, had a little retarded the Completion of the Note; and, after it was ready, I concluded that I should lose nothing by withholding it for a few Days, especially as the Marquis di Circello was incapable of attending to Business and had so informed me.

What will be the answer to the Note it is impossible to conjecture with any thing like Certainty. — It may be such as to make it necessary for me to reply to it; but the President may be assured that my further Stay in Naples shall be as short as I can make it.

I have the Honour to be — with the highest Consideration — Sir

(*private* Augᵗ. 24-16)[23]

WM. PINKNEY TO JAMES MONROE

Naples 29th August 1816[24]

My dear Sir

It is supposed here to be improbable that this Government will *at present* yield to our Demand about Murat's Spoliations; but it is impossible to ascertain with certainty upon what Grounds it will decline to pay. Those who undertake to conjecture differ

---

* I had reminded him of it by a private Note. — [This footnote is found in the original despatch. Editor].

22 Dated August 24th, 1816.

23 Date at heading of this despatch does not agree with this date at the end nor with the phrase (see above) "28th instant, yesterday.' '

24 This despatch, marked "private," was not published in *Message* (House Document No. 130). See note 20, p. 109.

112

among themselves. Extreme poverty will doubtless be one Ground, although not mentioned. The manner in which Murat applied the proceeds will I presume be another; and it is said that his dependent Situation with regard to France, and the fact (or rather an allegation) that he confiscated under the orders of Bonaparte, and that Bonaparte shared the Spoil, will be another. We shall see. — I am informed that the proceeds, as they came to the Hands of the Government, did not much exceed a Million of Dollars. — The *vessels* sold for very little and, although the Merchandize sold well, the fiscal System of the Country was then (as it is now) so corrupt in all its Branches that the Mass of the proceeds stopped *in transitu* and only an inconsiderable part got into the Treasury. —

You will perceive that my Note to the Marquis di Circello states that some of the Vessels are now in the possesion and service of this Government. I think there are three. What they will do with *them* I know not; but it is imagined that they will offer to restore them or to make Compensation to the Extent of their Value which is considerable. — My note says very little about those Vessels for obvious reasons.

Although my mission produced as I am told *some* sensation here (and the Commodore's making the Bay of Naples a rendezvous for the Squadron preparatory to his going to Sicily, perhaps produced more.)[25] I have been received with great Kindness and Distinction. The Commodore & the officers of the Squadron have also been received but those were no such Sensation. — I presented Commodore Chauncey and Commodore Perry[26] to the King, and they were as the Phrase is "graciously received." — The Captains would all have been presented if they had thought fit. — Mrs. Pinkney has been presented to the King — and we have all had as much attention as it is possible to show us by Invitations to Balls, galas &c. — Three Days ago Mrs. Pinkney & Myself had a formal audience of the Duke and Duchess del Genevese [sic][27] — She is the King's Daughter & he is the Brother of the King of Sardinia. They were very courteous. —

You will discover that my note to the Marquis di Circello of

---

25 See above note 16, p. 106, re: the sensation created.
26 Captain Oliver H. Perry of Rhode Island (1785-1819). In 1816-17, as Commander of the *Java*, Perry cruised in the Mediterranean. (*Dictionary American Biography*, 1934, XIV, 490).
27 According to the original invitation preserved in the United States National Archives the envoy extraordinary of H. M. the King of Sardinia informed Mr. Pinkney that the Duke and Duchess of Genovese would receive him and Mrs. Pinkney on Tuesday, 27th August, at 11 a.m. (See above, note 19, p. 108.)

the 24th Instant is in some Degree drawn up with reference to the sensation above mentioned — that is to say with great Care to avoid every thing like menace. — The subject of that Note is the most delicate & difficult that can be imagined. I found it quite a Task to write upon it in such a manner as to satisfy myself that I had gone far enough without going too far. — I hope that it will appear to the President to be a discreet Paper, and yet a firm and direct Exposition of our Case. — I have endeavoured to exhibit the Claim with all possible Strength, while I shunned whatever might produce Irritation or Ill Will. — I could only have made more of the Argument by making the Note ungracefully long. — A laborious view of the Subject would have been unsuited to a Note which merely introduced the Claim. — I think it a good Claim — and that it must finally succeed if it should even fail now. At any rate — our Citizens, who have been plundered, will be convinced by what is now doing that their Interests have not been neglected. —

As to the Commercial Subject, there is no Disposition here to make any arrangement with us. — The actual State of Things is too advantageous for them, and they have nothing to gain (according to their policy) by a Change. I will explain this hereafter.

We understand here that L^d. Exmouth[28] is expected in the Mediterranean to act at Algiers. There are not wanting persons who believe that our naval operations in these Seas are to be watched by His Lordship. — I suppose that to be idle speculation. —

My Mission has thus far been pleasant but it will be a severe Expence to me.[29] — The funds allowed will not be sufficient to

---

28 Edward Pellew, first Viscount Exmouth (1757-1833). English Admiral. He entered the navy in 1770. During the American Revolution, he distinguished himself for his bravery. Early in 1816 he was ordered to visit the several North African powers to obtain the release of all British subjects. This was readily granted by Algiers, Tunis, and Tripoli; but the dey of Algiers refused a request to abolish Christian slavery. Exmouth was then ordered to attack the Algerines. On Aug. 27, 1816, Exmouth sent in a note demanding, among other things, the abolition of Christian slavery and the immediate release of all Christian slaves. When no reply was received, Exmouth gave the signal to his ships to move in to the attack. The fire continued for eight hours, and the batteries and a great part of the town was silenced. The next day Exmouth received a message granting all his demands, and this was finally confirmed on the 29th. Some 3,000 slaves, mostly Italians and Spaniards, were liberated and sent to their respective countries. Thereupon Exmouth returned home. See: Edward Osler, *Life of 1st Viscount Exmouth* (1835); *Dictionary of National Biography,* London, Oxford University Press, 1921, XV, 711-715.

29 Theodore Lyman in his *Diplomacy of the United States* (381) table 2, records from official documents that for his mission to the Two Sicilies, William Pinkney received $9,000 for his "outfit" and $1,995.23 for "contingent expenses"— a total of $10,995.23. This, of course, was in addition to other sums paid to him

take me to St. Petersburgh; and when I get there the actual Salary will fall short of the Expence of the plainest Living, as I have been informed by persons at Naples who have lived long in St. Petersburgh.

P. S. I believe the Depot in Sicily will not be granted — but that it will be *kindly* refused.

WM. PINKNEY TO JAMES MONROE

Naples 6 September 1816[30] (Copy)

Sir.

I received from the Marquis di Circello, a day or two after its date, a letter of which a copy is enclosed,[31] respecting Commodore Chauncey's wish to have the privilege of a deposit of stores &c. in Sicily for the use of the American Squadron.

The Commodore seemed to go the length of desiring (as you will perceive by the enclosed copy of his letter to me of the 12th of August)[32] that he might be allowed to use as a place of deposit the public arsenal or dockyard at Messina or Syracuse. — I did not, however, convey his desire exactly in that form to this government; but, keeping back his letter, I stated his object generally, and at the same time referred the Marquis di Circello to what had been done in favour of our Ships in the ports of Sicily on former occasions.

As the Commodore's purpose won't extend beyond any thing which my Instructions authorized me to ask, and as, moreover, I am as anxious to commit the Government of the United States as little as possible, or rather to avoid committing it at all, I thought it right (as you are already aware) to communicate that purpose *informally* to the Marquis di Circello. — For the same reason (and also because I had kept no Copy[33] of my Note, *marked informal*, which simply reminded the Marquis that I mentioned the subject to him in a conversation understood at the

for services rendered in connection with his mission to Great Britain (1806-11) and Russia (1816-1818). Subsequently Pinkney served in the United States Senate from Dec. 21, 1819, to his death. *Dictionary American Biography*, 1934, XIV, 628.

30 This despatch was not published in *Message* (House Document No. 130). See note 20, p. 109.

31 See pp. 116-117.

32 See p. 118.

33 See Pinkney's "N.B." (page 119). Pinkney here followed the usual State Department procedure in keeping no copy, and forwarding none, of his 'informal' notes. Some diplomats saw fit to send copies of such notes for the record.

time to be of the same character) I repeated, in the reply which I afterwards sent to the Marquis's paper, that I had *so* communicated it. — A copy of the reply is enclosed.[34]

The Marquis's note declines the Commodore's proposal; but it is so unexceptioned [sic] in its tone, and perhaps in its substance too that it might probably have justified a less guarded answer than I felt disposed to give to it while the spoliation subject remained (as it still remains) open. — This note appears to make it unnecessary for me to procure (and I shall not therefore attempt to procure) any thing farther from the Marquis di Circello in the nature of assurance that our Ships of War shall be hospitably received in the ports of this Kingdom. — It amounts undoubtedly to such an assurance; and, as it has not offered an answer to a mere suggestion on my part (which, not only on account of its informality but also on account of its more extended purpose, implies no reciprocal pledge) it comes to us in the most convenient of all modes. —

I am in constant expectation of the Marquis's reply to my paper[35] of the 24th of August on Murat's Confiscations. —

I have the honour to be, with the highest Esteem and Consideration — Sir —

THE MARQUIS DI CIRCELLO TO WM. PINKNEY

(Enclosure with Mr. Pinkney's despatch of Sept. 6, 1816 to Mr. Monroe)

Naples 28th of August 1816[36]

The Undersigned Secretary of State Minister for foreign affairs had the honour to acknowledge to H. E. Mr. Pinkney Minister Plenipotentiary of the U. S. of America the Receipt of his note of the 22nd instant[37] in which was expressed the Wish of the Commodore of the American Squadron for the establishment of a Deposit of provisions at Messina or Syracuse for its use.[38]

In consequence of the Investigations had upon this subject the Undersigned regrets to be obliged to inform his Excellency that

---

34 See pp. 116-117.
35 See pp. 97-106 inclusive.
36 This note of the Marquis di Circello was not published in House Document No. 130. See above, note 20, p. 109.
37 The letter of the 22d is not found to have been included by Pinkney; nor is it elsewhere included in this publication of the Pinkney despatches.
38 For further information regarding this request, see the letter from Commodore Chauncey to Mr. Pinkney, dated Aug. 12, 1816. (See p. 118.)

such a demand is inadmissable as well with reference to the example which it would introduce in favour of all the Powers that have no Establishment in the Mediterranean, as on account of the State of Peace which exists between this Court and the Barbary Regencies. But this does not prevent that the American Squadron may have an agent in Sicily who may purchase on its account whatsoever provisions it may want; always however with a view to a particular Speculation and not to magazines established for the use of the Government of the U. S. and upon this express condition moreover that the articles composing such supplies shall be subject to all the duties which are paid by national Vessels, and foreigners; it being out of the power of this Government to grant any exemption which other allied and friendly nations do not enjoy. It is true that on other occasions there have been granted to the Ships of War of the U. S. of America[39] similar advantages but at that time this royalty was in a state of War (which it is not at present) with the Barbary Regencies, and therefore concurred with them to increase the means of offense against the common enemy, and by consequence not only were all these facilities given to them, but moreover several light vessels of this Royal Marine were placed at the disposal of the American Commanders.

These convincing motives leave no room to the Undersigned to doubt that H. E. Mr. Pinkney will be persuaded that it is only to be ascribed to the same that this royal Court is constrained against its wishes to decline complying with his Desire.

The Undersigned hopes to be more fortunate on some other occasion and in the meantime has the honour to repeat to H. E. the confirmation of his distinguished consideration.

---

[39] The Mediterranean Squadron was then made up of three frigates *United States, Constellation, Java,* and three sloops *Ontario, Erie,* and *Washington.* [Perrotta, *op. cit.,* 30].

117

COMMODORE I. CHAUNCEY[40] TO WM. PINKNEY

(Copy with Mr. Pinkney's despatch of Sept. 6, 1816, to Mr. Monroe)

U. S. SHIP WASHINGTON Naples Bay 12th August 1816[41] (Copy)

Sir

As it is probable that I shall find a port in Sicily more convenient for a deposit of Stores and a rendezvous for the Squadron under my command than either in Mahon or Cagliari I have to request that you will be pleased to obtain from His Sicilian Majesty's Government permission for the American Squadron in the Mediterranean to use the Arsenal or Dockyard at Messina or Syracuse for the Deposit of Stores &c — pledging myself that no injury shall be done to the place or buildings thus loaned to us.

It ought to be clearly understood that we shall be permitted to land and take off provisions and Stores (which are not intended exclusively for the Use of the Squadron) without hindrance or Molestation, and free from duties or imposts of any kind.

Your Excellency's early attention to this subject will greatly promote the people's interest, and add to the accommodation of the Squadron under my Command.

WM. PINKNEY TO COMMODORE CHAUNCEY

(Copy enclosed with Mr. Pinkney's despatch of Sept. 6, 1816
to Mr. Monroe)

Naples 30th August 1816 (Copy)

Mr. Pinkney presents his compliments to Commodore Chauncey, and is sorry that it is not in his power to transmit to him a more favorable answer than he now encloses[42] to the informal communication which Mr. Pinkney made to the Government here of the wish of Comm. Chauncey respecting a deposit of Stores &c. in Sicily.

He supposes it to be probable nevertheless that whatever may

---

[40] Commodore Isaac Chauncey, (1772-1840) of Connecticut. In 1815, he took command of the *Washington* and with this vessel as his flagship he commanded the Mediterranean Squadron in 1816-1818, and together with Consul William Shaler he negotiated a treaty with Algiers. (*Dictionary American Biography,* IV, 40). It was on the *Washington* that Pinkney and his suite travelled to Naples. See above, p. 90.

[41] See above p. 116.

[42] See pp. 116-117. Copies of this letter were sent both to Commodore Chauncey and to the United States Secretary of State.

be the repugnance of this Government to a *general* permission to use any of its dockyards, or Arsenals, or other places in Sicily, as established places of deposit for the provisions and Stores of the American Squadron, any *occasional* facilities that may from time to time be requested by the Commodore, will not be refused.

WM. PINKNEY TO THE MARQUIS DI CIRCELLO

(Enclosure with Mr. Pinkney's despatch of Aug. 30, 1816)

Naples August 30, 1816

Mr. Pinkney presents his Compliments to H. E. the Marquis di Circello and has the honour to acknowledge the receipt of his note of the 28 Instant[43] in answer to an informal communication from Mr. Pinkney to H. E. of a wish of Commodore Chauncey on the subject of a Deposit in Sicily for the accommodation of the American Squadron.

Mr. Pinkney would have been happy to find it stated in that note that the Commodore's desire in this particular was about to be gratified; but he will nevertheless take pleasure in transmitting a Copy of the Note to his Government which he is sure will duly appreciate the motives and sentiments which it suggests. — He will not fail moreover to make Commodore Chauncey acquainted[44] with its Contents.

He begs his Excellency the Marquis di Circello to accept the renewed assurances of his distinguished Consideration.

N.B. No copy was retained of the first informal Note[45] to the Marquis. It merely reminded him of an informal conversation on the Subject.

WM. PINKNEY TO JAMES MONROE

Naples 7 Septr. 1816 *Private*

My Dear Sir

We have just received here intelligence (by a British Frigate) of the late successful operations of L^d. Exmouth at Algiers,[46] of which you will be fully apprized before this can reach you. — The news is very good in many respects; but it will not have the best effect in the world upon my errand here. — Had the work been

43 See pp. 116-117.
44 This was actually done. See p. 118.
45 See p. 115.
46 See above, note 28, p. 114, regarding this exploit.

done by an American Fleet, it would have been another affair. — I should then have expected to close my Mission to Naples in the most advantageous manner. —

I learn from a quarter on which I rely that although my note of the 24th of August has (to use a common phraze [sic]) *plagued* these gentlemen a good deal, it has given no offense, and that I shall have my answer soon. It will not loiter long after the receipt of the above mentioned news: — I count upon being able to set out for Russia next week.

Will not L^d. Exmouth's Exploit at Algiers be likely to put an End to the necessity of maintaining an American Squadron in the Mediterranean, where certainly, in case of a sudden quarrel with an European maritime nation, our ships would be exposed to great Danger?

Every thing which I hear confirms me in the opinion that we shall not be wise if we do not use every exertion to form without delay a considerable navy but I should trust that this great purpose stands very little in need of a Demand for the Service of our Fleet against the broken Power of the Dey of Algiers, who seems now to have ceased to be worthy of producing an Exhibition of our Strength in those distant Seas.

P.S. L^d. Exmouth was so fortunate as to stop *in transitu* the money which was sent by this Government to Algiers under the Treaty[47] of last Spring. It is arrived here, to the great Joy of the King and his ministers.

WM. PINKNEY TO JAMES MONROE

Naples. Septr. 18th. 1816

Sir

I received on the 16th. Instant at night, from Mr. Harris,[48] the American Chargé d'affaires at St. Petersburgh, the Letter which is enclosed; and am about to send Mr. King, the Secre-

---

[47] A treaty of peace was signed with Algiers on June 30 and July 3, 1815 and was proclaimed on Dec. 26, 1815. For text of, and notes on this treaty, see: Miller, *op. cit.*, 1931; II, 585-594. Another treaty of peace and amity with Algiers was signed at Algiers, Dec. 22 and 23, 1816, but this was not proclaimed until Feb. 11, 1822. For text of, and notes on this latter treaty, see Miller, *op. cit.*, II, 617-644.

[48] John Levitt Harris, of Pennsylvania, U. S. Consul at Rotterdam from March 1, 1803 to Nov. 11, 1803. Consul at St. Petersburg Nov. 1803 to July 19, 1813. On July 19, 1813 he was appointed secretary of the joint mission for negotiating a treaty of peace and commerce with Great Britain. On April 26, 1816 he returned to St. Petersburg as U. S. Consul. He was appointed chargé d'affaires to France on Feb. 23, 1833.

tary of my Legation, with an answer, of which a copy is enclosed.[49]

Although the precipitate and most irregular Step, of suspending the usual intercourse with our chargé d'affaires upon the first intelligence of Kosloff's[50] arrest & Imprisonment, would justify the Government of the U. S. in being very lofty on its part, I presume that the inducements to manage upon such an occasion have appeared to be so powerful that the letter has been explained, and that there is an End of the difficulty which it has produced. — In my opinion, there was no ground on which the Emperor was authorized to take offence at all, still less to exclude the American Chargé d'affaires from Court. — But the goodwill of Russia is too important to us to be sacrificed to *Punebile*. [51]

I venture to hope that the President will approve the course which I take on this occasion. It seems to me to be clear that if the affair of Kosloff has not been adjusted to the Emperor's satisfaction I should act imprudently in going hastily on for the mere purpose of being affronted; and that if it has been adjusted (as I feel confident it has) I shall lose very little Time and shall arrive at St. Petersburgh according to the plan announced in my letter to Mr. Harris, very nearly as soon as if that affair had never occurred. —

Had the Emperor desired Explanations only, so as that it should be manifest that the Government of the U. S. had not

[49] On Sept. 17, 1816 Pinkney acknowledged to Harris the receipt of his letter of July 30 with enclosure. Pinkney stated that "the light in which the Emperor has seen the affair of Mr. Kosloff is deeply to be regretted . . . I am in possession of all the material papers belonging to the case, and consequently know, and am able to say with perfect confidence, that the Govt. of the U. S. had not, either in fact or constructively, any participation in the act of which the Emperor seems particularly to complain. — I am not, however, authorized to make a formal disavowal of that act, because, as I presume, it had not occurred to the Govt. that it could be necessary, or wd. be desired . . . It is plain upon the facts of the transaction that the Govt. of the U. S. gave no cause of offence to Russia, either by what it omitted to do or what it did . . ." MS National Archives.

[50] A letter from Harris, the American chargé in St. Petersburg, received September 16, stated that Pinkney's presence in the Russian capital was required on account of the strained relations with the Czar. Kosloff, the Russian Consul General in Philadelphia, had been arrested and tried by a civil court on a charge of rape. The Emperor took the incident as a personal insult. Since the Emperor refused to communicate with Harris, the latter appealed to Pinkney, whom he knew had been chosen to succeed him. Pinkney, he realized, was acceptable to the Emperor and therefore in a position to discuss the matter with him amicably. This letter made Pinkney anxious to leave for Russia. Perrotta, *op. cit.,* 35.

[51] *Punebile*: A word seldom used today; it conveys the meaning best approximated by the word 'contumacious', inclined to make trouble, to be 'touchy'. It is not as strong a word as 'belligerency' would have been in this context, and not so likely to give the impression of intent to affront the nation regarding whom it is used here.

been wanting in respect to him, the Papers in my possession would have enabled me to do all that he wished. But he wants Explanation and Disavowal *under express orders of our Government.* — I have no such orders; and I am not sorry that I have not; because at the Time of my Departure it was not known that Mr. Harris was forbidden the Emperor's Court; and certainly orders given without my Knowledge of that fact might have embarrassed me when I came to be apprized of it myself.

I have found myself obliged to remind the Marquis di Circello of my note of the 24th of August. — Enclosed [52] is a Copy of the promise which he has in consequence given to me that I shall have an answer in a few days. I expect to receive it today or tomorrow. — I trust therefore that I shall be able to set out towards Russia about the middle of next week.

I have the Honour to be, with the highest esteem and consideration.

THE MARQUIS DI CIRCELLO TO WM. PINKNEY

Naples, 16 Septr. 1816.[53]

The Marquis di Circello has the honour to inform His Excy. Mr. P. in answer to his private note of the 14th Instant that since the receipt of his note of the 24th of August he has not ceased to be occupied with the subject of it, and hopes to be able to give an answer to it in a few Days.[54] He profits of this occasion to renew &c.

THE MARQUIS DI CIRCELLO TO WM. PINKNEY

22 Sep^t. 1816[55]

The Marquis of Circello presents his compliments to His Excellency M. Pinkney, Ambassador of the United States to the Imperial Court of Russia; and being under a circumstance of conferring with him as soon as possible, would be happy to see His Excellency at his Office, hoping that it will be convenient in the course of the day.

---

[52] See below, this page.
[53] This note was not published in House Document No. 130. See also footnote 20, p. 109.
[54] See p. 125; also p. 126.
[55] This note, enclosed with letter of October 5, 1816, was not published in House Document No. 130. See also note 20, p. 109.

Wm. Pinkney to James Monroe

Naples, Sept. 24th. 1816.56

Sir;

I suppose it to be proper that I should send you the enclosed copy of a Letter which I have written, and think of sending to Commodore Chauncey,57 if the Squadron should still be at Messina, on the subject of some telegraphic Dispatches (recently received here and comunicated [sic] to me by the Marquis di Circello) announcing in a very vague manner the existence of Depositions at Messina between the Gentlemen of our Squadron and certain Englishmen, either on shore, or in Vessels in the Harbour. — It is to be presumed that the Thing is of no real importance, although it has moved them a good deal here (principally I doubt not because the English are said to be parties to it). — England is of great weight at this feeble Court.

I have the Honour to be, with the highest Esteem & Consideration

Wm. Pinkney to Commodore Chauncey

(Enclosure with Mr. Pinkney's despatch of Sept. 24, 1816)

Naples. 22d. Sept. 1816

My Dear Sir:

The Marquis di Circello, in the course of an interview to which he invited58 me this afternoon, informed me that he was about to send a courier to Messina upon the subject of some depositions which it appeared had taken place there between the Gentlemen of the American Squadron and certain Englishmen, either of the place or belonging to ships in the port, by which the tranquillity of Messina had been disturbed.59 — He read to me the substance of two telegraphic Dispatches recently received, which announced those Depositions and the concern which they had occasioned, but which gave no particulars from whence their cause nature or extent could be accurately ascertained. — He told me that they felt the greatest uneasiness here with regard to these Depositions; that the Americans were

---

56 This despatch was not published in House Document No. 130. See also note 20, p. 109.

57 This was sent. See following letter Pinkney to Chauncey, Sept. 22, 1816. See also p. 118.

58 See p. 122.

59 See pp. 133-134; and pp. 134-140 for Extract from a Report of the Prince of Scaletta, Governor of Messina, September 16, 1816.

their friends and the English their allies, and that it w^d. be extremely painful to the King's Government to interfere against either the one or the other; that, as he knew no more than the telegraphic communications contained, he was of course ignorant who was in the wrong, but that they were anxiously desirous that Messina should not become the scene of any Differences between those for whom the Government of this Country entertained and wished to show the utmost respect and kindness. The feeling which the Marquis manifested on this occasion was very strong; and you will I know take in good part that I avail myself of the earliest opportunity to suggest it to you . . . — Every body here has perfect confidence that you will use your authority as far as you can with propriety to put a Stop to the ill effects which could not fail to flow from the misunderstandings, whatever may have been their Cause. —

Aware as I am that the Gentlemen of our Navy are as remarkable for the correctness of their conduct as for their Gallantry, Skill and a Sense of Honour, I am persuaded that if any thing occurred at Messina to justify the imperfect Dispatch above alluded to, the Blame is not theirs. — Yet the danger of giving umbrage to the Sicilian Government by embarrassing it, and the Importance of gaining its confidence and good will by marked respect for its Peace and Jurisdiction, will I am satisfied have their just weight with you in regulating this matter. — At all Events it is proper that you should be apprized of the Sensations which this affair has already produced here, especially as it has been officially made known to me; and it is the sole object of this Letter to give you that Information.

For the rest, nobody is a better Judge than you are of what the case requires on your part.

Addressed
To Commodore Chauncey —
   or, in Case of his absence, to
   the Officer in Command, of the
   American Squadron &c.

   N.B. A Postscript to this Letter (dated Septr. 23^d. and written on the inner Enveloppe [sic]) informed the Commodore that the Marquis di Circello had just communicated to Pinkney a further telegraphic Dispatch, which imported that an English Schooner had been attacked under the Guns of the Town by the Boats (or a Boat) of the American

Squadron. — The Postscript merely added that this Dispatch had of course increased the uneasiness mentioned in the Letter. — The Postscript being written in a Hurry, no copy has been retained of it.

THE MARQUIS DI CIRCELLO TO WM. PINKNEY

Naples 27 Septr. 1816

The Marquis di Circello in reply to the private letter[60] of H. E. Mr. Pinkney, in which he was pleased to remind him of his official note of the 24th. of August last, has the honour to inform him that, notwithstanding the great anxiety of the Marquis di Circello to give the reply which he owes to the said note, he is not yet able to give it, since it must be the result of a reunion and accurate examination of all the information which the subject of that note requires, and for obtaining which orders have been given. — This may probably occupy several weeks more, and is of course impossible for him yet to fix the Epoch at which the said reply may be given, as Mr. Pinkney desires. The writer however assures his Excellency that, in case his situation should not permit him to wait for the said reply, he will make it his duty to forward it wheresoever he may indicate. —

In the meantime he profits of this occasion to have the honour to confirm to His Excellency the assurances of his distinguished Consideration.

WM. PINKNEY TO JAMES MONROE

Naples, Septr. 28th. 1816

Sir:

My Exertions have not yet been sufficient (although they have been unremitting) to obtain an answer to my note of the 24th. of August; and the Season is so far advanced that I fear I have only another week for further Exertions. If I do not set out for Russia without delay I shall subject myself to the Hazard of being confined in Italy by Rains and bad roads during a great part of the Winter. — It is my Determination, therefore to press immediately and finally for a categorical reply to my note, although I am persuaded that the Marquis is in no Situation

---

60 See the note of the Marquis di Circello to Mr. Pinkney, Sept. 16, 1816, p. 122 above.

125

to give it. — He must either reply at once, or show why he cannot. —

It has been mentioned to me, by those in whom I have confidence, that this Government has been extremely perplexed by the Demand contained in my Note, and has had it under constant and anxious consideration; that, fearing after much Consultation, to take the ground (suggested for it, as I think, in America) of the responsibility for such acts of Murat's Government as my note sets forth, it has been and still is searching for information as to *facts;* that diligent Enquiry, for example, has been made and is yet making for the original papers of the different Vessels and Cargoes for which we require compensation, or for such Evidence as might supply their place; and that it is probable that in the end an attempt will be made to encounter, at least a part of our Demand with proof (good or bad) that our Case is not altogether such as we suppose it to be *in its Circumstances.*

I am told that their search after the Papers of the vessels and cargoes is not likely to be very successful. — Very few, perhaps none, remain; and it is not easy to conjecture what satisfactory, or even plausible, Substitutes they can procure.

I wrote yesterday a private letter to the Marquis di Circello, urging a prompt answer to my note, and desiring that he would tell me, with view to preparations for my Departure (which of course he knew I could not much longer postpone) when I might count upon receiving it; but I now think it necessary to demand an Interview, with the same object, to take place either today or tomorrow.

WM. PINKNEY TO THE MARQUIS DI CIRCELLO

Naples. Septr. 30th. 1816 (Copy)

The Undersigned, Envoy Extraordinary of the United States of America, had the honour to receive last night the note of His Excellency the Marquis di Circello, bearing date the 27th. Instant,[61] upon the Subject of the Note of the Undersigned of the 24th. of August. —

The undersigned certainly regrets that the Government of His Sicilian Majesty has not been able already to honour him with a precise reply to that Note; and he regrets still more that,

---

[61] See p. 125.

126

on account of the difficulty of collecting the Information supposed to be necessary to a correct Decision upon the claim which it preferred, he cannot hope to have such a reply during the Time to which he is obliged to limit his present Stay in Naples.

He is perfectly sure, however, that the Epoch is at Hand when His Majesty's Government will be possessed of this Information, and when the Justice of the Claim of the Government of the United States in behalf of its injured Citizens will be fully perceived and distinctly acknowledged.

The Undersigned, in answer to that part of the Note of The Marquis di Circello which proposes to send a Reply, to the Note of the Undersigned of the 24th. of August, wheresoever the Undersigned may indicate, has the honour to state to the Marquis di Circello that, upon this point, as well as upon all such ulterior Steps as his mission and the Subject of it may be calculated to produce, the Undersigned will think it is his Duty to refer himself to his Government, which at the same time that it will give their due weight to the reasons which are now assigned for a short postponement of the Claim in question, will take such measures as it shall think the Case requires with regard to the future.

The Undersigned takes this occasion to renew to H. E. the Marquis di Circello the assurances of his distinguished consideration.

WM. PINKNEY TO THE MARQUIS DI CIRCELLO

Naples 30th. Sept[r]. 1816 (Copy)

The Undersigned, Envoy Extraordinary of the United States of America, being about to leave the Court of His Majesty the King of the two Sicilies upon the Business of his Government, has the Honour[62] to request that His Exc[y]. The Marquis di Circello will have the Goodness, to inform him at what Time His Majesty will honour him with an Audience.

The Undersigned avails himself of this opportunity to renew to H. E. The Marquis di Circello the assurances of his most distinguished Consideration. —

---

62 In House Document No. 130 (see note 20, p. 109) this word is "honor." In the original document the older spelling "honour" is found.

WM. PINKNEY TO THE MARQUIS DI CIRCELLO

Naples 1. October 1816. (Copy)

The Undersigned Envoy Extraordinary of the United States of America, has the Honour to request of H. E. the Marquis di Circello the usual passports for himself his Family & Suite and their Baggage &c.

It is his present Intention to go to St. Petersburgh by the way of Vienna; but it is possible that he may abandon that Route in favour of the Road through Berlin. — He wishes to set out at the End of this week.

He begs H. E. the Marquis di Circello to accept the renewed assurances of his distinguished Consideration.

WM. PINKNEY TO JAMES MONROE

Naples 1. October. 1816[63]

Sir:

The Emperor of Austria when he took possession of Venice,[64] obtained possession also of several Ships of the Line and Frigates which Bonaparte had built there, but (with exception of two or three of the Frigates) had not entirely finished. — The Emperor does not it seems aim at maritime power, and is desirous of having these Ships, either in their actual State, or completed, as the purchaser may think fit.

Lieut. General Baron Koller,[65] who is in high military command here, is charged with the Sale of these Vessels, and has requested me to offer them on his part to the Govt. of the U. S. — He has put into my hands Lists of them, with suitable Explanations, which are herewith enclosed. — The Ships of the Line (stated in the Lists to have Cannon) may be had without the Cannon, if that sh^d. be preferred, and so (as I think) may the Frigates. The prices are marked in the lists in Florins, which are worth about half a Dollar each. The Baron has suggested to me that the Neapolitan Govt. w^d. buy, but that it is too poor; and that the English talk of purchasing, but w^d.

---

[63] This despatch is not published in House Document No. 130.

[64] On October 17, 1797, the Peace of Campoformio between France and Austria gave Austria the territory of Venice as far as the Adige, with the city of Venice, Istria, and Dalmatia.

[65] Franz Koller (von). (1767-1826). Baron. Austrian Field Marshal. He died in Naples.

probably (I understood the Baron to say) demand to have the purchase money applied to some account to which the Emperor wd. not wish to apply it. The Baron tells me that he is not *specially* authorised to offer these Vessels to the *Gov*ᵗ. *of the U. S.* for that it did not occur to the Emperor's Gov., when the authority to sell was given to him, that there wᵈ. be any oppʸ. of proposing to sell to us; but that he is sure that it will be agreeable to the Emperor, and that personally he (the Baron) had rather we shᵈ. have these Ships than any other power. — He professes particular respect for our Country and I have heard does not like the English but after all I presume his object is to get our money. —

In Case the Govᵗ. of the U. S. shᵈ. desire to purchase the whole or any part of these vessels (and it may take exactly what it pleases and leave the rest, as the Baron assured me) it is expected that it will send a person skilled in naval architecture & Equipment to examine them before it bargains for them. The Baron states that they are amongst the finest Vessels in the world. — He states also that they may be finished by the purchaser (if it is thought best to buy them in their present State) or that the Austrian Govᵗ. will complete them at the prices marked. I suppose that they may be got below Prices at present required; but I did not think it wᵈ. be proper for me to enquire into that, or to do any thing more than receive the Baron's proposal and tell him I Wᵈ. send it to you; and that an answer would doubtless be returned either through Mr. Gallatin[66] or through me.

66 Abraham Alfonse Albert Gallatin, of Pennsylvania. (1761-1849). Secretary of the Treasury. In 1816, he was appointed minister to France, holding that office to 1823. From the diary kept by Gallatin's son and secretary, James, one gets the impression that official business was completely stifled by social amenities at Paris. In the main work of his mission, the claims for injury done to American commerce by the Napoleonic decrees, Gallatin made no progress with the successive ministries of Louis XVIII. See: Henry Adams, *The Life of Albert Gallatin* (1879); *A Great Peacemaker, the Diary of James Gallatin* (1914) covers the years of his father's diplomatic career. It is only fair, however, to call attention to the fact that much of the apparently 'social' intercourse described by Mr. Gallatin's son was due to the mode of the day of conducting all manner of semi-official intercourse and of meeting persons with whom matters of high scientific interest were constantly being discussed. To understand this aspect of the activities of Gallatin in France, one must recall that for two decades prior Mr. Gallatin had been in constant correspondence with the ranking scientists of the French Academy and his own scientific writings and studies were highly regarded by these men. Gallatin's former duties as Secretary of the Treasury had increased his scientific interest in the techniques of navigation both on the sea (as of value to the country's expanding commercial ships) and on land (in connection with the expansion of the United States Public Land Surveys). Gallatin himself was no novice in the matter of map drafting and his work attracted more attention abroad than at home. Scientific journals in France and other countries abroad gave considerable

If our Gov^t. sh^d. incline to treat for those ships or any of those Mr. Gallatin may be authorized to adjust the terms of payment through the Austrian Minister at Paris, or by correspondence with the Austrian government; but the *Purchase* must be made through the Baron Koller who will be at Naples.

I have thought it necessary to make this Communication to you, although I am aware of all the Difficulties in the way of deriving any advantage from it. — If the proposal of the Baron sh^d. not be approved, it may be politely declined. — I need not recommend that it may not so be dealt with, as to appear to be altogether slighted.

I have the Honour to be with the highest Esteem and Consideration —[67]

THE MARQUIS DI CIRCELLO TO WM. PINKNEY

Naples. 2^d. Octr. 1816

The Undersigned Secretary of State & Minister for foreign affairs, in reply to the official note of 30th. of last month, in which His Exc^y. W. Pinkney, Envoy Extraordinary of the U. S. of America has requested an audience of His Majesty The King of the two Sicilies, hastens to inform him that His Majesty will with pleasure receive him at the royal palace in Naples, either tomorrow or the next day (as may be most convenient to His Exc^y.) at half past eleven o'clock in the forenoon.

The Undersigned renews to His Exc^y. &c.

---

space also to other American scientific achievements, such for example as the Wilkes Exploring Expedition, and the work of David Dale Owen, brother of the minister to the Two Sicilies at a later date. Jefferson and Franklin, as well as Gallatin, found it well in the interest of their duties as ambassadors to France to play their due part in the court scenes of their day. There is not of any necessity any stigma attached to their diplomatic efforts in consequence of their conforming to the customs of the capitals where they were accredited. That Congress considered the nation's representatives abroad properly should conform to royal court practices in matters of ceremony, etc. (which of course implied attendance as Pinkney and the others well show), at all manner of social functions, is to be inferred from the continual granting of large sums to our diplomats for 'outfits' which would suffice to allow of their appearing in social functions in such costumes, and at such times, as their very presence and accrediting to the royal courts commanded of them.

67 Attached to this despatch, in the original, is a two-page document giving statistical information in tabular form on each of the frigates.

130

Naples 8th. October 1816.

Sir:

At the Interview of the 29th. of last month between the Marquis di Circello & myself he recurred to the Subject of the late Disturbances at Messina, which he had mentioned to me at a former Interview, as you will find explained in my letter to you of the 25th. of September and its Enclosure.

He said that he had now received an account of the particulars of those Disturbances, and that he intended to send copies of all the Papers to me.

It appeared from the little which he dropped on this Occasion that we were thought by this Government to be in the wrong in that affair, and that it was rather wished that we would avoid the Ports of Sicily in future. — Although I was displeased at this Intimation, and did not disguise my Dissatisfaction, yet, as I knew nothing of the Details of the Affair I thought it best to forbear much comment upon it.

Finding that I did not receive the Copies, of which the Marquis had talked before I had taken leave and had got my passports, I supposed that he had thought better of it and had changed his mind; but to my astonishment I received from him, late in the afternoon of the 5th. Instant, the letter and Enclosure of which Copies[68] are herewith transmitted. — I take for granted that no answer was expected, and that the letter was intended merely to be *shewn to the British Minister.* — I confess that this paper has provoked me, for it is unjust in itself and indecently parcial to the English; but I hope nevertheless that my answer to it (of which a copy is enclosed) is as a guarded a one as such a Thing deserves. The plain Insinuation of partiality which my reply contains, will not be related here, but they will not venture to show their Dislike of it. — The concluding words of my Reply appeared to me to be indispensible. — Such People ought not to be suffered to suppose that we will condescend to accept any Hospitality from them if it be not such as it ought to be. I set out tomorrow for Rome. —

---

[68] Note of the Marquis di Circello, Oct. 4, 1816, and its enclosure, which is the Report of the Duke of Scaletta, in two parts, dated Sept. 19th and Sept. 25th, 1816: that part of the Report dated Sept. 19th had enclosures together numbered No. 1, two depositions . . . see pp. 134-139; that part of the Report dated Sept. 25th, had enclosures No. 2. (the British Pro-Consul, Mr. Barker's letter) and No. 3, that of the U. S. Consul, John Broadbent . . . see pp. 141; also p. 132, note 70.

P. S. I ought to mention that I have found M. Hammett[69] (our consul here) uniformly ready to do me all possible Service officially & personally . He is an excellent officer and an amiable man. — The Papers belonging to the Claim against the Gov^t. of Naples will be left with him.

THE MARQUIS DI CIRCELLO TO WM. PINKNEY

(Enclosure by Mr. Pinkney on Oct. 8, 1816 to Secretary Monroe containing Reports of Prince Scaletta of Messina dated Septr. 19, enclosing Depositions of Septr. 16, and Septr. 25, 1816.)

Naples, 4th October 1816

Several unpleasant circumstances have taken place in Messina between certain English and American individuals. Altho' the government of his Majesty the King of the two Sicilies had been informed of this by means of the telegraph, it has, nevertheless, waited for a more distinct account. This having arrived & not a few facts having resulted from this information, charging the equipages (or crews) of the American vessels of war, anchored in that port, not only with violence against English individuals and merchant vessels of the English nation, but also with atrocities, and contemptuous conduct towards the sovereignty of the territorial authority, in defiance of the most cordial hospitality, that friendship and good understanding could possibly require; the undersigned, Counsellor & Secretary of State, minister of foreign affairs, feels himself obligated to lay an account of them before his Excellency, Mr. Pinkney, Envoy Extraordinary from the Government of the United States of America. The annexed sheets in which will be found a genuine exposition[70] of these occurrences, will fully inform Mr. Pinkney. The undersigned abstains

---

[69] Alexander Hammett, of Maryland, was commissioned consul of U. S. at Naples, April 9, 1809, to succeed Frederic Degan. Hammett was again commissioned on June 21, 1809, and again on April 20, 1816. He remained in the consular service at Naples until his retirement on Dec. 16, 1861. See section devoted to his Despatches, herein seq., when he acted *ad interim* as chargé d'affaires there.

[70] The enclosures to the letter of the Marquis di Circello are in the form of a Report of the Governor of Messina, Prince Scaletta, in two parts, dated Sept. 19, and 25, 1816, respectively; with the first part there is No. 1 enclosure, consisting of two depositions; with the second part No. 2 and No. 3 enclosures. For the reader's convenience these are identified by cross references to the pages in this present publication on which each of the enclosures will be found, and the enclosures themselves, as well as the report texts, which are continuous, save for the broken dating and the insertion of the enclosures, are identified in their heading notes. See above, note 68, p. 131; also below, p. 141.

from any observations. He is certain, that the heroic principles of justice which ought to regulate every government, and which distinguish Mr. Pinkney, will make him consider the conduct of those who have been parties in these outrages as very reprehensible, and will make him give such dispositions to these affairs as their gravity may demand.

The undersigned cannot, however, pass in silence, that part of the report of the Governor of Messina which relates to Com^r. Chauncey. The difficulties he made and the resistance he evidenced, in concurring on his part to restore and preserve the Public tranquility here occasioned the most serious sensations in the breast of the King. Mr. Pinkney cannot but agree that hospitality is impracticable when consequences of such serious importance may spring from it, and when so ill a return is made to the most friendly reception. The undersigned, therefore, expects from the wise discernment of his Excell^y. the strong measures that shall have the effect to secure, hereafter, public order. — That shall occasion the supreme rights of the sovereignty to be respected, not only in every thing that relates immediately to itself; but also in all that which the sovereignty itself owes to other friendly nations, whose subjects have a right to be protected and guaranteed from every insult in the Royal Dominions.

The underwritten has the honour to repeat to his excellency the assurances of his high consideration.

THE MARQUIS DI CIRCELLO TO WM. PINKNEY

[Enclosure with letter Oct. 4, 1816]

Extract from a Report of the Prince of Scaletta, Governor of Messina[71] to the Marquis di Circello, Secretary of State for Foreign Affairs

Messina 16 Septem. 1816

Excellency

By the telegraph I have briefly informed you of the disturbance between the English and Americans. I shall now offer you a minute relation of the whole. Early in the morning of the 12th instant a sailor belonging to one of the American Frigates went on board of an English merchant Brig. He was found in her (nel calare) hold, with some leather bundled in a pocket

---

71 Antonio Ruffo, Prince of Scaletta (1778-1846). In 1815 he was made Lieutenant General. In 1820 he served as Lieutenant General in Sicily. From 1822 to 1830 he was minister of war and of the navy. From July 13, 1830 to Nov. 12, of the same year, he was Captain of the Royal Guards.

133

handkerchief. This leather the English say he had stolen that very day and he had been *regalate* by an American sailor who happened to be on board of the Brig. The fact was, the English took the American belonging to the Frigate, stripped him, tied him up, flogged him and then kicked him overboard, *buttarlo in mare*. The sailor returning on board of the Frigate related the whole to his commander, who immediately, with other officers went on to the English Brig, which had now hoisted her flag and pendant. Fortunately, at that moment, the Captain of the port Lieut. Col. D. Litterio Natoli, happened to be passing there, and being informed of the circumstances that had occurred, he called the American Officers from on board of the Brig and conducted them to the house of their Consul. The Captain of the Port immediately informed me of what had happened, and I thought proper to defer the consideration of the affair until the American Commodore would return from Etna. In the meantime, however, I did not omit to treat with the respective Consuls. Yesterday, finally, I had a conversation with the American Commodore, who confined himself entirely to insisting that the Englishmen should be punished agreeably to the laws of this country, for a crime committed against its soverain [sic] authority. A conversation was then had with the British consul, by whom it has been accorded that he is ready to declare, or to make the Commander of the English Brig declare, as best shall please the American Commodore, that in the affair there has been no intention of offending the American Nation, as it was not known to what nation the American sailor belonged; that his being so severely treated was solely on account of his having been so found with stolen leather upon him: and that he was ready to consign over to the mate (*nostromo*) of the Brig to have him punished, for having failed in his respect to the Port. This accord I have communicated, thro' the medium of the American Consul, to the commodore, but I am not yet favored with his reply.

MEMORANDUM OF THE PRINCE OF SCALETTA
(Enclosure No. 1 (Copy) with Sept. 19, 1816.)

Messina 16: Sept. 1816.
British Consulate

Deposition sworn to by Nathaniel Tomy (nostro uomo mate) of the English schooner belonging to Marina in Malta, taken, attested and sworn to this day above written, before our W. W.

Barker for the information of the consular office, and of whatever other court, tribunal, or magistrate, and to have full & legal effect: which is as follows.

I Nathaniel Tomy, on my soul & by the omnipotent God swear that Wednesday (Giovedi) [sic] the 12th Sept. current, I saw on board of the Schooner Ann (Hann) a negro take from the deck a piece of leather, which as he had it, I had no suspicion he meant to steal. But not observing it afterwards I asked Mr. Richard Cornish, brother of the Captain of the Brig Ann who was on board of the same Schooner and who had also himself seen the negro handle the leather, "what had become of the piece of sole leather?" He replied, "I do not see it on deck where it was?" At this time the negro had hid it in his handkerchief, and was retiring from the vessel carrying it along with him. I accosted him and directed him to return it but he refused to do so. Then I in fulfillment of my duty, being charged with the vessel in the absence of Captain Bell, endeavoured to prevent him from leaving the ship, and the negro, making resistance, gave me a blow with his fist in the face, endeavouring at the same time to escape, but he was overpowered & arrested by the crew of the Schooner. Many persons, seeing from land the circumstances, came on board of the schooner which persons I then understood belonged to the American Squadron. These seized and the crew, saying, "flog him well, he is a thief — pay him for he is a disgrace to us, he ought not to go about plundering", & other words to that same effect. At this time Capt. Bell came on board & a little while after the negro was liberated, but being on the bridge of the wharf which leads to the shore, he was met and struck by a man, who I then understood, belonged to the American 74. who Kicked him, from the schooner & from that into the water (in mare).

I Declare further, on my oath before god [sic] as above, that the (riva) of our Schooner our inglish [sic] flag was hoisted at the suggestion of a man from the shore. In this affair I had no intention of offending any nation, authority or person whatsoever. I did not know to what country the negro belonged; and in punishing him, I thought I was only castigating a scoundrel, and should have done the same to any man, that I should have caught in the act of stealing & had the effrontery to give me a violent blow, on board of the same schooner, that I, in the absence of Captain Bell, commanded. So help me God.

(Enclosure with Memorandum of September 19, 1816, of Prince of Scaletta. Re-enclosed October 4, 1816 by the Marquis di Circello)

I John Bell Captain & Commander of the English Schooner Ann declare & swear on my soul, that being about sunrise on the 12th instant in the house of a Signor Modene in this city, I was called by my mariner Christopher Wood belonging to the said Schooner, to come immediately on board; he told me that a thief had been discovered on board stealing leather, which he had hid in his handkerchief and that he had also assaulted and struck the mate (nostromo) with his fist in the face. Understanding this, without any other reflection, I ran on board, where I saw a negro tied to the (sarse), and that the crew of my said schooner were flogging him, in which also I took a part, but I swear solemnly before Almighty God that I knew not to what country the said negro belonged, and that I had no intention whatsoever of offending any law, nation or person whatsoever, but solely to correct a thief found in the fact, with the plunder on him, and who had, besides outraged my mate. Immediately after my arrival on board the negro was put at liberty and passing on the wharf which leads to the shore, was struck by a man, who knocked him overboard (lo buttò in mare). This man I then understood belonged to the american 74.

I have been also informed that our British flag was hoisted to the (a riva) of my schooner by the direction of a man from the shore who cried hoist your flag, otherwise you will have a crowd of people on board. Immediately after an officer in the uniform of the United States came on board, saying "I am a Yankee, & you have flogged an American seaman, adding many offensive words, but I upheld that I did not know to what country the black man belonged. So help me God.

We certify that the foregoing depositions have been faithfully copied from the originals, written in the English Idiom, and remaining in the British consular office in this city of Messina & correctly compared & examined. In faith of which this day, Messina 17. September 1816.

[Report of September 19, 1816, of Prince of Scaletta]

Messina, 19th. September 1816

The affair relating to the American Seaman taken on board of an English Schooner and there stripped, flogged & kicked overboard, *buttato a mare*, was by me conciliated, as submitted in my last, and now, for the better information of your Excellency, I have inclosed under No. 1 the declaration on oath which I obligated the Captain of the English Schooner to make, which being presented to the Commodore, met with his approbation. Content with having succeeded happily in this accommodation I flattered myself with enjoying some moments of peace. But things have not so succeeded. The evening before last in a Billiard room the English and Americans attacked each other anew; and after having well bruised each other with fists they were separated by the arrival of the watch with a military patroll. At a very late hour of the same night, an american chirurgian asserts that in retiring to his vessel he was assaulted by a person whom he knew to be an Englishman, and to be Captain of the aforesaid schooner and by other English captains of Vessels; that in order to free himself from them, he discharged a pistol; but that he was slightly wounded by a pointed instrument in the right hand. This occasioned that he with other American officers and seamen, surrounded the said English schooner for the purpose of knowing from her captain, who was the person that had thus wounded him, as he who wounded him must have been known to the captain.

The captain on the contrary asserts, that the Americans intended to attack him while on board, and that for this, he had called to his aid the officers of neighboring british vessels — had armed, had prepared a cannon and stood ready with the match in his hand. The British Consul in the meantime being advised of the matter, expedited his chancellor assisted by the watch and patroll, and they succeeded in preventing the evil that at that moment was about to happen. At day break, the Consul came suddenly to me, to demand assistance for the English vessels, asssuring me that he should immediately send off an account of everything to Admiral Lord Exmouth. At the same time I assured him, that as far as depended on me, I would cooperate to restore peace between the English and Americans. I instantly had the American consul called, — had him informed by the British consul himself of all that had happened, and he besought him to go, in my name to the Commodore, and request, that after a given hour of the evening none of the crews (equipaggi) of his squadron, might be permitted to remain on shore, since, as my government was at peace with the two nations, I ought not to permit, in a port belonging to it, these continual

137

altercations, which might disturb the peace of the inhabitants, and might compromise the decorum of his Majesty. The reply was, that the Commodore had told him that he had not the power, to establish the regulation I desired. I, in reply, told him to inform the said Commodore, that in the year past I had seen same measure adopted by Captain Gordon,[72] and that in his absence, I had seen the same repeated by Captain Perry; but, at all counts however the case might be, I could not permit, in the territory of his Majesty that the tranquillity of two friendly nations, and of the peace of the inhabitants, should be disturbed: that, for this end, I was about to establish a very strong military patroll, which should patroll the whole night — should arrest all those individuals belonging to any nation whatever, that should be found on shore. If they should be officers, they would be conducted to the office of the guard, at the main guard: If soldiers or sailors to the prison; and that on the next day their conduct would be the subject of further enquiry.

I charged also the consul to relate all the foregoing to the Commodore but with sincere regret, I must inform your excel.ᵞ that this cold hearted man although I sent three times to him, requesting him to establish the above mentioned regulations; and altho' I made Lieut. Col. Natoli captain of the port, (whom I cannot sufficiently praise) assure him repeatedly that the latter measure would eventually be adopted, he was not to be moved. He even told Natoli, that if things went to a certain length and came to extremities, he should place his reliance on Providence. This occasioned me to call on him for the fourth time, and to declare to him that it was sufficient for me, that I had communicated to him my sentiments; that he was here, the representative of the American nation and that all responsibility must fall upon him.

I was required, in the mean time, both personally and by writing, from the British Consul, to prevent the machinations, which it was foreseen must occur and the evils of which have happened; because the Americans, in large parties, armed, were going about the wharves and particularly along side of the schooner in question. He made the English all retire on board of their respective vessels, and this was completely complied with. I directed that all the billiard rooms should be shut up until further orders — that 50 troopers with an officer and under the

---

[72] Captain Charles Gordon of Maryland. In 1816 he was on the *Constellation* in the Mediterranean. He died in 1817. (*General Navy Register and Laws . . . since 1798*. Washington, 1848, 52).

direction of Col¹. Natoli, should execute what I have above stipulated — that the watch and military patroll watch, and have closed at an early hour, all places in which a scuffle might possibly rise. Notwithstanding these measures, there were heard about 12 o'clock of the night of the 20th reports of loaded pistols discharged from a fishing smack in the port, which was then supposed to have been fired by some marine guards of the American Squadron. Shortly after shouts were heard toward the shore, which occasioned the Patroll to run there, where it found three American officers and the English Captain Bell[73] attacking each other in the most furious manner. The Captain of the Port succeeded in separating them, and conducted them into the Royal office of the high (or general) police, and there placed the Americans in one room and the English in another, & treated them all with supper.

In the mean time about ten or twelve American officers appeared at the aforesaid office, and without any regard to the place — to the constituted authority — or to the troops of his Majesty demanded the restitution of their companions, and enquiring in a high tone, why (according to their assertions) the British Captain had not also been arrested. The Captain of the port, to convince them that they were in error in this respect, said to them that English Captain, was in a room separate by himself. Pretending that they wished to be convinced of this, some American officers penetrated into the Room of Capt. Bell, and attempted to wound him. The secretary of the Captain of the Port, who was present having prevented the blow, another American officer attempted to make one at him, which was rendered ineffectual by the officer of the patroll interposing his arm; but he remained himself wounded in the hand. As soon as the Governor of Messina was informed of all these disorders he went to the place accompanied by the American Consul and the British pro-Consul. He proposed to both parties, either to accede to a mutual concession, or to attempt, by the way of Justice and law to repair their wrongs which they had received. The Ameri-

---

[73] An intensive search of the records of the War Office, London, still preserved in the Public Records Office, yielded no information concerning a Captain Bell of the British Army at Messina. The Bell referred to in this despatch may be identical with Captain John Bell, master of the schooner *Ann* of Malta, who was involved in a tavern brawl with certain U. S. officers at Messina on September 17, 1816, arising out of an accusation that he had ordered the flogging of a U. S. seaman. A full account of this incident is contained in a Despatch from the British consul at Messina, dated September 25, 1816, with various enclosures. This note was sent to the editor by the Under-Secretary of State of the War Office, London.

cans and English agreed to the first proposition, and were all remanded on board of their respective vessels.

[Continuation of the Report of Prince of Scaletta]

Messina 25th. September 1816

The British pro-consul had demanded of me by his letter, (a copy of which is transmitted to your Excell^y. in No. 2.)[74] security for the schooner of Capt. Bell, ready to depart from this port, and an analogous copy of which was sent by me to the American Consul; to which he favored me with a reply of assurance, which your Excell^y. will find in the annexed copy (No. 3.)[75]

Notwithstanding this assurance, the said vessel having hoisted sail for Malta at midday of the 22^d. on going out of the port, three launches of the American Squadron armed with cannon, gave her chase, and overtook her at the point of the Forti del Salvatori, boarded her, and demanded of Capt. Bell, the restitution of an american deserter, who was in the crew of the Schooner. Captain Bell immediately and without any resistance delivered up the deserter required, in compliance with a mutual convention, which exists between the nations & here generally unknown. But at this moment the American Frigate the United States, arrived from the port, with every hostile preparation — with batteries ready to open upon them, matches lighted, and with all the crew armed and arranged at the sides & on the masts — obligated her to return into Port & to anchor under the cannon of the vessels which were there at anchor.

This detail was not made known to me until after the return into port of the schooner; and the first movement of the americans determined me to remit to his Majesty a telegraphic account, which will have been noted by your Excellency.

At 3 post meridian of the same day an American Officer appeared on board of the said English vessel for the purpose of delivering to Capt. Bell a passport, in order that two frigates & a corvette, that had some few days before sailed on a cruise, might not molest him in the course of his voyage. It appears Capt. Bell refused it at first, but accepted of it [sic] the next day.

---

[74] See p. 141.
[75] See p. 141.

140

W .W. BARKER[76] TO THE PRINCE OF SCALETTA

[Enclosed with Memorandum of September 25, 1816, forming part of "Extract from Report of Prince of Scaletta" of September 19, 1816, and all with that of the Marquis di Circello to Mr. Pinkney of October 4, 1816.]

Messina, 20th. Sept. 1816. (No. 2 Copy)

Most Excellent Sir.

Captain John Bell commander of the English Schooner Anne, is ready to depart from this port, to prosecute his voyage. He fears, however, with some reason, according to the threats made him by the Americans, that in going out of the port, he may be overpowered by force. Hence I implore from the justice of your excell[y]. that protection that may guarantee the safety of the said captain & of his vessel. Persuaded of the Justice of your Excell[y]. I have the advantage of considering myself

LORD J. BROADBENT[77] TO THE PRINCE OF SCALETTA

[Enclosed with Memorandum of September 25, 1816, forming part of "Extract from Report of Prince of Scaletta" of September 19, 1816, and all enclosed with that of the Marquis di Circello to Mr. Pinkney on October 4, 1816.]

Messina, 25th Sept. 1816. (Copy)

Excellency

Replying promptly to the Letter with which you have honoured me inclosing me officially a copy of that of the British pro consul, Mr. William Barker, respecting the departure from this port, of Captain John Bell, permit me to observe, that the fear of the said captain springs alone from his own villanous conduct (cattiva condotta), but as the most perfect peace & friendship reigns between the two nations English & American, the official letter of the Signore British pro consul, is rendered superfluous. With all due respect and esteem, I am

---

76 William Wilton Barker was Pro-Consul at Messina from 1816 to June 28, 1826, when he was appointed Consul. He died on May 17, 1856.

77 John Broadbent of the Island of Sicily, commissioned United States Consul at Messina, on Mar. 20, 1805, and again on Jan. 17, 1806. He died at his post on Oct. 25, 1826. His successor, John Larkin Payson, of Massachusetts, was commissioned Mar. 3, 1827. (United States State Department, Official Consular List).

141

WM. PINKNEY TO JAMES MONROE

Naples. Saturday. Octr. 5th. 1816 [Despatch, unnumbered]

Sir:

On Sunday the 29th. of last month I had an Interview with the Marquis di Circello, in pursuance of the Intention announced in my last. — I pressed him for his promised answer to the note of the 24th of August, and insisted that if he could not reply to it immediately he would name the Time within which it was probable he could do so. — He said that an immediate answer was really impossible, and that he could not, without running the risk of misleading me, fix the precise Time for the giving of such an answer as sh^d. be categorical. — I asked the reason of this. He observed that the papers relative to the Vessels & Cargoes for which we now demanded an Equivalent had in Murat's time been scattered about in such a way that with all the Diligence they could use, they had not yet been able to collect them or such Information that might stand in their place; that all proper Steps had been taken by the King's Government for obtaining these papers and whatever else was connected with and material to our Claim, and that they hoped that they would soon be successful; that our Claim, apparently of large amount, was made upon those who confessedly had no participation in the transaction upon which it was founded; that it was therefore manifest they had all their Knowledge of those transactions to gain; that they were sincerely desirous of understanding them thoroughly; that, without all the Knowledge of the Circumstances of the case which could at this Time and by due inquiry be recovered, the King could not decide whether he was or was not answerable to us as we alledged; that a Decision would undoubtedly be hastened and made known to me as soon as possible and as he believed within a period of time not any means distant; but that I must perceive it was not in his power, without practising Disingenuousness, to assure me that this could be done in a few weeks. — In some further Conversation on this point I told him that I feared I should be obliged to leave Naples before his answer was prepared; and, as he knew that my ulteriour [sic] Destination was St. Petersburg, I informed him finally that I had determined to set out for Russia on Saturday the 5th. instant, (this day) unless by waiting a week or two more I could be sure of adjusting the Business of my mission. — He replied with his characteristical good-breeding that they should be ex-

142

tremely sorry to lose me, and that they hoped to have me with them for some time but that, if my Duty elsewhere called me away he would undertake to send the Answer to my note the moment it could be given, wherever I would indicate; that there was no probability that if I left Naples as soon as I spoke of, or even a week or two later, I should receive the answer here, but that if it *could* be given so promptly it *should*. — I rejoined that I doubted if without Instructions it would be well for me to receive the answer, after I had left the King's Court & Territories; that I confidently trusted the answer would admit our Claim (although we had no desire to urge them inconveniently as to Time or mode of payment or even to push the demand to its utmost Extent) but that, however little such a Result was to be expected, the answer might contest our Demand, or an important portion of it, in which case it was both my Duty & my Inclination to reply to the answer, and to maintain, as I did not fear to be able to do, the Grounds of fact and Law upon which I had already relied; and that this could not be done with advantage, nor perhaps with propriety, unless with the approbation of my Government, after my Departure for another Station. — The Marquis immediately expressed an opinion that I might regularly receive the answer after I had left the Neapolitan Dominions; and, in consequence of a question which I put to him in this Stage of the Conversation (whether it might not be more in Rule to offer to deliver the answer to whom and where the *Government of the United States* should think fit) he said that he should have no objection to any course which I preferred, but that he thought it would be best (*as being more respectful to me*) that he should undertake to send the answer as I should prescribe, especially as this Course essentially included the other. It would have been impossible for me to dispute an opinion referred to so civil a nature even if the matter had been worth disputing. — I do not think, however, that it was worth more words that had been bestowed upon it and I therefore left the Marquis to take his own way upon it, reserving to myself the Power of taking mine in due Season.

In the whole of this Conversation of which I have very shortly stated the Import not a Word was dropped by the Marquis condemning our Claim or intimating that it was likely to be rejected, although much what I said was calculated to provoke him to do so. — But again, he said nothing which amounted to an admission that the Claim would be acknowledged .

143

Before I went away I requested (and he promised) that he would write me a Note, expressing briefly what had passed between us; and in the Evening of the same day I received from him a Paper of which a Copy is among the Enclosures written and sent in consequence of that Request; but upon examining the papers I found that it referred to my unofficial letter mentioned in my last and not to our Interview, and moreover that it was dated the 27th. of September (perhaps a mistake for the 29th., or possibly my mistake of his figures) which was antecedent to the Interview. I took for granted, however, that the Marquis had understood me to wish that this mode should be adopted; and, as it was of no Importance, I did not put him, as at first I thought of doing, to the trouble of changing it. — I therefore founded upon it the three Notes (bearing Date, two of them, the 30th. of September, and the other the 1st. of October) of which copies are enclosed.

On the 2^d. Instant I received the Marquis's answer to my note of the 30th. of September which desired an audience of the King, and I took leave accordingly on Friday the 4th. Instant, one of the Days referred by the Marquis's Note to my Choice, as you will perceive by the Copy of it herewith transmitted. The King was polite and kind and conversed for some time with me on this occasion; but nothing was said by him which had any relation to the objects of my Mission.

Having received my Passports, my intention is to commence my Journey for S. Petersburg in a very few days. M^r. King left me for Russia about a fortnight ago, as my letters of the 18th. of September informed you he would and the Gentlemen attached to my Legation have gone before me to Rome where I hope to arrive on Thursday or Friday next.

I beg your attention, now, to a few words upon the Course which I have pursued as Envoy Extraordinary to Naples, and upon the actual position & prospects of the Claim which produced it.

My Stay here has perhaps been a little longer than was anticipated when I sailed from America; but upon a careful examination of my Instructions it appeared to me that I was directed by them to make the attempt to obtain an acknowledgement of our Claim upon this government as full & complete as possible without sacrificing to it the Interests of my Mission to Russia. — I have done this. As the Claim was of great Magnitude in a pecuniary sense, involved important principles, and turned

144

upon facts into which those with whom I had to deal had a Right to enquire, I could scarcely hope to bring it to an Issue of any kind within less than the two months which have elapsed since my first Reception. — With regard to my Mission to Russia I have yet made no Sacrifice. Independently of the explanations which I have had from Time to Time with Count Moconigo[78] [sic] (the Russian minister here) with regard to my own anxiety (conforming with the orders of my Government) to be in S. Petersburg without delay, those who have Experiences of the Road assure me that, if I had started sooner I would have been obliged to wait upon the Route for the setting in of the Frost, and that I should therefore have gained nothing. —

On the other hand, certainly, I could have no apology for protracting my Stay in Naples beyond the Time to which I have limited it. — My instructions, which are precisely what they ought to be, would not justify it. — By remaining here a few weeks more I should postpone for several months perhaps my arrival in S. Petersburg by losing the best Season for quitting Italy. —

Of the manner in which my negotiation has been conducted I have little to say. Avoiding Extremes of every kind I have sought to write & speak with politeness, but at the same time explicitly & firmly. My object has been to let the King & his Ministers understand that the Claim *must* be settled, and to place it upon such ground as to convince them that we are in earnest in considering them as our Debtors. — Without being studiously consiliatory [sic] I have forborne all Menace. They have indeed treated me & my errand with so much Respect that it would have been difficult for me, even if it had been wise and honorable, to endeavor to force the Claim upon them by arrogance and Harshness. —

I might indeed have contrived to display a more active & zealous Importunity than my Letters will be found to describe; but it could only have been that teasing Importunity which, wanting Dignity and unauthorized by usage, has nothing to recommend its Introduction into transactions like this. No proper opportunity has, I think, been missed to urge this government to a favorable Decision.

As to the footing upon which the Claim now stands and the Value of its future prospects, it is obvious that much has been

---

[78] Giorgio Mocenigo. (1762-1839). Count. Born in Zante. From 1790 to 1827 he was in the diplomatic service of Russia.

145

gained. — It has been presented (whether well or ill I dare not judge). It has been received in a becoming manner and entertained for Deliberation and Enquiry. The Way to ajustment [sic] has been prepared & smoothed. The great Principle on which the demand was rested by the Government of the United States is impliedly conceded, and at any rate has been greatly strengthened, by the forbearance of this Government, not only *in Linine* but even to the last moment of my mission, to deny it, with opportunity and every inducement to do so constantly presented to it. — It was to have been expected, and *was* expected, that the Court of Naples would resist at the Threshold a demand which, directly as well as implicitly asserted its responsibility for the violences and frauds of Murat. — It was its true Policy to repel such a demand at once (without reference to Details) if it meant to contest all the responsibility, upon which the Claimant altogether depended, and which formed in Truth the only dubious part of their Case. It was prepared to take that Course (as I was *well assured*) upon my first arrival. Yet it has not ventured to take it. — On the contrary, it has avowedly busied itself, since the presentation of my Note of the 24ᵗʰ. of August, in Efforts (which cannot be successful) to lay a foundation of *fact* for Distinctions that may give it a chance of escaping from our principle, which finally it declines to question. —

The Reasons suggested by this Government for a short postponement of its Decision are such as I suppose I could not have quarrelled with, without putting myself in the wrong. — They are perfectly respectful to the United States and of real weight in themselves. — Their Effect is to leave negotiation open, to give Encouragement to resume it, and, at the same time that they impart new Solidity to our Claim to render as acquiescence on our part in a brief ajournment [sic] of it, not only consistent with our Honour, but a Duty. In the meantime the two Governments are not brought to a disagreeable Issue as (if the Claim had been rejected without ceremony, or even with all the ostentation of civility) they might have been.

There is another light in which the matter may be considered. This government is the most corrupt in the world. An agent employed by the American claimants would now with reference to that consideration, have ground to stand upon. The claim has many a lodgement and has become respectable, and manageable and is in a state to receive that sort of aid.[79]

---

[79] In the original the entire paragraph beginning with "There is another light . . ." is also given in code which was so transmitted by Mr. Pinkney.

146

With all this to be sure the Government of the United States or its Minister has and can have nothing to do; but the claimants may be inclined to lay some stress upon it, and they are at liberty to manage their own affairs as they may; taking Care only not to connect their Government. —

In not consenting to receive the answer of this Government after my Departure from Naples I was a good deal influenced by the apprehension that they might possibly give me such an Answer when absent as they would not give me if present. — I desired, moreover, to insure to my Government a just control over the subject, and to the Claimants a clear stage for their own private Exertions. I thought that a more convenient resting point could scarcely be had, and that it would be better that I should afford time to advise upon the Case to those who had more Right than I had to dispose of it in future than that adhering to my Mission after I had separated myself from those to whom I was accredited, I should risk the Loss of everything by the Exercise of a very doubtful Authority under all sorts of Disadvantages. —

I have not Time to add to this Letter some miscellaneous Remarks & Information which occur to me, and a part of which would require to be in Cypher. From Florence perhaps I shall be able to write again by such an opportunity as may enable me to dispense with the Caution that it is necessary to observe. —

I ought to add however, that upon the Commercial Subject I did not renew my conversation with the Marquis di Circello, because it was evidently not worth while — of that more hereafter.

I have the Honour to be with sincere Respect and consideration your faithful & obedient servant

WM. PINKNEY TO THE MARQUIS DI CIRCELLO

Naples. 6 October 1816.

Sir:

The Undersigned, Envoy Extraordinary of the United States of America, had the Honour, in the course of the afternoon of yesterday, to receive the note of His Excellency the Marquis di Circello, Secretary of State and Minister for foreign affairs of His Majesty the King of the two Sicilies, bearing Date the 4th. Instant and enclosing several Documents, relative to a misunderstanding said to have taken place, between some of the officers of the American Squadron and certain Englishmen, at Messina.

147

The Undersigned laments sincerely that any such Incident should have disturbed the Quiet of Messina or given uneasiness to His Majesty's Government; but the Marquis di Circello will readily perceive that it is beyond the Power of the Undersigned to found upon it any other measure, for avoiding its recurrence, than that of referring His Excellency's Communication (which he will not fail to do immediately) to the Government of the United States, whose Respect for the Peace & Jurisdiction of friendly Sovereigns is equal to its Determination to exact the Respect which is due to itself.

The Undersigned has no other Knowledge of the Transaction in question than he has been able to derive from the Evidence (certainly incomplete and altogether unsatisfactory) which the Marquis di Circello does him the Honour to transmit to him when he is on the point of departing from Naples; and of course it would not become the Undersigned to enter at this time into any particular Discussion of their merits. — Yet he must be permitted to remark that the statements annexed to the note of the Marquis di Circello place in a very strong Light the moderation of Commodore Chauncey, if they represent (as the Undersigned believes them to do) that he was disposed to be satisfied with less than the punishment of both the persons (the master and mate of a Merchant Schooner) who presumed to beat in a brutal manner and otherwise to abuse, an American Seaman upon a petty charge, of which he may have been innocent, under the very Guns of the Squadron to which he belonged, and so immediately in the Neighbourhood of the Town of Messina that persons from its Shore were in a Situation to encourage this signal Contempt of all order and Decency.

The undersigned cannot refrain from expressing his Surprise at the Impunity which that acknowledged outrage, as disrespectful to the just authority of His Sicilian Majesty as it was insulting to the American Flag, appeared to have enjoyed, and at the extraordinary oblivion into which, as the Cause of all the discord that ensued, it seems to have passed, at the moment too when Expedients are to be devised for preventing such Discord in future, and when the Right of the Subjects & Citizens of States in friendship with His Majesty, to Security and protection from lawless violence in his Dominions, is so much insisted upon. — The undersigned is sure that it will occur to the Marquis di Circello that this Impunity, which apparently has continued until Punishment has become impracticable, was calculated not to

148

tranquillize but to exasperate the indignant feelings which the outrage itself was so peculiarly fitted both to excite and to justify. —

The Undersigned will take the Liberty to add that the established Reputation of Commodore Chauncey, not only for long tried gallantry and Devotion to his Country but for Soundness of Judgment and exemplary attention to all the Duties of his Station, with which no man is more familiar, would not prepare the undersigned to believe that he could ever be forgetful of what he owed to any Sovereign, in amity with his government, who should receive him into his ports with that impartial Hospitality which may be enjoyed without a Sacrifice of personal Honour or National Dignity; the only Hospitality that an American Commodore has ever been known to seek or would consent to accept. —

The Undersigned seizes this occasion to renew to His Excellency the Marquis di Circello the assurance of his distinguished consideration.

WM. PINKNEY TO JAMES MONROE

Naples. 9ᵗʰ. Octʳ. 1816. [Despatch, unnumbered]

Sir:

I believe I have omitted to mention that my letter to Commodore Chauncey (of which I enclosed you a copy in my Dispatch of the 24ᵗʰ. of last month) was sent to Messina, and that (the Squadron having sailed before it arrived there) it has come back to me. — In lieu of it I have enclosed to the Commodore a copy of the Marquis di Circello's communication to me of the 4ᵗʰ Instant, and of my answer of the 6ᵗʰ. I did not think it necessary, and indeed have not had time, to send him copies of the Documents transmitted in the Marquis's communication. —

Everything being now prepared for my Departure, I intend to begin my Journey tomorrow morning.[80] In passing through

---

80 When it became clear that Mr. Pinkney had failed to obtain the indemnity for which he had been sent to Naples, the English, who had evinced much apprehension, felt relieved. *The Niles Register* (XII, 139), a London paper, on Feb. 8, 1817, declared as follows:

"It is not true, and we are most happy it is not true that the Island of Lampedosa has been ceded to the Americans towards whom the government has behaved with great spirit. The former have in fact gained nothing from their mission to Naples. The Americans are certainly a rising people, but it is rather premature, we think, for them to begin the reaction of colonizing Europe."

A Neapolitan newspaper (an official organ) thus praised the achievement of

Rome, Florence, Vienna, & Berlin it will probably be decorous in me to seek to be presented to the Pope,[81] the Grand Duke[82] the Emperor of Austria,[83] and the King of Prussia.[84] I shall carry from hence the most advantageous Letters of Introduction to all these Places.

The Passports which I have found it is Rule to take from here are those of the Marquis di Circello, the Minister of Russia & the Minister of Austria. — They all describe me as the Minister of the United States at the Court of S'. Petersburg. — The little misunderstanding about Kosloff's affair does not appear to be known here, even to the Russian minister.

I have spoken in some of my letters to you of the Gentlemen *attached to my Legation.* — To prevent any misapprehension on that subject I ought perhaps to state that I have attached my son Charles and three other Americans (who accompanied me in the Washington) to my Legation and have permitted them to wear the diplomatic uniform as private secretaries; but neither the Government nor myself has anything to do with their Expences, except so far as *Charles*[85] is a part of my own Family. — These Gentlemen have added much to the Appearance and Respectability of my Mission, and I have had every Reason to be perfectly satisfied with them.

---

the King (*Niles Register,* XI, 307): "Naples, Oct. 18. Mr. Pinkney has taken leave . . . There is every reason to believe that all differences between the United States and our country are terminated. Our honor has received no stain, and it could receive none under a prince who is fully conscious of the dignity of his crown and the rank which his dynasty holds in Europe. Austria has shown upon the occasion that she was ready to support our just pretentions. It is thought that a treaty between our court and the United States has been proposed and that it will be very advantageous to us. Advantages have been guaranteed the Americans in the ports of Sicily."

81 The Pope was Pius VII, Barnaba Luigi Chiaramonti (1742-1823). Benedictine. Bishop of Imola. In 1785 he was made a Cardinal. Elected Pope in 1800.] In exile during the Napoleonic invasions of Italy. He returned to Rome in May 1814.

82 Ferdinand III of Lorraine (1769-1824) was the Grand Duke of Tuscany in 1816. He came to the throne of Tuscany in 1790, succeeding Peter Leopold who had become emperor. Ferdinand III was dethroned in 1801 by Napoleon I, and he retired to Würzburg. In 1814 he was restored as Grand Duke of Tuscany and the following year he returned to Florence. At his death in 1824, his son, Leopold II, succeeded him to the throne.

83 Francis I, Emperor of Austria, 1806-1835.

84 Frederic William III (1770-1840). King of Prussia 1797-1840.

85 Charles Pinkney of Maryland superseded William R. King, of Alabama, as secretary of the Legation in Russia on November 30, 1818. He acted as chargé d'affaires *ad interim* from Feb. 14, to Sept. 22, 1818, and from July 5, to Nov. 9, 1820.

Modena. Nov. 3. 1816. [Despatch unnumbered]
Sir:

I left Naples on the 10th. of last month, and have since got on as fast as I could to this place. — In the Morning I shall resume my Journey to St. Petersburg by the way of Vienna.

At Rome I became acquainted with the Cardinal Gonsalvi[86] [sic] (The Secretary of State and a very able man) who showed me all sorts of Kindness, and through him I had a long and very satisfactory private audience of the Pope at the Castello Gandolfo, in the neighbourhood of Albano, a few miles from Rome.

The Pope is an extremely interesting man from every view, and loses nothing by being approached. — His manner, which is very engaging, has the recommendation of announcing the goodness of his Heart. — As he talked to me in Italian (which I understand imperfectly when it is spoken, although I read it pretty well) and I talked to him altogether in French (which he understands about as well as I do Italian) I derived less Reassurance from his conversation than in itself it was calculated to give. It gave me great Pleasure nevertheless. —

No Person was permitted to be present at this Audience. — The "Monsignor" who conducted me into the Pope's Closet retired immediately, closing the Door, and passing through the anteroom (the door of which also he shut) into a large Hall where the Pope's attendants were in waiting and the Gentlemen who accompanied me remarked on my way to the Closet I was desired to leave my hat upon a Chair in the anteroom. As soon as I was introduced the Pope offered me his hand, which according to established usage I kissed. — Our conversation turned principally upon the political & moral State of the World upon the climate &c of Italy, and upon Rome antient and modern. — He spoke pleasingly and well upon all these Subjects, mixing up now and then a little French, for my benefit, with Italian. — When talking of our Country he did not omit to make me perceive that he was acquainted with its worth and that he held it in the highest respect. — We were seated during the whole of our Conversation. — When I was about to retire

---

[86] Ercole Consalvi, (1757-1824). He was a shrewd and energetic Cardinal Secretary of State (1800-23). In 1801 he concluded a Concordat with France. In 1816 he caused the approval and publication of "motu proprio organico" signalizing the triumph of ideas of tolerance. He was dismissed by Leo XII.

151

he invited me to stay to Dinner, and upon my excusing myself
he took me by the hand (after having first offered me his to
kiss as upon my Entrance) and conducted me out of the Closet
to the Door of the Antechamber which he opened. — The gentlemen who accompanied me were then introduced to him, in the
antechamber (as is customary) after which we left him. The
Monsignors (I think they are so called) of his Court were extremely civil, and urged me very strongly to dine at the Castello:
but as I knew that the Pope would not be at the table (he always
dines alone) I declined the Invitation, and returned to Rome.

I left Rome as soon as was in my power, (having however
first taken a rapid view, under the auspices of the Cardinal Secretary of State, of every thing in it which is worth seeing) and
arrived at Florence on the 25ᵗʰ. of last month. — One of my
carriages had suffered in our Journey from Rome, and was
found to require Alteration as well as Repair. This detained
me at Florence until the 31ˢᵗ when I set out for Bologna where
I stayed only a single night. —

I have a letter from Mʳ. King (dated at Vienna October
16ᵗʰ.) in which he tells me that the Passport of the Russian
Government and a letter from Mʳ. Harris, containing nothing
new, wait for me at Vienna. — Mʳ. King went on to St. Petersburg. — It appears from the newspapers that an American Corvette passed the 23ᵈ. of September with a messenger for St.
Petersburg. — I take for granted that this is connected with
Kosloffs [sic] affair, and of course that there is an End of all
Difficulty on that subject. — I shall consequently pass on to my
destination as rapidly as Roads, weather &c. permit. A few
weeks will I trust find me there. —

P. S. I hope you will receive in due season my last letters
from Naples intrusted to the care of our Consul there. — It is
impossible to make copies of them on the Road.

WM. PINKNEY TO JOHN QUINCY ADAMS[87]

St. Petersburg 27ᵗʰ. Febʸ. 1817. [Despatch unnumbered]

Notwithstanding the explicitness of my answer of the 30ᵗʰ.
of September of the last year to the proposal contained in the

---

[87] John Quincy Adams of Massachusetts. (1767-1848). In 1809 he was Minister
at St. Petersburg; he was Minister to the Court of St. James after the War of
1812; Secretary of State under Monroe 1817-1825; and President of the United
States, 1825-1829.

note of the Marquis di Circello of the 27th. of the same month, I had scarcely quitted Naples when he sent after me his reply to my note of the 24th. of August. — The obstacle which, while I was present, threatened to retard that reply for many a week and even for months, disappeared with a marvellous rapidity, after I had departed; for the reply passed me on the road to St. Petersburgh and arrived there before me. —

The Neapolitan Minister at this Court (to whom it was forwarded by the Marquis di Circello for the purpose of being delivered to me) manifested immediately upon my arrival here a very anxious desire that I should receive it. — He even *entreated* me to do so with such earnestness that it was not easy to resist. — I refused, however, to have anything to do with his packet, and assigned as my reasons, that I had ceased to have any right to meddle with the subject of my late mission to his Government, that the Marquis di Circello was distinctly told by me, when I found that I must leave Naples without an answer to my note, that I would not continue to correspond with him upon the Claim which it proferred, unless I should be instructed to do so by my Government, and that he could not but know, without the help of any body's information, that it was impossible that I should so soon be in possession of such instructions, even if the President approved of that course (as it was probable he would not for the conclusion of my Negotiation). — The Duke proposed finally to write me a Letter importing that he had the reply to my Note that he wished me to take it. — I assented to this, and the short Correspondence of which a Copy is enclosed[88] was the Consequence. —

If I had been perfectly sure that the reply was a favorable one and required no *further discussion* (which, indeed, I did not understand it to be the intention of the Sicilian Government to indulge me in) I would have received it. — The Celerity with which it had followed me, however, suggests the opposite presumption, and the Duke's desultory conversations with me as often as I met him (in which he talked as the Marquis di Circello was wont to do of the Poverty of his Master &c) did not weaken that presumption. Certain newspapers, too, professing to speak from authority, had affected to *quote* the Reply, as a refusal which had already been given to me. — You will find a Republication of one of these articles in the enclosures *"Con-*

---

[88] The four letters here referred to as enclosed will be found on pp. 155-158.

servateur Impartial," and will be satisfied that the Sicilian Government, or its Minister at Vienna or St. Petersburgh, has dictated the latter part of it. —

Upon the whole, having lost my power to deal with the Reply as its Contents might require, and fearing that it was not what it ought to be, I thought it my duty to insist upon the Impropriety of sending it at this moment to me (an Impropriety for which the Marquis di Circello could have no Motive that I ought to sanction) and upon that ground to decline to take it. — The Duke has shown uneasiness at this court; and I am not sorry for it. — His Government is a good deal disturbed by our Claim; and we hazard nothing (and may gain) by practising upon its anxiety within certain bounds, or even to any extent we think fit.

P. S.[89] 14th. May 1817 — Not having had any opportunity of forwarding this letter I have broken it open to say in a Postscript that I am this moment informed for the first time that Mr. Gallatin has long since (about the time of my arrival here) received the answer of the Marquis di Circello to my Note of the 24th. of August and has transmitted it to you.[90] My Informant thinks that the answer bears date the 13th. of October,[91] three days only after my departure from Naples. — It results, that the Sicilian Government, notwithstanding its declarations to the contrary, was prepared, or knew that it would be prepared, to give me the answer within the Time I had indicated.

The course which the Marquis di Circello has pursued of sending the answer to M[r]. Gallatin (who, as he had nothing to do with my negotiation, it was natural to fear would refer him to me) has a little surprized me; and at any rate I should have been glad to know the fact from M[r]. Gallatin at the earliest possible moment, for the regulation of my Conduct.

---

[89] This postscript is omitted from the printed version of the Message of President Monroe, as found in House Document No. 130. (See also note 20, p. 109).

[90] In reporting the matter to his government, Gallatin conjectured: "It may be presumed that the Neapolitan government delayed that note in order to prevent the possibility of a reply; their intention in communicating it to me was to hasten its transmission to you." Mr. Gallatin sent the Note to Secretary Monroe, Nov. 19, 1816 (See Despatches, France, XVII, by date; also Perrotta, *op. cit.,* 39-40.) This despatch of Mr. Gallatin was not published in the President's Message, dated Feb. 28, 1818. See House Document No. 130; and note 20, p. 109.

[91] The date on the reply was October 15th, not 13th, as here stated in the despatch. (See, below, p. 158.)

THE DUKE OF SERRA CAPRIOLA TO WM. PINKNEY

[Enclosure (1) with Mr. Pinkney's despatch of Feb. 27, 1817]

St. Petersbourg, ce 9/21 fevrier 1817

Monsieur —

J'ai reçu hier la lettre par laquelle votre Excellence a bien volu, repondre à celle que je lui ai addressée le 7/19 du courant; j'y ai vu les raisons par lesquelles Elle ne se croit plus autorisée a reçevoir la note responsive qui m'a été envoyée par le Ministre de Sa Majesté le Roi Mon Maître.

Votre Excellence comprendra facilement combien il aura été desagréable et pénible au Roi de n'avoir pas pu durant votre Mission à Naples faire donner une reponse a Votre Note du 24 Aout de l'année passée; mais cette Reponse, comme vous le savez vous même Monsieur, devoit être appuyée de pieces et de preuves qu'il etait assez difficile de se procurer, vu que l'evénement discuté avoit eu lieu, sous un Gouvernement étranger au présent. — Si ce retard a été pénible au Roi et à son Ministére combien ne le serait il pas encore plus, s'ils voyient la réponse arrêtée de nouveau. Je me fais donc un devoir, Monsieur, de vous engager à recevoir le paquet dont je suis chargé, au moins pour le transmettre a Votre Gouvernement. Vous satisferiez par là le desir de ma Cour, et feriez connoître au President des Etats Unis des raisonnemens fondés qui pourraient accellerer la fin de cette affaire. —

Profittant de l'offre que vous m'avez faite, Monsieur, je vous prie de vouloir bien me donner une Copie de la lettre du Marquis di Circello et de votre reponse du 30 Septembre; — Je vous en serai infinement obligé, Monsieur, et, en vous en remerciant d'avance, je saisis cette occasion pour vous réitérer les assurances de la Consideration très distinguée avec laquelle j'ai l'honneur d'etre

Monsieur,

De Votre Excellence le trés humble y
tré oblig. Serviteur[92]

WM. PINKNEY TO THE DUKE OF SERRA CAPRIOLA

[Enclosure (2) with Mr. Pinkney's despatch of Feb. 27, 1817]

St. Peterburgh, 21 Feb.y 1817 (N.S.) (Copy)

Sir.

It would really give me sincere pleasure to be able to conform to the Wish which Your Excellency presses upon me with so

---

[92] No translation appears to have been filed with this Note.

much earnestness; but I feel insurmountable Repugnance, arising out of what I believe to be a correct sense of my Duty, to giving any Sanction to the making of a Communication to me as if I were still the accredited Envoy of the United States at Naples. — I can have no Difficulty, however, in consenting to forward to the Secretary of State of the United States any thing which by order of your Court you may think fit to address to him.

What may be the Nature of the Packet which has followed me from Naples I do not know, and do not desire to know, further than that it is in answer to a Note written by me in an official character which I no longer possess. — I have the utmost Confidence indeed, that it proposes a fair Indemnity to our plundered Merchants, not only with reference to that part of the Spoil which (not having been sold by Murat) has passed into the hands of His Majesty the King of the two Sicilies and is now in his possession but with reference also to that larger portion of it which was converted into money. — But let it propose what it may it is not to me that it should address itself, at least until my Government is known to have given me such Instructions (which it has not yet had Time to give even if it be disposed to adopt that Course) as may justify me in receiving it and in acting upon it as its contents may require.

The Copies which you desire[93] are herewith enclosed. — They will satisfy you that the Marquis di Circello ought to anticipate the answer, which I now repeat, to your application.

I have the Honour to be, with the most distinguished Consideration, Your Excellency's Most Obedient Humble Servant

THE DUKE OF SERRA CAPRIOLA[94] TO WM. PINKNEY

[Enclosure (3) with Mr. Pinkney's despatch of Feb. 27, 1817]

St. Petersbourg le 19/7 Fevrier 1817[95] (Copy)

Monsieur,

J'ai reçu de ma Cour un paquet contenant une Note responsive á celle que Votre Excellence a adressée à Monsieur le Marquis

---

93 See reference to these in letter 9/21 Feb. 1817, of the Duke of Serracapriola (p. 155.) These copies are not repeated in this printing as they were in the original.

94 Antonio Maresca. Duke of Serracapriola. (1750-1822). Diplomat and statesman. He was minister plenipotentiary at St. Petersburg from 1783 to 1822. See "Il Duca di Serracapriola e Giuseppe De Maistre" in *Archivio storico per le provincie napolitane*, XLVII (1922) 313 ff, and in *Uomini e cose della vecchia Italia,*. Bari, 1927, II, 193 ff. (*Dizionario del Risorgimento Nazionale*, Milan, 1937, IV, 270).

95 English translation of this letter was printed in House Document No. 130.

di Circello en date du 24. Aôut de l'année passée, et qui n'a pas pue vous être donnée avant votre départ, a cause des Renseigne-mens et notices qui devaient être pris sur l'affaire dont vous avez été chargé par votre Gouvernement. —

J'ai l'honneur de Vous en informer Monsieur pour savoir si vous voulez la recevoir et prendre vos dispositions a cet egard. —

Agreéz en attendant les assurances de la consideration trés distinguée, avec laquelle j'ai l'honneur d'être.

Monsieur

de Votre Excellence

le tres humble et tres Obess^t. Serviteur

(Signed) Le Duc de Serra Capriola

A Son Excellence
Monsieur Pinkney
&c &c &c

WM. PINKNEY TO THE DUKE OF SERRA CAPRIOLA

[Enclosure (4) with Mr. Pinkney's despatch of Feb. 27, 1817]

St. Petersburgh, 20 Feby. 1817. (Copy)

Sir.

It would have been particularly agreeable to me to obtain, dur-ing the continuance of my functions as the Envoy Extraordinary of the United States at Naples, while I might regularly have taken and acted upon it, an answer to the note which in that character I addressed to the Marquis di Circello on the 24th of August of the last year; and I certainly spared no efforts for that purpose. — I found it impracticable, however, after the Importunity of many weeks, to obtain either an answer or the Designation of any precise Time within which I might be authorized to expect one; and, as my ulterior Duties here would not suffer me to wait at Naples for the issue of Enquiries & Deliberations of which avowedly the Term could not be fore-seen even by those who were engaged in them, I was compelled to leave unsettled the subject of my Note and to put an end to my Mission. — My Power to correspond with the Government of the King of the two Sicilies upon that Subject, or otherwise to assume an agency in it, has consequently ceased, and can only be revived by the President of the United States, from whom I derived it originally and to whom I have rendered an account of the Use which I was able to make of it. Whether it will be his Pleasure to renew it in any Degree, or in what other way he will think it proper to deal with the Subject, I have no means of knowing. — I know only that he has yet given me no orders upon it, and that there has not been Time for such orders. —

The Marquis di Circello must be prepared for this answer to your Excellency's letter to me of the 19th Instant, if he does me the honour to preserve any recollection of my Note to him of the 30th of September last, of which (as well as of his Note to me of the 27th of the same month) I shall be very willing to give you a Copy if you desire it.

THE MARQUIS DI CIRCELLO TO WM. PINKNEY

Naples [October 15, 1816] (Copy)

Altho' the Government of His Majesty, the King of the two Sicilies, was, from the first moment, in a situation to judge of the validity of the remonstrances and demands made by His Excellency, Mr. Pinkney, Envoy Extraordinary of the United States of America, in his note of the 24th August last, nevertheless, wishing to examine and discuss them under all their aspects of right and of fact, it has waited accordingly, until all the materials and lights were collected, proper to this end.

The many difficulties attending the search after those materials, owing to the change in the order of things, during which the facts occurred that have given rise to the demand of Mr. Pinkney, rendered it impossible for the Royal Government to reply to the note of his Excellency, before his departure from Naples.

Now, that the papers, and appropriate enquiries have shed the strongest light upon the affair in question, the Undersigned, Counsellor and Secretary of State, Minister of foreign affairs of his M. the King of the Two Sicilies, hastens to give, by order of his Sovereign, the following reply to Mr. Pinkney, requesting his Excellency be pleased to communicate it to his government.

All the arguments contained in the note of the 24th August look to the end of making his Majesty's Government responsible for the consequences of the Confiscation & Sale, whether just or unjust, of several American vessels & cargoes, which took place in Naples, while the Kingdom was held by Murat.

In support of this pretention, it is assumed, that the abuse of power and violation of good faith by which these arbitrary acts were committed, are of such a nature as to survive the political authority of the author of them, and that of course, as there accrued a right of reclamation against the Government of Murat, there exists one, also, against the present Government of the Two Sicilies.

His Excellency adds, that altho' the American Claimants have not the means of ascertaining to what uses the produce of the above mentioned sales was applied, yet, they may presume that it was expended in works and objects of public utility, or left in the public coffers, and therefore affirms that, under this point of view, likewise, his Majesty's government is bound to indemnify the victims of the Spoliations committed during the ascendancy of Murat.

Without undertaking to enquire whether a sort of succession or inheritance in legitimate and illegitimate governments, can be maintained upon good grounds, the undersigned will be content to remark, that whatever may be the opinion of publicists as to this point, no one has ever pretended to visit[96] the injustices of the contracts or deeds of usurpers upon the people subjected to their yoke, or upon the legitimate Sovereigns.

That theory would, indeed, be a disconsolate one which should extend the power of an enemy, not only to the consequences of fact, but even to those of right. The victory which restored the legitimate prince would be fatal to both, if it must have the effect of making him responsible for the acts of injustice and violence which the usurper might have perpetrated against foreign nations .

It avails not to say that these are of the description of obligations and engagements which survive the overthrow of the usurped dominion, as common to the nation over which that dominion was exercised.

This would be the place to determine whether we could reasonably qualify as an obligation, an engagement from government to government, nation to nation a mere right of reclamation, which according to the allegation of M. Pinkney himself, the United States kept in reserve to be exercised with Murat, had not his power been subverted.

---

96 "to visit" is used in the sense of "to reflect upon." The Italian original reads: "non si è mai preteso da alcuni di *fare rifluire* l'ingiustizia dei contratti o delle operazioni degli usurpatori su i popoli da essi sottomessi, o su i sovrani legittimi."

But the undersigned will simply ask his Excellency, if that very right is not to be regarded as null, seeing that the continual, strong, vehement demands officially made by the Consul General of the United States at Naples, upon the Ministers of Murat, for the restitution of the confiscated vessels and cargoes for compensation to the American owners, were rejected, or remained without a reply.

However this may be, it is always incontestable, that it is not against the actual governments of his Majesty, that a right to which he who created it, would not hearken, can be tried as it were in the nature of an appeal.

It is among the principles of reason and justice, that a Sovereign who never ceased to be in a state of war with the usurper of his dominions, and who, very far from having afforded grounds for presuming that his rights were waived, — as is asserted in the note of the 24th August, carried into effect, in concert with his ally, England, a powerful expedition in the Islands of Procida & Ischia nearest to the capital of his usurped kingdom, in the year 1809, precisely that in which the confiscation of the American ships at Naples took place, — it is among the principles of reason and justice that he should not be, on regaining his dominions in process of the war which had compelled him to absent himself from them, held responsible for the excesses of his enemy.

Let then the relations of the usurper with the Powers friendly or allied to France have been what they may, the inferences which the American Merchants may have drawn from them, in relation to the prosecution of their trade at Naples, should not be made to recoil upon the treasury of a Sovereign who, not only, did not shew any the least acquiescence in the usurpation, but did all that was in his power, and all that circumstances would permit to vindicate his abused rights.

There is still less foundation for the arguments brought forward in the note of the 24th August to prove that the Neapolitan Nation was, in some sort, a party to the measures by which the Americans suffered, & therefore liable, *in Solideum*,[97] for the consequences.

---

[97] "in solideum" etc. means "united in effort . . ." The Italian original reads: "Ancor meno fondate sono le ragioni che si adducono nella nota dei 24 Agosto per dimostrare, che la nazione napolitana sia stata in certo modo solidaria nelle misure prese a danni degli Americani, e che perciò sia rimasta responsabile delle conseguenze di tali misure."

If the inhabitants of the Kingdom of Naples could only have signified their wishes, there would undoubtedly have been for the maintenance of relations of justice and friendship with the Americans, the only nation which, by means of its neutrality, might provide a vent for the commodities accumulated thro' so many years in the Kingdom under the operation of the noted continental system of ruinous memory.

But everybody knows that the Neapolitan nation prostrated by a foreign dominion, is but the mournful spectator & first victim of the arbitrary acts which were daily committed. So far then, from being able to indemnify others, it would be exceedingly fortunate, if she could find means of compensating herself for the losses and immense injuries which she sustained during the occupation of the Kingdom.

These considerations would be more than sufficient to prove that the claims of the American Merchants cannot reach either the actual government of his Majesty, or his people.

But, to make the Demonstration complete, and to exhibit the question under all its aspects, the undersigned will admit for a moment, this absurd hypothesis, that the present Government of Naples stands in the place of that of Murat, & has succeeded to all his obligations.

The demand of Mr. Pinkney would not be, on this account, the less unsustainable, since the confiscation and sale of the American vessels & cargoes were acts which proceeded directly from the power & from the will of Bonaparte. There exists, in fact, in the archives of the Treasury, a Report of the Minister Agar[98] who presided over that Department in 1809, addressed to Murat who was then at Paris.

The Minister relates in this report, that two American ships had arrived at Naples, one from Salem, the other last from Algiers, laden with colonial produce, and that the necessary orders had been given to put the same under sequestration, conformably to the directions antecedently issued from higher authority with respect to the other vessels arrived at Naples before the departure of Murat for Paris.

He proceeds then to point out the great benefit which the Treasury would derive from opening the market to the colonial produce lying on board those ships, or in the custom-house of

---

[98] Jean Antoine Michel Agar, Count de Mosburg. (1771-1844). In 1800-01 he was Commissioner to the provisional government of Tuscany; later, he was minister of finance of Murat (1806-08) in the Grand Duchy of Berg, and from 1809 to 1815 in the Kingdom of Naples.

Naples, by the duties which would be collected upon the sale of it, and upon the export of the oils which the Americans would take as return-cargoes.

The Minister remarks, in fine, that the confiscation itself of the American vessels & cargoes was but a inconsiderable resource compared with the very great advantages which would have resulted to the Treasury, from an active American trade, could it have been tolerated in the ports of the Kingdom.

Murat did not deem himself authorized to decide in any way, and submitted the report to his brother-in-law Napoleon, who decreed in margin, that the vessels & cargoes in question should be confiscated, because the embargo laid in the ports of the United States induced him to believe, that the produce must be British property & its introduction into the Continent a breach, therefore, of his too famous Berlin & Milan Decrees.[99]

On the disclosure of this decision of Bonaparte in Naples, it was ordered, also that the proceeds of the sales should not be paid over to the Treasury of the State, but that a separate and special amount should be opened for them, which was done accordingly.

In order to understand well this distinction, and to be able to draw from it the consequences applicable to the case, it is useful to note that, during the military occupation of the Kingdom, there existed a Treasury, so called, destined to receive the public revenues & defray the public charges and as, among the latter, the support of the luxurious household of Murat was not the least onerous, accordingly, the sums allotted to this purpose were paid into the hands of a particular Treasurer, who disposed of this as his master directed.

Besides this particular chest into which, moreover, all the proceeds of the private domain were emptied, Murat established another by the name of separate account or fund, (*conto a parte*) as a receptacle for the sums arising from the sale of the vessels and cargoes confiscated in 1809 & 1812; and also for the profits of the Licenses which, in imitation of England & France he sold to the vessels entering & leaving the ports of the Kingdom.

---

[99] By the Berlin Decree (Nov. 21, 1806) Napoleon prohibited all intercourse with Great Britain and authorized the seizure of Englishmen and English property wherever found. According to the provisions of the Milan Decree (Dec. 17, 1807) any ship that touched at any English port or yielded to England's demands, lost the protection of her neutral flag, and could be seized as a prize. It also declared a blockade against all British possessions.

The new fund was always considered as appertaining to the extraordinary & private domain of Murat himself. An irrefragable proof of this may be offered. — The 1ˢᵗ article of one of his decrees of 25 April 1812, is conceived in the following terms. "The commission established by our decree of 30 Nov. 1811, for the purpose of liquidating the accounts of our Royal household, is, in addition, charged with examining the accounts of the vessels sequestered in our ports, regarded by us as the property of our extraordinary and private domain."

Besides, it is enough to read the account rendered, of the cashier of *the separate fund,* to know that the sums paid into it were dissipated in large fees to the favourites of Murat, in marriage-portions to some of his relatives, and in other licentious expences of Murat and of his wife, especially during their visit to Paris. It appears, moreover, that Murat having anticipated on said fund a sum of two hundred thousand livres on account of the Treasury, towards cost of the expedition with which, during several months, he menaced Sicily with an invasion from Calabria, the Minister of the finances lost no time in reimbursing the fund with proceeds of the public taxes.

From the foregoing statement, two important & obvious consequences are to be drawn.

The first is, that Murat only lent his name in the confiscation of the American Ships; as he did merely, in all the other measures pursued in Naples, during the occupation of the Kingdom. This was no mystery, nor could foreign nations be ignorant of it. Still less could they be unacquainted with the extent of the power which Bonaparte usurped in order to give all possible latitude of effect to his decrees of Milan and Berlin, in the countries over which he exerted his fatal influence.

Obstinate in his fantasies, absolute in his will, he studied only to enlarge the sphere of his favourite plan. A mere remonstrance on this head, if Murat had allowed himself to prefer one, would have cost the latter his crown. Holland furnished an incontestible example of this truth.

Murat, then, — let it be repeated — was but the passive instrument of the will of Bonaparte in the confiscation of the American ships and if this could give birth to responsibility, such responsibility should no longer be imputed to the country over which he reigned, and still less to the Government which has there resumed its lawful authority.

The other, and not less important consequence is, that the

163

Treasury which was the fund of the State, never enjoyed the proceeds of the confiscations, and that, instead of being employed to alleviate the burdens of the people, or applied to the improvement and embellishment of the country, as is supposed in the note of the 24th August, those proceeds only served to feed the caprices and the oriental pomp of the family of Murat and his adherents.

After this rapid & faithful exposition of facts, the undersigned will not enter upon the enquiry whether the American merchants would have been entitled to call for indemnity, if the power which commanded and executed the confiscation of their property had, unfortunately, continued to flourish.

He will go no further than to remark to M. Pinkney, that such a call could not affect the actual government of his Majesty, nor his people; and his Excellency & his government are too enlightened and too impartial not to be fully convinced of this, now that they can dwell upon circumstances which, perhaps, were not previously within their knowledge.[100]

The undersigned renews to Mr. Pinkney, on this occasion, the assurances of his most distinguished consideration.

---

[100] This assumption of the Neapolitan government, declaring itself in no way responsible for the depredations went far beyond the attitude of any other European state which admitted some complicity. Perrotta, *op. cit.*, 42, see also Theodore Lyman, *The Diplomacy of the United States* (Boston, 1826), 220-221. Not satisfied with the results of Pinkney's mission, on Jan. 30, 1818, Samuel Smith, of Maryland, introduced a resolution requesting the President of the United States to transmit to the House of Representatives "such information concerning the claims of the United States against Naples that might be communicated without injury to the public." *Annals of Congress,* 15th Congress, 1st Session, 832. Although President Monroe complied on Feb. 28, 1818, nothing further was done. The repeated protests of the merchants were of no immediate effect.

JOHN J. APPLETON
(April 12, 1825 to August 30, 1826)

H. CLAY[1] TO J. J. APPLETON

Department of State, Washington, 12. April 1825[2]

[Instruction, unnumbered]

J. J. Appleton Esquire[3]
Cambridge, Massachusetts.

Sir,

Since you left this place, it has occurred to the President that your services may be more useful to the public as Commercial Agent at Naples, than as Secretary to the British Legation, and he accordingly wishes you to accept that appointment.[4] The Agency will be temporary, but may end in a public Commission. The object of it will be to sound the Government of Naples as to the practicability of getting indemnity for our Citizens for their numerous and large claims upon that Government. It is the same as that on which Mr. Pinckney [sic] was once sent. Your compensation will be at the rate of $4,500 per annum. It will be some weeks before your Instructions can be prepared, and you may await their reception at Cambridge, or come here to receive them, as may be most agreeable. Your compensation will be considered as commencing from this day, if you accept the appointment.

---

1 Henry Clay, of Kentucky, was commissioned Secretary of State by President John Quincy Adams, March 7, 1825. Clay resigned March 3, 1829.

2 This communication and all other Instructions in this chapter (from the Secretary of State to Mr. Appleton) are found in bound volume of original records of the State Department. *Instructions to United States Ministers*, X (July 15, 1823-Dec. 30, 1825).

3 John J. Appleton (1789-1864). Although born in France, he was considered as a native of Massachusetts. He graduated from Harvard in 1813. He acted as chargé d'affaires *ad interim.* in the Netherlands from October 20, 1817 to April 18, 1818, and from May 5, 1818 to January 4, 1819. He was commissioned secretary of the Legation in Portugal, March 3, 1819; he acted as chargé d'affaires *ad interim* in June 1821. He was commissioned secretary of Legation in Spain, May, 1822; he acted as chargé d'affaires *ad interim* from March 2 to December 4, 1823. He left November 23, 1824. He was commissioned chargé d'affaires in Sweden May 2, 1826. He left there August 20, 1830. He acted as chargé d'affaires *ad interim* from September 20, 1833 to January 9, 1834.

4 In his *Memoirs* (Phila. 1877), vol. VI, John Quincy Adams refers at length to Mr. Appleton's appointment. Adams was President-elect at the time and was still Secretary of State.

165

J. J. APPLETON TO H. CLAY

Cambridge April 22ᵈ 1825[5].

Sir,

I had the honor of receiving, yesterday, your letter of the 12ᵗʰ Instant, informing me that it had occurred to the President since I left Washington that my services might be more useful to the Public as Commercial Agent at Naples than as Secretary of Legation to London, and that he wished me accordingly to accept that appointment.

Influenced by a sincere desire to be employed wherever my services may be most useful to my Country, I accept with pleasure the new appointment which the President is thus pleased to confer upon me, and shall derive great satisfaction if, by my best exertions in it, I can prepare the way for a settlement of the claims of our injured countrymen, and deserve the continuance of the confidence of the government.

Your letter being marked "Confidential" I shall not consider myself at liberty to disclose its purport until I know the further wishes of the Government.

As you have been pleased to leave it to my option, either to wait here for my instructions or to go to Washington to receive them, I have after reflecting seriously on the delicacy of the trust to be committed to me, thought that I might be better prepared for discharging it to the satisfaction of the government by an interview with you, and shall accordingly hold myself in readiness to proceed to the Seat of Government when I receive your directions to that effect.

H. CLAY TO J. J. APPLETON

Department of State Washington 12. May 1825
[Instruction, unnumbered]

Sir.

Some citizens of the United States have large claims upon the Government of Naples, founded upon the seizure and condemnation of their vessels and cargoes during the reign of Murat, in 1809. Mr. Pinckney [sic] was sent in 1816, on a temporary Mission to Naples, as Envoy Extraordinary and Minister Pleni-

---

[5] This despatch, and all other despatches and enclosures in this chapter (those from and to Mr. Appleton) will be found in the United States National Archives, Washington, D. C. in State Department General Records, Group 59. See, *Diplomatic Despatches*, Naples-Sweden, Feb. 8, 1825-Aug. 15, 1830, V.

potentiary of the United States, for the purpose of requiring indemnity and satisfaction for those claims. His mission was not attended with the success which the evident justice of the object of it, authorized us to anticipate. There have been received at this Department some communications from Mr. Hammett, the American Consul at Naples, importing that he had reason to believe a better disposition to render justice to the claimants, prevailed in the Government of Naples.[6] Whatever that may happen to be, it is the determination of this Government not to abandon those claims, but to continue to assert them until satisfaction is made for them. Their great amount, the long delay which has intervened since the wrongs were perpetrated, and the information derived from Mr. Hammett, justify the renewal of endeavours to obtain the indemnity which is justly due. But the President does not think it proper, at present, to send a Representative of this Government, cloathed with a formal commission. He has considered it better adapted to the circumstances of the case to appoint you a commercial Agent. I transmit, however, an informal Letter[7] of introduction to the Minister of Foreign Affairs of Naples, which you are authorised to present. The object of your Agency will be to ascertain, by such means as may appear to you best calculated to elicit, the present temper and disposition of that Government in respect to those claims. You will enquire of Mr. Hammett, on what ground he has formed the opinion that a better prospect existed for obtaining justice from Naples, and avail yourself of whatever information and assistance you can derive from him. You will let it be known to the Government of Naples that the United States still hold it responsible for the injuries inflicted upon their citizens, at the period, and in the manner, before mentioned, that this responsibility, far from weakening, acquires, in the view of the President, augmented strength, by the lapse of time, and that it never will be considered as cancelled, until full indemnity is made.

If you should conclude, from all the circumstances which you may be able, on the spot, to observe and weigh, that there is a reasonable hope of obtaining an acknowledgement of the obligation of Naples to pay the claims, and a provision for their pay-

---

[6] Ferdinand died of apoplexy on January 4, 1825. His son, Francis I, succeeded him. This fact together with the inauguration of a New Englander as President of the United States, two months later, again opened the question of indemnities. (See also Perrotta, *op. cit.*, 45).

[7] For the text of this letter of introduction, see below, p. 169.

ment, at even a distant day, a Commission will be sent you as Chargé d'Affaires, to agree upon a Convention for that object. If, on the contrary, no favourable prospect exist, you will return to the United States. The duration of your abode at Naples, is necessarily left to your discretion, to be regulated by all the facts that may present themselves. I herewith transmit you a copy of the instructions formerly given to Mr. Pinckney [sic], and the correspondence which passed between him and the Government of Naples; all of which are to be found in the 11th volume of Wait's *State Papers,* from page 486 to the end of the volume.[8] I also place under your care, to be used if necessary, the papers and documents in support of the respective claims.[9]

---

[8] *State papers and publick documents of the United States from the accession of George Washington to the presidency, exhibiting a complete view of our foreign relations since that time* . . . 3d. ed. Pub. under patronage of Congress. Including confidential documents, now first published. Boston, T. B. Wait and sons, 1819. 12 vols. Today Wait's series is considered full of inaccuracies and Gales and Seaton's *American State Papers* are preferred.

[9] With this instruction of May 12, 1825, the State Department sent to Mr. Appleton a List of the Captures, Seizures and Condemnations under the authority of the government of Naples. This list, in this volume, constitutes pages 172-173. The papers and documents in support of the respective claims were more numerous. These are mentioned as being "placed under the care" of Mr. Appleton, but their quantity, which was augmented from time to time, by the time Appleton left Naples, amounted to those contained in the "packet sealed with my arms", which Mr. Appleton left with Mr. Hammett, the United States Consul. This packet grew, with successive attempts to clarify the claims, and to get them indemnified, until there were successive 'packages' of such documents, most carefully transmitted by officials of the United States upon each change in the representative in Naples. Eventually these 'supporting documents for the claims' were laid before the Commission created by Congress to adjudicate the claims and to apportion the amount of the indemnity paid by the Neapolitan government. By the rules laid down for the conduct of the Commission's activities, these 'supporting papers,' along with those created by the Commission itself, including its journal, and its final report, were turned back to the State Department. Today these are to be found in the United States National Archives, Records Group 76: Boundary and Claims Commissions and Arbitration. In item 64 thereof the following are found:

Papers on claims, A-Z	11 vols.
Arguments before the Commission	1 (vol. #12)
Miscellaneous Papers	1 (vol. #13)
Journal and Appendix	2 vols. unnumbered
Report of the Commission	1 vol.
Dockets 1 and 2	2 vols.
List of Holders of Certificates	1 envelope
Six envelopes and miscellaneous papers	1 bundle of 6 envelopes.

The Report of the Commission was published, in 1898, by the 53d Congress, 2d Sess., incidental to *House Misc. Document No. 212, History and Digest of the International Arbitrations to which the United States has been a party.* By John Bassett Moore, U. S. Govt. Printing Office, Washington, 1898. 6 Vols. See therein, *V. Appendix G: The Neapolitan Indemnity: Convention of Oct. 14, 1832.* The final report of the Commission, as printed in this House Misc. Document No. 212, mentions "The list of awards made by the Board, following this report . . ." but in this printed version this list was not published. It is probable that the list referred to is that noted above as "List of Holders of Certificates — 1 envelope."

Your compensation will be at the rate of $4500. per annum, computing from the day of your acceptance of this Agency, to that of your return to the United States. Your reasonable expenses in going and returning, will also be allowed you, exclusive of those which may be incurred during your residence in Naples. Note. In a letter from this Department to Mr. Appleton, offering him the appointment, it is mentioned — "Your compensation will be considered as commencing from this day (12 April) if you accept the appointment," — consequently his salary account will be from the 12 April, 1825.

H. CLAY TO NEAPOLITAN MINISTER OF FOREIGN AFFAIRS[10]

Department of State, Washington 12. May 1825[11]

[Diplomatic Note]

Sir,

The President of the United States having thought proper to appoint John James Appleton for the purpose of conferring with the Government of Naples on the subject of Indemnities claimed by Citizens of the United States from that Government, in reference to the sequestration and confiscation of their property within the Neapolitan Dominions, I have to pray your Excellency

There is no evidence that this list was published at the time of the making of the awards. An earlier list of the claimants with a summary of the amounts claimed, and various other data relating to each claim made prior to Oct. 1, 1826, and for a supplement of 17 claims thereafter (100 claims in all), was published in House Document No. 68, 19th Congress, 2nd sess. This document comprised lists only, and included other lists of claims for France, Denmark, etc. These 100 claims (Naples) were also published in *American State Papers, Foreign Affairs*, VI, p. 384 ff. They obviously do not, in number of individual claims, constitute the whole number of 275 the Commission adjudicated and may not include all the vessels involved, or all the owners and shippers who suffered loss. (See later chapters of this work for the manner in which these claims were substantiated with much difficulty and considerable delay.) The amount actually granted to claimants individually was apparently never published, probably for reasons of policy, since the amounts varied greatly between claimants, both as to what they claimed and as to what they received; and certain firms, with numerous cargoes and vessels involved, had suffered far more than had others.

[10] According to the *Almanach de Gotha* (1827, 243.) the President of the Council of State and the Minister of Foreign Affairs *pro interim* was the Chev. Luigi de' Medici. On May 7, 1825, Secretary Clay had written a letter to His Excellency the Minister of Foreign Affairs at Naples, which, however, is marked cancelled. In it Clay notified the Minister that the President had appointed Appleton as chargé d'affaires at Naples. This letter did not make any mention of the specific purpose of the appointment. Credences, II, (March 10, 1825-Sept. 21, 1841).

[11] Credences, II, (March 10, 1825-Sept. 21, 1841). An earlier letter of credence, dated Washington May 7, 1825, is marked "cancelled." This text is slightly different.

to give him a reception corresponding with the entire confidence which this Government reposes, from an intimate knowledge of his excellent qualities, in his good faith and probity. He knows the concern the President takes in the friendship of the King of the Two Sicilies, and how desirous He is that all obstacles should be removed to the most friendly and harmonious understanding between the Government of the United States and that of Naples; and for that reason he is especially instructed by the orders of the President, to cultivate your confidence and freely to confer with you, concerning the nature and amount of the Indemnities referred to. He knows also my zeal to promote this understanding between the two Countries by whatever may depend upon my ministry; and I have no doubt that Mr. Appleton will so conduct himself as to deserve your confidence.

I avail myself with pleasure of this occasion to tender to your Excellency assurances of my high and distinguished consideration.

D. Brent[12] to J. Appleton

Department of State, Washington 14. May, 1825.
[Instruction, Unnumbered]

Sir,

The Secretary left the City this morning, on his journey to Kentucky, where he will probably remain till the month of July. Before his departure, he directed me to inform you, as I have the honour of doing, that your instructions are all prepared and signed by him, and that it is his wish you should come hither, as soon as you conveniently can, to receive them, that you may embark upon the voyage to Naples without any unnecessary delay.

J. J. Appleton to D. Brent

Boston May 24th 1825. [Despatch, Unnumbered]

Sir,

The letter with which you honored me on the 14th did not reach Cambridge until the 21st Instant. Letters to Boston are usually received on the fifth day from their date in Washington. The Postmaster has accounted for this difference, by saying that

---

12 Daniel Brent, of Virginia, was appointed chief clerk in the Department of State on September 21, 1817. He resigned on August 8, 1833, to accept an appointment as consul at Paris.

170

letters addressed to Cambridge leave the Boston Mail at Hartford, and take a circuit thro' the upper part of this State before reaching their destination. This being the case, it might be well, where despatch was an object, to address letters for Cambridge to the care of the Postmaster in Boston, who will forward them, on being so directed, to Cambridge on the day of their receipt, or that immediately following, by the mail which leaves this thrice a week[13] for that place.

You are pleased to inform me, under directions from the Secretary of State, that he signed my instructions as Special & Commercial Agent of the U: S: at Naples before he left Washington, and that it is his wish that I should go to receive them as soon as I conveniently can, in order that my departure may experience no unnecessary delay.

On receiving this notice I made arrangements for an immediate compliance with the Secretary of State's wishes, in consequence of which I may still reach Washington before the month expires.

J. J. APPLETON TO H. CLAY

Havre (France) July 15th, 1825 [Despatch, Unnumbered]

Sir,

I have the honor to inform you that I arrived here this morning after a passage of 29 days from New York. As soon as I can make the necessary arrangements, and provide myself with letters of introduction from my friends in London, I shall resume my journey to Naples, taking Paris and Geneva in my way.

Before leaving the United States, I had, in compliance with the wishes of the Department, an interview with M[r] Oliver of Baltimore, who put under my care, for his agent in Naples, a sealed package, containing, as he told me, Papers in support of his claims. He appeared much pleased with the early attention shewn to these claims by the new administration.

---

[13] A curious glimpse of the slower pace of those early days, for Cambridge was only just across the Charles River from Boston, yet, as we see in this text, it had mail only thrice weekly.

List of Captures, seizures and condemnations under the authority of the Government of Naples, transmitted to Mr. Appleton with the foregoing instructions.[14]

Names of Vessels	Names of Masters	Voyage	Cargo
Brig Alexander	Picket	From Newburyport to Naples	Am. & Col. Prod.
Schooner Alert	Gelston	N. York to Gallipoli	Fish & D°
" Amherst	Bradford	" " "	Fish
Brig Aurora	Bartlet	" " "	"
Ship Augusta	Moore	" " "	"
Brig Betsey (N° 1)	Tucker	Salem to Naples	Col. prod. & fish
Schooner Dove	Page	Salem to Civita vecchia	Dried Salt fish
" Dove	Thomas	" " "	Fish
Brig Emily (N° 2)	Waterman	N. Y. to Naples	Colonial produce
Ship Francis (N° 3)	Haskell	Salem to ————	Pepper
Schooner Fortune (N° 4)	Martin	" " "	Tobacco and cotton
Ship Henry (N° 5)	Gardner	Boston to Naples	————
Schooner Hamilton	Brown	————	————
Ship Hercules (N° 6)	West	Salem	Col. & India prod.
Schooner Hound	Warren	————	Col. & India prod.
Ship Jersey	Williams	N. York to Palermo	————
Sch.ⁿ John (N° 7)	Dixey	————	Col. & India prod.
Brig John	Currier	Newburyport	Fish
" Indiana	————	Baltimore	————
Sch.ⁿ Kite	Thompson	————	Col. & India prod.
" Louisiana	Mudge	————	————
" Louisiana (N° 15)	Newal	————	Fish & Col. prod.
" Mary	Larcom	————	Col. & India prod.
" Maria N° 9	Cleveland	————	D° & India goods

[14] This list subsequently was revised. Note that the *total* of claims here given *disagrees* with published lists. See House Document No. 68 and the final list as awarded. See above, footnote 9, p. 168; also below, footnote 13, p. 175.

When Captured or seized	Condemnation acquittal or release	Insured value of vessel and cargo	Remarks
1811	Confiscated	$34,000	Seized in Port
1810	"	66,000	D°
"	"	15,000	Confiscated in Port
"	"	15,000	D°
"	"	15,000	D°
"	"	70,245	D°
Oct. 1811	"	————	Seized in port — appears to be liberated
"	Restored	12,000	Confiscated in port
1809	"	110,000	Carried into Naples supposed by a Neapolitan privateer & sequestered
Jan. 25 1810	Confiscated	159,807	Seized in port
Feb. 13 1810	D°	25,000	Confiscated in port
Dec'. 1810	D°	39,067	Seized in port
1809	D°	135,000	Seized in port
————	————	————	Confiscated in port
————	Condemned	18,850	Taken by Neapolitan privateer
————	————	25,000	Taken in Port
————	————	22,000	Confiscated in port
————	————	50,000	Confiscated in port
1809	Confiscated	11,000	Seized in port
————	————	18,000	Confiscated in port
————	————	50,000	Captured by Neapolitan Gun Boats - vessel & cargo confiscated
Feb. 24 1810	Confiscated	90,000	Seized in port

Names of Vessels	Names of Masters	Voyage	Cargo
Schʳ Morning Star	Atkins	————	————
" Mary (N° 8)	Derby	————	Col. prod. & fish
Brig Mary Ann	Brown	Newburyport	Fish
Schʳ Nancy (N° 10)	Holman	————	Col. & India prod.
" Oceanus (N° 11)	Wilson	Boston to Naples	Am. & Col. prod.
Brig Orozimbo	Holden	Baltimore	Colonial prod.
Schʳ Ousetonack	Shefield	Boston to Naples	Fish, beef & Tobac°.
Brig Phoenix (N° 15)	Haskell	Boston	Ballast & cash
Schʳ Peace	Graves	————	Fish
Brig Perseverance	Foster	————	Col. & India prod.
" Radius (N° 15)	Lander	————	D°
" Romp (N° 12)	Lander	Salem to Naples	D°
" Ruth & Mary	Gardner	Philadelphia	Coffee
Suckey & Betsey (N° 13)	Hanscom	————	Colonial prod.
Schʳ Syren	Ianoren	————	Fish
Brig Sophia	Carman	Baltimore to Naples	————
" Two Betseys	Gardner	Beverly	Col. & India prod.
Ship Trent (N° 15)	Cavendish	Boston	D°
Schʳ Two friends	Lee	Beverly	Fish
Brig Victory (N° 14)	Felt	Salem	Col. & Ind. prod.
Ship Urania	Peck	N. York to Naples	D°
Schʳ William	Turner	————	Pepper & sugar
" Zephyr	Murphy	————	————

174

When cap-tured or seized	Condemnation acquittal or release	Insured value of vessel and cargo	Remarks
───	───	───	D°
Feb. 15 1810	Confiscated	30,000	Confiscated in port
───	───	36,000	Seized in port
1810	Confiscated	48,000	Confiscated in port
March 1811	D°	65,000	Seized in port
1809	───	105,000	D° Confiscated
1809	───	29,500	Confiscated in port
1808	Confiscated	7,600	Seized in port
───	───	18,000	Confiscated in port
1809	───	118,000	D°
1810	Condemned	30,000	D°
Dec. 1809	Confiscated	94,000	Seized in port
───	───	100,000	D°
Jan. 1810	Confiscated	5,500	Confiscated in port
───	───	28,000	D°
───	───	57,000	D°
Dec. 26, 1809	Confiscated	80,000	Seized in port
1809	D°	76,000	D°
1810	Condemned	18,000	Confiscated in port
Dec. 9 1809	D°	120,000	Seized in port
1809	Confiscated	80,000	D°
───	───	36,000	Confiscated in port
───	───	───	D°

Recapitulation[15] . In all 47....$2,163,069

[15] This total for the claims was only tentative at this time and the State Department expended much effort and published some advertisements in an attempt to get the claimants to justify all claims thoroughly. See later for Davezac's comment on delays and difficulties encountered in getting necessary "proofs" in Sicily.

J. J. APPLETON TO H. CLAY

Naples February 14. 1826.[16] [Despatch, Unnumbered]

Sir,

The object of this is merely to inform that I have had the honor of forwarding to you by another channel a full account of my proceedings in the Agency committed to me here. By that account you will see — that the purpose of the Government has been only partially effected — that our claims have again been explained fully, and urged with an earnestness leaving this Gov^t no hope that they will be abandoned — that altho' my exertions have not availed in obtaining a promise of indemnity they were for a while animated by the indecision of this Government, and only became entirely vain, when in a discovery of the extent of my powers they found reasons to presume that we had not yet the intention of pushing matters with them to extremity; but, especially, when in their communications with the French Government they found a pretext, and confidence for a further postponment [sic] of our claims.

Four confidential Notes, of which I have the honor of enclosing you copies, N° 1.2.3. & 4. will shew you distinctly the course which this business has taken. For a history of the circumstances which produced them, I have to refer you to the report of my conferences — of which, indeed, they are to be considered as parts. To render them intelligble [sic] however, in the event of this reaching you before that report, I will

---

[16] This despatch was received in Washington on May 20. On the previous day (May 19) the House of Representatives passed a resolution directing the Secretary of State to submit a "Schedule of the claims of the American citizens against the governments of France, Naples, Holland, and Denmark, which may be on file in the Department of State." Secretary Clay, as already stated, transmitted this report on January 30, 1827; on the 31st it was communicated to the House. (*American State Papers, Foreign Affairs*, VI, 384 ff). Conditions at Naples had not changed much since Mr. Pinkney had arrived ten years earlier. Francis I was a true Bourbon, from whom no change in the tyranny of his government could be expected. The new ministry was as lethargic as ever; de Medici, the Foreign Minister, as evasive and as subtle as Circello. (Perotta, *op. cit.,* 49). Twice earlier this matter of the Neapolitan spoliations claims had been before the Congress: *July 6, 1812: Message of the President, transmitting Report of the Secretary of State, showing captures, seizures and condemnations of American ships and merchandize, under authority of the Government of Naples. American State Papers, Foreign Affairs* III, 583 ff. (47 captures named as having been made by special decree of Murat. Total value cited as 1,830,781.95 ducats; the names of vessels are given). *Feb. 28, 1818* (communicated Mar. 2, 1818): *Message of the President, together with papers relating to the claims of merchants of the United States upon the government of Naples, in conformity with the resolution of the House of the 30th of January last.* (17 documents including Secretary Monroe's instructions to Mr. Pinkney).

merely say, that I had two conferences with Mʳ Medici (the Secretary of Foreign Affairs) before receiving his letter N° 2. — that in the first he had agreed to discuss amicably and confidentially the subject of our claims; and that altho' he betrayed a strong aversion to admit the abstract principle of responsibility for the acts of Murat, still he was so far from insisting upon it as a sufficient reason for not making them a subject of negociation that he said he would see whether the Council of State would give him a *basis* on which to negotiate. — that at the second interview, at which I had come with an expectation that he would suggest a *basis,* he had again insisted, on the irresponsibility of the King for the acts of Murat, and in explaining the principles on which the King had secured other rights acquired under those acts, regreted that our case could not claim the benefit of those principles, because the property *plundered* from us had been considered and employ'd by Murat as his private property. — that I declined assuming the obligation to shew the use made of our property thus plundered. That Mʳ Medici then urged the abandonment of our claims against France,[17] inferred from the conclusion of a Treaty of commerce with her, as a reason why we should abandon our claims against Naples — and finally that on being assured by me that our claims against France still subsisted he had concluded the conference by saying that the Council of State had expressed a desire to know, before they gave him a *basis* what France had done in relation to our claims, and that as it now appeared that his impressions were incorrect, he would write to the King's Ambassador in Paris, for information on the subject, and that our conferences might be resumed when he had received his answer.

Auguring no good from this reference of our claims to Paris, I endeavour'd to supersede its necessity by furnishing Mʳ Medici the correspondence, between Mʳ Gallatin and the French Government,[18] and pointing out particularly Mʳ Vil-

---

[17] President Jackson pressed France for payment of the bill standing against her for reprisals under Napoleon. Mr. Rives, whom he had sent to Paris, succeeded after much effort in inducing Louis Philippe to agree to pay 25 million francs for all our claims. Reparations in this case were mutual. The treaty signed July 4, 1831, provided that the United States reduce its duties on French wines and pay France 1,500,000 francs for failure to safeguard her property in Louisiana in violation of the purchase treaty. (Perrotta, *op. cit.,* 51).

[18] See: Beckles Willson, *America's ambassadors to France* (1777-1927) *a narrative of Franco-American diplomatic relations.* London, J. Murray, [1928,] 433 pp.

lele's[19] Note of the 6ᵗʰ of November 1822 as you will see by my note N° 1. This correspondence, the inspection of which did not produce the desired effect of reviving our conferences, was returned to me with his note N° 2. I sent him two days afterwards a view of the probable amount of the property taken from us, which he had expressed, at our last interview, a desire to possess. As it was furnished merely with the intention of making it a subject of discussion, and of shewing by a written document how far we had proceded in discussing our claims, it was intentionally rendered as imperfect and inconclusive against us as possible. — Indeed it contained no information which he had not before from the *"Conto Aparte."* These expedients to renew the conferences before he had heard from Paris proved unavailing. They had determined to be cautious — Altho' Mʳ Medici continued to receive me with great politeness he always declined entering upon the subject of the claims, until the answer from the Ambassador was received.

Having gone, however, to Mʳ Medici's house at his invitation, on the 27 of November he made known to me that in consequence of the information which they had received from their Ambassador in Paris it was not proper that they should now in any way *prejudge* the question with me, but that they ought to adhere strictly to the answer given 1816. This communication was at my request reduced to writing, and forms with a slight variation the contents of the paper N°. 4. You will observe that in neither of the notes addressed to me Mʳ Medici has taken his title of Minister of Foreign Affairs.

What has since occurred has not essentially altered the position of our claims. You will see however that I continued in my endeavours to strengthen the impression that instead of being prejudiced, our claims could only acquire more importance by the delay of this Government in settling them — and that I so far gained my object, that when I enquired of them whether they would give up those of our Vessels that still remained in the King's service, on the *owners'* applying for them; and whether they would furnish *me* with an account of the Sales of the Cargoes, and of the others confiscated by Murat, Mʳ Medici had, after consulting the Council of State, answered, that no

---

19 Villèle, Jean Baptiste Guillaume Marie Anne Seraphin Joseph. Count de. (1773-1854). French statesman. In 1821 he was minister of finance; in 1822, prime minister. See his *Memoires et correspondance.* Paris, 1888-90. 5 vols. See also: J. G. Hyde De Neuville, *Notice historique sur le comte de Villèle.* Paris, 1855; C. De Mazade, *L'opposition royaliste.* Paris, 1894.

resolution could be announced by this Government on either of these subjects, previous to our giving an answer to the Note of the Marquis of Circello. — You will finally learn from my report that as late as the 8th Instant, on my enquiring whether by refusing all further confidential conferences with me on the subject of our claims they had intended to close the door to an amicable settlement of the differences existing between the two countries, Mr Medici had replied that this was nowise the King's intention; that when the negociation between the two Governments was resumed, in an official form, perhaps some way might be found of arranging their differences — for example, *by referring them to a third Power.* Thus ended my last conversation with Mr Medici on the subject of the claims. The official correspondence between the two governments, to which he alluded, I should not have thought it proper to revive, even if the character with which I am clothed would have permitted it, without previously putting in your power to instruct me minutely upon the different points on which it might turn, by submitting the information which has now been obtained concerning the views and temper of this government in relation to our claims.

On comparing what has been discovered in the conferences with Mr Medici, with what has been obtained from other quarters I am inclined to believe that the disposition to attend to our claims which it was the object of my agency to ascertain confirm and improve, did really exist here at the period of my arrival — but I must also say that the circumstances under which it ceased to appear authorise me to state it as my firm opinion that it had not proceded from a growing sense of justice but from a complete misconception of the means which were now to be employed to enforce our claims — and of those by which they would be extinguished — above all from ignorance, uncertainty, or error, in relation to the state of our affairs with France.

In support of the opinion I have now expressed, I must add, that commercial letters which had preceded me here from different quarters had announced that the Government of the U: S: was about making a new effort in favour of its claims, and had augmented its Squadron in the Mediterranean to take justice in its own hands if that effort proved abbortive [sic]. Since my arrival our affairs have frequently occupied the attention of the Council of State where there has existed much alarm in relation to our intentions. I understand that the King went so far as to say "he would have no noise," and that he would make personally any sacrifice to avert reprisals upon the commerce of the country, already too reduced to bear a new blow. To this feeling of alarm I was probably also indebted for the extraordinary and unnecessary attentions that were shewn me by Mr Medici who treated me as one who at all events was to be propitiated.

That there was an idea of proposing a treaty of commerce as a partial or total extinguishment of our claims is not only proved by the belief expressed by Mr Medici, that our claims against France had been thus extinguish'd, but also by repeated suggestions to that effect made to me by the Count of Luchesi,[20] [sic] their Consul General to the U: S: whom I found on my arrival on the point of departing for his post, but who delayed his departure on various pretenses until the answer from France had been received.

I never doubted that the Count of Luchesi [sic] was charged by Mr Medici to ascertain on what terms we should be disposed to settle with Naples, altho' he always protested that he had no communication with his Chief on the subject. He takes with him the key of the King's private Cypher and is no doubt instructed to watch diligently the progress of the feelings of the American Government and People in reference to their foreign claims. This is a point, however, on which their anxiety must have diminished, for the Count has, since his departure, obtained permission to spend the remainder of the Winter in Europe. An increased confidence in their cause is a natural consequence of their having discovered, that it was common with France, who not only refused us justice herself, but exerted herself to prevent our obtaining it from others — I fear therefore, that unless we resort to the most unequivocal demonstration of earnestness, we shall not soon again have the benefit of the *only* sentiment on which we might reply, with certainty for a recognition of our rights — I have done what I could with propriety to prevent their believing that we would admit the subordination of responsibility, which they wish to establish between our claims against Naples and those we have against France; and

---

20 Count Ferdinando Lucchesi-Palli was at this time Consul General at Washington, for both the Two Sicilies and the Papal States. For his letters see chapter on Neapolitan Legation in Washington, D. C.

when Mr Rothschild,[21] their Banker, told me a few days since, that Mr Medici thought it would always be time to pay; I answered that he who paid last, would have to pay most. He has been informed by the Government of every step I have taken in relation to the claims, and as he has assured me that this Government would not borrow again, without the consent of his house, until the year 1827, I have but, little doubt, of his having used what influence he has, against us. He has, however, told me that, Mr Medici, expected some overtures from me in relation to a treaty of commerce.

What precedes and what is found in more detail in my principal report will I hope be considered as yielding all the information contemplated and required by the Government, to enable it to adopt suitable measures for the establishment of our rights against Naples. The more I have looked into the foundation of law and fact of these rights, the more I have been convinced of their validity. This conviction does not however leave me any hope that they can be established by the mere force of reason. Nothing of importance will be effected until a Negociator can come here, armed with the fixed purpose of his Government to redress itself, if in a given time, appeals to principles of justice prove ineffectual. — their maxim is that "they are always in time to pay." — The character of the King and Nation, will not however, render an actual resort to force necessary, the threat will be all sufficient — if they see that its execution is at hand. It was in this very bay of Naples, that commodore Martin,[22] in 1740, and commodore Campbell[23] shook a

21 Karl Rothschild. (1788-1855). Banker. Born at Frankfort; died in Naples. One of five sons of Meyer Amschel Rothschild who were all bankers. As director of the Neapolitan branch of the banking firm, Karl was well-known and influential at the Bourbon Court. For an account of this powerful financier, see Raffaele De Cesare, *La fine di un Regno*. Città di Castello, Ed. Albrighi e Segati, Naples, 1908; also E. Demachy, *Les Rothschild*, Paris, 1896; I. Balla, *Die Rothschild*, Berlin, 1912; E. C. Corti, *Das Haus Rothschild*, Leipzic, 2 volumes. An Italian edition of Corti's work was published by Mondadori, Milan, 1938. The Rothschilds are mentioned in all works dealing with Bourbon history, especially in very recent studies on Francis I and Ferdinand II, by Ruggero Moscati. The diplomatic correspondence of the period contains frequent references to the Rothschilds.
22 In 1742 Admiral Mathews in charge of the British Fleet in the Mediterranean was instructed by the Secretary of State to take action against Naples unless her King ceased to furnish troops to assist the Spaniards. On July 22, 1742, Mathews ordered Captain William Martin to go to Naples with directions that he was "to bring the King of the Two Sicilies to a just sense of his errors in having attacked in conjunction with the Spaniards the Queen of Hungary's territories in Italy." Martin delivered his message to the King and demanded an answer in half an hour. He got the King's promise to withdraw his troops. H. W. Richmond. *The Navy in the War of 1739-48*. Cambridge Press, 1920. 212 pp.
23 Possibly John Campbell. See John Charnock, *Biographia Navalis*. VI, 35.

firmer purpose, and firmer men than those who now govern the councils of Naples.

If there are circumstances which prevent our offering to this Government the alternative of "justice, or reprisals," a Minister here, be his talents what they may, will obtain nothing which you could accept. The most that he could do, would be to put the business *here,* and in the United States (for the cause I fear is to be won there also) in a state, to be acted upon, when circumstances favour. In either case you require to be served here, by one, who can speak, with more authority, than I can. There are resources here, of talent, subtilty, [sic] and skill, which will furnish ample employment to our most gifted and accomplished statesmen. It is not just, that the credit of the country and of the administration should be endangered, by reposing in hands, conscious of inability, to do it entire justice. I beg you therefore to consider me, as cheerfully abandoning any pretentions, which your letters might have encouraged; and as fully compensated for this proof of my attachment to the Administration, if I retain its confidence in some other post of less oppressive responsibility — I shall however comply with the Presidents [sic] desire in remaining here, until I hear from you, and then obey, to the best of my ability any orders I may receive connected with the public service on which I am now employed.

I cannot suffer myself to lose this or any other favourable occasion of acknowledging that I have been much indebted, since my arrival here to the information furnished me by Mr Hammett, who by his talents, and character, truly respectable, does credit to the country he represents.

J. J. APPLETON TO CHEV. DE MEDICI

[Enclosure N° 1 with despatch February 14, 1826]

[October 7, 1825]

Mr Appleton salutes respectfully H. E. the Chevalier de Medici and hastens to transmit to him a volume of official documents, containing the correspondence of which he has had the honor of speaking to him this morning. Without giving himself the trouble of looking thro the whole of it, H. E. will see by the letter of Mr de Villele under date of the 6. November 1822.

that the claims of the U: S: founded on acts of Bonaparte had not been absorbed in the Commercial convention concluded between the two governments on the 24 of June of the same year, but on the contrary that the Government of France then proposed to enter into a definitive arrangement, which should comprise on one side the said claims, and on the other those which France produced against the U: S: in consequence of her construction of the Louisianna [sic] Treaty. The refusal of the United States to admit any other construction of this Treaty than that which they had given it up to this day is, it seems, the only obstacle which prevents a definive [sic] settlement of the claims to indemnity between the two States.

Mr. Appleton will immediately make out also the list of the American Vessels confiscated by Murat and will do himself the honor of transmitting it to H. E. as soon as possible. —

He begs that H. E. would permit him, to renew the assurance of his most distinguish'd consideration.

CHEV. DE MEDICI TO J. J. APPLETON

[Enclosure N° 2. with despatch February 14, 1826]

Naples 13, October 1825.

The Chevalier de Medici has read attentively the letter of Mr de Villele of the 6th of November 1822 pointed out to him by Mr Appleton in the book which he has now the honor of returning to him. He has not found in it any but general expressions tending to make known the idea and the desire of the government of H. M. C. M. to embrace in a single negociation the mutual reclamations of the two States, and not yet any precise indication of what merely by way of argument of analogy had been maintained by Mr Appleton upon the sentiments of the French Government in relation to the object of Mr Appleton's discourse. And altho' what may be done by the French Gov't is not a point applicable to this Royal Court, because the political position of that Government in reference to the United States of America is entirely different, still as a full knowledge of what is in contestation between the United States and the French Government[24] in questions of origin prior

---

[24] The claims convention (and the duties on wines and cottons between the United States and France) was not proclaimed until February 2, 1832. For text of the treaty see, Miller, *op. cit.*, III, 641-651. In the Italian text, the initials H.M.C.M. in this paragraph, are transcribed as "Governo di S. M. Xma."

to, the restoration, and of the dispositions of the latter towards the former in reference to the said subjects may throw more light on the question and add new force to the determination of this Royal Court, the Chev' de Medici has lost no time in asking of the Prince of Castelcicala,[25] the Royal Ambassador in Paris, the fullest information upon this matter, and hastens to inform M' Appleton of it, reserving to himself to confer with him anew, as soon as the required information shall have reached him.

He profits in the meanwhile, very willingly of this occasion to express to him the sentiments of his particular consideration.

J. J. APPLETON TO CHEV. DE MEDICI

[Enclosure N° 3 with Despatch February 14, 1826]

Mr. Appleton presents his respects to H. E. the Chevalier de' Medici, and in compliance with his promise has the honor of transmitting to him a very imperfect Memorandum of the proceeds of the sales of American property affected by the ex-government of Naples. He also begs that H. E. would grant him a new interview.
the 12. Oct: 1825.

"Memorandum."

The total number of American Vessels and Cargoes confiscated by the ex-Government of Naples, in the Ports of the Kingdom, or taken and carried elsewhere by its Vessels of war, may be about fifty. Thirty of those Vessels and cargoes were

---

[25] Fabrizio Ruffo. Prince of Castelcicala and Duke of Calvello. (1763-1832). He was Neapolitan ambassador at London. At the outbreak of the French Revolution, he refused to represent his court at Paris, remaining in England to the year 1795, when he was recalled to become minister of foreign affairs. He was a member of the State Court for political offenders (Giunta di Stato per i Rei). As a State Councilor, during the revolution of 1799, he accompanied the King to Sicily where he [Ruffo] remained for two years. He was then sent on a secret mission to the Regent in England. In 1815, he was named ambassador to Paris; in 1816, he returned to London to negotiate a treaty of commerce; in 1820, he was removed from office. He died in Paris from the cholera. The Prince of Scaletta descended from a different branch of the same family. On Ruffo, see: Alessandro Cutolo, "La rivoluzione di luglio e il principe di Castelcicala." in *Archivio Storico Italiano*, 1933, 7th ser., XX, pp. 263 ff. This article is based on diplomatic documents. See also Antonio Capograssi, "L'Unità d'Italia nel pensiero di Lord W. Bentinck." in *Rassegna Storica del Risorgimento*, Rome, 1934, XXI; Berardo Candida Gonzaga, *Memorie delle famiglie nobili delle provincie meridionali d'Italia*. Naples, De Angelis, 1876-79, 6th vol., part 1. All the works on Bourbon history refer more or less extensively to the Prince of Castelcicala.

184

confiscated in a single day in virtue of the first article of the decree of the 12. of March 1810. It would appear from the information sought at the time, that the cargoes of these thirty Vessels were sold for a sum of 1830.781 ^{93}/100 Ducats, viz.

Hercules	D^s 170,303.76/100
Augustus	122,536.14/100
Zephyr	46,155.14/100
Sophia	47,707.50/100
Orozimbo	100,070.28/100
2 Betsyes	109,760. 7/100
Romp.	120,066.89/100
Kite	43,589.68/100
Victory.	117,780.94/100
Ousatonack.	9,834.64/100
Syren	20,00
Phenix	1,600
Emily.	98,889.71/100
Francis	153.757.96/100
Hound.	50,901.37/100
Dove.	84,405.75/100
Maria	73,339.83/100
Urania	47,254.30/100
Amherst	1,500.17/100
Ruth & Mary	100,000
William	33,047.31/100,
Fortune	27,577.40/100
Nancy Ann.	41,708.81/100
Mary (Derby)	30,022.7/100
Louisianna. [sic]	25,387.6/100
John	15,185.36/100
Luckey [sic] & Betsey [sic]	50,000
Hamilton	70,000
Peace	20,000
	————————————
Ducats.	1,830,781.93/100[26]

The correctness of the information which has been used in the formation of this list is not guaranteed. It is still more difficult to learn, even approximately what the subsequent confis-

---

[26] Compare prior totals, hitherto cited in this chapter, and see footnote 9 concerning reasons for the differences in these totals. See also this page "correctness not guaranteed" and why. Note value here is in ducats.

cation in Naples or else where, produced; yet it is not improbable from the bills of lading attached to the claims, that they yielded nearly in the same proportion, that is to say 1,200,000 ducats. It would be necessary also to ascertain what the Vessels, sacrifised like the cargoes to the wants of the moment, produced; and how far the spirit of plunder which had dictated the confiscations, communicating itself, to those, who had it in charge to realize their value, may have diminished their proceeds. It is to be presumed that if the search formerly ordered was now continued, means might be obtained of verifying the exactness of the data of this memorandum. The American Government has on its side all that it requires, to shew the amount of the losses of its Citizens.

THE CHEV. DE MEDICI TO J. J. APPLETON

[Enclosure N° 4 with despatch February 14, 1826]

Naples 28 November 1825.

The Chevalier de Medici has received the confidential letter which Mr Appleton has been pleased to write to him on the tenor of the conversation of Saturday last. Observing in it some difference in the expressions, altho' the sense is nearly the same, he hastens to note down word for word, what he finds in his minutes, in order that they may perfectly agree. They say "that in consequence of the information which we have just received from France I cannot enter upon conferences on the question without prejudging it: I can only therefore, refer strictly and literally to our Note of the year 1816."

The Chevalier de Medici improves this occasion to renew to Mr Appleton the assurances of his perfect consideration.

H. CLAY TO J. J. APPLETON

Department of State Washington 8. June, 1826.
[Instruction, Unnumbered]

Sir,

The only Letter received from you at this Department since your arrival at Naples, is dated the 14th of February of the present year, and was not received until the 20th ultimo. The one to which it refers, as having been forwarded by another

186

opportunity, and containing a full account of your proceedings in the agency committed to your charge at Naples, has not yet reached this Department.

Since a reasonable hope is no longer to be indulged, from the tenor and complexion of your communication, of your obtaining an acknowledgment of the obligation of Naples to pay the claims of our citizens upon that Government, even at a distant day, the President has concluded to postpone to a more propitious moment, the further prosecution of them. The purpose of this Letter is, therefore, to make known this determination, and to inform you that you have been appointed Chargé d'Affaires of the United States at Stockholm, in Sweden, whither it is the Presidents [sic] wish that you should lose no time in repairing. Your Commission, and an Introductory or Credential Letter from this Department to the Minister of Foreign Affairs at that Court, are, accordingly, herewith transmitted to you; to which are added a copy of that Letter, and the Duplicate of one to the Banker of the United States for this Department at Amsterdam, authorizing and instructing him to honour your Drafts for your outfit.[27] four thousand five hundred dollars, and your salary, as it becomes due, at the rate of four thousand five hundred dollars a year, and for the contingent expenses of your office. Your further and general instructions will be prepared with all convenient dispatch, and transmitted to the care of Mr. David Erskine,[28] our Consul at Stockholm, to await your arrival in that City. In the meantime, it is the wish of the President that, before leaving Naples, you should take care to impress upon the Government of that Country, through the proper channel, a due sense of the disappointment which is felt here at the unfavourable result of this renewed effort, on our part, to obtain the indemnity or a promise of it to which our citizens are so justly entitled from that Government, and to let it be distinctly understood that the future prosecution of these claims will be persevered in, and, for the present, is only postponed by this termination of your Agency, to enable you to fulfill the Presidents [sic] instructions, by repairing, without loss of time, to another post, where the public service requires your presence.

---

[27] See above, Mr. Pinkney, p. 114, for his comment on the inadequacy of the allowance for diplomats' "oufit."

[28] David Erskine was nominated consul of United States for Stockholm November 27, 1818; referred to Committee on Foreign Relations. He served to November 1836, (*Senate Executive Journal*, III, 142, 150, 152).

The compensation allowed you on your Agency at Naples will terminate on the same day that your salary commences as our representative at Stockholm.

J. J. APPLETON TO H. CLAY

Naples August 7th 1826. [Despatch, Unnumbered]

Sir,

I received yesterday the letter with which you honor'd me under the date of the 8th of June last, and will in compliance with its directions, immediately terminate my agency near this Government and proceed to Sweden to assume the new charge which the President has thought fit to confer upon me.

Altho' debar'd by the tenor of the Note of the Chevalier de' Medici, under date of the 28th November, from any further attempt to persuade him of the propriety of coming to some understanding with me in relation to the object of my agency, I have lost no opportunity of impressing upon him, and upon those who were supposed to exercise influence over the determinations of this Government, the idea that the United States were fixed in the purpose to prosecute their claims to a settlement; and founding myself on your orginal instructions, have never failed to represent these claims as gaining strength and increasing in amount by the delay of the Neapolitan Government in providing for them — It will now be my duty, in repeating these sentiments, to express the disappointment which the President has felt on learning that the new attempt he had made, thro' my means, to establish an understanding between the two Governments on a subject which must sooner or later be settled between them, had proved totally ineffectual: to announce his determination to persevere in the prosecution of the claims, which is only temporarily suspended by the termination of my agency. This communication will be made in writing to Mr Medici, and submitted to you with other Papers presumed interesting for the further prosecution of our claims, as soon as I can find a more suitable conveyance for them than the Neapolitan Post Office. As I intend taking a passage here, in the course of ten days, for Leghorn, it will probably be from this latter place that I shall next have the honor of addressing you, when I hope I shall have it in my power to mention the probable period of my arrival in Stockholm.

I cannot close this letter, without taking the liberty to request that you would express to the President my grateful sense of the honor he has confer'd upon me in the unsolicited appointment to the Court of Sweden, and assure him, that I shall endeavour to do justice to his continued confidence by devoting all my means to the promotion of the affairs he has committed to my charge.

J. J. APPLETON TO H. CLAY

Naples August 21, 1826. [Despatch, Unnumbered]

Sir,

I have the honor to enclose to you my account with the Department of State for my services and expenses in the Special Agency to Naples.

I have, in assuming a date for the commencement of my compensation as Special Agent to Naples, fixed upon that on which my salary of Secretary of Legation terminated. In doing this I hope I have rightly understood the intentions of the Government. Should the fact be otherwise my error will be easily rectified by substituting to the 12th of April, the 22nd the day on which I signified my acceptance of the agency. A corresponding correction will then, however, be required in my former account in order that no interval may exist between my Secretariship [sic] to London and my Agency to Naples. I have made my compensation to terminate on the 18th of August 1826, the day on which I asked my passports of the Neapolitan Government.

As your letter of the 12th of May 1825 informed me that my reasonable expenses in *going* and *returning* would be allowed me, I have charged to the Department the expenses which I incurred while actually travelling to this place. Having been obliged to make a visit to England after my arrival at Havre; to stay a few days at Paris, and at other places on the road, I have considered all the expenses then incurred as strictly for my own account, and have consequently thrown them out of that which I now present to the Government. In my anxiety to render my travelling expenses as light to the United States as possible, I came with the public coach as far as Chambery, where, this mode of conveyance failing me, I was forced to hire a vettura to carry me to Turin. At Turin I bought a cheap carriage and took post horses. After my arrival at Naples I

189

sold my travelling carriage, and finding that the difference between the price of purchase and that of sale, was 200 francs, I charged this sum to the Government. These explanations will I hope induce you to pass this part of my account. As your instructions promised me, also, my reasonable expenses in *returning,* I might, perhaps, with propriety, have charged to the Government the expense of my journey to Stockholm, which, embracing a distance by land of nearly 2200 miles will cost me not less than $1000. I was, however, unwilling to avail myself of this faculty to increase the expenses of my agency, especially as the outfit which is allowed me as Chargé d'Affaires to Stockholm, might be considered by the President as a substitute for the promised indemnity. I will submit it, however, to the consideration of the Government whether, subjected as I am to an expense of at least $600. more than I should have incurred in repairing directly to my post from the United States, I may not, in strict justice, Charge the United States with the same amount of expenses for my return from Naples as I actually incurred in coming, that is with the additional sum of $616.62. if your decision should be in the affirmative, the amount, which I have now the honor to present, may be so changed as to make my charge for travelling expenses $1233.24. instead of $616.62.

On my account for the contingent expenses of the office, no explanations, I presume, are necessary, further than to observe, that altho' I had no official character at Naples, and indeed no intercourse directly with the Department of Foreign Affairs, this was not considered sufficient to exempt me from the contribution which Mr Medici's Servants levy at Christmas & at Easter upon the Foreign Ministers. I paid to these servants $8.10^{cts}. which I have charged to the United States.

I have credited the United States with the money I actually received here for my drafts upon Baring Brothers & Co.[29] As in three different occasions, however, I had payments to make in England, I remitted my bills upon Messrs Baring and credited the U:S: with a sum of dollars equal to what those bills would

---

29 Alexander Baring. First Baron Ashburton (1774-1848). Financier and statesman. The eminent financial house of Baring Bros. & Co. was founded by Sir Francis Baring (1740-1818). The firm had numerous connections with the United States and Alexander was sent here to strengthen and extend its business operations. On the death of his father in 1810, Alxander became the head of the firm. In a letter dated Naples, Aug. 20, to Daniel Brent, Chief Clerk of the Department of State. Mr. Appleton stated that if the balance of the money due to him could not be remitted to Baring in London, he begged that the money be sent to Mr. Thomas Perkins of Boston, for his account. MS Diplomatic Despatches, Naples-Sweden, V. (Feb. 8, 1825-Aug. 15, 1830).

have produced here if negociated at the average price of the others. Having also received 220 pounds sterling from Messrs Baring, while in England, I credited the U:S: the corresponding number of dollars at the par of Exchange: what little advantage I might gain thereby being fully compensated by my continual losses in the exchange of money during my journey.

It only remains that I should ask you to be so good as to direct Messrs Baring Brothers & Co. to hold subject to my disposal the balance which shall appear to be due me by the settlement of my account at the Treasury Department.

General Abstract of disbursements made by John James Appleton, Chargé d'Affaires at Stockholm, and late Special Agent at Naples, From 12, April 1825, to 3, April 1827.[30]

Following sums disbursed by him as Special Agent to Naples From 12, April to 15, August 1826, p^r his Account N° 1 & Vouchers herewith — viz:

For Contingent Expenses —

Postage on public letters & documents p^r Vouchers N° 1. to 4	$52.55	
Franking	11.00	
Stationery p^r Vouchers N° 1 to 3	10.95	
Christmas and Easter gifts to the Neapolitan Minister's Servants..	8.10	82.60

For travelling Expenses —

From Cambridge M^s to Washington	$28.25	
" Washington to New York, including baggage	20.25	
" New York to Havre (including Steward of the Packet) ...144.00		
" Havre to Paris by the Diligence, seats for self & servant, transportation & baggage .... Francs............ 82.—		
" Paris to Lyons by D° D° D° ....298.—		
" Lyons to Chambery D° D° D° ....100.—		
Custom House fees at port Bonvoisin .... 10.—		
Expenses to Turin in a vittura [sic] ....240.—		
" to Genoa with post-horses ....116.—		
" to Sarzana .. D° ....102.—		
" to Pisa D° .... 77.—		
" to Leghorn D° .... 22.—		
" to Florence D° .... 88.—		
" to Aquapendente D° ....143.—		
" to Rome D° ....121.—		
" to Teracina [sic] D° ....113.—		
" to Naples D° ....110.—		
Personal Expenses on the road 242.80		

---

30 This abstract is included because of its interest in showing methods and costs of conveyance in continental Europe in the early part of the nineteenth century.

Tolls or fees to Officers of the Customs ....170.—
Repairs of his traveling carriage in Leghorn ....120.—
Loss upon the sale of same in Naples ....200.—

Francs.........2354.80=423.22
[Dollars $]   615.72
Carried Forward ....[$]   698.32

The following sums disbursed by him as Chargé d'Affaires at Stockholm from 18, August to 31, December 1826, per his Account N° 2. & Vouchers herewith — viz.

For Contingent Expenses —

Paid for 2 blank books—pr.	Voucher No. 1 .. Rix Dollars B^{co} ^{31}	2.00
" " D° — D°	" 2...... "	3.16
" " An inkstand ...	" 3...... "	2.00
" " A paper folder ..	" 4...... "	1.00
" " Wafers	" 5...... "	1.00
" " Paper & Wax ..	" 6...... "	17.00
" " A pair of Scissors	" 7...... "	1.00
" " A blank book ..	" 8...... "	2.08
" " Tape	" 9...... "	1.00

Rx. Dollars B^{co}....30.30

For New Year's Presents —

To the runners of the King & Prince ..... 10 .Rx.D'B° 18.—
" the under Officers of the Custom House 11 .... 10.—
" the Servants of ....D°...... 12 .... 2.—
" D° of the Dept. of Foreign Affairs 13 .... 10.—
" D° of the Post Office .... 14 .... 2.—
" D° of the King .... 15 .... 3.—

45.00

For 3 copies of the Treaty of Commerce between Sweden and England, forwarded to the Department of State—
Pr Voucher N° 16.... 1.12
For Postage on public letters & Documents — " — 17.... 90.44

Rx: D^s Banco.... 167.38
at 2.^{R} 32^{Sch} 11/12 to the Dollar is equal to......62.4?^{32}

---

31 *Rix Dollars Banco*: Rx Do Bo: Rx D. B. All these expressions have the same meaning, e.g., "dollars of the empire or realm." (Any of various German, Dutch, and Scandinavian silver 'dollar' coins, now nearly obsolete.) Since Mr. Appleton was accounting here for disbursements in Stockholm, here he meant the coin value of the last of these three countries. "Banco" indicated that the "standard or bank" value was to be understood here in contrast to the actual coins at 'state money' (depreciated) values, or in 'monies' d'accompte' or 'book values.' The 'banco' values fluctuated less often in foreign exchange and, therefore, afforded the diplomat a more stable unit of reporting his accounts.
32 The missing figures in the final column, where the Swedish values are translated into United States dollar values, were indistinct in the original, but, by careful reinspection, were decipherable, except for the last digit in the item at end

And the following sums disbursed by him as Chargé d'Affaires aforesaid (from 1. Jan: to 3. April 1827. P'. his Account N° 3 & vouchers herewith — viz).

For a translation of the Royal Report to the Storthing,

" Illumination on the evening of	P' Voucher N° 1 Rx D. B.	12.32
" the King's return from Norway	" 3.........	4.36
" Stationery	" 2.........	12.00
" Postage for January, February		
& March	" 4.........138.28	

Rx: D' Banco 188.00

At the exchange of 2ᴿ 33ˢᶜʰ 10/12 to the Dollar is equal to ...70.04

Dollars [U.S.] 830.83

J. J. APPLETON TO D. BRENT

Leghorn, August 30ᵗʰ 1826 [Despatch, Unnumbered] (*Private*)

Dear Sir.

Having had abundant proof in my relations with you of your general disposition to oblige, & particularly of your regard for me, I so far presume upon the continuance of these sentiments as to take the liberty to commit an affair to your care, in which without giving yourself much trouble, you may greatly oblige me — The case is this: My Uncle Thomas Appleton,[33] who is now Consul of the U:S: in this place, finding that the emoluments of his office will no longer cover his expenses, is desirous of being removed to the Consulate of Paris whenever it shall become vacant. This event, the declining health of the present incumbent induces him to believe cannot be far distant. He is aware that other applications will be made for that office, but believes, that, if his claims are fairly examined they will be found to outweigh those of any other candidate for it. His first application for the office at Paris, made in 1798, was back'd [sic] by names so numerous and respectable, that if it failed of being successful, it was because the existing state of our relations with France, rendered the appointment of a consul at that time in-

(62-4.-). The missing digit occurred just where the volume's binder had pierced the page with his sewing thread and the figure, in consequence, had disappeared. In the table that follows on this same page, note that the two columns do not correspond exactly, and that even the voucher numbers are not in order.

[33] Thomas Appleton, of Massachusetts, was appointed consul of United States for Leghorn on February 7, 1798. He retained this post until his death in 1840. Philip Mazzei in his *Memoirs* [New York, 1942] 391, 409, refers to Mr. Thomas Appleton.

expedient. Such at least was the answer it received from the then President, who in lieu of the appointment he had solicited gave him the consulate at Leghorn. During the 28 years that have since elapsed he has rendered important services to the commerce of our country and particularly by obtaining soon after his arrival the levy of the sequester which the French Military authorities had laid on all American property in the place. Having always devoted himself, exclusively, to his consular duties, he has had the satisfaction of *satisfying* those whom the laws of our country had placed under his protection, unwilling to leave this fact to his mere assertion, he confidently refers the Government for the impartial testimony of their officers who have from time to time commanded the Mediterranean Station. Under these circumstances he is no doubt entitled to the favourable attention of the President if an opportunity should offer of ameliorating his condition, which in consequence of the great diminution of the American trade to port, has now become any thing but eligible — May I then beg that, whenever you shall learn that the Consulate of Paris has vacated, you would make known to the Secretary of State and thru him to the President, my uncle's wishes, in order that they may consider him as an applicant for the office, and after comparing his claims as they are here explained, with those of other candidates, they may determine upon them what they shall think fit for the best service of the country — I ought not to omit to state that my uncle has deserved well of his country, by endeavouring to introduce into it the cultivation of many plants, to which Italy is indebted for her her [sic] wealth, & by seconding the progress of the fine arts. It may also promote his object to state, that the Commission under which he acts here as Consul of the U:S: is of a date anterior to that of any other of the same character, held by an American-born citizen.

I need not say that your kind attention to the contents of this letter when the contingency of making use of it shall occur, will be considered by me as a proof of your friendship & regard entitled to my most grateful acknowledgments.

J. J. Appleton to H. Clay

[Leghorn.] August. 30th 1826. [Despatch, Unnumbered]
Sir.
I had the honor on the 6th. instant to signify my grateful acceptance of the appointment which the President has thought

proper to confer upon me at the Court of Sweden, and have now that of informing you that I have brought my Agency at Naples to a close in the manner prescribed by your instructions of the 8th. of last June, and by reference also to those with which you furnished me on the 12th. of May 1825. You will find enclosed, (N°. 1)[34] a copy of the letter which I addressed to Mr Medici. Before sending him this letter, I made two unsuccessful attempts to see him. I did not expect that the situation of our affairs would be changed by a new interview, but I hoped that it might enable me to discuss the impression which my intended communication would make upon him. Having been denied this opportunity, I can add nothing to the information already submitted respecting the sentiments of this Government in regard to our claims.

I would have been gratified to have had it in my power to send you M^r. Medici's acknowledgment of the receipt of the note (N° 1) in which, I made known to him the views which you have taken of our claims; but as the Vessel in which I was to sail for this place would not retard her departure longer than the 21st. Instant, I was obliged to leave Naples before I had received it; not, however, before I had obtained a promise from M. Giraldi,[35] the Director general of the Department of Foreign Affairs, that it would be forwarded to me, here, so soon as my note, which was still in the hands of Mr Medici, should be sent back to the office. It was, also, from M. Giraldi that I received, on the same occasion, the Passport I had requested. On my arrival here on the 28th. instant I called at Neapolitan Consulate where the promised answer was to have been sent, but it had not yet arrived. If I should be obliged to leave this before receiving it, I shall direct M^r. Hammett to apply for it, and to transmit it to you, directly —

As during my residence in Naples I had had several confidential conversations with the Russian Minister Count Stackleberg,[36] on the subject of our claims, I thought it proper to make known

---

[34] See p. 199, below.

[35] The correct spelling is Don Ferdinando Girardi. Baron. (1760-1860). Director of the ministry of foreign affairs.

[36] The correct spelling is Gustav Stackelberg. (1766-1850). Count. Russian diplomat. Envoy extraordinary and minister plenipotentiary in Naples from 1819 to 1835. See: Ruggero Moscati, *Il regno delle Due Sicilie e l'Austria, Documenti dal marzo 1821 al novembre 1830*. Naples, R. Deputazione di Storia Patria, 1937. 2 vols. II, 378; Alfredo Zazo, *La politica estera del Regno delle Due Sicilie nel 1859-1860*. Naples, A. Miccoli, 1940, 203-204.

to him, previous to my departure, the substance of the last instructions I had received from you. This gentleman, who had always expressed wishes to see my endeavours to bring about an understanding between the United States and Naples, crowned with success, and had, also, as I was informed, early expressed similar wishes to Mr Medici, now seemed to regret, sincerely, that the object of my agency remained unaffected; ascribing, however, its failure to the short-sighted policy of the Neapolitan Government, who considered delay in every affair, as equivalent to success —

As Mr Medici had spoken freely of our claims I lost, on my side, no proper occasion to make out as favourable a case for them as my means would permit. Those who acknowledged their justice, (and I have found but few who thought that it could be seriously questioned) have generally concluded that the Neapolitan Government, wanting the disposition as well as the means, to satisfy us, would never do us justice so long as our claims against France remained unacknowledged. In reply I have observed that it was not only unjust, but bad policy in Naples, to postpone the payment of what she owed us, until an arrangement, (which must from the nature of their relations sooner or later take place), between the United States and France, would leave to Naples, without the power to defeat any longer our claim, and the United States without the disposition, which they now felt, to temper their pretentions to the circumstances of the Kingdom of the Two Sicilies. The members of the Diplomatic Corps with whom I had the most intimacy, (namely, the count of Flemming, Minister of Prussia,[37] and the count of Ficquelmont, that of Austria,[38]) have also been informed that the prosecution of our claims was only suspended to enable me to assume duties elsewhere. In this manner I have endeavoured to prevent any unfavourable impression in relation to the justice of our claims, from being made, by an apparent abandonment of them. Whenever it shall suit you to renew their pressure upon this Government no degree of energy which you may think

---

[37] Count Flemming, Prussian minister at Naples. *Almanach de Gotha,* 1827. 243.

[38] Ficquelmont, Karl Ludwig. Count. (1777-1857). Austrian general, secretary of state, and minister. In 1815, he was sent to Sweden as a special envoy; in 1820, in the same capacity, he was assigned to the courts of Tuscany and Lucca; and in 1821, to the court of Naples. In January 1829, he was charged with a special mission to the Russian court. In 1852, he was made a Knight of the Order of the Golden Fleece. C. Wurzach, *Biographisches lexikon der kaiserthums Oesterreich* . . . Vienna, 1858, IV, 221-223.

proper to display, will be considered either premature, or unnecessary, at any of the great courts now represented in Naples. It is now well understood that the Government of Naples is bound in equity as well as in justice to indemnify our Citizens. The property taken from us is known to have produced a sum, which, if it had been raised by loans at the time, would, at the rate at which the public securities were then negotiated, have fixed an Inscription on the great book of Naples of triple the amount, and which, with the accruing interest, would now constitute a public debt of 15 millions of Dollars, entitled to all the benefits of the recognition guaranteed by the Convention of Casalanza[39] to the debts of the State. I have not suffered our claims, however, to rest merely upon this ground of equity — for it is a view of the subject which concerns us less, than the government of Naples. Our claims would still be valid altho' we should be unable to show, (and this inability is a necessary consequence of the property; having passed out of our hands) that the present Government have been benefited by our losses. He that sues the heirs of a robber, cannot be obliged to explain in what manner the property taken from him had enriched the inheritances. It is sufficient if he prove the robbery committed upon him, and the transmission of the Robber's estate, to the persons from whom he claims. *Potier*[40] [sic] in his work on contracts, recognises it as an undeniable principle, that the claim of him who has been robbed (*spoliation*) should be preferred to every other exhibited against the estate of a robber. I have made use with success of the well known fact, that some of the Vessels taken from us by Murat were still in the naval service of Naples and had been so retained, notwithstanding their having been pointed out to this Government by M[r]. Pinkney as American property: and by that fact, have shown, that this Government has always considered, notwithstanding its official assertion to the contrary, the confiscations of Murat, made in Virtue of Public

---

39 See: Military Convention between the army of Naples and that of Austria at Cassa-Lanzy, the 20th May, 1815. In: George Frederic de Martens, *Nouveau Recueil de Traités d'alliance, de paix, de trève . . . et de plusieurs autres actes servant à la connaissance des relations étrangéres des puissances . . . de l'Europe . . . depuis 1808 jusqu'à présent.* Gottingue, Dietrich, 1871-41. 16 volumes. II, 279. See also note 63, pp. 278-279.

40 Robert Joseph Pothier (1699-1772). French jurist. In 1720, he was appointed judge of the presidential court of Orleans, a post which he held for fifty-two years. See: Pothier, Robert Joseph, *A treatise on maritime contracts of letting to hire.* Translated from the French with notes and a life of the author, by Caleb Cushing. Boston, Cummings and Hilliard, 1821. xxxvii, 170 p.

Decrees, and cloathed in all the usual forms of officiality, and executed by the ordinary authorities, as real acts of the State, which effected a legal transfer of property, and under which, it had acquired and retained; and not as acts of private robbery & piracy under which it would neither hold or acquire without becoming the robber's or the pirate's accomplice.

I left with M^r. Hammett a packet sealed with my arms, containing the papers in support[41] of our claims which were furnished me by the Department of State, with directions to hold them at your disposal. This gentleman has always shown himself disposed to lend to my efforts in favour of our claims the benefit of an intimate acquaintance with the circumstances under which they originated and of his long experience of the character of this Government and People. If it enters into the views of the President to send hereafter a Minister to Naples, I know of no person who could be of more assistance to the object of his Mission, in the capacity of Secretary, than M^r. Hammett, who, whether on account of his zealous and persevering services in the matter of the claims, or of his intelligence and integrity, is deserving the most favourable attentions from the Government. Should he be obliged to leave his consulate, which, no longer produces sufficient emolument to pay an office rent, I would wish to be considered as recommending him for any other more lucrative appointment for which he may apply, and the duties of which, I am sure, he will perform ably and faithfully. I should consider it, however, as a circumstance to be deprecated that one who is so well acquainted with everything relating to our claims against Naples should be constrained to part with them before they are acknowledged.

I have yet some documents[42] intended for your use, which, from want of time, I cannot now enclose, but which I shall take care to transmit to you from this Port. My account as Special Agent at Naples, with an explanatory letter[43] accompanies this dispatch.

---

[41] See Instruction, unnumbered, dated Washington, 12 May, 1825, from the Secretary of State to Mr. Appleton. These papers supporting the claims continued to be passed on from one representative of the United States in Sicily to the next, until the claims treaty eventually was signed. This 'packet,' which Mr. Appleton sealed and gave to Mr. Hammett's care, represents the second such packet we shall find referred to in this series of documents now published in this volume.

[42] It is not clear what documents here are referred to. They may possibly be those forwarded from Stockholm, see pp. 200-201 or the despatch abstracted in footnote 45, p. 200.

[43] See above, p. 189 ff. See also footnote 45, p. 200.

J. J. Appleton to Chev. De Medici

[Enclosure N° 1 with despatch from Leghorn, Aug 30, 1826]

Naples August 18th.1826 (Copy)

I have the honor to announce to your Excellency that my Agency in Naples for the prosecution of the claims of the United States has ceased in consequence of my having been appointed their Chargé d'Affaires in Stockholm.

The President has been greatly disappointed by the rejection of the overtures he had authorised me to make to H.S.M.'s Government for an arrangement of the differences that unfortunately exist between the two Countries. Fixed, however in his determination to hold the Kingdom of Naples responsible for the injuries it inflicted on the Citizens of the United States, he justly considers that responsibility as augmented by every new postponement of the duty it imposes on H.S.M.'s Government to provide for the aggrieved a full indemnity. These ideas have been repeatedly expressed in the interviews I had with your Excellency. It is with me a matter of deep regret that they have not availed in convincing H.S.M.'s Government of the impolicy as well as of the injustice of postponing any longer an adjustment of the points at issue between the two Governments.

It remains that, in compliance with my last Instructions, I should inform Y. E. that the President of the United States will persevere in the prosecution of their claims against the Kingdom of Naples, which is only for the present interrupted by the termination of my Agency to enable me to fulfil his intentions by repairing without loss of time to another post where the service of the United States requires my presence.

Having taken a passage for Leghorn, I must beg Y. E. to furnish me in addition to the Orders you have had the kindness to send me for my baggage, the Passport which I require.

I avail myself of this last occasion to offer to Y. E. with my grateful acknowledgments for the civilities of attentions of which you may made me the object, during my residence at Naples, the reiterated assurance of the profound respect with which I have to remain . . .

J. J. Appleton to H. Clay

Sir.
Stockholm. 5. Nov: 1826 [Despatch, Unnumbered]

I have the honor of enclosing to you a copy and a literal translation[44] of the note by which M^r. Medici has acknowledged the receipt of my letter of the 18th. of August last, announcing to him, the termination of my Agency and the view taken by my Government of its claims against that of Naples —

The Chev. De Medici to J. J. Appleton

[Enclosure with Appleton's to Clay, from Stockholm, Nov. 5, 1826.]

Naples 31. August. 1826[45]

The undersigned, Counsellor and Minister of State, charged ad interim with the Portfolio of Foreign Affairs has received the note by which M^r. Appleton has been pleased to inform him that he had been appointed chargé d'Affaires of the United States near H. M. the King of Sweden and that his Agency in Naples had in consequence ceased.

In presenting to M^r. Appleton his congratulations on this new mark of the confidence of his Government in his talents, the Undersigned has the honor to observe in reference to the sentiments of the President of the United States, to which the said note *alludes,* that as the nature of that affair does not regard the Government of his August Master, he cannot do otherwise than to refer to the verbal communication which he had the honor to make to M^r. Appleton under date of the 26th. of November of the last year: He, however, hastens to assure him, and begs that he would inform the Government of the United States, that H. M. will always avail himself with pleasure of the opportunity, whenever it shall be presented to him, to do what may be gratifying to the Government of the United States, as it is his intention to live with it, for their mutual advantage upon terms of the most perfect intelligence.

---

44 Translation only in this edition. See below, this page.

45 Mr. Appleton wrote to Mr. Brent (Naples, Aug. 20, 1826) requesting that whatever balance was due to him be remitted to Messrs. Baring in London, and, if this was not practicable, to Thomas Perkins of Boston, for Appleton's account. Diplomatic despatches, Naples-Sweden, V, (Feb. 8, 1825-Aug. 15, 1830).

JOHN NELSON[1]

October 24, 1831 to October 15, 1832

EDWARD LIVINGSTON[2] TO JOHN NELSON

Department of State, Washington, 27th Octr 1831. Instruction N° 1

Sir: —

The President having appointed you Chargé d'Affaires U. S. near the Government of His Majesty the King of the Two Sicilies, I herewith transmit to you,

1. Your commission.

2. A letter to the Minister of Foreign Affairs of His Majesty the King of the Two Sicilies, introducing you in your official character.

3. A passport for yourself.

4. A sample of despatch paper.

5. A letter of General Instructions, with documents annexed to it.

Amongst the last mentioned, you will find a letter to Alexander Hammett, Esquire, Consul of the United States at Naples, requesting him to deliver into your hands, a packet, with the private seal of Mr. Appleton, late Special Agent there, and left by him in Mr. Hammett's hands. This packet it is understood from Mr. Appleton's despatch, contains papers in support of our claim for indemnities for spoliations, which were furnished him by the Department of State.

As essential to the object of your mission the following works are furnished you, and are intended to be deposited with, and to form hereafter a part of, the archives of the Legation at Naples. Should you leave that place before the appointment and arrival of a successor, they are, together with the other part of the archives, to be left in the charge of the Consul.

1. Laws of the U. States — 8 vols. and Laws of the 20th and 21st Congress in four pamphlets.

---

[1] John Nelson, of Maryland, commissioned chargé d'affaires Oct. 24, 1831. His appointment was confirmed by the Senate on Jan. 7, 1832. He left this post about Oct. 15, 1832. See also note 55, p. 569.

[2] Edward Livingston, of Louisiana, commissioned Secretary of State by President Jackson May 24, 1831; commissioned as Envoy Extraordinary and Minister Plenipotentiary to France May 29, 1833, and retired that day from the former post.

2. Waites' State Papers—12 volumes.
3. Elliot's Treaties — One volume.
4. Commercial Digest — One volume.

As it does not appear from the records of this office whether any, or, if any, what portion of the public documents and books are among the archives of that mission, you will, as soon as convenient after your arrival at Naples, transmit to the Department a list of such of them as you may find there; and, if found deficient, the set will be completed by a supply which will, for that purpose, be sent to you from this office.[3]

---

[3] The remainder of this despatch comprises the ordinary subjects treated in Personal Instructions to our diplomatic agents abroad, such as uniform, allowance, &c, &c, and corresponds, *mutatis mutandi*, with those addressed to Mr. Hughes, (see below) with the exception of the List of Consuls, for which the following is substituted: "Alexander Hammett, Consul, Naples; Benj.ⁿ Gardner, Palermo; John L., Payson, Messina").

"Salary to commence 24.ᵗʰ Oct. 1831." (Annotation in red ink). The full text of Personal Instructions No. 1, to Christopher Hughes, dated 20th March, 1830. See *Instructions to United States Ministers, XIII,* 90-97. This included, among other matters, the very important instruction expressly forbidding the acceptance by representatives of the United States of any and all presents of pecuniary value, either upon the concluding of a treaty or upon the eve of their departure, the practice itself being stated to be common in Europe, but described as "exceptionable", and especially so in view of the fact that the U. S. Government would not in any way reciprocate such gifts at any time.

The final commentary in these Personal Instructions also is significant (p. 96):—
"The great inconvenience which is daily felt by this Department, in its correspondence with the Diplomatic Agents of the United States in foreign countries from the incomplete state of the archives of our missions abroad, has led to the recent adoption of regulations, which, it is believed, will greatly facilitate the transaction of business, both here and at those missions.

"A practice having prevailed at most or all of them for the Ministers, on their returning home, to withdraw from the Archives the original despatches of this Department, as well as the official communications which they may have received from the Governments to which they are accredited, as also the records of their official correspondence both with their own and the foreign Governments, it is understood that, in no case, henceforward, can this practice be approved by this Department. You will, therefore, have the papers of every description, being of an official character, and connected with the affairs of the mission, kept well arranged, so that easy reference may be had to them in all future time, and a record of your official despatches, letters, and notes, carefully and punctually made, all to be delivered to your successor, or left with the books and other archives of the Legation, for his use, in the hands of such person as may be designated by this Department.

"Minute as these particulars appear, they are found to be very essential to the good order and convenience of business in the Department."

(Signed) M. Van Buren

E. Livingston to J. Nelson

Department of State, Washington, 27th October, 1831. Instruction N° 2

Sir: —

The President has appointed you Chargé d'Affaires of the United States on a special mission to His Majesty the King of the Two Sicilies. The appointment is important to the country as well as to many of its citizens, whose interest is deeply concerned in the negotiation with which you are charged.

The facts on which the demand is based, which you are instructed to make, are simple — have never been disputed — and the right which is deduced from them, is founded on the clearest and best established principles of the laws of Nations. Hence it follows, that your instructions will be precise, but will require in their execution a steadiness of purpose not to be diverted from the object of your mission by arguments, however, plausible, or retarded by the usual resources of diplomatic ingenuity.

These are the facts. In the year 1809, while Joachim Murat was King of Naples, and neutrals were suffering under the operation of the English orders in council on the one hand, and the Berlin and Milan Decrees on the other, which last were enforced in the kingdom of Naples — American commerce was almost banished from the ocean, and few merchants of our nation dared to venture their ships in a trade so hazardous, and subject to so many vexations as that with any country in Europe, which was under the influence of France. Naples was one of these countries — being governed by a member of Napoleon's family, the two decrees before mentioned were strictly enforced in all its ports. The consequence was, that having no shipping belonging to the country, and having banished all neutral ships, the surplus produce of the country could not be exported, and fell in value, and foreign articles of the first necessity, rose to an exorbitant price — the natural and inevitable consequence of despotism was resorted to, combined with a faithlessness to which even despots have seldom had recourse. It appears that, on the 31st. of March, 1809, a modification of the Berlin and Milan decrees was adopted by the Government of Naples, which admitted certain enumerated articles imported in neutral vessels: but finding the Americans reluctant to place themselves in their power under the general promise of protection implied by this decree, a special invitation was made to the merchants of the United States, by a decree dated on the 30th. of June, 1809, and

203

officially communicated to their Consul, by which the Americans, by name, were promised the free disposal of their cargoes, if accompanied by the usual papers, provided they had not been in a port of Great Britain, or had not been visited by her cruisers. As soon as the tenor of this decree could be known, several enterprising merchants of the United States, putting faith in the promises it held out to them, fitted out vessels with rich cargoes for Naples. The first two or three that arrived were fairly dealt by; their cargoes were sold, their returns were taken in, and they were suffered to depart without molestation—but when, tempted by their show of good faith, an additional number had been drawn within their grasp, and the prey became worth taking, the whole were, by order of the King, seized, confiscated, and sold without a colorable pretext. The protests of their masters were disregarded; the complaints of the Consul treated for many months with contemptuous silence; and when at last an answer was given, the robbery was said to be justified by an Act of Congress passed on the 1st of March preceding, which forbade commercial intercourse between the United States and both France and England — an act not relating to Naples in the remotest degree and which having been passed four months before the decree inviting the American vessels into the ports of Naples, could never have justified the seizure of them after they came there. The number of vessels and cargoes thus faithlessly seized and sold was forty-nine,[4] as appears by the schedule (A) which is furnished to you. The masters of some of the vessels were even forced to draw bills on their owners, for the port charges. The crews to the number of several hundred, were left to starve, or be supported by the Consul of the United States, and although promised a conveyance to their country by the Neapolitan Government, the Consul was obliged to charter a vessel, at the expense of eight or ten thousand dollars, to carry them home. These facts are proved by the papers (B & C) delivered to you, and will be further substantiated, if need be, by the testimony of Mr. Hammett, our Consul at Naples ,who will give you every information you may require, to ascertain the amount of the losses of our countrymen, and to estimate the damages that may be due to them. Four other vessels, with their cargoes were also seized and sold, in the year 1812, under the like frivolous pretexts, by the same Government; the history of which last aggression you will find in the correspondence of Mr. Hammett, which is among

---

[4] Later schedules altered the number on the basis of fuller data.

the papers delivered to you with these instructions. This part of the transaction is remarkable from the circumstance that, at the time of this seizure, several other vessels under the American flag were also under prosecution, but the Consul of the United States being convinced that they were English property, and sailing under forged papers, frankly stated that fact to the Neapolitan courts. This open and proper conduct produced the condemnation of those vessels which had fraudulently assumed the use of our flag, but did not save those that were *bona fide* American property — so that their value must be added to the amount of the indemnity claimed. For this indemnity continued claim has been made — first by the Consul, Mr. Hammett, as you will find by his correspondence — afterwards, by the Special Mission of Mr. Pinckney [sic] in 1816 — and, subsequently, by Mr. Appleton, sent out as a special Agent for that purpose in 1825. The proceedings under three missions (D & E) form part of the documents accompanying these instructions. In them you will see that the facts of the seizure and sale of the vessels and cargoes are neither denied nor justified by the restored dynasty — but that they resort to the untenable ground, that the Government of Murat having been a usurpation, and he having dissipated the proceeds of the seizure, the present incumbent of the throne is not liable to our demand of indemnity; and under this pretext they have hitherto evaded the payment to which we are justly entitled.

Under these circumstances, which are here rather adverted to, than detailed, your mission has been resolved upon, for the purpose of making a strong and decisive attempt to procure a just indemnity to our injured citizens, and at the same time assert the honor of our country, which suffers every day that we delay to enforce the demand. The time and circumstances are considered favorable for prosecuting it. The time — immediately after France whose example was followed, and whose authority was relied upon, has yielded to the justice of our claims: — the circumstances — the commencement of a new reign, when the mind of a young Prince may be supposed more susceptible of the feelings of justice than that of his predecessor, soured by the misfortunes inflicted upon him and his family by the former occupant of his throne — and not least, the known determination of the President to suffer no wrong. You will therefore, at a convenient time, after the ceremonies of your presentation, enter on the business of your mission in a manner to convince the

Government of the Two Sicilies that we are in earnest in exacting the full indemnity so long due to our citizens. You will address a note to the Minister, in which you will express the sincere desire that the President feels, to cultivate a good understanding between the United States and His Majesty's Government, to unite them in the bonds of friendship by the means of commercial intercourse on liberal and mutually beneficient terms. You may say that you have powers for this purpose, you may describe, in proper terms, the increasing wealth, population, and importance of our country, and the opening that increase offers for an advantageous and continually augmenting commerce, with a country whose productions and manufactures, differing mainly from ours, would render the interchange of commodities gainful to both. You may exemplify this by referring to the wines, silks, and productions of the fine arts, of Italy for which the demand in the United States would be greatly increased by liberal arrangements of commerce: but you must add, that an indispensable preliminary, is the settlement of the long deferred claims of our merchants — That the President indulges the lively hope that His Majesty will at once perceive and acknowledge that the demand is well founded, and signalize the commencement of his reign by an act of justice, that will at once increase his reputation, secure the good feeling of a friendly power, and in the end promote an intercourse that in a single year will produce more advantage to his people than the whole amount of the indemnity demanded. Anticipate the objection that may be raised to our claim derived from the alleged usurpation of Murat, but say that the liability of the nation to make good all the engagements made; to redress all the injuries done; and to profit by all the just advantages acquired; by its Government *de facto,* is too well established in the code of nations, and too recently and generally exemplified in their practice to be now denied even in argument; — That one nation can only look to the acknowledged and peaceable possessor of the political and civil power in another; — That a contrary doctrine would produce a continual intervention between the independent powers, injurious to the right of self-government in each — a position which the United States will never assume with respect to other nations, nor suffer to be taken with respect to themselves: — That you are therefore, instructed to say, that it is confidently expected by your Government that this ground of opposition to our demand, will no longer be insisted upon, and as, from the documents relating to the affair, no other has ever been advanced, that you are persuaded that His Majesty's Government will be prepared to treat for the long expected indemnity without any unnecessary delay, and enable you to announce to the American merchants that the long period during which they have waited for justice, is at length drawing to a close; and to the Nation, that their reliance on the honor and good faith of His Majesty, has not been disappointed.

Convey, in strong but respectful language, the idea that it was a firm resolve of the President on his entering on the duties of his office, to assert in the most efficacious manner the rights and claims of the merchant class of his fellow-citizens upon foreign governments: that his avowed principle is, to make no demand not founded in justice; but as far as his functions will permit, to submit to no wrong: that he has carefully examined all the circumstances of our demand upon the Neapolitan Government: that the principle upon which it is founded appears to him incontestable; and that therefore your mission has been resolved on to bring it to a close, to the end that, if it should unfortunately happen (an event that he cannot bring himself to anticipate,) either that a satisfactory answer should be denied, or delayed, up to the period necessary for communication to Congress, he may submit to that body a statement of the demand he has made — and afterwards execute whatever measures they may deem it due to the protection of their fellow-citizens, and the honor of the country, to pursue.

This being a negotiation in which, of all our other foreign relations strength of argument and firmness of purpose are to be united with courtesy of manner and language, due as well to others as ourselves, we cannot but congratulate ourselves in your acceptance of a duty so important to private interest as well as public reputation, and which your talents render you so fit to perform.

It is far from the intent of these instructions to tie you down to the use of any particular expression, or even argument. Much must be left (and is confidently left) to your discretion. What is intended strongly to impress upon your mind, and through you upon the Neapolitan Government, is, that the period for procrastination is past — that every diplomatic evasion of the result will be considered as a denial — and that there is a necessity that a communication of the result should be made to Congress who, most probably will take such measures as will ensure full compensation.

207

Thus much for the general principle of the negotiation — should that be conceded, two modes may be suggested for the execution:

1. A mixed Commission, of which you have an example in the convention with Great Britain under the Russian award — and prior to that, in the commission created under Mr. Jay's Treaty.

2. The acceptance of a sum in gross, to be distributed among the claimants by a commission created by an Act of Congress.

The first would be attended with much inconvenience, particularly in a commission made up of men speaking different languages, and liable further to this objection that the rights of the parties will be subject to the decision of chance, where the commissioners disagree, as they most probably would on all material points.

The second, therefore, is to be preferred, and in adjusting the sum, you have strong grounds to go upon to demand a full compensation, — in the unparalleled perfidy and shameless rapacity of the act on which the demand is founded and which is acknowledged on the other part in the warning given by our Consul, by Mr. Pinckney [sic], and by Mʳ. Appleton, that they will be held responsible as well for the delay as for the original wrong, — and in the absence of any counter-claim, or reasonable excuse for the delay of justice — a claim for interest during twenty years, for the injuries offered to the seamen and merchants, and for the expenses to which the Government was put for sending them home — all these, added to the principal, will make a formidable amount, from which you may retrench until you come to a sum that will satisfy the claimants — which ought not to be much, if anything, less than the amount of the ships and cargoes. But you will take every precaution in your power to prevent the admission into your estimate of all unfounded claims, and to reduce exaggerated estimates to their just value.

The expenses of the Government in returning the seamen and supporting them, must be insisted upon as a point of honor from which no deduction is to be made.

Congress will probably remain in session until the first of May — the result of your mission ought to be known to them the beginning of April, and may be sent, if no direct opportunity offers, by one of the vessels of the Mediterranean Squadron, on the first of March at latest. You will not, probably, be at your destination before the latter part of December. You will have, therefore, not much more than two months to obtain a definitive answer, and you must very early in the negotiations take occasion to state that it will be required by that time.

As the sum demanded is large, and may be inconvenient to raise at once, you may agree to receive it in annual instalments, with interest, to the extent of four or six years.

You will of course use the arrangement with France as a precedent the more in point, because the refusal of that Power was heretofore strongly insisted on, as a reason why the Neapolitan Government should not be urged to a settlement. Should the difference between the amount demanded then and the sum afterwards accepted be urged as a reason for making a proportionate deduction in this case, you may answer that France had counter claims to more than the amount of the difference — that some of our claims there, though equally just, did not carry with them the same palpable evidence that supports those now in question.

Should the answer to your demand be a positive refusal, the main business of your mission will be at an end, and you will demand your passports and return.

The Secretary of the Navy will furnish you with an order to the commander of our Squadron in the Mediterranean, to furnish a vessel for your despatches, or your return.

Should, as it is expected, your negotiation for the arrangement of our claims, prove successful, and a disposition be shown to enter into a treaty of commerce, on equal and liberal terms, instructions will be sent out to you for that purpose.

You will be pleased to keep the Department advised of every thing, as well relating to your mission as to the political events in the Peninsula and the Levant, which you may suppose interesting to us; for which purpose it would be advisable to open a correspondence with Commodore Porter, at Constantinople, and our Consuls at Smyrna and the other Mediterranean ports.

A copy of the treaty lately concluded by Mr. Rives, on the subject of our claims, and that part of the correspondence in which he treats the question of the liability of the present for the acts of the former Government, are furnished to you — the first, in order to prove the acquiescence of France in the justice of our claims — the last, to show that the question of liability for the illegal acts of the Imperial Government was insisted on in argument, was made one of the turning points of the claim, and was finally abandoned as untenable.

List of documents accompanying the above despatch.[5]

A. Schedule of Vessels seized and sold.
B. Mr. Hammett's correspondence since 1809, in relation to the claims for spoliation.
C. Translation of such parts of the above as were written in the Italian language.
D. Copy of the Instructions to Mr. Appleton.
E. Extracts from Mr. Appleton's correspondence in relation to his Agency at Naples.
F. Copy of treaty with France of 4th. July, 1831.
G. Extracts from Mr. Rives' correspondence — such parts as bear upon the liability of the present French Government for the acts of the Imperial Government.

J. NELSON TO E. LIVINGSTON

New York Nov. 7. 1831.

My Dear Sir

I received this morning yours of the 4th.[6] covering a note of introduction to the Duke di Regina, who has been kind enough to furnish me with several letters to his friends at Naples. —

The mail did not bring me the promised order from the Secretary of the Navy — This I presume I shall receive tomorrow — Should it be delayed beyond the hour of the Packet's sailing, it may be forwarded on to me at London, under cover to Mr. V. Buren.[7]

In the hurry of my preparations I have omitted to make the *necessary* arrangements (if any were necessary on my part) in regard to newspapers &c. Will you do me the favor to direct

5 These enclosures are not printed herewith. For A-E, see below, Hammett and Appleton chapters *hic opus;* for F, see Miller, *op. cit.,* III, 641-651; For G, see Despatches France. This Instruction, with accompanying documents, was published in: *United States—Documents relating to the convention with Sicily.* In the Senate of the United States. Feb. 9, 1833. Senate Document No. 70. 22nd Congress, 2nd session. 54 pp.

6 This letter of Nov. 4th, is not found. Gennaro Capece Galeota, Duke of Regina (1799-1867). Neapolitan diplomat. He was appointed on Sept. 25, 1828, consul general in the United States of America with residence in Philadelphia. He was appointed Secretary of the Neapolitan Legation at London in 1832; he was consul general at Smyrna in 1840; from 1842 to 1845 he was secretary of the Legation at the Court of the King of Prussia.

7 Martin Van Buren, of New York, was commissioned envoy extraordinary and minister plenipotentiary to Great Britain Aug 1, 1831. He took leave March 19, 1832, his appointment not having been confirmed by the Senate. He was President of the United States of America, Mar. 4, 1837 - Mar. 3, 1841.

such to be sent to me, as may keep me advised of the progress of affairs at Home?

The elections now in progress in this State are exciting no feeling — Here the opposition is regarded as merely nominal.

I expect to sail at 10. to morrow and shall proceed to Naples, by the earliest opportunity which may offer after my arrival in England.

J. NELSON TO E. LIVINGSTON

Paris, Dec.ʳ 25. 1831

My Dear Sir,

Upon my arrival at London, I became satisfied that to proceed to Naples by the way of Gibraltar would expose me to unavoidable delays inconvenient to myself, and injurious to the public interests — This conviction determined me to pursue the route by Marseilles by which I shall be enabled to reach my destination earlier than by any other — I shall set out for Lyons tomorrow, and move onward, with all possible despatch, in the hope of accomplishing my journey in nine or ten days, unless I should be quarantined on my way, which is by no means improbable — I shall not fail to apprize you of my arrival, and promptly to press upon the Neapolitan Government the views of the President.

I have made the inquiries, to which you desired me to direct my attention, and find that the most convenient mode of intercommunication between Washington & Naples will be through the Legation — I would therefore respectfully suggest, that my despatches, papers &c be sent via Paris — No arrangement could be effected at London, by which to secure their prompt transmission.

J. NELSON TO E. LIVINGSTON

Naples. Jany. 31. 1832. [Despatch No. 1.]

Sir,

My letter from Paris, of the 25th of December, will have advertised [sic] you, of the motives which influenced me to decline the route from London by Gibraltar to this place. My determination was, on every account a fortunate one — Our fleet, being at Syracuse, a gratification of the object primarily in

211

view in suggesting an approach by the Mediterranean, would have been impracticable; and as arrival by Sea, in any other than a National Ship, would unavoidably have exposed me to the inconveniences of a vexatious and protracted Quarantine, not likely to be relaxed, because of the purposes which have brought me here —

I left Paris on the 27th of Decr. with the hope of reaching Marseilles in time for the Steam Boat, plying thence to this City; but, not withstanding, that I travelled night and day, I was unfortunate enough to lose the opportunity of her sailing by a few hours — Thus circumstanced, I was subjected to the necessity, of posting the whole route through Nice, Genoa, Pisa and Rome; so that with the most anxious diligence, I was not able to reach my destination 'til late in the night of the 19th last. On the 20th, and 21st I was necessarily occupied in seeking accommodations &c which having provided, I, on Monday, the 23^d. addressed a note to Prince Cassaro,[8] Minister, Secretary of State for Foreign Affairs, apprizing him of my arrival, and asking an interview, that I might present my letter of credence — This was granted me on the 25th; and Sunday the 29th, assigned for the ceremony of my presentation to the King, by whom, on that day, I was received, with much *apparent* cordiality.[9] I have today transmitted to the Secretary of Foreign Affairs, a note, explanatory of the object of my mission (a copy of which accompanies[10] this Despatch) — In this communication, I have pursued my instructions very closely, as you will perceive — I have done so not only because such a course consisted with the dictates of my own judgement, but for the additional and stronger reason, that

8 Antonio Statella, Prince of Cassaro (1785-1864). He was the son of Francesco Maria, the first Prince of Cassaro. Antonio Statella was sent as envoy extraordinary to Sardinia (Decree of Dec. 28, 1815); ambassador extraordinary to Spain (Decree of March 21, 1820); envoy extraordinary and minister plenipotentiary to Vienna (Decree of Oct. 22, 1826). He was minister of foreign affairs *ad interim* from Jan. 26, 1830; minister of foreign affairs from July 27, 1830 to March 20, 1840; finally from March 15 to June 25, 1860, he was president of the Council of Ministers of Francis II. On the Prince of Cassaro, see: Ruggero Moscati, *Il Regno delle Due Sicilie e l'Austria;* G. V. Carignani, *Paolo Versace, la sua vita e le sue missioni. Documenti e ricordi da servire alla storia di Napoli dal 1825 al 1860.* Naples, Tip. Unione, 1872; Ruggero Moscati *Ferdinando II di Borbone nei documenti diplomatici austriaci.* Naples, Edizioni Scientifiche Italiane, 1947. In this publication Cassaro's entire political career is traced and developed from unpublished documents in the Archives of Vienna and Naples.

9 Referring to the "apparent cordiality" the *American Annual Register* (1833, 20) explained it by suggesting that "the ominous name of Nelson for Naples was fraught with recollections of bombarded capitals and exacted indemnities. The great English admiral had been a terror in the Mediterranean as long as Murat and Napoleon were in power." (Perrotta, *op. cit.* 53).

10 See p. 214, below.

the President has, in his message,[11] referred to those instructions as specific, and to be implicitly obeyed.

How this note may be received, it is impossible for one to anticipate — I have not been here long enough to have had opened to me any sources of information, upon which I can rely — I presume that I may expect an answer in a few days. Should it be delayed beyond the week, I shall solicit an interview and endeavor to ascertain the purposes of the Government. The President may be assured, that the negotiation shall be expedited by all the means at my command; and that my inportunities [sic] shall not be spared to bring it to a speedy and successful conclusion —

I am apprehensive, however, that it may not prove practicable to accomplish this object, by the time limited in my instructions viz. the 1st. of March. Should a vessel be sent here, as was contemplated, by the Government, when I left Washington, destined to receive the result of the Negotiation, I shall take the liberty of detaining her for a few days, should circumstances render it expedient. Sailing hence by the 10th of March, she would be enabled to reach the United States, before the adjournment of Congress — This is a subject, however, in regard to which, I am wholly inadvised. — I have never received the promised order from the Navy Department. Of this I apprized you, by my letter from New York — I have thought it probable, that some communication on the subject, may have been had with Commodore Biddle,[12] to whom when a suitable opportunity offers I shall not fail to write for information. — In any event, I shall endeavor to keep you regularly advised of the progress of the Negotiation[13]—

---

[11] In his Third Annual Message, Dec. 6, 1831, President Jackson referred at length to Nelson's mission, adding: "and I feel the fullest confidence that the talents of the citizen commissioned for that purpose will place before him [His Sicilian Majesty] the just claims of our injured citizens in such light as will enable me before your [the Congress'] adjournment to announce that they have been adjusted and secured. Precise instructions to the effect of bringing the negotiation to a speedy issue have been given, and will be obeyed." See Richardson, *Messages of the Presidents*, III, 1113.

[12] James Biddle (1783-1848). Commodore. Born in Philadelphia. In command of the Mediterranean Squadron from 1830 to 1832, during which period he was a commisssioner to negotiate a treaty with Turkey.

[13] The detailing of a war ship to 'bring the treaty home' was sufficiently unusual an occurrence, in view of the rank held by Nelson, to indicate that there was urgency in getting it ratified in the United States. On this point and the state of public opinion at that time, see below, pp. 219-220. There is no intimation in this present despatch that the presence of the American Squadron in the Mediterranean or of this ship 'to convey the treaty home' had any ulterior motive; just what the orders to Commander Biddle may have been, at this time, is not

213

My instructions require me to transmit "a list of such of the public documents and books as may be found among the Archives of this mission." I have the Honor, to inform you, that I have upon strict enquiry ascertained that there are none such here, with the exception of the Documents furnished by the Department of State to Mr. Appleton, which have been delivered to me — Of these I shall transmit a list,[14] as soon as I have the requisite leisure, to prepare one.

Upon examining the Diplomatic trunk, with which I was furnished upon my leaving Washington, I have not been able to find "The Acts of both Sessions of the two last Congress" embraced in the enumeration of Books, contained in my instructions. This omission I regret, since, for the last Tariff Law,[15] I may have occasion and I am not sure that a copy can be procured here. It should be supplied by the first opportunity.

My accounts for the quarter ending in Dec[r]. I have not rendered, because, with the exception of the charge against the Government for my accruing salary, and an unimportant item of incidental expense, there was nothing to adjust —

I have received no communication or package from your department, since leaving Washington.

J. NELSON TO PRINCE CASSARO

[Enclosure with Nelson No. I of 31 Jan: 1832.]

Naples Jany 31, 1832 (Copy)

The undersigned, Chargé d'Affaires of The United States of America, in addressing to the consideration of his Excellency, The Prince of Cassaro, His Sicilian Majesty's Minister, Secretary

---

revealed in the State Department records, since his orders would be Navy Records. Patterson, who succeeded Biddle, felt he had had a share in Nelson's success. (See below, p. 333, note 122).

14 For this list see pp. 237-239.

15 The tariff law referred to here is that approved May 19, 1828, "An Act in alteration of the several Acts imposing duties on imports," 20th Cong. 1st Session, House. See *United States Statutes at Large,* for that Congress and session, Ch. 55, 1828: See also note (a) on page 270, therein, showing that this act of May 19th, 1828 was superseded by that of July 14, 1832, ch. 227, "An act to alter and amend the several acts imposing duties on imports." Two subsequent acts, of Mar. 2, 1833, and of Aug. 30, 1842, further modified the tariffs on imports. (The text of the act first mentioned above, may also be found in *Register of Debates in Congress,* 20th Cong. 1st Session, House, Appendix p. xv.).

214

of State for Foreign Affairs, a frank explanation of the duties, with which he is charged by the Government he represents, begs leave to reiterate the opinions already tendered of the unfeigned desire, of the President of the United States, to cultivate the most cordial good understanding, with his Majesty's Government; and, to express his Earnest solicitude, that the differences existing between the two nations may be so happily adjusted, as, to remove every just cause of irritation, calculated in the least degree, to disturb the harmony of the relations, which their mutual interests require, should subsist between them.

Under the guidance of these sentiments, ardently cherished, The President of The United States, has given it in charge to the Undersigned, to invite the attention of his Majesty's Government, to a consideration of the means of ensuring an extended commercial intercourse, upon mutually beneficial terms, between the Kingdom of the two Sicilies and the United States; and, for the furtherance of an object, so promotive of the reciprocal interests of both Nations, has invested the Undersigned with full power, to confer and treat with your Excellency, or such other person or persons, as may be designated for that purpose, by his Sicilian Majesty.

The President is persuaded, that, there is much in the relative condition of the Two Sicilies, and the United States, to invite to liberal commercial arrangements between them. Varying as they essentially do, in their productions and manufactures; yielding scarcely any thing in common, likely to bring their interests into competition or collision; an interchange of their respective commodities, upon liberal terms, could not fail to conduce to the advancement, of their reciprocal interests.

For the wines, fruits, silks, and works of Art of the Sicilies, your Excellency is aware, a considerable demand already exists, in the United States. With the advance of population and the accumulated means of enjoyment, this demand must necessarily proportionably, increase. That population now amounts to thirteen millions, and is augmenting with an unprecedented rapidity; is growing in wealth, and political importance; and animated by a spirit of enterprize, which impels it, in the pursuit of fair commercial advantages, to search the most distant seas. — To this spirit, the surplus productions of His Majesty's Kingdom, offer the ready means of extensive gratification; which, under the encouragement of judicious arrangements, could not fail, to realize to his Majesty's people, as well as to the citizens of the United States, the richest commercial benefits.[16]

Deeply impressed, however, as is the President with the conviction of the value of well adjusted commercial stipulations between the Gov[t]. of the Two Sicilies and the United States; and earnestly desirous, as he sincerely is, of subserving an interest so important, he, nevertheless, deems it an indispensable preliminary, to any negotiation in regard to it, that a satisfactory and just indemnity should be accorded by his Sicilian Majesty, to the American Merchants, whose vessels and cargoes were sequestered and confiscated in the ports of his Majesty's Kingdom, during the years, Eighteen Hundred and Nine, Eighteen Hundred and Ten, and Eighteen Hundred and Eleven —

In the discharge of the functions devolved on him, as their Executive Chief Magistrate, by the American people, the President of the United States has felt it to be a duty of primary and imperative obligation, respectfully, but decidedly, to assert upon all Foreign Governments the well founded claims of the Mercantile class of his Fellow Citizens. Acting upon the principle, repeatedly and frankly avowed to the world, of making no demand, not founded in justice, and, as far as may depend upon his agency, of submitting to no violation of the rights of his Fellow Citizens, he has carefully investigated the nature of the claims now preferred; and being satisfied upon a minute examination of all the circumstances with which they are connected, that the principle upon which they are based, is incontestable, has instructed the Undersigned to invite the prompt attention of his Majesty's Government, to a consideration of the subject; deeply interesting to a respectable class of American Citizens, and involving, in the view of the President, the Honor and dignity of the United States.

To the nature and history of these claims, considerable in number and amount; or to the acts of the Neapolitan Government, upon which they are founded, the Undersigned does not feel it incumbent on him, at this time, particularly to advert — They have been heretofore, repeatedly, brought to the view of the Sicilian Government, and are doubtless well understood by your Excellency — They are claims, founded upon admitted

---

[16] The commerce and navigation statistics of the United States in those years gave separate figures for Sicily and for Italy and Malta, but no separate entry for Naples. It is, therefore, not possible to estimate the value of the imports and exports from the Two Sicilies. See United States, House of Representatives. Treasury Department, 22nd Congress, 1st Session. Document No. 230.

216

wrongs; inflicted upon the innocent confidently reposing on the official assurances of the Neapolitan Government; allured within its territorial jurisdiction by solemnly proclaimed pledges of protection; and then, treacherously sacrificed to its pressing wants, in violation of every principle, of good faith and common honesty — Against these flagrant outrages upon the clearest rights of its citizens, the Government of the United States, by its agents, at the time of their perpetration, earnestly remonstrated; and has since kept the Government of The Two Sicilies, constantly apprized, that it should insist upon the render of a full reparation. For more than twenty years, which have elapsed, since the inflictions of the injuries complained of, all redress has been withheld— The President of the United States indulges the lively hope, that the period for their settlement has at length arrived; that His Sicilian Majesty will perceive that the demands are well founded; and that he will signalize his reign by an act of justice, that will redound to his own fame; secure the lasting good feeling of a friendly power; and lead to an intercourse eminently beneficial to his people; an intercourse, whose results will realize advantages, greatly transcending the indemnity now demanded.

The Undersigned is not unapprized of the objection, to the gratification of the claims now preferred, heretofore urged by the Government of the Two Sicilies, founded upon the alleged usurpation of Murat; which has been supposed to dispense it, from the obligation to make the reparation required — But the undersigned, without at this time entering into a detailed examination of the satisfactory reasoning, by which, it is vindicated, is persuaded, that the principles of the liability of the Nation to effectuate the engagements made; to redress the injuries inflicted; and to profit by all the just advantages acquired, by its Government *de facto* is too broadly asserted by all writers upon National Law, and too recently and generally, exemplified in the practice, of the Governments of Europe to be now called in question — Independently of all authority, it is verified and sustained by the most obvious considerations of Natural[17] Equity. The citizens of one Nation, in their intercourse with those of another, cannot be required to look beyond the acknowledged possession of the political and civil power, a contrary doctrine,

---

[17] In the original this word could be read either "national" or "natural." The second stroke of the 'n' in the final syllable 'nal' is barely formed, and there would seem to be better justification for judging that letter to be an 'n' than an 'r'. However, the sense is perhaps stronger with the word 'natural'."

introduced into the international code would be pregnant with the most fearful consequences; fatal alike to private interests, and the internal tranquillity of Nations; provocative of a continual intervention between independent powers, essentially subversive of the right of self-government — To a principle so radically vicious, the Government of the United States can never yield its sanction. It will never consent that it should be made applicable to its own interests; nor will it assume it, in regard to other nations —

Under the influence of these views, the undersigned is especially instructed, to communicate to the Government of his Sicilian Majesty the confident expectation of the President of the United States, based upon a full reliance on the enlightened wisdom of his Majesty's councils, that this ground of opposition to the demands now renewed, will no longer be insisted on; but that his Majesty's Government will be prepared, promptly to repair, the injuries, which have been so patiently endured; and for which a just indemnity has been so long withheld.

J. NELSON TO E. LIVINGSTON

(Unnumbered despatch, marked "private," sent with despatch No. 1, of same date).

Naples, Jany 31, 1832.

My Dear Sir,

I have hastily prepared the despatch[18] which you will receive with this, with a view to avail myself of an opportunity which offers by an American gentleman going direct to Paris, via Marseilles. I send it to Mr. Rives,[19] who will forward it, by the earliest packet. The mails are subjected to so unspairing a scrutiny by the police officers of this Gov^t., that I cannot hazard a communication with you, through their means —

My instructions authorize me to draw from my accruing salary and the incidental expenses of the Mission upon the U. S. Bankers, but they do not designate them by name. Am I to draw on Paris or London? I should prefer the latter, because my private funds have been deposited with Baring Bros. & Co. Have the

18 Despatch No. 1, Jan. 31, 1832.
19 William C. Rives, of Virginia, was commissioned envoy extraordinary and minister plenipotentiary to Paris, on April 18, 1829. He took leave on Sept. 27, 1832.

218

goodness to advise me on this subject and furnish me with the necessary letter of credit, if any be required.

I am endeavoring to possess myself of accurate information of the Statistics of The Sicilies, and shall avail myself of the earliest opportunity, after it shall have been obtained, to transmit it.

J. NELSON TO E. LIVINGSTON

Naples Febry 13, 1832 [Despatch No. 2]

Sir,

I had the Honor on the thirty first of January of transmitting to you, a copy of my communication, of the same date to the Prince of Cassaro, His Sicilian Majesty's Minister, Secretary of State for Foreign Affairs, explanatory of the objects of the Mission with which I have been charged. Having received no reply, I, on the ninth Instant, addressed to him a note, asking a conference, at such time and place, as his convenience might suggest. To this application the Prince responded on the morning of the Eleventh, inviting me to an interview at the Foreign Office at two o'clock, of the same day. Thither, I accordingly repaired —

The Prince opened the conference by observing that he had received my note of the thirty first of January, which he had laid before the King, who had directed it to be submitted to a council of Ministers — That he hoped the Council would soon assemble, and that I might expect a reply, when their deliberations upon the subject of the demands preferred by me were closed — That, if I desired it, he would officially acknowledge the receipt of my communication; but that he could not respond to its contents, 'til he had received the instructions of the Council.

I replied, that I did not care to receive a formal acknowledgement of the due delivery of my note, since his verbal assurance to that effect was satisfactory. That my principal object in seeking the interview, with which he had honored me, was to impress upon His Majesty's Government a sense of the importance of a prompt decision upon the demands preferred. That this subject of contestation had been long pending, between the Sicilian Government and that of the United States — That it was necessary it should be brought to a speedy close. That with a view to its final adjustment, my mission had been resolved on, in the confidence that this third diplomatic effort, originated

219

by the Government of the United States, at considerable inconvenience and expense, would avail, to the satisfactory settlement of the differences existing between the two Nations — That should this reiterated application for a just indemnity for the aggravated injuries inflicted upon the American Merchants prove fruitless, there was no reason to believe that it would be renewed. That the citizens whose property had been rapaciously wrested from them, were entitled to the efficient protection of their Government and that their interests required, that the gratification of the claims should be no longer postponed — I expressed my entire confidence in the sense of justice of His Majesty and his councils; and my firm persuasion that a candid examination of the principles upon which our demands were based, would be followed by a full reparation — I stated distinctly, and in emphatic tho' respectful terms, that it was my especial duty to press for an early and decisive reply to the demand I had made. That the State of public opinion in the United States, imperatively required, that the subject should be definitely disposed of — That the President in his message to Congress, had promised the communication of the result of the negotiation, with which I was charged, to that body, during the present session. That, to enable him to fulfill that pledge, I should despatch that result, a letter favorable or otherwise, to the United States, by the sixth or seventh of March. That by that time, therefore, it was indispensable that the views of His Majesty's Government should be understood; to the end, that the Congress of the United States, if called on to deliberate upon the subject, might be possessed of the fullest information, upon which to found the measures which their wisdom might suggest as proper to pursue.

In the course of the conference, I referred to the circumstances connected with the previous negotiations upon this subject; to the recognition of the principle of responsibility by the different governments of Europe; and more particularly to the example of France, whose views had been the topic of discussion between Mr. Appleton and the Chevalier De Medici, in Eighteen Hundred and Twenty five — The Prince here remarked that the communications of the Chevalier De Medici to Mr. Appleton upon this subject, must have been verbal ones, as the records of his department, which had been examined, contained no evidence of any that were in writing. I replied that they were partly verbal and partly in writing. He enquired if I had the copies of any notes from De Medici to Mr. Appleton — I answered yes, of one — He asked if I would object to his seeing it — I replied, That I should not; That in the pursuit of a just object, I had no concealments to practice, and that a copy should be furnished, for his inspection. That altho' it did not, in terms, rest the course of the Sicilian Government upon that which should be pursued by France, yet that the pendency of the discussion with the French Government, was seized on by the Chev^r. De Medici, as a reason for postponing the consideration of the American claims; and that, connected with his verbal assurances, unquestionably given to Mr. Appleton, it did, in my view, commit the Govt. of His Majesty to a favorable consideration of our demands.

The Prince then remarked that he had not seen a copy of our Treaty with France,[20] nor did he understand exactly its character, but he had no doubt that it could be procured from Paris — To obviate this pretext for delay (for such I think under the circumstances it was not uncharitable to consider it) I apprized him of my having a copy, which I offered to communicate to him, in confidence — He begged that I would do so, and said that he would make known my solicitude for an early reply to the King — and, that I might expect it in the course of the next week. —

Thinking the opportunity a favourable one, to obviate any difficulties of a financial character which might be suggested, I referred to the supposed pecuniary embarrassments of the Sicilian Government and expressed the willingness of the Government of The United States to make such reasonable arrangements in regard to the payment of our claims, should their justice be recognized, as least heavily to press upon his Majesty's treasury — This suggestion the Prince said, he would communicate to the King —

He manifested much anxiety to know, what commercial arrangements I was authorized to propose — To his earnest and

---

[20] The United States negotiated with France, on July 4, 1831, a treaty of claims and of duties on wines and on cottons, etc. (For text see Miller, *op. cit.* III, 641-651). With this despatch No. 2, Feb. 13, 1832, Nelson sent to Livingston a copy of his (Nelson's) note to Cassaro, Naples, Feb. 13, 1832, enclosing "a copy of a convention between France and the United States, as agreeable to the wish expressed by His excellency at the interview." It would seem that this was done to register at once, with his government at home, the fact that Prince Cassaro had made this expressed request for the text of the treaty with France. Nelson's note, sent with the copy of the treaty with France, will be found, below, p. 223, March 12th. The "enclosure," — viz. the treaty text itself, is omitted as not directly germane to our topic. (See also note 22, p. 224).

repeated enquiries upon this subject, I replied, that in the present stage of the negotiation I could not confer with him, in regard to commercial interests— That the settlement of the reclamations of the American Merchants, for the confiscation and sale of their vessels and cargoes, was a sine qua non; an indispensable preliminary; and that I had so explicitly assured His Majesty's Government, in my note of the thirty first of January —

Recurring to the subject of our claims he remarked, that he supposed I was aware, that the proceeds of the sales of the American property had been applied by Murat, to his private purposes — I answered that I knew nothing about their application; nor did I deem it at all material, in regard to the claims of the American Merchants, to ascertain how those proceeds had been appropriated — That I was prepared, I thought, to satisfy him that the validity of our demands could in no wise depend upon the result of such an enquiry — That the property of our citizens had been taken from them under the authority of official decrees, executed by public officers, acting in the name and under the sanction of the Neapolitan Government — The Prince here interposed the remark, that he was not prepared to enter upon the discussion of the question, nor should he be, 'til he had received the advice of the Council — I replied, that I should be ready, at all times, to confer with him, and in answer to an enquiry as to the extent of our claims, stated my willingness, upon his application, to afford him such information, as I possessed, of the amount, upon the payment of which, the Government of the United States, felt it to be due, to the just demands of its Citizens, to insist —

Having accomplished the object for which this interview was sought, and received a renewed assurance, that the reply to my note should not be postponed beyond the next week, I took my leave —

The promised reply, I shall doubtless receive in a few days; from the tone and tenor of which an inference, as to our prospects, may be safely deduced — At present, I have no information of the views of this Government, upon which to found an opinion —

E. LIVINGSTON TO J. NELSON

Department of State, Washington, 25th Feb.ʸ 1832. Instruction N° 3.

Sir: —
Your letter, dated Paris, 25ᵗʰ. December, 1831, has been received. Your early arrival in London was known by a letter from Mr. Van Buren, and your detention in or between those capitals, which we are convinced must have been unavoidable, is, nevertheless, a subject of some regret, considering the very short time allowed for your negotiation. But the President relies with confidence on your known diligence and talent, to make up for any inevitable delays which the prosecution of your journey may have presented. He approves of the change of route you have adopted, and hopes to hear favorable account of your mission before the rising of Congress. The important matters before them, I think, will render an adjournment before the latter days of May highly improbable.

I think I neglected to send to you, at New York, the order from the Navy Department to the commander of the Mediterranean Squadron, to despatch a vessel for the United States whenever you should direct it. That omission is now supplied.

No addition to, or alteration in, your instructions has suggested itself since your departure, except the circular which you will herewith receive.

You will have the goodness to inform Mr. Hammett that his letters of the 24ᵗʰ. August and — October, 1831, have been received — that, the President duly appreciates his services, and that application has been made to Congress for the passage of a law that will put it in his power to compensate them.

J. NELSON TO E. LIVINGSTON

Naples March 12, 1832. [Despatch No. 3]

Sir,
In my despatch of the thirteenth of February[21] (a duplicate of which is herewith transmitted) I had the honor to communicate the substance of a conversation, which I had held with the Prince of Cassaro in an interview, with which I had been favored on the Eleventh. In compliance with his expressed wish, and my own promise, I, on the Monday following, furnished him with a copy

---

21 See above, p. 221, footnote 20.

223

of our convention with France (a Transcript of my note covering the Treaty, you will find among the papers accompanying this despatch, marked *A.*) Not having received the reply to my communication of the thirty first of January which had been explicitly promised I availed myself of a casual meeting, on the evening of the Eighteenth of February, at the apartments of the King, to remind The Prince of Cassaro of his engagement; and to express my regret that it had not been fulfilled. He evidenced a good deal of embarrassment, earnestly assuring me, to use his own language, that it was not his fault; that the President of the Council had not convened that body, as soon as he had expected, but that it would assemble on Monday (the 20th) when the answer to our demands should certainly be communicated to me. I expressed my anxious desire to receive it, and my apprehension, that longer delay might be regarded by the Government of the United States, as indicative of an indisposition in His Majesty's councils, to do justice to our Merchants; and coerce it, to resort to measures which it was solicitous, if possible to avoid. This last assurance like that tendered in the conference of the Eleventh of February remains unredeemed —

On the Twenty fourth of February, I received from the Prince of Cassaro a note dated on the Twenty second[22] (of which *B* is a copy) acknowledging mine of the thirteenth — In this communication, as you will perceive, he does not even refer to my note of the thirty first of January — This circumstance, connected with others, unofficially communicated to me by those in whom I have confidence, satisfied me of the indisposition of this Government to enter upon the discussion of our claims, and determined me to address a second and strong application, in an official form, to the Secretary for Foreign Affairs. In pursuance of this resolution, I transmitted to The Prince of Cassaro on the Twenty seventh of February, a note of which *C* is a transcript — I confidently hoped that this earnest appeal would have entailed the reply which had been, before, twice promised; and which, looking to the nature of the demands and the opportunity for their thorough investigation, which has been afforded, this Government cannot be unprepared to furnish — In this expectation,

22 On Feb. 22, 1832, the Prince of Cassaro wrote to Mr. Nelson acknowledging the receipt of a copy of the convention between the United States and France. Neither the *note* of Prince Cassaro, nor the treaty text are here included, because only indirectly related to the negotiations with the Two Sicilies through Prince Cassaro's interest in the text of the treaty with France. Both texts are in the original Records volumes in United States National Archives.

however, I have been disappointed. I am still without an answer, either to my note of the thirty first of January or to that of the twenty seventh of February.

Notwithstanding these repeated dis-appointments, it was my design, upon the approach of the period limited by my last note to the Prince of Cassaro to have sought a second personal interview with him, when to my utter surprize I was informed, that he had left Naples for Sicily where he was likely to be detained for some time. Of his intention to be absent from this City, I had not received the slightest intimation; and altho other considerations are alledged to have influenced his visit to Palermo, there is good reason for the belief that the opportunity it afforded, of avoiding the necessity, with some shew of excuse, of answering the demands I had preferred, was not entirely unappreciated — Information derived from various sources, satisfies me, that it is the policy of this Government in reference to the claims of our Merchants, to postpone the negotiation as long as practicable — By deferring the discussion, it hopes to render impossible the anticipated action of Congress upon the subject, during its present session; and to place itself in a position, which will enable it to avail itself of any circumstances, which may occur, to justify the further postponement of its consideration hereafter — That it will gratify our demands, in the end, is generally supposed, but that it will put off the evil day, as long as consists with its own security, I have every reason to believe —

Letters from Commodore Biddle, having apprized me of the destination of The Ontario, for this port, I resolved to make another effort, to ascertain the view of the Sicilian Government upon the subject of our claims and accordingly, on the ninth Instant addressed to the Duke of Gualtieri,[23] President of the Council, to whom, the Portfolio of the Department of State for Foreign Affairs, has been committed, during the absence of The Prince of Cassaro, a communication of which I transmit a copy marked D — The Ontario arrived on the same evening — On the next day, I received a note, bearing date on the ninth, of which E is a copy — It is entirely evasive of my enquiry — My desire was to know whether a reply to my notes of the thirty first of January and twenty seventh of February might be expected in

---

[23] Don Carlo Avarna. Duke of Gualtieri. (1757-1836). The title of Duke of Gualtieri was bestowed on Bartolomeo Avarna in 1797 for services rendered to Ferdinand I. Don Carlo was a member of the Pari of the Kingdom, Councilor of State, Minister of Sicilian Affairs from June 5, 1822 to June 16, 1824. He was appointed President of the Council of Ministers on Dec. 23, 1831.

time for transmission by the vessel whose arrival I anticipated —
The answer is, perhaps (forse) it may be furnished, before the
return of The Prince of Cassaro from Sicily.

The President, I trust, will be satisfied that no proper effort
has been unessayed by me, to meet his expectations and to bring
this negotiation to a speedy issue. That my exertions have failed
to accomplish the object of my mission within the period contemplated by my instructions, I most deeply regret. I have every
confidence, however, that this failure will be readily referred
to its true cause; the predetermination of this Government, to
avoid the discussion of our claims, as long as it *may*, and to pay
only when it is convinced, that it *must*.

I shall, of course, continue to press for the determination of
this Government, whose reply, when received I shall avail myself
of the earliest opportunity, to transmit to you.

Very soon after my arrival, I wrote to Commodore Biddle,
who was then, as he is now, at Syracuse, to ascertain whether he
had received orders from the Navy Department, to furnish me
with a vessel, for the conveyances of the despatches, which my
instructions, require me to transmit to the United States. His
reply under date of the fourteenth of February apprized me that
he had received none, but that my assurance that they were
intended to be forwarded was to him a sufficient justification, for
detaching a ship for the purpose; and that he shall despatch one
to this Port, early in March — The Ontario has accordingly
arrived — I have had some doubts, whether, in the present stage
of the negotiation, I ought to engage her in the service, to which
she is destined. But, after the maturest reflection, looking to the
nature of my instructions, and the utter impracticability, of putting you in possession of the information, now communicated, by
any other means within my control, I have been conducted to the
conclusion that the public interests require that she should sail —
I expect her to leave Naples to morrow, and trust that she will
arrive in the United States sufficiently early to accomplish the
purpose for which she is despatched, and to leave time for
Congress, before its adjournment (should the President[24] deem
it proper to invoke the aid of the Legislature in behalf of the
claimants) to adopt such measures, as may be calculated, to
ensure to our injured citizens adequate redress —

---

24 James Richardson. *Messages and papers of the Presidents,* cites no presidential message regarding the claims against Sicily during the period Jan. 1, 1832-
Dec. 17, 1832.

Every thing is quiet in Italy; and notwithstanding the occupation by France and Austria of different portions of the Papal territories,[25] it is confidently believed, that nothing is likely to occur, to disturb its repose.

J. NELSON TO PRINCE CASSARO

(Enclosure "C" with Despatch No. 3).

Naples February 27, 1832.

The Undersigned Chargé D'Affaires of The United States of America, takes leave to invite the attention of His Excellency The Prince of Cassaro, His Sicilian Majesty's Minister Secretary of State for foreign Affairs, to the note which he had the Honor to address to the consideration of His Excellency on the thirty first of January, in relation to the reclamations formed by the Government of the United States against that of the Two Sicilies, for the seizure, confiscation and sale, of the vessels and cargoes of the American Merchants, by the Neapolitan Government during the years Eighteen Hundred and ten, Eighteen Hundred and eleven, and Eighteen Hundred and Twelve.

In again pressing this subject upon the consideration of His Excellency The Prince of Cassaro, the undersigned is impelled by a sense of what is due alike to the Government he represents and that to which he has been accredited; by the sincere desire, that His Sicilian Majesty should be distinctly possessed of the views and expectations of the President of the United States, in regard to these reclamations; preferring as the Undersigned does, to expose himself to the possible imputation of importunity, rather than to leave the slightest room for misapprehension, as to the objects and precise purposes of the Mission with which he has been charged —

Of the cordial disposition of The United States to maintain and cultivate with the Two Sicilies, the relations of Amity and Concord; and of their settled repugnance to the adoption of any measures calculated to interrupt the interchange of those offices

---

25 The liberals in the Papal States staged a violent demonstration against foreign domination, and hoisted the flag of democracy and nationalism. Similar disturbances broke out in Parma and Modena. Soon, however, Austrian troops reestablished the old order, but Louis Philippe, to prevent Austrian domination, stationed a French garrison in Ancona which remained, despite the protests of the Pope and of the liberals, until 1838. See Cicognani's despatch to Martin Van Buren, dated Rome, Feb. 21, 1831 in Stock, *Consular Relations*, etc. 33-34; 34n.

of good Understanding, of which their mutual interests prompt the liberal indulgence, no clearer exemplification could be afforded, than that which is furnished by the course they have pursued, in relation to the demands, now preferred.

Of the justice of those demands, the Government of the United States has never doubted. It has at all times been impressed with the firmest conviction, that they rested upon principles of public law, so obviously clear, as to command themselves to general sanction; and so cardinally important of observance in the intercourse of Nations, as to render it a common interest, that they should be universally acknowledged — This conviction, always clear, The Prince of Cassaro is aware, has been recently fortified and strengthened by the recognition of its justice by some of the leading powers of Europe, who have yielded to a sense of their obligation to repair injuries inflicted upon American Commerce, under circumstances infinitely less aggravated, than those which give character to the Neapolitan confiscations. For in some of the cases alluded to, the wrongs inflicted and for which redress has been stipulated, were effected through the instrumentality of decrees, wearing, at least, the semblance of regularity, however really violative of the well defined rights of neutral Commerce, while those, for the reparation of which the Government of The United States appeals to that of His Sicilian Majesty, were wantonly committed, in lawless disregard not only of those rights, but of all the conceded obligations of good faith and National Honor.

More than twenty years have elapsed since the perpetration of these flagrant outrages — Within that period, the Government of the United States, has originated three Special Missions, at considerable inconvenience and expense to ask at the hands of the Sicilian Government a reasonable redress. Two of these have proved fruitless. That the efforts made in Eighteen Hundred and Sixteen and Eighteen Hundred and Twenty Six should not have availed to the adjustments to which they were directed, was regarded by the Government of The United States, in view of the principles in contestation, not only as a subject of profound regret, but of just and unaffected surprize. To the history of those negotiations; or to the causes of their failure to effectuate the arrangement contemplated in their institution, it is foreign to the design of the Undersigned at this time particularly to refer — They are adverted to, solely, as illustrative of the anxious desire, unceasingly manifested by the Government of The United

228

States, by patient and peaceful appeals, to the sense of justice of that of the Two Sicilies, to remove those causes of dissension between the two nations, which have already engendered strong feelings of irritation; and which, if suffered longer to exist, it may be feared will fester into an acrimony fatally destructive of the harmony of the relations which it is the interest, as it should be the aim of both parties to preserve — To obviate a result so much to be deprecated, and to which The President of The United States cannot look but with real concern, the Undersigned has been charged with the duty of recalling to the recollection of His Sicilian Majesty's Government, the well-grounded causes of complaint of the American Merchants, and once more, to seek the atonement which has been so long and injuriously withheld.

In the discharge of this duty in that spirit of respectful frankness, which it is the unaffected wish of the Undersigned to maintain in his intercourse with His Sicilian Majesty's Government, he cordially disclosed to The Prince of Cassaro in the interview, with which he was honored on the Eleventh instant, the pressing considerations which enjoined it upon him, to urge his Excellency to a prompt reply to his note of the thirty first of January — In answer to this communication, the Undersigned was gratified to receive the assurance, that the Views of the Government of His Sicilian Majesty would be made known to him during the following week. That assurance for reasons no doubt abundantly sufficient, to justify the delay of which the undersigned does not wish to complain, has not been fulfilled — The reply has not even yet been received. Thus circumstanced the Undersigned deems it necessary to repeat, That to the demands, which it has been the duty of the Undersigned to prefer, the President of The United States, indulges the expectation that a decisive reply will be promptly returned; That to enable him to fulfill his intentions and to meet the expectations of the American claimants, it is necessary, that the Undersigned be apprized of the determination of His Majesty's Government, by a very early day in the next month, when it will become his duty to despatch the result of this renewed application to The United States — That this is indispensable to the end, that, should the Government of the Two Sicilies unfortunately persist in withholding the demanded reparation, The President of The United States may be enabled to redeem the pledge contained in his last annual message by submitting its refusal to Congress, now in session, to whom, under the circumstances, it will belong, in the exercise of their Constitutional discretion, to prescribe the measures to be pursued, for the vindication of the violated rights of their Fellow Citizens, and the maintenance of the Honor and dignity of the Nation.

The undersigned avails himself of the occasion to reassure the Prince of Cassaro of his readiness at all times, to enter into such explanations of the views of the Government of the United States, in relation to the claims in question, as it may be desirable to the Government of his Sicilian Majesty to receive; and in conference or more formal discussion, to expose the principles upon which they are based, and by which their justice and Equity are vindicated — And he begs leave to reiterate the expression of his earnest hope that his Majesty's Government, bringing to the consideration of these demands, the spirit of candor and justice, by which it is distinguished, will perceive the propriety of according to the suffering victims of wrongs of unparalleled atrocity, a full, fair and satisfactory remuneration.

J. NELSON TO THE DUKE OF GUALTIERI

(Enclosure "D" with Despatch No. 3)

Naples, March 9, 1832.

Sir,

I had the Honor, on the thirty first of January last, to address to his Excellency, The Prince of Cassaro, an official note, explanatory of the objects of my Mission to the Court of His Majesty, the King of the Two Sicilies. On the eleventh of February, I was informed by him, that my note had been laid before His Majesty, who had directed it to be submitted to a council of Ministers; and that I might expect a communication of the views of The Sicilian Government upon the subject, to which it referred, in the course of the following week. On the Twenty seventh of February, I took the liberty, in a second official note, to remind The Prince of Cassaro of the assurance I had received, and, that it had not been fulfilled; and, to suggest the urgent considerations which constrained me earnestly to press for an immediate reply to the demands, which I had preferred — I regret to say, that to neither of these notes, have I received an answer.

I beg leave now to inform your Excellency, that I am in the expectation of the arrival at this port, in the course of today, of an American vessel, which it will be my duty, forthwith to despatch to the United States; That it is my design to detain her, only so long as absolutely necessary for the preparation of my official communications to my Government; and that the principal object of her return to America, is to convey to the President and Congress of the United States, information of the progress of the negotiations committed to my charge.

Permit me to enquire, whether I may indulge the hope that the decision of His Majesty's Government, in relation to the claims of the American Merchants, will yet be communicated to me in such time, as to enable me to avail myself of the present opportunity, to transmit it to the United States.

To His Excellency
   The Duke of Gualtieri
      Counsellor of State, President of the Council of Ministers
      &c &c &c

THE DUKE OF GUALTIERI TO J. NELSON
(Enclosure "E" with Despatch No. 3)

Naples, March 9th 1832.

Family affairs of great importance, obliged the Prince of Cassaro, Minister Secretary of State for foreign Affairs of his Sicilian Majesty, to go for a few days to Palermo, at the moment he was preparing to answer the notes addressed to him by Mr. Nelson, Chargé D'Affaires of the United States of America in date of the 31st. of Jany. — and the 27th. of Febr^y. last. The Undersigned counsellor Minister of State, President of the Council of Ministers who has been entrusted by the King, with the Portfolio of Foreign Affairs, during Prince Cassaro's short absence, deems it his duty to acquaint Mr. Nelson with this circumstance and to assure him that had it not been for the above named unforeseen occurrence the solicitude he expressed in his second note for a consideration of the first, would have been at this time fully satisfied. The undersigned must at the same time assure the Chargé D'Affaires in relation to the esteemed note he has done him the honour to address him under this date that such answer shall be made to him without delay and *perhaps* even before the return of Prince Cassaro. In the meantime he avails himself of this opportunity to renew to Mr. Nelson the assurances of his particular consideration.

For the Minister, Secretary of State for Foreign Affairs, absent,
      (Signed) The Duke of Gualtieri

231

J. Nelson to E. Livingston

Naples March 12, 1832.[26] (Despatch, Unnumbered, Private)

My Dear Sir,

My despatches, which have just been made up, will apprize you of every thing material, in relation to the negotiation which has been entrusted to me — Various suggestions have been made to me, as to the course which this Government is disposed to pursue, but they are so contrarient as to entitle them to little consideration, notwithstanding that they are derived from persons likely to be informed of its views and purposes — It is supposed by many (for the negotiation is a subject of general speculation) that it will propose a reference of subsisting differences to some third power — Should such an offer be made, in the absence of instructions upon the subject, I should feel much embarrassed — I could not accede to it, and should not choose to assume the responsibility of rejecting it, without referring it to the consideration of the President. I should be pleased to be possessed of the views of the administration in reference to such a proposition, in order that, if tendered, I may be enabled promptly to accept or decline it —

My own settled persuasion is that a reply to my notes will be delayed, as long as possible, and when given, that it will be so framed, as studiously to avoid the discussion of the questions involved in the negotiation — I do not believe that the Government has sufficient firmness, whatever may be its inclinations, to give a positive answer of refusal to our demands — I am quite clear, however, that if it yields, the result will be referrible, rather to its apprehensions, than to its sense of justice — The most effectual means of bringing the negotiation to a close, *within any reasonable time,* will be to satisfy His Majesty, of the power of The President to resort to measures of coercion, if redress is longer with-held — An act of Congress investing the Executive, with authority, to employ Naval force, to enforce our just demands, if satisfactory arrangements be not concluded by a limited day, would avail to the prompt accomplishment of all our purposes — Any thing short of this, I fear, will encourage the belief, that this negotiation, like that of Eighteen Hundred and Sixteen and Eighteen Hundred and Twenty five may be dismissed, without hazard to Sicilian interests.

---

[26] Perrotta, *op. cit.,* 56, quotes this letter in part, but his text differs slightly from that given here which is from the original document.

The revenues of His Majesty, are ample — He is quite able, to pay if he must — The debt of the Government, it is true, is large, but its means, are more than sufficient, to meet all its engagements — It is buying in its inscription debt every week — Twenty four Millions of Ducats, is the estimated amount of its clear income — Its debt, is nearly, one Hundred Millions, bearing an interest of five per cent — Its stock is worth about seventy eight —

The military force maintained by the Government, is enormously disproportionate to its means, or necessities — It now amounts to between Forty and Fifty Thousand men, who are represented to be good soldiers, upon parade, but very inefficient upon a field of conflict — about one sixth of this force, is made up of Swiss Regiments —

The Sicilian Navy is very inconsiderable — Two men of war one of which is unseaworthy, and a few frigates, badly equipped constitute the whole marine of the Kingdom. The commerce of the Two Sicilies, might be completely cut up, if it were necessary to resort to a system of reprisals, by the ordinary force of the United States, in the Meditteranean.

The arrival of the Ontario, at this port, has been delayed, by circumstances which Captain Gordon[27] will explain to you. I have felt the less difficulty, in despatching her to The United States, as he informs me that, without specific orders to the contrary, she would at any rate have returned home in the month of May. As the navigation of the Mediterranean is precarious, and it is not impossible that a communication through Havre, may anticipate the arrival of this vessel, it is my intention to forward you duplicates of the despatches now sent, by an opportunity which I hope to avail myself of on the 20ᵗʰ of this month. In the mean time I shall endeavour to see the Minister for Foreign Affairs, and will communicate to you the results of the interview.

---

27 William Lewis Gordon, (-1834). Naval officer. He was appointed Midshipman from Virginia. On March 29, 1831, he was ordered to the Mediterranean for command of the *Ontario*. He was later transferred to the Rendezvous at Baltimore where he died. In his letter dated May 4, 1832, from Hampton Roads, addressed to the Secretary of theNavy, Levi Woodbury, Gordon announced the arrival of the *Ontario* in the United States, after passage of 49 days from Naples, via Gibraltar. Gordon explained that the *Ontario*'s return "at a period so much earlier than the term of service would have authorized, is in consequence of an application from our chargé d'affaires at Naples, to the Commander-in-Chief of the Squadron in the Mediterranean, for a public conveyance of important despatches to the United States . . ." Information supplied by John B. Heffernan, Captain, United States Navy, Director, Naval Records and Library.

I beg leave to recommend the case of Mr. Hammett to your favorable consideration. His situation here, has imposed upon him much both of labour and expense, in his zealous exertions to preserve to our Merchants, the property which has been cruelly wrested from them — He is richly entitled to a liberal compensation, which I hope the gov'. will in some way extend to him. His circumstances are necessitous, and it is unjust that energy and time should have been employed in the public service, without remuneration.

I have received no letters from your department since my arrival in Europe. For the want of the necessary authority, I have not drawn from my accruing salary, or the contingent expenses of the Mission — I hope soon to receive the necessary advice on this subject.

Mr. John Van Buren,[28] who arrived at Naples, a few days since, brought me intelligence of the rejection of his father's nomination. This information surprized me very much. It is calculated to mortify Mr. Van Buren, tho' I have no doubt, that, in the end, it will benefit him, politically.

Have the Kindness to present me respectfully to The President and Mr. McLane,[29] and believe me to be, D'. Sir

Your obed'. Serv'.

E. LIVINGSTON TO J. NELSON

Department of State, Washington, 6 April, 1832. Instruction N° 4.

Sir: —

It is with great pleasure that, by your despatch N°. 1, we have yesterday heard of your arrival at Naples. Your note to the Sicilian Government is approved, and, it is hoped, will have the desired effect. From the close connection between the courts of Naples and Madrid, the former will probably be involved in any war in which the latter may be engaged; and our last

---

[28] John Van Buren (1810-1866). Lawyer, politician, born in Kinderhook, New York. The son of Martin Van Buren, eighth president of the United States. In July 1831, he was admitted to the Bar, and one month later he sailed with his father to London to become an attaché of the American legation. He became a favorite at the English court. Before returning to America, he travelled on the continent, and in 1838, he again visited England and Ireland. *Dictionary American Biography* (1936), XIX, 151-152.

[29] Louis McLane (1786-1857), of Delaware, a cabinet officer and diplomat. In 1831, he was recalled as minister to London and was made secretary of the treasury. He was commissioned secretary of state, May 29, 1833; resigned, June 30, 1834. *Dictionary American Biography* (1933), XII 113-115.

advices render it almost certain that if Don Pedro's demonstration against Portugal should be carried into effect, it will be the signal of hostilities between France and Spain; in which England on the side of France, and the northern powers on that of Spain, will eventually be engaged. This state of things, or the apprehension of its occurrence, cannot be favorable to your negotiations; and it will doubtless have been an additional reason for urging its conclusion.

A letter of credit on the Bankers of the United States at London, is now enclosed, and another copy will be sent with a duplicate of this despatch. You will transmit it, with your signature at foot, to Messrs. Baring, Brothers & Co^y. who will, as directed, honor your drafts.

Herewith you have a duplicate of my despatch N°. 3, — and of the order to the commander of the squadron in the Mediterranean, which is referred to in it.

The probability of a late session of Congress increases every day, and it is almost certain that they will not adjourn before the last of May — so that if the result of your mission has been put off till the last of March, it will probably reach us in time, for ratification, if favorable, or for ulterior measures, should the Sicilian Government have refused to do us justice.

J. NELSON TO E. LIVINGSTON

Naples April 23, 1832.[30] [Despatch No. 5].

Sir,

I have the honor to transmit herewith (marked A)[31] a list of the Documents referred to, in my Despatch of the thirty first of January.[32] In addition to these, which had been committed to the charge of Mr. Appleton by the Secretary of State, I have received from Mr. Hammett, and the claimants, sundry papers, relating to the confiscation of The Victoire, The Urania, The

[30] The No. 4 Despatch, Mr. Nelson to Secretary of State Livingston, Mar. 31, 1832, transmitted a statement of Nelson's accounts for adjustment by the Treasury. 'Adjustment' meant the routine review of accounts to determine if all the items of expense were 'allowable' by law and treasury regulations. The account, once 'adjusted,' passed on to the proper division of the Treasury for payment. Each account received a number and today, by such numbers, all old accounts of individuals with the United States are still presumed to be on file with the General Accounting Office of the Treasury.
[31] See pp. 237-239.
[32] See above, p. 214.

Globe, The Ruth and Mary, The Nancy-Anne & Alexander, The Augusta, The Pocahontas, and The Sophia.

I had an interview with The Prince of Cassaro on the fourth instant, in which I renewed my application for a reply to my notes of the thirty first of January, and Twenty seventh of February; and expressed my regret, and disappointment, in not having received the communication, which he had promised me, in time for transmission by The Ontario — He answered that he was much concerned that our demands had so long remained unheeded; that the situation of his family, had rendered his absence, in Sicily, unavoidable, at a time, when his attention would otherwise have been directed to their consideration; that he had just returned; that he was, then, very much engaged, in making becoming preparations, for the solemnization of the nuptials of The Princess D. Maria Amalia with D. Sebastiano Gabriele, of Spain; that as soon as the ceremony of their union (which was to take place on the following Saturday) was performed, he would devote himself to the subject of the American claims, and that my notes should be, thereafter, immediately answered.

Mr. Gardner,[33] our Consul at Palermo, having arrived at Naples on the seventeenth, on his way to The United States, I addressed a private note to The Prince of Cassaro on the day following, apprizing him of the circumstance and of my desire to embrace the opportunity of sending his long delayed reply, to Washington. Of his answer (marked confidential) I now forward a copy marked B.[34] The groundless pretext for further postponement, suggested in this note, unequivocally evidences the settled design of this Government, to protract the negotiation, to as late a period, as consists with a sense of its own security — The opinion, that this purpose is cherished by His Sicilian Majesty's advisers, I have expressed in my former despatches; and the experience of every day's intercourse with them, fortifies my conviction of its justice —

You will not fail to observe the mode of expression, adopted by The Secretary in his note (preliminare risposta). It would seem to indicate, that the answer to be given, is not to be definitive; and of course that it will not be a decided negative to our demands — What its character may be, it would be need-

---

[33] J. B. Gardner, of Massachusetts, was nominated consul of the United States at Palermo, Dec. 13, 1825; consent was voted by the Senate, Dec. 19th. He served in this post until his death in September, 1837.

[34] For enclosure "B" see p. 240.

less to conjecture — I have received many suggestions, from various sources, on the subject; but they are so contradictory, and the information they profess to convey, has been so indirectly obtained, that they afford no satisfactory data, upon which to form an opinion. A thorough investigation of the claims, and of the principles upon which they are based, has entirely satisfied me, that no just or tenable ground can be assumed by this Government, which will warrant a refusal to gratify them —

I am solicitous to learn that The Ontario has reached her destination in safety, and in time to meet the views of The President. I shall await advices from Washington with an anxious impatience.

The appearance of the cholera in France has induced this Government to impose a quarantine (which is strictly enforced) upon all vessels, goods, and persons, coming thence, into the Kingdom of The Two Sicilies, by land or by Water. The apprehension, that this terrible pestilence may make its way into Italy is not an unreasonable one; and it may well be feared should the measures of precaution which have been adopted prove ineffectual, that its ravages will nowhere have been more signally or fatally marked, than in a population, which, extreme poverty and filth, render especially obnoxious to its attacks —

(Enclosure "A" with Despatch No. 5)

List of Documents[35] delivered to J. Nelson, Chargé D'Affaires of the U. S. at Naples, referred to, in Mr. Appleton's despatch to The Secretary of State, dated Leghorn, Aug'. 30, 1826.

No. 1

Papers exhibiting claims of Joseph Peabody and Gideon Tucker, for the Brig *Betsey* and Cargo &c.

---

[35] This list of 22 documents delivered to Mr. Nelson by Mr. Appleton, is identified on its docket side of the sheet as "Enclosure A" with Mr. Nelson's Despatch No. 5, dated April 23, 1832. Mr. Appleton, when about to relinquish his post in Naples, had placed the documents in Mr. Hammett's care for safekeeping. It is not clear, without full checking of the individual papers, whether any other 'claims' or papers relating to claims already filed had been meanwhile placed in the hands of Mr. Hammett, as United States Consul; it is, however, noted that a ship *Victoire* is named in the Hammett list; whereas, in this Nelson list, there is a ship (No. 14) *Victory,* and there is no information at hand as to whether this is merely a difference in spelling or refers to two vessels. "Proofs" were filed for more vessels than were ultimately recompensed, since the Commissioners disallowed some of the claims. For some of the claims, the original set of "supporting documents" were several times augmented to amplify the evidence in one way or another.

237

No. 2

Claim of Gordon S. Mumford and Geo. Rossier & Roulet for the Brig *Emily* and Cargo &c.

No. 3

Claims of Joseph Peabody and Gid". Tucker for The Ship *Francis* and Cargo.

No. 4

Claim of Jery. L. Page & others, in behalf of the owners &c of the Schooner *Fortune* &c.

No. 5

Claim of Jery L. Page for The Ship *Henry* and Cargo.

No. 6

Claim of Nath'. West for The Ship *Hercules* and Cargo.

No. 7

Claim of W". Reed &c owners of The Schooner *John* and Cargo.

No. 8

Claim of John Fairfield and others, in behalf of the owners of the Schooner *Mary* &c.

No. 9

Claim of the Owners of the Cargo and Schooner *Maria* &c.

No. 10

Claim of Thorndike, Deland and others, in behalf of the owners of The Schooner *Nancy* &c.

No. 11

Claim of Jery L. Page for the Schooner *Oceanus* &c.

No. 12

Claim of Nath'. Silsbee in behalf of the owners of the Brig *Romp* &c.

No. 13

Claim of Stephen White in behalf of the owners of the Brig *Sukey and Betsey* &c.

No. 14

Claim of Dutch & Deland in behalf of the owners of The Brig *Victory* &c.

No. 15

Letter of Wm. Gray to Secy of State, dated May 10, 1816, transmitting claims for the Ship Trent, Brigs, *Radius,* *Phoenix* & *Louisiana.*

No. 16

Claim of J'. Thorndike for the Brig, *Two Betseys.*

No. 17

Claim of D°. for The cargo of The Sch". *Mary.*

No. 18

Claim of D°. for The Schooner, *Dove.*

No. 19

Claim by P. C. Brooks and W^m. Ward in the case of The Sch^r. *William* & Cargo.

No. 20

Letters and papers from Geo. Cabot concerning The Schooner, *Maria.*

No. 21

Claim by C. Bradbury, for The Schooners *Oceanus, Maria, Morning Star, Urasia,* and *Amherst.*

No. 22

Copies of Memorials, Letters &c of the Merchants of Boston, Balt°., &c to The Pres^t. U.S. dated 1815, 1816.

PRINCE OF CASSARO TO J. NELSON

[Enclosure "B" with Despatch No. 5]

Naples April 18ᵗʰ 1832 (Confidential)

The Prince of Cassaro has received a note bearing date of the present from Mr. Nelson in which that gentleman expresses a desire to take advantage of the American Consul's proposed journey to Genoa in order to transmit to the President of the United States some reply from the Government of His Sicilian Majesty *preliminary* to the business with which Mr. Nelson is charged.

The Undersigned regrets that it is out of his power to comply with Mr. Nelson's request as the *Preliminary answer* which he desires has not yet been submitted to the approval of His Majesty whom the many cares of the State prevent from giving attention to it. The Undersigned however hopes that, he shall soon be able to satisfy Mr. Nelson by sending the reply referred to and takes the present opportunity to assure Mr. Nelson of his high Consideration.

J. NELSON TO E. LIVINGSTON

Naples 16 May 1832. [Despatch No. 6]

Sir,

I have the Honor to acknowledge the receipt of your letter of the 25th of February,[36] with its enclosures.

I had an interview with The Prince of Cassaro, on Monday, the 14th instant. It was sought by me, with the purpose of unequivocally manifesting my decided dissatisfaction with the course which has been pursued by this Government, in relation to our claims. Upon calling at the Foreign Office, I found the Secretary engaged with a council of Ministers. After the lapse of a few minutes, however, he entered his room saying "I beg your ten thousand pardons; I am really ashamed that your notes have not been answered; but I assure you it is not my fault. When I went to Sicily, I expected that the answer would have been prepared and presented to you by the Duke of Gualtieri,[37] to whom, the King, during my absence, had committed my port-

---

[36] See Instruction No. 3, Feb. 25, 1832, p. 223.
[37] See above, p. 225, this chapter, note 23.

240

folio, and was surprized, on my return, to find that this duty, had been neglected"

I replied, that to me it was a subject of unaffected concern, that the demands, which it was the object of my notes to prefer against the Kingdom of The Two Sicilies, had failed to engage the prompt attention of His Majesty's Government; that, after the promises which I had received from time to time; that the views of His Majesty with regard to them would be communicated to me, I had just reason to complain, that the reply had been so long with-held; and that I was not sure, that instead of continuing to press the claims upon the notice of a Government seemingly indisposed to consider them, it would not better consist with the dignity of the Nation I represented, and with my own duty, to take my leave of the Sicilian Court; but, that I entertained a strong repugnance, to the adoption of any course, which might wear the appearance of harshness; or to break off a negotiation, which I trusted would yet terminate satisfactorily to the Government of the United States. That to accelerate so desirable a result, I had solicited the present conference, with a view of once more urging His Majesty's Government, to an immediate and favorable consideration of our demands; and that it would be gratifying to me to be informed, at what time, I might with confidence expect to be advertised, of the issue of their examination —

The Prince remarked, that the answer to the notes which I had addressed to His Majesty's Government, ought certainly to have been given; that it should not be much longer delayed; that it would be communicated, he believed, in a few days; to this, however, he could not pledge himself; but he would give me his word of honor that I should receive it, in the course of the present month; and after a moment's hesitation, added "I will state to you frankly, that I have prepared an answer, but the Council, to whom it has been submitted, have not approved of it, and insist upon its being remodelled; it must therefore be written over again. The Council is now in session, and occupied with this business." —

In reply to a remark of mine, that I presumed the Government had determined upon the principles, which were to form the basis of the proposed answer, accompanied by the expression of my earnest hope, that they would present no insuperable barrier to an amicable accommodation. The Prince observed, That His Majesty did not hold himself responsible for

241

the acts of Murat, and that the answer would chiefly rest upon that principle; that the Government of Murat was one of usurpation, the wrongs of which the present King was under no obligation to redress — I answered, That against the present King, as an individual, the Government of The United States, preferred no claims; That its demands, existed, and were prosecuted against The Kingdom of Naples, and against His Majesty, as the head and organ of that Kingdom; and that I hoped to succeed in persuading His Excellency whenever he would afford me the opportunity, that the principle which he had indicated, as the basis of the proposed reply, was altogether untenable; that it was directly opposed, by the best established principles of international Law; by the authority of publicists of acknowledged reputation; and by the practice of most of the powers of Modern Europe. That the recent example, furnished by our convention with France, was decisively affirmative of the doctrines, maintained by the Government of the United States; and that I was much deceived, if the History of the Two Sicilies since the restoration did not furnish evidence of their having received the sanction of the Government of His present Majesty, as well as of that of his predecessor.

The Prince expressed his desire, that the principles involved in our claims, should be fully discussed, saying, that in due time an opportunity for their investigation should be afforded, when it would give him great pleasure to hear and weigh any suggestions, I might have to offer; but he was quite sure, that there was nothing in the History of the Neapolitan Government, since the restoration, to give countenance to the doctrines upon which our claims are founded. That the example of France, he held it to be inapplicable, to the case of the Two Sicilies, inasmuch as the political relations of the two governments towards the United States, were essentially different. But, said he, "waiving this discussion for the present; what are the acts of the Government of the Two Sicilies, which you design to invoke in aid of your demands?"

To this question, I replied, by enquiring, whether at this moment His Majesty had not in his service several of the vessels seized and taken from the American Merchants, by the acts of fraud and rapine, of which the Government of the United States complained? and whether, His Majesty's Government, while it availed itself of the benefit of the acquisitions of Murat, could consistently seek to disregard the obligations, or to throw off the burthens, which his reign imposed?

The answer of the Prince to these inquiries, evinced, by its manner, his extreme embarrassment, "The ships," he said, "we are willing to give up." They ought to have been surrendered long ago. I don't know; I can't think why they have not been restored."

I observed that the offer of their restoration was made at a very late hour, and to such as did not duly appreciate the sense of justice and good faith of His Majesty's Government, it might, even now, seem to be dictated, by a consciousness, that their continued possession was incompatible with the principles, sought to be maintained by it —

The Prince interrupted me, by remarking that the vessels had never been demanded; to which I made the obvious reply That admitting that they had not been specifically demanded, The Sicilian Government had been apprized of the means by which they had been acquired; and that with that knowledge and the opportunity of at least tendering their restoration, of which it had not availed itself, it had asserted to, and exercised a right of property over them, by their employment for nearly seventeen years in the public service. But, that, in point of fact, they had been demanded and that their restoration to their original owners had been declined, by the Government of the Two Sicilies. That, not only, had Mr. Pinkney in his note to the Marquis Di Circello, of the 24th of August 1816, pointed them out as American property; but that Mr. Appleton, had, in tersus, desired to know of Mr. De Medici, whether upon application they would be given up, and had received a negative answer —

The Prince professed not to recollect, that the vessels had been referred to in Mr. Pinkney's note, which, he said, he had read three or four times; and observed, that there was nothing in the records of his Department, to show, what had passed between M^r. De Medici and M^r. Appleton. "*But,*" said he, "*we have no money — not a farthing. What can we do?*"

I repeated what I had stated in a previous interview, that the Government of the United States had no desire to harrass that of the Two Sicilies; and that I was authorized to make such arrangements, in regard to the payment of our demands, if their justice was acknowledged, as would, at the same time, satisfy the reasonable expectations of the claimants, and subserve His Majesty's convenience.

The Prince again adverted to the subject of a commercial treaty, which, he said, His Majesty was willing to conclude upon liberal principles; that he placed a high estimate upon the good opinion of the Government of the United States, and was prepared to enter into such arrangements, calculated to promote an extended commercial intercourse with its Citizens — To these and other observations of the like tenor, I could only reply that I was not authorized to confer with him, in regard to commercial interests, until a satisfactory adjustment of our demands for restitution had been effectuated.

In this interview, I did not deem it proper, (if it had been practicable to have engaged the Secretary in such a discussion) to enter into any detailed examination of the principles involved in this negotiation. I believed it to be more prudent, to wait the receipt of the answer, in the preparation of which His Majesty's advisers have experienced so much difficulty. This will disclose the views of the Sicilian Government, and uncover the grounds of difference between us. These, once defined, there will be no difficulty in bringing the negotiation to an early and definite issue.

My impression is, that no attempt will be made, to justify the confiscations. The perfidy and enormity of the act, of which we complain, will be fully conceded. That our Merchants have been wronged; and that their claims for indemnity, might, with justice, have been prosecuted against the Government of Murat, will not be denied. But this Government will insist upon its irresponsibility upon the principles assumed by the Marquis Di Circello, in his note of the 15th of October 1816, addressed to Mr. Pinkney — That these are fallacious, I am persuaded, I shall have no difficulty in satisfactorily demonstrating —

The satisfaction of our convention with France, has caused this Government great concern. The Secretary for Foreign Affairs has large estates in Sicily, and is deeply interested in its commercial prosperity — If the Government of The United States feels, that it is unfettered by the provisions of the 7th article of The French Treaty (and I presume it is) I have the strongest reason for the belief, that important concessions may be obtained, by offering to place the wine trade of this Kingdom upon the same footing with that of France.

It is my intention, upon the receipt of the answer to my notes of the 31st of January and 27th of February, to prepare and present, an immediate and full reply; and to follow it up by personal conferences, until, the views of this Government shall have been decisively ascertained.

J. NELSON TO E. LIVINGSTON

Naples July 12, 1832.[38] Despatch No. 8.

Sir,

I have the honor to acknowledge the receipt of your communication of the 6th of April,[39] covering a letter of credit on Messrs. Baring Bros. & Co. of London.

In my despatch (no. 6) of the 16th of May, I apprized you of the promise of the Secretary for Foreign Affairs, to furnish me during that month, with a reply to my notes of the 31st of January, and 27th of February. This I received on the second day of June, and now transmit a copy marked A.[40] It substantially re-asserts the principles, assumed by the Marquis Di Circello, in his note to Mr. Pinkney, of the 15th of October 1816. This "refusal" to satisfy our claims, if it had been given at an earlier period, I should have regarded as sufficiently "positive" to have justified me, in at once demanding my passports, and returning to the United States. But as I am in the daily expectation of receiving your instructions,[41] in reply to my despatches

---

[38] July 1, 1832, No. 7 Despatch, Mr. Nelson to Mr. Livingston, transmitted a statement of his accounts for the quarter ending June 30, 1832, for settlement.

[39] In his Instruction No. 4, April 6, 1832, to Mr. Nelson, Secretary of State Livingston acknowledged receipt of Mr. Nelson's Despatch No. 1, and enclosed to Mr. Nelson a letter of credit on United States bankers in London. This Instruction also transmitted duplicates of Instruction No. 3, from the State Department, and of the earlier omitted order to the Commander of the American Squadron in the Mediterranean. It also informed Mr. Nelson on the probable continuance of the current session of Congress until the last of May. (See *Instructions to United States Ministers*. XIII, 287-288.)

[40] See pp. 248-253. Mr. Nelson's notes of 31st Jan. and Feb. 27th, to the Prince of Cassaro are printed in Senate Document No. 70, 22d Congress, 2d session, pp. 22-26.

[41] Some idea of the delays involved in diplomats' communication with their home government, and the consequent extent to which they were constrained to face the problems of their post alone, may be gained from the fact that the month before this Despatch No. 8, of Mr. Nelson, his chief, Mr. Livingston, was writing in his Instruction No. 5, dated June 11th: "Your despatch No. 3, dated the 12th of March, was received by the *Ontario*, on the 6th of May last. Having since been in daily expectation of hearing from you, further instructions have been delayed until this moment, when the sailing of the *United States* obliges us to found them on the information given by you at that time when your last was written . . . . Neither the dignity of our Government, nor the duty it owes its citizens, will justify any further delay; and that you are therefore instructed to demand an explicit answer, whether the Neapolitan Government will make satisfaction for the seizures made by Murat of the property of American citizens, and take measures for the prompt and full payment of the same; that the frigate *United States*, despatched to demand this answer, will wait twenty days to receive

by The Ontario, I have felt it to be my duty to await their arrival; and in the interim, to use my best efforts, to impress this Government with more just and liberal views, upon the subject in controversy. My answer to Prince Cassaro's note, dated on the 29th of June (a copy of which, is likewise herewith communicated, marked B.) [42] will fully explain my impressions, in regard to the principles, upon which he relies. I am without the hope, however, that any change in the determination of this Government, will be effected by discussion — Nothing short of actual force; or the decided manifestation of a resolution to resort to reprisals, will influence it to do justice to our abused citizens. It has neither the power, nor the inclination to resist such a manifestation; but it calculates, confidently, on the continued forbearance of the American Government; and will, I fear, persist in withholding all redress, as long as mere negotiation is employed to enforce its rendition —

I called to see the Prince of Cassaro on the third instant. My note of the 29th of June, had not then been laid before the King. It was necessary that it should be first translated, and before this could be accomplished, His Majesty left the Capitol upon a visit to the province of Abruzzi, whence he is not expected to return, before the third day of the next month. The Secretary assures me, that very soon thereafter, he will decisively inform me, whether there is any probability of a change in the King's views and determination.

In the course of the conversation, to which this interview gave rise, the Secretary observed, that no step was taken in the pending negotiation, without consulting the Council of State, and that, in what passed between us, I must regard him, as speaking

it, and if, at the expiration of that time, a satisfactory answer is not given and proper provision made for the payment of our citizens, that you are directed to ask for your passports to return to your country, and that the President will then take such measures as his constitutional duties shall direct. After the delivery of this note, you are to depart at the specified time, or sooner if an unsatisfactory answer shall have been given; and you are to consider no answer satisfactory that does not assume the responsibility of the present Government for the acts of Murat against American commerce while he was King of the country, and that does not pledge the faith of the Government to nay the *whole* value of the vessels and cargoes seized, the expenses of the masters and agents in claiming the property, and the charges to which the Government was put in supporting the American seamen belonging to the confiscated ships, and their conveyance home. The whole to be assessed by an impartial and mixed commission, or compromised for a sum in gross which you may judge will be satisfactory to the claimants. This instruction is of course on the supposition that, previous to the receipt of it, you have made no arrangement under your former instructions."

42 See pp. 254-283. Mr. Nelson's answer to the above note, was dated June 29, 1832. Printed in Senate Document No. 70, 22d Congress, 2d session, p. 31-50.

unofficially; and immediately afterward enquired, whether, if the principles in contestation, were yielded by the Sicilian Government, that of the United States, would consent to receive works of art, in payment of the demands of its Citizens. I replied that I had no authority to conclude such an arrangement. He then said, "We have no money; and it is impossible for us to pay in money." The reiteration of this statement induced me to remark that, it was very extraordinary, that whilst in our previous interviews, the refusal to justify the claims of our Merchants, was constantly put upon the ground of the inability of the Sicilian Government to pay, in the written answer to our application for redress, they were professedly resisted upon the principle of its alledged irresponsibility for the acts of Murat — That neither position was defensible; the one being as unfounded in point of fact, as the other was untenable upon principle. That the Sicilian Government, if willing, was abundantly able to pay, that it was every week amortizing portions of its public debt, and that for the effectuation of that object, the appropriation had been recently doubled. That it applied more money to the purpose of purchasing and extinguishing its inscription debt, than would suffice, within the term, to which a credit would be extended by the Government of the United States, to satisfy the full amount of the demands of its Citizens — That, at all events, if the real motive for declining an arrangement, was to be found in the financial condition of the Sicilian Government, candor required that the refusal to pay, should, in our official correspondence, be placed upon its true ground. To these remarks, The Prince gave no direct reply, but observed, That the Government of the United States, insisted upon the legitimacy of Murat's rule, which His Majesty could never acknowledge — This I denied; and entered into a detailed exposition of the Principles upon which our demands are based; referring him to my note of the 29th of June, which, owing to the pressure of current business, he professed not to have read. He repeated that he could not undertake to pledge the Government to the adoptions of any specific measures; but promised, that the King should be consulted as early as possible and his final determination promptly made known to me.

I am awaiting advices from Washington, with much impatience. We have a rumor here, that an American ship was to have left Mahon for this port, during the past week. If this be so, I trust that she will bring to me such despatches as will relieve me from all difficulty, as to the steps I should take under existing circumstances.

THE PRINCE OF CASSARO TO J. NELSON

[Enclosure "A" with Nelson's Despatch No. 8, July 12, 1832]

Naples — 30 May 1832.

The Undersigned has the honour of informing Mr. Nelson that his notes of the 31st January and the 27th February last have been submitted to the King of the Sicilies, who is highly gratified by the assurances of the President of the United States of his desire that a friendly intercourse should subsist between the two Countries. His Majesty is no less anxious for the fulfilment of that wish and sincerely congratulates His Excellency upon the present flourishing condition of the United States and their prospects of future greatness.

His Majesty did not however expect to see revived the old controversy respecting the pretended claims of American merchants as he conceived that it had long since been set at rest by the powerful arguments which had been adduced against the justice of those demands; but in order to give an additional proof of the sincerity of his feelings towards the United States, he has deigned to command that the question be examined anew with strict attention to the most minute circumstances, so that he might be himself completely informed as to the facts and thereby enabled to determine what is required by justice and the Laws of Nations. The repeated discussions which were rendered necessary by this command interrupted too as they were by other and equally urgent business together with the absence of the Undersigned have made impossible to give M^{r}. Nelson an earlier reply. Those investigations being now terminated the following observations are now transmitted by order of His Majesty.

From an attentive examination of M^{r}. Nelson's note it appears that he undertakes to establish this principle —that citizens of one country in their intercourse with another cannot be expected to look beyond the acknowledged possession of the political and civil power — from this principle it follows of course — that he who is in acknowledged possession of the sovereignty of a country should be regarded by foreigners as the legitimate sovereign thereof.

248

Hence it is pretended that Murat having pledged his faith to the Americans his act is to be obligatory on the Nation over which he then ruled and on its legitimate sovereigns after their restoration to the throne.

Adhering to this principle the Undersigned considers as capable of demonstration that no indemnification is due to the American merchants for the losses they sustained, inasmuch as they were wrong in confiding in Murat whom they ought not to have viewed as the absolute entire and supreme possessor of this kingdom. In proof of this it will be proper to recapitulate the circumstances under which Murat reigned, and from which it will be seen that the Continental portion of the Neapolitan dominions was at that time only a great feud of the French Empire.

On the 15th of July 1808, Joachim Murat was invested by his brother-in-law Napoleon with the title of King of Naples which was made heriditary [sic] in his lineal male descendants, in failure of whom the crown reverted to him who had bestowed it on to his legitimate natural or adoptive successors. To the crown of Naples was added the dignity of High Admiral of France.

The Supreme Sovereignty of Naples consequently resided in Napoleon, by virtue of which he directed the political relations of the kindom [sic] with other countries just as he did those of the various States over which he had unjustly and forcibly placed other individuals of his own family. It was upon the strength of this supremacy that he issued the atrocious Berlin Decree extending to the kingdoms of Spain, Naples, Etruria, and Holland, and shortly after, that other monument of his arbitrary disposition the Milan decree.

These are points in history of the truth of which no one doubts nor did the American merchants doubt that the above mentioned Decrees applied to themselves likewise for they did not immediately dispatch cargoes for Naples. — Mr. Nelson asserts that they demanded security. No evidence of this however has been found among our archives notwithstanding the most diligent search. From whom could they receive such security? from Napoleon or from Murat? Certainly from Napoleon as Murat was merely the executor of those execrable decrees in Naples. If Napoleon's command was paramount throughout the whole extent of the French Empire in such a case as this, certainly the possession of that part of the sovereignty which regulated said political system resided in Napoleon and not in Murat.

Hence according to Mr. Nelson's own principle the American merchants erred in trusting to Murat; who as was clearly shown in the note of M^r. Pinkney did not dare disobey the inexorable Napoleon and therefore confiscated the American vessels notwithstanding his word had been pledged for their safety.

It is needless to allege that the Americans did not know who was the absolute entire and supreme ruler of the State, the authority which was to secure the fulfilment of the contracts. M^r. Nelson cannot but perceive that when a country is occupied by a Foreign force a distinction should always be made between that force and the citizens of the country, who being incapable of resistance have unavoidably fallen under the power of the conqueror. Persons at a distance, out of the reach of violence and at liberty to act as they please can and ought before they trust the occupier to examine carefully into his situation and calculate the chances of having their contracts fulfilled; this being done they can neither plead force nor ignorance and have no one to blame but themselves if those calculations are disappointed. If their speculation succeed so much the better for them [;] if it fail they alone should bear the loss.

Moreover in those days of sadness who was ignorant that Napoleon urged on by insatiable ambition and considering the whole continent too small a theatre for its display had conceived the wild idea of destroying the naval supremacy of Great Britain and for that purpose claimed the right of dictating to all the other states of Europe? Who did not know that he alone was the author of the Berlin and Milan Decrees and that the kings of his creation had nothing to do but merely signing their names to those arbitrary ordinances? How then can Murat be viewed as independent of Napoleon and of the French Empire, and as being the unrestricted possessor of the sovereignty of Naples.

There was yet another thing wanting; Murat should have been recognised not only as Sovereign *de facto* (which meant nothing more than occupation *de facto* in his case) but also as Sovereign *de jure;* he should have been admitted as Legitimate. Now setting aside the investiture by Napoleon he had not another foundation for his right than that of conquest, which according to all the most distinguished authorities on National law conveys no valid title unless it be followed either by a treaty of peace with or by the entire submission of the Sovereign disposed [sic]. Now it is well known that neither of these things took place; that Ferdinand the legitimate Sovereign of Naples and of Sicily remained constantly at war with Murat up to the day when he resumed possession of the whole kingdom. Murat was never the acknowledged possessor of the sovereignty of Naples all his acts being constrained and protested against by the legitimate ruler of the country. If therefore, the Americans entered into contracts with Murat (even leaving out of the question the fact that he was merely a Lieutenant of Napoleon) they ran the chances of war to which they were exposed by the doubtfulness of that person's political character and they shewed a particular want of caution in not considering the obvious uncertainty of his situation at that time. This being the case upon what grounds will it be pretended that the legitimate Sovereign or the Neapolitan Nation should indemnify them for losses occasioned either by the violence or want of faith of Murat.

The admission of such pretensions would be fraught with the most dire evils. One of the obvious consequences would be that every Prince who has been for a time dispossessed of his dominions would in addition to the evils of such spoliation be obliged on his restoration to make good the engagements of the usurping Party although the benefits resulting from those engagements had fallen entirely on that Party. Again — it is a fundamental principle of the Laws of Nations, that Sovereigns and Nations are to be considered as individuals acting under the law of Nature applied to Nations — now if the claims of the Americans were just, it would be also just, that when a robber has entered a man's house and has thence stolen property not only belonging to the owner of the house but also to his neighbors he should be obliged in addition to his own loss to make good to his neighbours that which they had lost.

Every unprejudiced man will agree that the Americans acted with the utmost imprudence; Murat had been on the throne of Naples scarcely a year, and adding the period of Joseph Buonaparte's reign the country had not been occupied by the French three years. War was actively going on between Murat and King Ferdinand; so that the occupation had received validity neither from time nor from the tacit acquiescence of the legitimate Sovereign; The contest between the latter and the usurper was most desperate and those who treated with the one exposed themselves to all the hazards of such a contest. It is absurd to

251

insist that either party should be at any period or in any case answerable for obligations contracted by the other.

The Americans were at that fatal time, prevented by circumstances from trading to any advantage with Europe; their productions were rotting on their hands, and they probably conceived that it would be the lesser evil to expose them in a country occupied by foreigners and thus run the risk of losing them than to remain unemployed. In so doing they were either imprudent or unlucky; they were more than imprudent, they were obstinate, for after having been once deceived they shipped again and again for this port — Now is it just that the Neapolitans or their king should pay the penalty which they incurred by so doing?

The Americans have asserted that the seizures were made beneficial to the Neapolitans; this it would be impossible for them to prove, for it certainly was not the case. The documents and registers of the period shew that the whole product of the prizes went into the private purse of Murat who considered it as his own property. Neither Naples nor King Ferdinand received any portion of it, and it would be contrary to every principle of justice that they should be forced to pay for what they never received.

It is hard indeed that such a demand should be made upon a kingdom which for ten years groaned under that desolating Continental system which occasioned the very evils for which the Americans require satisfaction; from a kingdom which is still loaded with taxes and debts, caused by the violence and rapacity of the French; from a kingdom which — though thus weighed down by its own misfortunes yet viewed the injustice committed on the Americans with the greatest sympathy, ardently desired to enter into amicable relations with the United States. — It is most hard to make this demand of a king who after so many years of exile and suffering recovered his kingdom at the expense of heavy sacrifices through the assistance of his august allies —

This plain exposition of the facts is sufficient to prove untenable the other principle which Mr. Nelson endeavoured to establish — viz — that the existing government is bound to fulfil the engagements of the preceding; for the Prince who recovers dominions to which he has never renounced the right can never be said to *succeed* the invader.

Nor can the fact that other nations have acquitted claims of this nature be admitted as of consequence; as circumstances very different from those under which Naples is placed and views and interests of another character, may have counselled such a measure. So far from destroying the validity of the objections it does not even weaken them —

Such is the result of the examinations which have been made by order of His Majesty; and the Undersigned flatters himself that when M^r. Nelson shall have pondered on the arguments advanced as well as on those contained in the reply to M^r. Pickney's note, he will be inclined to use his influence with the President of the United States, and that one so distinguished for impartiality as his Excellency will see that the American merchants however deplorable be their case have no claim for indemnifications upon this Government, or upon its king according to sound principles of National Law or of that common justice which he to whom are committed the interests of a country is most especially bound to observe.

The Undersigned has the pleasure of adding in the name of his Sovereign that although His Majesty by no means admits the justice of the claims of the Americans, yet as he wishes to give to the esteemed President a clear proof of his scrupulous delicacy, and to render apparent his desire for entering into friendly relations with the United States, he has commanded that if there should be among the vessels composing the royal navy any of those which were seized by Murat they shall be instantly returned or their value paid to the owner. —

His Majesty conceives that his generous determination will prove to the Government of the United States the sincerity of his wish for the establishment of an intercourse with the United States which will prove advantageous to both parties.

The Undersigned embraces the present opportunity to convey to Mr. Nelson the assurances of his particular consideration.

J. NELSON TO THE PRINCE OF CASSARO

[Enclosure "B" with Despatch No. 8, July 12, 1832][43]

Naples, June 29, 1832

The Undersigned Chargé D'Affaires of The United States of America, in acknowledging the receipt of the note of His Excellency, the Prince of Cassaro, His Sicilian Majesty's Minister, Secretary of State for Foreign Affairs, bearing date on the thirtieth day of May,[44] in reply to the notes of the Undersigned of the thirty-first of January[45] and twenty-seventh[46] of February last, begs leave to express the unfeigned satisfaction, with which he has received the assurances therein tendered, of the readiness of His Excellency to consider and discuss the reclamations claimed by the Government of the United States, against that of the Two Sicilies, and of the willingness of His Majesty, to allow for the benefit of the claimants every indemnity, which shall be shewn to be supported by the principles of National Law, or recommended by considerations of justice, and Natural Equity. These are the foundations upon which in the apprehension of the Government of the United States, the claims in question repose; the principles by which they are fortified and sustained. They are those, by which alone, it desires that their validity shall be tried, and the Undersigned therefore cheerfully unites with his Excellency, in referring their decision to the arbitrament of the high sanctions thus invoked; in the persuasion, that animated by a reciprocal disposition to conform to their dictates; and a sincere inclination to bring the question in contestation between the two governments, to a favorable issue, an adjustment mutually honorable and satisfactory may be attained, and that to secure a result so desirable, it is only necessary, that the liberal purpose indicated in the notes of His Ex-

43 This Enclosure 'B' with Despatch No. 8 of Mr. Nelson, is the one which constituted his masterwork while in the post at Naples, for in it he established, in lengthy and carefully thought-out logic, the full case for the American claims, supporting his argument with aptly chosen quotations from the works of learned international lawyers whose works still are standard after nearly 200 years. This letter is further noteworthy as being the one which Mr. Nelson, after he had started home, with the Treaty achieved, claimed had been distorted, in publication under the auspices of the Senate. (For this matter, see Mr. Nelson's letter of March 2, 1833, p. 333).

44 Printed (translation) in Senate Document, No. 70, p. 27-30; see post, Mar. 2, 1833 to D. Green, the printer, and Mr. Nelson to Mr. Livingston, March 16th.

45 Printed (translation) in Senate Document, No. 70, p. 22-24.

46 Printed in Senate Document, No. 70, p. 24-26.

cellency, should be accompanied by a frank impartiality of judgement, and a candid examination of the facts and circumstances involved in the controversy. —

Before proceeding to a consideration of the various suggestions, by which, His Excellency seeks to shew the irresponsibility of His Majesty's Government for the American confiscations, the Undersigned feels it to be incumbent on him, to notice the expression of surprize, imputed to His Majesty "that this old controversy (l'annosa controversia) [sic] should have been revived by the American Government, which he supposed, to have been put at rest by the strength of the arguments by which, on another occasion, the claims of the American Merchants have been combatted." That the "arguments" referred to may have been satisfactory to the mind of His Majesty, it is not for the Undersigned to question. But it is his duty to aver, that their conclusive sufficiency to relieve the Government of The Two Sicilies from the obligation to accord the indemnity demanded, has never been acknowledged by the Government of the United States; and to insist, that the course pursued by that Government discloses, no circumstances calculated to fortify such an impression; none to encourage a belief, that for the multiplied and flagrant wrongs, inflicted upon its betrayed citizens by the Neapolitan Government, it has at any time, entertained a design of renouncing a claim for adequate redress. On the contrary, from the date of the perpetration of these aggravated injuries, up to a very recent period, by its Consuls, Ministers and agents, it has kept the Government of The Two Sicilies constantly warned of its inflexible purpose, to persist in the assertion of these demands.

Nor is the Government of The United States, chargeable with the delay, which has procrastinated their adjustment. This is justly referrible to another and a different agency. In proof of this, the history of the negotiations successively instituted for the settlement of these claims, is confidently appealed to. It will testify, that, to the application first preferred by the United States, after the restoration, the Government of The Two Sicilies did not find it convenient to reply, until, from the circumstances in which he was placed, an examination of that reply by the American minister, had become impracticable; that in Eighteen Hundred and Twenty five "the controversy" was "revived" by the American Government, and that the discussions consequent upon this renewed application for redress, were suspended at the instance of the Sicilian Government, for reasons, to which, is the sequel of this note, the Undersigned will take occasion particularly to refer. That "the controversy" has become "old" is not therefore imputable to the Government of the United States. That it has not been prosecuted with a more impatient zeal has been owing to its acquiescence in that policy of the Two Sicilies, which has hitherto postponed its adjustment; to its solicitude that in the relations subsisting between the two countries, a spirit of harmony should be assiduously cultivated; and to its determination, as far as it depended on its agency, that this desirable condition of their intercourse should not be heedlessly disturbed.

As the discussion to which the note of His Excellency invites the Undersigned is necessarily connected with the facts and circumstances, upon which the American reclamations have been founded, he begs leave succinctly to recapitulate them, with such references to their nature and dates, as may serve to obviate misconceptions and to afford a clear view of the merits of this controversy.

The Decree of Berlin was issued by The Emperor of the French, on the twenty first day of November Eighteen Hundred and Six; that of Milan on the Seventeenth day of December, Eighteen Hundred and Seven. These decrees were reenacted by the Government of the Kingdom of Naples, the first on the Twentieth day of December, Eighteen Hundred and six; the last, on the ninth day of January Eighteen Hundred and Eight. They were professedly retaliatory to certain orders of blockade proclaimed by Great Britain; and is now universally conceded, were, like the measures which furnished the pretext for their enactment, grossly violative of the rights of Neutral Commerce. The operation of these decrees, and orders, was disastrously fatal to American interests. Under the joint action of their indefensible provisions, the commerce of the United States, was banished from the Ocean. Nor was the unfriendly influence of the policy which enforced them, felt by those only, against whose interests, they were especially directed. The Government of the Kingdom of Naples itself, discovered, in process of time, that a system, which rendered impracticable the exportation of its own surplus productions, and raised, almost indefinitely, the price of foreign articles of first necessity, in its markets, could not be profitably persevered in; and accommodating its measures to its necessities, it, on the thirty first day of March Eighteen Hundred and Nine, adopted a modification of its policy, so far as to permit the importation into its kingdom, of certain articles, in neutral vessels. The decree, announcing this relaxation, was followed by an order of Council of Great Britain, of the Twenty Sixth of April, Eighteen Hundred and nine, excepting from the operation of her system of blockade, the ports of Naples, and other portions of Italy. To the ports of this Kingdom therefore, there was then, licensed, in the enumerated articles, a neutral trade, which all nations, maintaining a non-belligerent character, were, implicitly invited to prosecute. The affect of this partial relaxation of its policy, seems however, not to have corresponded with the expectations, under the influence of which, the Neapolitan Government had adopted it. The American Merchants, unwilling to expose their property to the hazards, to which, the still subsisting restrictions, upon a free commercial intercourse with this kingdom, subjected it, hesitated to avail themselves of the proferred indulgence. To overcome this repugnance; and to encourage a trade, which it was so much the interest of the Neapolitan Kingdom to cultivate, and extend, Joachim the first, on the thirtieth day of June Eighteen Hundred and nine, passed a special decree, by which American vessels were declared to be exempted from the operation of the letter of the blockade Laws; and were authorised to import into this Kingdom not only the articles enumerated in the Decree of the thirty first of March preceding, but the additional articles of Rice and Staves; Peruvian bark and other medicinal cargoes; Georgia, Louisiana, and Carolina Cotton; Java Coffee and Sugar. And that nothing might be wanting to give assurance to the American Merchants, for the safety of the trade to which they were thus solicited, the Marquis de Gallo,[47] the then Secretary for foreign affairs, by the order of the King on the first day of July, Eighteen Hundred and nine, addressed a communication to Mr. Dagen Esquire, the Consul of the United States, declaring it to be the determination of His Majesty *as a general measure* that all American vessels which should arrive in this Kingdom, with direct expedition and positive destination for its ports, should be freely admitted. Provided, they should be furnished with the proper certification of the origin of their cargoes, and with the requisite papers of navigation in due order; and provided also, that they should

---

[47] The Marquis of Gallo is the same person who later became the Duke of Gallo. See note 9 on page 98.

not have become liable to the Royal Decree of the twentieth of December, Eighteen Hundred and Five, and the ninth of January Eighteen Hundred and Eight, relative to the English trade and that of the Neutral powers. These decrees, were only communicated to the merchants of the United States, who eager to realize the advantages which they proferred; with a relying confidence in the integrity of the Government, by which they had been promulgated, despatched their ships, freighted with valuable cargoes, to the unsealed ports of the Kingdom of Naples. The first that arrived were hospitably received; permitted to land and sell their goods and to return without molestation. But others, considerable in number and value, although strictly conforming to the requirements of the Decrees above recited, were unfortunately rich enough to tempt the cupidity of the Government, by whose orders, they were perfidiously seized, sequestered, confiscated, and sold, without colourable pretext; their officers oppressed and persecuted; and their crews turned adrift, to perish in a strange land, or to be returned, as they eventually were, to their native country, at the expense of the American Government.

These acts of atrocity and outrages, the Sicilian Government has never sought to vindicate or excuse. His Excellency, in his note of the thirtieth of May, professes not to justify them. They are reprobated alike by the Government of the United States, and that of His Majesty; by the party complaining, and that against which the complaint is preferred; by the representative of the victims of the practised rapacity on the one hand, and the responsible representative (as the American Government maintains) of the wrongdoer on the other.

The only question in contestation, therefore, is this; whether the sufferers of these admitted injuries, are bound, as His Excellency asserts, to regard them as "misfortunes to be deplored" or whether as the Government of The United States insists, they may not rightfully consider them in the light of wrongs to be redressed, by the Kingdom of the Two Sicilies.

The pretensions of the American Government are affirmative of three propositions:

1st That its citizens, during the years Eighteen Hundred and Nine and afterwards, were engaged in a lawful trade with the port of the Kingdom of Naples, in the persecution of which, their property to a large amount, was forcibly and injuriously seized, confiscated and sold.

2nd That the injuries of which they complain proceeded from the Government of the Neapolitan Kingdom.

3rd That the Kingdom of Naples having committed the wrongs, is bound to redress them; and that no change in its system of Government, or in the person of its rulers, can dispense it from this obligation.

The truth of the first of these propositions has not been denied. The proofs of its verity are written[48] within the reach of the Neapolitan Government, and shew[49] it to be undeniable.

The second and third are controverted. These it is the design of the Undersigned to vindicate and sustain, and in investigating the principles upon which they are based, respectfully to examine the positions, assured by His Excellency in his note of the thirtieth of May, and to submit to the view of His Majesty's Government, some of the many considerations, which, in his apprehension, incontestably shew, that, those positions interpose no well grounded defence to the American demands.

To support the second of the propositions, above asserted, the Government of the United States, does not feel itself called on to maintain, that the Neapolitan Government at the epoch to which this discussion refers, was strictly legitimate. Whether it was, or was not, is, in its view, wholly immaterial in relation to the present controversy. It limits its assertion, therefore, to the fact that the political affairs of the Kingdom of Naples during the period covered by the American confiscations, were under the direction of an Established Government; that Murat was its King de facto[50]; and that in the exercise of its sovereign power, the injuries, for which redress is demanded were perpetrated.

The proofs, sustaining these positions, are many and various; and, as conclusive, as they are notorious.

His Majesty, Ferdinand, the first, was driven from the throne of Naples, in the year Eighteen Hundred and six. He sought a refuge from the power of the conqueror, in the island of Sicily, where, under the protection of his ally, he remained in security until Eighteen Hundred and fifteen, when he was happily restored to the dominion, from which he had been expelled. In Eighteen Hundred and Eight, Murat under the title of Joachim,

---

[48] This word "written" does not appear in printed Senate Document No. 70, concerning which see above, note 44, p. 254.

[49] This word is spelled "show" in Senate Document 70.

[50] This phrase is italicized in Senate Document 70.

the First, was proclaimed Sovereign of the Kingdom of Naples, and invested with full regal authority. From the period of his investiture, up to that of his expulsion from the Kingdom, in Eighteen Hundred and fifteen, he wielded within its limits, all the powers, and asserted all the prerogatives of royalty. The Government, of which he was the acknowledged head, was complete in its organization, and efficient in its action. It had its ministry for internal and external affairs; its army; its Navy, and its custom-houses. Officers were appointed and dismissed; orders proclaimed and enforced; and decrees promulgated and executed in its name. Justice was administered, and commerce regulated under its auspices. Taxes were imposed and collected, and the public treasures disbursed, in subservience to its authority. In all its various departments; Civil and Military; judicial and ecclesiastical it was operated, within the bounds of its asserted sway, without molestation. The Neapolitan people acquiesced in its authority, and yielded to its rule an approbatory submission. During the extended term of its existence there were no rebellions amongst its subjects, seriously to threaten its stability, but its powers were everywhere recognized and by everybody obeyed. In a word, it was regarded and dealt with, as a Government, authoritative and established.

This Government, moreover, was, with a single exception, recognized by the leading powers of Europe, with which it interchanged the ordinary diplomatic courtesies. It received and entertained Ambassadors, Ministers, and Consuls; and was itself represented, in the persons of its accredited agents at foreign Courts. It stood, in the view of the world, in the attitude of a Government, independent and worthy of a place in the great community of Nations.

Nor was it, as His Excellency intimates, the Government of a mere military occupation. It had none of the attributes of such a rule. It professed not to repose on Military power, however it may have defended itself by its means. It was fixed, not temporary; civil, not military. In the mode of its action, as well as the means of its operation, it was administered by the accustomed instruments of established civil sway.

And are not these conclusive evidences of the existence of an established Government in this Kingdom, during the incumbency of Murat? of a Government, capable of acting upon the interests of others, and responsible for its wrongs? with which of the powers of sovereignty, was it not clothed? which of its privileges did it not enjoy? will it be seriously contended, that its commercial policy was not subject to its control? The very circumstances connected with the already detailed transactions, will refute such an assumption. It was in the exercise of this undoubted function of Sovereignty, that Joachim modified the commercial system of this Kingdom, in the manner already stated. *The decrees announcing these modifications were in his name, and authenticated by his Ministers.*[51] They professed to emanate from the Neapolitan Government; and were respected and dealt with, as its acts. And when the property of the unsuspecting victims of an unprecedented atrocity, was allured within the perfidious grasp of this Government, the same Sovereign function was faithlessly emanated in its seizure, condemnation, and sale. *The decrees of confiscation of the American vessels and cargoes, were promulgated by the authority and in the name of Joachim, the first, and authenticated by his Ministers; and the sales directed by his arbitrary edicts were conducted and consummated by the officers of the Kingdom of Naples.*[52] They were, therefore, the acts of its Government, and for which, upon the plainest principles, it was responsible.

His Excellency nevertheless asserts that the Government of Naples, at the period to which this controversy relates, was not *de facto*[53] in Murat; that the Kingdom itself, was but a fief of the French Empire, the supreme power over which, was in Napoleon, to whom the American confiscations were justly attributable.

The considerations adduced in support of these positions, the Undersigned, will now proceed to analyze and examine, premising, however, that even if they could be successfully maintained, he does not perceive or admit, that they would materially vary the question of the responsibility of this Kingdom for the acts complained of, since if these proceeded from the Neapolitan Government, the nation represented by it, would according to his view, be equally answerable, whether the powers of that Government, were in the hands of Napoleon or Murat. It is not pretended, that there was an amalgamation of the Governments of France and Naples. They were under the Dominion of different laws, administered by officers deriving their authority from different sources. Nor is it pretended, that the American confiscations avowedly proceeded from the Government

[51], [52], [53] These sentences and phrases are underscored in copy with Mr. Nelson's original despatch No. 13, and italicized in Senate Document No. 70.

of France; the Undersigned has already shewn that they were acts of the Government of Naples, and enforced by its power; *and he is prepared to maintain that if Naples was governed as a separate Kingdom, no matter by whom, and the powers of its Government were enacted to the prejudice of the American Merchants, the Nation is responsible for its acts, and bound to redress the injuries it has inflicted.*[54]

But are the positions of His Excellency sustained by the evidence, to which he has appealed for their support? The Undersigned thinks not.

The provisions of the Act of Bayonne,[55] of the fifteenth of July, Eighteen Hundred and Eight are supposed by His Excellency, to furnish proof of the dependance of the Kingdom of Naples, upon the Empire of France. That act declared, Joachim Napoleon, King of Naples and Sicily from the first day of August Eighteen Hundred and Eight. It settled the crown upon him and his male descendants, natural and legitimate, in a direct line, and in the order of primo geniture to the perpetual exclusion of female descendants, and with a reservation of a right in Queen Caroline[56] to the throne, should she survive her husband; with a reversion to Napoleon and his male descendants, natural and legitimate, or adopted, in the event of Joachim's dying without issue, capable of taking under the settlement; and in default of such heirs of Napoleon as well as of Murat, it provided that the crown should descend to the male heirs of Joseph,[57] King of Spain, Louis, King of Holland, and Jerome, King of Westphalia successively. It likewise declared that the title of grand admiral of France should be preserved (conservera) to Joachim, and should, thereafter, be attached to the Neapolitan crown.

Such being the tenor of the act referred to, the Undersigned confesses, he is at a loss to understand, how its provisions can

---

54 See above, note 51, 52, 53.

55 Napoleon retaliated with the promulgation on April 17, 1808, of the Bayonne Decree, with which he ordered the seizure of every American vessel in the ports of France. Note the discrepancy in the date of the Bayonne Decree.

56 On Jan. 20, 1800, Carolina Annunziata Bonaparte (1782-1839) married Joachim Murat. She assumed the title of Countess of Lipona. They had four children: — Prince Napoleon Achille (1801-47); Lucien Napoleon Charles, Prince of Pontecorvo (1803-78); Letizia Giuseppina (1802-1859); and Luisa Giulia Carolina (1805-1889).

57 Joseph Bonaparte (1768-1844), elder brother of Napoleon I, was made, on July 7, 1808, King of Spain and of the Indies. Louis Napoleon (1778-1846), third brother of Napoleon I, was from 1806 to 1810 King of Holland. Jerome Napoleon (1784-1860), youngest brother of Napoleon I, was King of Westphalia from 1807 to 1813.

be supposed to yield a support to the proposition of His Excellency. Applying to them the customary and well established rules of interpretation, it is respectfully suggested, that they distinctly refute it.

What was the effect of this settlement? Was it not to divest Napoleon of his title (whatever that may have been) to the crown and Kingdom of Naples, and to transfer it to another? Was it not, to invest Joachim with full royal authority, as far as the Emperor of the French had the competency to confer it?

The Undersigned humbly apprehends that by force and in virtue of the settlement, Joachim, was relatively to Napoleon at least, the rightful Sovereign of the Kingdom of Naples. That until the occurrence of the revoke, *and in the actual circumstances of the parties to the settlement,* most improbable contingency, upon which the reversion depended, Napoleon had no claim and could exert no power over this Kingdom; and that the right to the throne, confessed by it, was in Joachim, absolutely and unconditionally. *His tenure rested upon no contingency. The settlement imposed no restrictions upon his power; no limitations upon his authority. It recognized no condition of dependence; and devolved no duty incompatible with the free exercise of the Sovereignty, it conferred.*

This act therefore, instead of subserving the purpose, for which it has been invoked; instead of showing a reservation of the Supreme authority of the Acts of Napoleon, evinces its unshackled transfer to Joachim, who continued in its exercise, until by the pressure of a foreign force, he was compelled to relinquish its enjoyment.

Nor can the proposition of His Excellency devise any aid from the circumstances connected with the promalgation of the Berlin and Milan Decrees. Apart from the fact, that they preceded the reign of Joachim, who but enforced their provisions, as of Laws, which he found in operation upon his accession to the throne, they never professed to enact the authority, imparted to them, by the note of His Excellency. They did not purport, to be obligatory upon the Neapolitan Kingdom. Neither the decree of Berlin, nor that of Milan, was per se proprio rigore, of any force within its jurisdiction. To render them operative within its limits, it was indispensable that they should be re-enacted by its Government. They were thus re-enacted; and afterwards enforced, not as decrees of the French Empire, but as those of the Neapolitan Kingdom. The Undersigned will not worry the patience of His Excellency, by an argument to prove, that if, at the time of the promulgation of these decrees, Naples had been politically incorporated with France, no agency on its part could have been required, to give force to Laws, which were equally obligatory upon every portion of the Empire, which they assumed to control. The very fact, therefore that its authority was invoked to impart efficiency to those decrees, goes distinctly to demonstrate the separate, independent political existence of the Neapolitan Government.

And these conclusions are in strict accordance with all the public acts of Napoleon, which as far as they are known to the Undersigned, verify the position he maintains. His Excellency well knows, so decided was the policy of The French Emperor in this regard, that, in the original settlement of the crown of this Kingdom upon Joseph and his legitimate heirs male, he cautiously incorporated the proviso "that the crowns of France and Naples should never be united on the same head"; and that after Murat's investiture, he continued to bear public testimony to the independence of the Neapolitan Government, by the relations he maintained with it; represented as his power always was, at the Court of Naples, in the person of a diplomatic functionary, whilst that of Murat, was in like manner represented at the Court of France.

But it is alleged, that notwithstanding these ostensible indications of Sovereign power, Murat was in point of fact, the mere, passive instrument of Napoleon; and that in decreeing the confiscation of the American property, he but acted in obedience to the will of the French Emperor; or in other words, that he yielded to an influence, which he could not successfully have resisted.

The Undersigned does not doubt, that in its general policy, the Neapolitan Kingdom may have felt and submitted to the influence of France. It resulted, perhaps, as a necessary consequence from the circumstances which united the two nations. They were engaged in a common war, against a formidable enemy; and were bound together by bonds of the most intimate alliance. The incumbent of the throne of Naples was deeply interested in the prosperity of France, and was likely, for the purpose of perpetuating his own dominion, to yield a hearty concurrance, in any policy which might be calculated to strengthen Napoleon's power. Besides, he owed the throne he occupied to the favorable opinion of the Emperor, and a sentiment of gratitude would naturally prompt him, to subserve the views of his benefactor. But whilst the Undersigned admits the probable, general existence of this influence, he perceives nothing in the circumstances connected with the American confiscations, to create a belief, that they were acted upon by this indirect power; or that they were superinduced by any other influence, than the pressure of Murat's necessities, which he determined to supply, even at the expense of a Nation's faith solemnly pledged. By what motive, could Napoleon have been prompted, in encouraging the seizure of the property of the American Merchants? *The trade, in the prosecution of which, they were engaged did not interfere with his policy.* The British orders of blockade which it was the aim of his system to counteract, had caused to interrupt neutral intercourse with the ports of this Kingdom. *Nor could he have been instigated by a desire of pecuniary gain; because the spoils derived from these acts of foul enormity, were not applied to his use, but were appropriated to the exclusive purposes of the Neapolitan Kingdom and its Monarch.*

Conceding however the existence and enaction of the imparted influence, in the condemnation of the American property; and what is to be inferred from the concession? That it relieved Murat and his government from a just responsibility for their acts? Such a principle will not, surely, be seriously insisted upon. To maintain that a Government regularly constituted, universally recognized, and operating all the wonted functions of Sovereignty, may release itself from responsibility for its official acts, by interposing a plea of the alleged influence of a foreign power, would be, to license every Government to trample upon the most sacred rights of others with impunity. Under the operation of such a principle, if it could be made practically available, all international intercourse would be rendered insecure and circumvented by hazards, against the latent action of which, the most cautious vigilance could not guard. Nor would the evils resulting from its establishment be less extensive in their application, than fatal in their tendency. Looking to the political condition of Europe as it at present exists; as it has existed for centuries, and as, in all human probability, will long continue to exist; to the unequal distribution of its wealth and power, between the large states and the small; the strong and the weak; and estimating the influence, which all History teaches, is unavoidably incidental, particularly in seasons of general commo-

265

tion, to the relations of springing from such inequalities, and His Excellency will at once perceive, that the doctrine and a consideration, if acknowledged, would leave but few modern states liable for their acts.

If an established Government, in the exercise of its Sovereign power; distrustful of its own judgement, or willing to win the favorable opinion and support of a powerful neighbour, or ally; or, instigated by the suggestions of an unworthy fear, or a sordid interest, chooses to submit itself to foreign influence; it is a result, against which strangers cannot guard, and for the consequences of which, they cannot be answerable. The motives, which may induce such subserviency; the extent of its operation, or the mode and manner of its action, are alike beyond the knowledge and controwl [sic] of their powers. They have neither the right to institute, nor the means of rendering available, an enquiry into these hidden influences. They cannot be required to look beyond the official acts of such a Government, which they are not justified in regaining, but bound to treat as the emanations of a responsible authority.

The Decrees confiscating the American property, *were officially the acts of the Neapolitan Government.* They avowed its authority; they were clothed in its sanctions, and enforced by its power. Through its agency, therefore, the injuries, for which atonement is now sought, were inflicted; and from it, the victims of those injuries had an unquestionable right to demand redress.

The Undersigned has thus briefly, but he trusts, not inconclusively, replied to all the material suggestions, contained in the note of His Excellency, which are applicable to the second proposition. He has shewn that during the period to which this discussion relates, the interests of the Kingdom of Naples, were directed by a Government, regularly organized and established; that Murat was its King; that the confiscations complained of proceeded from its authority; and that under whatever advice or influence, they may have been decreed, they were nevertheless, the acts of the Neapolitan Government and for which it was responsible. It remains to enquire, whether the responsibility of the Government of Murat, for the wrongs shewn to have been committed by it, has devolved upon that of His present Majesty. That it has, the Undersigned is persuaded, may be rendered apparent, by a recurrence to principles incontestably established; by the authority of publicity of acknowledged reputation, and by the confirmatory practice of most of the powers of Modern Europe.

266

The following are the principles maintained by the Government of The United States —

That a nation is a moral power, capable of contracting obligations, and of committing wrongs. That as a moral person, it is bound to perform the one, and to redress the other. That this obligation is independent of, and remains unaffected by changes in its actual government. That whoever comes to the possession of its sovereign power, takes it subject to this obligation. That, neither a revolution in a State, nor a change in its rulers, or the form of its Government can dispense it, from the Duty of its performance; but, that as long, as the Nation exists, the obligation exists; and that even in the case of Conquest, its validity remains unimpaired.

It further maintains, that the acts of the rulers of a State, while engaged in the exercise of its Sovereign powers, are the acts of the State itself. That to constitute them such, it is sufficient, that they proceed from its *actual Government,* without reference to the source or tenure of its authority. That this is especially true in regard to the action of a Government upon the interests of strangers. That foreign nations, in their dealings with States, may enough regard the undisturbed possessions of the Sovereign power, as its rightful possessions; and that this duty results from their obligation to forbear from all interference, with the internal policy of such States.

It believes, that these principles are consonant to reason; that they are recommended by considerations of public convenience; and that apart from the protection afforded by their application, there can exist no security in the intercourse of Nations. It maintains, that the establishment of a different doctrine would draw after it, the most pernicious consequences. That under its sanction, every revolution in a Government, would avail to cancel the obligations of the Nation represented by it. That by inviting on the part of foreign traders, an inquisitorial scrutiny, into the origin and sufficiency of the titles of its rulers, the independence of every State, would be ceaselessly invaded, and its internal tranquillity constantly disturbed. That, in a word, it would provoke a continual intervention between independent powers, and thus essentially subvert all the rights of self-government.

Applying these principles to the case of the American claimants, it insists, that from Eighteen Hundred and nine to Eighteen Hundred and fifteen, Murat was the actual possessor of the Sovereign power of the Kingdom of Naples. That its Government was in his hands. That as its ruler, he represented its political power. That his public, political acts, were the acts of the Neapolitan Nation. That the American confiscations were his acts, because the decrees which enforced them were issued in his name and by his authority; and were executed by the power of his Government. That they were, therefore, imputable to the Neapolitan Nation. That being founded in manifest and admitted wrong, the Neapolitan Nation was morally bound, to repair the losses occasioned by them; and that the Nation, which contracted this obligation, notwithstanding the change in its ruler still exists, and through his Majesty's Government, which represents its power, is now bound to redeem it.

The Undersigned has said that the principles contended for by the American Government are sustained by "the authority of publicists of acknowledged reputation.["] In support of this position, he refers His Excellency to Vattels[58] Laws of Nations Book 1, cl. 4, Sect. 40, and Book 2. chapt. 18, Sect. 324. as explanatory of the representative relations, subsisting between a Sovereign and his subjects; of the obligations growing out of those relations, and of the duty of their fulfillment, by the Nation, to which they attach. A satisfactory discussion and supposition of the whole doctrine applicable to this controversy, His Excellency will find in Baron Puffendorff's[59] invaluable treatise, on the rights of Nature and of Nations. The author, in Liv. 8 ch. 12, Sect. 2. uses the following decisive language —

"De ce que nous venons de dire il paroît comment on doit resoudre une question proposée par Aristote, savoir si, lors'qu'un Peuple passe, du gouvernement absolu d'un monarque, ou d'une oligarchie, au gouvernement populaire; l'etat ainsi devenu libre doit garder, les Traites, les contracts, et les autres actes du Roi, ou des grandes, sous la domination desquels il etoît auparavant?[60] Ceux qui soutensiant la negative, se fondoient, sur ce que l'etat ne pouvait etrê tenu que de son propre fait, n'etait pas obligé d'accomplir les engagements d'un monarque absolu, ou d'un petit hombre de grands, dont l'autorité avoit été fondêe uniquement sur la force, et non pas rapportée à l'utilité publique; de sorte qu'alors ce n'etoît pas proprement un Etat; Mais c'est là sans contradit

---

[58] Vattell (von), Emmerich (1714-67). Swedish jurist, son of a Protestant minister, he was born in Couvet (Neuchatel). He served as a jurist in several European countries after finishing his studies at Basel and Geneva. He is best known for his work *Droit des gens ou principes de la loi naturelle appliqués a la conduite et aux affaires des nations et des souverains.* Neuchatel, 1758, 2 volumes. This work has been published in many editions, both in French and English translations. The first American edition was published in 1796. See also note 61, p. 270).

[59] Puffendorf, Le Baron de. *Le Droit de la Nature des gens* . . . Tr. from the Latin by Jean Barbeyrac. 1771. In this edition the quotation cited appears in v. 2, bk. 8, ch. 12, sec. 2, p. 607. Mr. Nelson, however, more probably, quoted from

une raison bien frivole. *Car une tête malade ne laisse pas pour cela d'être une tête; ainsi ce que les chefs de l'etat ont fait, quelque vicieux et dérégléz qu'ils fussent, est censé fait par tout le corps de l'Etat.*"

The principles asserted in the foregoing extract, His Excellency will not fail to perceive, are substantially, if not precisely those, upon which the American demands are supported. — The writer maintains, and illustrates his view by a very strong example, that the acts of the Government of a State, are the acts of the State itself. — That no revolution or change in the Government, can discharge the State from the obligations, which the acts of its rulers have imposed on it. That the "responsibility of *the State reposes upon the facts, of the actual existence of the Government, without being in any wise affected, by its organization or character.* That whether rightful or otherwise, its obligation is not varied. That, in the significant language of the author, "although the head may be sick, it does not therefore cease to be a head"; and that a Government founded *on mere force,* is as competent to charge the nation ruled by it, as if it were legitimate.

Nor can the force of the reasoning, or the weight of the high authority, by which it is sustained, be weakened, in its application to the present controversy, by an attempt to shew [sic] that the Government of Murat, was founded in usurpation — Without stopping to enquire into the nature of Murat's title to the throne of Naples, which the Undersigned may well admit to have been defective, relatively to Ferdinand, its legitimate Sovereign, he insists, that as its actual, undisturbed possessor, the Government of the United States, and its citizens under its protection, were justified in dealing with him, as with the rightful Sovereign; and that all the obligations growing out of their intercourse with his Kingdom, were as binding upon the Neapolitan Nation, as if it had been under the rule of Ferdinand himself. The nation was the same by whomsoever it may have been governed; *and it was with the Nation, and not its Governor, in his personal capacity, that the American Merchants maintained their intercourse.* —

So fixed and cardinal indeed, is this principle, in the view of

---

the Amsterdam edition in French, 1712, with Barbeyrac's notes. This was in the United States Legation's files. See below, Throop chapter, pp. 400-401.

60 The text of this quotation thus far only is quoted in Perotta, *op. cit.* 60; the remainder of the quotation, as here given, direct from Mr. Nelson's despatch (the original manuscript despatch) follows the text as found in the several editions of Puffendorf, allowing however for slight variations in the Puffendorff texts, as comparing them with Mr. Nelson's quotation, which variations, however, are apparently merely slight printers' errors in the spelling.

writers upon public Law, that even in the case of admitted usurpation, as understood by them, it is unequivocally asserted. Vattel in his treatise upon the Laws of Nations distinctly affirms it. In Book 4. ch. 5 devoted to the discussion of the rights of States to receive and entertain public Ministers, which he determines to be an incident of Sovereign power, he considers the question, *"whether foreign Nations may receive the ambassadors and other ministers of a Usurper* and send their ministers to him?"[61] When he then decides "In this particular foreign powers take for their rule, the circumstance of actual possession, if the interests of their affairs so require; *and indeed there cannot be a more certain rule, or one that is more agreeable to the Law of Nations, and the independence of States. As Foreigners have no right to interfere in the domestic concerns of a nation, they are not obliged to canvass and scrutinize her conduct, in the management of them, in order to determine how far it is just or unjust. They may, if they think proper, suppose the right to be annexed to the possession."*[62] Even admitting then Murat to have been a Usurper, the American Merchants were justified in treating with him as with a legitimate Sovereign. They had not the right to "canvass or scrutinize" his title to the throne, which he occupied; but were bound to suppose "the right to be annexed to the possession" of the powers of Government. It would be superfluous to add, that the power then to treat, necessarily implies the validity of the obligations, which the intercourse imposed, and as these attached to the Nation, the Nation was and will remain responsible for their fulfillment.

And His Excellency will find this view of the subject supported by Puffendorff in the third section of the chapter already referred to, in which he asserts and illustrates the doctrine contended for by the American Government; maintaining, that it is reasonable, that the acts and engagements of a usurper, after he has been driven from his usurped dominion, should be regarded as obligatory upon the nation represented by him; and distinguishing

---

61 Quotations verified to Emmerich de Vattell, *The Law of Nations.* Translated from the French, Phila., Nicklin and Johnson, 1829. The quoted passage appears in Bk. 4, ch. 5, sec. 68, p. 519.

62 Quoted material here differs slightly from the original text. The translation from the original text is as follows: "Here foreign powers, if the advantage of their affairs invites them to it, assume possession; there is no rule more certain, or more agreeable to the law of nations and the independence of them. As foreigners have no right to interfere in the domestic concern of a people, they are not obliged to canvass and inspect its economy in those particulars, or to weigh either the justice or injustice of them. They may, if they think proper, suppose the right to be annexed to the possession."

270

between the power of a restored Sovereign, even those acts of a usurper, which affect the internal interests of the Kingdom, *which he admits may be abolished,* and those, that relate to the interests of strangers, *which he decides to be beyond the controul of the new government.*

With this brief exposition of the views of the American Government, the Undersigned, deferring for the present a reference to the examples drawn from the History of Modern Europe, which are believed to give to them a decided sanction, will proceed to examine the suggestions, by which, His Excellency, in his note of the thirtieth of May has assailed them.

In the first place, it is alledged "that admitting Murat's independence of Napoleon and the French Empire; and conceding, that he was, at the time of the depredations complained of, in the full enjoyment of the Sovereignty of Naples, yet that his acknowledgement by the expelled Sovereign, was necessary to render such possession *rightful* without which, the present Government of Naples cannot be held responsible for his wrongs." This proposition if sustainable, the Undersigned admits, would furnish a satisfactory answer to the demands, which it has been made his duty to bring to the view of His Sicilian Majesty's Government. *But it assumes the whole question in controversy.* It takes for granted, that which is distinctly denied; and which, it is incumbent on the Government of His Majesty, in evidence of its irresponsibility, to prove. It is supported by no authority, and in the apprehension of the Undersigned, none can be found to sustain it. The Government of The United States disclaims all obligations on its part, to shew, that the authority exercised by Murat over this Kingdom, was rightful. *The responsibility of the Sicilian Government for his acts, depends, in its view, in no degree, upon the character of that authority.* However defective may have been his title to the throne, which he occupied, its *actual incumbency and the exercise of the Sovereign power of the Government* as has already been shewn, authorised foreigners, to regard, treat, and deal with the Nation, through him, as though a rightful Sovereign. To support the American claims, therefore, it suffices to shew the existence de facto, of the Government of Murat. And to constitute such a Government, it will not be pretended, that "the acknowledgement of the expelled Sovereign" could have been necessary, because being founded upon mere possession, and disconnected from all question of right, it might,

271

as in truth it did, exist in defiance of the more legitimate claims of another.

His Excellency next maintains "that Murat (putting aside his investiture) had no other more *specious title* to the throne of the Kingdom of Naples, than that of a conqueror; and that conquest, in the opinion of accredited publicists, is not consolidated, unless followed by a treaty of peace, or entire submission on the part of the Sovereign, who has lost his dominions." To this position, the undersigned apprehends it will suffice to oppose the reasoning employed in reply to the last. *This controversy does not turn upon a question of title; but upon one of possession*; and to fix the possession of the powers of the Neapolitan Government in Murat, it will not be contended, that "the acknowledgement of the expelled Sovereign" was necessary. It might have been requisite to "consolidate" and perfect his *title*; but his incumbency could not be the less *actual,* because his right remained unacknowledged by Ferdinand.

The undersigned readily concedes, that, notwithstanding the actual, established possession by Murat, of the powers of the Neapolitan Government, the right to reclaim and recover his lost dominion, existed and might properly have been asserted by the expelled Sovereign; and that this right could have been extinguished only by the suggested alternatives, of treaty, or entire submission. Ferdinand's claim to the throne of this Kingdom, continued to exist, notwithstanding its conquest and possession by another. As against him, the conquest could be consolidated "only by his own consent, express, or implied. As long as this was with-held, he had a right to use such means as he could controul, to recover the possession, which he had lost. But His Excellency will perceive, that there is nothing in the principle thus stated, at all inimical to the pretensions of the American Government. *It has never asserted the legitimacy of Murat's title; or that Ferdinand had relinquished his claim to the throne.* The right to recover the Kingdom might well have existed in Ferdinand, whilst its actual inclusive possession was in Murat. — The Government of Murat may have been illegitimate and usurped as against Ferdinand, whilst, as the Undersigned has already shewn, *being established, it was endowed with full political capacity relatively to Foreign States.* —

Nor is the aspect of the question at all varied by the consideration, that Ferdinand did in fact, continue to assert his claim to the Neapolitan Kingdom, since its assertion did not disturb

272

the possession of it, by Murat. From the period of his repulsion up to that of his restoration, Ferdinand remained a stranger to the actual government of Naples. His authority was not recognized within its limits. His claim existed; but it was latent and entirely disconnected from the possession. The powers of the Government was in other hands. *Murat reigned de facto.* There was no conflict of jurisdiction within the kingdom but all its interests were directed and controuled by a power, active efficient and enclusive.

The doctrine of the American Government is said to be inadmissible because of the mischievous consequences with which, it is supposed to be pregnant, the most obvious of which is represented to be "that a Prince temporarily dispossessed of his kingdom besides the misfortunes and calamities, consequent upon the suspension of his authority, may *at his own expense,* atone for the damages, done to Foreigners, by the Usurper on occasion of the effected usurpation;" and the unreasonableness of visiting upon the restored Monarch such a responsibility, is illustrated, by the supposed case of "The Robber" "Nonius" and his "neighbours" —

The reply to these suggestions will be as brief, as the Undersigned trusts, it will be satisfactory. *The imputed consequences cannot flow from the doctrine asserted by the Government of the United States.* His Excellency's argument is founded upon a misapprehension of the nature of that doctrine. It confounds the *individual* with the *State — Against the first,* no claim has been preferred by the American Government. *It is from the last, from the Nation,* that it seeks the required reparation. It is not to Ferdinand the second, in his personal capacity, that an appeal for redress has been presented; nor is it expected, that the just demands of the American Merchants will be satisfied out of his private funds; but the claims are advanced against the Kingdom and against His Majesty, in his political capacity, as its organ and representative; and the indemnity, insisted on, is sought from the treasury of the Nation.

And is it unreasonable that the Nation should redress the injuries, which, it has, itself inflicted? The wrongs heaped upon the American Merchants, did not proceed from Murat in his private and personal capacity — Individually, he was impotent and harmless. But in his public, political capacity, *as the Representative of the Neapolitan Nation and armed with the power of its Government,* he was competent to enormities which he

273

perpetrated. By the agency of the Sovereign power of the Neapolitan Kingdom, the wrongs complained of, were consummated. That Kingdom was therefore the aggressor; and from that Kingdom the aggrieved seek a retribution. —

The application of these obvious principles to the case put by his Excellency, will furnish a ready solution of the difficulty, it suggests. "The Robber" and "Nonius" are *but one and the same political person,* because each represents the nation. The State, by its agent "The Robber," acting in its name, and with its power spoils "the neighbours" and the State, by its agent "Nonius" is bound to make a suitable reparation. *The Nation cannot free itself from the responsibility, imposed on it by one agent, by acknowledging another. It cannot acquit itself of its just obligations, by a change in the persons of its rulers.*

His Excellency intimates that the losses sustained by the American Merchants should be quietly borne by them, because they were the fruits of their own imprudence, in dealing with a Government, so unsettled as was that of Naples; and a reference is made to the war, alledged to have been vigorously prosecuted by Ferdinand for the recovery of the Kingdom, to shew their temerity in having dealt with its possessors. The undersigned has no desire, because he holds such an investigation to be entirely foreign to the controversy, to enter upon a review of the incident of the war referred to. As he has already had the honor to state, with whatever vigor it may have been prosecuted, it had not the effect of unsettling Murats [sic] possession of the Sovereign power. But the Undersigned is not aware of any effect, which from its nature or the measures employed for its accomplishment, could have held out a reasonable hope of even partial success, to the expelled Sovereign, after the date of the expedition set on foot against the Islands of Ischia and Procida, in Eighteen Hundred and nine. From that period, the Undersigned has always supposed, that the object of His Majesty's most anxious solicitude, was to preserve the possession of Sicily, which he held under the protection of the formidable Naval power of his ally; that his position was one of defence, not of offence; and that, looking to the condition of the fortunes of the belligerent parties, there was much strange reason to have apprehended the loss of Sicily to his Majesty, than of Naples to Murat. Nor has the history of that eventful period led the Undersigned to believe, that the fortunes of Murat, were as unstable, as His Excellency seems to have supposed them. It is, at least certain, that the possession of

274

the Neapolitan Kingdom was retained by him, from Eighteen Hundred and Eight, 'til eighteen hundred and fifteen; and so firmly had his authority been established, that as late as December, Eighteen Hundred and fourteen, when the colossal power, which conferred upon him the crown, had crumbled into ruins, the separate political existence of the Neapolitan Government and of its King, was recognized and reasserted, in the face of Europe, by some of its leading powers. — And was it extraordinary that the American Merchants should have regarded such a Government, as established, and as competent to deal for and bind the nation represented by it? or that yielding to its treacherous solicitations, they should under the plighted protection of its decrees, have presented a trade with its ports? They found it, in the actual possession of Sovereign power; engaged in the exercise of all its functions and recognized by the Governments of Europe. And is it strange, or to be imputed to them for reproach, that when the nations, by which it was surrounded, with every means of forming an accurate judgement, saw enough in its actual predicament to certify its established political existence that American traders, removed by thousands of miles from its operations, and without the advantage of those means of investigation, should have treated it as a Sovereign power, and acting upon a faith in its official promises, have placed themselves within its grasp? That in point of principle they were justified in the course pursued by them, the Undersigned has already shewn; that in availing themselves of the right to pursue it, they acted with all the precautions which a proper prudence would have prescribed, the history of the transactions, will abundantly testify.

But it is said that the American Merchants in engaging in the trade, in it's results, so disastrous to their interests, were prompted by a spirit of speculation, and that, as in the event of its having proved profitable, they would have enjoyed its advantages, they should patiently submit to the losses incurred, in its unsuccessful prosecution. Admit that they were prompted by this spirit of gain. It was a laudable spirit. It is that which gives impulse to all commercial adventure. — It was a spirit of honest gain which sought not its gratification, in the invasion of the rights of others; and if in prosecuting the trade, thrown open to them in the ports of this Kingdom, they had encountered the reverses some times incident to commercial enterprises; if the State of the markets had been such, as instead of acquiting their toils and hazards in anticipated profits, to have exposed them to loss, the character of the American Merchants, afford a sufficient guarantee that the sacrifice would have been borne by them, without reprising. — But their losses were of a different description, and inflicted upon them, by the hand of Governmental power, in defiance of the clearest right, and of every principle, which should be held sacred in the intercourse of Nations. Of such injuries it became them to complain; and for their redress, it is natural, that they should invoke the aid of their Government, which owes, and will extend to them and to their interests, an efficient protection.

The position next assumed by His Excellency, in his note of the thirtieth of May, is this; "That the present Government of Naples, ought not to be held responsible for the American confiscations, because their proceeds instead of being applied to the public Service were converted by Murat, to meet his private expenses. That the Kingdom of Naples, having derived no advantage from the acts complained of, is not bound to indemnify the sufferers."

This proposition, the undersigned apprehends, is susceptible of two obvious and equally satisfactory answers.

The first is one of principle. The validity of the claims of the American Merchants, in no degree depends, upon the direction given to the fruits of the confiscations in question. *Their demands are founded, upon the seizure, condemnation, and sale of their vessels and cargoes.* The injuries inflicted upon them, consisted in the acts, by which, their property was fraudulently and forcibly wrested from their possession. The wrongs were consummated from the moment that they were arbitrarily deprived of that which belonged to them. The loss was then incurred; and to the sufferers, it was a matter of little concern, whether the proceeds of these acts of more than piratical atrocity, were appropriated to public or to private uses; to worthy or to unworthy objects — In either case, they were equally the losers; and the losers by the acts of the Neapolitan Government.

Upon what principle of common justice, can it be contended, that the right of the American Merchants to redress is weakened by Murat's alledged abuse of his public trust, in the appropriation of the proceeds in question? They had no power to controul their application; no competency to designate the objects, upon which they should be expended. If Murat really mis-applied them, it was in the exercise of powers, which his possession of the King-

276

dom enabled him to exert. And if the Government of Naples, was of such a character, as to invest its Sovereign with an unchecked controul, over the public funds, it would be strange indeed to maintain, that the possession of the power of their application, should be chargeable upon innocent strangers, to the relief of those, by whom it was conferred.

The second answer to His Excellency's proposition, is, that in point of fact, the Kingdom of Naples has derived an advantage from the spoliations of Murat.

A portion of the property confiscated, has unquestionably been appropriated to the public use. This will not be contested. It is a matter of notoriety. Six or seven, or more, of the American vessels, immediately after their seizure, were devoted to the Naval service of the Neapolitan Government. Some of these, even now, bear the flag of His Majesty, Ferdinand the Second. For more than twenty years they have contributed to the convenience, and added to the Marine force of this Kingdom. How many of them yet exist, the Undersigned does not profess to know, nor has he cared to enquire. He does know that for three successive reigns, since the period which restored the family of His present Majesty to the throne of Naples, they have been held and claimed, as the nation's property, and applied to the Nation's service.

And how was the residue of the American property disposed of? It was sold by the order of the Neapolitan Government. Its proceeds, it is now said, were appropriated to meet the personal expenses of the King. Admit that they were thus applied; that in the language of the Marquis de Circello, they but served "to feed the caprices and the oriental pomp of the family of Murat and his adherents" and will the concession justify the inference, deduced from it by His Majesty's Government? On the contrary, it is not apparent, that, however they may have been applied, the proceeds of these spoliations, have redounded to the relief, and ensured to the benefit of the Neapolitan people?

Murat was the reigning Sovereign of this Kingdom. At it's [sic] monarch, he had the power to controul and direct the application of its public treasures. These were properly applicable, not only to the public service, strictly so called, but to the support of the King and his household. The dignity of the Government required, that the privy purse of the Sovereign should be liberally supplied and as there was no other source, from which the necessary means could be obtained, the public funds were ordinarily chargeable with its wants. When, therefore, those wants were gratified by the appropriation of the proceeds of the American confiscations, it is manifest, that to an equal extent, the public treasury was releived. [sic]

Whatever therefore may have been the character or extent of Murat's expenses, they have been such to a certain amount by the means of the American Merchants; and to a like amount, at least, has the Neapolitan Nation been benefitted. Rapacious, as this alledged usurper is justly represented to have been; and regardless, as he unquestionably was, of his highest duties to the Nation, whose destinies he controuled, there was nothing to restrain the wasteful expenditure of the public treasures, which he is said to have so profusely dissipated. And is it not obvious, if the means of gratifying his "oriental pomp" and of "feeding his caprices" had not been opportunely furnished by the possession and sale of the American property, that they would have been sought in the ordinary revenues of his people? That he did not hold these sacred; or as above the reach of his royal power, we have the evidence of the Sicilian Government, itself, to prove. And would not the same unrestrained boldness, which prompted him, upon another occasion to cause "to be transferred Two Hundred thousand livres from the public treasury, to meet expenses, which he had incurred upon the credit of his private funds" have directed, in the absence of the American property, to the like sure source of supply? The American property then, has taken the place of the Neapolitan treasury. It has supplied means, which otherwise must have been drawn from the Nation. It has borne the burthens of this Kingdom, which it has protected, from the wasting and oppressive influences, of a reckless dissipation of it's [sic] means.

Nor in the apprehension of the Undersigned, has the benefit realized by the Neapolitan Nation, from these confiscations, been limited to the mere nominal amount of their proceeds. A recurrence to the history of the eventful period, in which these transactions occurred, will shew, that the like sum, if it had been raised upon the credit of the Government, must have imposed on the Kingdom, a much more oppressive burthen; which, with the debt, that actually encumbered its resources at the restoration, under the protection of the provisions of the treaty of Casa Lanza,[63] would have been entailed as a lasting charge upon the National prosperity.

---

[63] The treaty of Casalanza (May 20, 1815) was concluded between the Austrian General (Count Neipperg) and the defeated Neapolitan commander (Colletta). The Emperor of Austria, through his agent, personally guaranteed that "nobody

And is it "hard" that the Neapolitan Nation should be asked to return to the suffering citizens of America the value of the property, of which they have been so injuriously deprived and the benefit of which, it has so obviously realized? Upon every principle not only of strict right, but of liberal Equity, these citizens are justified in appealing to His Majesty's Government for redress. Would it now indeed be "hard" if, by the denial of the demanded indemnity, any of the victims of these cruel wrongs should be permitted, longer to pine in want, and remain exposed to the evils and sufferings of a hopeless bankruptcy? The Undersigned has too strong a confidence, in the high sense of right of His Majesty's Government, for a moment to suppose, that it will permit itself, to become the instrument of so unfeeling an injustice.

The undersigned has thus hastily adverted to the contents of His Excellency's note of the thirtieth of May, and endeavoured to shew, that there is nothing, in the positions it assumes, to impeach the validity of the American demands. It becomes his duty, now to demonstrate, that the doctrine contended for by the Government of the United States, has been recognized and acted upon by the leading powers of Europe. —

This position, he has heretofore had the honor to advance, and as it has not been questioned, he might well content himself with its reiteration. But as it is his wish, that the justice of the preferred demands, should be fully manifested; and their validity completely illustrated, to the view of His Majesty's Government, he begs leave to direct the attention of His Excellency to some of the examples, by which their justice is sustained. —

Amongst these, the most prominent are furnished by the provisions of the Nineteenth article of the Treaty of Paris, of the

shall be persecuted for opinions or conduct previous to the establishment of Ferdinand IV on the throne of Naples;" "full and entire amnesty, without any exceptions or restrictions;" that "the sale of property is irrevocably preserved;" that "the public debt will be guaranteed;" that "any Neapolitan shall be eligible to civil and military offices and employments;" that "the ancient and the new nobility shall be preserved;" that "every soldier in the service of Naples, who shall take the oath to King Ferdinand, shal be maintained in his grade, honors, and stipends." The full text of the treaty is published in Felice Turotti, *Storia d'Italia dal 1814 al 1854.* Milano, 3 vols., 1856, I, 241. On the treaty, see William R. Thayer, *The dawn of Italian independence,* Boston, Houghton, Mifflin Co., 1892, I, 147; *Dizionario del Risorgimento Nazionale,* Milan, Vallardi, 1931, I, 177; Pietro Colletta, *Storia del reame di Napoli dal 1734 sino al 1825,* Milano, 1848; Pietro Colletta, *Memoria militare sulla campagna d'Italia dell'anno 1815.* See also note 39, p. 197.

30th of May 1814;[64] by the stipulations, which ordered the restored Monarch to the throne of France, responsible "for all property, real or personal of British subjects, which had been unlawfully confiscated since 1792"; by the provisions, and especially the third article of the Convention of Paris, of the 20th of November 1815,[65] to which the allied powers gave their United Sanction; and by the special convention between France and the Senate of Hamburg of the 27th of October 1816[66]— To the foregoing examples, extracted from the history of Modern Europe whose pages are crowded with evidences, equally strong, in support of the principle involved in the American claims, the Undersigned deems it sufficient simply to refer, in the persuasion that his Excellency, familiar as he doubtless is, with the history of the important transactions to which they relate, will at once perceive, that they distinctly affirm the doctrine, in contestation. He will barely remark, that they are founded upon the admitted responsibility, of the restored Government of France, for the acts of Napoleon, during the period of his usurpation of its sovereign power.

But there is a more modern example, to which the Undersigned, feels himself justified in inviting the especial attention of His Excellency, since its claims to the consideration of the Sicilian Government, rest, not only upon its intrinsic applicability to the merit of the present controversy, but upon circumstances, which should invest it, with peculiar authority, in the view of His Majesty's councils. His Excellency doubtless understands, that the Undersigned alludes to the example afforded, by the late convention between France and the United States, of which, he has already had the Honor, to furnish a copy.

This is a convention of indemnity, for spoliations committed by the French Government, during the reign of Napoleon, upon American commerce. The claims for which it stipulates redress, after having been fruitlessly prosecuted against the Imperial Government, were, upon the restoration, advanced against that

---

64 Mai 30 1814, Traité de paix signé entre la France et l'Autriche et ses allies à Paris le 30 Mai 1814. See: Martens, George F. de, *Supplement au Recueil des Principaux Traités*. Goettingen, 1802-42, II, 1814-15 inclusive, 1-15.

65 Convention of Paris. Nov. 20, 1815. Convention conclué en conformité de l'article neuvieme du traité principal et relative aux reclamations provenant du fait de la non execution des articles 19 et suivans du traité du 30 mai 1814, entre la France d'une part, et l'Autriche, la Prusse, et la Russie et leurs alliés de l'autre, signié a Paris le 20 Nov. 1814. See: *Ibid.*, II, 691.

66 Convention entre la France et la ville de Hambourg conclué à Paris le 27 Oct. 1816, relativement à la banque de Hambourg. See: Martens, George F. de, *Nouveau recueil de traités d'alliance*, 1817-41, III, 1808-1818, inclusive, 91.

of His Majesty, Louis the 18th; and continued to form the subject of negotiation with the French Government, up to the fourth day of July, Eighteen Hundred and thirty one, when the treaty under consideration was concluded. *They were resisted upon the ground assumed by His Excellency, that Napoleon, who had committed the injuries complained of, was a usurper, and that the succeeding Governments were not answerable for his wrongs.* This was the principle upon which the negotiation turned. It was deliberately discussed, *and abandoned by France, as untenable.* It is therefore a direct authority, in support of the proposition advanced by the American Government.

This example, however, according to the view of His Excellency, is entitled to no consideration, and will be permitted to exert no influence upon the determination of His Majesty's Government, because, as His Excellency alledges, different circumstances, views and interests may have led to the acknowledgement by France of the American claims. In what that difference of circumstances, views and interests is supposed to consist, His Excellency has not explained. The Undersigned must be permitted to express his belief, that none such exists.

However disposed the Government of the Two Sicilies may now be, to disregard the example of France, in this negotiation, it has, heretofore itself appealed to it, for the purpose, at least, of postponing the consideration of the American demands. As recently as the 13th of October 1825, *it believed,* that "a full knowledge of what was in consideration, between the United States and the French Government, in questions of origin prior to the restoration, and of the dispositions of the latter towards the former in reference to the said subjects might throw more light on the question and add new force to the determination of this Royal Court." *Under the influence of this belief, it suspended the negotiations then pending. Under the same influence it declined, afterwards, to renew them during Mr. Appleton's residence in Naples.* Apprized of the determination of the Sicilian Government to await the receipt of this "full information" the President of the United States, deemed it respectful, not to press upon the Neapolitan Kingdom, the claims in question. He acquiesced in the wish it had suppressed that their consideration should be suspended 'til the result of the negotiation with France, could be ascertained. That concluded, he is now prepared, through the Undersigned, to furnish "the full information, which was so solicitously enquired after in Eighteen Hundred and Twenty

281

five — But that "information" is adverse to the views and interests of the Sicilian Government; and is now discovered, not to be calculated "to throw light on the question" in controversy, and because it will not "add new force to the determination of this Royal Court," it is to be entirely disregarded. The Undersigned cannot persuade himself, that His Majesty's Government, always animated by a spirit of liberal equity, will feel itself justified in thus summarily disposing of an example, which presents so many commanding claims to its respect.

In concluding this note, the Undersigned prays leave to suggest to His Excellency, that the History of the Two Sicilies, may perhaps itself, afford evidence that the principle asserted by the United States, however theoretically denied, has been practically acknowledged, by the Neapolitan Government. Proof of this, it is believed, may be found in provisions of the convention of Casa Lanza, of the 20th of May and the Royal proclamation of the 22^d. of August 1815, which guaranteed the debts of the State, a part of which had been contracted during the incumbency of Murat. If the restored Government of Naples, was, thus bound to make good the contracts of "the Usurper" with those, who voluntarily loaned the State their money whilst under his rule; the Undersigned is acquainted with no principle of public Law, or common justice which would not extend the obligations of indemnity, to those, whose property against their consent, by a kind of forced law, was converted, through the agency of the constituted authorities, to the purposes of the Kingdom.

The same principle has been distinctly and broadly assented by the Neapolitan Government, in its dealings with a part of the identical property, wrested from the American Merchants, by Murat's confiscations. How has the Government of His Majesty acquired; or how did that of his predecessors obtain, a title to the American vessels, employed in the Sicilian Service? The original proprietors never voluntarily parted with them. They have received for them, no equivalent. They were torn from their possession, forcibly and tortuously. Yet the Sicilian Government for the seventeen years which have elapsed since Ferdinand's restoration, has held and employed them, as the property of the Kingdom. *It has been apprized of the means, by which they were acquired, and with a knowledge that they were the fruits of "the Usurper's" rapacity, it has constantly asserted its title to them, and used them as its own.* Now, surely, if the restored Government may profit of Murat's acquisitions, it must be answerable for his wrongs. It cannot, consistently, maintain that it may avail itself of his gains for the benefit of the State, and at the same time throw off the burthens, which his reign imposed on it.

Will it be said that the vessels in question, have been retained in the Sicilian service, because their restoration has not been demanded? Such an intimation has already been informally given to the Undersigned, but it is without foundation. *The vessels have been more than once demanded.* And in one case, that of the Brig Emily, a written memorial has been presented to the proper department of the Sicilian Government, asking its restoration to the original proprietors. *And it was positively refused.* Proof of this, the Undersigned will be prepared to produce, whenever it may be required.

In reply to the suggestion contained in His Excellency's note "That His Majesty will cause enquiry to be made, whether there are in his Royal Navy, any captured American vessels, and if there be, that orders will be given that they be promptly restored, or their value paid" the Undersigned feels it to be his duty to state, that his instructions contemplate no partial arrangement of the claims, against His Majesty's Government. They rest upon a common principle, and the Government of The United States expects, that all will be provided for in a single convention. Still, if for the vessels, which have been employed in the Sicilian service, His Majesty's Government shall tender a sufficient recompense, the Undersigned will not decline its acceptance. But to be sufficient, in his view, it must cover, not only the value of the captured vessels, *in the port whence they sailed,* at the time they were taken, but the interest upon that sale, from the time of their seizure up to the day of payment. And in receiving such a sum, in discharge of the particular claims, of the proprietors of the vessels in question, the duty of the Undersigned will oblige him to require, that its acceptance shall be accompanied by an explicit declaration that it shall not be construed, to weaken or impair, in any wise affect the residue of the American demands, upon a satisfactory adjustment of the whole of which, the Government of the United States will never cease to insist.

The Undersigned eagerly avails himself of the occasion, to renew to the Prince of Cassaro, the assurances of his high consideration. —

THE PRINCE OF CASSARO TO J. NELSON

(Enclosure with Despatch No. 9,[67] of July 28, 1832).

Naples July 17th 1832.

His Majesty having deigned to appoint Don Antonio Girardi,[68] as his Consul General in the United States of America, in place of the Cavalier Capece Galeota, who has been removed to another situation, the Undersigned has the honour of informing Mr. Nelson of the fact, in order that he may communicate it to his Government.

The Undersigned would also take it as a favour, if M^r. Nelson would use his interest to procure an exequatur for Signor Girardi, as soon after his arrival at his post as may be convenient.

The Undersigned willingly embraces the present opportunity of renewing to M^r. Nelson the assurances of his particular consideration.

J. NELSON TO E. LIVINGSTON

Naples Septr. 3, 1832. [Despatch, Unnumbered, Private]

My dear Sir,

I have transmitted to Mr. Appleton,[69] our Consul at Leghorn, a bundle covering despatches No. 7 and No. 8, to be forwarded, by The Indiana of New York, which I am informed will sail for the United States in a few days. I have been anxiously seeking an earlier opportunity of possessing you of these papers, but none has offered.[70] There are at this season of the year, no persons travelling to Paris, to whom they could prudently, have been entrusted, and they are too voluminous for convenient trans-

---

[67] Despatch No. 9, July 28, 1832, not here reproduced, was from Mr. Nelson to Mr. Livingston, covering the letter sent with this enclosure. In it Mr. Nelson also informed Mr. Livingston of Mr. Girardi's appointment as Consul General of Naples to the United States.

[68] Antonio Girardi. Chevalier and diplomat. In 1831, he was consul at Malta. By the decree of May 29, 1832, he was appointed Consul General in the United States of America, with residence at Philadelphia. From 1833 to 1834, he was Consul General at Tunis.

[69] He was the uncle of John James Appleton, Nelson's predecessor at Naples. See note 33, p. 194.

[70] After the departure of the *Ontario,* none of Mr. Nelson's despatches were sent to Mr. Livingston until Sept. 15, because of lack of conveyance. Perrotta, *op cit.,* 61.

mission by the mails. Lest they may not reach you, as early as I have every reason to expect, I avail myself of the ordinary channel of communication to apprize you of their import.

Despatch No. 7, has relation to my accounts, for the quarter ending, the thirtieth of June.

Despatch No. 8 is accompanied by the answer of this Government to my notes of the 31st of January and 27th of February last. It bears date on the 30th of May, but was not received 'til the 2ᵈ. of June. It is in effect, the answer of Circello to Mr. Pinkney's note of 1816. It rests its denial of the responsibility of the present Sicilian Government for the acts of Murat, upon two grounds.

First, that he never was de facto, the King of Naples; that the acts of confiscation complained of emanated from Napoleon and that France alone is responsible for them, Murat, being in regard to them, but the passive instrument of the Emperor.

Secondly, That conceding Murat to have been invested with complete sovereign power, yet that it was founded in usurpation and that the restored dynasty is not answerable for his wrongs.

These positions are supported by various suggestions of fact and argument specious and plausible. — No attempt is made to justify the confiscations; on the contrary they are denounced as indefensible. The note concludes with an offer to deliver up the American vessels now in the Sicilian service, or to pay their value. —

To this paper I sent in a reply (a copy of which you will receive with despatch No. 8) on the 29th of June, in which I have discussed the several questions presented, in detail. I have endeavoured to shew, that the Govᵗ. of Naples from 1808 to 1815 was in Murat. That he reigned de facto. That the confiscations of vessels and cargoes of our citizens, were the acts of the Neapolitan Govᵗ. for which the nation was responsible; and that the responsibility having once attached to the Nation, adheres to it, in despite of the changes which have occurred in its Govᵗ. & rulers. To this offer to deliver up the vessels or pay their value, I have replied that my instructions contemplated no partial arrangement of the claims preferred; but that should the Sicilian Govᵗ. tender a sufficient recompense for any part of them, I should not decline its acceptance; that to be sufficient in my view, however, it must cover not only the value of the vessels at the time of their seizure, in the port whence they sailed, but the interest upon that value up to the time of

285

payment; and that its acceptance, in discharge of the particular claims, must be accompanied by an explicit declaration that it shall not operate, or be construed to impair or affect the residue of our demands, upon a satisfactory arrangement of the whole of which, the U. States, will not cease to insist. —

To this note I have received no answer. — I have had repeated conferences with the Prince of Cassaro, since its date, from which I have collected enough to satisfy me, that this Government, will with-hold all redress, until measures of coercion are resorted to. — I have been urgent in my applications for a reply to my last note, which has been repeatedly promised me, but has not yet been given. My impression is, that it is not the intention of this Government to answer it; or if it does, that it will be, barely to say, that it has effected no change in His Majesty's views. — I shall not have so long waited for it, had I not expected despatches from Washington. Should I receive none by the middle or close of the present month, I shall feel it to be my duty, unless some alteration in the determination of this Government, is indicated, to demand my passports and return to the United States. I have no advice from your department of a date later than the 4th of April.

In my despatch No. 8 I have referred to His Majesty's absence from Naples, upon a visit to the province of Abruzzi, whence he was not expected to return before the third or fourth of August. On the 25th day of July, [1832], however, The Brandy-wine and Constellation[71] came into this port. The consequence was that an

---

[71] At this time the United States was sending some of her newest and best known sloops of war and frigates to the Mediterranean. In the first half of the year 1832, Biddle was in command, with the Brandywine as his flagship; on June 23d, Patterson was appointed to relieve him as Commodore of the Squadron, with orders to rendezvous at Port Mahon, Minorca, the larger of the two Balearic Isles, conveniently handy to Naples. (See Navy Department Records, in the United States National Archives, Officers, Ships of War. No. 20, Woodbury to Patterson, date cited). On June 11th, the Secretary of State (See Instructions to United States Ministers, XIII, Livingston to Nelson) had instructed Nelson that, "the Frigate United States despatched to demand the answer of the King in regard to payment of the indemnity will wait twenty days to receive it, and if . . . a satisfactory answer is not given . . . you are directed to ask for your passports .). . and the President will take such measures as his constitutional duties require." Patterson's flagship was this United States, and this ship it was which carried to Nelson these Instructions of June 11th.

Meanwhile, in the United States, the readying of the United States, the Delaware, and others for sea duty at short notice, caused rumors to fly thick and fast. Nor was their destination unknown; for both newspapers the Globe and the National Intelligencer, deemed to reflect closely government viewpoints, engaged, in May, in lively, and opposing, printed interpretations of what all this activity of the Navy portended, the Intelligencer asking pointedly, and with the reinforcement of comment by Niles Register (a Baltimore paper, almost as widely read on government matters and public affairs) : — "What business have our vessels of war with

express was despatched to His Majesty, who returned two days afterwards. The point is, that great uneasiness was felt, upon the Occasion, and vigorous preparations made for the defence of the City, which its inhabitants had the weakness to suppose, was about to be attacked. The Ships have since sailed; and the alarm subsided with their departure. —

I am without American papers, since March, and of course

---

diplomatic negotiations?" See *Niles'* comments on these and other articles, in *Niles Register,* May 19, 1832, XLII, 211).

The Mediterranean Squadron also included, at this time, the *Ontario,* the *Boston,* the *Constellation,* the *John Adams,* and the *Concord* — an impressive array and even if not all lying in Naples' harbor, sufficiently near, and well-known, to be seriously impressive. On October 2d, Nelson, in his Despatch No. 10, mentioned with satisfaction that "The ships of the American Squadron, the *United States, Brandywine, John Adams,* and *Concord* are here" [i.e. in Naples' harbor]. Eight days short of the allotted "twenty", Patterson — on the *United States* — was advised by Nelson of the signing of the convention by Cassaro and himself, and thereupon Patterson wrote to the Secretary of the Navy: — "It is admitted by Mr. Nelson that the appearance of the Squadron in this bay has had great effect in producing so favorable a result." (See *Captains' Letters,* Patterson to Woodbury, Oct. 13, 1832.). On October 14th, within the hour of the signing, Nelson sent off, via Marseilles, his Despatch No. 12, with the 'triplicate' copy of the convention text. Then on the morning of the 15th, Nelson himself, in the *Concord,* set sail with the precious signed "memorandum copy", headed for Portsmouth, where the ship arrived on December 5th. Then followed the necessary Congressional action, described in footnote 79, pp. 293-294; the Presidential Proclamation that, as of Aug. 27th, the Treaty was "in force", which had only occurred after the ratifications had been exchanged on the preceding June 8th; and by the following November 30th, 1833, of those many vessels in the Mediterranean ere the treaty was signed, there remained under orders there, only the flagship, *United States,* the *Constellation,* and these two now reinforced by the newly arrived, newly conditioned *Delaware.* The *John Adams* was there but under orders for home; the *Concord* and the *Boston* were already in their home ports for repairs; and the *Brandywine* lay in the Brooklyn Navy Yard, being coppered. (All these details are gleaned from the *Records of the United States Bureau of Naval Personnel, Record Group 24, Logs of Individual Vessels.* These documents are now at the United States National Archives.)

With further reference to the movements of the frigate of war, *United States* there is information as follows: In the postscript of an Instruction of the State Department addressed to G. W. Sullivan, Bearer of Despatches to Spain (letter of June 7th; P. S. June 11th: see Instructions to United States Ministers, XIII, 311-312): "Since the date of the preceding instructions it has been determined that you embark on board the frigate *United States* which probably sails from New York in the course of this week, and take your passage in that vessel for Gibraltar, where you will be landed . . . you had better make definite arrangement with the commanding officer of the frigate . . . A letter from the Secretary of the Navy, to Captain Patterson, Commander of the Mediterranean Squadron, who goes to that sea in the frigate *United States,* authorizing and directing him to give you a passage is herewith furnished you." The *United States,* which at this period was the flagship of Commodore Patterson of the Mediterranean Squadron, was an old ship, but had been remodelled and refitted. Being a slow ship she was nicknamed, "Old Wagon." She lasted, with the aid of numerous rebuildings, until the Civil War, and was one of the ships scuttled and sunk when the Federals abandoned Norfolk Navy Yard, April 20, 1861. She was, however, a very famous ship, owing to her capture of the British frigate, *Macedonian,* Oct. 25, 1812. See: Howard Irving Chapelle, *The History of American Sailing Ships.* New York, Norton & Co., 1935. See also the index to this work, for other Navy (sail) ships of various classes, mentioned in these despatches.

entirely in the dark, in regard to events that are transpiring on the other side of the Atlantic. This is a serious grievance, which, however, I see no means of correcting.

I am promised an interview, with Prince Cassaro, to-morrow, when I have the expectation, that he will disclose to me the final determination of the Sicilian Gov.ᵗ Should he do so, I shall apprize you of its import. —

I send this by a casual opportunity to Rome, to be mailed there for Paris. I can entrust nothing to the mails of this Country. —

J. NELSON TO E. LIVINGSTON

Naples, Oct. 2. 1832.[72] [Despatch No. 10.]

Sir,

I have the Honor to acknowledge the receipt of your despatches of the 11ᵗʰ. and 16ᵗʰ. of June, which were delivered to me by Commodore Patterson,[73] on the 11ᵗʰ. of Septʳ. On the 12ᵗʰ. in pursuance of your instructions, I addressed a strong note to the Prince of Cassaro, who immediately invited me to a conference. I have since been favored with several interviews, in all of which I have earnestly endeavoured to impress the Sicilian Government, with a just sense of the importance of an immediate adjustment of our differences, and at one time, indulged the hope that the object of my Missions would be satisfactorily attained. I regret, however, to inform you that in this expectation I have been

---

[72] In his Instruction No. 5, June 11, 1832, to Mr. Nelson, Secretary Livingston acknowledged the receipt of Despatch No. 3, mentioning that the President, under the existing circumstances, had deferred making a communication to Congress relative to our claims on Naples. Nelson was instructed that, should the reply prove unsatisfactory, or be delayed beyond the twenty days the ship *United States* was detailed to wait for that reply, he [Nelson] was to ask for his passports and return home at once. (See *Instructions, United States Ministers*, XIII, 314-315. This volume is in United States National Archives).

In Instruction No. 6, dated June 16, 1832, Secretary Livingston chided Mr. Nelson upon the fact that nothing had been received since that despatch of his numbered '3', expressing also his disappointment and anxiety for information relative to the status of the negotiation. Again he referred firmly to Instruction of June 11th, and requested Mr. Nelson to write frequently and in duplicate. Then he softened this prick to the distant diplomat's pride, by adding assurance of the confidence of the Government in his zeal and ability to effect the object of his mission. As we have already seen, the problem for Mr. Nelson, was in part one of sufficiently frequent and dependable conveyance for despatches of such confidential nature and also of the length of time consumed in those days in a trans-Atlantic voyage.

[73] Daniel T. Patterson. (1786-1839). From 1832 to 1836 he commanded the Mediterranean Squadron, after which he was, until his death, commandant of the navy yard at Washington, D. C. *Dictionary American Biography*, 1934, XIV, 301. Also, see above, pp. 286-287, note 71, end of note.

disappointed. With an avowal of it's [sic] willingness to settle our claims, this Government, yesterday assumed such grounds in regard to the indemnity to be accorded, as to constrain me to put an end to the negotiation. — I have accordingly demanded my passports. — The largest sum offered by the Prince of Cassaro, falls so far short of our demands, as to justify the belief that this Government has never sincerely contemplated an amicable arrangement. —

I design sailing for the United States, by the end of the present week; and hope to reach Washington, by the middle of November,[74] when I shall have the honor of presenting to you a detailed report, of every thing that has transpired in relation to my mission, since the date of my despatch No. 8. In the mean time I forward this despatch, in duplicate, by the way of Havre and London, in order that you may be apprized as early as possible of the result of the negotiation. —

The American Squadron consisting of the United States, Brandy-Wine, John Adams and Concord, is still here. — The John Adams will sail for Mahon, touching at Marseilles, to-night; The Concord for Portsmouth, as soon as I have had my audience of leave.

J. NELSON TO E. LIVINGSTON

Naples Oct. 8, 1832. [Despatch No. 11.]

Sir,

I have the Honor to inform you, that after I had received my passports, which my last despatch apprized you I had demanded, and on the very day assigned for my audience of leave, I received a note from the Prince of Cassaro, in which he stated, that urgent duties would prevent the King from seeing me according to appointment, and suggested the expediency of another interview on the following day. — To this proposal I, of course, acceded, and have been constantly occupied since in the business of my negotiation, which, I have great pleasure in informing you, has been brought to an issue, highly favorable, as I think, to the interests of the claimants. The Treaty is now preparing and will be signed in a day or two. In the mean time

---

[74] The Concord with Mr. Nelson and his full report (see his Despatch No. 13 and Enclosures, q.v., p. 293 ff.) reached Portsmouth, December 5th — too late to enable the President in his Annual message of December 3rd to announce that the treaty had been concluded, although as the text of that Message reveals he anticipated that such would soon occur.

I have obtained from the Secretary of Foreign Affairs a written statement of the terms of the settlement. —

By this agreement, this Government stipulates the payment of Two millions, one Hundred and fifteen thousand ducats, in installments, with interest.[75] — This sum, I believe, will very nearly cover the principal of all the just and well founded claims. Mr. Hammett, who is familiar with the whole subject, thinks it quite sufficient to satisfy them all.

The negotiation has been a very arduous one; but if the result should prove satisfactory to the Government of the United States, I shall find in its approbation, a full remuneration for the toils and vexations to which I have been exposed during its progress. It was closed only an hour ago. With a view to possess you of the information, I am anxious to avail myself, if possible, of the Havre Packet of the 20th for the transmission of this despatch, which has necessarily been hastily prepared.

The Concord will sail for the United States, as soon as the treaty is signed.

J. NELSON TO E. LIVINGSTON

Naples Oct. 14, 1832.[76] [Despatch No. 12.]

Sir,

I have the Honor to enclose herewith the copy of a convention of Indemnity, executed to-day. The Concord, which I expect to sail for The U. States to-morrow, will convey to you the Original.

---

75 This sum, here stated in haste, by Mr. Nelson, on October 8th, to be sent via the Havre packet, was a million ducats less than the figure he had handed to the Prince of Cassaro on Sept. 17th, prior (see pages 308, 309, 311). It also was less, by the exact amount of the United States government claim for transportation of the American seamen, than the amount finally agreed upon when the convention was signed, October 14th (See *Memorandum copy*) of the *Convention*, p. 291, in Article 1st of the Convention text). This despatch (No. 11) was published in United States — Documents relating to the Convention with Sicily. In the Senate of the United States, Feb. 9, 1833. 22nd Congress, 2nd session. Document No. 70, 54 pp.

76 Naples, Oct. 5, 1832, two letters, one from the Prince of Cassaro to Mr. Nelson and the other from Mr. Nelson to the Prince of Cassaro regarding a farewell audience with the King are omitted.

[Memorandum text of the Convention as signed by the Prince of Cassaro[77]] (Copy)

[Enclosure with Despatch No. 12, October 14, 1832].

Convention between the Government of the United States of America, and His Majesty the King of the Kingdom of the Two Sicilies to terminate the reclamations of Said Government, for the depredations inflicted upon American Commerce by Murat, during the years 1809, 1810, 1811 and 1812.

The Government of The United States of America and His Majesty the King of the Kingdom of the Two Sicilies, desiring to terminate the reclamations advanced by Said Government against his Said Majesty, in order that the Merchants of the United States may be indemnified for the losses inflicted upon them by Murat, by the depredations, Seizures, confiscations and destruction of their vessels and cargoes, during the years 1809, 1810, 1811 and 1812, And His Sicilian Majesty desiring thereby to strengthen with the said Government the bonds of that harmony, not hitherto disturbed; The Said Government of the United States and His aforementioned Majesty the King of the Kingdom of the Two Sicilies have with one accord resolved to come to an adjustment, to effectuate which they have respectively named and furnished with the necessary powers, viz.: the said Government of the United States, John Nelson, esquire, a citizen of said States, and their Chargé d'Affaires near His Majesty the King of the Kingdom of the Two Sicilies, and His Excellency D. Antonio Maria Statella &c &c &c His said Majesty's Minister Secretary of State for Foreign Affairs &c &c who[78] after the exchange of their respective full powers found in good and due form, have agreed to the following articles.

Article 1st.

His Majesty the King of the Kingdom of the Two Sicilies, with a view to satisfy the aforesaid reclamations for the depredations,

---

[77] It will be noted that this Memorandum text, which was what Mr. Nelson and the Prince of Cassaro had signed on Octobed 14th in Naples, differs slightly from the text sent to the House with House Document No. 60, the reason, of course, being that in the interim the Senate, before "consenting" had "advised" to the extent of certain alterations in the wording.

[78] See printed version of this Convention as sent to the House, House Document No. 60, 22nd Cong. 2nd sess., Jan. 24, 1833, Message of the President transmitting a copy of a Convention concluded . . . Oct. 14, 1832. Also see above, note 77.

sequestrations, confiscations and destruction of the vessels and cargoes of the Merchants of the United States / and for every expense of every Kind whatsoever incident to or growing out of the claims / inflicted by Murat during the years 1809, 1810, 1811 and 1812, obliges himself to pay the sum of Two Millions one hundred and fifteen thousand Neapolitan ducats to the Government of the United States, Seven thousand six hundred and seventy nine ducats part thereof, to be applied to reimburse the Said Government for the expense incurred by it, in the transportation of American Seamen from the Kingdom of Naples during the year 1810, and the residue to be distributed amongst the claimants by the Said Government of the United States in such manner and according to such rules as it may prescribe.

Article 2^d.

The sum of Two millions one hundred and fifteen thousand Neapolitan ducats agreed on in article the 1st. shall be paid in Naples, in nine equal installments of two hundred and thirty five thousand ducats, and with interest thereon at the rate of four per centum per annum, to be calculated from the date of the interchange of the ratifications of this Convention, untill the whole Sum shall be paid. The first installment shall be payable twelve months after the exchange of the Said ratifications, and the remaining installments, with the interest, successively, one year after another; The said Payments shall be made in Naples, into the hands of such person as shall be duly authorised by the Government of the United States to receive the Same.

Article 3^d.

The present Convention shall be ratified and the ratifications thereof shall be exchanged in this Capital in the space of Eight months from this date or sooner if possible.

In faith whereof the parties above named have respectively subscribed these articles, and thereto affixed their Seals. Done at Naples on the 14th. Day of October One thousand eight hundred and thirty two.

Signed / Jno. Nelson   (Seal)

Signed / The Prince of Cassaro   (Seal)

J. NELSON TO E. LIVINGSTON

(See also enclosures "A" through "P")

Naples Octr. 15, 1832 [Despatch N° 13.]

Sir,

My despatch No. 12 under yesterday's date will have possessed you of a copy of the Convention of indemnity, concluded with the Sicilian Government on the 14th Instant. I have the Honor herewith to present you the Original.[79]

---

[79] This Despatch No. 13, worded as if to be sent, was actually carried home by Mr. Nelson himself, when he left Naples on the *Concord,* a ship of the United States Mediterranean Squadron, under orders to sail to Portsmouth. Already, in his Despatch No. 12, hastily sent to catch the Havre Packet of the 20th — a more expeditious means of getting mail back to Washington — Mr. Nelson had sent his triplicate copy of the text of the Convention. The text he himself carried, that enclosed with his Despatch No. 13, and carried by the *Concord,* he designated the 'original' text; this now is called the *'memorandum copy'* or 'official text of the convention.' It, however, is not the Treaty Text (the Document) itself, for that text was the one ratified later, and made the basis of the Proclamation by the President of the United States and by Decree of the King of the Two Sicilies. With Despatch No. 13, Mr. Nelson also enclosed another text, namely, his Draft of a Convention, which he had handed to the Prince of Cassaro for the latter to present to the Council of Ministers of the Neapolitan Government. This draft text, considerably altered in phrasing, and specifying a larger indemnity total than was eventually agreed upon, was accompanied by a Memorandum showing the calculations by which Mr. Nelson arrived at the total of indemnity asked for; it was dated Sept. 17, 1832. The text, as "Memorandum Copy," and that of the triplicate sent off an hour after the signatures of Mr. Nelson and the Prince of Cassaro had been placed thereon, were both dated October 14th, the date of the signing, and Oct. 15th, for the letter sent with the former, viz., Despatch No. 13. From Mr. Nelson's letter of the 7th of December (pp. 331-332) written from Boston, we learn that the *Concord* had made Portsmouth somewhat earlier. If then, the copy of the treaty text, sent via Havre, had indeed been more expeditious, President Jackson would not, it seems, have had to state in his Annual Message, dated December 3d, communicated December 4th, that the "Government of Naples had still delayed the satisfaction due to our citizens, but at that date the effect of the last instructions was not known. Despatches from thence are hourly expected, and the result will be communicated to you without delay." In a further Message of Dec. 17th, the President communicated to the Senate the text of the Convention. A rare printed copy of this text, alone, is found in the Archives of the Senate, together with the manuscript copy that was sent by the State Department to the President, and by him with his Message and bearing in pencil the evidence of how the text was assigned to the printer's typesetters. This printed text (treaty only) bears the legend, *Convention between the Government of the United States of America and His Majesty the King of the Kingdom of the Two Sicilies, 22nd Cong. 2nd sess. Confidential No. 3. In the Senate of the United States, Dec. 17, 1832, Read and referred to the Committee on Foreign Relations and ordered to be printed in confidence for the use of the Senate.* (This pamphlet, two pages, is found in the United States National Archives, Executive and Legislative Records Division, *Senate, Class 22B-B7, Two Sicilies*). On December 31st, the Senate, by Resolution at the instance of Mr. Forsyth, of the Foreign Relations Committee, called for all the correspondence pertaining to the Convention, and also for the Instructions which had been sent to Mr. Nelson. On January 14th, President Jackson complied with this request, but added an emphatic caution that in this correspondence there were "confidential reports concerning the Neapolitan officers, which were never meant for the public eye, and that might, if printed, accidentally find their way abroad and thereby em-

In my communication of the 12th. of July (Despatch No. 8) I apprized you of the absence of His Sicilian Majesty from this capital; and of the expectation that he would return to it, by an early day in the next month. He arrived on the 29th of July. On the 8th of August I called on The Prince of Cassaro, in the hope that he would be prepared to redeem the pledge given to me on the 3^d. of July, to make known to me the final determination of this Government upon the subject of our demands. In this expectation I was disappointed. I found him more than usually reserved, and wholly indisposed to entertain the subject of our claims. Even when pressed by my enquiries, he answered briefly and evasively. He professed to regret that His Majesty had not yet decided upon the answer to be returned to my note of

barrass our ministers in their future operations in foreign countries." Further, the President recommended "such discrimination be made as to avoid that inconvenience." See: United States: Convention: United States and the Two Sicilies. *Message from the President of the United States. Transmitting a copy of a convention between the United States and the Kingdom of the Two Sicilies.* Jan. 24, 1833, referred to the Committee on Foreign Affairs. United States Executive Document No. 60. House of Representatives, 22nd Congress, 2nd session, II, 2 p. The Senate, receiving this message on the 16th of January, proceeded on the 19th of January to "advise and consent to the ratification of the convention." (Thirty-nine Senators concurred. See, *Senate Executive Journal,* IV, 301).

The Senate having passed upon the treaty officially, and the House of Representatives having implemented it in due course on March 2d, the matter of the exchange of ratifications proceeded under the orders issued on January 29th, 1833, to Auguste Davezac, United States Minister to the Hague, who was directed to proceed to Naples and attend to the securing of the ratification by the Neapolitan King, in exchange for the ratification signed by the President of the United States. This took place on June 8, 1833, but not until this signed document had been delivered to the President did he issue, on August 27, 1833, his Proclamation of the text of the treaty, with the statement that it was from that date in force. This proclamation text, for the first time, gave both the English and the Italian texts, in parallel columns.

Eleven months later, on May 13, 1834, the President again communicated to Congress "copy of a convention . . . to terminate the reclamations . . . for the depredation upon American commerce by Murat . . ." The text, both in English and Italian, of the convention as proclaimed was incorporated in this Message of the 13th of May, as communicated on the 14th. Thus was closed, so far as the United States itself was concerned, the long cycle of official procedures required to create its share in the birth of a new item in international law. From the point of view of the claimants, however, the matter was still far from closed, for there remained still the work of the Board of Commissioners, appointed under the Act of March 2, 1833, and the long tedious process of supporting and adjudicating the individual claims, all of which must be brought within the total amount of the indemnity agreed to in the convention. For a general account of that process, see Miller, *op. cit.* III, 718-721. For a list of the individual awards, of which there were some 275 approved, see House Document 242, 24th Cong. 1st sess., Letter from the Secretary of State, in compliance with a Resolution of the House the 23d instant, letter dated Apr. 27, 1836. For further details as to the international financing of the payments from the Neapolitan Government and the measures used to protect the interest of the claimants in the devious transactions of international exchange, see Senate Document 351, 25th Cong,. 2d sess., *Report of the Secretary of the Treasury, in compliance with a resolution of the Senate of the 16th of February last, in relation to the payment of the French and Neapolitan indemnities,* dated March 30, 1838, read and ordered to be printed.

the 29th of June, which he, however, promised should be communicated to me in a few days. I urged him to assign some fixed period, by which I might hope to be informed of this determination, but without avail. He could not undertake, he said, to pledge himself to any given day, but that it should be furnished without delay, and that he would do every thing in his power to bring the negotiation to a speedy termination.

Things remained in this condition until the 29th of August, when I addressed to the Prince a note soliciting an interview, which he assigned for Monday the 3^d. of Sept^r. (copies of my note and of his reply are herewith communicated marked A.B.)[80] Upon calling at the Foreign office according to this appointment, I was concerned to learn that the Secretary was absent, being detained at his country seat by the extreme illness of The Princess, who died on the same evening. This event, of course, forbade any further advance on my part, until the arrival of "The United States" by which I received your despatches of the 11th. and 18th. of June. These were handed to me by Commodore Patterson on the 11th of Septr. On the 12th. I addressed to the Prince of Cassaro a note of which C.[81] is a copy and to which he, on the same day, returned a reply. Of this and of my answer D.[82] and E.[83] are transcripts.

The interview of the 14th, if not entirely satisfactory, was such as to encourage the hope, that an adjustment of our long standing differences was not altogether impracticable. The Prince opened the conference by remarking that it had been his purpose on the 3^d. of Septr. to have disclosed to me, frankly, the liberal views of His Majesty with regard to the American claims, but that this purpose had been postponed by the severe visitation under which he was still suffering; that he had been commanded by the King to inform me that although he could not assent to all the principles maintained in my note of the 29th of June, yet, that solicitous to preserve the most amicable relations with the Government of the United States, upon the good opinion of which he placed the highest estimate, he was willing in a spirit of compromise, to pay a gross sum, in satisfaction of the American demands.

I replied that the principles upon which our claims rested were such as the Government of the United States could never

---

80 "A" and "B" are not printed in this edition.
81 For "C", see pp. 305-306.
82 For "D", see pp. 306-307.
83 For "E", see p. 307; and see p. 297, regarding "F" and "G".

renounce; that I had endeavoured in my note of the 29th of June to demonstrate their soundness; that, no answer had been returned to that note; that the grounds assumed in it were such as I believed to defy successful assault; and that in addition to the authorities by which it's reasoning was fortified, I might safely appeal to the relations maintained by the Kingdom of the Two Sicilies with that of France, in evidence of the justice of our demands. The Prince interrupted me, by remarking, that there were principles avowed by Republican and Constitutional Governments, upon which pure Monarchies could not safely act, but that the decision of His Majesty superseded the necessity of their further discussion; that the only question now to be settled between us was one of amount; and that this must be adjusted with a liberal reference to the pressing necessities of His Majesty's Kingdom. I answered, That in any propositions which I should submit to His Majesty's Government, I should be governed by a sense of what was due to those whose interests had been confided to my charge; whilst I had every disposition to meet in a liberal spirit, the purposes now avowed by His Majesty's Councils; that the injuries upon which our claims were founded, had been long since inflicted, and as all our previous applications for redress had been dis-regarded, it was equitable that the claimants should be remunerated, not only for their original losses, but for the injuries resulting from the delay in repairing them. The Prince replied with much decision, that His Majesty's Government could not for a moment entertain any proposition, embracing a demand of interest; that the financial condition of the country was so depressed as to render the gratification of such a demand impossible; and that upon principle, interest was not demandable upon an unliquidated claim. — To these remarks I urged in answer, that the financial difficulties of the Sicilian Kingdom furnished no excuse for withholding from our Merchants their just demands; that their property had been seized and converted to its purposes by the Neapolitan Government, more than twenty years ago, and that it was reasonable and just, that for its use, an adequate return in the form of interest should be made; that the circumstance of the demands remaining unliquidated, by no means weakened the claim to interest, since that was owing to the refusal of the Sicilian Gov'. to settle them, the Government of The United States having been always willing and ready to adjust them. —

The Prince referred to the example furnished by our negotiations with other Governments of Europe, against none of which, he said, had a claim of interest been preferred; that in the case of France our claims had been of as long standing, as were those against Naples; and yet that in our negotiations with that power, interest had not been demanded; that if the demand was persisted in, the result must be to defeat any arrangement, His Majesty preferring to expose himself to the hazard of any sacrifice, rather than to yield to it. —

I disclaimed in reply all knowledge of the particulars of the demands preferred against other powers, but continued to assert the equity of the allowance as against this Government, until perceiving the utter hopelessness of the effort to secure it, I promised the Prince of Cassaro to reflect upon the propriety of with-drawing it.

The Prince after begging me to reduce the demands to the lowest possible sum, remarked, that His Majesty expected that I would be prepared to conclude a Treaty of Commerce upon terms of a liberal reciprocity. — I replied, that I had no specific instructions upon the subject, and might find it necessary to refer to the Government of the United States before I formed such a convention; but that as soon as the question of indemnity was settled, I should be prepared to confer with him, upon the subject of our Commercial relations, and to do, what under the circumstances might be just and proper. He said, that it was in every respect desirable to His Majesty that a commercial arrangement should be at once concluded. He begged that I would call again on the following Monday, when he would be glad, he said, to receive any propositions which I might be disposed to submit, remarking, that as His Majesty was absent from Naples and would not return before the 19th, and as no definite arrangement could be concluded in his absence, the loss of the intervening day could be of no importance. —

I accordingly called on Monday and left with the Secretary the memorandum and draught of a convention, of which F.[84] and G.[85] are copies. These he promised immediately to submit to the Council of Ministers, and to His Majesty upon his return to Naples, and to apprize me of the result with the least practicable delay. —

---

[84] For enclosure "F" see pp. 307-310.
[85] For enclosure "G" see pp. 310-312.

On the 22ᵈ. of September I received the note of which H.[86] is a copy, inviting me to a conference on the 25th, when the whole subject of our claims and the Commercial relations ot the Two countries was brought under review and discussed. — The Prince referring to the memorandum I had left with him, remarked, that in the calculations I had submitted as the basis of my proposition, I had entered into a computation of interest, which as he had before apprized me, His Majesty could never consent to allow, and which he had been led to hope from our previous interview, would not be insisted on. I replied that although in the memorandum referred to, interest had been calculated, it had not been urged as a demand against the Sicilian Government; that it had been waived however, not because I doubted of its justice, but because I was willing to yield something to the compromising spirit, which had been manifested by His Majesty; that it's equity was demonstrable, but that, the decisive determination of the Sicilian Government not to treat upon it as a basis, and my own acquiescence in that determination rendered it's further discussion superfluous. — The Prince then remarked, that His Majesty's Government had been in correspondence with that of France, with a view to ascertain the principles, upon which our claims had been adjusted by the Convention of July 1831;[87] that in the protracted negotiation with that Government interest had never been demanded by the Government of the United States; that the original claims amounted to Seventy five Millions of Francs,[88] from which the American Government eventually deducted two-thirds, and that even with this abatement, the claims owed their recognition to the active interference of Genˡ. La Fayette in their behalf; that at all events it was reasonable that a proportionate deduction should be allowed on the claim against His Sicilian Majesty's Government; that the course pursued by France had been urged as an authoritative example in regard to the principle involved in the negotiation; and that when His Majesty consented to yield to its authority in this respect, he expected that it would be conceded to be applicable in all these. That the claims preferred exceeded the amount actually received by

---

[86] Enclosure "H" omitted from this version; as also the letter of Sept. 29th. See footnote 107, p. 312.

[87] For text of Convention between the United States and France (July 4, 1831), concerning claims, and duties on wines, cottons etc., see Miller, *op. cit.*, III, 641-651.

[88] For a full discussion of the French claims, see *Annals* of 22nd Congress, 2d session, 202-297.

Murat from the sale of the American property, to the payment of one third of which, His Majesty would not object.

To these remarks I replied, that I was not particularly informed as to the amount of the claims originally advanced against the Government of France; that I beleived [sic] it to have been greater than the sum stipulated to be paid by that power; but that there was a marked difference between these claims and the demands against the Government of Naples, both in respect to the claims themselves and to the relations subsisting between the two countries and the United States; that of the claims against France, many were involved in doubt and that the amount of those that were just was in some degree conjectural, whilst those against the Two Sicilies were supported by the clearest proofs, and susceptible of an accurate ascertainment by reference to the records of the United States Government; that besides France had counter claims to a large amount against the Government of the United States, which were proportionally reduced, and that the Convention was the result of a liberal adjustment of various and conflicting pretensions, whereas His Majesty had no such claims or pretentions to set off against our demands; that in offering to receive the sum proposed by me as the basis of a compromise, I had been controuled [sic] by a view of the amount supposed to have accrued to the Government of Murat from the American confiscations; that my estimate might not be stricly accurate, but if erroneous, that it was easy for His Majesty's Government to correct them; that I had no desire to press my demand, which was not strictly just, and that if the records of the Sicilian Government were thrown open to me, and I could be convinced that less than the estimated amount had been received by it, I would cheerfully submit to the proper deduction. —

To an enquiry as to the amount His Majesty proposed to offer in satisfaction of our demands, The Prince answered, that he was not then authorised to tender any specific sum, but that he would be prepared to do so, on the next or ensuing day; that he trusted it would be such as I would accept; but if otherwise, he presumed I would transmit it to my Government and await its decision. I replied, that an inadequate proffer would leave me no alternative but to demand my passports; that I needed no further instructions, being already authorised to conclude the negotiation upon fair and liberal terms, which however would not be extended beyond the period indicated in my note of the 12th Ins^t.

The Prince dwelt with much earnestness upon the financial difficulties of the Kingdom, assuring me of its extreme embarassment [sic] and of the impossibility of His Majesty's paying the sum demanded; and urging me to reduce the amount. Averring that I had already reduced it below the just claims of our Citizens, I avowed my willingness to afford further evidence of a disposition to deal liberally, by consenting to receive Three Millions of Ducats, putting the payments upon the footing of those provided for in the Convention with France. He said that he would consult the King and let me know his views on the subject; remarking at the same time that he did not think it would be possible to prepare a Treaty by the period limited in my notes. — I suggested, that, it would be very easy, as the Convention would consist of but two or three articles, which could be arranged in an hour, after the sum to be paid, should be agreed on. His answer to this remark, greatly surprized me. His Majesty, he said, expected that the Commercial Convention to be concluded between the Two Governments, would be embodied in the same Treaty. I protested against this, reminding him of my having constantly declined to connect the subjects of Commerce and Indemnity in the negotiation; — and assuring him, that although prepared to place the Commercial relations of the two countries upon a footing of the most liberal reciprocity, that the Government of the United States would never consent that the payment of its demands should be in any wise dependent upon such an arrangement; that the subjects were entirely distinct in their nature and must be separately disposed of, that of Indemnity, first; that of Commerce, afterwards. —

On the 29th of Septr. The Prince of Cassaro transmitted to me a note (of which (I) is a copy)[89] inviting me to an interview on the following day, when he informed me that he had consulted with the King, to whom my proposition had been submitted and by whom he was authorised to propose a compromise, to which he thought I ought to accede; or, if I did not feel myself authorised to close with it, that I ought at least to transmit it to Washington for the President's consideration; that, looking to the demands originally preferred against France, and to the sum eventually accepted, the King thought Eight

---

[89] See Note 107, p. 312. The text is not included in this printing.

Hundred Thousands Ducats a liberal proffer; and that he was willing, to acquit himself of all further responsibility, to pay that amount. He added, that the Minister of Finance had made a hasty examination of the records of his Department, and was satisfied that the sum realized by Murat from the American confiscations was considerably below that stated by me; and that the amount now offered, was proposed as justly proportionate to that accepted under the French Treaty. —

I need scarcely say that this proffer was promptly rejected. — I expressed my surprize that it should have been made and my conviction that His Majesty's advisers did not expect it to be acceded to; adding that if in tendering it, the object was to protract the negotiation, it was an act not to be attained, since as His Majesty well knew, my instructions were peremptory in requiring my departure from this Court by a given day, unless a satisfactory adjustment was in the meantime accomplished; that even under different circumstances, I could not have consented seriously to have submitted such a proposition to my Government, and that if it was the purpose of His Majesty to adhere to it, I should consider the negotiation at an end, and at once demand my passports. — I again referred to the subject of the negotiation with France, and repeated the explanations given in a previous interview, in regard to its character and the circumstances under which it was concluded, for the purpose of shewing the points in which it differed from the pending controversy.

The Secretary adverted anew to the pecuniary embarassments of this Kingdom; to the weight of taxes by which it was oppressed, and to its inability to pay the sum of Three Millions, and said, that His Majesty had determined if I insisted upon my proposition and in demanding my passports, that he would send a Chargé D'Affaires to the United States to negotiate further on the subject. He begged that I would reduce the demand to the lowest sum I would be willing to receive, and said, he would again see His Majesty and endeavour to dispose him to an accommodation but, that the sum of Three Millions transcended the means of the Gov^t. and could not be paid.

In reply, I reviewed the whole ground of controversy, and vindicated the claim I had preferred, but at the close of the interview, proposed as my ultimatum the sum of Two Millions Five Hundred Thousand ducats, which I believe to be quite sufficient to cover the principal of all the just claims. To this

301

demand I warned The Prince of Cassaro of my purpose to adhere and desired that he would give to it a definite and early reply, which he promised to communicate to me on the following day at one o'clock.

Of the result of the conference of the first of October, you have been already advised by my Despatch No. 10. It left me without the hope of being able to effectuate the desired arrangement; the Prince of Cassaro having assured me, in the most decided terms, of the fixed determination of His Majesty not to advance upon his offer of Eight Hundred Thousand ducats, and to transfer the negotiation to Washington, should I persist in declining its acceptance. Upon receiving this assurance, I avowed to him my purpose of at once demanding my passports; and in pursuance of that purpose, on the same day addressed to him notes, of which K. and L. are transcripts. Copies of his replies, dated on the 2^d. of October and received on the 3^d. are likewise herewith communicated marked M. N.

These last notes had not been delivered to me an hour, before I was honored with a visit from the Austrian Chargé D'affaires.[90] He appeared to be minutely familiar with the whole course of the negotiation, which he said might yet be terminated amicably, if I would consent to postpone my departure from Naples for a month. This I assured him I should not do; that my arrangements for taking leave were completed, and that I should certainly embark on Saturday the 6ᵗʰ. Instant. He had scarcely left me, before I was called on by a Sicilian Nobleman of much influence with the Government, who earnestly implored me not to persist in my determination, and expressed his conviction that if I would remain a fortnight longer, a satisfactory adjustment might be brought about. He zealously urged the various considerations, which had been previously advanced by the Prince of Cassaro, to induce me to abate from my demand, and to accept the proposal of the Sicilian Government. — These visits were repeated on the following day, when I was again

---

90 Ludwig Freiherr von Lebzeltern. (1774-1854). Austrian statesman. His first diplomatic assignment was at the Austrian embassy in Lisbon. Later he was secretary at the chancery in Rome, and still later he became a special envoy and minister at St. Petersburg. He was then sent to Naples as envoy. C. Wurzbach, *Biographisches lexikon* etc. 1865, XIV, 281-283. See also: Friedrich Christoph Schlosser, *Geschichte des 18 und des 19 Jahrhunderts bis zum Sturz des Französischen Kaiserreichs mit besonderer Rücksicht auf geistige Bildung.* 2nd. ed. in 6 vols. 1836-1848. 5th ed. in 8 vols. 1864-1866. In the third edition, volume 7, see 858ff, 862, 969, 1060. English translation: *History of the eighteenth century and of the nineteenth till the overthrow of the French empire.* London, Chapman & Hall, 1843-1852, 8 volumes.

urged to defer my departure. It was not difficult to perceive, that these applications, although presented by the individuals before named, proceeded in fact from the Sicilian Government. I resolved so to treat them, and therefore informed the Austrian Chargé d'affaires, that if it was the wish of the Prince of Cassaro to renew the negotiation and to make to me any new propositions, and he would *officially* request me to delay my embarkation, that I would consent to remain a few days longer; but I desired it to be distinctly understood, that I should interpret such a request as indicative of liberal purposes on his part, and that it would be complied with under no other or different impression; That the propositions heretofore submitted were totally inadmissible and that no others offered in the same spirit would be entertained by me. —

On the morning of the 5th, previously assigned for my audience of leave, I received from the Prince of Cassaro a note of which O.[91] is a copy, to which I returned the reply Marked P.[92]

The interview to which I was thus solicited, was a protracted one; devoted to the discussion of various propositions, involving all the considerations connected with the pending controversy. The first offer made by the Prince of Cassaro was to pay one Million of Ducats. — This was promptly rejected. He then offered twelve Hundred thousand, which was likewise declined. The sum of Fifteen Hundred thousand and eighteen hundred thousand ducats were successively proposed, discussed and dissented from. Eventually and as his ultimatum, he offered Two Millions, which I declined to accept, insisting upon Two Millions and a half. — The Prince, expressed his apprehension that the negotiation would again be broken off, as His Majesty could not be induced to advance beyond the Two Millions, and professed deeply to deprecate such a result. Concurring [sic] with him in this sentiment and fearing, from the temper displayed, that such might be the consequence of an obstinate adherence to my proposition, I intimated to the Secretary the possibility, if the sum of Two Millions, Two hundred and fifty thousand Ducats was proffered, that it might be accepted. This, he declared, he had no authority to offer, but that he would consult His Majesty on the subject, and apprize me of his determination on the following day.

I was concerned on the morning of the 7th to learn that His

---

91 "O" is not published in this volume.
92 "P" is not published in this volume.

Majesty was resolved not to recede from the ground taken on the preceding day, and the more, as I was aware that his engagements at Capua would require his absence from the seat of Government, during the week, and that, if the arrangement was not concluded by the next day, a protracted delay might be the consequence. This conviction led me to urge the necessity of an immediate disposition of the subject, and finally to agree to receive the Sum of Two Millions, One Hundred and fifteen thousand Ducats.

A new difficulty now presented itself. The Prince insisted upon introducing Commercial stipulations into the Treaty. — This I firmly resisted and the requirement was ultimately abandoned. —

The times and terms of payment were next to be adjusted. — I proposed five years. This Government twelve. — I, five per cent interest on the installments; the Sicilian Government appealing to the provisions of the Convention with France, insisted upon reducing the note to four percent. The arrangements eventually concluded, are to be found in the Convention.

Owing to his Majesty's absence from Naples, the Treaty was not signed 'til last night. —

In submitting this result of my mission to the President, I deem it superfluous to enter into any detailed exposition of the principles which have governed me in the conduct of the negotiation. These are sufficiently developed in the correspondence, which I have had the Honor already to transmit to you. I have a consciousness that I have left nothing undone, which it was in my power to effect. I have pursued the object of the negotiation committed to my charge, with an assiduity corresponding with the solicitude, which it was natural I should feel for its success; and an anxiety, that the confidence reposed in me by the Government of the United States, so far as depended upon my zeal and industry should be found, not to have been misplaced.

That I should have been gratified to have secured a larger sum than that stipulated to be paid is true: but as this was not practicable, I trust that the arrangement will prove satisfactory to the claimants. At all events, in view of the circumstances connected with this long-pending controversy, I have not felt myself prepared to assume the responsibility of rejecting an adjustment, which I believe to be highly advantageous to the parties interested, and in reference to the consequences, incident to it's failure, of great importance to the Government of the United States.

In extending the payment[93] beyond the period of six years, I am aware that I have transcended the letter of my instructions, but as the time was pertinaciously insisted on, and the installments have interest, I have not regarded the matter as of sufficient importance, to justify me in declining an arrangement, in other respects satisfactory.

J. NELSON TO THE PRINCE OF CASSARO

(Enclosure "C" with Despatch No. 13, of October 15, 1832).

Naples Septr. 12, 1832.[94] (Copy)

Sir,

When I had the honor to present my note of the Twenty ninth of June, in reply to that of your Excellency of the thirtieth of May last, I was assured that it would receive, from His Sicilian Majesty's Government, the prompt attention which was due to the important interests to which it relates; and which from uncontroulable [sic] circumstances, had been denied to my earlier applications in behalf of my injured Fellow Citizens. — In the interviews, with which your Excellency has since favored me, these assurances have been repeatedly renewed. — In that of the Eighth of August, in a reply to my urgent request, I received an explicit promise, that the definite determination of His Majesty's Government upon the subject of the American demands should be communicated to me in a few days. That promise has not been redeemed. More than two months have elapsed since the date of my note and, the assurances tendered remain unfulfilled. —

It becomes my duty once more to present the subject of this negotiation to your Excellency's consideration. —

I have already had the honor to communicate to your Excellency, the expectation of the President of the United States, that a full and satisfactory indemnity would be readily accorded by His Sicilian Majesty's Government, to the American Merchants, for the wrongs inflicted on them by the Government of Naples,

---

93 See Miller, *op. cit.*, III, 718-721.
94 Letters from Mr. Nelson to the Prince of Cassaro of Aug. 29, 1832, (Enclosure "A" with No. 13) and from the Prince of Cassaro to Mr. Nelson of Sept. 2, 1832, (Enclosure "B") regarding an interview, are omitted. The death of a princess was also mentioned.

during the reign of Murat. — In the thorough conviction of the responsibility of the existing Government of the Two Sicilies for those wrongs, and in the confidence inspired by His Sicilian Majesty's known regard for justice, The President, notwithstanding the unexpected delays, with which the application for redress has been met, has continued to cherish the hope, that eventually it would not be with-held; and in the indulgence of that spirit of forbearance, which has so long and signally marked the course of the American Government in regard to the claims in question, has been unwilling, whilst that hope remained unextinguished, to adopt any step, that would evince a distrust of His Sicilian Majesty's desire to do, what Justice and Equity alike demand. — But neither the dignity of the Government of the United States, nor the duty it owes to its citizens, will justify or sanction submission to further delay. I am therefore specially instructed to demand an explicit answer to the following enquiry. —

Will the Government of His Sicilian Majesty render satisfaction for the seizures and confiscations made by the Neapolitan Government during the reign of Murat, of the property of American Citizens; and take measures for the prompt and full payment of the same?

I am further instructed to apprize His Majesty's Government, that the Frigate "United States" now in the port of Naples, has been despatched to receive the answer to this specific demand; that she will wait for it Twenty days; and if at the expiration of that time, a satisfactory reply shall not have been given, and proper provision made for the payment of the claims preferred, I am directed to ask for my passports to return to the United States, when it will devolve on the President to take such measures for the vindication of the rights of his Fellow Citizens as his constitutional duties shall direct.

THE PRINCE OF CASSARO TO J. NELSON

[Enclosure "D" with Despatch No. 13, of Oct. 15, 1832]

Naples Septr. 12, 1832. (Copy)

Sir,

I have the honor to acknowledge the receipt of your kind letter of this day.

When I begged you *last* time to call at the Foreign Office I had a mind to explain to you frankly, the definitive intentions

306

of His Sicilian Majesty on the subject of the American claims, but the dire and as well as unexpected misfortune that befell me and my family on that very day, (the loss of my dear wife) prevented me of course, from the pleasure of an interview with you, and it has brought a new but short delay to the settlement of a business, The United States attach so much importance to.

Now though my health has no little suffered of such a cruel stroke, and that I am still plunged in the deepest affliction and sorrow, however in consequence of your urgent application, I am ready to receive you at my house, on Friday or Saturday next, as it will be more convenient to you, at one o'clock.

J. NELSON TO THE PRINCE OF CASSARO

[Enclosure "E" with Despatch No. 13, of October 15, 1832]

Naples, Sept'. 13, 1832. (Copy)

Sir,

I had the Honor last evening to receive your Excellency's note of yesterday. —

Deeply sympathizing, as I sincerely do, in the poignant affliction, with which your recent loss has overwhelmed your family, nothing but a strong sense of public duty, could have influenced me at this moment to ask your attention to official concerns. — But the instructions received by me on Tuesday, are of such a nature, as to require, that I should lose no time in bringing the negotiation entrusted to me, to a close. —

I shall therefore avail myself of the opportunity of conferring with your Excellency on Friday, at the hour indicated in your note of the 12th Instant. In the meantime I beg leave to assure your Excellency of the unaffected Esteem, with which I am,

Memorandum of Am^n. Claims (Copy)

[Enclosure "F" with Despatch No. 13, of October 15, 1832]

Documents and papers have been furnished Mr. Nelson, shewing the seizure by the Government of Murat, from the year 1809 to 1812 (both inclusive) of Fifty one American vessels, the cargoes of all of which were confiscated and sold. That there were others, there is every reason to believe. Some five or six of the vessels, embraced in the schedules furnished to Mr. Nelson, after a temporary detention, were returned to their owners.

The information possessed by the claimants, of the amount for which their property was sold, is necessarily imperfect. The Sicilian Government has the means however of correcting any inaccuracy, which may exist in their estimates. It is quite certain, that the vessels and cargoes disposed of, were brought into the market under the most depressing disadvantages, and that much less was realized by their sale, than their real value.

Mr. Nelson finds upon recurring to Mr. Appleton's note to the Chev^r. de Medici, of the 12th of Octr. 1825, that forty nine vessels and cargoes were estimated by him to have sold for Three Millions, thirty thousand, seven hundred and Eighty one Ducats and ninety three grains. The sale of Fifty one Cargoes, and of the vessels not restored, added to the value of those, retained in the Sicilian service, Mr. Nelson, upon the data in his possession, estimates at Three Millions, one Hundred Thousand Ducats. —

Besides this amount, realized from the sales, the Neapolitan Government received for Port duties, quarantine fees, and other expenses, about Fifty Thousand ducats. The actual loss to the claimants, therefore, in money, was Three Millions, one hundred and fifty thousand Ducats.

These losses were incurred more than twenty years ago. The larger portion of the property was sold under the decree of the 12th of March 1810; the residue in 1810, 1811, and 1812. The sales were made in despite of the protests of the American Counsul, and the remonstrances of the masters and owners. Reparation was immediately after, and has been since repeatedly demanded — Upon principles of strict right therefore, the claimants are entitled to be reimbursed not only the original value of their property, but the interest on that value.

Assuming the period of computation as of the 17th Septr. 1812, (before which all the sales were made) and calculating the interest at five per c^t. per annum (the rate paid by the Neapolitan Government on it's [sic] public debt) and the following would be the result.

Amount of proceeds of Ducats[95]

sale, Port duties, &c &c	3,150,000
Int. for 20	
ys at 5 pr. ct.	3,150,000

Ducats 6,300,000[96]

making the claims amount to Six Millions, three Hundred thousand Neapolitan Ducats — And this without taking into account the expense of supporting the seamen, the loss of freights, and the vexations to which the claimants were necessarily subjected.

In addition to this sum there is a small claim of the Gov^t. of the United States, for the cost of transporting to their country, some of the seamen thrown adrift, at the period of confiscations in 1810, amounting agreeably to the Consul's certificate to 7,679 Ducats,[97] which with the sum above stated, would make the gross aggregate of Ducats 6,307,679.[98]

This statement is submitted by M^r. Nelson, to shew the amount, which the Government of the United States, if disposed to demand rigid justice, at the hands of the Neapolitan Gov^t. might reasonably expect to receive. —

---

95 The value of the Neapolitan ducat in American money, at this time, was $.835, or approximately four-fifths of a dollar. From 1812 to the date of this treaty in 1832 there had been a range of variation of the ducat, on foreign exchange, of from 80 cents to $1.25. Therefore, this treaty was concluded when, the ducat being low, the sum collected would mean proportionately higher value to the claimants. See later, how this worked at the date of settlement of the claims. For further data on the fluctuation of exchange for Naples money, see (*Universal Cambist and Commercial Instructor* by Patrick Kelly, Headmaster of Finsbury Square Academy, Mathematical Examiner to Trinity House. London, 1811; 1821; 1825; 1831; 1835; 1842 editions), and the combined Steele and Kelly works, edited, 1846, by Wm. Tate; see also Blunt, *Shipmasters Assistant,* 1848, 1851.

96 Compare Ducats 6,307,679 given below; see also p. 311, the 'draft' figure.

97 This claim by the United States Government itself suffered no alteration at any time in the negotiations, nor in any of the various preliminary texts of the treaty. It is found in House Document 60, 22d Cong. 2d sess. as sent to the House on Jan. 24, 1833, also in the proclaimed text, with the message of the President on May 14, 1833, as published in House Executive Document 414 of that date. The claimants, on the whole, fared virtually as well, it being calculated that about 94% of the total claimed amounts was compensated; but the government's claim (for transporting seamen home) was like the private claims settled (paid) at slight discount.

98 This total amount asked, was eventually compromised at approximately one half the sum asked. Note that (see page 308) Mr. Nelson here was including 20 years interest at 5%; in the final accounting the interest was figured on a different basis. Note, too, that in the text of the treaty the reference to the total amount varied as betwen 579 and 679 as the last three figures to the right. (As proclaimed, the figure here was 679).

M^r. Nelson has assurred [sic] the Prince of Cassaro, however, of his willingness to meet the Sicilian Government in the spirit of compromise which it has manifested, and of his readiness, frankly and at once to disclose the sum he would be prepared to accept in full settlement of all the American demands. In this spirit, M^r. Nelson offers to receive the sum[99] of Three Millions, one hundred and fifty seven thousand, five[100] hundred and seventy nine ducats; to be paid at the time, and in the manner indicated in the accompanying draft[101] of a Convention,[102] to be concluded within the time, to which, the Prince of Cassaro is already apprized. Mr. Nelson is limited by special and peremptory instructions.

Naples, Septr. 17, 1832.

[Enclosure "G" with Despatch No. 13, October 15, 1832]

Draft[103] of a Convention of Indemnity between the U. States of America, and His Majesty the King of the Kingdom of the Two Sicilies — (Copy)

---

99 Approximately one-half the figure called that of 'rigid justice' by Mr. Nelson in his Memorandum and Draft for the Prince of Cassaro to present to the Naples Council of Ministers, gives at first glance the impression that in the end the United States took payment in full but without interest. This was not the case. For full concept of how the matter was worked out in actual handling of the payments from Naples, see Miller, *op. cit.*, III, 718-721; also Moore, *History and Digest of International Arbitrations*, V, 4581-4589. Published as House Miscellaneous Document, 53d Cong., 2d sess. vol. 39, same paging. Also see 25th Cong., 2d sess. Senate Document 351, Serial No. 317, *Report of the Secretary of the Treasury,* March 30, 1838. Also 44th Cong. 2d sess., Executive Document No. 38. The final report of the Commissioners, dated March 17, 1835, is given in Moore, *op. cit. super,* last three pages. This was the report of the adjudication of the claims; it yet remained for the Treasury to continue to collect the installments from Naples, and then to distribute *pro rata* to the 275 claimants, for list of whom see Document 242, 24th Cong. 1st sess. Dated April 27, 1838, Claimants' names and amounts, totalling $1,925,034.68.

100 Note here the use of the figure 579, as compared with 679 two paragraphs above. See note 98, above regarding same.

101 Draft text will be found, below, enclosure "G."

102 For source references to the various versions of this Convention developed during subsequent negotiations see note 79, above, p. 293-294, and the following note 103.

103 The frequency with which this treaty text has been published, and the several stages it went through in its procedural course before it assumed its final, proclaimed form with full force of law, makes it desirable that one compare these several texts. Thus alone can the significance of the changes be clearly grasped. For modern printing of the final form alone, see Miller, *op. cit.,* III, 711-722, also an older, but official printing in volume *Treaties and conventions of the United States and the other powers.* United States Government Printing, 1889; also see United States *Statutes at Large* VIII, *European Treaties,* 1853, 442-444.

The United States of America and His Majesty the King of the Kingdom of the Two Sicilies, desiring to maintain upon a stable footing, the connexions of good understanding, which have hitherto subsisted between the two countries, have resolved to adjust, upon principles of Equity, the reclamations formed by the Government of the United States, upon that of the Two Sicilies, for seizures, sequestrations, confiscations, and destruction of the property of Citizens of the United States, made by the Neapolitan Government during the years 1809-1810-1811-and 1812; and have named for the purpose of effecting said adjustment, on the part of the United States, John Nelson, a citizen thereof and their Chargé D'Affaires, near His Majesty, the King of the Kingdom of the Two Sicilies, and on the part of His said Majesty, His Excellency, The Prince of Cassaro, His Said Majesty's Minister, Secretary of State for Foreign Affairs, &c &c who after having exchanged their full powers found in due form, have agreed upon the following articles. —

Article 1st.

His Majesty, the King of the Kingdom of the Two Sicilies, in order to liberate the Government thereof fully and entirely, from all the reclamations preferred against it by Citizens of the United States and the Government thereof, for unlawful seizures, sequestrations, confiscations or destruction of the vessels and cargoes of such Citizens (and of every expense of every kind whatsoever incident to, or growing out of the same) made by the Neapolitan Government, during the years 1809-1810-1811-and 1812, engages to pay the sum[104] of Three Millions one Hundred and fifty seven thousand, five[105] hundred and seventy nine Neapolitan Ducats, to the Government of the United States; seven thousand six hundred and seventy nine ducats, part thereof, to reimburse the said Government of the United States for expenses incurred by it, in the transportation of American seamen from the Kingdom of Naples, during the year 1810, and the residue thereof to be, by said Government of the United States, distributed amongst those entitled, in such

---

[104] Compare the sums mentioned on pages 292, 308, 309; also see that mentioned in the treaty as proclaimed (House Executive Document No. 414, 23d Cong. 1st sess., Art. 1st of the Treaty).

[105] For process of adjudication of the claims, under the Act of March 2, 1833, see above, note 79, pp. 293-294.

manner and according to such rules[106] as it may think fit to prescribe. —

Article 2ᵈ.

The sum of Three Millions one hundred and fifty seven thousand, six hundred and seventy nine Neapolitan Ducats, stipulated to be paid by the first and foregoing article shall be paid at Naples in five annual installments of Six Hundred and thirty one thousand five Hundred and thirty five Neapolitan Ducats and Eighty grains each, into the hands of such person or persons as shall be authorised by the Government of the United States to receive the sums. The first installment shall be paid, in one year next after the exchange of the ratifications of this Convention and the others at successive intervals of a year one after another 'til the whole shall be paid; the said installments each to bear an interest of five per centum per annum from the date of the interchange of the ratifications aforesaid 'til paid. —

Article 3ᵈ.

The present Convention shall be ratified and the ratifications shall be exchanged at Washington, in the space of Eight Calendar Months from this date, or sooner if possible.

In faith of which the parties, in the preamble hereto named, have respectively signed these articles and thereto set their seals.

Done at Naples the [blank] day of September, Eighteen Hundred and Thirty Two.

J. NELSON TO THE PRINCE OF CASSARO

[Enclosure "K" with Despatch No. 13, of October 15, 1832][107]

Naples Octʳ. 1ˢᵗ. 1832. (Copy)

Sir,

The determination of His Sicilian Majesty communicated to me this morning having extinguished all hope of an amicable accommodation of the differences subsisting between the United States and the Kingdom of the Two Sicilies, I have the honor

---

106 These rules were established during the sixth session of the Board of Commissioners, and were published on January 24, 1835, in the form of "principles governing the making of the awards." They may be found in Moore, *op. cit.,* V, 4585; (Miller, *op. cit.,* does not give them).

107 Enclosures "H" and "I" are here omitted. These were two notes from the Prince of Cassaro to Mr. Nelson, dated Sept. 22d (Enclosure H) and Sept. 29th (Enclosure I). There was no enclosure marked "J.'

to request of your Excellency my passports and such orders in relation to my baggage, as I may require. It is my intention to take passage on The United States Ship Concord, which will sail hence by the end of the present week.

In making this request I beg leave to repeat what I have had the honor so often verbally to communicate to your Excellency that in the propositions which I have submitted to His Majesty's Government for the adjustment of existing differences, I have been actuated by an earnest desire to meet the views and to yield to the pressure of the alledged necessities, of His Majesty; and that under the influence of this inclination I have reduced the demands much below the amount justly due to the American claimants. — These propositions preferred in a spirit of liberal compromise, having been rejected by His Majesty, I feel it to be my duty to declare no longer obligatory upon the Government of the United States, which, remitted to it's original rights, will hold The Sicilian Government responsible for the whole value of the vessels and cargoes seized by Murat; for the expense of the masters and agents in claiming the property; for the charges to which the American Government has been put, in supporting the American seamen belonging to the confiscated ships and their conveyance home, and for any expense which may be hereafter incurred in the further prosecution of the claims of its citizens.

J. NELSON TO THE PRINCE OF CASSARO

[Enclosure "L" with Despatch No. 13, of October 15, 1832]

Naples, Octr. 1, 1832. (Copy)

The Undersigned Chargé D'Affaires of the United States of America, being about to return to his country under the instructions of his Government has the Honor to request that His Excellency The Prince of Cassaro will inform him at what time His Sicilian Majesty will honor him with an audience —

The Undersigned avails himself of this opportunity to renew to His Excellency The Prince of Cassaro the assurance of his particular consideration —

THE PRINCE OF CASSARO TO J. NELSON

(Enclosure "M" with Despatch No. 13, of October 15, 1832)[108]

Naples 2nd October 1832.

The Undersigned has received Mr. Nelson's note of the [blank] and has the honour of sending him herewith a passport agreeably to his request, and of informing him that proper arrangements have been made for the free imbarcation [sic] of his suite and baggage.

The Undersigned however declares to Mr. Nelson, by order of the king, that although he may have thought proper to quit the country, yet the Sicilian Government does not consider the negociation terminated; as His Majesty actuated by that spirit of conciliation, which forms so distinguishing a trait in his character, has conceived certain propositions, which being similar to those agreed upon in the late convention, between France and the United States, seem likely to accommodate the existing differences.

His Sicilian Majesty urged by a sincere desire to maintain and strengthen his amicable relations with the United States and to dispel the existing difficulties is determined to bring the affair in question to a conclusion, and as the departure of Mr. Nelson will render that impossible here, His Majesty will send immediately to the United States a diplomatic agent furnished with proper instructions and with the power necessary for making a treaty, and thus ending the negociations here begun.

Having thus communicated to Mr. Nelson the determination of His Majesty the Undersigned renews to that gentleman the assurances of his esteem.

J. NELSON TO E. LIVINGSTON

U.S. Ship Concord At sea Oct. 20 1832. [Despatch No. 14]

Sir,

Of the solicitude of the Sicilian Government to connect the subject of a Commercial Treaty with the late negotiation, my despatches, heretofore communicated, have fully apprized you.

---

[108] Enclosure "N" with Despatch No. 13 is here omitted. This was the Italian (and the English translation) of the note from the Prince of Cassaro to Mr. Nelson, Oct. 2, 1832, expressing the King's willingness to grant an interview to Mr. Nelson on the following Friday. (For Enclosures "O" and "P", with Despatch No. 13, see above, notes 91, 92, p. 303.)

Although indisposed, as I was unauthorised by my instructions, to embarrass the question of indemnity by such a connexion, I became convinced very soon after my arrival at Naples, that the interests of our commerce and navigation might be essentially promoted by proper commercial arrangements, between the United States and the Sicilies; and with a view to possess myself of such details as might prove useful in any future intercourse with the Government of that country, I, on the 24th of August, addressed a circular to our Consular agents at Naples, Palermo and Messina, of which I have the Honor now to furnish a copy marked A.[109] The replies of those officers are herewith likewise communicated marked B. C. D.

From the information contained in these papers you will perceive, that our commercial interchanges with the ports of the Sicilies are extremely limited; and that our trade is almost wholly confined to the importation into the United States of the silks of Naples, and the wines and fruits of the Island of Sicily— Our exports to the Kingdom being merely nominal —

This depressed condition of our commerce with the Sicilian Kingdom, is mainly referrible [sic] to two causes; First to the unreasonable rigor of the sanitary regulations which are found to be exceedingly inconvenient to American vessels; and secondly and principally, to the discrimination in the duties upon imports, in behalf of certain privileged nations, of which this is not one.

The quarantine regulations are controuled [sic] by a board of Health established at each port of the Kingdom; whose decisions are very capricious, and altho' their requirements are often relaxed in regard to the vessels of England, France and Sardinia, they are always vigorously enforced, and with less reason, against those of the United States.

As explanatory of the origin, nature, and extent of the privileges secured to the commerce of England, France and Spain, I have the honor to present you, with this Despatch,

---

[109] The seven enclosures with this Despatch No. 14, will be found as follows: — A, pp. 322-323; B, p. 323; C, 327; D, 329; E and F are treaties with England and with France, and in this printing are omitted, since they are not apropos to the Two Sicilies (See note 119, p. 329, below). "G," the draft text of the commercial convention, prepared by Mr. Nelson, pp. 318-322. These enclosures all are copies. The originals of these documents were all left by Mr. Nelson with Mr. Hammett, as part of the archives of the American Legation at Naples, for use of his successors. These documents now, however, have long since been returned to the United States. The Neapolitan Legation was closed when the whole of Italy became united, and Rome became the seat of United States diplomatic approaches to that country.

copies of the Treaties existing between those countries and the Kingdom of the Two Sicilies, marked E. F.[110]

The necessary and unavoidable operation of these stipulations is to exclude from the ports of the Sicilies all American Vessels. The differences of ten per centum in the duties against them, renders it impossible to American merchants to participate profitably in Sicilian commerce. — We have in consequence no direct trade of any value, with that country. American vessels desiring to load its fruits, wines or other productions, are subjected to the necessity of discharging their own outward cargoes at Leghorn, Genoa, or some other Mediterranean port, and of proceeding thence to Palermo or Messina in ballast.

England enjoys a monopoly of the most important branches of the commerce of The Sicilies. In the articles of Coffee, Sugar, and Colonials generally; in Cotton twist, Iron, Fish, and various manufactures her Merchants prosecute a direct, brisk and highly profitable trade. The condition of her Commercial marine, renders the privileges secured to Spain almost valueless; and France has failed to avail herself, to the extent of her capabilities, of the advantages it offers to her commercial enterprize.

There can be no doubt, that an arrangement which should place our commerce with the ports of the Sicilies, upon a footing equally favorable with that of England, would eminently subserve the interests of our Merchants, whose position and enterprize would enable them successfully to prosecute a most profitable trade with that Kingdom. Independently of Colonials, which they might advantageously supply to a large amount, it is believed that it would open a market of no inconsiderable extent, for our cottons, rice, fish and other productions —

That it would be practicable to effectuate such an arrangement I have the fullest confidence. The present Government of Naples professes an anxiety, which I believe is really felt, to unfetter it's commerce from existing restraints, and to encourage a competition which it perceives must result in the increase of it's revenues, whilst it will subserve the more important interests of it's [sic] subjects, who are consumers of the imported articles —

Nor are the means of accomplishing this object, limited to those considerations, which address themselves to the judgment of His Sicilian Majesty. We have it in our power to constrain

---

110 These enclosures "E" and "F" are here omitted. See above note 109, page 315.

the adoption by him, of liberal views on this subject.— Sewing-silks, wines, and Fruits, constitute most important items in the foreign trade of the Sicilies. — Of these, a considerable portion finds it's market in the United States, the duties upon which may be so regulated, as measurably to coerce the Neapolitan Government to place our trade upon a fair footing. —

A few weeks before my departure from Naples, yielding to the pressing solicitations of the Minister for Foreign affairs, I drafted a convention of Commerce and Navigation, a copy of which accompanies this despatch marked G.[111] — It was submitted to His Sicilian Majesty with the information, that I was unin-structed upon the subject, accompanied by the expression of a belief, that it embodied principles which would receive the sanc-tion of the Government of the United States. It's leading object, was to put our commerce, in all respects, upon the footing of that of the most favored nation. — It was for several days under the anxious consideration of the Council of Ministers, by whom it was eventually referred, for more particular examination, to the Minister of Finance. — The day before my embarkation The Prince of Cassaro renewed to me the assurance that His Majesty was disposed to deal liberally with the subject, but stated that particular circumstances, the nature of which he did not disclose, would necessarily postpone a definitive action with regard to it, for some months; and upon the occasion of my taking leave, in adverting to my informal propositions the King begged me to understand that he had not decided to reject them; adding that they should receive the attention, which was due to the important interests to which they relate. —

In obedience to my instructions, before leaving Naples, I delivered to Mr. Hammett our Consul at that Port, a Trunk containing the books furnished me by the Department of State; the original papers connected with the negotiation, and a record of my correspondence with the Neapolitan Government, as well as with that of the United States. —

The documents relating to the claims of our merchants I have with-drawn, with a view to deposit them in the State Department, where they may be procured by those interested —

---

[111] See pp. 318-322 for the draft text of the commercial treaty.

Draught of a Commercial Convention
[Enclosure "G" with Despatch No. 14, October 20, 1832][112] (Copy)

The United States of America and His Majesty the King of the Kingdom of the Two Sicilies, being desirous to make firm and permanent, the peace and friendship, which happily prevail between the two Nations, and to extend the Commercial relations which subsist between their respective territories and people, have agreed to fix, in a manner clear and positive, the rules which shall in future be observed by the parties respectively, by means of a Convention of Friendship, commerce and navigation. — With that object, the President of the United States of America has conferred full powers on John Nelson, a citizen of said States, and their Chargé d'Affaires near His Majesty, the King of the Kingdom of the Two Sicilies; and His said Majesty has conferred like powers on the Prince of Cassaro his said Majesty's Minister, Secretary of State for Foreign Affairs &c &c &c who after having exchanged their said full powers, found to be in due and proper form, have agreed to the articles following.[113]

Article 1

The contracting parties desiring to live in peace and harmony with all the other nations of the Earth by means of a policy, frank and equally friendly with all, engage mutually not to grant any particular favor to other nations, in respect of Commerce and navigation, which shall not immediately become common to the other party, who shall enjoy the same freely, if the concession were freely made, or on allowing the same compensation, if the concession were conditional.

Article 2.

The contracting parties being likewise desirous of placing the commerce and navigation of their respective countries on the liberal basis of perfect equality and reciprocity mutually agree that the Citizens and subjects of each may frequent all the coasts and countries of the other and reside and trade there in all kinds

---

[112] This draft of proposed commercial convention bore no title on the copy which Mr. Nelson sent with his Despatch No. 14, dated on the Ship *Concord*, at Sea, Oct. 20, 1832. This fact distinguishes this draft outwardly from the earlier draft of the Indemnity Convention, sent with his Despatch No. 13. (See pp. 310-312).

[113] This particular convention of friendship, commerce and navigation, was never concluded since the first treaty of this kind with Naples was not signed until Dec. 1, 1845. See later in these despatches.

318

of produce, manufactures and merchandize; and they shall enjoy all the rights, privileges and exemptions in navigation and commerce, which native citizens or subjects do or shall enjoy, submitting themselves to the Laws, decrees, and usages, there established, to which native citizens or subjects are subjected. — But it is understood that this article does not include the coasting trade of either country, the regulation of which is reserved by the parties, respectively, according to their own separate Laws.

Article 3.

They likewise agree that whatever kind of produce, manufacture or merchandize, of any foreign country can be, from time to time lawfully imported into the United States, in vessels belonging wholly to the citizens thereof may be also imported in vessels wholly belonging to the subjects of the Kingdom of the Two Sicilies; and that no other or higher duties upon the tonnage of the vessel or her cargo shall be levied and collected, whether the importation be made in the vessels of one country or the other, and in like manner that whatever kind of produce manufacture or merchandize of any foreign country can be, from time to time, lawfully imported into the dominions of the Two Sicilies, in the vessels thereof, may be also imported in the vessels of the United States; and that no higher or other duties upon the tonnage of the vessel or her cargo, shall be levied and collected, whether the importation be made in vessels of the one country or of the other. — And they further agree that whatever may be lawfully exported from the one country in its own vessels, may in like manner be exported or re-exported in the vessels of the other country. And the same bounties, duties and drawbacks shall be allowed and collected, whether such exportation or re-exportation be made in vessels of the United States or of the Two Sicilies. Nor shall higher or other charges, of any kind, be imposed in the ports of one party, or vessels of the other, than are, or shall be, payable in the same ports by native vessels —

Article 4.

No higher or other duties shall be imposed on the importations into the United States of any article, the produce or manufacture of the dominions of His Sicilian Majesty; and no higher or other duties shall be imposed on the importation into the said dominions of any article the produce or manufacture of the

United States, than are or shall be payable on the like articles, being the produce or manufacture of any other foreign country. Nor shall any other or higher duties or charges be imposed in either of the two countries on the exportation of any articles to the United States or to the dominions of His Majesty the King of the Kingdom of the Two Sicilies, respectively, than such as are or may be payable on the exportation of the like articles to any other foreign country. Nor shall any prohibition be imposed on the exportation or importation of any articles the produce or manufacture of the United States, or of the dominions of the King of the Kingdom of the Two Sicilies, to, or from the States or territories of the United States or to or from the said dominions, which shall not equally extend to all other nations. —

Article 5.

The United States and His Sicilian Majesty mutually agree, that no other or higher duties, charges, or taxes of any kind, shall be levied in the territories or dominions of either party, upon any personal property, money, or effects, of their respective subjects or citizens, on the removal of the same, from their territories or dominions reciprocally, either upon the inheritance of such property, money or effects, or otherwise, than are or shall be payable in such states upon the same, when removed by a Citizen or subject of such state respectively. —

Article 6.

The citizens or subjects of each of the contracting parties shall have power to dispose of their personal goods, within the jurisdiction of the other, by sale, donation, testament or otherwise, and their representatives, being citizens or subjects of the other party shall succeed to their said personal goods, whether by testament or ab intestato; and they may take possession thereof, either by themselves or others acting for them and dispose of the same at their will, paying such dues only as the inhabitants of the country, wherein such goods are, shall be subject to pay in like cases; and if in the case of real estate the said heirs should be prevented from entering into the possession of the inheritance on account of their character of aliens, there shall be granted to them the term of three years to dispose of the same, as they may think proper, and to with draw the proceeds without molestation and exempt from all rights of detraction, on the part of the Government of the respectives States. —

Article 7.

The wines of the Kingdom of the Two Sicilies from and after the exchange of the ratifications of the present convention, shall be admitted to consumption within the states and territories of the United States, at duties which shall not exceed the rates following — By the gallon (such as is at present used for the measurement of wines in the United States) whether imported in bottles, cases or casks, in addition to the duties on bottles, when so imported [blank] cents —

Article 8

It is mutually understood that the stipulations in the preceding articles contained, secure to the vessels and cargoes of the United States, brought into the ports of His Sicilian Majesty's Kingdom, every deduction and abatement from the established duties, which are or may be allowed to the vessels and cargoes of His Sicilian Majesty's subjects, or of any foreign nation whatever. —

Article 9.

His Sicilian Majesty stipulates that from and after the exchange of the ratifications of the present convention, no longer or other quarantine shall be imposed on any American vessel or cargo coming into the ports of His Sicilian Majesty's dominions from the United States, than is or may be imposed on the vessels and cargoes of the most favored nations coming from any other Foreign country; provided every such vessel shall be duly furnished with a certificate of the good health of the port, from which such vessel shall sail, duly verified by His Sicilian Majesty's Consul or Vice-Consul residing in such port, if any there be; or if there be no such consul or vice consul there residing, then by the collector of said port under his official seal and provided also, that in case such vessel shall not be provided with such certificate, verified as aforesaid, His Sicilian Majesty shall be at liberty to adopt such regulations in regard to such quarantine, as to him may seem fit and proper.

Article 10.

To make more effectual the protection which the United States and His Sicilian Majesty shall afford, in future, to the navigation and commerce of their respective citizens and subjects, they agree mutually to receive and admit Consuls and Vice

Consuls, in all the ports open to Foreign Commerce, who shall enjoy in them all the rights, privileges and immunities of the Consuls and Vice Consuls of the most favored nation; such contracting party, however, remaining at liberty to except those ports and places, in which the admission and residence of such consuls and vice consuls may not seem convenient —

Article 11.

In order that the Consuls and Vice-Consuls of the contracting parties may enjoy the rights, privileges, immunities and exemptions, which belong to them by their public character, they shall before entering on the exercise of their functions, exhibit their commission or patent in due form to the government, to which they are accredited, and having obtained their Exequatur which shall be granted gratis, they shall be held and considered as such by all the authorities, magistrates, and inhabitants in the consular District in which they reside —

Article 12.

The present convention shall be in force for ten years from the exchange of the ratifications thereof and further until the end of one year after either of the contracting parties shall have given notice to the other of its intention to terminate the same

Article 13.

This convention shall be ratified and the ratifications thereof exchanged in the City of Washington within eight months from the date hereof, or sooner, if possible —

In faith whereof &c &c

J. NELSON TO A. HAMMETT

[Enclosure "A" with Despatch No. 14, of October 20, 1832][114]

Naples Augt. 14, 1832. (Copy)

Sir,
I am desirous of ascertaining the extent and condition of American commerce in the different ports of this Kingdom, and will be obliged to you for such information on the subject as you may have it in your power to furnish.

114 These enclosures with Despatch No. 14, although here printed out of chronologic order, follow the order as filed in the bound volume of Despatches in the United States National Archives. See above, note 109, p. 315.

What number of vessels have cleared from the port of Naples, for the United States, during the past year?

How many of these were American and how many Sicilian or of other Nations?

What were the articles of which their cargoes were composed, and what their probable value?

What have been the extent and nature of the importations into the port of Naples, in American bottoms, during the same period?

What are the disadvantages which American commerce encounters in it's [sic] intercourse with Naples, and which it would be competent, by Treaty stipulations, to remove?

Are there any, and if any, what American productions, whose introduction into the ports of the Sicilies, merits encouragement, and which proper commercial regulations could successfully foster?

Any suggestions which your long acquaintance with the trade of the Sicilies may enable you to offer, will be thankfully received and duly weighed. — I shall be glad to learn, also, the general character of the Sicilian commerce with other nations, and with whom it is chiefly prosecuted. I beg that your reply may be as prompt as your leisure may permit.

A. HAMMETT TO J. NELSON

(Enclosure "B" with Despatch No. 14, of October 20, 1832)

Consulate of the U. States Naples 27, August 1832.

Sir,

In reply to your letter of the 14th inst. I have the honor to inform you that no vessel has cleared from Naples for the United States during the past year nor has there been any importations in American bottoms during the same period. It would seem in consequence, that no commercial relations exist between the two countries, but this is not in reality the fact.

It is known to you that England, France, and Spain obtained by treaties with this Government some years past, ten percent diminution on the duties in honor of their respective flags, to the exclusion of those of other nations, which prior thereto, were treated almost upon an equal footing with them. The Captains and Merchants of the latter held in little account the right of visit or search, for it could then be rendered null by a few dollars. But when the three favoured nations by giving up their free flag, or right of exemption from search of their merchant vessels and receiving in lieu thereof, the aforesaid diminution of duties, were placed in the enjoyment of so positive and certain an advantage it was evident from the very moment, that there remained no other alternative to others but to abandon altogether the ports of the Kingdom: so that, in fact, there is seldom seen here even a merchant vessel belonging to other nations than to England or France. Though Spain has equal advantages, yet from the circumstances in which she has been placed of late years, her merchants, captains seldom visit the Ports of the Kingdom.

These partial advantages lasted several years to the protection of English and French commerce when the Government of Naples at last opened their eyes to see their own merchant vessels rotting in Port and their Captains and sailors fast approaching, for want of employment, to want and pauperism. It was then decided to grant the ten per cent diminution on the duties likewise to their own vessels, extending it to the produce and manufactures of every country from whatever port they came, whilst the vessels of the three nations before mentioned were restricted to their own produce and manufactures respectively to obtain the said diminution. They each however got it sometimes fraudulently, by previously changing the packages as for example putting Havana Sugars in English on French Casks.

Some years after, His Sicilian Majesty, with a view of encouraging distant voyages, extended the diminution in favor of such national vessels as might be employed in them, to thirty p. cent on the duties. Many voyages have been undertaken, principally to the Brazils, and brought a prosperous issue, and it is reasonable to expect, that others, under such encouragement, will follow. If none of these have been made to the United States, it is to be attributed to the counter sailing duties and tonnage there, so that they send their sewing silks, the most important articles of trade between this country, your own, to the ports of Leghorn and Marseilles, to be there reshipped on board American vessels, as on the other hand are frequently reshipped in those ports on Neapolitan vessels, to enjoy the ten p. cent diminution of duties in their favor at Naples, part of the cargoes imported in such ports by American vessels. It is to be observed, that such reshipment of sewing silks is very often made for Neapolitan account, whilst the reshipment of part of her American cargoes is seldom or never made for account of our own

324

merchants, being sent here, either by the merchants themselves of those places, on own account, or by orders of those at Naples.

Such being the circuitous route of the trade between the two countries, I have no data to form a just idea of its value. I believe however, that what is sent from Naples to the United States in this indirect way, far exceeds in value what is imported from thence. And this arises perhaps from the richness of the article of sewing silks which can be expeditiously sent by the Steam Boats, whilst bulky articles cannot be forwarded by similar conveyances.

A direct communication would then seem to be reciprocally advantageous. The extra freight, expenses, and commissions payable at the intermediate port, would, in this way, be avoided. By a direct intercourse, too, the productions of the growth and industry of the United States might find a limited market here, if the regulations and high duties to which they are subject were removed. Tobacco is a monopoly of the Government, and it is not to be expected they would relinquish so productive a branch of Income. Were the trade free, much however would be consumed. As it is two or three cargoes of our tobacco are supplied annually through a House at Genoa to give force and fragrance to their own, which is principally cultivated in the province of Lecce. Cotton too, might be imported were the duty small. That raised in Sicily and the Province of Salerno is at present, worth $40. per Cantar or 196 wt English.[115]

The rice consumed comes from Lombardy and Piedmont, and to a limited extent, that of the Carolinas might often find a sale The article was formerly cultivated in the province of Salerno, but has been discontinued since some years by order of the Government.

This is a large market for dried, smoked, and pickled fish. The whole trade is in the hands of the English who send here not less than 100/M quintals Codfish annually besides several cargoes of pickled herrings. American codfish is well known at Naples, but there is a decided preference given to the English cured. The latter being smaller, more dried, and less salted, than the American, imbibes more water and thus turns to better account of the retailers, who besides look out the heaviest water to soak these fish in. It also keeps longer. The difference in price cannot be less than 70 to 80 Cents p. Quintal in favor of the English.

---

[115] On the margin of the original document there is this note: "Duty 21 D°. Cantar, 9 cts. per lb."

These four articles are all important to our country and it cannot but be desirable to procure a market, however limited for them. There are several of the articles of our soil that would also answer but which from their minor importance, it is deemed unnecessary to mention.

The Commerce in Colonials at Naples being common with the rest of the Italian ports and so well known, require no explanation. England and France chiefly supply the country with all they want. The first sends her manufactures, Cotton twist, Crushed Sugars, Hardware, Iron, lead, fish, &c &c to the amount of about two millions pounds sterling. Of these, more than a third in cotton twist[116] alone, the annual consumption being near fifteen millions pounds sterling: Can we not market it as good and as cheap as the English? One hundred swift vessels from 150 to 200 tons each come here annually in this trade. The second (France) does not send more than twenty five small vessels annually from the port of Marseilles, however many Neapolitan vessels come from thence with colonials, hides, both raw and tanned, manufactures of Paris and Lyons, in return for cargoes of oil, skins, staves, figs, raisins, tartar, liquorice, raw silks, grain, &c. But the imports from France do not amount to more than a third of the value of those from England.

The larger size Neapolitan vessels likewise go to Bergen for stockfish, to the ports of the Baltic with cargoes, of olive oil, and sometimes to England, besides to South America. The rest, or smaller ones are confined to the Mediterranean. I dare say the oil and the other may arrive to 120/M [120,000] tons. There is too a considerable coasting trade.

I do not feel, Sir, that [anything] else be necessary in reply to your said letter than a few observations on their quarantine regulations, which are often capricious and bothersome. American vessels when they visited this port direct from those of the United States, were sent to the island of Nisite without regard to Bills of Health and the most positive assurances of the health of the port from whence they came to perform a quarantine of 21 days with susceptible goods & 14 days with insusceptible and this in both cases, after the landing of the goods, an operation often rendered tedious for the express purpose of increasing the expenses. In any commercial treaty, if such should come to be made, it will be necessary to provide particularly against such abuses as well as the charges to which they lead.

---

116 Marginal note reads: "Duty 12 cts pʳ. lb."

I believe, Sir, that I have given you a general view of the commerce of Naples, if not sufficiently satisfactory for all your purposes, at least as far as my present means of information afford. We have no statistical work on the commerce of the Kingdom and you know well enough by this time, that information can only be got secretly and by paying for it.

J. B. GARDNER[117] AND L. PIRANDELLO TO J. NELSON

[Enclosure "C" with Despatch No. 14, of October 20, 1832]

Palermo, August 27th, 1832.

Sir,

In reply to your regarded favor of 14th inst., I have to communicate to you the following particulars respecting this Island, which I think may be interesting.

The American Commerce has been rather extensive during the past year; twenty eight vessels have imported here Mahogany, Rum, Nails, Staves, Logwood, Tobacco, Wax, Rice, Pitch, Rosin &c. to the amount of 20647 dollars, & cleared out for the U. S. with productions of Sicily Soy Wine, Rags, Shurmac Liquorice paste, Manna, Feathers, Lemons, Oranges, Cantharides, Squill, Anchovies, Oil, Sulphur, Walnuts, Filberts, Cork, Silks, Almonds, Argol &c amounting to 260,786 Dollars; no Sicilian vessels, or of any other Nation, has gone out to the U. S. last year, but generally not more than two or three of the former make these voyages as it is the case in this year. Imports in American vessels are limited, on account of French & English flag having ten p. cent allowance on duties of goods of their productions, brought here, which, being very high in general, it makes a great difference to Merchandise, & American produce cannot be put in competition with those of the above nations. It would be also in my opinion a good prospect of business, should the duty on our wine be reduced in the U. S. as it being abundant here, shipments of consequence can be made out, it would employ many Americans yearly, as they are always prefered for such voyages.

The ports touched by Am". vessels are Palermo & Messina, & very seldom Trapani for Salt & Barrilla, or Girgenti for Brimstone. Sicilian Commerce is most extended for England, France,

---

117 On Mr. Gardner's appointment, see above footnote 33, p. 236.

& Genoa, & very little for other nations, the business however with England is much continued. Tobacco has always been carried here in abundance from the U. States, but, since the new duty has taken place, very little has come in; it pays D^{ts}. 28 p. cantar for leaf, and D^{ts}. 56 p. C^r. for manufactured, so that, if a reduction on the duty could be obtained from our [sic] King, it would make it an object to revive this business.

The long quarantine fixed to vessels from U. S. is a great obstacle to Commerce, as they are obliged to perform it in other ports of Italy (where is much less) with great expense; in Naples is 14 days, & here is 28 days for vessels & 40 for goods; to avoid this inconvenience, I have made sundry application to this Deputation of Health, & received verbally in answer, that in America, no deputation is fixed to survey, as it is the case in all ports of Europe; So that I never had redress even when vessel brings certificates fr. the Sicilian Consul, or other authorities of the perfect state of health; to the contrary, when in cases of any suspect, quarantines from England or France are prolonged, immediately on the Consul's demand to the minister in Naples, the affair is examined, & consulted, & quarantine is reduced from those places, that gives no founded [sic] suspect of any sickness; at this moment vessels from Baltimore or Philadelphia are not admitted on account of the cholera; this affair is not a little against U. S. commerce observing you, however, that a restriction with the U. S. as well as with all other places, is raised in a great part from the miserable state of this market.

I beg you to excuse the insufficiency of the above considerations, which are all I am able to give you, trusting, that will be of some use to your purposes.

I. L. Payson[118] to J. Nelson

(Enclosure "D" with Despatch No. 14, of October 20, 1832)[119]

Messina 15th. Septr. 1832

Sir,

Indisposition is the cause of my not having replied at an earlier period to your communication of the 14th. Augt.

From the within documents you will ascertain the extent of the commerce between the U. S. & this port, which has perceptibly increased for the past six years, & would have been more extensive the past season, were it not for the impediments caused to trade by the rigorous sanitary regulations.

Since the reduction of the Port Franco of Messina in 1826, to Government Warehouses, the trade with the United States has been almost exclusively confined to Exports or produce of the Island, the amount of imports in the U. S. vessels since the above period will not average one year with another over *$5000* while the average Amount of Exports for the past 3 Years will exceed the value of *$150,000* Yearly.

Previous to the above named restrictions, the importations were far more numerous, at which period the Porto Franco was open to the City of Messina, and the import consumption duty only 1% upon a Tariff Valuation. The existing custom house regulations and heavy duties upon imports will account for this falling off in importations and indeed these remarks will apply in general to the foreign Trade particularly that with England. —

The Privileged flags are the English, French, and Spanish, which enjoy a reduction of 10% upon the amount of duties paid by other nations — particulars of which you will also see from the enclosed statement, to say upon Coffee an English flag would pay £4.24.4 p. Cr. of 175 lbs., the American flag £5.10.4 p. Cr.;

---

118 I. L. Payson, of Massachusetts, nominated consul of the United States for Messina, Sicily, on March 3, 1827. He held office until Dec. 1845.

119 Enclosures "E" and "F" with Mr. Nelson's No. 14 (and here omitted) are printed copies of other treaties entered into by the Kingdom of the Two Sicilies. Copies of these texts are in the United States National Archives. "E" is the "Treaty of Commerce & Navigation between H.B.M. & H.M. the King of the Two Sicilies, together with a separate and additional Article thereunto annexed, signed at London, Sept. 26, 1816, presented to both Houses of Parliament by Command of the Prince Regent, May 1817." London, Printed by R. G. Clarke, Cannon Row, Westminster, 4 pp. 8°. "F" is "Ferdinando I, per la Grazia di Dio Re Del Regno Delle Due Sicilie di Gerusalemme &c &c &c . . . o concessioni godevano ne' Nostri domini i bastimenti coperti delle bandiere inglese, francese e spagnola . . . Convenzione con la Inghilterra . . . convenzione con la Francia (Feb. 28, 1817) convenzione con la Spagna (Aug. 15, 1817) . . . 20 pp., 4.°"

the articles enumerated are those generally imported from the U. S. adapted for the consumption of the place. —

Several attempts have been made to introduce the manufactures of the United States into use, but thus far without much progress; the difference of duty is certainly one great obstacle, add to which the Qualities of our Cottons are too good for this Market & buyers will not pay the difference while they acknowledge their superiority; hence we are unable to compete with those of England, made up expressly for the market; still then does appear an opening for similar Importations, could our commercial relations be placed upon a similar footing with those of the most favored Nations; while a long time must elapse before the manufactured stuffs of the United States can be brought in competition with those of England, France & Germany with which, the place is mostly supplied. These remarks are more particularly applicable to Sicily. —

Of Staves there is an occasional importation from the United States; the supplies are mostly drawn from Calabria & Sicily with which those from America cannot compete. Naval Stores form an an article of Importation, though to a very limited extent, as also Tobacco, which however being a Gov^t. monopoly cannot be ranked with other produce. —

It is difficult to foresee the immediate advantages that Commerce would derive from a treaty with this Gov^t. though there cannot be any doubt of our own imports in general becoming much more extensive than they now are, perhaps the produce of the United States might not be materially effected for the present, still the carrying trade with American vessels must be increased, by which the introduction of Colonials & the like, would have a tendency to reduce the balance of trade more in favor of the U. S., thus enabling importers to provide for their return cargos by taking in Exchange for same the produce of the Island which at present is paid for in effective, brought by the vessels, or by Credits, that generally terminate in loss; taking into view the Exchanges between the U. S. & Europe & those in this Country & Europe. — During the last five years, three Sicilian vessels have left this port for America, the value of each cargo would not exceed $5000. —

By the recent Tariff to take effect in the United States in March next, it appears there is a reduction of duties on many of the exports from Sicily, among which however is not enumerated that of Wine, the heavy duty on which in the U. S. amounts to a prohibition of the article from this Island. — And it does appear, this branch of trade is deserving of particular notice. — The description[120] of common Wines are very numerous, & of excellent quality and generally can be shipped from Sicily on more favorable terms than the French or Spanish & were the duties on the same to correspond with the French, the exportations to the United States would be thousands annually, whereas under existing restrictions it must become quite a dead letter. — The Wines of Naples come under the denomination of Mediterranean Wines upon which the duties are much less than those of Sicily, these remarks are particularly applicable to the Red Wines of Sicily, to which subject permit me to recommend your particular attention. —

The Tonnage duty upon all foreign vessels is the same. —

In my intercourse with this Government I have in every instance found the facilities afforded to the interest of the United States to be strictly compatible with the good faith existing between the two Nations. —

It has not been in my power to procure satisfactory information upon the general trade with other Nations, that with our own country will rank about the fourth, taking first England of which flag about *150* vessels annually arrive here, most of which head for the United Kingdom after which comes the Kingdom of Sardinia, Austria, & the Low Countries, then the United States.

The foregoing remarks apply alone to the trade of Messina. —

J: NELSON TO E. LIVINGSTON

Boston 7th Dec[r]. 1832 (Private)

My Dear Sir,

I take pleasure in informing you, that I arrived at Portsmouth, in the Concord, on the 5th. having concluded[121] a convention of

---

[120] i.e., "the varieties of."

[121] Mr. Nelson was highly pleased with his success in concluding the convention. Commodore Patterson too was elated, especially since he had contributed to its success. Writing to his superior officer, the Secretary of the Navy, on October 13 (note this date was the day before the treaty was signed) Commodore Patterson said: — "It is admitted by Mr. Nelson that the appearance of the Squadron in this bay had great effect in producing so favorable a result." (United States Navy Records, in United States National Archives, *Letters, Officers: Captains' Letters; Patterson to Woodbury, Oct. 13, 1832.* For contrasting comment in the *American Annual Register,* 1832, and in the *London Globe* see Perrotta, *op. cit.,* 71-72.

331

indemnity with the Gov^t. of Naples on the 14th Octr. As I expected to present to you the Treaty in a few days, I omitted to write from Portsmouth. — My exhaustion and fatigue have obliged me to stop here; I hope however to reach Washington, in all next week. — I have only to add, that I have seen Mr. West and others of the claimants who are *entirely* satisfied with the result of the Negotiation. Mr. West thinks that the sum secured will more than pay, the principal of the just claims, by Twenty per cent. —

I have had a boisterous and very uncomfortable passage, and of consequence have suffered much, and am still indisposed.

E. LIVINGSTON TO J. NELSON

Department of State, Washington, 11th. Jany. 1833. [Unnumbered]

Sir: —

Be so obliging as to inform me whether it is your wish to return to Naples in the same character in which you were first sent? The immediate object will be the exchange of ratifications of the treaty which you so ably negotiated. It will, however, be considered as a continuance of the same mission, and of course no outfit allowed. Should it not suit your convenience or wishes to return, a special authority for the exchange will be despatched by a messenger.

E. LIVINGSTON TO J. NELSON

Department of State, Washington, 17 Jany. 1833.

Sir: —

On the 11th. instant I addressed you a letter, for the purpose of ascertaining your intention respecting the exchange of the ratifications of the treaty with Naples. Having received no reply, which fact induces the supposition that the letter may have miscarried, and a decision on your part being urgent, I send you a copy of it, and will thank you for an answer as soon as convenient.

J. NELSON TO E. LIVINGSTON

Frederick March 2, 1833.

My Dear Sir,

Mr. Forsythe was kind enough to forward to me, to-day, a copy of the Document touching the convention with the King of the Sicilies, printed by the Senate's order.[122] I find upon referring to it, that it contains three of my notes to Prince Cassaro, one of which and that the most important, dated 29 June 1832, has been so inaccurately printed as completely to disfigure the argument it was designed to present. — There is scarcely a paragraph, *or sentence,* into which some error has not crept. In this form, it is certainly calculated to do me great injustice with the public. I do not know how it may be corrected, but if it be practicable, I think that I may reasonably expect that it will be done. —

Will you do me the favor to look at this Document, and to ascertain whether in the copies transmitted to the Senate, these errors exist? I take it for granted that they are ascribable to the negligence of the press.

It is mortifying to me, that this note certainly prepared with some labor, should go to the public in the mangled condition, in which this Document presents it.

E. LIVINGSTON TO J. NELSON

Department of State, Washington, 8. Mar. 1833.

Dear Sir: —

I have looked at the document mentioned in your letter of the 2ᵈ. instant, and find that your note has been wretchedly mangled in the printing, but have not yet had it in my power to compare

---

[122] There was passed on Feb. 9th, 1833, (*Senate Journal,* IV, Appendix, p. 286; *Senate Executive Journal,* p. 30) an "order to remove from the seal of secrecy, and to be printed, the following documents communicated to the Senate on the 16th of January in compliance with a resolution of the 31st of December:—
"Instructions of the Secretary of State to Mr. Nelson, Nos. 2 and 5, of 27 Oct. 1831 and 11th June 1832;
"The correspondence between Mr. Nelson and the Prince of Cassaro, minister of foreign affairs of the kingdom of the Two Sicilies, viz:
"Letters of Mr. Nelson dated 31st January, 27th February, 29th June, 1832.
"Letter of the Prince of Cassaro dated 30 May 1832
"Despatches Nos. 10 and 11, of Mr. Nelson to the State Department, dated the 2d and 8th October, 1832,
"And that they be printed for the use of the Senate."
(See also further regarding the printing of these letters, footnote 124, pp. 334-336).

it with the copy sent to the Senate: But as the rule of the Department is to let no papers go out, without a strict examination, I take it for granted, that all the errors are typographical. I know of no other remedy, Congress having now adjourned, than that of publishing the errata in a newspaper. This will be a very imperfect mode of correcting the evil, but it is the only one that occurs to me, and I will have it done if you desire it.

J. NELSON TO E. LIVINGSTON

[Re: Errors charged in printing Note of 29 June, 1832, to the Prince of Cassaro. Enclosed letter of D. Green, Printer]

Frederick 16 March 1833.[123]

My Dear Sir,

Upon my return from Balt°. a day or two since, I found your favor of the 8th. The errors in the printed Document are so numerous and important, as to render it impossible to correct them, by the mere indication of them, as errata, in the News-papers. Besides, you are aware that in the shape this note has assumed, unless something be done to prevent it, it will be bound up[124] in the public Documents and then do me lasting injustice.

---

[123] Mr. Nelson, now having completed his mission to Naples, was resting at his home in Frederick, Md., awaiting further proposals, but keenly aware that the written evidence of his diplomatic work had somehow not been printed so as to give the public a true record of his correspondence with the Neapolitan Government. His letter of the 2d of March had made this plain, and at Mr. Forsyth's suggestion, he had written to the printer, who had referred him to the State Department. But the dates of both his letters, here included, make it plain that, together with the date of the Senate's "ordering" of the printing he complained of, this incident itself could not be considered responsible for his refusal to return to Naples to secure the ratification of the treaty.

[124] The question as to what printed text Mr. Forsyth actually showed to Mr. Nelson — that which Mr. Nelson made the basis of his charges in his letter of March 2d — leads to interesting facts about the printing procedures of those days in regard to Congressional documents. Investigation of the original records, and comparison of these with the various printed versions, shows that the texts of the treaty (as at various stages of the negotiations and subsequent consideration in Congress, in both Senate and House, as well as when finally proclaimed by the President and subsequently so reported to Congress) were separate publications of the treaty text alone. Th story of the publication of the correspondence regarding the convention with the Sicilies is as follows, and the dates involved are to be carefully noted:

The letters whose text Mr. Nelson complains, on March 2d, had been "inaccurately printed" were those he had enclosed with his Despatch No. 13, and which, arriving with himself on the *Concord*, at Portsmouth, approximately Dec. 5th, 1832, had also been among those Notes, Despatches, etc. which the President, on January 14th, 1833, in compliance with a Resolution of December 31st, had communicated to the Senate, and were by the Senate referred to the Committee on Foreign Relations; on January 19th, the Senate had voted to "advise and consent to the ratification of the convention," on January 24th, the Presi-

The note as published is not the note presented by me to the Neapolitan Gov'. — and I think it due to me as well as to the public that a paper, professing to proceed from the Gov'., should not be permitted to remain before the country in the mangled

---

dent had communicated the treaty, minus any of the correspondence, to the House, which having had the matter under advisement in its own Committee on Foreign Affairs had brought forth the implementing Act of March 2d, 1833, providing for the appointment of a Board of Commissioners to adjudicate the claims.

When the President communicated the letters to the Senate, he had been at some pains to caution that ". . . they are written by the agents of the United States to their own government with a freedom, so far as relates to the officers of that of Naples, which was never intended for the public eye, and as they might, if printed, accidentally find their way abroad and thereby embarass our ministers in their future operations in foreign countries, I respectfully recommend that in printing, if deemed necessary, such a discrimination be made as to avoid that inconvenience, preferring this course to withholding from the Senate any part of the correspondence." (See Message of January 14th, communicated January 16th). No order to print the correspondence at all is found at this time.

On February 9th, however, and while the House was considering what form the implementing act should take (the act was passed on March 2d) the Senate, on motion of Mr. Forsyth, ordered the removal of the seal of secrecy on certain specified documents in this correspondence, and ordered them to be printed "for the use of the Senate." This phrase, in those days, usually meant the printing of a small 'separate' issue, sometimes specified as to number, usually 100 copies, which were in the nature of 'working copies' for Senators' use during the discussions on the floor or in committee; and of such nature may have been the copy shown to Mr. Nelson which prompted his protest letter of March 2d, to Secretary of State Livingston, especially since, on March 16th, Mr. Nelson refers to it as not yet "bound up in the public documents."

In the form actually "bound up" we find the same set of letters listed as is mentioned in both the *Senate Journal,* IV, App. 286, and the *Senate Executive Journal,* page 30, under date of February 9th, in both cases, in the order to "remove secrecy" and "to print." Thus "bound up" these letters comprise Senate Document 70, of the 22d Congress, 2d session "for the use of the Senate." 54 pp. This writer has not been able to locate a copy of the printed version to which Mr. Nelson took such severe exception; nor has he been able to discover any evidence, to date, either in printed form, or in the original documents in the United States Archives, that any 'separate' (as hypothetically assumed might have existed, and have been the one handed Mr. Nelson by Mr. Forsyth) ever existed. That it may have existed, and having been found to have been full of errors, thereupon recalled from (or never have reached the hands of) the Senators is another possibility within the general pattern of printing difficulties of that day.

Careful comparison of Mr. Nelson's Notes to the Prince of Cassaro, especially that of the 29th June, 1832, of which he most vehemently protests its misprinting, shows that the printed version in Senate Document 70, as found "bound up" in the public documents series, and bearing the labels of the Senate Chamber and the Senate Library, varies scarcely at all even in spelling and punctuation, and not at all materially in phrases or meaning, from the original of that note comprising Enclosure B, with Mr. Nelson's Despatch No. 13. Reference, further, to the texts of this Note to the Prince of Cassaro, as sent with the President's Message (and therefore originating as copies made in the State Department for the President's transmitting to the Senate) shows that these texts also, which are the ones sent to the printer and bear the printer's endorsements of names of his typesetters who were to handle the several sections of this printing job, — agree, virtually verbatim, with Mr. Nelson's own Despatch No. 13, enclosure B and similarly for the other letters, of which Mr. Nelson complained as to their misprinting. The only hint given by this file to the possibility that these letters went twice to the printer, is the fact that two manuscript copies of them are found in *Senate, Class 22B-B7,* and that the printers' names endorsed thereon,

condition, in which the Senate's document presents it. If it cannot be otherwise put right, I shall be constrained to cause it to be reprinted at my own expense —

At the suggestion of Mr. Forsyth, with whom I met in Balt°., I addressed last week, a note to D. Green the Senate's printer, a copy of whose reply, I take the liberty of enclosing to you. You will perceive upon examining it, that he refers the errors to the Department of State. — Now although confident that they are attributable exclusively to the carelessness of his office, I will be obliged to you, if you will cause the necessary comparison of the Documents to be made, and apprize me of the result.

I am sorry to trouble you on this subject. If the errors were few or unimportant I should be careless about them. But they are such, as uncorrected, are calculated to prejudice me before the public. There is not a paragraph in the printed document which does not mis-represent me, in so far as the note of the 29th of

---

in assigning the work, appear to be different on the two sets of the letters in question. But mystery remains, owing to the further fact that both these sets of the manuscript letters (those from which the seal of secrecy was removed on February 9th, as above cited), are as virtually verbatim, to the Nelson enclosures with his Despatch No. 13, as are these same letters found in the "bound up public documents" in Senate Document 70. Therefore, unless and until, and if ever possible now after passage of more than a century, an actual 'separate' printing of the letters, on Senate order (there was only the one order, that of February 9th cited above) turns up from some obscure pamphlet collection, perhaps still personally owned, there will be no way of knowing just what, in detail, were those 'errors in printing' which Mr. Nelson on March 16, 1833, claimed, with particular reference to the Note to the Prince of Cassaro of June 29, 1832, was "not the note presented by me to the Neapolitan Government," and that in this Note "there is not a paragraph in the printed document which does not mis-represent me . . . the more remarkable as all other portions of the Document have been printed with unusual accuracy." The printing of documents in loose pamphlet form, preliminarily, and then, with same title page, but sometimes altered text (due to official action meanwhile) has been known to occur in the ordinary course of procedure. This occurred, without change of the text, in the case of the Treaty text itself, as sent to the Senate, December 17th, 1832, (see footnote 79), and could have similarly occurred in the case of these Despatches and Notes "released" for publication on Feb. 9th, 1833. No other explanation seems logical, for the allegations in Mr. Nelson's letters of March 2d and March 16th; and since the copy Mr. Nelson criticized was handed him by the chairman of the Senate's Committee on Foreign Affairs, Mr. Forsyth, it is also reasonable to suppose, but none of the misprinted copies was ever put into the hands of the Senators. In this supposed case, the entire issue may possibly have been destroyed, a reprint correctly made, and that then, the form found as Senate Document 70, of the 22d Cong. 2d session, 'for the use of the Senate', ordered printed February 9, 1833, may have been the only version, in print, that ever was in any way really circulated. At this late date, the problem involved here is of small moment, but the attempt to ascertain the facts is enlightening as to printing procedures of that early period, and as to how supposedly justified protest over inaccuracies of printing could be handled with as much aplomb as were international affairs.

June[125] is concerned. This is the more remarkable as all other portions of the Document have been printed with unusual accuracy.

D. GREEN[126] TO J. NELSON

(Enclosure with Mr. Nelson's of March 16, 1833)

Wash.". 8 March 1833. (Copy)

Sir,

The copy of the correspondence to which your note of yesterday refers has been returned to the Senate. If you will do me the favor to note the errors I will have the copy and the printed Doc.ᵗ compared, and if the fault is attributable to my office, I will cause a reprint at my own expense, provided the errors are to the extent your letter indicates; otherwise you must obtain your object through the State Dep.ᵗ where I presume the errors originated in copying.[127]

---

[125] See above, enclosure "B" with Despatch No. 8 (pp. 254-283). This was Mr. Nelson's master effort in striving to achieve the signing of a treaty: his long discourse on points of the 'law of nations' involved in this case of the Murat spoliations. Compare this "Enclosure B" text, with that of printed Senate Document 70, 22d Cong., 2d session, February 9, 1833.

[126] Duff Green was one of the public printers in Washington. The print of Senate Document 70, containing the letters in question, as found in the Public Documents Series, does not individually bear the printer's name; but the title page to the whole volume, Serial 230, from Senate Chamber Library, and now in the United States National Archives Library, bears the imprint "Printed by Duff Green, 1832." This date is governed by the date of beginning of the Second Session of the 22d Congress. The dates of the individual documents contained in the volume are indicated on their several title pages, that for Senate Document 70 being February 9, 1933. The title there used was "Documents relating to the Convention with Sicily." The treaty text itself is not included therein.

[127] As to the lack of errors in copying see footnote 124, above, in this chapter. The question remains open, as to what errors occurred, or to whom attributable.

AUGUSTE DAVEZAC[1]

January 30, 1833 to February 19, 1834

E. LIVINGSTON TO A. DAVEZAC

Department of State, Washington 7th. March 1833. No. 16.

Sir:

You will herewith receive a Special power to exchange the ratification of the convention with Naples, by the President, for that of His Majesty the King of the two Sicilies.

The Treaty thus ratified on our part, having been transmitted to you by Mr. Mark, our consul at Ostend who sailes [sic] on the 8th. February in the Liverpool Packet, will probably have reached you before this despatch. The letters which accompanied it will have prepared you for these instructions, which are, that you proceed in the most expeditious manner to Naples, and on your arrival request an interview with the Minister for foreign affairs, to whom you will present your powers for exchanging the ratification and request that an early day may be assigned for the purpose. In order to accelerate this exchange, you may say that as soon as it is effected, you have powers to negotiate a commercial Treaty on terms mutually beneficial to the two countries. A copy of the law for carrying the convention into effect, accompanies this despatch. You may show this as a proof of the confidence felt by this Government, that no unnecessary delay will take place on their part. In making the exchange you will pursue the form herewith sent to you.

You may draw on our bankers for such sum as may be necessary for your expences going to, remaining at, and returning from

---

1 Auguste Geneviève Valentin D'Avezac (1780-1851), born in Santo Domingo, lawyer and diplomat. After his return from France where he had gone to study, he settled in New Orleans, La., where he acquired distinction as a criminal lawyer. He became secretary of the legation at The Hague, Aug. 11, 1829 and promoted to chargé d'affaires to the Netherlands, on Oct. 15, 1831. On Jan. 30, 1833, he was appointed special diplomatic agent to the Two Sicilies and empowered to negotiate a treaty of general commerce. On this mission he remained a year in Naples, returning to The Hague about Feb. 19, 1834. He retired from the Netherlands' legation, July 15, 1839. He returned to the Netherlands as chargé d'affaires, April 19, 1845, and remained in this position until September 1850. Although Davezac signed his name *Davezac* and was addressed by the State Department as *Davezac,* the *Dictionary of American Biography* (1930), V. 89, spells the name D'Avezac, Auguste Geneviève Valentin (1780-1851). For biographical information on D'Avezac see: Charles Howens Hunt, *Life of Edward Livingston* (1864), N. Y., Appleton Century, p. xxiv, 448 *passim;* Louise Livingston Hunt, *Memoir of Mrs. Edward Livingston* (1886) I, p. 182; Henry Stuart Foote, *The Bench and Bar of the South and Southwest* (1876), VIII, 194-264; *United States Magazine and Democratic Review,* Feb. 1845; New York *Herald,* Feb. 16, 1851.

Naples, not exceeding four thousand five hundred dollars, of which power to draw notice is given to our bankers at London, on which place it is supposed your drafts may sell to better advantage than at Amsterdam.

You will advise the Department of your departure progress and arrival at Naples, and write by duplicate.

When the exchange of the ratification is completed you will immediately despatch the certified copy, by a special messenger to this Department, or if a proper person cannot be found to make the voyage, you will send it by some safe person to our Charge d'affaires at Paris, requesting him to put it in safe hands to be conveyed here, or if the Brandywine Frigate should not have sailed, when you arrive, you will send the accompanying order to the Commander of our Squadron in the Mediterranean, and keep that vessel to carry home, the treaty. In all events giving notice by triplicate to this Department of the day at which the exchange took place. You are particularly instructed to lose no time in having this done, as you will perceive by the treaty, that the payments are to date from that day.

You will also herewith receive a full power to conclude a commercial Treaty with His Majesty the King of the Two Sicilies, according to the instructions, which, if possible, will accompany this despatch, but if not, will be sent you immediately after.[2]

A. Davezac to E. Livingston

Legation of the U. States at Naples
June the 10th 1833 [Despatch No. 1]

Sir,

In compliance with your instructions, I lose not a moment in informing you that the ratification of our Treaty[3] with Naples, was exchanged on the 8th of June at the hour of Two in the afternoon at the Foreign Office between me and the Prince of Cassaro. I enclose a Copy of the Procés verbal in which you will

---

2 These instructions were not sent therewith, but followed in Instruction No. 17, dated March 13, 1833. It carefully specified the conditions which the United States was willing to accept in such a commercial treaty and urged haste in forwarding the text if such a treaty were concluded by Minister Davezac, but warned him not to hold up the sending of the ratification document to wait for the negotiation of the commercial treaty.

3 This was the Convention concluded on October 14, 1832, by John Nelson, dealing with indemnity for the Murat spoliations. Mr. Nelson had been offered the privilege of returning to Naples for the formalities of its ratification by the Neapolitan Government but had refused, and Mr. Davezac was asked by the State Department to leave temporarily his post at the Hague for this duty. This instruction No. 16 by Secretary Livingston is found in Instructions, Netherlands, XIV, 2-3.

find some slight departure from the form you sent me with my instructions. They are so unimportant that I did not think it worth insisting on preserving the precise wording you had directed, particularly when it was observed, that the act proposed was in strict conformity with the form of similar instruments made on like occasions at their Chancerys. In fact, I was too eager to conclude to dispute on forms when the substance was fully attained. There were many here who would have wished that some obstacle had arisen in the way of the execution of this Treaty by this Government. I will send the original procés Verbal and the ratified Treaty itself either by the Brandywine, if it be still on this Station, which I will know in a day or two, or by a special messenger in some of the modes you have pointed out.

A slight indisposition by compelling me to borrow the aid of M^r. Hammett's pen, prevents me, in respect to that Gentleman's delicacy, to express in a letter dictated to himself, as fully as I intend to do, in another dispatch, the high sense I entertain of that meritorious functionary. I wrote from the Hague as you directed, previous to my departure; of my progress, I had not time to give you any account, it was so rapid through Belgium and France. I arrived at Naples on the 24th. of May. All business in the offices of the Government was suspended, owing to the approaching nuptials of the King's sister, a lovely and blooming Princess, with the Grand Duke of Tuscany. On the 7th., the marriage ceremony was celebrated, and on the 8th. affairs having resumed their wonted course, the ratifications were exchanged as I before stated, so that, on my part, there has not been the loss of a moment to bring to a conclusion the business confided to my charge.

In one of the Triplicates of this despatch you will find the observations made by Mr. Hammett on the subjects to which the memorandum you sent me referred; and likewise a list[4] made by him of the confiscated American vessels, with the dates of their arrival. Every step will be taken to answer satisfactorily all the queries contained in said memorandum. Directions have already been given by Mr. Hammett to the Notary here to prepare copies of the Acts executed in his office. Expenses must be naturally incurred in obtaining these copies, as well as to

[4] This list was sent with Mr. Davezac's Despatch No. 2, by hand of Lieutenant Harwood. See below, pp. 346-353. It was certified by Mr. Hammett, the American consul, whose observations are found in his letter to Mr. Davezac, June 18, 1833. See p. 353.

procure and send the documents which may be found at any of the offices of Government. I will also be under the necessity, if the Brandywine be not on this Station, to disburse the money required to send you the Treaty by a special messenger. This I will procure from Mr. Willink on whom I am authorized to draw for contingent expenses for the Netherland Legation. Presents to Menials, as Mr. Nelson must have apprized you, are expected here, and will of course be given. All these will be charged regularly and certified by Mr. Hammett.

Of the other business given to me in charge, I can only say now, that I have every reason to expect a favorable conclusion.

Procés Verbal of Exchange of Ratification, signed by A. Davezac and Prince Cassaro, June 8, 1833.

[Sent with Mr. Davezac's Despatch No. 1, June 10, 1833, triplicate.]

The Undersigned having received full powers from their respective Governments to proceed to the exchange of the ratification of the convention concluded, and signed on the 14th of October 1832 between the United States of America, and His Majesty the King of the Kingdom of the Two Sicilies, at Naples, for the purpose of terminating the reclamations of the Government of the United States for the depredations, seizures, confiscations and destruction of American vessels, and their cargoes, made by Murat,[5] have met at the office of Foreign Affairs, and the said ratifications having been read, have exchanged the same in the manner adopted in such cases.

In witness whereof, the Subscribers have signed in both languages, the present act (procés verbal), and affixed to it their respective seal at Naples the 8th of June 1833.[6]

Signed, August Davezac   The Prince of Cassaro
    (Seal)   (Seal)

---

[5] "It is interesting to note that the Bourbon court never accorded the title of 'King' to Joachim Murat." (Perrotta, *op. cit.,* 81).

[6] The original, in English, of the Procés Verbal of the ratification of the Convention is bound as an ordinary document in Italy I, Despatches Naples, No. 2. The United States today has only a positive photostat of the Italian version, of which the original is in the Archives of the Italian Government at Rome. (Notation in record volume of United States State Department, at United States National Archives). Another copy of this Procés Verbal will be found, herein, as Enclosure No. 5, with Mr. Davezac's Despatch No. 2, dated June 20, 1833 (see below, p. 354).

A. DAVEZAC TO E. LIVINGSTON

Legation of the United States of America at Naples,
June 20, 1833. [Despatch No. 2] via Lt. Harwood. (Confidential)

Sir,

In conformity with the instructions given in your despatch of the 7th. of March last, the Brandy Wine having already left this station, on her way home, I determined to send you the ratified copy of our Treaty with Naples, by Lieutenant Andrew Allen Harwood,[7] who was recommended to me, by Commodore Patterson, as an officer worthy of being entrusted with the care of that Document, in order to take it to the United States, as a special messenger. The short acquaintance I have, myself, formed with Lieutenant Harwood, has so favorably impressed me, as regarding his talents and acquirements, that I take the liberty of inviting on him, the attention of the Department. You will find enclosed, a copy of his instructions,[8] in relation to the duty which he has undertaken to perform, in which you will observe, that I have only stipulated his receiving, in compensation of his services, the usual retribution. — Moved in circumstances of the like nature, I enclose, likewise, my account[9] with the duplicate receipt for the sum I have advanced him to enable him to proceed to America, as well as that which I have disbursed to pay for the Notarial Acts (which I herewith transmit to the department, as directed), in order that I may be instructed, whether the amount is to be charged, as contingent expenses of the Hague Mission, or whether you intend, that I should draw for the same, on Baring and Co: on a distinct head, for the contingent expenses of my Special mission here. In execution of the intention of the Department, there will be further expenses incurred; thereupon, it is proper that I should be informed of the determination of the Government on the Subject.

---

[7] Andrew Allen Harwood (1818-   ), naval officer, was born in Pennsylvania. He was appointed midshipman, Jan. 1, 1818. He was commissioned as lieutenant March 3, 1827; he served on frigate *United States,* Mediterranean Squadron, 1832-1833; he was detached as special messenger to bring home the ratified treaty with Naples. He returned again (1835-1837) to the Mediterranean Squadron. He commanded the frigate *Cumberland,* Mediterranean Squadron, 1853-1855. He was commissioned Rear Admiral, Feb. 16, 1869. Lewis R. Hamersly, *The Records of Living Officers of United States Navy and Marine Corps.* 1870, 37-38.

[8] See below, p. 354.

[9] This account and Lieutenant Harwood's receipt were forwarded to the Treasury; the advance was $400.00. (See p. 354).

I have received, from Mr. Rothschild,[10] the well-known banker of this City, a letter which I have the honor to transmit, remarking at the same time, that Mr. Rothschild, — in addition to the influence of his wealth, has no inconsiderable political weight in this Government, and, therefore, may be useful to us in the negotiation in which we are engaged, at this time.

I have frequent conferences with the Prince de Cassaro on the subject of the intended Commercial Treaty; he is eager to bring that to a fortunate issue, as he did the one which I exchanged with him, some days since. He says, that he can foresee no obstacle to the accomplishment of his wishes, and — of mine, except that which arises from their revenue being farmed out for a period which will not expire before next September twelve-months. The treaty must therefore, stipulate, that its clauses will not be in force until after that time. As we have not yet put any thing on paper, I must wait a greater maturity in our negotiation before I am more explicit. You may rest assured, however, that I will be guided by the spirit, and letter of my instructions.

I discharge a pleasing duty, now that I can write, in stating that I derive the utmost aid from the talents and experience of our Excellent Consul, Mr. Hammett, who, not only knows all that relates to the commerce of the Kingdom, but is also well informed as to the character and views of the leading men, at this Gov.ᵗ

Civita Vecchia, as may be seen in any good map of the French Empire, published after the Papal dominions had been swallowed up by Napoleon, was a part of the Department of Rome, and never subject to the authority of Murat.

I have ascertained, that this Government would have no objection to pay the indemnity by issuing stock-notes. If any thing of the kind be intended, it would be necessary to send me instructions, as to the mode in which it is desired that this should be executed.

There has been a conspiracy discovered here, of a nature extremely alarming to the Government.[11] It was intended to make

---

[10] Karl Rothschild. On him see note 21, p. 181. For his letter see p. 345.

[11] The conspiracy was headed by Cesare Rossaroll, a corporal in the second regiment of the guards. Together with Lieutenant Francesco Angelotti and Vito Romano, Rossaroll first planned a military plot which was to do away with the King in January or February 1833 when the King was to go to the Teatro Fiorentini at Naples, but then it was postponed to April 1833, on the occasion of the King's trip to Caserta. The plot was carried out in May 1833, under tragic circumstances

way with the King, and to react, as regards the Foreign Troops, the Bloody Tragedy of the Sicilian Vespers: The chiefs, two non commissioned officers, finding their plans betrayed to the Police, fired at each other, standing breast to breast, one, was shot dead, the other, it is believed, will not survive the desperate wound he has received. Many of the presumed acomplices [sic] have since been arrested. This conspiracy was evidently connected with that which has thrown such deep roots thro' the whole Piedmontese Army,[12] as to make it doubtful, whether His Sardinian Majesty can, now, continue with any safety, to keep on foot a National Army.

As I was about closing this despatch, a N°. of the English News paper "The Times" was brought to me, in which I have just perused, with the utmost indignation, a statement, by an anonimous [sic] correspondent of that paper, of a pretended conversation had with me, at Benpiles, which has not the slightest foundation in truth. I thought, at first, of addressing to the editor a letter giving the direct lie to his correspondent, but, on further consideration of the matter, I came to the conclusion to remain silent, rather than engage in a polemic with a writer who had not signed his name to his communication.

Prince de Cassaro, has been exposed to the bitter animadversion of courtiers, for the Treaty he signed with Mr. Nelson; and even the Chargé d'Affaires of Austria, who advised the King to yield, has been accused of having sacrificed an *old city* to a *new - friend!* but, the Prince has triumphed over his adversaries, and holds his power, now, with firmer hands than he did not long since.

Commodore Patterson,[13] who has been here a few days, with

---

when the conspirators were discovered by Paoletti, the banner carrier, who, feigning to take part in the movement, revealed the would-be regicides who were apprehended at the Maddalena bridge at Naples. Rossaroll was condemned to death on December 13, 1833. See: Giuseppe Paladino, "Una congiura mazziniana a Napoli nel 1833." *Archivio storico per le provincie Napoletane,* Naples, 1924, X, 287; Nicola Nisco, *Ferdinando II° e il suo regno.* Naples, Morano, 1888, 29; Wm. R. Thayer, *The dawn* etc. I, 409.

12 The disturbances in Piedmont in 1833, inspired by Mazzini, resulted in the death sentence of many liberals who had participated in the revolt. Jacopo Ruffini, a friend of Mazzini, and a leader in the uprising, committed suicide in a prison in Genoa.

13 The squadron no longer caused consternation in Naples. The men were cordially received. Commodore Daniel Todd Patterson (1786-1839), especially, was shown every courtesy. Patterson had taken part in the war against Tripoli in 1803, when he was imprisoned for almost two years. During the negotiations to enforce claims against Naples, his squadron gave effective aid by entering the Neapolitan harbor one ship after another, until all six were assembled. *Dictionary American Biography* (1934), XIV, 301-302. (See above, note 71, pp. 286-287; note 73, p. 288).

344

the United States, and the Constitution, was visited, yesterday, by Prince Cassaro, and three of his daughters: he left the United States, greatly pleased with the manner of his reception, by the Commodore, and the officers; and, more and more impressed, he said to me, with the idea, that, with a nation possessing, such a navy, was the interest of Naples, to cultivate the most friendly relations.

Memorandum of the documents accompanying this despatch . . .

N. 1. a letter to me from Mr. Rothschild

N. 2. Copies of Protests.[14]

N. 3. Mr. Hammett's letter to me, the receipts of the Notary, the receipt of Lt. Harwood for the sum advanced to him, on account, on my account.[15]

N. 4: Copy of my Instructions to Lieutenant Harwood.

N. 5. Procés Verbal of the exchanges of ratifications.

C. M. ROTHSCHILD[16] TO A. DAVEZAC

[Enclosure No. 1 with Mr. Davezac's Despatch No. 2.]

Naples, 4 June 1833.

Sir,

In our last conversation you was so kind to inform me that the Government of the United States of America has not yet any Banking house here or in any other place of Italy for the managing of those affairs which the pecuniary and commercial concerns of the said states may require in these countries. I therefore take the liberty to offer my best services to this purpose especially as the commerce of the United States is encreasing [sic] with this part of Europe.

I shall feel myself highly honored by any order or business I

---

[14] Enclosure No. 1, see below, this page, and Enclosure No. 2, pp. 346-353, consist of list of the claims, in terms of the cargoes of the several despoiled vessels. Since the protests referred to by Mr. Hammett (see his letter, p. 353) are not found in the bound volume of despatches, they were probably at once transferred to the committee considering the claims. For Enclosure 3, see p. 353; for Enclosure No. 4, see p. 354; for Enclosure No. 5, see p. 354.

[15] The receipts of the notary and of Lt. Harwood are not found with these despatches. They would have been forwarded by the State Department, in due procedure, to the Treasury Department, since they involved matter of accounts with the government.

[16] See above, note 10, p. 343.

may be entrusted with from your Government and you will be persuaded that my position on this place as well as the several Establishments of our different houses enable me to attend to the management of those affairs in such a manner as to give the utmost satisfaction.

Note of the American vessels and cargoes confiscated at Naples.[17]

[Enclosure N°. 2 with Mr. Davezac's Despatch N°. 2]

1809[18]

Augt. 27 schr. Hamilton, W. Brown
1111. Tunisian quintals Coffee, 28 boxes Sugar.
Crews adventure
8 Boxes Amer[n]. Codfish & 7 Barrels leaf Tobacco.

---

[17] It is to be noted here that each of the lists of these claims, as found in the despatches, represents a different angle of approach to the problems they presented. The text of the convention, having provided for a lump sum indemnity payable to the United States Government, and Congress having implemented that convention by setting up a Claims Commission to adjudicate the amounts payable therefrom to the individual claimants, this present list represents compliance with the State Department's request for still more details and in notarized form, to enable the Commissioners to proceed to determine how to distribute the monies obtained from the Neapolitan Government in behalf of the claimants. The itemized claims, as finally published, with claimant's names and amounts adjudicated to each, was published as House Document 242, 24th Cong. 1st sess. Serial No. 291. 6 pp. Letter from John Forsyth, Secretary of State, to the Hon. James K. Polk, Speaker of the House of Representatives, April 27, 1836, transmitting "A list of the Awards of the Commissioners on Claims arising under the convention with the King of the Two Sicilies." Of the approximately 250 claimants listed, 102 were either executors or administrators of the estates of the original claimants. It had taken but a year to adjudicate the claims, but it had taken from 1809-10-11 to 1832 to get the Neapolitan Government to agree on the convention. Mr. Pinkney's first diplomatic efforts dated from 1816.

[18] Dates of vessels' arrival at Neapolitan ports are indicated in the first column. See page 340. Just what purpose this particular list was intended to serve is not clear on the face of the evidence; but since there is no mention of the cargo values in this list, it was perhaps called for as further means of identification of the vessels' several cargoes. In the list of final awards, in House Document 242, referred to in the preceding note, it is evident that claims were laid for certain kinds of damages for one voyage of a vessel, and for other damages on a different voyage, which would call for the most complete details that Mr. Hammett could secure evidence to support. The final column of the list is of value as showing the extent to which products of the West Indies as well as from the American mainland, were being carried at this period to the Mediterranean markets.

Sept. 13 ship Hercules, E. West

735 Boxes Sugar, 106 Hhds. and 1 Barrel Sugar, 130 Boxes Tea, 47 Tierces: Bark, 5 Hhds. & 22 bags coffee, 1 Hhd & 5 Balls Tobacco, 44 Boxes Codfish, 10 Barrels Rum, 205 Bales nankeens.

"   " Ship Augusta, J. H. Moore

2649 Bags Cocoa, 33 Bags Coffee

Sept. 30 Schr. Zephyr, J. Murfey

78 Boxes Sugar, 50 quintals logwood, 102 Barrels Coffee & 446 Bags. Ditto.

"   " Brig Sophia, S. Carman

110 baskets Javesugar, 800 Bags Bourbon Coffee, 100 Bags ginger, 1 ton 8 Cts. logwood. Belonging to the mate 2 Barrels Tobacco.

Oct. 16 Ship Margaret, W. Fairfield

Compromised with the owners of the French Privateer which captured all the Acts passed between them & the Captain in the French Consulate.

Nov. 5. Brig Orozimbo [sic], R. Holden

690 Bags & 101 Barrels Coffee, 286 Boxes Sugar, 3 Hhds. Rum, 9 tons logwood, 120 Bales Nankeen, 5 Hhds. Wax, 7 Hhds. Tobacco & 6381^w Cassia.

1809

Nov. 30 Brig Two Betsys, J. Gardner

35 Hhds. & 6 Blls. Martinique Sugar, 198 Boxes H. Sugar, 16 Bales F^r. Incense, 6 Bales myrhh [sic], 26 Seroons Indigo, 30 Bales Moka Coffee, 30 Barrels & 332 Bags Cocoa, 1000 Bags or 634 Quintals pepper, 44 Butts pepper belonging to the crew 6 Cases H. Sugar, 29 Bags Coffee, 1 Hhd. leaf Tobacco 6 Kegs Tobacco, 1 keg Cocoa, 1 Bag Coffee.

347

Dec. 2 Brig Romp, W. Lander

239 Boxes & 50 Hhds. Sugar, 371 Bags Coffee, 102 Blls. coffee, 667 Bags pepper, 157 Bags Cocoa, 3 Hhds. Cocoa, 3 cases gum, 2 Bundles Cassia, 3000 pieces nankeens.
Belonging to the Crew, 59 bags & 8 Blls. coffee, 25 boxes Tea, 20 Blls. Salmon, 3 Boxes Codfish, 4 Seroons Indigo, 6 Tons logwood & 3 Blls. Cocoa.

Dec. 9 Sch^r. Kite, A. Thompson

75 Boxes sugar, 26 Tieras, 28 Blls. & 102 bags coffee, 200 Bags pepper, 300 bundles cassia, 11 bales wax, 12 bales salsaparilla, 10 Hhds tobacco, 4600 w. logwood belonging to the crew. 10 boxes Sugar, 2 barrels Indigo 3 Blls. cloves, 5 Blls leaf tobacco.

Dec. 14 Brig Victory, J. Felt

163 Hhds. 42 Blls & 20 Boxes sugar, 25 Bags, 53 casks & 32 Blls coffee, 200 Bags pepper, 135 Bags Cocoa, 20 Blls Colombo root.

Dec. 19 Ship Trent J. Cavendish

121 Hhds & 4 Blls Sugar, 203 Boxes Sugar, 21 Blls & 164 Bags Coffee, 75 Bags Cocoa, 358 Bags ginger.

1809

Decr 30 Scho. Ousetonack, W. Sheffield

1895 Quintals Codfish, 25 barrels beef & 34 Boxes tobacco

The following vessel was taken by the Neapolitan Gun Boats and carried to Civita Vecchia Cargo as correct as possible.

Sch^r Mary - Larcom

87 Boxes, W. & 65 Boxes B. Sugar, 851 Bags Sumatra pepper, 7 Bales G. cotton.

Jan. 7 Sch' Syren J. Janiron
2068 quintals Codfish, 50 kegs salmon, 6 Blls fish oil & 4 Blls beef.

Jan. 9 Brig Phoenix, S. Haskell
In ballast with some cash.

Jan. 15 Scho. Peace, W. Graves
1800 Quintals Codfish.

Jan. 22 Brig Emily, D. Waterman
20 Hhds, 322 Blls Sugar, 54 Bags Cassia, 205 Bags pepper, 17 Hhds, 47 Tierces 176 Bags Coffee, 313 Bags Cocoa, 13 Tierces Cloves, 5 Cases Indigo, 11 Casks Indigo & 6 Tons logwood.

Jan. 26 Ship Francis, W. Haskell
500,076 ʷ pepper.

Feb. 1 Sch' Hound N. Warren
350 Bags Coffee, 183 Boxes Sugar, 12 Cases Cassia, 3 tons or 218 pieces logwood.

Feb. 7 Sch' Dove D. Thomas
1236 Quintals codfish

Feb. 12, Sch' Maria R. Cleveland
24 Hhds Tobacco, 2 Casks wax, 23 Tons logwood, 352 Bales & 65 small Bales nankeens.

febʸ 12 Sch' Urania J. M. Peck
8000 pieces nankeens, 7 Boxes nutmegs, 19,000 ʷ. Coffee, 230 Boxes Camphor, 1200ʷ. Cloves, 4000ʷ. Cassia

" 13 Sch' Amherst G. Bradford
1448 Quintals Codfish

" " Brig Ruth & Mary W. Gardner
200 000ʷ. Coffee

" " Sch^r William L. Turner
100 Boxes Sugar and 880 Bags Pepper

" " Sch^r Fortune S. Martin
65 Hhds Tobacco, 60 Bales Cotton, 25 Tons logwood, & 2000 Staves

" " Sch^r Nancy J. Holman
70 Boxes Sugar, 74 Hhds 125 Bags & 4 Casks Coffee 85 quintals Codfish, 22 Bales nankeens, 1 Ton logwood, 5 Bales Bark, 9 Barrels & 70 Bags Cocoa, 4 Blls Cloves

" 15 Brig Nancy Ann M. Brown
3200 Quintals Codfish

" 16 Sch^r Mary Jno Derby
109 Boxes, sugar, 19 Bales Cotton, 11 Bales Bark, 8 Boxes gum, 775 quintals Codfish, 9 Bags Coffee, 9 tons logwood, 39 Bags pepper & 18 Boxes Codfish.

1810

Feb. 17 Sch^r Louisiana T. Newhall
18 Hhds Sugar, 47 Bags Cocoa, 915 quintals Codfish, 7 Tierces, 5 Bags & 34 Hhds Coffee, 12 Blls coffee and 11 Tons logwood.

Feb. 20 Brig John Ed. Currier
2,200 quintals Codfish

April 16 Sch^r John P. Dixey
322 quintals Codfish, 10 Hhds Tobacco, 33 Hhds & 9 Blls Sugar, 18 Hhds, 28 Blls & 109 Bags coffee, 672 Tons logwood.

April 16 Brig Betsey An^d. Tucker
274 boxes sugar, 488 Bags Cocoa, 16 Hhds Coffee, 2 Tons logwood belonging to the Captain

350

34 Boxes Sugar, 4 Bags Coffee, 19 Boxes
Sugars.
belonging to the Mate and Sailors,
25 bags coffee, 18 Boxes codfish

Nov. 9 Ship Victress   Jn°. O. Roosbach
In Ballast

Dec. 6 Ship Henry B. Gardner
51 Hhds tobacco. 105 Tons 11 Cw^t. logwood, 150 Bags Coffee, 33 Bales Cotton,
30 Boxes Brown Sugar, 5 boxes & 5
Seroon, P. Bark; 194 Bags Race ginger,
8 Cases and 1450 Bundles cassia, 20 Bales
nankeens, 6 Cases Indigo, 8 Cw^t. 2 q.
14 ^{w}. whalebone
To the Mate
20 quintals codfish

1810

Dec. 31 Brig Alexander W. S. Pickett
1460 quintals Codfish, 210 Bags Coffee

1811

Jany 31 Sch^r. Oceanus W. Willson
39600 P^s. [pieces] Nankeens, 13,894 ^{w}.
Indigo, 2814^w. P. Bark, 715^w. nutmegs,
356^w. Cloves, 90 Cw^t. o. 24^w. Sugar, 9350
Cocoa, 215^w. cassia, 4 Tons fustic and 72
ton [sic] Nicaragua wood.

1812

Febr. 19 Brig Golden Age W. Fairfield
723 Barrels pilchards

Mar. 2 Ship Pocahontas I. Sherburne
3000 quintals Codfish, 4000 staves.

Mar 19 Ship Admittance P. Sprague
1176 Hhds Pilchards

Mar 19 Ship Boston W. Bain
1003 D°. D°

Mar 19 Ship Concord   S. Storm
                        1350 D°. D°.

Mar 19 Ship Horace   W. Appleton
                        1383 D°. D°.
                        25   D°. To the Captain

April 16 Sch'. Playmate H. Bancroft
                        A quantity logwood belonging to a Tuni-
                        sian taken by a French privateer & com-
                        promised.
1812

Apr. 26 Scho Mary Jn°. Drew
                        3200 hard Spanish Doles on board, bound
                        to Messina was set by the current on the
                        coast of Calabria Seized by order of Gen.
                        Manhes, & ordered to Naples, but
                        wrecked on the passage.

                    Note of Cargoes at Gallipoly
1809

Dec. 29 Brig Suckey & Betsey, W. Hanscom,
                        84 Boxes or 211C. 31rot. Sugar
                        26 Hhds. or 157.86 D°.
(5 Hhds Sugar lost   200 bags or 90.16 pepper
in the Lighter while 20 Hhds. ⎱
unloading)   41 Blls. ⎰ or 125.38 Coffee
                        21 Bales or 13,29 Cassia
                        22 Hds [sic] or 161.31 Tobacco
                        16 Hhds, or 86.07 codfish
                                    29.16 logwood
1810

May 18 Brig Radius B. Lander
                        72 Boxes Sugar, 26 Hhds. 14 Blls., 2 Bags
                        Coffee, 135 Bags pepper, 100 Boxes
                        herrings, 20 Hhds Codfish, 47 Cant. Log-
                        wood, 34 C. 55 wt. Iron hoops, 20 Blls
                        alewives, 10 Blls. Mackerel, 5 Blls. Sal-
                        mon, 6 Hhds 2 Blls Rum, 17, 260 pipe
                        staves, 318 or 27,000 feet plank, Mara-
                        lone W.

352

Sept. 4, Sch'. Alert   C. A. Gilston

> 53 Boxes sugar, 100 Bags Coffee, 48568
> Codfish, 110 C. Longwood, 30 C. yellow
> wood, 50 Blls salmon, 90 C. Iron hoops,
> 19 C. whalebone.

Consulate of the U. States of America
   Naples.

These are to certify, that the above list contains to the best of my knowledge an exact account of the packages, with the nature of their Contents, composing the cargoes of the American vessels, siezed and confiscated at Naples or in the Kingdom thereof.

> Given under my hand and Seal of office in Naples aforesaid this fifth day of July A.D. 1833.

Alex'. Hammett   [Seal]
U. S. Consul

A. HAMMETT TO A. DAVEZAC

[Enclosure No. 3, with Mr. Davezac's Despatch No. 2]

Naples 18 June 1833
Dear Sir,
   I have the honor to hand you the authenticated copies[19] of the Protests and Acts made for the American vessels and cargoes before the Notary and Chancellor to this Consulate, with his note of expense amounting to D 107.40.
   My fees thereon would be One hundred and eighteen dollars, but as perhaps the Secretary of State does not expect to pay them, you will be pleased to mention the circumstance to act as he likes. Those of Gallipoli and Civita Vecchia[20] will be handed you when received.

---

[19] Copies as called for in State Department Instruction to Mr. Davezac, Mar. 7, 1833. Although not couched in 'protest' wording, this listing of the cargoes may have been a summarization of the data in such protests; or the protests themselves, as full copies thereof, may have been turned over to the Commissioner appointed to consider the claims, as suggested in note 14 above and merely the tabulation therefrom retained in the State Department's file. What the procedure was at this point is not clear.

[20] Civita Vecchia was at this point a part of the Department of Rome, of the Papal States, and never was subject to Murat. (See above, text, p. 343).

A. Davezac to Lt. A. A. Harwood[21]

[Enclosure N° 4, with Mr. Davezac's Despatch N° 2]

Legation of the United States of America at Naples
June the 18th. 1833. (Copy)

Sir, having been directed by the Secretary of State, in his despatch of the 7th of March last, to send the ratified copy of our Treaty with Naples to America, by a Special Messenger, and being informed by Commander Patterson that you were willing to undertake to perform that duty, I commit herewith to your hands, having felt confidence in your prudence and discretion, a Box, containing the said Treaty; and also a packet, enclosing despatches, the one and the other, addressed to Edward Livingston Esquire Secretary of State of the United States, which you will, with all possible haste, proceed to deliver to the Department of State, at Washington. In addition to your necessary travelling expenses, you will receive from the government the compensation usually allowed for services of the nature of that which you have undertaken to perform. The Sum of four hundred dollars is now paid you, on account.

Exchange of Ratification of Convention

[Enclosure N°. 5 with Mr. Davezac's Despatch No. 2.][22]

The Undersigned having received full powers from their respective Governments to proceed to the exchange of the ratification of the convention concluded, and signed on the 14th. of October 1832 between the United States of America and His Majesty the King of the Kingdom of the Two Sicilies, at Naples, for the purpose of terminating the reclamations of the Government of the United States for the depredations, seizures, confiscations, and destruction of American vessels, and their cargoes, made by Murat, have met at the Office of Foreign Affairs, and the said ratifications having been read, have exchanged the same in the manner adopted in such cases.

---

21 On Lieutenant Harwood, see above, p. 342, note 7.

22 This text is the same as that found with Mr. Davezac's Despatch No. 1 from Naples, (for which see above, p. 341) and accounts for the use of the word 'triplicate' with regard to that earlier copy in Mr. Davezac's Despatch No. 1. See in the State Department's annotation at head of No. 1, on p. 341.

In witness whereof, the subscribers have signed in both languages, the present act (procés verbal) and affixed to it their respective seal at Naples the 8th. of June 1833.

Auguste Davezac   The Prince of Cassaro
[Seal]   [Seal]^{23}

A. DAVEZAC TO L. MCLANE

Legation of the United States of America - Naples
August the 20th 1833 [Despatch No. 3]

Sir,

I had the honor of receiving, some days since, your despatch N°. 21, bearing date the 29th. of May, in which you were pleased to inform me of your having been entrusted, by the President of the United States, with the charge of the department of State. Allow me, Sir, while I felicitate you on this high evidence of the President's just appraisement of your talents and experience, to express the pleasure it affords me to renew an acquaintance which, tho' brief, had impressed me with feelings of deep respect, and grateful recollections.

My negotiations, with this Court, continue slowly, but with every prospect of being brought to a successful issue. Our Treaty, with Russia,^{24} which you advisedly sent, opportunely arrived. It will have great weight in the determination of this Government, particularly, as Count de Stakelberg [sic], the Russian Minister,

---

23 These two seals, affixed to the Procés Verbal bring to notice two things: — first, the beauty of the designing of that day, both in Naples and in the United States, if Davezac's seal was made there. Mr. Hammett's seals, too, both his official and his personal one, were of fine design; second, it is here to be noted that the seals of Mr. Davezac and of the Prince of Cassaro were used as personal seals attesting their signatures, but were not to be construed as 'official seals', since for a document such as this convention even the 'ratification' document was regarded as still a preliminary document. The use thus of personal seals by the two governments' representatives subtly indicated that the signatories, though acting in their official capacities, did so within certain limitations on their acts; and that only when the treaty should be officially proclaimed by both the President of the United States and by the King of the Two Sicilies did it become international law. It was only to the Proclamation making the Convention a law, that the great seal of the United States would be affixed, and likewise, in Naples, the seal of the King.

24 On December 18, 1832, the United States had concluded a treaty of commerce and navigation with Russia. A separate article, signed at the same time, provided that certain stipulations with other powers were not to be invoked. For the text of this treaty, in English and in French, see Miller, *op. cit., III,* 723-740.

355

urges the King to follow the example of the Emperor Nicolas, by drawing closer the ties of friendship with our Government.

The political plot of upper Italy, by occupying much of the attention of ministers, has had the effect of retarding the conclusion of our affairs: but you may be assured, that I will soon, further send you such a Treaty as you directed me to make, or be on my way back to the Hague.

As I was given to understand, that this Government will not consent to insert, in any Treaty, stipulations at variance with their sanitary laws; and, being aware, that one of the obstacles in the way of a direct commerce, between this Kingdom and the United States, is the long, and expensive quarantine to which vessels arriving here from America, are subject, I have conversed with several of the members of the *Magistracy of Health,* in order to devise some means of mitigating the rigor of their enactments. They all agreed in stating, that having no regular correspondence with any well-known *board of Health,.* in the United States, they were always uncertain, for want of information on which they could rely, how to act; and, therefore, obliged, as the only safe mode, to enforce the quarantine regulations of which I complained. This, I communicated to the Department in the hope that they may determine on some means to suggest to the several boards of Health, of our principal ports, the propriety of establishing a correspondence with that of Naples.

I have the honor of forwarding, to the Department, as I was invited to do, several Naples *Prices General* — (*No. 1*) of the latter months of the year 1809, of the earlier months of 1810, and one of January 1811, the period of arrival and confiscation of the greater number of American vessels, in this Kingdom; and a Note (No. 2) of American vessels and cargoes confiscated at Naples. I send likewise a duplicate of my account.[25]

---

[25] *Prices General* were printed public announcements by the Government of the Two Sicilies, and therefore a good basis for considering what profit Murat may have made of his confiscations of the American goods. None of the enclosures here mentioned are herein reproduced.

A. DAVEZAC TO L. MCLANE

Legation of the United States of America at Naples
October 19, 1833 [Despatch No. 4.]

Sir,

It cannot be, I assure you, a greater disappointment, to you, to receive a despatch, from me, bearing the date above, and containing no definitive statement of the result of my negotiation here than it is, to me, to write it; and yet, I can truely [sic] say, the four months I have spent here, have not been idly consumed: the fact is that, (as the communications of my predecessors, at this Court, must have informed you,) business is carried on thro' so many intermediary agents, that tho' Ministers be incessantly at work, affairs, nevertheless, do not progress. In continuing my stay here, I have exercised a discretion which, I thought, was left to me, if not by the express words, at least, by the spirit of my instructions. I was of opinion, that, as the Government had incurred the expense of a mission to this Court, I ought not to leave unfinished one of the objects.

They had contemplated, while there remained, & as I believed, a probability of effecting it, in a reasonable delay. The event will, I hope, justify me, in having so acted, for, in the conference I had, yesterday, with the minister of Finance,[26] at the request of Prince di Gassaro [sic], in order to give him some information of which he stood in need, with regard to our last tariff, having observed, that I must return to my Post at The Hague, at the end of the present month, he earnestly urged me, not to take such a ship; assuring me, that the objections to a Treaty of Commerce with America, which had hitherto proceeded from him, would now be changed into the most active efforts to bring the matter to a prompt, and favorable issue, as a proof of which determination, he added, that The Director of the custom house had received order to wait on me, on the ensuing morning, in order to reduce to writing, in the form of articles, the stipulations previously discussed between him and me, and which he now was disposed to accept, as the ground work of our intended

---

26 The Minister of Finance was Marquis Giovanni d'Andrea (1776-1841). (*Almanach de Gotha*, 1833, 250). He occupied important positions in the government of the Two Sicilies, including judge of the *Gran Corte* (1803), judge of the court of appeals (1808), director general of post-office (1815), minister of finance (1821-1822; 1830-1841). During this last period he was also minister of ecclesiastical affairs. He was able to carry out important and useful public reforms. See, Paolo Spada, *Della vita del marchese Giovanni D'Andrea*, Naples, 1842; *Dizionario del Risorgimento Nazionale*, Milan, 1930, II, 827-828.

Treaty of commerce. Accordingly, I have had, this morning, a long conference with the Chev^r. di Ligore,[27] the person designated by the Minister, in the course of which the negotiation, hitherto so tardive, has progressed in a way that leaves me, now, but little doubt of final success. I will endeavour to so conduct the affair as to be able to send you the Treaty (if my hopes be not blighted) early enough to allow the President to speak of it, in his next Message to Congress.

I entreat the Department to remember, that I have paid, out of my own funds, four hundred dollars to the Special messenger by whom I sent them the ratified Treaty of indemnity. It becomes the more urgent to give direction, either to Mr. Baring, or Mr. Willink,[28] to repay me this sum, that I may, again, be under the necessity to make a like disbursement, for a like purpose.

The Death of the King of Spain has produced here, as all over Europe, a deep lamentation. The King of Naples, is making great efforts to free himself from the ominous Treaty stipulations with France, England and Spain; and to break the bonds of tutelage, by which he has been held, by Austria,[29] ever since the occupation of Naples by the forces of that power.

England, is very jealous of the object of my mission here: but, tho' it was not possible to keep from her minister the knowledge of our views, I have succeeded in inducing a belief, on their part, that I had been unsuccessful in my attempts at negotiation.

It is but an act of justice, which I feel a lively pleasure to perform, to note to you, Sir, that our meritorious Consul Mr. Hammett, has given me, with the utmost zeal, the useful aid of his experience, and of his knowledge of both of the public men [sic] and of the commerce of this Kingdom. The services which he has rendered to our country, on former occasions, are important; and, I know, from the communications of your predecessor, appreciated as they must be, by the department. Allow me, Sir, to say, that, should our relations with this Court become of such a nature as to induce the President to nominate a minister resident for this kingdom, M^r. Hammett is qualified, by the

---

[27] He was probably Raimondo de Liguoro who, in 1860, was minister of finance.

[28] Wilhelm Willink Jr. was banker of the United States in Amsterdam.

[29] In July 1820, a Carbonari revolution broke out in Naples which forced the king to grant a liberal constitution to his subjects. Revoking the constitution, the king soon invited the Austrian army to suppress the uprising with the result that in March 1821, absolutism was restored in Naples.

urbanity of his manners, his collegial education, and his habits of affairs, to occupy the place of Secretary of legation to that mission.

A. DAVEZAC TO L. McLANE

Legation of the United States of America at Naples.
January 21, 1834. [Despatch No. 6][30]

Sir,

I have the honor to acknowledge the receipt of a duplicate of your despatch N°. 85, in the margin of which, it is noted, "that the original was sent to Amsterdam": as the duplicate, however, was transmitted to me, here, I perceive, with great pleasure, that you had anticipated the possibility of my having been detained, at Naples, longer than you had expected. I proceed to explain the causes of that delay in the accomplishment of your views, and the fulfilment of the hopes I had previously expressed of a more prompt result.

The manner of doing business here, it is proper to state, in justice to myself, lest it should appear as if I had not urged the negotiation with sufficient energy, is such as to render the making of any treaty a difficult task; and, as this Government had never made a treaty of commerce with any nation, the want of a precedent, in their own diplomatic records, rendered the task, confided to me, one attended with the most tedious delay. The Minister of Finance, having claimed the initiative of the negotiation with me, on the ground that, as a treaty of commerce must necessarily affect the revenue of the Kingdom, the laying [sic] down of the principles on which it's [sic] chief stipulations were most felt, of course, within the attributes of his department, I was under the necessity to discuss, first with the Chev. Legori, named by him to that effect; and lastly, with himself, every article alternately proposed; and each stipulation, thus discussed and preliminarily agreed to, had to undergo a re-examination, in the council of Ministers; a Council before which, all affairs of what ever nature, originating in any of the several departments of State, are regularly brought for discussion; and, as each minister urges then, the priority, and superior importance of the business of his own department, it not un-

---

[30] Despatch No. 5, missing here, is another copy of Mr. Davezac's instructions to Lt. Harwood, for text of which see p. 354, above.

frequently has occurred, as regards the Treaty, that a week intervened, between the time when an article, agreed upon, was sent to the Council, and that, when it returned, either with their sanction or with direction to endeavour to have it altered, or modified in the mode determined on, by the majority of the Ministers.

Had my instructions limited my stay at Naples to a certain and determined date, I would even then, have felt some doubt as to the propriety of my having unfinished the negotiation commenced, when I had the King's own declaration that "He wished to have a Treaty made with America, and that he had ordered his ministers to proceed to the framing of it, with all convenient celerity;" but, as the silence of the department, on that head, implied a discretionary power, to act for the best, according to my own view of the probability of final success, I resolved, not to yield the ground to the English minister, who, aware of the object of my mission here, through the indiscretion of the subordinate agents of this Government, left no means untried to thwart my efforts. The oppening [sic] of this market, yet unexplored, in some measure, by American commerce, to the activity of our citizens, is an object which I thought was worth attaining, at the expense of some delay, leaving my motive to be judged of by one accustomed to take a wide and liberal view of things.

I have the promise of Prince di Gassaro [sic], that all will be terminated before the 20th of this month; and, should my exertions be crowned by success, aware as I am of the importance of your having the treaty before Congress adjourns, I will, as directed by my instructions, send it by a special messenger.

I have the honor to transmit the copy of a communication from Prince di Gassaro [sic], in which you will perceive that this Government is very desirous to pay, at once, in consideration of a heavy discount, the sum due to the United States, in virtue of the stipulations of the Treaty of the 14ᵗʰ of October 1832. I inclose likewise a letter to me, from our Consul Mr. Hammett, relating to one of the confiscated vessels.

THE PRINCE OF CASSARO TO A. DAVEZAC
(Enclosure (1) with Mr. Davezac's Despatch No. 6, January 21, 1834.)
Napoli 14 Dicembre 1833 (Copy)

The Royal Government desirous of fulfilling it's obligations towards the Government of the United States of America, established by the Convention with the same concluded on the

360

14th October 1832, and consulting on the other hand it's own interests and, the economy which it's straitened finances dictate, finds itself in the condition to propose to the said Government, the prompt payment of all the sums which in virtue of the said convention it is bound to pay them in the space of nine years, at fixed instalments. This payment would be executed either in money, or in inscriptions of rent, but the Royal Government would [want] an abatement of twenty five per cent, which facility might put it in the condition to fulfil the offered payment. —

The Undersigned Minister Secretary of State for Foreign Affairs hastens to manifest this proposition to Mr. Davezac charged with a special mission of the Government of the United States, and begs him to communicate it to his Government, and in season to inform him the reply which he shall receive from the same.

A. HAMMETT TO A. DAVEZAC

(Enclosure 2 with Mr. Davezac's Despatch No. 6, January 21, 1834.)

Naples 14 Jany. 1834.

Dear Sir,

By a letter of Mr. George Law[31] from Washington, dated the 18 Novem'. last, it appears that in one addressed to you, and which you forwarded to the Secretary of State, I said that I knew nothing of the Brig Globe and cargo. Such declaration had thrown discredit on the papers respecting the capture & condemnation of the property. I again repeat, as regards either, I am entirely ignorant, for it was before I was consul at Naples, and occurred out of my consular district and therefore could know nothing. "That if the privateer was French, no light could be obtained here of the capture, if Neapolitan, the Tribunal of prizes at Naples could alone afford it," was added under the idea at the time, that your application, as well as my own might obtain the papers and sales generally relating to the confiscated property. Therefore, I did not then apply directly to the President of such Tribunal, about this vessel and cargo, which I have now done, stating to him all the facts. Perhaps the motives of refusal

---

[31] George Law was an attorney and agent for the brig *Globe*. He also served as counsel for a number of ships in connection with the settling of the claims against France. Adelaide Hasse. *Index to United States Documents Relating to Foreign Affairs, 1828-1861*, I, 672.)

by this Government, unfelt by him individually, may not prevent him to furnish the proof required. If disappointed, I will write to Corfu, though I have little hope of succeeding there.

My services having been general for all the American property, I only turned my attention to particular cases when requested to do so, as it was useless, as long as the principle of restitution remained disputed. Besides, as for these interests I had made considerable pecuniary sacrifizes, I was not in state to continue them. I declare, however, that the phrase complained of was never intended to create a doubt of the loss of the property by capture, but simply that the facts were unknown to me and that if the proofs were to be had here, to indicate where they might probably be found. — If I can get them from the President of the Tribunal of prizes, a gentleman whom I know personally, I will pass them to you to be forwarded with all despatch to the Secretary of State. In a contrary case, I shall beg you to be pleased to address a note for them to the Minister of F. Affairs.

With the request, that you will send this explanation immediately to the Department at Washington, I have the honor to remain, Dear Sir, Very respectfully,

A. DAVEZAC TO L. McLANE

Legation of the United States of America at Naples,

February 19, 1834. [Unnumbered Despatch]

Sir,

I have the honor to acknowledge your despatch of the 26 of December last, and to inform you, that, in conformity with your instructions, having ascertained that there was no reasonable prospect of concluding a treaty with this Government, within the time you have expressed, I have asked from the King an audience of leave, in which I will deliver to him the President's letter, and make the communication which you direct, as regards the motive of my departure and the intention of the President as to future negociations.

I must have ill expressed my determinations, in relation to the proposal made to me unofficially, by this Government, on the subject of the convention of the 14th. of October, 1832, since he understood my letter as conveying the idea that I had entered into negociations tending to alter, or modify, the stipulations of this Treaty, as I have in fact, expressly refused to do anything in the matter except to transmit, as I did with one of my

362

despatches, their offer to pay the amount due by them, at once in consideration of a deduction which, as I expressed in my letter to you, I thought and trust that the American government would not agree to. This Government far from entertaining the hope of obtaining any alteration of the stipulations of the Convention, have made arrangements to affect the first payment. This will fall due on the 14ᵗʰ. June next; and will have it ready to be paid to the person who may be charged to receive it; this fact shows that I never gave them any reason to believe that the American Government entertained the intention to modify the Treaty of indemnity.

In obedience to your instructions, I intend to return to the Hague thro' the Tyrol, the most economical and expeditious route. In my next communication I will inform you of what will have taken place in my audience of leave.

A. DAVEZAC TO J. FORSYTH[32]

Legation of the United States of America to the Netherlands.

December 18ᵗʰ 1834 [Despatch No. 111 (Davezac, *Netherlands*)]

Sir,

In conformity with your directions, I now proceed to lay before you an historical account of my negociation with the Government of the King of the Two Sicilies. A return of the malady to which I have alluded in my last communication, prevented my doing it as early as I had expected to do at the date of my last despatch, as it left me (tho' secure, my physician assures me, of another attack) in a state of weakness, till within a very few days, such that, during it's continuance, I was advised to avoid all business.

---

[32] John Forsyth (1780-1841). Born at Fredericksburg, Va. After his graduation from Princeton in 1799, he studied law and was admitted to the bar in 1802. In 1808, he began his political career with his appointment as attorney general of Georgia. He was successively a representative, United States senator, governor of Georgia, minister to Spain, and secretary of state. He held this last post from June 27, 1834 to March 4, 1841. These years were important in American diplomatic history for it was under Forsyth that the disagreeable contest with France over the treaty of 1831, and the grave question of admission of Texas into the Union was settled. See: Stephen F. Miller, *The Bench and Bar of Georgia* (Philadelphia, 1858), vol. II, gives an excellent sketch of Forsyth's career. See also: Jennie Forsyth Jeffries, *A history of the Forsyth family* (Indianapolis, 1920); E. I. McCormac, *American secretaries of state and their diplomacy.* (IV, 1928); *Dictionary of American Biography* (1931), VI, 533-535.

I take the liberty to state that circumstance in order to explain my delay in obeying the directions of the department.

After the exchange of the ratified Treaty of which I was the bearer, for that which I have had the honor to transmit to the Government; and after having been assured, by the King himself, that he persevered in the intentions he had expressed to my predecessor, I devoted some time to enquiries necessary to obtain a full knowledge, not only of the actual state of our commercial relations with Naples, but also of the various interests and influences, likely to stand in the way of the success of my negotiations: As to the first, I found that, except with Sicily, where we carried on an active and extensive trade, American ships had almost entirely forsaken the ports of the kingdom, unable to contend with England, protected, as the navigation of that power is, by a deduction in their favor, as well as in that of France, and Spain, of ten per cent on the duties paid by other Nations; As regards the others, I was not long in discovering, that I would have, as adversary, a powerful body of Messapolioti,[33] who had staked their fortunes on the continuance of the protection given to their manufactures, against rival productions, by high duties. In Naples, as in every part of Europe, which has been even for a short time subject to French dominion, or influence, during the prevalence of the continental System, manufactures have grown up under the shade, either of absolute prohibitions, or of very high duties, which made all competition hopeless. Agriculture too, had been encouraged to grow produce hitherto obtained from foreign markets, and great landed proprietors now claimed to be maintained in the possession of advantages which, they contend, belong to them as it were, by possession rights. The Cotton, for example, cultivated in the vicinity of Naples, and in some of the Provinces, is inferior in quality to that of the United States, and therefore could not be produced by the farmers, to any profit, but for the protection it receives from the enormous duties laid on that of foreign growth. The same interest I would have to contend against, as to the free introduction into the Kingdom of our raw cotton, would, I was aware, be enlisted in opposition to every attempt to open the Neapolitan market, either to our cotton twists, of such num-

[33] The reference here seems to be to the people called the Messapii, a people of the Ionian peninsular region in the time of Herodotus who described them as living in what now is the southeastern part of Italy. Later the name was also applied to the Calabrians. See a long article about these peoples, under "Messapi," in the *Enciclopedia Italiana*, Rome, 1934, XXII, 947-949.

bers as are spun at Naples, or, to our domestics[34] of qualities similar to their own: yet, knowing that, in opposition to these interests, I would have with me, the wish of the King to do away a monopoly which he considered as ruinous to the general agriculture of the country, while it enriched only a few great land owners, and some foreign capitalists, supported by public opinion, which, even at Naples, is not altogether unattended to, I did not despair of success. The view I had taken of the natural wealth of that beautiful country, of it's arts, of it's flourishing tho' ill directed agriculture, and of it's means of furnishing to our trade, in exchange of the produce of our commerce and industry, that of it's favored climate and soil, made me the more determined to leave no exertion untried to obtain the end the government had in view in the mission given to my charge.

On the 7th. of July 1834 I had an interview with Prince di Cassaro, the minister of foreign affairs. After reiterating in the name of the King, the assurances I had received from His Majesty's own lips, of his desire to enter into a treaty of commerce with the United States of America, the Prince said, that his personal views were in perfect accordance with those of the King, and that I would find him as anxious as myself to place the commercial relations of the two countries on the plane which their mutual and well-understood interests, required them to be. He presumed, he added, that Mr. Nelson's project of a commercial treaty contained all the stipulations, which, on the part of the United States, it was intended that it should embrace. I expressed, in reply, the pleasure I felt at the declaration he had been pleased to make, both as to the King's intentions and as to his own favorable sentiments in relation to the advantages likely to result from closer commercial relations between our respective countries; I observed that, as he had conjectured, the Project presented by Mr. Nelson contained the stipulations which was desired to make the basis of the negotiation: (but, as my in-

---

[34] A term used in the cotton trade to designate unbleached cotton yard-goods of rather coarse texture and grade. Such goods were sold in considerable quantity by United States cotton manufacturers in early years before the American dyes industry had developed to the point where printed or colored cotton goods could be sold economically when in competition with the English mills' products. Originally, these goods were made solely for domestic trade and hence received this designation which persists to this day on some of the unbleached muslins, as for instance those known as unbleached sheeting which the trade knows as "domestics." The term here, in this despatch, is aptly used in connection with the manufactured cottons, of which first are mentioned the 'twists' or cotton yarns, and the reference in the same sentence to 'numbers' has to do with showing that yarns of various strengths and sizes were in competition with similar 'numbers', i.e., types of yarn, made abroad.

structions told me, if I found, on the part of the Neapolitan Government any disinclination to the articles relating to neutral rights, to omit them,) I enquired, from the ministers, what was his views as to those articles: he replied, without hesitation, that they were disposed to examine the project with the articles in question, remarking, at the same time, that Naples, not being a great naval power had no interest opposed to principles tending to extend and enforce neutral rights: There was one Nation, however, he said, ever jealous of stipulations relating to neutral rights being embodied into a new treaty, whose influence, he acknowledged, was great, and dispersed, thro' the agency of their merchants, among every class of society, except that whose interests the King was determined to free from the bondage of monopoly and restrictions. The influence of that nation, and of their friends, would be exerted, he knew, to defeat the Treaty. On my remarking, that the negotiations on which we had entered, might be kept secret, since there had been no avowed motive of my mission in Naples, but that of exchanging the ratified Treaty — and as my protracted residence, at Naples, after attaining that object, would naturally be attributed to the desire of seeing more of the country, or to an unwillingness to encounter the fatigue of a journey, back to the Hague during the excessive heat of an Italian summer. The Prince interrupted me, saying, that the project promoted by Mr. Nelson had already been made known to the "Commission of Commerce" in order to obtain their opinion on the subject; that the same project, reproduced by me, with such modifications to it as I might propose would again be presented to their examination. That secrecy under such circumstances of previous publicity, and at Naples, where foreign Ministers had such means of knowing all that it was their interest to know, was out of the question; the Prince, in conclusion, observed, that he would enjoin all the persons to whom the subject had been disclosed, if the fact of a negotiation having been commenced had been divulged, as he feared it had, at least, to be silent, as to the points to which it related.

I left Prince de Cassaro favorably impressed as regarded the views he personally entertained on the subject of the proposed Treaty; but, a very short stay at Naples had sufficed to convince me, that his influence with the King was on the decline; I knew, that the marriage of His Sovereign with a Sardinian Princess,[35]

35 King Ferdinand II married, on Nov. 21, 1832, Marie-Christine (1812-1836), the daughter of King Victor Emmanuel of Sardinia. A year after her death, on Jan. 9, 1837, he married Queen Marie Thérèse-Isabelle, Archduchess of Austria, daughter of Archduke Charles.

had been determined on, and concluded without his participation, and that his enemies at Court had succeeded in representing him, to the King, as one devoted to another's interests more than to those of his own country. Still he continued in office, and when, aware of having no longer the full confidence of his Sovereign, he tendered him his resignation, he was urged to remain at the head of the Cabinet, with the flattering declaration that his services could not be dispensed with. In a court, where favor is ever fluctuating, and among a people so long under the directing influence of Austrian politics, the momentary displeasure of the King against a minister, who may be considered as the representative of the System of the three great northern powers, could not be viewed as decisive of his fate, and it was the opinion of Count Stakelberg, the Russian Minister, that the Prince would, in a short time, regain, in spite of the situation of France, his former influence over the King.

In consequence of the invitation of the Prince, I transmitted to him, a transcript of Mr. Nelson's project of a Treaty, with the modifications directed by my instructions. On the following day, I met Prince di Cassaro, at the house of his daughter the Princess di Tinase.[36] He took me aside, and after stating that the projet of a treaty would shortly be presented to the "commission de commerce," he observed, that the greatest obstacle to the success of the negotiation, was the advantages entrusted, by Treaty, to France, England and Spain, of a diminution of ten per cent, in favor of their navigation, or the duties paid by other nations in the ports of the Kingdom; that, there was not a Napolitan [sic] but felt the weight of that humiliating concession, to those three nations, but that some of the King's ministers, and among them, the Marquis d'Andrea, the Minister of Finance, at the same time that he confessed this concession to be onerous to the Treasury, and destructive to the commerce of the country, entertained doubts as to their being at liberty, without violating the faith of

---

[36] The Prince of Cassaro had no daughter with the title of Princess of Tinase. However, the files of the Neapolitan ministry of foreign affairs has this information: "On Sept. 9, 1838, the Marquis Crosa, minister at the Sardinian Legation at Naples, transmitted to the Prince of Cassaro, a copy of a letter which Count Solaro della Margherita had received from Madrid. The letter, dated Aug. 18, 1838, informed Count Solaro della Margherita of a serious wrong committed by a police commissioner, who, accompanied by several detectives and aids, had presented himself at the Italian hospital, and after asking for the keys of the tomb or pantheon, ordered the demolition of the walls of the tomb, treating with irreverence, 'among other things, the remains of the dead buried there and ordering the opening of the casket of the daughter of the Prince of Cassaro.'" This information is found in Folder 2038 in the Reports of the Ministry of Foreign Affairs in the *Archivio di Napoli.*

a treaty, to grant the same advantages to other nations, in compensation of some concession made in favor of Napolitan [sic] commerce, or to render it illusory for the free power now possessing it, by granting it to every other nation. The Prince advised me to seek an opportunity of conversing with the Marquis of Andrea, on that subject, assuring me, that it would give him no jealousy that I should do so, convinced as he was, that, the influence of that minister would weigh heavily against the treaty, I should oppose it: but he said it would be best to defer the interview until after the commission of trade had made their report, which, he feared, would not be before the end of September; When I exclaimed against such a delay, he observed that, at Naples, it was impossible to get any thing done promptly; but that he would urge the chief of the commission to act with all possible celerity in reference to the matter.

Weeks after weeks, I received from the Minister of foreign affairs, assurances that the expected report would be favorable; an opinion which I did not share; some person well informed, as the event showed, having warned me, that the influence of the ministers of England,[37] and France,[38] had been successfully exerted among the masters of the board of trade: Prince Cassaro insisted that my informers were mistaken; and remained confident of the result — until the report was made, not in direct terms against the policy of forming a commercial treaty between the two nations, but advising to delay entering into any engagement of the nature proposed, with any foreign power, changing the existing tariff, until after it had been revised and modified,

---

37 John Ponsonby, Viscount Ponsonby (1770?-1855). Diplomat. Before his appointment to Naples, he was envoy extraordinary and minister plenipotentiary at Buenos Aires and Rio de Janeiro. In 1830, he was sent to Belgium in connection with the candidacy of Prince Leopold of Saxe-Coburg to the throne. and remained in Belgium until Leopold was elected king of the Belgians on June 4, 1831. Viscount Ponsonby was envoy at Naples from June 8, to Nov. 9, 1832, ambassador at Constantinople from Nov. 27, 1832 to 1841, and ambassador at Vienna from Aug. 10, 1846, to May 31, 1850. Although he had great influence, his conduct as an ambassador sometimes occasioned embarrassment to the ministry. He was, however, a keen diplomat of the old school, a shrewd observer, and a man of broad views. See: Augustus Loftus, *Diplomatic Reminiscences,* London, 1892, I, 129-130; *Dictionary of National Biography,* 1921-1922, XVI, 86.

38 Latour-Maubourg, Just Pons Florimond de Fay, Marquis de. (1781-1837). French diplomat. He entered the diplomatic service under the Consulate, serving as secretary of the embassy at Copenhagen, and later at Constantinople (1806), and minister plenipotentiary at Stuttgart (1813). After the Restoration he continued to serve as minister plenipotentiary at Hanover (1816) and at Dresden (1819). In 1823, he was appointed ambassador at Constantinople. In 1830, he was sent as ambassador to Naples and finally in 1831 to Rome. *La Grande Encyclopédie,* Paris, 1894-1895, XXI, 1017.

in the way intended by the Government. The minister of foreign affairs, expressed his astonishment that commercial men should have come to such conclusions; adding, that he would take the earliest opportunity to advise the King to direct him to proceed on with the negotiation. The reports made by commissions were viewed as decisions, and he had no doubt, he said, but that his opinion would prevail, particularly as the minister of finance, whom he advised me to see, was, of late, favorably disposed on the subject of a Treaty with America. Previous to a determination on the steps proper on this occasion, I requested the Prince to ask an audience for me from the King. His Majesty received me, as he has ever done, with the greatest affability, enquiring, as he usually did, of the President's health; After expressing my acknowledgements, I stated the regret I experienced that so little progress had yet been made in the negotiation for a Treaty of commerce, which His Majesty had assured me he was desirous to make with the United States. The King replied merely in the words following "J'entretiens toujours les même sentiments que Je vous ai deja exprimé; je parlerai au Prince de Cassaro, afin que l'affaire marche plus vite à l'avenir." His Majesty then spoke of the number, unusually great, of Americans who had visited Naples of late, observing that he was pleased that so many of them had travelled in his dominions.

Encouraged by these royal assurances, which I hastened to communicate to Prince di Cassaro, who said that the King had given him directions in conformity with them, I readily accepted an invitation of the Minister of finance, the Marquis d'Andrea, to meet him at his office, or to call on him at his own house whenever I felt so inclined, and waited upon him, on the 6th of October, he began the conversation by saying that I had perhaps been impressed with the opinion that he was opposed to a commercial treaty between the United States and Naples; that such was not the fact, and that he was happy of an opportunity of declaring it to me; that it was time, that, as the Government of the Two Sicilies, had never entered into any treaty of that nature — with any one nation, he thought that every step taken, on so important a subject, ought to be deliberately weighed; that he wished to see his way clear, as to the means of facing the public expenditure, paying the Army, the interest of the debt, and the sum which would shortly be due to the United States; That, if he were convinced the stipulations proposed would not drain the treasury, and undermine the credit of the state, he would, instead of being the adversary, as he was represented, of closer commercial relations, become the warmest advocate of a Treaty establishing them.

I said to the Marquis, in answer, that the Government of the United States asked, from that of the Kingdom of the Two Sicilies, no commercial advantage except in reciprocity; that, for every concession, they offered a concession in return; That, if my Government had authorized me to negotiate on the subject of a Treaty of Commerce, it was because His Majesty, the King of the Two Sicilies, had, himself, expressed to my Predecessor at this Court, Mr. Nelson, his willingness to enter into negotiations to that effect; that, with regard to what His Excellency had said of his fear of draining the Treasury, by lessening the duties on articles imported into the Kingdom, in consequence of similar diminutions being made, in America, on articles the growth of the Nepolitan [sic] Soil, the fruit of their industry, or of their arts, experience had shown, both in the United States, and in such of the European states as had acted on liberal principles of reciprocity, like that which we offer to Naples as the rule of our commercial relations, that, far from diminishing, such reductions had even increased the amount of duties received; that this was the natural consequence of increased demands, the constant concomitant of lessened duties. The Marquis observed, in reply, that he adopted most of my views; but, as regarded the deduction of ten per cent in favor of England, France and Spain, he was fearful that, unless conceded for a valuable equivalent, England, and perhaps, France also, might make it the ground of angry remonstrances; That, as I must be aware, the Kingdom was vulnerable on the one hand; and that great Prudence was required on the occasion: but, nevertheless, as the King was determined to have a Treaty of commerce with America, he would do all in his power to lay aside existing obstacles; that I must not be discouraged by the delay: that it was unavoidable, in relation to a matter of such importance, in a country when there was no precedent of a Treaty of the kind . . .

After proceeding thus far, in this narrative, I became so fatigued and exhausted, that I must delay the conclusion till the next mail day.

A. DAVEZAC TO J. FORSYTH

Legation of the United States of America to the Netherlands

The Hague, January 12, 1835. [Despatch No. 112.]
(Duplicate) Confidential

Sir,

Being now perfectly recovered from the malady which had so long preyed on me, I resume the interrupted narrative of my negotiation with the King of the Two Sicilies.

. . . The Minister assured me, that Prince di Cassaro, and him, acted in perfect Harmony of views, independent of all tratories[39] of power or of influence, and content only to serve their King and their country — He was prepared, he said, to reduce to one half the existing duties on our Cotton, Tobacco, rice, Tar, and other articles the growth of the United States; that he would even agree to allow Tobacco (a determined quantity) to be deposited in the Custom House, at Naples, under conditions to be hereafter stipulated; — but, that in consequence of these concessions, we must, on our part, favor their wines, brandy, sewing silks, &c. As to their Silks, in general, he knew that they were, like most of other articles of the growth of the Kingdom, free of duties, under the provisions of the last Tariff, and therefore, our concessions should be on the articles he had enumerated: I remarked, in answering this last observation of the Minister, that the reciprocity which we proposed to establish, by Treaty, would secure Naples, while it continued in force, against all possible changes of our tariff, and, therefore, give them an advantage, in our markets, over those nations subject to its fluctuations: The advantage to which I referred, the minister said, was illusive, we had, in fact, paid all our debt; and, unlike the other nations of the world, what we had to fear was that our Tariff, even as revised, would bring too much, not too little in the Treasury. Their wine brandy and Sewing silks! Those were

---

[39] This metaphorical use of the word "trattories" is very apt here. The trattorius is a 'grassy way', i.e., an easy mode of approach, in short, the minister here was saying that it was not his easy access to the King that influenced the attitude of himself and his colleagues. The trattorius was the public grassed road, of which many existed from ancient days, in Italy. These were the roads followed by sheepherders with their flocks, leading to the higher summer pastures. They were kept traditionally grassed and not used for wheeled vehicles, so that the flocks in their long trek to high pastures, might have feeding grounds all the way; also so that the hooves of the sheep, which in Italy were of a strain not suited to hard rocky or beaten-hard roads, might not be injured by rough travel, and so derogate the sheep's health by sore hooves or contagious hoof diseases brought about by the cracking of the hoof due to hard travel.

371

the articles they would insist on to be favored, in reciprocity of their diminishing the high existing duties on tobacco, cotton, rice, and some of the numbers of cotton twists which we manufactured, and which their own manufacturers did not produce: Then our conversation was interrupted, by the Minister, who said, that he had an appointment which called him away; but, before we parted, he reiterated, with great warmth, the assurances of his desire to constitute, to establish between our respective countries, commercial relations which, he knew, would be equally lucrative to both. I hastened, immediately after this conversation, to communicate, to Prince di Cassaro, what had passed between me and his Colleague. He seemed pleased that I should have found him so favorably disposed, because, he said, the King had great confidence in his knowledge of all motives relating to commerce: During the months of July, August, and September, no business of any kind is transacted by ministers; promises may indeed be obtained, to silence remonstrances against unreasonable delay, but their execution is never seriously intended or confidently expected by such as are aware of the official usages of the Sicilian Court. It even, therefore, was superfluous to report to you the various steps I took; the number of interviews I requested and obtained, from Prince di Cassaro; always urging him to give me a final answer, and claiming from his candor to say whether his Government continued desirous of entering into a Treaty of commerce, on the basis of reciprocity? declaring my determination to return to my post at the Hague, as soon as I should become convinced of the impossibility of accomplishing the end of my mission: On all such occasions, the Minister of Foreign Affairs invariably declared that, tho' they were obstacles in the way, they were not of a nature so serious as to make him doubtful of a favorable result. He confessed, that great exertions had been made, and still continued, on the part of the persons interested in preserving prohibitions, and high protecting duties, to defeat our negotiations. He gave me to understand that, England, and France showed themselves jealous of the friendly aspect of our relations, but he insisted, that perseverance and above all, patience at delay, in a country where the last had become a habit in the transaction of most state affairs, would surmount all difficulties; He alluded to his negotiations with my predecessor, which had been brought to a close at the very moment when it seemed the most unlikely that it would terminate as it had done. Alluding once to that treaty, he said that,

372

tho' his adversaries had severely blamed him for advising it, the King had determined that he would execute it, with his characteristic good faith, and that it was his wish (the King's) to pay the total sum stipulated, if I were authorised to make a proper deduction, as a compensation for prompt payment; That, if I were not, he would transmit to me, in order to be laid before the President of the United States the Proposals of his Majesty's government in relation to the subject.

As I was not uninformed of the obstacles to which the minister of foreign affairs alluded, I endeavored in reply, to guard him against the means that were made use of to excite alarm among the Timid and unreflecting by threats of the displeasure of England and of France, in presenting to him that both those nations were too much occupied in preserving their own internal peace to seek a cause of dispute with a friendly power, in their exercising the clear right, which every state confessedly possess, to grant commercial advantages in return of concessions of a like nature made in favor of their Trade. I held out to him the prospect, not only of the immediate profits to their agriculture, of an increased demand in our markets, and in those of the American Republics that our commerce and navigation supplied, but also of that which would be the consequence of the rapid spread of a taste for all the productions of their soil, their manufactures and arts, as soon as they could be known and dispersed in the countries frequented by our Ships; contrasting the slowly increasing population of the Two Sicilies, with that of America, multiplying in a proportion unexampled in the history of the world, I remarked that, to America, the advantages arising from the proposed treaty, would remain almost the same, during the time it continued in force, while, on the part of Naples, there would be a continual increase of those secured to their trade by the ever-augmenting number of the consumers of their produce, in the United States. I urged him, for the attainment of an end, promising to his country such an extension of wealth and prosperity, to press the negotiation, persuaded, as he must be, that when such a treaty as that which I had proposed was made public, the clamours of anxious adversaries, and selfish monopolists would be lost in the general applause of enlightened and patriotic men: nor did I fail paying to the Prince the praise due to the firmness he had displayed during his late negotiation with Mr. Nelson, in doing what he knew to be just, uninfluenced by the adversaries he had encountered and spurned.

On the occasion when the offer of paying at once, the indemnity stipulated, by the Treaty, was made, I declared that I had no power to move on the subject, adding that I could transmit to my Government the proposal to which he had alluded, for their consideration.

The negotiation proceeded in the manner I have related above (condensing the substance of many conversations I had with Prince di Cassaro) always with such a near prospect of success as to make it my duty, as I thought, not to break them off, while the King himself, and his Minister of Foreign Affairs, assured me that, by continuing them, the object which the two governments sought to obtain, would be attained within a reasonable delay, untill [sic] I received the despatch of the Department which directed me to deliver my letter of recall to the King and immediately to return to my Post, at The Hague, unless I had reasonable ground to believe the negotiation would be brought to a close within a specific time. I communicated this order of the President to the Minister of foreign affairs, who, even then, assured me that he had well founded hopes of a successful issue, if I would defer my departure to the time limited by my instructions. This I declined, persuaded, tho' I have never entertained a doubt of his sincerity, or of that of the intentions which the King had expressed to M^r. Nelson, and reiterated to me, that it would not be in his power to carry his views into execution in the delay to which he alluded, and therefore requested him to obtain, for me, an audience in order to deliver to the King the President's letter, and take leave of his Majesty. That day, as the Minister had given me to understand would be the case, was designated to a period corresponding with that limited by the department, in order, he said, to endeavour, in the mean time, to get over the difficulties thrown, by some of his adversaries, in the way of his success, in an affair which, they knew, he had so much at heart. These hopes the Minister persisted to indulge to the last, and even when I took leave of him, he expressed a confident belief that, had I been allowed, by my instructions, to have remained some months longer, at Naples, the object of my mission would have been obtained.

I cannot conclude without expressing the opinion that the intentions of the King, and the inclination of the people, were made to yield to the intrigues of a rival power; but, that unsuccessful as they were, the negotiations that have taken place, have so acted on public opinion, as to render more easy the

374

attainment of the result, which it was not my fortune to accomplish, on a future occasion. The experience I had gained, as to the manner in which affairs are conducted at the Court of the Two Sicilies, lead me to believe that, when the powers of Government pass into the hands of a minister possessing greater energy of purpose than Prince Cassaro, negotiations may be renewed with greater probability of success, particularly if the Nepolitan [sic] Government can be induced to treat at Washington, instead of Naples; as the necessary powers and instructions can be sent to their consul general in the United States, without awakening the jealousy of Great Britain: The good faith of the King when a treaty, made in conformity with his instructions, shall be offered to his sanction, will induce him to disregard every effort tending to it's rejection. The arts of designing advisers may prevent his entering into engagements which his own judgement [sic] approves, but they will never succeed in causing him to violate his word.

It will ever be, Sir, a subject of deep regret to me, that I have not succeeded in executing the views of the government in the Mission with which I was charged; but I find a consolation in the conscience that I have exerted my best ability in order to obtain, for my country, the advantages of a reciprocal trade with Naples on the principles of mutual concessions; and in the persuasion that, what I have done during my residence there, in removing prejudices, and remedying the misinterpretations of envious rivals, will ultimately serve to hasten the time when the relations of that country, and the United States shall be placed in the situation required by the wants and interests of both.

ENOS THOMPSON THROOP[1]

(February 6, 1838 — January 12, 1842)

E. T. THROOP TO J. FORSYTH

Owasco (N. Y.) May 9, 1838.

My Dear Sir

I have the honor to inform you, that, my private affairs being arranged, I shall leave this place (my home) on Saturday the 14th. inst. for the city of New York to prepare for embarcation on my mission to Naples.[2] The necessary preparation in the City will require several days, but I hope to be ready by the 24th instant, and have requested my friends in the city to endeavor to secure me a passage in the Liverpool Packet, to sail on that day.

You were good enough to give me my option to take my outfit in treasury notes, or in a bill upon the Government bankers in England. Not being much conversant in such matters, I replied that I should prefer it in treasury notes. On reflection I have altered my opinion, and I will take, in preference to any thing else a bill on London. As one inducement for this choice, but not the only one, I suppose that the outfit will be due me in Europe, & that the bill will be for the whole amount there, without any deduction for the difference in Exchange. But to prevent mistake, I repeat the idea, that if I am mistaken in this, I still prefer to have my outfit in a bill on London.

I do not know, & I shall not until I reach N. York, how numerous my suite will be. I take from this place a young lad of eleven years of age, & may have added three other persons. I give this information now, particularly in regard to my pass-port, the form of which & it's purposes I do not precisely understand. If it is sufficient, in general terms, to embrace myself & four persons, besides Servants, I shall be glad to have it for-

---

[1] Enos Thompson Throop, of New York, Jurist and Congressman, was commissioned chargé d'affaires Feb. 6, 1838. He left the service on Jan. 12, 1842. For biographical studies on Thropp, see: *Dictionary American Biography* 1936, XVIII, 510-511; *Sketch of the Life of Governor Throop*, Cayuga County Historical Society, collections no. 7, (1889); J. S. Jenkins, *Lives of the Governors of the State of New York* (1851), 478; C. Z. Lincoln, *State of New York; Messages from the Governors* (1909), III, 269; L. M. Sears, "The Neapolitan Mission of Enos Thompson Throop, 1838-1842." *New York State Historical Association, Quarterly Journal, Oct. 1928*, IX, 365-379.

[2] Instruction No. 1 to Throop was not issued until nine days after this letter; there had evidently been verbal arrangements made earlier, as may be inferred from the second paragraph of the letter.

warded to me in that form; if not, I will give more precise directions from N. York. On this subject will you have the goodness to direct M`r`. Markoe,[3] or the proper clerk, to write me, with as little delay as possible, that I may be informed soon after I reach the City.

I shall be in the City of New York to receive all communications which may be directed to me, until the period of my departure from the country.

J. Forysth to E. T. Throop

Department of State. Washington, 18 May 1838. [Instruction No. 1.]

Sir,

The President, by and with the advice and consent of the Senate of the United States, having appointed you their Chargé d'Affaires near the King of the Two Sicilies, I transmit to you with this despatch —

1.—Your commission.[4]

2.—A letter of credence addressed to the Minister of Foreign Affairs of Naples.

3.—A full power.

4.—A special passport for yourself and suite.

5.—A letter of credit on the Bankers of the United States in London, authorising them to pay your drafts for your outfit, and your salary as becomes due, with the contingent expenses of the mission actually incurred, which, however, are limited to the sum of $500. In availing yourself of this authority you will be careful not to exceed, in the amount drawn for, the sums to which you may be entitled in account with the United States at the respective dates of your drafts.

6.—A set of printed personal instructions prescribed by this department for the government of all the Diplomatic agents of the United States abroad.

7.—A printed list of the Diplomatic and Consular Agents of the United States in foreign countries.

8.—A list of the documents and books furnished by the Depart-

---

[3] Francis Markoe, Jr., of Pennsylvania, Clerk in the Consular Bureau, Washington, 1835; Clerk in Diplomatic Bureau 1837-57? United States *Official Register* 1831-61.

[4] Commission was dated Feb. 6, 1838.

ment for the use of your Legation. [This list was placed in Mʳ. T's hands before he left Washington.]⁵
9.—Two reams of despatch paper.
10.—A cypher to be used in your correspondence when special secrecy is required.

Your compensation, as fixed by law, is at the rate of $4500 per annum, with an outfit equal to a year's salary, and a quarter's salary for your return to this country. By a general rule the compensation of diplomatic representatives commences on the day of their leaving their residence to proceed upon their mission. In your case it will commence on the 14th day of May 1838.

On your arrival at Naples you will ascertain whether any books or papers of the former Legation still remain in the care of the Consul at that place, and take charge of any which may be found giving notice thereof to the Department, and describing them.

J. FORSYTH TO E. T. THROOP

Department of State. Washington 19 May 1838. [Instruction No. 2.]

Sir,

Information of your appointment as Chargé d'Affaires of the United States, having been already communicated⁶ to you, it is the President's wish that you should repair as early as possible and by the most direct and elijible [sic] route to the place of your destination, where it will be your general duty to superintend the interests of the United States and of their citizens, and to promote by all your exertions, the accomplishment of such other objects, deemed of essential importance to the commercial interests of this country, as will form the subject of the present special instructions. The disposition expressed on a former occasion by the Government of the Two Sicilies to enter into commercial relations with the United States has led to the establishment of the present mission, and furnishes at the same time a well grounded hope that you will be successful in effecting arrangements mutually beneficial to the Two countries.

Upon your arrival at Naples, which will be your place of residence, you will as promptly as may be convenient deliver

---

⁵ Words in brackets are a State Department annotation on the Record Copy of this Instruction No. 1. Compare the first section of list of documents and books Throop turned over to Boulware, his successor. See, below, p. 511 ff.

⁶ Instruction No. 1, to Mr. Throop, see Enclosure I, May 18, 1838; for which see p. 377.

your letter of credence to the Minister of Foreign Affairs of the Two Sicilies. You will then request an audience of the King, and upon your introduction you will express to His Majesty in proper terms the ardent desire of the President to cultivate friendly relations, and to cherish the utmost good will and a liberal intercourse between the United States and the Two Sicilies, which it is his wish, and will be his aim by all the means in his power to strengthen and perpetuate.

The chief object of your mission, that which forms at present a subject of deep interest to this Government, and to a numerous and respectable class of the citizens of the United States is the condition of our tobacco trade, and the best methods by which it may be relieved from the restrictions which have been laid upon its introduction into Europe, and increased consumption of the article produced. With this despatch you will receive a copy[7] of the instructions of this Department to Mr. Wheaton[8] our Minister to Berlin which will serve as your guide as far as they may be applicable. You will also receive the Report of the Select-Committee[9] of the House of Representatives at the

---

[7] This enclosure is not reproduced in this printing.

[8] Henry Wheaton, of New York, was commissioned chargé d'affaires at Berlin on March 3, 1835; he was commissioned envoy extraordinary and minister plenipotentiary on March 7, 1837. Presented credentials as such on Sept. 29, 1837. He was empowered to treat with Bavaria, Hesse Cassel, Saxony, and Würtenberg, concerning the abolition of *droit d'aubaine* and taxes on emigration and with Hanover concerning commerce and navigation. He took leave July 18, 1846. (Hasse, *op. cit.*, part 3, 1822-1823). See also note 84, p. 593.

[9] U. S., Reports of Committees, 24th Congress, 2d Session. House of Representatives Report No. 239. Tobacco. Feb. 18, 1837. *The report of the select committee to which were referred the memorial of the tobacco planters, and the resolutions of the General Assembly of the state of Maryland, upon the subject of high rates of duty, and restrictions imposed by foreign governments upon American tobacco.* On this subject, the *Niles Weekly Register,* May 27, 1837, fifth series, No. 13, II, 195, wrote as follows:
"Tobacco: The committee on behalf of the tobacco planters and others interested in the trade, to wait on the president of the United States and to present to him certain resolutions passed by a meeting of the planters of Prince Georges county, held on the 4th instant, made the following report . . . the president remarked . . . that he had already caused many steps to be taken to promote its prosperity and success. In particular our ministers to England and France had been furnished instructions on the subject, these instructions were also in course of preparation for our minister in Prussia, and that Mr. Joshua Dosge, a gentleman of great practical information in this business, who had been appointed as a special agent to assist Mr. Wheaton (the minister) in relation to it, would sail with instructions without delay. He also said that no minister to Austria had been appointed as yet, and that for special reasons he did not desire to make that appointment earlier than the next meeting of congress, but that no injury would probably result to the tobacco trade from this delay, as he intended in the interim to send an agent to that country whose duty it should be to collect all the material facts and the information which he could in respect to it. The effect of which would be to render more easy and certain of success the efforts which our minister would be instructed to make when sent . . ."

379

Second Session of the Twenty-fourth Congress upon this subject. The joint resolution recommended by that Committee which will be found appended to their Report from want of time or some other causes was not acted upon by the Senate; yet it was passed as a separate resolution by the House of Representatives, and it is not doubted that the Senate concurred with that body in its wishes on the subject, as a considerable sum was allowed by Congress in the general appropriation bill, with a view as was understood, to the appointment of special Agents to negotiate with the Governments of those countries in which American tobacco is subjected to duties and restrictions, and in which the United States have no accredited Representatives and provision was also made for missions to Austria[10] and Prussia,[11] it is believed with a special view to the extension of this particular trade. Since that period circumstances have occurred[12] which plainly show that there is no abatement of the interest felt upon the subject, and that the benefits expected to flow from successful negotiations with the different European governments respecting this commodity are regarded as of no ordinary value. You will, therefore, bear this in mind and if you can procure any information, general or particular, in relation to the trade in tobacco, communicate it immediately to this Government with such observations as may be prompted by your own Knowledge, and by the inquiries you may make in respect to a matter that so deeply concerns the United States. Should the present tariff, or custom's regulations be found to bear, in practice, more heavily upon American than other tobacco, or prove otherwise injurious to the interests of our citizens, you will without delay, use your utmost endeavors to procure by all the means in your power such a modification of the present system as shall seem best calculated to remedy the evil.

The present moment being considered favorable to the formation of a commercial treaty between the United States and the Two Sicilies, I am directed by the President to charge you with the execution of this duty in which it is to be borne in mind by you that the article of American tobacco is to form a promi-

10 Nathaniel Niles, of Vermont, was appointed special agent to Austria, on June 7, 1837, with a letter of credence to the minister of foreign affairs, to procure a modification of the duties and restrictions on the importation of American tobacco. His functions ceased on the arrival of Mr. A. Muhlenberg, who was commissioned envoy extraordinary and minister plenipotentiary on Feb. 8, 1838, and took leave, on Sept. 18, 1840.

11 This was the mission entrusted to Henry Wheaton. See footnote 8, p. 379.

12 See above, note 9, p. 379.

nent item. As long ago as 1831, when M^r. Nelson was sent on a special mission to demand indemnity for losses sustained by our citizens, during the reign of Murat, the attention of our Government had been turned to this subject, and M^r. Nelson was informed that if the negotiation with which he was then charged should prove successful, and a disposition should be showed by the Government of the Two Sicilies to enter into a treaty of commerce on equal and liberal terms, instructions would be sent out to him for that purpose. Such a disposition appears to have been entertained by that Government, but a desire was at the same time manifested to connect the subject with that of the claims, an arrangement to which M^r. Nelson was not authorized to accede. This is supposed to have been one of the principal causes that prevented the immediate conclusion of a Convention.

M^r. Nelson returned to the United States, and M^r. Davezac our Chargé at the Hague was specially commissioned to exchange the ratifications at Naples of the treaty of Indemnity which had been recently concluded, and to form a treaty of Amity, Commerce and Navigation with the Government of the Two Sicilies for which purpose particular instructions were given him under date of the 13th of March 1833. On the 20th of June Mr. Davezac wrote that he had had several conferences with the Prince of Cassaro, on the subject, who was apparently desirous of bringing the negotiation to a favorable issue, and who represented the only obstacle as arising from the circumstance of the revenues being farmed out for a period which would not expire until near the end of 1834. In subsequent despatches Mr. Davezac held out hopes of his succeeding in the negotiation, but the procrastination and slowness of the Neapolitan Ministers, of which he complained, induced this Government to direct him on the 26th of December 1833, to leave Naples, and repair to the Hague, if there should be no reasonable prospect of his concluding a treaty within ten days from the receipt of the despatch, and he was instructed upon taking leave to say to the King of Naples, that the President did not intend to abandon the idea of a commercial treaty with him, but that he would at some convenient time renew the negotiation. Mr. Davezac accordingly returned to the Hague whence he wrote to the Department soon after his arrival announcing that fact, and transmitting a copy of a note addressed to him on his departure by the Neapolitan Minister in which a hope was expressed on the part of the King that the negotiation, which had been interrupted, might be renewed.

The foregoing presents a brief narrative of the attempts formerly made to conclude a treaty of commerce with the Government of the Two Sicilies, and of their failure; although it was obvious to both parties that their mutual interests would have been essentially promoted by the accomplishment of such an object. Since this suspension the motives and inducements to form a closer connexion by means of a treaty have continued to exist with undiminishing, indeed with increasing force, and the President conceiving the present time propitious to the renewal of negotiations, wishes you to regard this as the most interesting object of your mission. In the commercial arrangement which you are thus authorized and instructed to endeavour to conclude, you will be careful in the first place to secure upon the most advantageous terms the admission of American tobacco into the ports of the Kingdom of the Two Sicilies. In extending the treaty to other objects you will next proceed to the general trade between the two nations observing not to enter into any stipulations which will interfere with the existing obligations of the United States to other countries. A full power to conclude a treaty of commerce and navigation with the Two Sicilies will be found in despatch [13] N°. 1.

The commercial policy of the United States, as is well known to you, is founded upon the broadest basis of equal advantages and fair reciprocity. The various public acts of the Legislature, especially those of 1824 and 1828,[14] which embody the leading features of our system, and have placed it on its present simple and liberal footing, will be a safe and ample guide for your Government in the execution of the duty which is now confided to you. This principle upon which you will first endeavour to negotiate is that on which the act of Congress of 1828 was based. You will find it unfolded in the Third, Fourth, and Fifth articles of the Treaty concluded in 1828 with Brazil,[15]

[13] Instruction No. 1 from the State Department to Mr. Throop, for which see above, pp. 377-378.

[14] See an Act to amend the several acts imposing duties on imports. Approved May 22, 1824. United States 4 *Statutes at Large*, 25-30; also *Annals of Congress*, 18th Congress, 1st sess. House, XLII, col. 3221.); and later, An Act in alteration of the several acts imposing duties on imports. Approved May 19, 1828. United States, 4 *Statutes at Large*, Ch. LV, 270-275; also see *Register of Debates in Congress*, 20th Cong., 1st sess. House, IV, part 2, Appendix, p. xv.

[15] On Dec. 12, 1828, at Rio Janeiro, the United States and Brazil concluded a Treaty of Peace, Friendship, Commerce and Navigation. (Miller, *op. cit.*, III, 451-476; for Miller's notes on this treaty, *ibid*, 476-484.)

which presents our System in its full extent as to the equalisation of duties on tonnage and imports, whatever may be the nature and origin of the cargoes or from whence imported. Should it be found impracticable to conclude a Convention upon the broad ground of the act referred to, you will assume, as the principle of the negotiation the provision of the act of 1824, — which you will find contained in the treaty with Mexico of 1831.[16]

You may propose ten or twelve years for the duration of the Treaty, and, provided the Plenipotentiary acting on behalf of the Two Sicilies will consent, it would be agreeable to the President to have a clause inserted similar to that in the Convention with Mexico, that the treaty shall remain in force until the end of one year after either of the contracting parties shall have given notice to the other of its intention to terminate the same, each party reserving to itself the right of giving such notice at the end of the term for which the treaty is to be made to endure.

I transmit with this despatch a copy of several documents of which a list is annexed.

List of documents[17] accompanying the above despatch.

1. Circular to Ministers &c.		28 March 1833.
2. Prince of Cassaro to Mr. Davezac	(translation)	7 June 1834.
3. Mr. Davezac to Mr. McLane		26 June 1834.
4. Mr. Forsyth to Mr. Davezac		29 August 1834.
5. Mr. Morelli to Mr. Forsyth	"	31 March 1836.
6. " " " " "	"	31 Oct. 1836.
7. " " " " "	"	12 June 1837.
8. " " " " "	"	17 June 1837.
9. " " " " "	"	5 July 1837
10. Mr. Dayton to Min. of Foreign Affairs of Naples		6 July 1837.
11. Mr. Morelli to Mr. Forsyth	(translation)	25 Sept. 1837.
12. " " " " "	"	17 Oct. 1837.
13. " " " " "	"	18 Oct. 1837.

---

[16] On Apr. 5, 1831, the United States of America and the United Mexican States concluded a Treaty of Amity, Commerce and Navigation. Subsequently, on Sept. 17th and Dec. 17th, 1831, two protocols, respectively explaining and amending the agreement, were offered by the Mexican government and accepted by the American, and eventually incorporated in the text of the treaty. (Miller, op. cit., III, 599-634; for Miller's notes on the treaty, ibid, III, 633-640). An additional Article to this treaty, there being 34 articles in the body of the treaty, provided for the suspension, for six years, of the provisions of articles 5 and 6 of the Treaty.

[17] For these documents see Davezac chapter, hic opus.

14.	Mr. Morelli to Mr. Forsyth	(translation)	13 Nov. 1837.
15.	" " " " "		" 28 Feb. 1838.
16.	Mr. Hammett to Mr. Forsyth		1 Feb. 1838.
17.	Projét of a treaty by Mr. Nelson		1 Feb. 1838.
18.	Mr. Forsyth to Mr. Morelli		25 March 1836.
19.	" " " " "		12 April 1836.
20.	" " " " "		24 May 1836.
21.	" " " " "		14 June 1837.
22.	" " " " "		7 July 1837.
23.	" " " " "		12 July 1837.
24.	" " " " "		29 Sept. 1837
25.	" " " " "		25 Oct. 1837
26.	" " " " "		17 Nov. 1837.

E. T. THROOP TO J. FORSYTH

New York, May 20, 1838.

Dear Sir,

I had the honor to inform you, by letter from my residence at Owasco, of my intention to leave for this city on Saturday last, to embark on the 24ᵗʰ. instant in the Ship Sheffield for Liverpool. I accordingly arrived in that city last tuesday [sic] morning; but not having yet received my instructions from the Government, I have been compelled to relinquish the accommodations reserved, conditionally, for me in that ship.

I shall remain here until my departure on my mission, unless otherwise directed; but under the impression that an early embarcation will best meet your wishes, I have taken my passage, unconditionally, in the Packet Ship Sheridan, which will sail from this port for Liverpool on the first day of June next.

I shall be accompanied by a nephew, eleven years of age, and two ladies.

E. T. THROOP TO J. FORSYTH

New York May 23, 1838

Sir,

I have the honor to acknowledge the receipt this day, by mail, of my commission as Chargé d'Affaires of the United States near the King of the Kingdom of the Two Sicilies, with the accompanying documents.

I return, enclosed, the duplicate of my letter of credit on the Bankers of the United States, at London, for my outfit, salary and contingent expenses, as requested.

I shall have occasion to use a small portion of my outfit here, and to render it available if it is necessary that I should draw for the amount I wish to use, and accompany my draft with the letter of credit. To be prepared for any accident which might occur in parting with my letter here, I should like to have a duplicate of it to take with me. Have you any objection to furnish me with a duplicate to be used in the possible contingency suggested?

E. T. THROOP[18] TO J. FORSYTH[19]

Southampton (England) July 21, 1838

Dear Sir,

Pursuant to my arrangements, of which I had the honor to advise you, by my letter from New York of the 20th of May last, I embarked in the Packet Ship Sheridan for Liverpool, on my way to Naples, on the second day of June last and reached the port of destination on the twentieth day of the same month.

My principal object in passing through this Kingdom was to arrange my money affairs with the Bankers in London, on which I was furnished with a letter of credit for my outfit & salary, to purchase my uniform, books & other things necessary for an outfit so far as they could be purchased to advantage there, to arrange with a proper agent for the regular transmission to me of letter, newspapers, stationary [sic] books &c which should reach that city or be provided for me there, and finally, during my short stay there, to form such acquaintances with the diplomatic corps at that court, as might be useful to me in the discharge of my duties, at my destined station.

On my arrival at Liverpool I found the Kingdom entirely engrossed with the approaching coronation of Queen Victoria,[20]

---

[18] Letter, New York, June 1, 1838, from Mr. Throop to Mr. Forsyth informing the Secretary of State that he is leaving this day on the ship *Sheridan* for Liverpool, is omitted. Mr. Throop asked that the *Globe* and *The Democratic Review* be forwarded to him, if admissable.

[19] Instruction No. 4, Washington, June 28, 1838, from Mr. Forsyth to Mr. Throop asking that he transmit the President's letter to the King of Naples regarding the birth and subsequent death of a royal Princess, daughter of the Count of Syracuse, is omitted. Secretary Forsyth acknowledged the receipt of the Prince of Cassaro's note concerning the style of address of letters of ceremony addressed to the President.

[20] Queen Victoria (1819-1901) was crowned Queen of Great Britain and Ireland, etc., on June 20, 1837.

which was then to take place on the twenty eighth of that month, and I learned, that the mechanics of the Metropolis were employed, and the houses of entertainment preengaged. This information was confirmed by a letter which I received from M^r. Stevenson,[21] in reply to one I addressed to him from Liverpool, and it determined me not to hasten to the City. I however kept on my way, and reached London on the twenty seventh, where, during several days, without making myself known to any persons,[22] except M^r. Stevenson, I was employed in the business of preparation which had brought me there.

I called upon Messrs. Rothschild, and was informed by them that they had refused to accept my draft upon them, made at New York, on account of their not having received any advices of my letter of credit from the Government. The bill had not been returned & I prevailed upon them to honor the letter of credit which I bore to them. They told me that they had not been in the habit of recognizing letters of this description which were not transmitted to them directly by the Government, & I found afterwards, that my draft, before it was dishonored, had been the subject of a correspondence between them & A. Stevenson before my arrival, who had advised them to accept it. On my leaving the City they (the Bankers) gave me credit for the balance of the outfit, altho' they had not then received the expected communication from the Government.

I was enabled to leave London yesterday, and I arrived here this day, for the purpose of taking my passage in the steam boat for Havre, on my way to Paris, where matters connected with my preparations and correspondence with the Government, will require my stay for a few days. I determined upon this route to Paris as the most easy and expeditious, and also, that I might see our Consul at Havre, through whom probably newspapers and other large packages unfit for transmission by mail, may be advantageously forwarded.

On Wednesday the eighteenth I attended the levee at St. James, in my official character, & was presented to the Queen.

Before I left London I formed the acquaintance of the Count

---

21 Andrew Stevenson, of Virginia, was commissioned envoy extraordinary and minister plenipotentiary to London, March 16, 1836. He took leave on Oct. 21, 1841. He was empowered on Nov. 27, 1837, to negotiate with Greece concerning commerce and navigation.

22 Since Mr. Throop was not accredited to the British Court, he apparently was not invited to the coronation. This fact and his own sense of fitness may well have moved the diplomat to delay his arrival in the midst of the festivities.

de Ludolf,[23] the Sicilian Minister at that Court, who received me with great kindness, and volunteered a letter of introduction to the Prince of Cassaro: who, I was glad to learn, is still at the head of foreign affairs at Naples. Whatever may be transmitted to me through our Legation at London will go into the hands of Mr. Miller, a Bookseller & Stationer there, with whom I have had several interviews. The chances of sending by private conveyance to Naples from that City will be much less frequent than from Havre or Paris, through our Legation in France. But as there is no difficulty in forwarding from London such things as we prefer to pass by mail, and as the intercourse between England & our Country is becoming frequent, rapid & certain by means of the successful experiment of crossing the Atlantic by steamer, it may be best to send letters, requiring expedition, through that channel. On the subject, I shall be able to give more satisfactory advice, after I have been at Havre & Paris.

I was informed by an attaché to the Sicilian legation at London, that, altho' their government was ostensibly bound by treaty to favor the commerce of England, France, and Spain, yet by a secret article they were at liberty to extend the same advantages to other nations. I hope I shall find this to be true, and that the treaties with the before mentioned favored nations do not exist as any barrier against negotiations with us.

I shall write you again from Paris, and in the meantime, I have to assure you of

My high consideration and regard —

[23] Giuseppe Costantino Ludolf (1787-1875). Count. Illustrious Neapolitan diplomat. He completed his education in Vienna, Constantinople, and S. Petersburg. In this last city he began his diplomatic career as attaché to the Neapolitan Legation. After the entrance of the French in Naples in 1806, he enlisted in the Russian army, fought at Friedland, and was wounded. He remained in Sicily with the Bourbon Court to the restoration. He then resumed his diplomatic career and was sent successively as envoy extraordinary to Constantinople (decree of May 25, 1816), chargé of a temporary mission to Vienna in 1821, envoy extraordinary and minister plenipotentiary at St. Petersburg (decree of May 2, 1824), minister plenipotentiary at Rome (decree of Dec. 31, 1831) where he remained to 1848. In that year he was recalled to Naples and later sent to Paris and London on a delicate mission to uphold the rights of Ferdinand II on Sicily. When absolutism was restored, he returned to Naples and although he did not participate actively in public life, he remained at court as a King's Councilor. In 1859, he went to Russia to announce the accession to the throne of Francis II. In 1860, he withdrew to private life in Tuscany. See G. Gallavresi, "Un ambassadeur italien sous l'ancien régime." *Revue d'Histoire Diplomatique*. Paris, 1905; the Ludolf papers in the archives of the Società Storica Napoletana; Irma Arcuno, *Il regno delle due Sicilie nei rapporti con lo Stato Pontificio 1846-1850*. Naples, Perrella, 1933; Ruggero Moscati, *Austria, Napoli, e gli stati conservatori italiani (1849-1852)*. Naples, Società Storica Napoletana, 1942; Ruggero Moscati, *Il regno delle Due Sicilie e l'Austria*, etc.; Giuseppe Paladino, *La rivoluzione del 15 maggio 1848 a Napoli*. Città di Castello, Ed. Albrighi e Segati, 1920.

E. T. THROOP TO J. FORSYTH

Milan September 2, 1838.
Dear Sir,

I have the honor to inform you, that I reached this city on the night of the 30th. ult°. from Paris by the way of Geneva, and that my arrangements are completed for continuing my journey to Naples, tomorrow, by the way of Rome. My stay at Paris was longer than I intended, but not more so than was necessary to complete my arrangements.

At Havre I saw our consul M^r. Beasley,[24] who very readily consented to take charge of my correspondence with the Government, and to forward my letters by mail, and newspapers, & other matters, not proper for the mail, by such other casual conveyances as should present themselves. After an interview with Gen. Cass,[25] at Paris, I came to the conclusion to advise you to use M^r. Beasley as the medium of correspondence between us.

Since I left Paris, I have obtained information which I sought for in vain at London, Havre & Paris, that a pretty brisk trade is carried on between Liverpool & Naples, and that a vessel leaves Liverpool as often as every three weeks, and makes the voyage to Naples, in about thirty days. I have made the acquaintance of Mr. Samuel Dutton jun^r. of the house of McNair & Dutton, Liverpool (No. 30 Water Street) from whom I obtained this information, and whose connexion with the trade of the Mediterranean has made him familiar with the navigation to Naples. M^r. Dutton has agreed with me to forward, by the earliest opportunity, all such matters, as may be sent to the care of McNair & Dutton. That house is entirely English, but I have travelled with M^r. Dutton, and I am sure that I cannot be deceived in him, and I have no doubt, that he will execute with scrupulous fidelity and punctuality any commission with which he may be charged by the Government or myself.

Permit me, therefore, to request you to send to the care of the house mentioned my newspapers & other things, which you do not mean to have forwarded by mail through Europe, and

---

24 Reuben R. Beasley, of Virginia, was appointed United States Consul for Havre de Grace on Dec. 19, 1816 in place of I. C. Barnet. Beasley served until Feb. 26, 1845 when he was removed. (U. S. Senate, *Executive Journal*, II, 62; VI, 399). Havre de Grace is the older name for the city of Le Havre, Department of Seine Inferièure, in France.

25 Lewis Cass, of Ohio, commissioned envoy extraordinary and minister plenipotentiary to Paris on Oct. 4, 1836. He took leave on Nov. 12, 1842.

to M^r. Beasley my letters intended for the mail. I believe that all despatches of importance would be more certain of safe conveyance through that channel and in order to place myself more fully in possession of it I have requested Mr. Dutton to give letters of introduction to me at Naples, to all such captains of vessels, sailing between the two cities, as he considers trust worthy. It occurred to me that it might be proper to have every thing directed to our consul at Liverpool, which is destined to pass through the house of McNair & Dutton, but the fewer hands packages pass through the less damage there is, from accidents or carelessness.

I go from here in a vetturino [sic]. This is a slow conveyance, but the only one which presents the means of a comfortable progress through this country, except a post chaise. I am informed that at this season no business is transacted at the Court at Naples, but that the King withdraws from the city; and I perceive that the expected event, the birth of a child,[26] which has hitherto kept him near Naples, has occurred, so as to leave him at liberty to follow his willingness in regard to a summer residence. There is therefore no need of extraordinary exertions on my part to reach my post at the earliest date; still I consider it my duty not to linger on the way, nor to deviate from my route.

The Emperor made his Grand entry into the City, as King of Italy,[27] yesterday, preparatory to his coronation, which will take place on the Sixth instant.

E. T. THROOP TO J. FORSYTH

Naples October 2, 1838. [Despatch No. 1]

Sir,

By my letter of the 2nd of September, from Milan, I had the honor to inform you of the course and incidents of my journey, and of the arrangements I had made for opening a safe and expeditious channel of correspondence between the Government and myself. I have nothing to add on the latter subject, now, except that letters will pass more rapidly through our legation at London, by means of the facilities of steam navigation, than by any other channel, and upon all accounts I think that the

---

26 Prince Charles Louis, Count of Trani, was born on Aug. 1, 1838. He was the son of King Ferdinand II and Queen Marie Thérèse-Isabelle.

27 Ferdinand I (1793-1875) of Austria. Son of Francis I. He was crowned on Sept. 6, 1838, at Milan, King of Lombardo-Venetia.

preferable course for all letters intended to be forwarded through Europe by mail.

I left Milan on the third day of September in a vetura, [sic] passing through Bologna, Florence and Rome, & reached this Capitol [sic] on the evening of the 25th of the same month.

At Bologna, I was attacked, and delayed a day, by a complaint which had some of the alarming symptoms of the cholera; brought on as I feared, by traversing during the heat of summer, and while the process of rotting hemp was going on, [on] the beautiful and fertile plains between Milan and that City. The Symptoms abated, and I hastened to reach a purer atmosphere, by ascending the mountains, in the prosecution of my Journey, which I finished without any farther personal inconvenience from climate or disease. I spent four days at Florence, and about the same time at Rome.

In the course of my progress to this, my place of destination, I did not deviate from the ordinary direct rout, but I did not travel with post haste, nor with that expedition, which might have been reasonably employed, if our relations with the Sicilian government had been such, as to require immediate negociation; but having been apprized by the letter of M^{r}. Davezac, one of my predecessors here, that business was not transacted at this Court, during the months of July, August, and September, I felt assured that I should be better qualified to fulfil the expectations of the Government, if I should avail myself of the opportunities, presented by moderate expedition, to observe the productions of the country through which I was to pass, and the manner, habits, and political relations of its people and Governments. The Government to which I am accredited, I need not say, has intimate relations of various kinds with the several Governments, who divide the power over all the Cisalpine regions.

Having reached this Capitol [sic] on the evening of the 25th, on the 27th I addressed the following note to the Prince of Cassaro: —

"E. T. Throop, appointed chargé d'affaires of the United States of America, near His Majesty the King of the Kingdom of the Two Sicilies, hastens to inform His Excellency, the Prince of Cassaro, Minister Secretary of State for Foreign Affaires, of his arrival at this Capitol [sic], and begs the favor of him to inform him when he can have the honor of an interview to present his letter of credence.

E. T. Throop avails himself of this occasion to assure the Prince of Cassaro of his most distinguished consideration. Naples September 27, 1838."

To which I received during the same day the following reply: —

"The Prince of Cassaro is very glad to hear the arrival at Naples of M^r. E. T. Throop, appointed Chargé d'Affaires of the United States, at the Court of the Two Sicilies, and will feel very happy if M^r. Throop will do him the honor of a visit tomorrow at one O'clock, at the foreign office.

The Prince of Cassaro begs M^r. Throop to receive the assurance of his distinguished consideration. Naples, September 27, 1838."

At the hour appointed, I attended at the Foreign Office, and delivered my letter of credence, & was received by the Prince of Cassaro with kindness. He informed me that the King was then at Messina, whence he would return in the course of four or five weeks, and that I should not be able to have an audience with him before that time; but that, in the meantime, I would be entitled to all the consideration of an accredited minister, except in such matters of Etiquette, which would require repetition after my reception by the King.

I took the occasion to express my gratification at finding him still at the head of foreign affaires, [sic] as he had left a favorable [sic] upon all who had preceded me here; and I thanked him particularly for his courtesy, in replying to my note in the language of my country.

I took the liberty at this interview of making several necessary inquiries of him in regard to the ceremonials to be observed, on my arrival, towards the personages of dignity, who surrounded the Court, both domestic and foreign, and received a very polite communication from him on that subject during the day, communicating the desired information. —

I have the honor, also, to acknowledge the receipt of a despatch[28] from the Department of State, *marked no. 4,* dated 28 June 1838, covering a letter from the President to His Majesty the King of the Two Sicilies, an open copy thereof for the Minister, and instructions in relation to their delivery. In

---

[28] Mr. Throop still does not correctly name the communication from the Department of State. Here he should refer to Instruction No. 4.

fulfilment of my duty in relation to them, I enclosed the letter & copy to the Prince of Cassaro with the following note. —

"Naples September 29, 1838

The Undersigned, Chargé d'Affaires of the United States, has the honor to transmit, herewith, to His Excellency The Prince of Cassaro, a letter from the President[29] of the United States for his Majesty Ferdinand the Second, King of the Kingdom of the Two Sicilies, in answer to his Majesty's letter, addressed to him on the 30th of March last, communicating the fact that, Her Royal Highness the Countess of Syracuse gave birth to a Princess on the 23[d] of March last, whom, it had pleased God, to call to Himself, on the 29th of the same month, and also a copy of the same.

The Undersigned is also directed to inform His Execellency, the Prince of Cassaro, of the receipt, at the Department of State, of his letter of the 12th of May last, in reply to a communication, dated on the 6th of July last, from M[r]. Dayton, then acting Secretary of State, who was directed by the President to explain to the Government of the Two Sicilies in a distinct manner the reason why letters of Ceremony were to be addressed to the President of the United States alone and, at the same time, to acquaint His Excellency of the satisfaction which is felt by the President, at the assurance given by your Excellency, that this style of address shall in future be adopted by the Royal Chancery.[30]

The Undersigned has great pleasure, in availing himself of this occasion, to renew the assurances of his most distinguished consideration. E. T. Throop."

To His Excellency The Prince of Cassaro
Minister of Foreign Affaires. &c &c &c

In passing through Tuscany, I learnt that the Grand Duke had recently published an ordnance,[31] containing 287 sections, relating principally to the administration of Justice in his

---

[29] See p. 395. The Prince of Cassaro's calling him "President of the Congress" was not (p. 396) to be taken too lightly!

[30] "Punctilio" was not all on the side of the Royal Court. It would seem that the young Republic too could insist on due observance of its dignity!

[31] The reference is to the organic law of the new Tuscan tribunals which was published *motu proprio* on Aug. 2, 1838. On the law, see: *L'analisi della legge organica dei nuovi tribunali toscani*. Florence, Stamp. Granducale, 1838, 43 pp. 8°. This work contains officious explanations on the judiciary reform. See also, A. Zobi, *Storia civile della Toscana*, Florence, Molini, 1852, IV, 494-499.

dominions, with a preamble, in which he avows a determination to establish, in the Grand Dutchy [sic], a uniform plan of administration of Justice,[32] founded upon principles best adapted to the present state of society &c. I have procured a printed copy[33] of it, which I will forward to the Department by the first private opportunity.

I have not yet read it through, but the preamble expresses very liberal feelings towards individual rights, and the great scope of the ordinance [sic] is to enable his subjects to appeal from tribunal to tribunal, without bringing their causes before the Duke himself. It establishes the administration of Justice as a right & not a matter of grace. Although he still retains all the Legislative power in his own person, yet this may be looked upon as a measure, by which he has divested himself of the power over private causes. There is importance attached to this measure, if the information I have received is true, from the circumstance, that similar measures are under consideration with the Kings of Sardinia & Naples. But my information is not sufficient to speak upon the subject.

I have taken possession today of the rooms which I am to occupy here, but I have not yet been able to receive and open the boxes, which contain my books, documents, and stationary [sic]. The paper I now use, is some that I happened accidentally to have in my portfolio, and not that intended for dispatches. Every thing which has been forwarded to me from the United States and Europe in boxes, has arrived, except one, with Books & stationary [sic] from London, which is daily expected. I have not yet had time to open the diplomatic trunk, remaining here with the Consul.

On my arrival I was promptly attended by our Consul Mr. Hammett, to whose obliging disposition, knowledge of public & local affairs here, and readiness to aid me by his personal services I am already much indebted. I shall in future, also, be obliged further to avail myself of his services and knowledges which which [sic] it would be difficult for a diplomatic representative to enter advisedly upon his duties.

---

[32] Ever since the publication in 1764 of Cesare Beccaria's *Dei Delitti e delle Pene*, the Grand Dukes of Tuscany had introduced important penal and legal reforms aiming to improve the administration of justice in Tuscany. These reforms received widespread attention everywhere, including the United States. Cfr. G. Baldasseroni, *Leopoldo II granduca di Toscana e i suoi tempi*. Florence, tip. all'Insegna di S. Antonio, 1871; A. Zobi, *Storia civile della Toscana*, Florence, 4 volumes.

[33] This printed copy was not found in despatch volume.

Before I left our country I was made acquainted with Mr. Hammett's useful services heretofore, during his long residence at this post, and beleived [sic] then, as I am now convinced, that he has a pretty large, just claim upon the government for monies actually expended and services actually rendered, for which he has received no compensation. I am informed that he has a claim pending before Congress for compensation, which I hope and trust will succeed in attracting the particular notice of Congress; for it is not consistent with the spirit of justice which guides the counsels of our nation, to refuse reasonable compensation to public servants for actual services, when facts are made known to them, and they are convinced that the claim is neither fraudulent nor exaggerated. In Mr. Hammett's case it is as important that justice should not be delayed, as that it should be ultimately done.

I trust that these remarks in favor of an old and faithful public servant, who is not present to press upon the consideration of the Government his claim, will not be considered misplaced or intrusive.

E. T. THROOP TO J. FORSYTH

Naples November 5, 1838 [Despatch No. 2.]

Sir,

In my dispatch, bearing date October 2nd ult$^\circ$. I had the honor to inform you of the absence of the King in Sicily and of his expected return in the course of four or five weeks. He is still absent, and, by the last account, he was at Palermo, where he had recently arrived. It was rumored here that he would return to the Capitol by the 12th of the present month, and to ascertain the truth I obtained an interview with the Prince of Cassaro. He informed me that intelligence had been received of the King's arrival at Palermo but not of the time when he would return, but that he might reasonably be expected about the middle of the present month. It is now rumored that he will not be here until Christmas.

Having presented my credentials on my arrival to the Prince of Cassaro, I afterwards called to pay my respects to the Queen Mother, who presides at Court during the absence of the King, and afterwards attended two courts on gala days where I had an opportunity to meet the foreign Ministers as well as the

Royal personages and State Officers. I had previously left my cards for the foreign Ministers & received theirs in return.

Although I have not thought it expedient, or even proper, in my present situation, to make any advances towards negociation upon my subject, yet I have made the best use, in my power of the time & opportunities, afforded by my position to inform myself of facts which may be useful hereafter. There is so little published, and so few persons here who interest themselves in public affairs, that the process of acquiring knowledge of the internal affairs & statistics of the Kingdom, is very slow and difficult for a stranger unaccustomed to the habits, manners, and language of the people.

My dispatch N°. One contains a copy of my note to the Prince of Cassaro which accompanied the transmission of the President's letter to the King, in reply to the information of the Parturition of the Countess of Syracuse, in which, in compliance with my instructions, I made known to the Prince the satisfaction with which the President received his assurance, that in future communications, the Royal Chancery would correct its address of letters of ceremony to the President of the United States.

I was not merely astonished but somewhat confounded in receiving a note from the Prince of Cassaro in which he acknowledged the receipt of the President's letter, describing him as the President of the Congress of the United States. It was difficult for me to beleive [sic], from the friendly manner in which I had been received by him, that he intended a wanton insult to my government, such as I should have construed his note to be, if it had been designedly written in the offensive form; and on the other hand, it was equally difficult to suppose, that, under the circumstances, it could have been the result of accident. The fact of the recent return here of Morelli,[34] mingled in my suspicions. I determined, however, to treat it as an inadvertency, & to give the Secretary an opportunity to explain if he would. I thereupon addressed to him the following note:

---

[34] Domenico Morelli. Neapolitan diplomat. On October 24, 1832, he was appointed consul general in the United States of America with residence in Philadelphia; in 1838 he was transferred as consul general of the second class to the Kingdom of Greece with residence at Athens; on December 16, 1840, he returned to Naples on leave, and on Feb. 27, 1845, he was appointed envoy to the Regency of Tripoli. For his correspondence with the State Department, see last chapter in second volume.

"Unofficial"

Mr Throop Chargé d'Affaires of the United States of America presents his most respectful compliments to the Prince of Cassaro, Minister Secretary of State of foreign Affairs, and takes the liberty to call his attention to that part of his note dated the 2nd of October instant, in which the P. of C.[35] informs M^r. Throop of his readiness to submit to his Majesty the King, as soon as he should return here, the reply of the President *of the Congress* of the United States of America (del Presidente del Congresso degli Stati Uniti d'America) of the parturition of S. A. R. la Contessa di Siracusa.

Mr. T. begs leave to remind the P. of C. in this unofficial note, that he has the honor to represent here, "The President of the United States, as the Executive head of the American government; and not the President *of the Congress* of the United States; and there is no officer of the latter title connected with it's [sic] government. Mr. T. is conscious that the error is inadvertent, & that he need only point it out to the Prince of Cassaro to have it promptly rectified.

Mr. T. learnt, with pain, that the absence of the P. of C. from the grand circle at the grand gala yesterday, was owing to sickness. He hopes that the indisposition is not severe, and that the P. of C. will soon be restored to health.

Mr. T. returns his thanks to the P. of C. for his prompt and very polite reply to his note of inquiry concerning the proper time and manner of paying his respects to the dignitaries of this Royal Court, and he seizes the occasion to renew to the P. of C. the assurance of his distinguished consideration. Naples October 5, 1838."

I thought it best to send an unofficial note, as it would leave me at liberty to assume such a tone in an official one, if one should be necessary, as circumstances might require.

A day or two afterwards, I received an application from a clerk in the office of foreign affairs for leave to withdraw the note, stating the irregularity was an error entirely of his own. I afterwards received the following note of the same date in it's [sic] place.

Translation. Napoli 2. Ottobre 1838.

The Undersigned, Minister Secretary of State for foreign af-

---

35 In the actual Note Mr. Throop would, of course, not have abbreviated thus a minister's name and title.

fairs will be anxious to put in the possession of his Majesty the King his August Lord, as soon as His Majesty shall have returned here, the answer of the President of the U.S. of America to the communication of the parturition of S. A. R. the Countess of Syracuse, which Mr. T. Chargé d'Affaires of the Gov.^t of the U. S. transmitted to him by his official communication of the 29 of Septr together with the usual copy (or copy for his use).

He hastens to acquaint Mr. T. with it, and renew to him the assurances of his special[36] consideration.

Signed, Il Principe di Cassaro"

It is generally believed that there is not an entire good understanding between the Prince of Cassaro, and the King, and remarking upon one occasion, upon the absence of the Secretary of State from Court, the gentlemen to whom I addressed myself alluded to the resumed estrangement, and hinted that his absence was owing to dissatisfaction, rather than sickness, the alledged cause. That he was sick at the time I had occasion to know, and I hope that the public is at fault in regard to the supposed misunderstanding between him and the King, as he seems to be a fair man, and is spoken of here by foreigners as the best disposed person in the Cabinet. It is alledged [sic] that one cause of the King's displeasure is a belief, that he yielded[37] too much in the indemnity Treaty between this government and ours, and that the sum they stipulated to pay was more than we were honestly entitled to.

The Regio Magistrato di Sanità (or board of health) of Genoa, following the example of Trieste, Marseilles &c. opened their ports on the first day of October last, to the immediate entry of all goods, arriving from North and South America, with a clean bill of health, and in addition thereto, a certificate from their consul at the port of departure, or in case of no consul being there, the certificate of some other European consul, residing at that place, proving that the place was free from contagious disease, & particularly the yellow fever. I am told, tho' not with sufficient authority to vouch for its truth, altho' I beleive [sic] it, that Leghorn has done the same thing.

---

36 The Italian version shows the word used was "particular" rather than as translated "special" consideration.

37 See this chapter, pp. 466, 467, 469, which indicate that the Prince of Cassaro was eventually forced to leave the Court because of his sympathy with the American point of view.

The board of health in this city have had the subject before them, in a modified form, but have not yet come to a decision. It was proposed to relinguish the Quarantine in relation to unsusceptible Goods, and the question resulted in a tie. This is a City with a very large and crowded population, and the authorities, not without reason, are particularly alive to the approach of contagious disease; yet it is supposed, that, on more reflection, and with a board entirely full, they may yet adopt the modified measure, as one free from danger.

I alluded to the subject in an interview with the Prince of Cassaro a few days since, with the hope of obtaining something authentic in regard to the views of the Government, but he seemed unconscious of any movement, and suggested the propriety of my addressing him a note upon the matter. This I declined on the ground of it's [sic] not being my object in alluding to it, to make it a matter of negociation.

In truth, it is a question which in the present state of our commerce with them, does not interest us, as no American vessel has entered this port, direct from home, for many years. The last one here arrived in December, with coals from Liverpool. We have but few articles, the produce of our industry which can find a market here, while these people produce much that we want. Our Commerce will not be vastly benefitted by any treaty which does not allow us to carry to them the productions of other countries. I hope this government may be made to see their advantages in such a Treaty.

The King has recently interfered with the manufacture of sulphur in Italy so as to reduce the annual production of the article, and thereby enable the persons at present engaged in that business, to realize large profits from the increase of price expected to result from a scantily supplied market. For this measure he received a large compensation, I beleive [sic] 300,000 ducats a year, by persons engaged in the manufacture.[38]

This measure affects British interests in two ways, first, by interfering with what they are disposed to call the private property of British subjects, who have invested capital in the manufacture; and secondly, by increasing the price of an article greatly used in manufactures. In the last point of view other countries are interested as Mount Etna & it's [sic] vicinity is the great

---

[38] For information concerning the sulphur monopoly see: Great Britain, *Accounts and Papers 16-17 Trade, Navigation, misc.* 1840, XLIV, 447; also: Great Britain, Reports of Commissioners, 1840, XXI, *Report on the commercial statistics of the Kingdom of the Two Siciiles* by J. Macgregor.

storehouse of that article, whence it is exported to all ports of the world.

The British minister, M^r. Temple[39] is not here, but M^r. Kennedy[40] the Chargé *ad interim* is making a serious question of it. I am told that the King treats it as rather an impertinent interference with the domestic arrangements of his Kingdom. The British representative on the other hand, in order to maintain his ground, shews a disposition to mock the *divino jure regum* and deny the absolute right of the King to dispose at will, of the property of subjects, and especially of British subjects, who, relying upon the inviolability of private rights, have entered into the Kingdom with their capital skill and industry to employ them in the trade. How far he will venture to press, in diplomatic correspondence, the doctrines he holds in conversation, or how far they will be sanctioned by the British government, remains to be seen; but he will find it difficult to compel the King who is obstinate and tenacious of all his rights, to retrace his steps.[41]

I send herewith, an inventory[42] of all the public property delivered to me, here, as belonging to the Legation. It was in a trunk left with M^r. Hammett, sealed by Mr. Davezac.

In comparing the books forwarded to me here from the department with the list I missed Seybert's[43] and Pitken's[44] statis-

---

[39] Temple, Hon. Sir William. K. C. B. He was attached to the embassy at The Hague from Jan. to Sept. 1814, and to the Congress at Vienna, Sept. 1814. He was appointed secretary of legation at Stockholm, Oct. 10, 1814; at Frankfort, July 29, 1817; and at Berlin, Nov. 4, 1823. He was appointed secretary of embassy at St. Petersburg, Jan. 1, 1828. He was Précis Writer to his brother, Viscount Palmerston, from Jan. 5, 1831 to Sept. 15, 1832. He was appointed minister plenipotentiary at Dresden, Sept. 18, 1832, and envoy extraordinary and minister plenipotentiary at Naples, Nov. 27, 1832, and held the post to 1856. He was made a K. C. B., March 1, 1851. He died on Aug. 24, 1856. See: Frederic Boase, *Modern English Biography,* 1901, III, col. 910.

[40] John Kennedy was secretary of legation in Sicily, 1832-44, and also acted as chargé d'affaires at Naples during Mr. Temple's absence June 10, 1838-March 2, 1840. (*British Diplomatic Representatives 1789-1852,* Royal Historical Society, L, 134.)

[41] A good study on Anglo-Italian relations during this period is one by Alfredo Signoretti, *Italia e Inghilterra durante il risorgimento.* Milan, Istituto per gli Studi Politici e Internazionali. 1940, 369 pp.

[42] See inventory following; and next later one, below, this chapter, p. 511 ff.

[43] Adam Seybert. *United States statistical annals embracing views of the population, commerce, navigation, fisheries, public lands, post-office establishment, revenues, mint, military and naval establishments, expenditures, public debt and sinking fund of the United States of America founded on official documents commencing on the fourth of March, 1789, and ending on April 20, 1818.* Philadelphia: Thomas Dobson & Son, 1818. See also note 144, p. 513.

[44] Timothy Pitkin, (1766-1847). *A statistical view of the commerce of the United States of America including also an account of banks, manufacturers and*

tics, — the first vol. of the Laws of U.S. and two or three volumes of documents. The first volume of the Laws I was able to supply from the books here.

I have not received any periodical or newspaper from the United States since I left London.

My last dispatch received from the Department is marked N°. 4. and bears date the 28 June last.

N.B. The ship from London, in which was shipped the stationary [sic] I ordered, when there, has just arrived in this port, but I have not yet received my box, and have no suitable envelope paper.

Mr. Throop is desired by M^r. Hammett to present his profound respects to Mr Forsyth, and to express his hopes that the Secretary will have the goodness to remember his claims.

Inventory of Public Property Remaining with the Legation at Naples delivered to me by M^r. Hammett the U. S. Consul in a sealed trunk deposited with him by Mr. Davezac.

1. A Seal.
2. The first seven volumes & an Index of the Laws of the United States.[45]
3. The 1 & 2 volumes of Waits [sic] State papers.[46]
4. Two old volumes, printed 1712 of *Le droit de la nature et des Gens par Puffendorf.*[47]

internal trade and improvements together with that of the revenues and expenditures of the general government accompanied with numerous tables. New Haven: Durrie & Peck, 1835. An earlier edition of Pitkin's work was published in Hartford, Charles Hosmer, 1816; another edition was published in Hartford, printed by Hamlen & Newton, 1817, 445 pp.

[45] The first six volumes of the *Laws of the United States* (Bioren & Duane edition, Colvin editor) were in 1827 increased to seven volumes; the seventh was published by Peter Force, 1827, and comprised the Index prepared by Samuel Burch, on order of the House, one of the best covering the period of years included. The Index was also published separately from the set of the *Laws,* 1828, 361 p., issued by the Law Library of Congress and covering 1789-1828, *Laws and Treaties.* Samuel Burch was Clerk of the House.

[46] These *State Papers* were repeatedly published by Thomas Wait and his two sons, each of the early editions including new materials while republishing what had earlier been published. The third edition comprised 12 volumes. The first edition of but 9 volumes, was published by Act of Mar. 25, 1816. Peter Force also published a series called *State Papers,* of which 6 volumes were on Foreign Relations. See Poore's *Catalogue of Government Documents,* p. 19 (Act of March 2, 1833).

[47] In his original work on the *Law of Nations,* written in Latin, 1694, the Baron Pufendorf used but one 'f' in his name's first syllable. Mr. Throop, in common with most French and English translators of the Baron's work, spells the name Puffendorf. This simple difference has caused much confusion in the cataloguing of the many editions of the many translations of this work into various languages, especially when the difficulty of distinguishing editions has

5. A manuscript book, partly filled by Mr. Nelson with the records of his mission.
6. A few bundles of papers.

Naples November 5, 1838.

E. T. Throop

E. T. THROOP TO J. FORSYTH

Naples December 6, 1838.[48] [Despatch N°. 3]

Sir,

In my last dispatch, dated the 5ᵗʰ ult°. I had the honor to inform you of the continued absence of the King, and his expected return to the capitol in the course of a short time. He has not

led to the publisher's playing up the name of translator, editor, commentator of new editions, rather than the original author's name, or even the re-use of the exact same title. This edition which Mr. Throop refers to finding in the 'diplomatic trunk' was the Amsterdam (3rd) edition of 1712, in French (and Mr. Nelson, see p. 268, quotes from it) with annotations by M. Barbeyrac. In Amsterdam in 1688 appeared an edition in Latin: Samuelis Pufendorfii. *De Jure naturae et gentium, libri octo. Editio ultima, auctior multo, et emendatior. Amstelodami, apud Andream ab Hoogenhuysen,* 1688. 4 p. l., 928 [8] p. 22½ cm. Copies of these editions, as well as more than 20 other editions in various languages, are to be found in or listed by the Library of Congress. The latest of these is that issued by the Carnegie Foundation for International Peace as No. 17 of their *Publications,* 1934. It is to be noted that the English editions are translations sometimes from the Latin, sometimes from one or the other of the French editions; again they are editings from earlier English editions. The American editions, until this latest in 1934, have been largely from the English edition of Chitty, with 'cases' cited closer to the memories of the readers of their current generation of lawyers. Each of the many editions of this work is notable for containing a great many contemporary illustrations, making more apt the points of international law originally voiced by Pufendorf, but 'dressing' the exposition of these with more and more modern cases by way of elucidation of the legal discriminations and principles outlined in the work. The ancient and honored position of this long series of repeated publications of the legal principles enunciated by the Baron Pufendorf makes it the more unfortunate that the series as a whole is not generally appreciated because of the great scattering of the volumes even in larger libraries that do possess many of the editions. This is due to the spelling of the name, primarily; also, to the fact that some titles and cover titles have used the names of the translator-commentators, who have amplified the case-illustrations, without greatly changing the main body of the legal doctrines of Pufendorf. Certain slight differences in the wording of the title itself, in various translations, especially the secondary ones, also has added to the propensity for the volumes to get separated in cataloguing, as library cataloguing methods have altered with the passage of so many years. Further separation today is noticeable, owing to the propensity to deploy such old volumes to 'rare book divisions' rather than to keep them in the general collections on international law. From the point of view of these despatches from Naples, it is of interest to note that, thus early, our ministers, and indeed the State Department itself, which then had but recently added the Pufendorf work to its own library, was sending it forth as an integral part of the 'diplomatic trunk' to implement the thinking of its diplomats abroad.

[48] Instruction No. 5, Nov. 24, 1838, was from Secretary Forsyth to Mr. Throop, transmitting the President's note of ceremony, congratulating the King of the Two Sicilies on the birth of a son, Prince Charles Louis.

yet returned, nor is it certainly known how much longer he will remain absent, although there seems to be a well founded beleif [sic] that he will be here about the middle of the present month.

For the reasons mentioned in my former dispatches I have not thought it expedient to allude to any matter of negociation with the Minister for foreign affairs, and he seems to be equally reserved.

The following correspondence has taken place between us concerning the claim upon our government of an Italian by the name of Gaetano Carusi,[49] who, as a subject, has invoked the influence of the Neapolitan government upon his application for releif [sic]. Supposing it probable from the terms of the note, that Carusi is now in the United States, and perhaps a naturalized citizen, I made a preliminary inquiry of the Minister as to the fact of his present residence. The correspondence is as follows:

"Napoli 24. Novembre 1838. Il Regio Suddito Signor Gaetano Carusi per effetto di convenzione passata in Catania nel 1804 col Capitano I. Hall commandante una frigata Americana vanta un credito di più centenaja di dollari sopra i primi tre anni di servizio da lui intrapresi come Capo-bandista et non compiuti per un congedo forzoso datogli dal Capitano, avanti il termino prefisso.

Reclama egli contro i maltrattamenti, le ingiurie ricevute e contro la insidia tesagli di distrarlo dalla patria con illusorie promesse congedandolo con anticipazione.

Domando [sic] quindi un compenso pe' dispendi sofferti, per aver consumato quanto possedeva ad oggetto di provvedere ai suoi mezzi di esistenza, ed infine per la perdita a cui soggiacque de' suoi effetti che venner gettati a mare dal bordo della fregata Chesapeake ove egli trovavasi inbarcato nel 1807 allorchè la stessa fu smattata da una frigata Inglese nella vicinanza di Baltimora.

---

49 See: United States 23d Cong. 1st sess. House, Reports vol. I, No. 180, Jan. 15, 1834; 24th Cong. 1st sess. House Reports, No. 86, Jan. 6, 1836; 23rd Cong. 1st sess. *House Journal*, Dec. 12, 13, 16, 1833; Jan. 16, 1834; 24th Cong. 1st sess., *Senate Journal*, April 6, May 19, June 30, 1836; 29th Cong. 1st sess., *House Reports*, IV, No. 745, June 17, 1846. For a brief sketch of Gaetano Carusi, his children and band, see Giovanni E. Schiavo, *Italian-American History*. The Vigo Press, N. Y., 1947, 290-291. Mr. Schiavo spells the name Caruso, and explains that it became Carusi later. Gaetano Carusi is described as the organizer and first leader of the United States Marine Band. The Italian text of the following letters contains several obvious mispellings which have not been marked with a [sic].

Duolsi in ultimo dell'inadempimento di un secondo contratto fatto col Generale in Capo dell'armata James Wilkinson col quale gli venner promessi $200 al mese pel mantenimento suo e di sua famiglia a condizione di organizare [sic] et dirigere una banda di 20 individui. La banda sarebbe stata messa in piedi, il servizio prestato per sei mesi, ed il Carusi non avrebbe raccolto che colonnati 100 in virtù di soscrizione fattasi da varii uffiziali commossi a favor del Carusi e indisposti del procedere del generale.

Da questi titoli sorgono le domande del Carusi per oltre colonnati 5,000 fra sorte et interessi per lo periodo di anni 30 elapsi.

Parecchie circostanze, et tra le altre l'ignoranza della lingua non permisero al Carusi di produrre davanti il Congresso le sue ragioni primi del [sic] anno 1829.

Fu nel 1836 che la Camera de' Deputati penetrandosi della giustizia, e delle circostanze del Carusi passò un bill al suo favore di $1000, ma la Camera del Senato fu al contrario avviso, et le speranze de Carusi per questo lieve soccorso non giunsero a realizzarsi.

Trattavasi questo anno di riprodurre l'affare del Carusi, et l'onorevole Senatore Isacco McKim avrebbe assunto l'incarico della mozione.

Il sottoscritto Ministro Segretario di Stato degli affari Esteri nel consegnare in questo esposto la sostanza delle reclamazioni di quel Reggio Suddito, richiama sull'assunto seriamente l'attenzione del Signor Throop, Incaricato d'affari degli Stati Uniti d'America interressandolo perchè mediante la valevole interposizione de' suoi uffici al governo Americano prenda in accurato esame le ragioni et la compassionevole posizione del Carusi, rendendogli quella giustizia che gli è dovuta; e intanto il Sottoscritto non lascia di ripetere al Signor Incaricato d'affari le proteste della sua distinta considerazione

(Signed)   "Il Principe di Cassaro."

"Naples November 28, 1838

Mr. Throop chargé d'Affaires of the United States of America has the honor to acknowledge the receipt on the 26th inst. of the Prince of Cassaro's note dated the 24th inst; and he would be much obliged to the Prince of Cassaro, if he will inform him whether Gaetano Carusi, whose claims upon the American government form the subject of that note, is at present a resident of this Kingdom or of the United States. Mr. Throop avails himself of this occasion to renew to the Prince of Cassaro the assurance of his most distinguished consideration.

(Signed) "E. T. Throop."

"Napoli 29. Novembre 1838.

Il Sottoscritto Ministro, Segretario di Stato degli Affari Esteri, replicando alla nota che il Signor Throop, Incaricato d'affari degli Stati Uniti di America gli ha diretto sotto la data del 28. Novembre cadente ha il pregio di manifestarle che il Signor Gaetano Carusi trovasi stabilito negli Stati Uniti, et le ultime reclamazioni recan la data di Washington.

Il Sottoscritto proffitta [sic] di questa opportunità per ripeter al Signor Incaricato d'affari i sensi della sua distinta considerazione."

(Signed) Il Principe di Cassaro."

"Naples 30 November 1838.

The Undersigned Chargé d'affaires of the United States of America understands the case of M^r. Gaetano Carusi as presented to him in the note, which he has had the honor to receive from his Excellency the Prince of Cassaro, bearing date the 24th of November instant, is as follows:

That Carusi, now a resident of the United States, but a native of this Kingdom, claims compensation from the government of the United States for unrequited services rendered, and certain damages sustained by him, in the non-fulfilment of certain contracts alledged to have been made by him while a subject of his Majesty the King of Two Sicilies with certain Naval & military officers in the American Service.

It is also stated that Carusi caused his claims to be laid before the Congress of the United States, at it's Session in the year 1836,[50] and that the House of Representatives passed a bill allowing him $1000 which did not become a law in consequence of the non-concurrence of the Senate.

It does not appear by the statement whether Carusi's claim was considered and rejected by the Senate, as not being meritorious, or not authenticated by proof, or whether, being presented to that body out of season, it was suffered to fail for want of time to investigate its merits.

---

50 See below, p. 405.

If M^r. Carusi, by voluntarily entering into the service of the government of the United States has suffered wrongs, all the means of redress are as accessible to him as to a citizen, and in applying to the Legislature, instead of the Executive branch of our government he has selected, without doubt, the proper tribunal for the redress of his grievances.

M^r. Throop does not hesitate to assure the Prince of Cassaro that any claim upon the justice of the government which M^r. Carusi may present to Congress, cognizable by that high body, at the proper time, and duly supported by proof will command it's prompt attention and assent.

It will afford M^r. Throop great pleasure to communicate to his government the wishes expressed on this subject by the Prince of Cassaro, and he has no doubt that they will receive the attention due to the high and respected source from which they emanate: The Undersigned avails himself of the occasion to renew to the Prince of Cassaro the assurance of his distinguished consideration. Signed   E. T. Throop."

I took the pains to look up the proceedings in Congress at the Session of 1836 upon this case, and found the facts stated by the Prince of Cassaro substantially correct. Document 86 House of Rep^s. I Sess. 24 Cong. (See Reports of Committees) is the Report[51] in this Case. It is brief and states that Carusi and his three sons, were employed as musicians by the officers of the Mediterranean Squadron for three years, and went with them to America, and were abandoned there before the time had expired, and without a fulfilment of the contract. Although the officers had no authority to make such contracts, the committee reccommended [sic] an allowance of $1000 which passed the house without objection. Four days before the close of the season the bill was taken up in the Senate, and on motion of M^r. Calhoun ^{52} laid upon the table.

As this matter has been brought to the notice of this government, and maintain the proceedings quoted a case of naked injustice and is a matter of small account, I venture to ask whether, to take from this government the power to point to this case as an act of bad faith, it is not of sufficient importance to de-

---

51 For other reports, see above, note 49, p. 402.

52 John C. Calhoun, of South Carolina, (1782-1850). United States Congress, 1811-17; Secretary of War, 1817-1825; Vice-president, 1825-32; United States Senate, 1832-43, 1845-50; Secretary of State, 1844-45. *Biographical Dictionary of American Congress*, 1774-1927, United States Government Printing Office, 1928, 777.

mand more attention on the part of the Executive, so as to expedite the progress of the bill for releif [sic] through Congress. If it should ever be alluded to here again, I should dispair [sic] of making this government, where every thing depends upon the will of the Executive, comprehend the causes which deny or retard the liquidation of the claim. —

I have received from M^r. Marston[53] our Consul at Palermo a letter concerning his Exequatur of which, and my reply, I send copies herewith marked A. and B.

I have no copy of the letters given the department of State on this question, but having an impression that the tenor of them is as I have stated to M^r. Marston, I do not feel authorized to open the matter with this government.

By the 41st. Article of the Report in relation to the Consular establishment, it is made the duty of every consul to appoint consular agents for every port within his district at which he does not reside, whose acts are to be considered as the acts of the consul, so far as regards his own government. This consular agent as I understand the views of the department, is in fact a mere clerk of the consul, holding no official relation to the government, and signing not his own name, but the name of the consul, in all official transactions in which he is the agent. Where, as is the case here, there are several distant ports within the same district such persons, or others clothed with more official authority, are required to give the necessary official ubiquity to the Consul.

But the government here have interposed, what seem to me to be, insuperable obstacles in the way of this arrangement. I understand that it has determined that no person shall exercise consular functions, within the Kingdom, whose authority from his own government to do so has not been recognized by this. Mr. Hammett at Naples and Mr. Payson at Messina, have received Exequators coextensive with their commissions which enable them to place at their respective outposts the consular agents authorized by our law; but as regards M^r. Marston, whose commission is vague, like those of M^r. Hammett & M^r. Payson, but like theirs was intended to embrace a district with more than one port, this Government refuses to give an exequatur

---

53 On J. M. Marston, see note 14, p. 25. See also *Senate Executive Journal*, V, 31, 32, 42.

to extend beyond the port named in his commission, to wit Palermo.

And they are all embarrassed in this manner: First, the local authorities are commanded not to recognize the agents of M^r. Hammett and M^r. Payson, and therefore they cannot transact business with the local authorities, and the consular functions are virtually suspended at those ports, and, in the next place, M^r. Marston being restricted to his port, has no authority even to act himself, at other places.

In order to remove these impediments this government requires, I understand, that the consular commissions shall contain a clause authorizing the consuls to make the appointments required by the 41st and 42nd articles; in which case the local authorities will be directed to respect their acts.

It might reasonably be inferred, that the law directing consuls, to appoint such agents and to give notice of such appointments to the resident minister of the United States, and the local authorities of the place, was meant to provide for something more than a mere clerk, having no existence even by name, in the discharge of his duties, and that some act of recognition by the local authorities might be required.

If we maintain the position that no recognition of these Agents, on the part of this government is necessary, I do not see that we can find fault with it for refusing to transact business with them, as such agents, if it chooses to take that ground. In its present position we can scarcely hope ever to bring this matter to a close by negociation with this government; and our commercial interests, at the out-posts, dependent upon consular interposition must in the meantime suffer.

The only way that I see open to remove this difficulty, if it is admissable, is to alter the form of the consular commissions; and in doing so another source of embarrassment to our consuls here, and of confusion among themselves might be obviated. From the vagueness of Commissions making the jurisdiction dependant [sic] upon the proximity of the ports to the consuls [sic] residence, an inconvenient arrangement of districts and a clashing of authority sometimes occur. If the commission should name the two extreme ports, and include all the coast between them, it would establish certain limits. It is sometimes difficult without a survey to determine to which consul a port belongs; and it very often happens that the duties may be more conveniently performed by a remote than by the nearest consul. For example: I understand from M^r. Hammett that he has until recently considered the whole coast of the southern point of the peninsula of Italy within his district, but some of its ports are nearer to M^r. Payson on the other side of the Strait, in Sicily. He beleives [sic] that it is more convenient for him, residing at the seat of government, to discharge the duties of some of those ports than for M^r. Payson. I do not mean to give this otherwise than as ilustration, and as the views of M^r. Hammett.

I hope to receive instructions in this matter.

On the 28th ultm°. the board of health of this city passed a resolution requiring the same quarantine for cotton, and other susceptible American goods, coming here from the ports of France, Austria, Leghorn and Genoa, as if they came directly from American ports. I am assured from a source almost official, that during the next month, some resolution on the subject of quarantine, favorable to importations from America will be taken.

The Sulphur question between England and this government[54] is not yet settled; and I infer from the addresses which the King is receiving during his present tour in Sicily, signed by persons interested in the manufacture, and published in the official journal in this City, approving of his measures, that he does not mean to retract. It was reported that an official communication, direct from the foreign office in London, was dispatched to this government, couched, in strong, perhaps menacing terms. That the story is not entirely without foundation I infer from M^r. Kennedy's reply to a question which I put to him that the matter was not now in his hands. It is also said, but I cannot vouch for its truth, that the English government has proposed a commercial treaty, which has not been well received here.

I have received no dispatches or other things from the Department since my last.

J. M. MARSTON TO E. T. THROOP

[Enclosure 'A' with Mr. Throop's Despatch No. 3, December 6, 1838.]

Consulate of the United States of America. Palermo. Nov. 19, 1838.

Sir,

I noticed sometime since your appointment as Chargé D'Affaires of the United States near the King of the Two Sicilies, and have been informed of your safe arrival at Naples.

---

54 Re: sulphur question, see footnote 38, page 398.

It becomes necessary for me to address you the present upon the subject of my Exequatur as consul of the United States for this port and District, which I have not yet received, although my commission was presented to his Excellency the Lieut. General of Sicily in February last immediately after my arrival at my post. The reasons of the delay in not granting the customary Exequatur as assigned by the Minister of Foreign Affairs of this Kingdom are these, that my patent does not express in so many words, the faculty of appointing vice consuls, or commercial agents for the United States, at the several outposts, which are nearer to Palermo than to the residence of the other consul of the United States of the United States [sic] in the Island, M^r. Payson at Messino [sic], nor does it name the ports and places within the Consulate. These facts I am aware of, and in conversation upon the subject, with the Secretary of State in this City, we came to the understanding of awaiting your arrival at Naples, and that if you should give such explanations as should be satisfactory the required Exequatur as Consul General would therefore be given to me. The government of the United States have two Consuls General[55] in Sicily, one resident in this city, and the other in Messina, who have exercised the power as intended to be granted in their patents of the appointment of Vice Consuls or Consular Agents in all other ports required, but such appointments have never been legally recognized by this government for the same reasons as stated in not granting my Exequatur such appointments when made ought certainly to be fully acknowledged by the Authorities of this Country. I was allowed to enter upon the duties of my office on the 29th. March last, through a temporary Exequatur from the Lieu^t. General of Sicily[56] until I should receive the full recognition. The offer of an Exequatur for this party only, was made to me, which I respectfully declined to accept, as not being in accordance with the intention of the Government of the United States in my appointment, and I was at the same time

---

[55] As a matter of fact, the United States at no time had "consuls general" in Sicily. In 1838 there were, however, consuls at Messina, Palermo, and Naples. Mr. Throop is accurate in stating that they could appoint vice-consuls, but such were directly responsible to the consul and he, for their acts and duties, to the government in Washington. The exequatur applied to the consul and through him to his appointed assistants.

[56] Onorato Gaetani, Duke of Laurenzana (1770-1857). He was highly esteemed for his straightforward character. In 1821, he was a candidate for the post of minister of the police, and had the Duke of Ascoli declined the appointment, Gaetani would have obtained the post. In 1838, he was appointed Lieutenant General of Sicily. *Almanach de Gotha*, 1840.

informed that it was similar to those my predecessor and M^r. Payson had acted upon.

In consequence of the above arrangement, made with the Secretary of State I have not as yet acquainted our government of the delay thinking it would be unnecessary as you would probably be able to place the matter satisfactorily before the minister, and prevent the necessity of referring it to the Department at home.

I understand that the ports and places embraced within my jurisdiction are Terranova on the South part of the Island round by the West as far East as Cefalù inclusive and all Islands adjacent thereto beyond the ports mentioned to the East come under the Consul in Messina.

E. T. THROOP TO J. M. MARSTON

[Enclosure 'B' with Mr. Throop's Despatch No. 3, December 6, 1838.]

Legation of the United States Naples November 28, 1838.

Dear Sir,

I hasten to acknowledge the receipt of your letter of the 29th inst. & to reply to it's contents.

Being at Washington last Spring and looking over the Archives connected with this Legation, I found that the matter of Exequaturs to consular agents had been a subject of diplomatic correspondence between our government and this. My reccollection [sic] is, that the question, as it exists in your case, was presented by the Neapolitan government to ours on the occasion of an appointment of a consular agent made by M^r. Hammett, who asked for an Exequatur, and it was refused.

On that occasion it was represented to our government that by the laws of this Kingdom no consul could be recognized by the local authorities in the discharge of consular functions, who had not received an Exequatur, and that no Exequatur to consular agent would be issued unless the power of the consul to make such appointments was expressed in his Commission.

To this representation the Secretary of State responded: That a consular agent is not an official person, but the personal representative of the Consul who appoints him, and who is responsible for his acts, and that therefore his official recognition by the government within whose dominions he resides is not necessary; and he accompanied his reply with a copy of the law in relation to the 41st. article as explanatory of his views.

410

I give the above as my reccollection [sic], yet it may not be entirely accurate.

As Mʳ. Hammett as well as yourself have been in collision with the authorities here, and your views as well as his seem to be at variance with those entertained at the department, it appears to me, that any correspondence on my part, with the authorities here, would tend only to involve the question in greater perplexities, and that it is best not to agitate the matter again until we can receive instructions upon it from home. I shall therefore, without delay, state the question to the Secretary of State, and ask for instructions.

I trust I do not mistake your idea in supposing that you do not, at present, desire to have the question discussed on your right to an Exequatur co-extensive with your commission, without embracing in it the power to nominate agents, clothed with official authority.

E. T. Throop to J. Forsyth

Naples January 7, 1839. [Despatch N°. 4.]

Sir,

The King reached this capital, on his return from Sicily, on Saturday the 22ⁿᵈ day of December last; and on the 24ᵗʰ of the same month I addressed a note to the Secretary of State for foreign affairs of which the following is a copy.

"Naples December 24. 1839. The Undersigned Chargé d'Affaires of the United States of America, having been informed that his Majesty the King has arrived in this Capital, is desirous of being presented to pay his respects to him, at the earliest possible period. He therefore has the honor to request his Excellency the Prince of Cassaro Minister, Secretary of State for foreign Affairs to ask for him an audience of his Majesty, and to inform him at what time his Majesty will be pleased to admit him to that distinguished honor.

The Undersigned would also esteem it a favor if the Prince of Cassaro would allow him an interview before his presentation. And he avails himself of this occasion to renew to the Prince of Cassaro the assurances of his high consideration and regard.

signed   E. T. Throop.

I received in reply the following note:

Napoli 28 Dicembre 1838. The Undersigned Minister, Secretary of State of foreign affairs has read the respected letter, written to him on the 24th of this month by M^r. E. T. Throop,, chargé d'affaires of the United States of America, and informs him, that he will present M^r. Throop to Their Majestys, the King and Queen, according to the sovereign orders received, on the first of January, at the circle which, on account of that anniversary, will take place at the Royal Palace at 11½ o'clk A. M.

Mr. Throop is master of the services of the Undersigned whenever he shall manifest a desire for them, as often as he pleases. He will be, therefore, particularly, at home, tomorrow, Saturday, at one o'Clk P. M. In the meantime the Undersigned renews to him the sentiments of his particular esteem and consideration. (Signed) Il Principe Cassaro

On the 30th of December, I found the Prince of Cassaro at his home, and I informed him, that as the King had determined to receive me at a Court Circle, I wished to know what would be the ceremony, and whether his Majesty would expect from me the accustomed address on the reception of a diplomatic representative from a foreign power. He replied that as I was accredited to the Minister of Foreign Affairs, and had entered upon my duties, and was to be presented at a full court, an address which would have been expected at a private audience, would be out of place.

After having disposed of this matter I took the occasion to say, that I had not spoken to him on any subject connected with my mission, as it seemed to me premature to open any negociation before I had been admitted to an audience with the King; but that I desired, after that ceremony should be through, to have an interview with him, on the subject of a commercial treaty. That it was, as I believed a plain matter, presenting but few points, and one upon which I thought, that we could have no great difficulty in coming to an understanding. He replied that he hoped so, and that he would be very ready to converse with me on the subject, at any time; but that it was best to make no appointment, until after the holy day amusements and ceremonies should be passed.

I answered that it was not an affair of immediate urgency, but as he was probably aware, other persons near the throne were desirious of taking an agency in framing a treaty between us, but I refused to give an ear to any suggestions of that nature, and desired to have my correspondence on the subject entirely with him.

I took it for granted that he understood my allusions, as the Minister of Finance had thrust himself into all previous negociations, and was ambitious to get the matter into his own hands, of which the Prince of Cassaro could not be entirely ignorant. The suggestion I saw had it's intended effect, and he replied with more than his wonted energy, that he thought it would not take us long to make a Treaty, and that very considerable progress had been made in one with Mr Davezac before he left. I purposely avoided any remark upon the last allusion, changed the conversation, and soon took my leave.

On the first of January, I met the Prince of Cassaro at Court, and was presented by him to the King and Queen, but as neither of them speak English, and I dare not venture conversation in any other language,[57] what passed between us was interpreted by the Minister. The King said that he hoped my coming here would promote the interests of both countries. I replied, that I was commanded by the President to assure his Majesty of his earnest desire to cultivate the utmost good will, to enlarge the intercourse, and to strengthen and perpetuate the most friendly relations between the United States and the Two Sicilies. To which he replied that he thanked the President, & reciprocated the sentiments.

After the King had passed I turned to the Prince of Cassaro & said, that the King had a disposition to look personally into all his affairs as I was informed, and that if, after a proper understanding between us, he could be induced to give some attention to the examination of the terms of a treaty, the labor of conducting one would be very much releived [sic] of it's difficulties. He replied that he thought it might be done.

On the third instant, I met the Prince of Cassaro at dinner with the Austrian Minister,[58] and before we separated I alluded again to our intended conferences, and he said, that he would be willing to meet me at any time, either at his house, or at his office, and that I would find him any day between the hours of one and three o'clock. He said we would take up the treaty

---

57 It was not until some years later that a spoken knowledge of foreign languages was required of United States diplomatic representatives.

58 The Austrian minister was Count de Lebzeltern Collenbach (Franz). His title was envoy extraordinary and minister plenipotentiary. (*Almanach de Gotha*, 1840). See note 90, p. 302.

which had been partly agreed upon with Mr. Davezac, and examine it and see how far it's terms are acceptable. To this renewed suggestion I found it necessary to reply & said, that I had no objection to that course, but that I was not prepared to say anything in regard to that projected treaty, as it had not been communicated to me in my instructions, and I doubted, from the total absence of any remarks upon it, whether it, or any of it's provisions had been communicated by Mr. Davezac to our government. I added that my idea was, that it would be better in the first place to consider, without the embarrassment of details, the principle which should form the basis of a treaty; and if we would agree upon that, the filling it up would be a light labor.

My view in all this is, in the first place, by canvassing the principle of a perfect reciprocity in all things, to uncover all the impediments in the way of making a liberal treaty. I shall hope by these means, to obtain a view of the engagements of this government, with other nations particularly the English, French and Spanish, and get an insight of the interpretations which they themselves give to their compacts with them. In the next place, to get before the King, if possible, a view of all the advantages, so very obvious, which he may derive from a direct trade with us; and if I make the impression upon him which I hope to do, it will not only enable me to expedite the conclusion of a treaty, but it will forestall the influence which may be employed to embarrass the negociations both by the Minister of Finance, and the diplomatic agents of other governments. All this I wish to effect before others are aware that any negociations are on foot, or at least, of the form in which they are progressing.

The Minister of finance can get possession of the subject, officially, only when it is put into the form of a treaty, and according to the course of these matters, submitted for examination and remark to a board of which he is the head. When it goes into his hands he, as well as his board will be apt to look at it only as a matter of revenue, and as it may affect the interests of the farmers; and from what I learn of his character in regard both to capacity and disposition, I believe nothing would be gained by attempting to conciliate him, or by yeilding [sic] to his approaches.

I do not know, that there is any ground for the rumor I mentioned in a former despatch that there was not a good un-

414

derstanding between the King and the Prince of Cassaro, but I am convinced that the Minister has it in his power to retain his place if he chooses, & I do not beleive [sic] that he has any intention to retire. He is a man of very fair intentions, and I beleive [sic] desirous to conclude a treaty. The King is quite disposed to manage all the affairs of his kingdom with as little interference as possible, or reliance upon his ministers. It is therefore that I am anxious to enlist him in the matter at an early stage of the regociations.

I am apprehensive that I shall find the Treaty partly agreed upon with Mr. Davezac an obstacle to my progress at the outset, which may require considerable time to remove. It is looked upon by the Prince of Cassaro as a thing almost concluded, and it is no easy matter to change the current of the thoughts of these people. The terms, altogether, are too much in favor of the commerce of this country, and some of them are absolutely inadmissible; yet having been passed upon here, by all the departments, I am prepared to expect that they will be tenaciously adhered to at the first.

I shall postpone for a few days my interview in order the better to arm myself with statistics of commerce, of which I am convinced no great knowledge exists on the part of those with whom I am to treat. I feel it also important not to press with an ardor which may give the impression that we consider a treaty with them as a matter of vast importance to us.

The Treaty with England stipulates, for a deduction of ten per cent on the *amount of duties* on the importation of the merchandize or productions of Great Britain & Ireland, and her colonies, possessions & dependencies. Although there is an article in the same treaty which saves to this government the right to grant similar privileges to other nations, yet I understand that by a secret article in the treaty with Spain, which secures to that nation the same privileges, the British government claims by its stipulation to be placed on the footing of the most favored nation, a perpetual exclusive right to the ten per cent deduction.

This government to favor it's navigation allows a heavy deduction, about thirty per cent, from the duty on all goods imported in Sicilian Ships. Under this encouragement some refined sugars have been recently introduced from Boston in Sicilian Ships, and I find that English merchants have become alarmed lest American and other merchandize may be introduced by

415

these means, at a rate lower than British productions,[59] and thus it's trade be indirectly deprived of the advantages secured to it by the treaty. There is some ground for this apprehension, and I am told that it is a subject connected with the sulphur business, of angry remonstrance on the part of the British government, and that they hold in regard to it strong and menacing language. They insist that it is a violation of the Treaty.

These matters together with a recent order prohibiting the exportation of wheat and other grain, before the expiration of the time fixed by a previous order, by which it was allowed, with wheat in the hands of British purchasers here to the amount of several hundred thousand dollars, ready to be shipped, have somewhat disordered the good understanding between the two governments.

In my last I mentioned a rumor, that Breat Britain had tendered a commercial treaty, which was not well received. The response, which rumor attributed to the Minister of Finance, was in classic language, that he looked with suspicion upon the tender of such specious favors. I believe that some advances towards a commercial treaty have been made from that quarter, and that in view of the matters I have mentioned, the British government would be willing to exchange its present treaty for one more liberal in it's [sic] principles.

I have received, this day, by the way of Liverpool, under cover from the Department of State a copy of the convention with Texas for running the boundary line,[60] and a copy of the Treaty with the Peru-Bolivian confederation.[61] I also received, by mail this same day, the London Times, containing the President's message, which I read with very great satisfaction, and immediately sent with a proper prostestando as to the comments, to the Prince of Cassaro for his perusal.

I have been very unfortunate in this dispatch paper which I got in New York & which I find very difficult to write upon.

---

[59] See: Great Britain. *Accounts and Papers. Revenue, population, commerce. 1844.* XLVI, 217. This publication contains various accounts relating to the trade, shipping, value of imports and exports of the Two Sicilies, 1837-40.

[60] On April 25, 1838, the United States concluded a treaty with the Republic of Texas, concerning the boundary. For text see: Miller, *op. cit.*, IV, 133-134; notes by Miller, *ibid.*, 134-142; map, 144.

[61] On Nov. 30, 1836, the United States concluded a treaty of Peace, Friendship, Commerce, and Navigation with Peru-Bolivia Confederation. For text, see: Miller, *op. cit.*, IV, 71-96; notes by Miller, *ibid,* 96-106. This treaty was proclaimed on Oct. 3, 1838. Because of alteration in the political situation in Peru, this treaty, though proclaimed, was only partly operative. See Miller, *ibid,* IV, 106.

I shall be obliged to procure better paper. The ship, which contains some books which I left in London with my agent to be forwarded, without delay, and my stationary [sic], is now at Quarantine in this port, and I have not been able to obtain a delivery of the articles.

My account of contingent expenses up to the thirty first day of December will be made out and forwarded, as soon as I receive from London the account there, which I have directed to be forwarded to me up to that date.

E. T. THROOP TO J. FORSYTH

Naples February 6, 1839 [Despatch N° 5]

Sir,

By the last dispatch, which I had the honor to transmit, I informed you that the Prince of Cassaro was ready to fix upon a day for an interview on the subject of a commercial treaty. I did not ask an early appointment for the reason mentioned in my last, and also for another which still exists and prevents me from now urging any thing upon the particular attention of the Minister of foreign affairs. I allude to the existing carnival, during which every body is absorbed in amusements, and is both unwilling and unfitted to consider business matters presenting much of importance or perplexity. It will end with the twelfth day of the present month, and be followed by a season of abstinence both in diet and amusements better fitted to the consideration of important State affairs.

Nevertheless I asked an interview which was fixed for the twenty-sixth of January, at the Minister's house. I opened the conversation by saying that it was understood by my government when Mr. Davezac took his leave of this Court, that the subject of a commercial treaty was to be kept in view, and that his Majesty had expressed a desire to resume the negociation at a future time. That it was the policy of our government to regulate its commercial intercourse with other nations by compact, and that in accordance with that policy, it desired a treaty with this government, if one could be arranged upon terms which would promote the interests of both, and that this desire, connected with the favorable disposition manifested by his Majesty was the principal inducement for my appointment to this Mission. That when I alluded to a treaty on a former occasion he spoke of one partially agreed to with Mʳ. Davezac, but I had no instructions in relation to it, and that I inferred therefrom that the records of our department of State furnished no evidence of any terms of a treaty which had been considered and assented to, growing out of M^r. Davezac's negociation.

He replied, that it was true that the disposition existed on the party of the King to make a treaty, and that the terms of one had been discussed, and nearly all assented to, and that they were upon the point of concluding one when Mr. Davezac was suddenly called upon to leave this Court and return to his post at Holland. That M^r. Davezac brought with him, on his arrival a letter by which he was accredited to the King, and on his taking leave he presented a letter from General Jackson[62] the President to the King, in which he informed him of the necessity for the withdrawal of M^r. Davezac, and of his wish to renew the negociation at a future day, in which the King concurred. He then asked me if I had not found among M^r. Davezac's papers the project of the treaty to which he alluded. I replied that I had found a paper in the Italian language, which purported to be a treaty, but that it was connected with no memorandum, shewing that it had been considered, or any part of it agreed to. That he said must be the paper, as the articles had been drawn out fairly, and at full length.

I then told him, that I had examined that paper, and if he was right in his conjecture, I felt bound to say, that the relations which we endeavoured to establish with foreign powers, and which we had provided for in most cases by the treaties we had made with them, was upon the most liberal principles of commercial intercourse, and that some of the Articles of this projected treaty, conflicting with our engagements to other powers, could never receive the sanction of our government.

He then asked me what would be my choice in conducting the negociation, whether to continue it where it was left by M^r. Davezac, or to begin it anew. I replied that upon the supposition that what I had seen was M^r. Davezac's treaty I should certainly choose to commence the negociation anew; and in doing so I would ask him to look first at the basis of a treaty upon the most liberal principles of reciprocity. He said he had no objections to that course, and that he would take the orders of the King upon the subject.

He then asked me what treaties we had with other nations.

---

62 Andrew Jackson was President of the United States from March 4, 1829 to March 4, 1837.

I mentioned Austria, Prussia, Russia, the Hanseatic Republic, Sweden and Denmark, most of which were of recent date; and that they were liberal and generally (that with Austria for example) established entire freedom and mutuality. That we had treaties also with England and France, which were reciprocal but restricted, owing probably to the inherent nature of our intercourse with them.

He then said you would propose a treaty like that you have with Austria.[63] Yes, I replied, as far as regards the general principles. We can examine the basis, leaving details for after consideration, and if our views harmonize we will see if there are any obstacles in the way of carrying them out, and endeavor to remove such as we may discover.

I then asked him if there was any thing in their treaties with other powers, England, France or Spain, which would interfere with the basis proposed: —

To which he replied, that on a compromise of some claims growing out of ancient relations, this government had stipulated to favor the commerce of the nations named by a deduction of twenty per cent upon their duties. I told him that I had seen the treaty with England, and that this government reserved the right to grant similar privileges to other nations. He said that was true, but that there was a secret article in the treaty which did not appear in the printed copy. I told him that I understood that such an article accompanied the treaty with Spain, and that England claimed the benefit of it, under their right to be placed upon the footing of the most favored nation. He said that the treaties with the three powers were exactly alike, and that he would collect them together some day and shew them to me.

I then observed, that the stipulation in the English treaty was in favor of British productions only, and not of their navigation,

---

[63] A treaty of commerce and navigation between the United States and Austria had been concluded on Aug. 27, 1829. Miller, *op. cit.*, III, 507-517; notes by Miller, *ibid*, 516-521. A treaty of commerce and navigation (16 Articles) with Prussia, signed in Washington, May 1, 1828; ratifications exchanged at Washington, March 14, 1829; proclaimed March 14, 1829. Miller, *op. cit.*, 427-439; notes by Miller, *ibid*, 440-445. Russia signed a convention for the settlement of claims, March 17, 1828. Miller, *op. cit.*, 421-425, but on Apr. 27, 1824, had signed a treaty of navigation, fishing, trading, and the Northwest coast of America. Miller, *op. cit.*, 151-155; Miller's notes on the treaty, *ibid.*, 156-162. Under date of May 19, 1828, there was enacted a United States Statute for punishment of contraventions of the fifth article of the treaty between the United States and Russia. 4 *Statutes at Large*, 276. Sweden and Norway signed a treaty of commerce and navigation on July 4, 1827. Miller, *op. cit.*, 283-301; notes by Miller, *ibid.*, 301-308. Denmark signed a treaty of friendship, commerce and navigation, on Apr. 26, 1826. Miller, *op. cit.*, 239-243; notes by Miller, *ibid.*, 243-248.

and that I did not see how the granting of similar privileges to the productions of other countries could interfere with their engagements with England.

He seemed to reflect upon this, as upon something new to him, but I was at a loss to determine whether he was struck with the truth of the remark, or whether he was pondering upon something in the Secret Article which destroyed the force of it. That the latter might be the case I apprehended from a reply of Sir Frederick Lamb,[64] who happened to be here, to a remark I made to him for the purpose of ascertaining the value which the British government place upon their privilege. I said him [sic], I do not see that this privilege in favor of your commerce is of much importance — None in the least was his reply, except that we can annoy them with it, and if they grant privileges to you, or to any other nation, we will be entitled to the deduction of the ten per cent upon such privileges.

I undertook to point out to the Prince of Cassaro some of the benefits to this country from a direct commerce with ours. That as a nation we were great consumers of foreign articles; and that nearly all the productions of this Kingdom, agricultural, mineral and manufactured which are the materials of it's [sic] export trade were not produced by us but enter into our consumption. — That we draw our supplies of them principally from the Mediterranean, but that the Kingdom of the Two Sicilies furnish only a very small proportion of them. I then enumerated some of the principal articles, such as silks, wines, oils, almonds, fruit, fresh & dry, sulphur, Barilla &c. which they now have in abundance, and many more articles, now of little consideration, but which they have the means of producing, and which would grow into importance under the impulses which the industry and the ingenuity of their people would receive, from the demand augmented by a new market. I observed, that this Kingdom from it's fruitful soil, mild climate, active and ingenious population and favorable commercial position ought to command the supply of our wants in those articles which it produces in common with France, Spain, Greece, Turkey and the Levant; but that our importations were now chiefly from those countries and England

---

64 James Frederick Lamb, third Viscount Melbourne and Baron Beauville (1782-1853). Diplomat. In 1811 he was secretary of legation; in 1812 he was minister plenipotentiary *ad interim* at the court of the Two Sicilies; in 1813 he was in Vienna; from 1815 to 1820 at Munich; from 1825 to 1827 in Spain; in December, 1827, he was sent to Lisbon as ambassador. In 1831 he was appointed ambassador at Vienna where he remained until 1841, when he retired. (*Dictionary National Biography*, London, Oxford Press, 1921-22, XI, 429-30.)

— That France and England enjoy the largest portion of this trade, because they receive the productions of our soil and industry and our trade with them is a profitable exchange of commodities. — That in enumerating the Articles which we produce for exportation it will be seen that little else than our Tobacco and Saltfish can be brought to this market; and that, rice, flour, pork and all other articles of provisions are produced cheaper here than with us, and that the small amount of cotton which they might want for the supply of their manufactories would do but little towards furnishing outward cargoes to our ships, on voyages here to purchase their productions. — That our ships now hardly ever visit the ports of this Kingdom, this side of the Straits, nor their ships our ports. — To change all this we must be invited to come to them, and to enable us to do so we must be permitted to load our ships wherever we can find Cargoes.

To all this he listened with apparent approbation and assent.

After promising to send him our Treaties for perusal, and a brief note of our commerce in some of the principal productions of the Countries, bordering on the Mediterranean, we parted with an understanding that we would have another interview at a future day.

I have not yet sent either the Treaties or the note, intending to reserve them until after the termination of the Carnival. I intend then to ask an interview in which we will examine both their and our treaties, and when I hope to have a better view of the ground to be occupied in the future progress of the negociation.

I have nothing to communicate of general affairs worthy your attention, or as affecting our interests here. Nothing further has been done in relation to the Quarantine.

Since my last dispatch I have received four copies of the acts of the last Session of Congress; two of them without direction and one for the Secretary of Legation at Naples, and the other for the Secretary of Legation at Texas, one of which I have given to the Consul. I have also received a copy of the Treaty with Greece.[65]

I am informed that a treaty has been negociated between our Government and Sardinia,[66] and the late Sardinian Secre-

---

[65] On Dec. 22, 1837, the United States concluded a treaty of commerce and navigation with Greece. For text see, Miller, *op. cit.,* IV, 107-121; notes by Miller, *ibid.,* 122-124.

[66] On Nov. 26, 1838, the United States and the Kingdom of Sardinia concluded a treaty of commerce and navigation. For text, including a Separate Article, see Miller, *op. cit.,* IV, 145-161.

tary[67] of Legation at this Court who is about to return to Turin, has promised to inform himself and send me a memorandum of it's [sic] principal provisions.

I have no acknowledgement of the receipt of any of my letters addressed to the Department from this Capital or from any other part of Europe.

My account of Expenditures from the contingent fund is not transmitted herewith, because my agent at London, (M^r. Miller) has neglected to send me his part of the account up to the first of January, as he had promised to do.

E. T. THROOP TO J. FORSYTH

Naples March 6. 1839. [Despatch No. 6.]

Sir,

I have the honor to acknowledge the receipt from the Department of State of Dispatch N°. 5, dated 24th Novr. 1838, forwarded by McNair & Dutton from Liverpool, which came to hand on the 19th February.

I transmitted the President's letter addressed to the King and the copy of it which accompanied that dispatch to the Minister of State for foreign affairs with a note of which the following is a copy.

"Naples February 26 1839.

The undersigned Chargé d'Affaires of the United States has been commanded to convey to His Majesty a letter from the President of the United States in reply to a communication from

---

67 The Secretary of the Sardinian Legation at Naples was Manfredo Bertone de Sambuy. Chevalier. After having served as diplomatic attaché at Munich and The Hague, he was appointed, on June 11, 1836, secretary of the Legation at Rome, and in Febr. 1837, chargé d'affaires at Naples. After 1838, he became secretary of that Legation; and after Apr. 18, 1838, following the departure of Minister Pallavicini, de Sambuy remained as Sardinian chargé d'affaires at Naples, continuing in this capacity to July 12, 1838, when he informed the Bourbon Government that Nicolò Crosa di Vergagni had been appointed as the new Sardinian envoy extraordinary and minister plenipotentiary at Naples. On June 1, 1838, de Sambuy was also appointed chargé d'affaires of His Royal Highness the Infante Duke of Lucca. On Sept. 13, 1839, de Sambuy was replaced by the Marquis Doria di Dolce Acqua as secretary of the Sardinian Legation at Naples. From Mar. 28, 1841 to May 9, 1843, de Sanbuy was chargé d'affaires at St. Petersburg, later he was chargé at Lisbon, and still later he was charged with a special mission to Madrid. After leaving the office of the Secretary of Foreign Affairs, he was appointed envoy extraordinary and minister plenipotentiary and, on Oct. 17, 1848, he was accredited to Munich and Dresden, whence he was recalled on Dec. 10, 1850. On Oct. 30, 1851, he was accredited to Rome, but was recalled on Dec. 2, 1852. He was retired on Dec. 23, 1855. *Archivio di Stato*, Naples, Foreign Affairs — Folder No. 2038.

422

His Majesty, announcing the fact that Her Majesty the Queen had given birth to a Prince on whom has been conferred the name of Luigi Maria. In fulfilment of this duty he has the honor now to transmit to his Excellency the Prince of Cassaro, Minister Secretary of State for foreign affairs the said letter and a copy of the same. — And he has the satisfaction at the same time to renew to his Excellency the assurances of his most distinguished consideration: signed, E. T. Throop."

To which I received the following reply:

Napoli 28, febbraio 1839.

The Undersigned, Secretary of State for foreign Affairs will (with eagerness)[68] hasten immediately to place in the hands of the King his master, the letter which M^r. Throop Chargé d'Affaires of the United States of America forwarded with his note of the 26 inst. addressed to his Majesty from the President of the United States in answer to the Communication made to him of the fortunate delivery of her Majesty the Queen.

And he renews to him the sentiments of his particular esteem and consideration. Signed, Il Principe di Cassaro."

In the further prosecution of the negociation for a commercial treaty I sent, on the second day of March instant, to the Minister of foreign affairs, the 8th volume[69] of the laws of the United States, that he might peruse in it, our treaties with Austria, Prussia, the Hanseatic Republic [sic][70] and Sweden and Norway, and I accompanied it with the following note and memorandums.

"Naples March 2, 1839.

M^r. Throop chargé d'Affaires of the United States presents his compliments to His Excellency the Prince of Cassaro and has the honor to send him a volume of the laws of the United States, in

---

[68] The original manuscript shows a faint line drawn through the words within the parenthesis in the English translation of the letter made by Mr. Throop in his own hand. The line drawn through the words "with eagerness" indicates that Mr. Throop himself realized that he had overemphasized the Prince's attitude, thereby crossing out that phrase and substituting the words "hasten immediately."

[69] Bioren and Duane edition, see below, note 73, page 425.

[70] The Hanseatic League comprised the Republics of Lübeck, Bremen, and Hamburg, often referred to as the Hanse Cities or the Hanseatic City States.

which he will find the Commercial treaties[71] made between the
United States and Austria, Prussia, The Hanseatic Republic,
[sic] Sweden and Norway. In an accompanying memorandum
M^r. T. has noted the pages in the book where these several
treaties are to be found, the years in which they were conducted,
and those principles established by them which M^r. T. wishes
to bring to the notice of the Prince of Cassaro.

A treaty was concluded between the United States and Russia
in the year 1832 embodying the same principles, with some variation in regard to port charges and tonnage. Mr. T. cannot, at
present, lay his hands upon the book containing that treaty, nor
upon one containing a treaty with Denmark, on account
of the derangement of his library by his recent change of residence; but he will have the honor of submitting them in a few
days to the Prince of Cassaro, together with a copy of a treaty
recently concluded with Greece.[72]

M^r. T. also sends herewith a memorandum of some of the
articles of merchandize which the United States import, produced
principally in the countries bordering upon the Mediterranean;
and in fixing the amount has taken the year 1836, as affording
a fair average.

Mr. T. will be particularly obliged to the Prince of Cassaro,
if he was find [sic] upon some day, as soon as it will suit his
convenience, when M^r. T. may have the honor to wait upon him,
and examine with him the treaties herein alluded to as also to
pursue the conversation upon the subject introduced in the last
interview.

---

[71] See for these treaties (texts only) *United States Statutes at Large, VIII,
European Treaties* Prussia—Treaty of amity and commerce, July 11, 1799 (text
in English and French, on facing pages), 162-177; *ibid.,* 378, Prussia, — Treaty
of commerce and navigation, May 1, 1828; *ibid.,* 398, Austria, treaty of commerce and navigation, Aug. 27, 1829; *ibid.,* 366, Hanseatic Republics of Lübeck,
Bremen and Hamburg — Convention of friendship, commerce and navigation,
Dec. 20, 1827; *ibid.,* 346, Sweden and Norway. Treaty of commerce and navigation, July 4, 1827. For these treaty texts, with historical notes on the negotiations,
see Miller, *op. cit.,* II, 433-456; III, 427-445; 507-521; 387-404, and additional
article to 1827 Hanseatic treaty, signed June 4, 1828, *ibid.,* 447-450; Sweden
and Norway, *ibid.,* 283-308.

[72] The treaty of commerce and navigation was concluded between the United
States and Greece, Dec. 10-22, 1837; see *Statutes at Large,* VIII, 498-509; also
Miller, *op. cit.,* IV, 107-124. On November 26, 1838, a treaty of commerce
and navigation had been concluded with Sardinia. See *Statutes at Large,* VIII,
512-523, including the 'separate article'; Miller, *op. cit.,* IV, 145-169.

Memorandum.

Year
1829. Treaty with Austria, see
    page 946.[73]
1828. Prussia p. 924.
1827. Hanseatic Republic
    p. 896.
1827. Sweden and Norway,
    p. 868.

The treaties referred to in the margin have the same fundamental principles.

The preamble of the treaty with Austria shews the intentions of the parties to have been the adoption of entire freedom of navigation and a perfect reciprocity.

1. By Art. 1. the same privileges in Commerce are secured to the inhabitants of each Country in the ports of the other, as are enjoyed by the inhabitants of the same country in their own ports.
2. By Art. 2. the same tonnage and port charges in each others ports are to be levied upon Vessels arriving, belonging to the two parties without discrimination.
3. By Art. 3. & 6. the same with regard to imports, exports, bounties & drawbacks.
4. By Art. 4., which is an explanatory article to remove all possible misapprehension, it is declared that these favors are to be enjoyed in each others ports, whether the Vessels or their cargoes arrive from their own or from foreign ports.
5. By Art. 5. the productions of each country are to enjoy in the country of the other party the same privileges as to duties, exportations and importations which are enjoyed in that country by the most favored nation.

A treaty in all respects similar was concluded with Denmark[74]

---

[73] The 8th volume of the *Laws of the United States* is here referred to in the Bioren & Duane edition, as is shown by the page citations. This is *Laws of the United States*, Mar. 4, 1827-1833, including all European, Barbary and Indian treaties, negotiated and ratified within that period, and several other valuable documents which have resulted from or are connected with Acts of Congress and treaties, with copious notes and references. Washington, printed by W. A. Davis, 1835, vol. 8. Our footnote references to vol. 8 of the *Laws of the United States* refer to the 1853 edition, published by Little Brown & Co. of Boston, and edited by Richard Peters. This edition (1853) restricted itself to the texts of the treaties, whereas the 1835 B & D edition in its vol. 8 gave notes and references. The 1853 edition of the *Laws* is also called familiarly, the 'stereotyped edition.'

[74] No treaty was concluded with Denmark in 1822; this date has been verified by Mr. Throop's original despatch and is found to be 1822. What he should have made reference to, in this context, was the treaty of commerce and navigation concluded with the United States in 1826, for which see *Statutes at Large*, VIII, (1853 edition), 340-345; also Miller, *op. cit.*, III, 239-248. The treaty in 1830 dealt with claims.

in 1822 — and it is said that one has been recently negociated with Sardinia upon the same terms.

Naples March 2. 1839

A statement of certain Articles of merchandize imported into the United States of America, annually, being productions principally of the countries bordering upon the Mediterranean.

Value in Dolls. [sic]

Silk goods (other than India) $19,357,000
from France $15,131,000
    England 3,310,000
    Italy & Sicily 446,000

                                $18,887,000

Sewing Silk 669,000
    France 205,000
    England 131,703
    Italy & Sicily 346,690

                         $688,832[75]

Goods composed of Silk & worsted 3,171,000
    from France 2,329,227
    England 784,313

                    $3,113,540

Wines, Gall^{s}. 7,564,784 ....$ 4,282,451
    France Gall^{s}. 3,680,826 $2,077,800
    Sicily 534,407   207,642

          Gall^{s}. 4,215,233 $2,285,442

The residue is the production of Spain, Austria, Germany, Italy & other countries bordering upon the Mediterranean.

Spirits (not manufactured from grain) ....$ 1,538,770
    France .... G^{s}. 17,835....$16,247
    England .... 9,370.... 8,976
    Sicily .... 57,497.... 37,490
    Italy .... 38,016.... 25,515
    Trieste .... 35,898.... 27,351
    Greece & Turkey ... 12,731.... 9,287
    Spain .... 41,264.... 31,663
    Malta & Gibraltar .. 16,130.... 12,390

        G^{s}. 228,740 $168,919

---

[75] Total should read $683,393.

```
Sulphur  ...................................  $130,000
    France  ........................  33,750
    England  .......................  14,686
    Italy  ..........................  29,619
    Sicily  .........................  29,616
    Trieste  ........................  13,658
                                     ─────────
                                      $121,329
Barilla  ....................................  144,000
    England  .......................  19,741
    Teneriffe & Canaries ............  90,000
    Madeira  .......................  13,750
    Italy  ..........................   9,784
    Sicily  .........................   7,955
                                     ─────────
                                      141,230
Dried  fruits  lbs.  27,507,409  ...................$ 1,731,936
    Almonds  .....................$414,641
    Currants  ....................  91,096
    Prunes  ......................  63,209
    Figs  ........................ 135,072
    Raisins  .....................1,028,000
        From  Italy  ...........$  16,400
              Sicily  ........   26,000
              Trieste  ........  106,000
              Turkey  ........  140,000
```

Dye woods & stuffs - opium - coarse wool - jewelry - plain glass-
ware - paper hangings - vinegar - cordage hemp & Fresh fruit,
are among our importations & some of them to large amount.

Naples March 2. 1839.

My object in making the above statement of our commerce in the
Mediterranean was to lay before the Minister a table in which he
could see at a glance: first, that the Kingdom of the Two Sicilies
does not furnish our trade with its proper proportion of those
productions, and what countries in its vicinity are its competitors,
and securing our trade by a more liberal policy; and secondly,
that such of its productions as reach us come indirectly through
England and France, to the prejudice of Neopolitan [sic] industry & navigation.

On the fifth instant I met the Prince of Cassaro at an evening party, and for the purpose of drawing him into some conversation, I reminded him of my having sent him[76] a book containing some of our Treaties.

He seemed very ready to speak upon the subject of our negociation, and in the most friendly and frank manner said, that a treaty with us would depend very much upon the result of the negociation now pending with England. That the present obstacle was the existing treaty with England, and the English had submitted to them a project for a commercial treaty in which they proposed to relinquish their present advantage of ten per cent reduction upon the duties of importation. That if this government should accept the proposal it would be an act changing their entire policy, and they would be open to treaties with all other governments upon liberal terms. It seemed to me that he was pleased with the idea, and I received from the conversation an impression that the arrangement would be made.

I did not fail to hint that the policy of free trade was gaining ground, and had been adopted, in some shape, by nearly all the European nations; and to suggest the advantages which the Kingdom of the Two Sicilies, from its advantageous commercial position in the centre of the Mediterranean designed by nature as a depot and mart of it's productions, would derive from the adoption of that policy.

The British government has learned that it is easy for this government to evade their treaty, and deprive them of all the advantages stipulated, by measures avowedly to encourage their own navigation; and their present movement confirms the opinion which I expressed in a former dispatch, that they would be willing to relinquish their exclusive privileges for the more certain advantages of a free and open trade.

Sir Frederick Lamb, who accounted to me for his presence here, by a desire to winter in a better climate than Vienna, is charged, I find, with the negociation, while M^r. Temple, the resident Minister is in England, & M^r. Kennedy, the Secretary of Legation is the ostensible representative. Sir Frederick is unquestionably the abler man, and he will endeavor to secure, in lieu of whatever he relinquishes some equivalent favor; but if he can obtain none I am confident that he will accept an unqualified reciprocal treaty.

It will be my endeavor to watch it's progress, and see that nothing is acceded [sic] to which may enterfere with our trade,

---

[76] See above, page 423.

and aid in bringing to a conclusion such a treaty as can be won only by vanquishing the prejudices of these people, and which will leave a door open to the friendly reception of a proposition from us for a treaty upon the same basis.

To place myself in a position to keep the negociation in sight I repeated to the Prince of Cassaro an observation, which I formerly made, that it did not seem to me, that the British treaty stood in the way of a treaty with us, and I obtained from him a renewal of his promise to shew me the Secret Article and to explain to me all the difficulties growing out of it.

If, as I anticipate matters shall so shape themselves here, that this government will tender us a treaty of reciprocity, there are some very important details to be considered, in regard to which I desire to have the views of the government. I allude particularly now, to the duties upon wines and sewing silk on their importation into our Country, and to the introduction of tobacco here.

The preference secured to French wines in our treaty with France, is limited to 1842, and if nothing better can be done, we may stipulate to place the wines of this Kingdom upon the most favored footing, and postpone its operation until the year 1842.

[Tobacco here is a government monopoly, from which it derives great profit, and which it would relinquish with the greatest reluctance. However small may be the prospect of success, it's importance to us makes it worthy of a struggle.] Sewing silk is the great stable commodity of this part of the Kingdom, which finds it's way to our market, of which about seven hundred and fifty thousand dollars worth comes to us directly & indirectly. The heavy duty under which it now labors is under process of reduction by the working of our compromise tariff law, so that in 1842 it will be limited to twenty per cent.

I am not aware of the exact ground of the policy of our government in imposing a heavy duty upon sewing silk, while it admits to entry silk goods free of duty. If it was to give protection to a branch of industry at that time struggling to establish itself in the Eastern States, it may be important for me to know whether the same reasons exist for continuing the policy which influenced the adoption of it. As tobacco is almost the only production of our industry which is sure of finding a market here, and sewing silk is the most important article to Naples with which it furnishes us, they may be brought to bear upon each other in settling the terms of the treaty. The recent great efforts made to introduce the culture of silk with us have been

429

successful in the sterile plains of New Jersey & farther south along the sea coast; and this takes from the subject, it seems to me, the sectional character it had at the time of the last adjustment of the tariff.

I do not know how much importance this subject has with this government, but, as this is the only country in Europe which produces sewing silk for market, our duty seems to be invidious, and at war with the principles of free trade which we endeavor to inculcate with them.

I take the liberty to allude to this matter now in the hope that the government will put me in possession of it's [sic] views upon that and other important topics before it may become necessary to discuss them.

I send herewith my account of expenditures of the contingent fund made up to the 31ˢᵗ Decʳ. last.

E. T. THROOP TO J. FORSYTH

Naples, April 22ᵈ, 1839.

Dear Sir,

Mʳ. Persico[77] is very anxious to obtain an answer to his application for leave to use the marble of Ravaccioni for his group instead of the Statuary marble mentioned in his contract.

He says that the marble of Ravacconi [sic] is free from defects, more compact than the other kind, and is used by artists for Statues designed for exposure to the weather.

The Statuary marble he says, is not to be had, and he can do nothing towards his work until he receives an answer. I write this at his earnest request.

E. T. THROOP TO J. FORSYTH

Despatch N°. 7. [No date][78]

Sir

I have the honor to acknowledge the receipt of bundles of newspapers forwarded from the Department, completing the files of the Globe to the 14ᵗʰ of January. Also a bundle, con-

---

77 Luigi Persico was an Italian artist in the United States. See, *Enciclopedia Italiana*, 1933, XIX, 1037; William Hensel, "An Italian artist in old Lancaster, Luigi Persico, 1820." A paper read before the Lancaster County Historical Society, March 8, 1912. Lancaster, Pa., (New Era Print. Co.) 35 p. See also Boulware Despatches, *hic opus*, pp. 529, 542, 552, 556.

78 Although this despatch [No. 7] is not dated, a notation indicates that it was received by the State Department on June 2, [1839].

taining Seybert's, Pitkins[79] and Watterston & Van Zands[80]
statistics. They were forwarded to me by McNair & Dutton of
Liverpool and reached me in good condition. I have nothing else
from the Department since my last dispatch. My dispatch N°. 6
was mailed here the 12th March; and it was accompanied by my
account of contingent expenditures made up to the 31st of December. My account for the last quarter is delayed for vouchers
from London not yet received, and will be made out and forwarded as soon as I am possessed of them.

I closed the history of my negociations here, in the last
dispatch with the information that the Prince of Cassaro had
promised to shew me the secret article in the treaties with
England, France and Spain, and to explain the difficulties growing out of it.

I afterwards asked an interview of him and he agreed to see
me at the foreign office on the 16th of March. He was engaged
with Sir Frederick Lamb and M^{r}. Kennedy when I arrived. After
their departure I saw him, and he commenced the conversation
by repeating the remark, that the obstacle to a treaty with us was
the treaty with England, and if that should be removed they
would be open to treat upon liberal terms. As I was anxious to
ascertain, as near as possible, the terms upon which the English
proposed to treat, to find out if they designed any shackles upon
this government to embarrass it's [sic] negociations with others, I
enquired of the Minister whether the English claimed any equivalent for the privileges they proposed to Surrender. He replied
that they did not, but that their object was to get rid of the
discriminating duties, and port charges, so as to place their
vessels in the ports of this Kingdom upon an equality with
those of the nation.

I then remarked to him that I supposed the treaty, if one
should be made would be so shaped that the British could have
no pretence for claiming the ten per cent upon the grounds of
their rights as one of the most favored Nations: and I then

---

[79] For Seybert, see note 43, p. 399; for Pitkin, see note 44, pp. 399-400.

[80] Watterston, George (1783-1854) and Nicholas Biddle Van Zandt, *Tabular
statistical views of the population, commerce, navigation, public lands, post office establishment, revenue, mint, military and naval establishments, expenditures and public debt of the United States.* Pubd. under the patronage of the
Congress of the United States. Washington, printed by J. Elliott, 1829. 135 pp.,
23$^{1}/_{2}$ x 29 cm. See also, *Continuation of the tabular statistical view . . .* Washington, Way & Giddeon, printers, 1833.

inquired whether a treaty with England would remove all the difficulties, or whether it would not also be necessary to consult France and Spain. His reply was, that France would be called into consultation, and that no difficulty was apprehended from Spain.

I remarked that the Government of Spain was in that disordered state that it might be difficult to negociate with that nation, or at least to bring a matter of that kind to a speedy issue. He said that this government had never recognized the existing government of Spain, but that the British would undertake to arrange that matter, and obtain the consent of Spain. I then put this question to him: Suppose that a treaty shall not be made with England, is there any thing in your existing relations with them which prevent you from allowing the deduction of ten per cent upon British productions, say of the West Indies, brought here in American vessels, inasmuch as your engagements with them are in favor of their industry and not of their navigation? He answered by saying, that the secret article secured the advantages to their navigation also; and he produced the treaty & read the secret article with every thing that bore upon it:

The Secret article, so far as it interests us, is this in substance, and nearly in terms: That if the Sicilian government shall, at any time grant a reduction of duties to any other nation, it shall, at the same time make a similar reduction in favor of Great Britain, so that they shall always enjoy the advantage of ten per cent.

This is evidently no extension of the original grant, but was rendered necessary by the circumstance that the ten per cent was to be deducted from a tariff then existing. It was a provision against any future reduction of their tariff which might nullify the grant. I suggested this to the Minister who seemed perplexed at not finding the article as full to the point as he had supposed, and said that it had always received that construction, but, if I wished, he would have that question put to the Minister of Finance. This I declined for several reasons: that which I assigned to him was, that if a treaty should be concluded with England, all difficulties would be removed; but if none should be made, it would then be in time to consider what could be done without interfering with their engagements. The reason, however, which principally operated with me was, that I had previously, indirectly, procured his opinion, & found that his views of the force of the treaty conceded [sic] with those of the Minister of foreign affairs.

432

The opinions of this government on these questions are influenced by a dread of the English power, and the determined tone in which that government presses upon this it's complaints & views; and I esteem it almost a hopeless job to induce this government to give any new construction to the existing treaty with England which would vary, prejudicially to English interests, the practice here. Unless it should resolve (a thing not to be expected) to put the English power at defiance, however plainly their rights to place by treaty their commerce with other nations upon a liberal footing may appear upon the face of their treaty with England, I entertain but little hope of inducing them to act upon those rights. I look therefore with anxiety & hope to the termination in a treaty, of the pending negociation.

Yet the prospect of such a result is not as favorable at present, as once it seemed to be. The merchants have been consulted and they are so sensible of the injurious effect upon their interests, as well in trade as navigation, of an arrangement which would admit British ships upon a footing of equality with their own, that they have advised against the Treaty. The Ministers are divided I am told. The Prince of Cassaro with a majority of the Cabinet are in favor of it, and the Minister of finance with the minority in determined hostility. The latter functionary is uncompromising in every thing, is a vigilant revenue officer, and has much influence with the King. But an impression has been made upon them, that they are becoming isolated in their policy.

The merchants are favorably disposed towards us, and such is the general feeling, but they dread the English, & would be unwilling to admit any nation to an equal participation in privileges in the ports of this kingdom.

Whatever may ultimately take place, I apprehend that nothing will be immediately effected, as this government is given to procrastination, and a measure which is to change a policy settled for ages, and about which opinions are divided, cannot be suddenly adopted by a government of so little energy as this. Sir Frederick Lamb is gone, whether impatient of the delays he has encountered or not, I cannot say, but there is a rumor that he is to be succeeded by a secret negociator of more skill and knowledge of detail, who has been employed as an adjunct, in the treaties recently made by the British at Constantinople & Vienna.

I ventured to ask M^r. Kennedy a few days since, what progress he was making with his treaty, & he seemed to be quite out of humor at the delays and obstacles they had encountered, and said

433

that it required not only patience, but the most enduring patience to effect anything. His bile, however, seemed more disturbed at the little progress he had made in getting satisfaction for the matters of complaint they had to make, partaking more of a private than of a public nature, I suppose, the wheat & sulphur questions.

I told him that I was anxious that he should conclude a treaty, & would do all in my power to help him forward. He replied that the same dispositions prevailed in the other Legations, and that their negociation was regarded as the pioneer. They wanted, he said, only an unrestricted trade.

The negociation has been, and will be continued in able hands, and I am not without apprehensions of a ruse, covered by their assumption of the obligation to procure the adhesion of Spain. Should a treaty be made to take effect at it's execution, England might find its interests in preventing an arrangement with Spain. While pursuing it's trade under a new treaty, she might urge upon the government of the Two Sicilies it's obligations to Spain, while they remain unchanged, to prevent it from according liberal terms to other nations. They would be very apt to take that ground in relation to a treaty with us, whom they fear as competitors, more than any other nation, and whose negociation they look upon with no friendly eye. If in this manner they could effect delay, they would, in the mean time, become masters of the commerce of the country.

Their principal inducement to the present negociation, in which they magnanimously proffer a relinquishment of the preference they now enjoy in these ports, and ask in return, merely, that their ships may enter upon the same conditions as national ships, is to monopolize the entire trade of the country, by suppressing it's navigation, which, under the encouragement now extended to it, begins to shew some enterprize in distant voyages. In effecting this object they will be careful not to leave an opening; if they can possibly avoid it for a rival like us, whose power of competition is so fully understood.

Desirous to impart to the Minister of foreign affairs my fears upon this subject, I resolved to ask another interview with him, at the earliest period. I meet [sic] him on the evening of the 24th March, & requested him to appoint a time, when he would receive me at his own house, & he fixed upon the Wednesday following. To sound him a little in anticipation, I asked him if it was true, as I had been told, that Sir Frederick Lamb had departed. He replied that he had but that the negociation was still going on. I alluded to Spain, & inquired whether they should make it a condition with England, if they affected a treaty, to obtain the consent of Spain; to which he replied "not at all — we care but little for Spain, and we are not at present upon good terms with' at government. ["] This reply made me still more anxious for the interview, as we could carry our conversation no farther, being surrounded by other persons.

I hardly need say to you, that the cause of legitimacy secures the good will of this government to the camp of Don Carlos of Spain, notwithstanding that the Queen is of this family.

At the hour agreed upon the 28th. of March, I attended at the house of the Prince of Cassaro, but he had just received a summons from the King to attend him, immediately, in counsel, and was occupied in his preparations. At a subsequent time I arranged another meeting with him at the foreign office, at which I attended, but he was then at the Palace with the King, and I have not been able to see him since.

The Arch Duke Charles of Austria[81] has been on a visit here, who, independent of claims to attention from his distinguished personal character, is father of the Queen, and has been treated by the King with the most assiduous Courtesies, and deferential respect. There seemed to be but little time during his stay for the King, or his officers of State to devote to any affairs which were not connected with his visit.

I intend soon to see the Minister of foreign affairs, and as all discussion on the basis of a treaty is, from the position of affairs, necessary [sic] suspended, I shall endeavor to draw him into discussion upon collateral matters. If it should terminate merely in discussion, it shall afford me an opportunity for official intercourse with him.

I shall ask a modification of their laws in regard to the introduction of tobacco into the Kingdom, upon the ground that such a treaty as we offer is so favorable to them, and of so little value to us, that it merits some equivalent; at least, that the few articles we have to bring to this market should not be subjected to extraordinary burdens.

It may perhaps be expedient to give them to understand, that we have it in our power to adopt countervailing measures, and may resort to them, if we do not find a liberal disposition

---

[81] Charles (Archduke). Duke of Teschen (1771-1847). He was born in Florence, the third son of Emperor Leopold I. He was a famous Austrian general.

435

towards us on their part. I am pleased with the move made by M'. Benton[82] on this subject, as it appears to me that our government has so far extended its relations with foreign governments, as to be in a position to take strong grounds with those who manifest a want of liberality; and this government is one with whom energetic measures might be more persuasive than reasoning.

It is exceedingly gratifying to my pride as an American Citizen to see the attitude which the government has taken in regard to the contested boundary, and the unanimity with which it is supported by the nation. —

E. T. THROOP TO J. FORSYTH

Naples May 9. 1849. [Despatch No. 8.]

Sir,

Since the last dispatch which I had the honor to direct to you, I have had the desired interview with the Minister of Foreign Affairs, and I hasten to lay the result before you.

Pursuant to a previous appointment I met the Minister at the foreign office on the 7ᵗʰ of May instant. On opening the conversation, I told him that I was anxious to have something favorable to communicate to my government in regard to our negociation, and that I should be most particularly happy to be able to give it assurances of a reasonable prospect of transmitting a treaty to be laid before the Senate at the opening of the next Session of Congress. I inquired if the negociation with England was still on foot. He replied that it was, and that he should probably be obliged to go to Vienna during the latter part of the present month to meet Sir Frederick Lamb and bring the matter to a conclusion. The King he said was convinced.

I found in the further progress of the conversation that the cabinet had been in session that morning, and had received a report favorable to the new policy, from a commission which the King had created a few days before, for the special purpose of examining the question. The Commissioners were three Citizens

---

82 Thomas Hart Benton (1782-1858). He was a Democratic senator from Missouri, 1821-51; Missouri Compromise Democrat to 33rd Congress, 1853-55. (*Biographical Dictionary of American Congress*, 1774-1927, United States Government Printing Office, 1928, p. 695.) He compiled fourteen volumes of *Abridgement of Debates of Congress* based on Thales and Seaton's *Register of Debates, the Annals of Congress and Notes on Debates*, by John C. Rives. Published, N. Y., 1860-61.

of Naples, not of the Council, & who were supposed to understand the trade and interests of the country. I was apprized of their appointment at the time it took place, and their individual views, from a quarter to which it is not necessary now to allude. I inquired of the Prince of Cassaro whether the Minister of finance had yeilded [sic], and understood from intimation rather than directly, that his opinions were unchanged, but that he would make no resistance.

I then asked him whether France had yet been consulted, and hinted, with all the delicacy possible, the danger of concluding a treaty with England without the previous consent of Spain. He said that nothing had yet been done with France; and that no treaty with England would take effect without the concurrence of Spain.

I infer from all this: that this government is prepared to take the great step, and change it's policy, and that it's first treaty (necessarily preliminary to every other) is to be concluded under the advice of Austria. The French have in fact no Minister here.

Casimir Périer[83] is a young man, and came here commissioned chargé d'Affaires, as locum tenens, to await the arrival of the Duke of Montebello,[84] who had been appointed Minister, but who, on account of the state of political affairs at that time in France, had thought it better to go into the Chamber of Deputies and remain a short time there. France will consequently be represented on this question at Vienna; and the meeting I conclude is to be fixed for the first of June.

While Austria may act as a mediator, she also will be interested

---

[83] Périer, Auguste Victor Laurent Casimir (1811-1876). French politician and diplomat. Entering the diplomatic service in 1832, he later, in 1839, was first secretary in Russia, and in 1843, minister plenipotentiary in Hanover. During the disturbances of 1848, he supported the policies of Guizot. In 1849, he was elected to the Legislative Assembly, taking an active part in the parliamentary debates. He opposed the coup d'etat of Dec. 2, 1851, and he withdrew to private life, devoting his time to studies on political economy. See: Martel, Eloge funèbre de Aug. Cas. Périer (Sénat, séance July 6, 1876; Aug. Collin, Notice sur Casimir-Perier. Nogent-sur-Seine, 1876); Eng. Choulet, La famille Casimir-Périer (Grenoble, 1894); Grande Encyclopédie, no date, XXVI, 377.

[84] Lannes, Napoléon Auguste, Duke of Montebello (1801-1874). French diplomat. In 1828-29, he was attached to the embassy at Rome under Chateaubriand. As a reward for his support of the July Government, he was sent to represent France in Denmark (1833), Prussia (1833), Switzerland (1836). In 1839, he served in the ministry of foreign affairs. An ambassador at Naples, he negotiated the marriage of the Duke d'Aumale (1844). He was minister of the navy and colonies from May 1847 to Feb. 1848. In 1849, he served in the Legislative Assembly where he opposed the policies of the Elysée. He protested against the coup d'état of Dec. 2, 1851, but later supported the Empire which he represented (from 1858 to 1866) at Saint Petersburg. He was appointed senator in 1867. Grande Encyclopédie, no date, XXI, 923-924.

in seeing that the Sicilian Kingdom is left free, and take care that there be no entanglement on account of the manner in which their affairs with Spain are left. She also will be the first to avail herself of the disenthralment of this government, and will conclude a treaty with it, before they separate.

Under other circumstances I should apprehend that the claims of Spain would be treated with too little regard, not as respects herself, but as regards the use which the English might make of it, as I have before mentioned. I inquired of M^r. Kennedy, a few days since, whether Spain was willing to treat, and by the tossing of the head and other significant signs he conveyed to me the idea of an utter contempt for her claims.

To resume the narration of our conversation, — I told the Prince of Cassaro that I should be glad to discuss with him the terms of a treaty between our two governments, to be considered cotemporaneously [sic] to that with England — that I did not see how it could interfere, and that it might perhaps be auxiliary. He said he had no objection, and asked me if I would make him propositions; but he intimated, at the same time, more emphatically than he had done before, the great probability that matters would be brought to a close with England early in June, and that it would be advisable to await that issue.

I then reminded him, that a treaty, should one be made with us, would be so much in their favor, that they had so much to send to us, and we so little of domestic products to return, that I should like to know what equivalent they could give us. — That almost our only production of any value, adapted to their market was tobacco, and that is was now excluded by a monopoly. That it was a subject of deep interest with us, and one which I was specially charged by my government to press upon their consideration; and I wished to know whether the government would relinquish the monopoly, or was prepared to make some arrangement by which we should be able to bring them that article.

He answered that we would be able to bring them West india [sic] and other foreign productions, and that they would place our commerce with them on the same footing with their own. That tobacco was a source of great revenue to the government, and that it would be utterly hopeless to attempt to induce them to relinguish the monopoly. That we might make some arrangement concerning it as respects Sicily, and a depot, and that we might contract to sell to the government. — That for himself

438

individually he was for a free trade, and was opposed to all monopolies, but that it was impossible to induce the government to concur in these views. I told him that I should make this a question of importance; and had made these suggestions now, in order that the subject might be under consideration. I added that measures had been taken by Congress to have the state of our commercial relations with foreign governments before them at their next Session, in order to adapt our laws to the state of things they might find existing with the several governments; and that this made me more anxious upon the subject of their tobacco regulations, which operated so severely upon one of our most important staples.

I learn that the exclusive privilege of cultivating and selling tobacco has been sold to Torloni,[85] the Banker at Rome, who pays for it an annual sum of one million four hundred thousand Ducats. No person plants or imports, or sells without his permission. With such a system established, and a King who is somewhat remarkable for his attention to revenue, it argues no extraordinary discernment to be able to foretell that little can be speedily accomplished to ameliorate the system.

I have now the matter in my hands to propose a treaty when I choose, but I think it best to delay until after the meeting at Vienna. I have already accomplished part of my object in having brought to the consideration of the minister the prominent topics, and in obtaining the indirect assurance, as I have above narrated, that in the event of their being released from the existing obligations to England, they will place our commerce with them upon the most liberal footing. In the meantime and before I put any thing into writing, I shall reflect upon the details, and I have a hope, too, that I shall be made more fully acquainted with the views of the department.

I have received nothing from the Department since my last dispatch.

---

[85] Don Alessandro Torlonia (1800-1886). The second son of the banker, Giovanni Torlonia, who was the first to receive the title of nobility. The Torlonia Bank was founded in 1814. Pope Gregory XVI, recognized Alessandro as Duke of Cesi and as Marquis of old Rome, and as Prince of Civitella Cesi. Although opposed by the members of the government, he financed the drainage of Lake Fucino. Encouraged by King Ferdinand II, Don Alessandro bought half of the shares of the society that was to carry out the project and succeeded, thanks to his wealth and enterprising spirit, in terminating the work which was first started by De Montricher, a Frenchman, and later completed by Bermont and Brisse. For this, Don Alessandro, in 1875, was given the title Prince of Fucino. He declined all titles in favor of his daughter, Annamaria, who married Giulio Borghese. In that same year, the latter assumed the name Torlonia with all the attributes of the title. See Raffaele De Cesare, *La fine di un regno,* II, 81 ff.

Naples June 10, 1839. [Despatch No. 9]

Sir

After the conversation with the Prince of Cassaro which I had the honor to detail to you in my last dispatch, I thought a week or two might be well spent in seeing the Country, which surrounds the City. In the meantime I supposed that the minister, as he contemplated at our last interview, would have departed for Vienna, and that something decisive would be known in regard to the English treaty. On my return, after a fortnight's absence, I found him still at home, and much agitation in the City, in regard to the treaty.

I had an interview with him, on the sixth (6ᵗʰ.) of the present month, by appointment at his own house. I told him that as our negociation was, in some measure dependant [sic] upon that with England, I was anxious to know if any thing had yet been concluded. He said that it was necessary to pass the treaty through all the forms, and submit it to the examination of various bodies, and therefore nothing had yet been concluded: but that it had received the consideration of commissioners, and other boards, and it was now in a state to submit to the council of ministers. He gave me no farther particulars, but a pretty direct assurance, that the treaty would be made: "and then," he said, "we shall have got rid of all the obstacles, and will be prepared to make a liberal treaty with you." I told him, that from what had passed between us before I left the city, I supposed that he would have been at Vienna on my return. He seemed somewhat surprized, and did not at first remember that he had intended to go there, but recollecting himself, he said that it was thought probable that he might go to Vienna to meet Sir Frederick Lamb.

I then remarked that France was yet to be consulted, and that I was told that the Duke of Montebello was to come here; and asked if he was soon expected. He said, that he would come here as soon as this government should appoint a minister to the french [sic] court, that the death of Count Ludolf, who had received a commission to go there, had left a vacancy in that legation.[86]

---

[86] After the death of Count Giuseppe Costantino Ludolf, the Neapolitan chargé d'affaires at Paris was Don Luigi Carafa of the Dukes of Traetto. (?-1840), one of the principal representatives of the noble Carafa family. A diplomat of the Bourbon Court, he was secretary of the Royal Legation at the Holy See. By the decree of May 29, 1830, he was appointed chargé d'affaires ad interim. By the

It seems, that the negociation with England was not advancing, at the time of my previous interview with the Prince, as fast as he then supposed. Being sincerely desirous to bring it about, and having, on that day, received in Council a report of the Commissioners in it's [sic] favor, and carried a vote against the opinion of the minister of finance, he supposed that all the difficulties at home were overcome. But the minister of finance is obstinate, almost ferocious, prejudiced, persevering and able; and is supported by the shippers and merchants of the Capitol [sic] who fancy that a treaty would be ruinous to their interests. I have avoided from the beginning any intercourse with him, and prevented the reference of any thing to him from the department of State, by which he could become acquainted with the fact, that I was attempting to negociate. I learned his character, and hostility to the commercial treaty immediately on my arrival, and was more upon my guard against him, from ascertaining that he was watching me, and anxious to get the negociation into his hands, that he might crush it at the outset. I gave his agents to understand that a treaty was not necessary for us, and that I came here with no particular design to make one; but that I was ready to treat whenever the government here should manifest a disposition to form a compact with us upon the liberal terms which we offer to all nations.

I have kept myself entrenched behind the English negociation, against which the Minister of finance is expending his force and influence, while I have labored to impress upon the King, and the people an idea of the advantages which this nation would derive from a free commercial intercourse with us. There is now an active inquiry into the means of our trade by official agents, as well as individuals; and while commercial men are bitterly hostile to the English treaty, an opinion is silently making its way among them, and beginning to manifest itself, friendly to a treaty with us.

On the 3rd. of this month I was informed, that a remonstrance against the treaty with England, signed by between four and five

decree of Aug. 9, 1832, he was appointed chargé d'affaires at the Court of the Emperor of Austria, a post he held to Aug. 5, 1834. On Jan 11, 1835, he was appointed chargé d'affaires to the Sublime, Ottoman Porte with headquarters at Constantinople. However, on Feb. 8, 1835, he was still in Naples waiting for another appointment. In August 1835, he was sent to Paris to carry out the work of that mission. In 1836, he was chargé d'affaires at Paris, and, as ambassador, he remained in Paris to July 17, 1840, when he was recalled to Naples. On Aug. 6 1840, he was appointed Secretary General of Banks and of the general administration of the currency. *Archivio di Stato,* Naples — Scrivania di Razione, Assienti, vol. 1003, 108; vol. 1006, 15; vol. 1007, 9.

hundred merchants and shippers, would be presented that day, to the King and Council. I called aftewards at the house of the Prince of Cassaro, and was informed by his Servants, that he had been sent for by the King in haste, and had gone to meet him in Council. I was afterwards told that the Council was equally divided, four and four, but that the King remained in favor of it.

There are undoubtedly difficulties yet to be surmounted, and the treaty may not be so near a conclusion as the Secretary of State fancies, or we may desire. It somewhat depends upon the firmness of the King. The opposition here will be continued and France is still to be consulted. It is not the habit of France to jump at once to a treaty. In the end, however, a treaty will be concluded. On the evening of the fifth instant I found M^r. Kennedy getting into his carriage to visit the Prince of Cassaro on business, and he invited me to accompany him. I accepted the invitation, and on the way I congratulated him upon the prospect of speedily concluding a treaty. But, I remarked, France has not yet given her assent, will there be any difficulty there? After some hesitation he answered that he did not think there would be any, but that he believed this government had a right to make a treaty with whomever it pleased.

At my interview with the Prince of Cassaro, I volunteered a renewal of my promise to submit to him a project of a treaty, and gave him a list of all the articles of domestic origin which we are in the habit of bringing to this country, and requested him to procure a statement from official sources of the amount of those articles which are annually imported into this country. I wish to fix his attention to the subject for the purpose of asking a reduction of the present duties.

My late excursion was into the proximate provinces of Principato citra and ultra Terra di Lavoro, and along the Liris to Fucino, through one of the vallies of Abruzzo. It is the country of the ancient campania felix, bordered by the mountainous region of the Samnites and Volsciani. The fertility of the country (now bearing its grain crops to maturity) not only exceeds anything that I have witnessed elsewhere, but it is beyond any thing that I had imagined. The campagna felice, which extends ten or twelve miles in all directions from Naples, is a plain covered with exuberant crops of wheat, flax, hemp, indian corn, and all kinds of esculent vegetables, and provender, under fruit, mulberry, poplar and other kinds of trees, sufficient, in full leaf, to shade the ground, and each supporting a vine,

442

festooned from tree to tree. It is all, as indeed is all the Country I have seen, under garden culture, and when the crop, indian corn for example, is sufficiently open to admit of it, another crop such as beans, or turnips and sometimes both, are cultivated with it. The indian corn is planted, usually, in rows about eighteen inches apart, and is never allowed to grow without another full crop. The Seasons admit of constant cultivation, and when one crop is removed from the ground another is immediately put in its place. The valleys between the mountains connected with the plains, are of equal fertility until they rise to an elevation so high as to be injuriously affected by the moisture and cold. The mountain sides are also extremely fertile up to the foot of the bare rocks which usually form the apex. The mountains pour upon the valleys everliving streams of water, which furnish the power to move machinery, and impart fertility to the soil by means of irrigation.

Half a century ago there was scarcely a safe carriage road in the Kingdom; now (with the exception of about thirty miles from Sora to Fucino, which I was obliged to travel on horseback) I was enabled to perform my whole rout [sic] upon royal roads, graded to a very gentle elevation, wide and macadamized, or covered with gravel and rolled hard & smooth. Independently of the leading roads from Naples South into Calabria, East to the Adriatic, and North into the heart of Abruzzo ultra, there are various other connecting ones, constructed upon the same model, and with the same care. Along the valley of the Liris, [sic] above Sora, where from the earliest ages there has been nothing better than a very bad horse path, a road has been determined upon and marked out.

The ruling passion of the present King is supposed by many to be avarice, but he is pushing vigorously the construction of these roads, and seems to have a passion in other respects for embellishing his Kingdom.

There is a board and a gradation of officers for the laying out and constructing roads. A rout [sic] and plan is determined upon by the board, and the province through which it runs is compelled to construct it under the superintendance of the government officers.

The intercourse which is promoted by these roads is producing a perceptible change in the industry, and in the manners and habits of the people. The country affords great facilities for manufacturing. It has ample supplies of water, and is exempt

443

from the evils of frost & ice — Building materials are abundant everywhere; these volcanic regions afford a cement more durable than any other; and the people are active, healthy, ingenious, and ind[ust]rious. The "dolce far niente" is a fable, as far as my observation extends, for I have never witnessed more industry, or vigorous labor, than among the peasantry of Italy. Provisions are abundant; the other wants of life are easily supplied; and labor must always be cheap. The greatest and most solid structures can be raised at small expense, and there is nothing to affect their durability.

Upon a Stream in the neighborhood of Salerno there are several establishments, which have had their beginning within a few years, principally six years, and are now extending themselves, for the manufacture of cotton, wool, and iron, with the latest English machinery, conducted for Swiss proprietors with Italian partners. They spin cotton twist and print calicoes. In one of the establishments, which confines its operations to spinning, the superintendant told me, that he had in operation 8400 spindles and worked up 16,000 weight of the raw material every week. In another establishment, connected with the dyeing and printing, there was a building for spinning which I did not enter, but I should suppose from its appearance, that it would work up about the same amount of material as the other.

I am told, I do not know with what truth, that these establishments are not doing well for the owners; but if it is so, it is only the usual incident of new enterprizes with inexperienced hands. I do not for myself see why these manufactures should not florish [sic] here, if they are not kept in check by a fear of the insecurity of property from the nature of the government. If they should florish [sic] the time is not far distant when they will demand a supply of our cotton. Cotton is an article produced by themselves, nearly to the amount of their present demand, but they will bye and bye require a better kind than this Country produces; and indeed the soil which will produce cotton is so prolific, that it may be cultivated to better account in the production of other things.

I have received nothing from the Department since my last dispatch.

Naples July 17, 1839. [Despatch N°. 10]

Sir,

The subject of a treaty with England having passed through all the forms required, the main question has been decided in the affirmative. I suppose the decision to be final, although I am told that the Minister of finance is still making active resistance, as he declares, under that faint hope of success which unextinguished life inspires. The last Council, that of the Ministers, resolved in conformity to the King's opinion by a decided majority. I congratulated Mʳ. Kennedy upon having carried the question, and he replied by saying "that the King & council had determined to make the treaty;" but said he, it is very strange that having come, to that determination, they should still delay executing it.

I have heard many rumours and cannot say precisely why it is, that the consummation of the treaty is delayed; but I infer from my knowledge of this people, and from all I have heard, that the delays arise, first, from the hesitation with which this government comes to a final and irrevocable action in foreign policy, second, from the still active opposition of the minister of finance, and lastly from there being some details yet to be considered. I beleive [sic] also that it is the intention now, that when all the difficulties are overcome here, to have a meeting, with Sir Frederick Lamb and that the treaty will be consummated under the superintendance of Austria.

I do not doubt that the treaty will be made, but I do not feel justified in saying any thing in regard to time.

Having followed up the negociation with England until it had reached the point stated above, I considered the time propitious for presenting in a form to be laid before the King, and to be considered, the views of our government with regard to a treaty. I therefore drew up, and sent on the eighth day of July instant, to the Prince of Cassaro a project of a treaty, a copy of which accompanies this dispatch marked A: and I sent with it a note, a copy of which also accompanies this dispatch marked B. —

I have no doubt that my proposition with regard to tobacco will excite surprize, and it is probable that I shall not soon receive a formal answer.

445

The Globe[87] of April 22 has just reached me, containing the Report in the House of Representatives of Feb. 25 on the subject of the tobacco trade.[88] It affords me great pleasure to find the course I have pursued in this matter so well supported by the views presented by the Committee. I still receive my newspaper by the dilatory conveyance of ships from Liverpool & the Globe mentioned is the last date which has come to my hands. I have directed my New York papers to be sent for me to Havre by every packet: thence they will come to me through France by mail. I should be glad to receive the Globe by the same rout, [sic] directed to Mʳ. Beasley, as I continue very much behind in intelligence, particularly in regard to what is transacted by the government.

I shall consider it my duty to press the tobacco question to the utmost point, and if I fail in effecting any arrangement, I shall still hope to have done something towards success at a future day. The present advantage which I shall risk at any rate, from the posture in which I have placed that question, and the others associated in it's class, will be to divert the attention of this government by means of existing questions, from the practicable questions of the treaty, so that they may be yielded,

---

[87] The *Congressional Globe* was one of the predecessors of the present-day *Congressional Record* and served the same function, that of reporting the proceedings and debates in Congress. The first of these was the *Annals of Congress*, which covered the period Mar. 3, 1779 to May 27, 1824, but was not published until ten years from the end of that period, 1834-1856, being its publication years, 42 volumes; then followed the *Register of Debates in Congress*, 29 volumes, published by the same publishers. Beginning in 1834, and continuing until 1868, 82 volumes of the *Congressional Globe* were published, also under authority of Congress, the work being issued under the auspices of the Library of Congress and covering the proceedings and debates of the 23d Congress 1st session, to the end of the 42d Congress, 2d session. J. C. Rives was the printer of these issues. In 1880, the 46th Congress, 2d session, called upon the Public Printer of the day, J. D. Defrees, on April 28, 1880, to report to the Senate concerning the condition of the stereotype plates of the *Globe*, the quantities of the back numbers on hand, and the custody of the plates purchased from Rives and Bailey, etc. See 46th Cong. 2d sess., vol. II, *Letter concerning the Stereotype Plates* of the *Congressional Globe*, May 19, 1880; *Senate Miscellaneous Documents*, 92.

[88] See 25th Cong. 3d sess., vol. II, *Reports of Committees, House, Select Committee Report No. 310, Feb. 25, 1839; Report on the Tobacco Trade.* 11 p., 8°. This report recommends that the President direct the diplomatic agents of the Government to use their efforts to obtain a diminution of the duty imposed by the Governments of Europe upon tobacco exported from the United States. The tobacco question remained a live issue in the United States. On May 1, 1840, at the Convention of Tobacco Planters from all parts of the country, Mr. Dodge, who had been appointed by the government to report as special agent concerning tobacco trade conditions in Europe, gave the tobacco planters a long report on his findings abroad. See *Niles Register*, May 30, 1840, 201-203, and the speech of Mr. Triplett, member of the Select Committee on Tobacco, as printed on the June 6, 1840, issue of *Niles Register*, 211.

without a tedious process of negociation to which this government is prone.

Commodore Hull[89] is here with his Ship, having sent the Cyane on a tour of observation to Palermo, where there has been recently some disturbances by robbers. He intends to go East in a few days.

The War, which it is understood has commenced between Turkey & Egypt is the topic now of conversation in the diplomatic circles, but I can communicate nothing interesting on the subject which you will not get better from other quarters.

I have received a note, of which the following is a copy.

Napoli 8. Luglio 1839.

Essendo sua maestà la Regina felicemente pervenuta agli alti mesi della sua gravidanza, la Maestà del Re Suo Augusto consorte ha ordinato, che le ne desse conoscenze [sic] alle corti esteri per mezzo dei rispettivi loro ministri accreditati presso la sua real persona, nella certezza in cui ch'esse vorranno prender parte a questo lieto avvenimento che colma di giubilo gli amati suoi popoli.

A tal'effetto quindi e con infinita sua soddisfazione il Sottoscritto Ministro Segretario di Stato degli affari esteri ne rende consapevole il Signor Enos T. Throop Incaricato d'affari degli Stati Uniti d'America pregandolo nel tempo stesso a gradire le proteste ch'ei gli rinnova della sua particolar considerazione.

(Signed) Il Principe di Cassaro.

The event mentioned in the preceding note will probably retain the Court, during the season at the Royal residence of Capodimonte in this City, where the Royal family is, at this time. But the weather has now become so warm as to begin to produce the enfeebling effects of the uninterrupted warm weather of this climate and a disinclination to business. I do not look for any vigorous diplomatic action on the part of this court, until the return of cooler weather in the fall.

---

[89] Joseph Bartine Hull, born in Westchester County, N. Y., on Apr. 26, 1802. He was attached to the frigate *Potomac,* Mediterranean Squadron, 1834-37. He retired on July 16, 1862.

Project of a treaty of Commerce between The United States of America and his Majesty the King of the Kingdom of the Two Sicilies.[90]

The United States of America and his Majesty the King of the Kingdom of the Two Sicilies equally animated with the desire of maintaining the relations of good understanding which have hitherto so happily subsisted between their respective states, of extending also and consolodating [sic] the commercial intercourse between them; and convinced that this object cannot better be accomplished than by adopting the System of an entire freedom of navigation, and a perfect reciprocity based upon the principles of equity equally beneficial to both countries, have in consequence agreed to enter into negociations for the conclusion of a treaty of commerce and navigation, for which purpose the President of the United States has conferred full powers upon Enos T. Throop Chargé d'Affaires at the Court of his Majesty the King of the Kingdom of the Two Sicilies, and his Majesty the King has conferred like powers upon, . . . [blank space] and the said plenipotentiaries having exchanged their said full powers found in good and due form, have concluded and signed the following articles:

Art. 1. — There shall be between the territories of the high contracting parties a reciprocal liberty of commerce and navigation. The Citizens and subjects of their respective states shall mutually have liberty to frequent and enter the ports, places, rivers and territories of each party, wherever foreign commerce is permitted, and reside and trade there in all kinds of produce, manufactures and merchandize; and they shall enjoy to that effect, the same security, protection and privileges, as Citizens or Subjects of the country wherein they reside, on condition of their submitting to the laws, decrees and usages there established, to which native citizens are subjected.

Art. 2. Vessels of the Kingdom of the Two Sicilies arriving, either laden or in ballast, in the ports of the United States of America, and reciprocally, vessels of the United States of America arriving, either laden or in ballast, in the ports of the dominions of the King of the Two Sicilies, shall be treated on their entrance, during their stay, and at their departure upon the same footing as national vessels, coming from the same place, with respect to

---

[90] The treaty negotiations were protracted, since the treaty was not concluded until Dec. 1, 1845.

the duties of tonnage, light houses, pilotage and port charges, quarantine and charges incident thereto, as well as to the fees and perquisites of public officers, and all other duties or charges of whatever kind or denomination, levied in the name or to the profit of the government, the local authorities, or any private establishment whatsoever.

Art. 3. All kinds of merchandize and articles of commerce, either the produce of the soil or industry of the United States of America, or of any other country which may be lawfully imported into the ports of the dominions of his Majesty in vessels of the Kingdom of the Two Sicilies may also be imported in vessels of the United States of America without paying other, or higher duties or charges of whatever kind or denomination, levied in the name or to the profit of the government, the local authorities, or of any private establishments whatsoever, than if the same merchandize or produce had been imported in vessels of the same kingdom. And reciprocally, all kinds of merchandize and articles of commerce the produce of the soil, or of the industry of the dominion of his Majesty, or of any other country which may be lawfully imported into the ports of the United States, in vessels of the said States, may also be imported in vessels of the Kingdom of the Two Sicilies without paying other or higher duties or charges of whatsoever kind or denomination levied in the name or to the profit of the government, the local authorities, or of any private establishment whatsoever, than if the said merchandize or produce had been imported in vessels of the United States of America.

Art. 4. To prevent the possibility of any misunderstanding it is hereby declared that the stipulations contained in the two preceeding articles are to their full extent applicable to vessels of the Kingdom of the Two Sicilies and their cargoes, arriving in the ports of the United States of America, and reciprocally to vessels of the said states and their cargoes arriving in the ports of the dominions of his Majesty whether the said vessels clear directly from the ports of the country to which they respectively belong, or from the ports of any other foreign country.

Art. 5. No other or higher duty shall be imposed on the importation into the United States of any article the produce or manufacture of the dominions of his Majesty; and no other or higher duties shall be imposed on the importation into the dominions of his Majesty of any article the produce or manufacture of the United States, than are or shall be payable on the

449

like article, being the produce or manufacture of any other foreign country. Nor shall any prohibition be imposed upon the importation or exportation of any article the produce or manufacture of the United States, or of the dominions of his Majesty, which shall not equally extend to all other nations.

Art. 6. All kinds of merchandize and articles of commerce, either the produce of the soil, or of the industry of the United States of America or of any other country, which may be lawfully exported or reexported from the ports of the United States in national vessels may also be exported or reexported therefrom in vessels of the Kingdom of the Two Sicilies, without paying other or higher duties or charges of whatever kind or denomination levied in the name and to the profit of the government, the local authorities, or of any private establishments whatsoever, than if the same merchandize or produce had been exported or reexported in vessels of the United States of America.

An exact reciprocity shall be observed in the ports of the dominions of his Majesty the King of the Kingdom of the Two Sicilies, so that all kinds of merchandize and articles of commerce, either the produce of the soil, or the industry of his Majesty's dominions, or of any other country, which may be lawfully exported or reexported from the ports of the kingdom of the Two Sicilies in national Vessels may also be exported or reexported therefrom in vessels of the United States of America, without paying other or higher duties in charges of whatsoever kind or denomination levied in the name and to the profit of the government, the local authorities or any private establishments whatever, than if said merchandize or produce had been exported or reexported in Vessels of the Kingdom of the Two Sicilies.

And the same bounties & drawbacks shall be allowed, whether such exportation or reexportation be made in vessels of the one party or the other.

Art. 7. It is expressly understood and agreed that the coastwise navigation of both the contracting parties is altogether excepted from the operation of this treaty, and of every article thereof.

Art. 8. No priority or preference shall be given directly or indirectly by either of the contracting parties, nor by any company, corporation or agent, acting on their behalf, or under their authority, in the purchase of any article of commerce lawfully imported, on account of or in reference to the character of the vessels, whether it be of the one party or of the other, in which such article was imported, it being the true intent and meaning of the contracting parties, that no distinction or difference whatsoever shall be made in this respect.

Art. 9.   If either party shall hereafter grant to any other nation any particular favor in navigation or commerce it shall immediately become common to the other party freely, where it is freely granted to such other nation, or on yielding the same compensation when the grant is conditional.

[Art.]⁹¹ 10. — The preceeding articles to be so modified, as not to infringe upon the privileges granted to France by the United States in regard to their wines, until the expiration of the term stipulated in the treaty, which will be the second day of February 1842.

[Art.] 11.   The duties on Tobacco, Cotton and other articles the production of the industry of the United States to be so arranged and modified that they may be imported into the Kingdom of the Two Sicilies. —

In view of the distance between the two countries and the consequent long voyages and the difficulty therefrom of adapting cargoes to the market: and the utter impossibility of an infectious or contagious disease being transported, without manifesting itself during the voyage, articles embracing the two next following subjects are proposed, to wit:

[Art.] 12.   Reexportation without duty or with drawback.

The right of entering for the purpose of re-exportation, within the term of [blank space] years, all kinds of merchandize and articles of commerce, lawfully imported into the Kingdom of the Two Sicilies in vessels of the United States of America; and reciprocally all kinds of merchandize and articles of commerce lawfully imported into the United States in vessels of the Kingdom of the Two Sicilies, shall be allowed on placing such articles of merchandize in secure deposits, and paying the duties thereon to be returned on re-exportation or without payment of duties — and each government shall proceed without delay to establish and prescribe such rules as it may deem expedient to regulate and secure the privilege of re-exportation, and to prevent it's [sic] abuse.

[Art.] 13. — Quarantine.

---

⁹¹ Bracketed word is omitted in the original, i.e., the numbers alone are given for articles 10 through 13.

Vessels arriving direct from the United States to a port in the dominions of his Majesty, or direct from a port in his Majesty's dominions to a port in the United States, furnished with a certificate of health from the competent health officer of the port whence they took their departure, and countersigned by the consul of the other party residing at that port (if there shall be such consul there) certifying that no malignant or contagious disease existed at that port, shall not be subjected to any other quarantine than such as may be necessary for the visit of the health officer of the port, at which they may have arrived; but shall, after such visit be permitted immediately to enter and discharge their cargoes: Provided always that it may be found that no person has died on board, or been affected during the voyage with a malignant or contagious disease; that such vessel during the passage shall not have communicated with any vessel, liable itself to undergo quarantine; and that the country from which the vessel comes shall not have been generally regarded at the time, so infected or suspected that it had been previously necessary to adopt a regulation by which all vessels coming from that country are to be regarded as suspected and subjected to quarantine.

In addition to the foregoing it is proposed to insert the usual articles —

1. — For the protection of vessels in the ports of each other —

2. — The protection of persons and their business and effects under the jurisdiction of each other — and to secure them and their representatives in the alienation, devise and descent of their effects.

3. — To secure protection and assistance to vessels and their cargoes driven by pursuit of enemies, pirates, stress of weather or otherwise into each other's ports, or shipwrecked upon the coast.

4 — To adopt the principle that free ships make free goods. — to define a blockade, and declare what articles are contraband. —

5. — For consuls resident in each others [sic] ports.

452

[Enclosure B with Mr. Throop's Despatch No. 10, July 17, 1839.]

Naples July 8. 1839.

The undersigned, chargé d'Affaires of the United States of America has the honor to transmit herewith to his Excellency the Prince of Cassaro, Minister, Secretary of State for foreign affairs, a note of the matters, which he proposes as the basis of a treaty of commerce between the United States and the Two Sicilies.

As the first nine propositions are the usual provisions of a treaty upon the principles of equal advantages and fair reciprocity, he has put them into the form of treaty stipulations. If the principle be admitted the details will require no material alterations.

The restrictions and high duties imposed upon the importation into this Kingdom of the few productions of the United States adapted to this market are so much in contrast with the liberal terms upon which the government of the United States admits to consumption the varied and valuable productions of this Kingdom and so at variance with the liberal principles of commercial intercourse, which are now fast extending their influence over the civilized world, that his Majesty cannot fail to acknowledge, at once, the propriety of modifying them as proposed in number Eleven.

Without a scala franca, or the privilege of re-exportation, it is quite obvious that the direct trade between the United States and the Two Sicilies will labor under great disadvantages to the prejudice of both countries. The great extent of Ocean to be traversed will not permit an immediate supply of whatever the market may unexpectedly demand: months must intervene. If cargoes from America be permitted freely to enter on payment of duties to be refunded on reexportation, under official inspection of unopened packages, there will be less hesitation on the part of the subjects of his Majesty in American ports on their return, or Americans on their outward voyages, to load their ships with such articles as can be best purchased, with regard to the kind and quantity. The advantages to this Kingdom in having a supply on hand to meet casual wants: and the employment which would be given to labor and capital in making the great commercial cities of the Kingdom places of deposit, and the resort of purchasers from abroad, are not to be overlooked. His

Majesty must see that there will be a struggle in the Mediterranean ports, under the new and more liberal system of commerce to secure the advantages of the long voyages and rich trade with the United States, and that they who practice the most discreet liberality will enjoy the greatest share of it. His Majesty's government is too enlightened to admit of a doubt, that he will avail himself of the vast resources of his Kingdom, and it's commanding position in the centre of the sea, to make it what nature designed it to be, a depot and mart of the productions and merchandize of the Mediterranean. In Article twelve, relating to drawback of duties, and in the next subsequent one, thirteen, the undersigned offers an arrangement, which he believes will promote the interests of the Two Sicilies; and which contemplates nothing more than mutuality, by establishing in this Kingdom regulations similar to those now in operation with success and safety in the United States. Goods entered on their arrival for reexportation, may be reexported at any time within three years; and vessels from any quarter of the Globe are permitted to enter immediately after proper examination by health officers, unless under circumstances leading to suspicion.

With regard to the other matters, the Undersigned does not consider it material to say anything more at present, than that they are subordinate in interest, although of much importance in themselves, and that they may be discussed and arranged after the principal propositions shall be disposed of.

In respect to the main feature of the treaty, which the undersigned now offers, he feels sure that the time has arrived when it is unnecessary for him to urge upon his Majesty or your Excellency a single argument in favor of it's adoption. It is a principle which has been tendered by his government in all it's negociations with foreign powers from the time of the first organization, altho' it is only of late years that it has been admitted to it's full extent as the basis of treaty stipulations. He is now proud to observe, that it's [sic] adaptation to the mutual wants, the prosperity and amicable intercourse of nations has in the progress of knowledge & liberality, been universally admitted; and that his government has been enabled to arrange it's commercial relations with nearly all the governments of Europe in conformity with it.

During the short time that the undersigned has had the honor of residing at this Court he has noticed with admiration, the great works of public utility in progress in this Country, worthy of it's past ages of glory; and how sensitive in the plenitude of it's [sic] capabilities, this country is to the general influences which set it's [sic] springs of productiveness in motion. He hopes that the same enlightened counsels which have given an impulse to industry by interior arrangements will embrace the opportunity now presented of adopting into the foreign policy the principle of perfect reciprocity; a principle which embodied in a treaty with the United States will open to his Majesty's subjects a wide field for their enterprize, industry and ingenuity. To add force to this view he need only say, that the people of the United States are great consumers of all the production of this Kingdom, and if encouraged to look to it for supplies they will stimulate it's industry to more extensive and varied productions.

It is not the intention of the undersigned in this note to enter into a discussion of the topics presented by this project of a treaty, but he deems it his duty to mention a subject with which he is charged by his government as one of the deepest importance. He alludes to the exclusion from this Kingdom by a monopoly and excessive duties, of the only staple article of the United States which might offer itself to any considerable amount of value in this market. He alludes to Tobacco.

He is aware that it is a subject deeply interesting to the revenues of this Kingdom, and that his Majesty's Government is not the only one in Europe which persists in the same policy. He trusts, however, that when his Majesty has further considered it in it's bearings upon new relations with other powers, he will be convinced that both his revenue and the wealth of his Kingdom will be increased by such a modification of his laws in this respect, as will divest them of their injurious operation upon the trade and harmony of the two countries. The dark ages of national intercourse are fast disappearing before the intellectual illumination of the present day; and the system of particular monopolies which interfere with a free commerce between nations, in articles which are the production of the industry of each, is destined soon to the same tomb with other commercial restrictions. The exact time of the removal of this obstacle to free trade between nations will be marked as an epoch, in which shall have been cast off the shackles of prejudices in favor of long standing measures, grown into abuses from having survived the occasion of their adoption. The undersigned trusts, that his Majesty will see the subject in the same point of view, and identify his reign with this epoch, by being the first to abandon a monopoly, violating the first principle of reciprocal advantages in international commerce, and operating with particular hardship upon a nation disposed to extend its relations with his dominions, and to place them upon the most equal, amicable and durable foundations.

The President of the United States, being animated by the most friendly sentiments towards this Government whose justice and good faith he is proud to acknowledge has charged the undersigned to tender to it a treaty, which in it's basis secures reciprocity, and in it's [sic] provisions the most favorable relations.

In the performance of this duty, rendered more agreeable by the uniform kindness which he has experienced in his intercourse with your Excellency, the undersigned avails himself of the occasion to renew to your Excellency the assurances of his most distinguished consideration and regard.

E. T. THROOP TO J. FORSYTH

Naples September 2. 1839. [Despatch No. 11.]

Sir

I send herewith my accounts and vouchers for the six months, ending on the 30th of June last. A delay in the receipt of my voucher from London for the first quarter of the present year having occurred until near the termination of the second, I thought it better to bring the two quarters into the account; but a similar cause in respect to the account of the second quarter has delayed me until this time.

I have nothing new to add in reference to our negociations. The treaty with England sleeps under the nursing of a committee which is charged to report such alterations in the tariff as will adjust it to the provisions of the treaty. Remonstrances have been presented recently to the King, but received by him in such a manner as to shew that his opinion is not to be changed. The last remonstrance, I am told, was returned by him to the petitioners.

The usual relaxations from business at this season, and particularly during the months of September and October, will be augmented this year by the festivities attendant upon the accouchement of the Queen, which is now daily expected. It would surprize me, if the English treaty should be finally acted upon before the end of the next carnival, although the Minister of foreign affairs has it much at heart, and I am told that all the obstructions, both here and with France, are in a fair way to be speedily removed.

I have recently made two or three attempts to have a conversation with the Prince of Cassaro but have not found him at home. It was my intention to prevail upon him, if possible, to discuss with me in writing, preliminarily, the tobacco question. I should endeavor to lay before the King arguments to prove, that his revenue, as well as the industry & trade of his Kingdom, would be improved by a change in his system from a monopoly to the imposition of a reasonable duty; and I should avail myself of the occasion to shew how vitally this question affects our commercial relations with him. I shall embrace the first opportunity to have this interview with him.

I have forwarded my dispatches from here regularly according to their numbers, but I have had no acknowledgement from the department of the receipt of any of them.

I received yesterday, by the way of Liverpool the acts and resolutions of the last session of Congress, and a file of the Globe down to the 3ᵈ. of June. Permit me to renew the request I made in my last dispatch that the Globe be sent to me by each Havre packet.

E. T. Throop to J. Forsyth

Naples September 23, 1839. [Despatch Nº. 12]

Sir,

We are now in the season when but little business is usually transacted; and all the persons connected with the Court have been occupied with the expected accouchement of the Queen. That event has now occurred, and the Queen has made her subjects very happy by giving them another Prince. In this state of things I have not thought it best to press our affairs upon the government, although I have called several times to see the Prince of Cassaro, and have found him either engaged or absent. At my request he appointed yesterday to see me at his house; but when I went there I found him engaged with the Austrian Minister and the resident agent here of Don Carlos of Spain, and I did not go in.

I think it very probable that the disastrous state of the affairs of that Prince, at this juncture, who is looked upon here as the true Sovereign of Spain, will, for a time, occupy much of the attention of this court, as his cause has been always warmly espoused by the King and supported by his treasures. I think it probable that he will seek an asylum here. The failure of Don Carlos throws the King of Naples out of the line of succession.

As I did not see the Prince of Cassaro yesterday, he called upon me at my house today. I explained to him that I had been anxious for some time past, to have a free conversation with him upon the topics in the project of a treaty which I had submitted to him; and particularly upon that part of it, which relates to a modification of their duties and laws regulating the introduction into this Kingdom of merchandize the production of our country. — That the few articles we were permitted to bring here were loaded with duties, ranging from seventy to two hundred per cent, while we impose moderate duties upon the importation of three or four articles only, produced in this kingdom and admitted every thing else free of duty. — That this inequality was unjust, and ought to be remedied; but that our importations into this Kingdom were so small, that the grievance was nothing compared to the injury which we sustain by their refusal to permit us to trafic [sic] in tobacco, one of the most important staples of our country. — That this matter was in no wise dependant upon the existing or contemplated treaty with England, and that this government was entirely free to negociate with us upon it.

He observed that among the difficulties that surrounded this subject there was this: that the monopoly of tobacco had been given on contract for a period which had not yet expired probably by some years. I remarked that this need not prevent our discussing the subject or it's [sic] intrinsic merits and if there was nothing improper in the request, I would be obliged to him if he would furnish me with a memorandum of the unexpired term of the contract, the amount of revenue which the King receives from it, and the amount of tobacco consumed in the Kingdom.— That upon this data I should like to present to his Majesty my views of the policy of a change in his System, with the hope that I should be able to convince him, that opening to us the trade in tobacco would both increase his revenues and promote the industry of his kingdom. I therefore proposed that as a preliminary we should discuss that question. I told him that the trade was now all on one side, and of very little importance to us, unless we could have some farther encouragement to come here with our productions. I added, also, that the question was assuming a serious aspect in our country, and that it was agitated in both houses of Congress, whether it was not our duty to adopt a countervailing tariff against those countries who refuse to admit our tobacco, and give us no other equivalent advantage in trade.

He replied that they would be very willing to look over the tariff which affected the importation of our produce and make reasonable reductions; and that he would very cheerfully furnish me the information I desired, and consent to enter into the preliminary discussion as I proposed: but, he said, the tobacco was a difficult question, that it was an old established source of revenue, and, although he would be very willing to see the monopoly abolished, the proposal would be fiercely opposed by the minister of finance, and he feared that I would find insuperable difficulties with the King. Still he was willing to give me every facility for making an impression upon his Majesty — he would furnish me with the information as soon as he could collect it, and after a few weeks we would enter upon the subject. I told him that I should not dispair [sic] of being able to convince his Majesty, as he had shewn himself, by his assent to the principles engrafted into the treaty with England, capable of rising above the prejudices in favor of long established Systems, which require reform.

He informed me that the difficulties were overcome both with England and France, and he knew of nothing to prevent the conclusion of the treaty, and expressed a beleif [sic] that it would soon be executed.

I have received nothing from the department since my last dispatch.

E. T. THROOP TO J. FORSYTH

Naples December 12, 1839. [Despatch No. 13]
Sir,

I have delayed writing for a longer time than usual, in the hope of having something important to communicate in relation to the negociations here, but affairs still remain without material change.

Shortly after the date of my last letter, a M^r. McGregor,[92]

---

[92] John Macgregor (1797-1857). Statistician and historian. In 1837, he represented the British Government in the negotiations with the Kingdom of Naples for a revision of the commercial treaty of 1816. In 1840, he was one of the joint secretaries of the Board of Trade. He was joint author with James Deacon Hume of a vast work on the commercial statistics of all nations. *Dictionary National Biography*, 1921-22, XII, 540-1. See note 2, p. 602.

a person without diplomatic rank, but an individual much employed by the British government in negociating it's commercial treaties, arrived here, and continued until about the middle of the last month in correspondence with this government on the subject of the treaty, which it seems had not been well understood although the Prince of Cassaro had so considered it. He has not returned to his government with the result, which is so variously understood by the public here, as to have an unfavorable effect upon commercial activity. The Prince of Cassaro has again assured me that the terms of the treaty are agreed upon with M^r. McGregor, but he added that it was necessary to submit it again to the king for his approval.

One, and probably the principal difficulty has been to adjust the sulphur question, which has been insisted upon by the English government and strenuously resisted by this, not only as a matter of interest, but also as a matter of pride. The King is unwilling it should be understood that he has, at the demand of another power, revoked a measure which belongs properly to the internal regulations of his government, and therefore he will be slow to assent. Nothing however has occurred to shake my beleif [sic] in the opinion I have uniformly expressed, that the treaty will be ultimately concluded; but the circumstances alluded to above, will probably retard, for some time to come, it's final execution.

I have endeavored, whenever an opportunity has occurred to press the Prince of Cassaro to some action upon our proposed treaty, but there is an evident reluctance to touch it, until the affairs with England are closed, and I have not beleived [sic] that it would promote our interests to be importunate. On the 25th of September last I sent him the following note. —

"Sir, In pursuance of the understanding at our interview, a few days since, I now have the honor to put into writing my request, that your Excellency will furnish me with a statement:

First of the amount of the annual consumption of tobacco in the Kingdom of the Two Sicilies.

Second of the amount which is paid into the royal treasury by the contractor, and the expenses which are properly chargeable as a deduction from that amount, shewing the nett [sic] proceeds.

Third the term unexpired of the existing contract.

As I explained to your Excellency, it is my object to use the information desired, as the basis of an argument to satisfy his

Majesty's government, that a change in the policy of this Kingdom in regard to that article, placing the introduction of it upon a footing more satisfactory to the United States, would not prejudice his Majesty's revenues. I avail myself of the occasion to renew to your Excellency the assurances of my high consideration."

I have not yet received any reply to this note. On one occasion when I reminded the Prince of this note, he answered that he was collecting the information and would send it to me. On another occasion when I repeated the suggestion that we might discuss the propriety of readjusting the tariff and that this matter was not entirely dependant [sic] upon the conclusion of their treaty with England, he expressed a desire to defer it upon the ground, that the conclusion of the treaty with England would not be much longer delayed, and that they could not reduce the duty upon any thing without at the same time, reducing the duty on the same article ten per cent in favor of English commerce. I did not think it politic to press the subject any farther at that time, but advisable to wait the course of events.

In the meantime, I have reason to beleive [sic] that the government is not entirely negligent of it's [sic] relations with us. I find that some subordinate officers of the department of foreign affairs are making inquiries in relation to the various suggestions which I have made. Whenever the proper time arrives, I shall not hesitate to speak to this government with as much energy as the occasion may require.

I have received nothing from the department since my last dispatch.

The Channel by which I have hitherto received the Globe newspaper is so circuitous, that I do not receive it until three or four months after it's date. The Havre packets afford the most speedy conveyance and I would be much obliged to you if you would direct it to be forwarded by that route.

E. T. THROOP TO J. FORSYTH

Naples January 21, 1840.[93] [Despatch No. 14]

Sir,

The Journals in France and England have announced the return of M^r. McGregor to England with a treaty agreed upon be-

[93] Instruction dated Jan. 13, 1840, from Secretary Forsyth to Mr. Throop asking him to transmit the President's letter to the King of the Two Sicilies regarding the announcement of the birth of his son, Prince Alberto Maria Francesco, is omitted.

461

tween that Country and this; but there is nothing material in relation to the negociations through McGregor, to add to my last dispatch. An affair, however, has occurred which may somewhat embroil the negociations, and postpone still farther their consummation.

I mentioned in my last dispatch that "the result (of Mr. McGs negociation) was so variously understood by the public here as to have an unfavorable influence upon commercial activity." The official Journal of the 16ᵗʰ. December contains a sovereign rescript, in which, after reciting that his Majesty had received in the Council of State the petition of the merchants in all parts of his Kingdom, the opinion of the Council of the Administration of indirect taxes, and of the Administrative Chamber of Commerce &c. also the opinion of the *Consulta Generale* of the Kingdom, proceeds as follows:

"si è benignata di permettere, che i benefici accordati alla real bandiera col Sovrano Rescritto del 15 aprile 1837 per le navigazioni del Baltico, et nei mari delle Indie orientali ed occidentali, siano prorogati senza limitazione di tempo, salvo a rivocarli quanto piaccia a S. M.; previo avviso da darsene al commercio sei mesi primo [sic] per le Indie orientali ed occidentali."[94]

This rescript, giving assurance to the navigating interests of the Kingdom that he would not revoke the decree giving thirty per cent preference to the royal flag in its commerce in the East and West India seas, and in the Baltic, without a notice of six months for the Baltic, and one year for the East and West, seemed to me to indicate that the treaty with England was not agreed upon and to throw doubt upon the intentions of the King.

On the 18ᵗʰ Decʳ. I meet [sic] the Prince of Cassaro and apprized him of the inference I had drawn from the promulgation of the rescript. He told me that it meant nothing, that the King's mind was unchanged, and that there had been intrigue employed in procuring it. It was plainly to be perceived, that the decree had been issued without consultation with him, and that he was piqued at it. "You know," said he, "that the treaty is drawn up and agreed upon." "I am happy to hear it," I replied. "Yes," says he, "it only requires to be laid before the

---

94 His Majesty has benignly granted that the benefits allowed to the royal flag by the sovereign rescript of April 15, 1837, for navigation in the Baltic, and in the seas of the East and West Indies, be extended indefinitely; it is understood however, that these benefits may be revoked whenever it may please His Majesty. It is also understood that in the case of the East and West Indies a notice must be issued to commerce six months previously.

King for his approval and signature." "But," I remarked to him, "does not the sulphur question yet remain an obstacle?" "Oh no," he said, "that thing will now, very shortly, be disposed of."

In truth, the Prince of Cassaro, prompted by his feelings and interests as a Sicilian, has it much at heart to open a free commerce with the Kingdom, and has shewn much more than his accustomed energy in prosecuting his views, and has, as I am told, threatened to resign if he fails in carrying his measures. He has the King on his side, but the crafty, obstinate and persevering Minister of finance is constantly at work, by means direct and indirect, to counteract him. What I suspected from the beginning I am now positively assured is true, that the parade of deliberation and consultation spread out in the preamble of the rescript is a mere cloak for the minister of finance, who procured the King's assent to it, without consultation with any body. He did it, no doubt, with the design to embarrass the negociations with Great Britain; and to place the King in a situation to render him unjust towards his own Subjects, if he should carry into immediate effect the treaty as now understood.

There is nothing in all this, however, which may not be overcome, but I fear obstacles and delay from a quarter where the Prince of Cassaro foresees no difficulty. This government has nothing yet from France, except a general assurance of concurring with England in a treaty. I put the question to the Prince of Cassaro, and he told me that Casimir Perier had shewn him a letter from Louis Philippe to that effect: As the assent of France is indispensible, it is probable, that this subject mingles itself with the affairs now under discussion between Great Britain and France. I take it for granted that France never yields, at the request of other powers, to a change in their relations, without at least negociating and asking something new as an equivalent. The Duke of Serracapriola[95] has held, for a month past and longer, the ap-

---

[95] Nicola Maresca, Duke of Serracapriola. (1790-1870). He was born in St. Petersburg and died in Portici. He began his diplomatic career as private secretary of his father who was ambassador at St. Petersburg, and was a member of the staff of the Neapolitan Legation at St. Petersburg from 1811 to 1822, except for brief absences. In 1812, he was raised to the position of Chamberlain of King Ferdinand; in 1814, he preceded his father to the Congress of Vienna. He returned to Naples in 1816. In 1820, he was charged by the Regent Francis and later by the King to return to Russia to collaborate with his father to justify the measures taken against the Carbonari. By the decree of Sept. 30, 1839, he was appointed envoy extraordinary and minister plenipotentiary to Paris to solve the sulphur dispute. On Nov. 14, 1847, he was appointed Lieutenant General of Sicily, a post which he never held because, meanwhile, he was charged to form the first constitutional cabinet. He was President of the Council of Ministers from Jan. 27 to

pointment of Minister to France; and it is understood that on his arrival at Paris the Duke of Montebello will come here: but he has not yet gone, nor is the time of his departure fixed.

The opinion I hinted in my dispatch of Septr. 2, (no. 11) that notwithstanding the then favorable posture of affairs, the treaty with England would not be finally concluded until after the next Carnival, is now almost prophecy fulfilled. We have just entered upon the Carnival season and the treaty is far from being adjusted. A change has recently taken place in the ministry which may have an effect to delay still farther, although I think it cannot ultimately defeat the treaty with England. The Marquis of Pietracatella[96] has been advanced from the post of President of the *Consulta generale,* to that of President of the Council of Ministers, made vacant by the death of the Marquis of Ruffo.[97] He is of the old school, and as Minister of State has uniformly resisted the new policy. He was a member of the Commission issued by the King to examine and report upon the treaty with England, and the report, submitted to the King in it's favor, was contrary to his opinion. As he succeeds to the place of an advocate of the treaty, his accession makes a difference of two votes in the Council of Ministers. He is a man of acknowledged learning and capacity, one of the first in the Kingdom; and as his temperament is rather unsocial, and his

April 3, 1848. Later, from 1849 to 1860, he was Vice-president of the Consulta of the Royal Domains on this side of the Faro. Meanwhile, however, in 1856, he was sent on an extraordinary mission to Russia. He was a member of the Council of Regency which Francis left behind him in Naples in 1860. After the constitution of the Kingdom of Italy, he retired to private life. Sources: Private archives Maresca di Serracapriola at the home of the Duke of Salandra. Bibliography: H. Gustave, *Notice Biographique sur la vie et les travaux de monsieur le duc de Serracapriola.* Paris, 1842, passim; Benedetto Croce, *Uomini e cose della vecchia Italia.* Bari, Laterza, 1927, II, 193 ff; Giuseppe Paladino. *Il 15 maggio del 1848 a Napoli.* Ed. Albrighi e Segati, Milan, 1921, 42 ff. On Antonio Maresca, the father, see note 94, p. 156.

96 Giuseppe Ceva Grimaldi, Marquis of Pietracatella. (1777-1862). Neapolitan nobleman and a prominent personality of the period. He was superintendent of the Great Archives (Grande Archivio). In 1821, he was appointed State Councillor, to which post he was reappointed in 1824. In 1826, he was appointed a Visitor of the provinces of Principato Ultra Capitanata, Terra di Bari, and Terra di Otranto. From Nov. 21, 1830 to Dec. 23, 1831, he was minister of the interior, president of the general advisory body of the Kingdom; and from Jan. 14, 1840 to Jan. 27, 1848, he was president of the council of ministers. The *Almanach de Gotha* (1840, 218) lists the Marquis of Pietracatella as Councillor of State, Minister of State, and President of the "Consulta Generale" of the Kingdom.

97 Girolamo Ruffo, Marquis, (-1829). He belonged to a branch of the noble family to which the Prince of Scaletta and the Prince of Castelcicala also belonged. He was minister of the Royal House to Sept. 9, 1832, and councillor and minister of state without portfolio. After May 18, 1836, he was *interim* President of the council of ministers. The *Almanach de Gotha* (1840, 218) lists the Marquis of Ruffo as Councillor of State, Minister of State, and President of the Council of Ministers *ad interim*.

manners reserved, it is not expected to him to yeild [sic] his opinion or waive his opposition. I do not consider his promotion, however, as any evidence of a change on the part of the King in his views; he is committed to the new policy in a way that he cannot depart from it.

I asked the Prince of Cassaro if I might take the liberty to call his attention to my note, requesting information of the state of the tobacco contract; and he replied, that he had the information collected ready for me, and would send it in the course of two days; but I have not yet received it.

The following correspondence has taken place in relation to the claim of Carusi.

Napoli 28. Novembre 1839. Il sottoscritto Ministro, Segretario di Stato degli Affari Esteri con nota del 24 Novembre passato anno, nell'intertenere il Signor Throop Incaricato d'Affari degli Stati Uniti di America sulla natura de' reclami prodotti dal Regio Suddito Gaetano Carusi, lo pregava ad interessarsi della di lui posizione commiserevole, ed intercedere presso il Governo Americano, mediante i suoi valevoli uffizî a pro del Carusi quella giustizia che gli si competea.

Niun riscontro finora essendo pervenuto dal Signor Incaricato d'affari, e d'altronde facendo il Carusi iterate istanze per la definizione di questo affare, dietro la quale egli si augura di venir tratto dallo stato d'indigenza in che trovasi per le perdite che assicura di aver sofferte, il Sottoscritto ha il pregio di rivolgersi novellamente al Signor Throop per rammentargli la cosa; e coglie questa occasione per rinnovargli le proteste della sua distinta considerazione.

Signed. Il Principe di Cassaro.

Naples December 19, 1839. The Undersigned chargé d'affaires of the United States of America, hastens to reply to the note of his Excellency the Minister, Secretary of State for foreign affairs of the 28th. of November last on the subject of the claims upon the American government of Gaetano Carusi.

It will be reccollected [sic] that Carusi, although a native born subject of his Majesty, has voluntarily resided for the last thirty years or more, under the protection of the government of the United States, subject to it's laws, and participating in all the rights of an American citizen, in respect to any claims he may have upon the government or individuals. If he has any just claims upon the American government, the consideration of them belongs to the legislative department, and not to the Executive, and he has very properly called the attention of Congress to his case. No citizen has a right to petition the President of the United States for redress in a like case, or even to ask the influence of the Executive department.

The undersigned had the honor of expaining this matter to his Excellency the Minister Secretary of State for foreign affairs, by his official note of the 30th. of November 1838, and at the same time to inform him that from respect to the high official source from whence he was requested to interest himself in behalf of Carusi's claim, he would communicate the matter to his government. This he did by an official letter of the sixth of December following. The undersigned seizes the occasion to renew to his Excellency the Prince of Cassaro, the assurances of his most distinguished consideration.

Signed — E. T. Throop

You will perceive that I was in no haste to reply, and that my answer is laconic.

The mail is in today without bringing the message, and without news of the Steamer Liverpool. My newspapers now arrive regularly by the way of Havre.

E. T. THROOP TO J. FORSYTH

Naples March 25, 1840. [Despatch No. 15.]

Sir

There is a new face upon affairs here; and the Prince of Cassaro has resigned.

From the period of the date of my last dispatch until within a few days past, knowing that the Prince of Cassaro was much perplexed with his foreign affairs, and that nothing material was going forward, I refrained from alluding to our negociations.

Mr. Temple having recently returned to his post, and I having heard that there was excitement in the King's cabinet in consequence of a communication from him, I said to the Prince in a crowded room, "Is there any thing new in your relations with England." He replied with embarrassment after a little hesitation, that affairs were going badly, and that he would talk with me about them. In the course of the following week I was told that the Prince had refused to sign some Communication dictated by the King, and had expressed his readiness to resign. I called immediately at his house and left a note requesting him to fix a time when he would see me. In the course of that day (the 21st March inst.) I received a note from the Prince of Scilla & Duke of S. Cristina[98] informing me that the King, having accepted the resignation of the Prince of Cassaro, had charged him with the portfolio for foreign affairs: and I received another from the Prince of Cassaro to the same effect.

Being desirous to know the exact truth as well as to pay my respects to the fallen Minister, whose virtues had secured my esteem, I called at his house the next day & was admitted to see him. After I had expressed my regret and sympathies he said, ["]perhaps you do not know all the circumstances["]: — I replied that I did not. He then said that in the course of their correspondence with England, the King had required him to sign a paper at variance with what he had promised both verbally and in writing and with the sanction of the King: and that he had replied that his Majesty might remove him from office, or imprison him, but that he required of him that which he could not in honor and would not do. He added with feeling that he had maintained through life the character of a man of honor, and that he did not mean at this time to forfeit it.

I learnt from him also, that the occasion of the rupture was a demand of the British government, that the sulphur monopoly should be broken up, and that British subjects should be paid large damages, which they claim, for the interruption of their business; accompanied by a threat that they would remedy themselves by force, if the demand should not be complied with. The King took offence at this, and directed an answer that he would not rescind his acts in regard to the sulphur. It was this reply which the Prince of Cassaro refused to sign, having promised before, by authority from the King, that the monopoly should be broken up.

That I should not be misled by rumor in regard to any of the facts, I paid a visit to Count Lebzeltern, the Austrian Minister, who, I was aware from his age, experience, position and long residence, at this Court must be intimately acquainted with all

---

[98] Fulco Ruffo di Calabria. Prince of Scilla, Duke of Santa Cristina. (1773-1852). Diplomat, councillor of state and ambassador to Spain. He became a prominent political figure after the crisis of March 1840. He was minister of foreign affairs from March 20, 1840 to Feb. 1848. He left the diplomatic service at the time of the sulphur crisis. The *Almanach de Gotha* (1840, 219) states that he was also Councillor of State.

the facts. He informed me that the terms of the treaty stipulated with McGregor embraced their commercial relations, and relinquished on the part of Great Britain their claim to ten per cent, which was so embarrassing to this government; but that one of the inducements to the British government for making this treaty was their desire to break up the sulphur monopoly, and that promises to remove this difficulty had been made before and cotemporaneously [sic] with the more formal act concluded with McGregor. The King had constantly hesitated to give an official sanction to the act while the British were amused with promises. Instructions from the British government to make the peremptory demand mentioned preceded, a short time, the arrival of M^r. Temple, and Mr. Kennedy was induced by the Prince of Cassaro not to present it, under the beleif [sic] that the King was upon the point of complying, and that this demand might irritate the King and make a new embroilment. M^r. Temple on his arrival, and seeing the debates in parliament, considered it his duty to delay no longer.

I am not sure that I have sufficiently explained the sulphur question, heretofore; it is simply this:

The fifth article of the treaty of 1816 between Great Britain and the Two Sicilies secures the privilege to British subjects to reside within the Two Sicilies, to occupy dwelling and ware houses, to dispose of their personal property of every kind and description, by sale, gift, exchange or will, without the smallest loss or hindrance given to them. — they are to be exempt from military service — they are to pay no taxes but such as are paid by the most favored nations within the dominions of Sicily — they are to be subject to no vexatious search or visits — and to no arbitrary examination of their books papers or accounts. His Sicilian Majesty guarantees to them residing in his dominions the preservation of their property and personal security, in the same manner as those are guaranteed to his subjects, and to all foreigners belonging to the most favored and most highly privileged nations.

Under this treaty individuals and companies of british [sic] subjects established themselves in Sicily, in the business of manufacturing sulphur. Nearly two years since the King granted to a company, composed principally of french [sic] Carlists, the privilege of vending all the sulphur manufactured in Sicily, and of limiting the amount to be made so as to enable them to fix their own price upon the article. The manufacturer was not

468

entirely absolutely prohibited from sending his productions abroad, but there was a very heavy duty imposed upon it's [sic] exportation by him, part of which went as profits to the Company. For this privilege the King receives a large bonus.

The British government complains (with what justice it is not for me to say) that this interference with the manufacture of sulphur by the British subjects settled in Sicily is an infraction of the treaty. The Marquis of Pietracatella, now President of the Council of Ministers, whom I have before mentioned as hostile to the commercial policy of the Prince of Cassaro still remains of the same opinion but he is in favor of rescinding the sulphur contract, and warmly sustained the Prince in the Council. This fact I get from the Prince himself.

It is said, and I beleive [sic] truly, that when the Prince of Cassaro refused to sign the King required Pietracatella to sign it as President of the Council; and that he retired to his house after the Council broke up and sent to the King his resignation as the alternative if he persisted in demanding his signature. The King was unwilling to part with Cassaro, and sent the Minister of grace and justice, and the Minister of police both of whom are members of the Council of Ministers to persuade him to remain in office: on seeing them enter his apartment he said, perhaps you have come to conduct me to prison, if such is the will of his Majesty I am ready.

The Prince has the sympathy of all the diplomatic corps.

· All now is battle & preparation for war, and the King has, with the greatest activity sent troops & munitions of War to Sicily, determined, as he says, to resist, force by force. In the mean time he sends as Minister to England, one of his courtiers the Prince of Castelcicala,[99] who has the merit of speaking the English language, and of knowing some of the English, having faught [sic] and been wounded on the Continent under English Generals; accompanied, in an unofficial character by a lawyer

---

99 Paolo Ruffo. Duke of Calvello and later Prince of Castelcicala. (1791-1865). He was born in Richmond, England, while his father was minister of the King of Naples in England. Educated at Eton, he fought at Waterloo in the ranks of the British army, acquiring the habits and manners of a true Englishman. Entering the diplomatic career, he was chargé d'affaires at Berne from 1824 to 1829. From Sept. 24, 1841, to 1852, he was envoy extraordinary and minister plenipotentiary at London. In March 1853, he was entrusted with an extraordinary mission to Francis Joseph. From May 1855, to May 16, 1860, he was lieutenant general and commander of the forces in Sicily. On his education, see: Raffaele De Cesare, *La fine di un regno*, etc., passim; for his diplomatic activity, see: Ruggero Moscati, *Ferdinando II° di Borbone nei documenti diplomatici austriaci.* 78 ff. On his father, Fabrizio Ruffo, see note 25, p. 184.

of some merit and talents. At the same time the Duke of Serra-capriola has orders to embark immediately for France.

The habit of this government is procrastination, and nothing is ever brought to a close by negociation. I said to Count Leb-zeltern that I supposed we had an interest in common on the question of the Commercial treaty, and that I had relied upon it's being concluded, more upon the influence which his government might have over the King, than upon his own energy to adopt measures so strong as to change the long established policy of his Kingdom. He replied that the Austrian interests in favor of a free trade were six times greater than ours, and that they had been negociating for it twenty two years without success.

With such a disposition on the part of Austria it is my impression that this rupture will bring about the conclusion of the treaty. The British government have the power to force compliance, and will do it if they are not checked, by the conti-nental powers. If the King had simply put himself upon his dignity as an independent monarch, and had demanded a recal [sic] of the menace without replying to the demand; and if he is right in treating the question as an interference by England in the internal administration of his government, he might have invoked the other powers to interfere and to interpose a shield against his powerful foe. There is no power in Europe that would like to see Sicily under the influence of Great Britain. As it is, I beleive [sic] that the immense power of Austria, guided by it's present able councils, will be wielded if necessary, to bring about an accomodation, which will leave Naples open to her Commerce.

The Prince of Scilla who is now charged (not appointed Secretary) with the portfolio of foreign affairs is old and has lived retired; I do not know him personally. He was never distinguished, but he answers the present purpose of the King. The withdrawal of the Prince of Cassaro is a great loss to the King, and there is no one in his Council able to fill his place. He has had much experience in public life, having represented this Court at Madrid and Vienna before he entered the King's Council. He is courteous in his manners and frank and honorable in his disposition. The young King needs such a Counsellor near him. I hope that he will return to his post after the present dif-ficulty shall be settled; but Count Lebzeltern thinks that he will not.

It seems superfluous for me to add, that further direct negocia-tion on our part must await coming events.

I have the honor to acknowledge the receipt of the letter from the department of the 13th. January 1840 enclosing a letter from the President to the King, which I transmitted with a note dated the 6th. March to the Minister of foreign affairs. I received an acknowledgement of the receipt of it, with information that it had been laid before his Majesty, dated the 10th. of March. As it is desirable to make as little bulk as possible, I do not transmit copies of these notes, nor of those of ceremony which have passed between the present & late ministers and myself on the occasion of the change.

As the letter of January 13 is marked N° 6 and I do not find N°. 5 among my papers I fear that one has miscarried.[100] It acknowledges the receipt of all my dispatches except N°. 3. That dispatch referred to the claim of Carusi, and treated on the subject of the consular establishments in the two Sicilies.

E. T. Throop to J. Forsyth

Naples April 6. 1840. [Despatch N° 16.]

Sir

As the Steam Ship will leave Portsmouth on the 1st of the next month, and the roads must have suffered by the rain and snow, which has continued to fall, with little interruption up to this time, through the month of March, I think it prudent to avail myself of this mail to forward a dispatch. In a few days I will have the honor to write to you more fully, in the hope that my letter will reach London in season for the same conveyance.

The King is pushing forward his preparations for war with great vigor. He has already thrown about 20,000 troops into Sicily, and he displays much activity in personally superintending the operations. The Duke of Serracapriola has gone Minister to France, and the Prince of Castelcicala to England; but the person I mentioned in my last as about to accompany the latter has not gone. Dispatches have been sent to Russia, and probably to the other European Courts. The Prince of Cassaro was waited upon the evening before last by an officer, who conducted him out of the City with orders, it is said, to escort him to Foggia, a town in the Province of Capitanata near the Adriatic Sea; there to remain a prisoner of State.

The answer to the demand of the British government, which

---

[100] Instruction No. 5 was not found.

it is said the Prince of Cassaro refused to sign, has not been sent, and I am not certain that any answer has yet been returned. A reply, however, embracing the views of this government, has been drawn up and presented in a pamphlet form,[101] a copy of which I will forward to you at a future time. It is written with good sense, and briefly and clearly states the arguments upon which this government denies the right of the British to intermeddle with the Sulphur monopoly. It States,

1. That the granting of monopolies is an act of sovereignty, which no other nation has a right to complain of, and instances the various monopolies which the British government has granted.

2. That the limits to production established by the Sulphur monopoly, abridging the rights of proprietors, is a prudential and proper restraint, to prevent the exhaustion of monies: drawing a distinction in this respect between the productions of the soil, and those of mines.

3rd. That the treaty of 1816 secures to British subjects no other rights or privileges than the Subjects of the most favored nations enjoy.

E. T. Throop to J. Forsyth

Naples April 8. 1840. [Despatch N°. 17.]

Sir

Wishing to avail myself of the mail to apprize you of passing events, and fearing to trust to it any thing improper to be read by the authorities here, I had the honor of transmitting a brief notice of events by a dispatch dated the 6th. instant. As the Steam boat for Marseilles leaves this port tomorrow, I intend to improve the opportunity to write you more fully upon the same topics, in the beleif [sic] that it is still in season for the Steam Ship, which will leave Portsmouth on the first day of May.

A British armed Steam boat from Malta has been lying here for three or four days. It is understood that it came here for the purpose of receiving dispatches from the Minister, and that it arrived about the expiration of the time[102] given by the british [sic] Minister to this government to reply to his note. Yesterday morning the Prince of Scilla, Minister for foreign affairs had an interview with the British Minister, at the house of the latter, and in the afternoon, the British Minister carried in person, his dis-

---

101 The copy of this pamphlet was not found.
102 Only one British vessel needed!

patches fixed by a Clique who now surround & possess exclusively the ear of the King, who have private reasons for not wishing the sulphur contract to be rescinded, and whose private interests would be promoted by a War. I shall be understood when I say, that the Sulphur contract was gained by a bribe of several hundred thousand Ducats, shared among others by the King's confessor, the Minister of the Interior, and the Commander in Chief of the King's army; and that no fortunes are now made here except by bribery or plunder.

I am told that the Prince of Cassaro received with great calmness the order to prepare to leave Naples within two hours, and said to his family who were weeping around him: "Be comforted! this is proof that I am not among the worst men in Naples; if I were I should have remained in office.["]

I have said that the King may probably loose [sic] the services of Pietracatella from his Councils. He has commenced an heroic career, and it is to be hoped for the honor of human nature, that he has enough of the Roman in him to hold out. He as President of the Council of Ministers has maintained the doctrine, that the Monopoly is an invasion of those rights of the Proprietors which nature gives them, and which despotic power should respect: and he appalled his associates in the Council by telling his Majesty, that under constitutional governments the people can remedy themselves by calling the ministers to account, but that under a despotic government the ministers are bound, in duty, to interpose themselves as a shield against oppressive acts by the King. And he having refused to attend a subsequent council, the books containing the proceedings and among other things a question mooted by the King, whether Cassaro should be sent into exile, he refused to sign the book, sent on his own resignation, and with it as the page to the King, that if his Majesty decided to exile Cassaro, he should beg the favor to be exiled with him. His resignation was not accepted, he afterwards attended the Council, and the day before Cassaro was arrested, and after a conference of some hours with a confidential agent of the King, he said to a friend that the sky was beginning to clear up. Cassaro was arrested on the King's own motion, without again consulting the Council. Pietracatella was ignorant of it, yet he was acting in the Council at the last intelligence I had of him. I think, however, if he should be inclined to bend to the storm rather than encounter destruction, that he will find it impossible to do so with his opinions and his mould of mind.

As to the issue: my opinion is, that the war will be a short one. Sicily wants but a protector to revolt from this government; and it's dissatisfaction cannot fail to be increased by the treatment of Cassaro, who is a Sicilian and of one of the most noble and ancient families of the Kingdom. He represented them at this Court, his place is now filled by a Neopolitan [sic], and the King has thrown in upon them an army of Swiss and Neopolitans [sic]. Throughout the Kingdom, on this side of the Strait, there is discontent which is shared by the troops and they will not fight. In my opinion five thousand English troops, perhaps less, landed at three or four different points, in this part of the Kingdom, would render the King as powerless as if he was fixed by a magic spell. He would discover that resistance by force was useless, and he would place all his hopes upon being sustained by the European powers. As I have given my opinion in a former recent dispatch, upon the course these powers would pursue, and seeing no reason to change it, I will not trouble you with a repetition.

I sum up by saying that it will depend upon England whether there shall be hostilities, and we should be prepared for such an event. I shall immediately apprize Commodore Hull[103] of the state of things here.

This affair has not only postponed our negociation, but has put it in a much worse condition. It is supposed by some that the King was never sincere in making a treaty with England. I think otherwise: Cassaro beleived [sic] that all the difficulties with the King were overcome; and that with a little more patience on the part of England, he would have signed the treaty and rescinded the contract. Indeed I am well assured that the King had actually signed and placed in Cassaro's hands an order to rescind the sulphur contract, but that he was startled at the enormous demands which the English were prepared to present for damages; and was beset by the persons around him, who had shared in the bribe, and wished to be protected in what they had received.

Cassaro can never come into favor again. If in concluding eventually a treaty the British should consider themselves bound to see him (who has suffered by his fidelity to his engagements with them, and who with large possessions is actually poor, and in want of the salary of which he has been deprived) in some way provided for, he may perhaps be restored to his salary, but never probably to his place or influence in the cabinet. The place

---

103 See above p. 447 and note 89 thereon.

of Minister of foreign affairs will probably be occupied by one of different views of commercial policy.

We have had the promise of a treaty of reciprocity; a treaty which has always seemed to me of little value unless it provides for the introduction into this Kingdom of our productions upon a footing approaching to equality, in respect to duties, with the introduction into our Country of the productions of the Two Sicilies; or, unless it should leave us at entire liberty to operate through our tariff upon the interests of this Kingdom. In regard to the first proposition I hoped to gain something through the liberal views of the Prince of Cassaro; and in regard to the other it is a question whether our tariff measures shall precede or follow a treaty. It is very certain that this government supposes that we have need of those productions of theirs which we admit free of duty, or we would not place their admission upon so favorable a footing.

E. T. THROOP TO J. FORSYTH

Naples April 14. 1840. [Despatch N°. 18.]
Sir,

As another Steam boat leaves this port for Marseilles, today, by which I can send a dispatch out of the Kingdom, without trusting it to the post office, and as it is yet in Season for the Steam Ship of the 1ˢᵗ. of May, I avail myself of the occasion to inform you of what has transpired since my last.

It is now rumored in this City, that the difficulties are settled; and the rentes, or government Stock, which fell from 105 to 98 & below, were yesterday again at 104 without sellers. I have learned from the very best source of information: that the rumor of a speedy adjustment is not without foundation: my informants [sic] words are "It is probable, nay, I may say almost certain, that in a few days the causes of war will be removed." From what I have gathered in the same conversation, and from other sources, I infer, that the persons who hold the Sulphur monopoly contract are desirous to relinquish it, fearing that it would prove an unprofitable speculation if a war, or an interruption of commerce should grow out of it. I think, therefore that it will soon be announced that the Sulphur monopoly is at end; and probably a duty will be laid upon the article sufficient to compensate the monopolists, and defray certain other expenses which have been incurred on account of it.

This alone will not satisfy the British for they claim *damages*; and in proportion as the fear of the English residents in this Kingdom, of a sequestration of their property, in consequence of hostilities diminishes, their clamors will increase that their government shall insist upon damages. Whether the King of the Two Sicilies is prepared to advance this step, or not, it is not worthwhile for me, in the present state of my information, to advance an opinion. When he once begins to yeild [sic] he will find himself urged forward by the strongest impulse of his nature; I mean avarice; as the amount necessary to satisfy all claims is trifling, compared with the expenses to which even the present state of thing subjects him. The duties of all kinds levied here, are as much as the Kingdom can well bear; and as a despotic monarch, the King exercises the right of placing in his private coffers, all the revenues which are not required for the public service. By a System of retrenchment, and economy in his household and official expenditures, amounting to parsimony, he has his coffers full of money, and no other passion can long resist the feelings with which he must see the golden heap rapidly diminishing. I avail myself of this occasion to give you these traits of character, to which I have not deemed it prudent before to allude.

I have never supposed that it was the intention of the British government to make war, but that they thought it would be sufficient for the Lion to shew his teeth and claws. Having however threatened force unqualifiedly, I have supposed that if the King should not succumb, the question with them would afterwards be, not so much whether their treaty had been violated according to the laws of nations, as whether the other powers of Europe would permit them to employ force. What might eventually be the course of the European powers I will not conjecture, but I have the same unquestionable authority to which I have before alluded, for saying, that the King of the Two Sicilies will receive no countenance, in his present position, from the governments in whose protection he would principally rely.

The Sulphur question and the treaty question as I mentioned in my last are now independent of each other, and if this King should comply with the demands of the British in regard to the former question, I do not beleive [sic] that the latter government would ratify the treaty stipulated with McGregor without further provisions. Nor do I beleive [sic] that this government, with it's [sic] reformed Cabinet, will as formerly, be disposed to open it's

476

trade with the world upon the footing of reciprocity. Pietracatella, notwithstanding his bravery at the outset, still remains in the Cabinet, a deadly foe to all innovations.

Since Cassaro has fallen[104] it is the aim of all his enemies to gather and heap upon his head, all the sins with which he has at any time been charged; and it is perhaps unfortunate for us, that he is now again accused of having weakly yeilded [sic] to our indemnity claim, and also of having given more than was our due. The accusation receives force by the use which the English have made of it, during the present difficulty, more, I beleive [sic] with the design of doing us injury than of promoting their own cause by argument.

Our negociation is now interrupted, and I do not know when it can with advantage be renewed. I have received no answer to my note of the 8th of July last, which accompanied the project of a treaty, copies of which I had the honor to transmit to the department with my dispatch N°. 8. I have been waiting for a more favorable opportunity to press for a reply. I doubt whether the attention of this government can be drawn to it, with any degree of favor, until we put ourselves in a better condition to demand it. I beleive [sic] it is necessary to carry into effect Mr. Benton's[105] measures, in order to awaken the attention of the government; our existing tariff laws certainly place us in an unfavorable position here, for negociation. I am prepared to expect that the first question which will be put to me on resuming the negociation, is, what will you give us in return for that which we may relinquish in favor of your commerce; and it will be very difficult to make the government understand that it has the consideration in hand.

E. T. THROOP TO J. FORSYTH

Naples May 11. 1840. [Despatch N°. 19.]

Sir,

When I had the honor to write my last dispatch it was generally beleived [sic] here, that all differences had been adjusted between Great Britain and this government, and all fear

---

104 For events surrounding the Prince of Cassaro's fall, see above, this chapter, pp. 469, 472, 473, 474; he was relieved from exile, see below, Despatch No. 28, May 2, 1841, pp. 501-502.

105 For excellent biography with steel engravings of Senator Thomas Hart Benton (1782-1858), see: *Appleton's Cyclopedia of American Biography* (1888) I, 241-243. See also note 82, p. 436.

of hostilities had been dismissed. After a few days, however, it was announced that cruisers from the English fleet had captured some Neapolitan Vessels, and sent them into Malta. This proved true, and an English armed Steamer kept moving actively about the bay, and frequently came into the harbor, sometimes lay under the guns of the fort, and without interruption kept up intercourse with the City, and on one occasion offered to land persons taken from captured Vessels, but this was prohibited.

On the 25th. April an armed French Steamer arrived; that evening the King laid an embargo upon the English Vessels, about seven or eight in number, then, in this port, and removed them within the harbor, close under the guns of his armed ships; the next day another french Steamer arrived; in the evening the English ships were released; and the next morning it was announced that the french government[106] had offered it's mediation, which had been accepted by both parties, and that the captured Ships on both sides were to be released.

I send herewith a paper containing an article which appeared in the government Journal of the 28th April which was prepared under the eye of the King, and had his sanction, in which it is declared that the difference between the two governments had been satisfactorily terminated by a *voluntary* and kind offer of the King of the french to mediate between the parties, which had been accepted by England, and which his Majesty had not hesitated to accept, and that the negociation was to be conducted at Paris. It also states that by a preliminary arrangement the vessels seized on both sides are to be given up.

This Article produced much agitation here. In the first place, I understand that the French chargé called upon the Minister of foreign affairs to protest against that part of it which states that the offer of mediation was voluntary on the part of France, affirming that it had been solicited by Naples. Next the British Minister called to complain that it misrepresented the preliminary agreement, affirming that the captured Neapolitan ships were not to be surrendered, but to be held to abide the event. And lastly, the Austrian Ambassador loudly complained that the King should have abandoned his natural ally Austria, the protector of Italy, and forgot his duty to the holy alliance, and thrown himself into the arms of a constitutional government.

The English have discontinued Captures, but they have not given up the captured ships. Every thing is in doubt, there is no

---

106 See: Grosjean, *Les relations de la France avec les Deux Siciles*. Paris, 1888.

confidence in the public mind, and commerce is almost at an end. The same confusion prevails in the King's council as every where else. The Prince of Scilla who holds the port folio of foreign affairs is a mere man of straw; he takes no responsibility, nor does the King exact any from him. A Priest by the name of Capriola,[107] who has heretofore been the private secretary of the King, has been put in the office, as under secretary, with the understanding that he was to control the office, but he has not given the King entire satisfaction, nor is there entire harmony between him and some of the members of the Cabinet. The King has a great disposition to manage affairs himself, and finding them not to go well, he finds fault with his ministers, many of whom are corrupt and guilty & stand trembling for their fate.

There was nothing in the way of rescinding the Sulphur contract, and upon it's being known that the King has resolved to do it, the opinion was generally entertained, and among others by the Austrian Minister, that every difficulty would be settled. What caused the breach in the negociations which resulted in the reprisals by the English, I do now know certainly, but I suppose it to have been the extravagant demands of the English for damages. The Austrian government did not wish a rupture, and I beleive [sic] that it's influence was exerted here to induce the King to comply with the English demands. In this it may have been moved somewhat by a desire to get rid of the embarrassing English treaty, but principally by much more important considerations connected with the political relations of Europe.

Negociation here is now at an end, it being transferred to England & France; and the King departed yesterday, with the

---

107 Giuseppe Caprioli (1794-1870). Priest. He was charged with the Protocol of the Council of State. He was private secretary of Ferdinand II from 1831 to 1841, exercising an ever increasing influence on the King. Together with Mgr. Cocle, Archbishop of Patras, Father Caprioli became one of the most powerful men in the Neapolitan court. He was one of the most courageous accusers of Lebzeltern who was suspected of being the leader of a movement, among the diplomatic corps accredited to Naples, hostile to the sovereign. Although he did not agree with the Prince of Cassaro, Father Caprioli tried to mitigate the political excesses of Ferdinand II. He was one of the principal authors of the conciliatory policies toward the liberals which the Bourbon King exercised at the beginning of his reign. Father Caprioli brought about closer relations between Naples and Sardinia, having been chiefly responsible for the marriage of the King to Maria Cristina of Savoy. After the crisis of 1840, he hoped to keep control of the foreign policies of the kingdom, by supporting the name of the Prince of Scilla, Fulco Ruffo. But having become a *persona non grata,* Father Caprioli was not able to attain his purpose, and was replaced by Don Leopoldo Corsi. Father Caprioli was vice-president of the general advisory body (Consulta Generale) of the Kingdom from April 1841 to Feb. 1848. See: V. Riccio, "Un segretario di Ferdinando II°." in *Saggi Biografici,* Milan, 1924, passim; Ruggero Moscati, *Ferdinando II° di Borbone,* etc., 24, 25, 42, 47, 48.

Queen, for Sicily, to review his troops there, and return in the course of ten or twelve days. He likes to be with his army, & to move secretly, and it is my opinion that he will not return very speedily to his capital.

I am watching with anxiety the progress of the boundary question with England. However ignorant of the subject all other Englishmen may be, English statesmen know well how unfounded their pretentions are. And it appears to me that they will follow the obvious dictates of wisdom and purchase of Maine[108] the territory North of and including their road, rather than go to war, or refer to an impartial tribunal the exact question of boundary; and I am not sufficiently conversant with the subject to see why Maine, or the United States, should not be willing to accept such an arrangement. The navigation of the St. John's, I suppose, can be acquired only by negociation or conquest. I cannot perceive that our government can have any interest in cutting off the communication between Great Britain and the province, for in time of peace the money expended by the British government in its northern colonies promotes the industry of the Union, and in time of war it will depend entirely upon the disposition of the Canadas whether the attempt to sever them would be judicious or not. But if Great Britain chooses war I am not among those who think, that a war at this time, is the greatest calamity which could befal [sic] us.

I have the honor to send herewith my accounts of contingent expenses for the last two quarters of the year 1839, and I have the first quarter of the present year ready except that it is deficient in the items from London. It is the difficulty of getting my account in season from London which I offer as my apology for not being more prompt in forwarding my accounts. My previous accounts have not been acknowledged, and I am desirous of being informed, with as little delay as is compatable [sic], whenever there is anything objectionable in them as to items or proofs. I wish to avoid the embarrassment of meeting them at a future day.

I have received no communication from the department later than that numbered 6. —

---

108 This boundary question was settled by the Webster-Ashburton treaty between United States and Great Britain on August 9, 1842. This brought to a close a dispute that had been going on since the treaty of peace in 1783. For text of treaty see: Miller, *op. cit.*, IV, 363-477.

E. T. THROOP TO J. FORSYTH

Naples June 15. 1840. [Despatch N°. 20]
Sir,

Nothing very material has occurred to change the state of things here since the last dispatch which I had the honor to send you, but I write now, not only to say this, but also to correct the numberless false reports which may reach you through the Gazettes.

The Duke of Montebello is here as *Ambassador* and charged, as I understand, with the mediation, but it is very difficult to find out precisely how it progresses, as much secrecy is observed by all interested, and many rumors constantly agitate the public mind. These rumors are often contradictory but their tenor is generally some new version of the final adjustment of the controversy: that the captured vessels are to be restored, and that the british [sic] fleet, lying at the port is about to take its departure. Nevertheless, the merchant vessels do not return, nor does the fleet depart.

I endeavored to improve the opportunities which I have had within a few days past to converse with M^r. Temple on the subject; and I found from the conversation that nothing had yet been concluded, and that from the difficulty of bringing this government to action, he apprehended much delay. I was most anxious to ascertain whether the commercial treaty would be consummated with the other affairs; but all that I gathered from him was that McGregor came here merely to give advice, and procure information but that he was not clothed with any powers to negociate and that what he concluded was unauthorized, and his conduct disapproved.

From another individual whose means of information warrant me in relying upon the accuracy of his statement, I gather facts at variance with M^r. Temple's statement in regard to the want of authority on the part of McGregor. Sir Frederick Lamb preceeded [sic] McGregor here, with the powers of Ambassador, and all the principal topics of the treaty were discussed and agreed upon. When he departed he promised to send McGregor, who is a man of detail, to arrange and put into form the minor matters. This corresponds with my understanding of it as the negociation progressed, and the assurances which I received from time to time from the Prince of Cassaro. Immediately after Sir Frederick Lamb went away the Prince informed me that the

481

treaty would soon be concluded, and he expected to meet Sir F. Lamb at Vienna to sign the articles. Something occurred to interfere with that arrangement; and when afterwards McGregor came here and the treaty was put into form, the Prince beleived [sic] that nothing was wanting to consummation except the formality of the King's signature.

I am told from the same source of information to which I have last alluded, that there is the strongest reason for beleiving [sic] that the sulphur difficulties, the matters under the mediation of France, will be arranged in the course of ten or twelve days;[109] that Lord Palmerston[110] now regrets his hasty violent measures and would be very happy if they could be sunk in oblivion; and that instead of the £1000 a day claimed for damages amounting to several hundred thousand pounds in the aggregate, they will be content with a small sum say 10 or even £8000. If this be true I can readily beleive [sic] that the difference will soon be compromised, as the King had determined to cancel the Sulphur contract at the outset, and that it was a thing conceded in submitting to the mediation. The contractors in that case will exact a large equivalent for their contract, but it can be raised by a duty upon the Article.

I am told also that the Prince of Cassaro will be recalled from his exile within a few weeks, and elevated to a higher rank than he had hitherto attained, that of Counselor of State, and that the portfolio of foreign affairs will probably be restored to him. This is an event much to be desired, as it would bring back to us a hope of renewing with success our suspended negociation for a commercial treaty. The present chargé of the portfolio is a most inefficient personage.

I send herewith marked A. & B. the Copy of a note from the Minister of foreign affairs and my reply, in relation to some

---

109 The issue of April 24-30, 1840, No. 16, of the *Giornale del Regno delle Due Sicilie* (which was enclosed) announced, under date of April 28, that negotiations between England and Naples to settle the sulphur dispute were under way. The account given in this issue is incomplete since some of the sheets of the paper are missing.

110 Henry John Temple. Third Viscount Palmerston in the peerage of Ireland. (1784-1865). Statesman. He spent much of his youth in Italy. He was in charge of the foreign office from 1830 to 1841, except for a brief interval in 1834-35, during which Peel held office. In 1840, he was responsible for the instructions on the conduct of the negotiations with the Government of Naples regarding the sulphur monopoly. Under Palmerston the prestige of England was greatly enhanced throughout Europe. He pursued a strong foreign policy. He was ever in sympathy with the cause of Italian independence. In 1848-49, he favored secretly the revolutionary governments of Italy and Hungary. *Dictionary of National Biography*, 1921, XIX, 496-513.

disorderly conduct, at a public house, charged upon two American officers of the Sloop of War Cyane, recently here. I consider it a captain's affair and have so treated it. The Minister was induced to make the complaint on the representation of the young gentleman sitting in the Coffee house, who felt himself offended at one of the officers elevating his feet upon the table where he was sitting, and on remonstrating was followed with abusive language. I was told that one of the two was an Englishman and the other an American, probably an officer of marines; and I was pleased with the opportunity of throwing the *onus probandi* upon the other party. I should have beleived [sic] them both officers of the English navy, who were willing to throw the odium of their own misconduct upon the Americans, if it were not for the national trait displayed in the affair.

I have the honor to forward my accounts for the first quarter of the present year.

I have received two boxes of books, documents of the two last Sessions of Congress.

THE PRINCE OF SCILLA TO E. T. THROOP

[Enclosure 'A' with Despatch No. 20, June 15, 1840. Copy]

Napoli 28 Maggio 1840. Verso le ore 12 della sera del 24 corrente, due officiali Americani ebbri essendo nella bottega di Caffè, sita sotto l'Albergo Reale ruppero quivi co' loro bastoni i Cristalli della porta, e poscia impresero a percuotere parimente i tubi di lumi, ed uno di questi venne ridotto in pezzi, alcuni dei quali caddero su di un Gentiluomo, sito colà. — Colui se nè [sic] dolse, ma urbanamente rilevò loro la sconvenevolezza, et passò in altra Stanza. Gli uffiziali seguirono a molestarlo, allora il gentiluomo disse loro, che compativa lo stato loro di ebbrezza. In questo mentre giungeva l'Uffiziale di Polizia, ed avvertitine gli uffiziali andarono via. Il Ministro di Polizia dispose che l'indomani un Ispettore si recasse a bordo la Corvetta per reclamarne al Comandante, ma il legno era partito. Il Sottoscritto, Consigliere, Ministro di Stato, Incaricato del Portafoglio degli affari Esteri si sollecita informarne il Signor Throop, Incaricato di Affari degli Stati Uniti di America, rilevandogli questo spiacevole avvenimento, il quale avrebbe potuto avere ingrate conseguenze a danno degli autori, et la prega voler disporre che in occorrenze di approdi di legni da guerra americani non si rinnovino, onde evitare maggiori disordini a scapito della pubblica quiete.

Il Sottoscritto confida che le sue premure saranno gentilmente secondate dal signor Incaricato, cui ha l'onore di rinnovar le proteste della sua particolare considerazione.

Signed — Principe di Scilla, Duca di Cristina.

E. T. THROOP TO THE PRINCE OF SCILLA

[Enclosure 'B' with Despatch No. 20, June 15, 1840. Copy]

Naples June 3, 1840.

The Undersigned Chargé d'affaires of the United States of America seizes the earliest moment to reply to the official note, which he had the honor to receive on the 1st. instant from his Excellency the Minister of State, charged with the portfolio of foreign affairs, dated the 28 ultimo, complaining of certain outrages, committed at a coffee house in the Capital by persons supposed to be two American officers. The Undersigned assures the Minister that he does but justice to his disposition in supposing, that he is ready to afford all the aid in his power in preventing, suppressing and punishing disorders by Americans, who may be so forgetful of their duties, as to occasion any disturbance of the public peace, while temporarily here; and it is with particular mortification that he was informed that American naval officers were charged with having so misdemeaned themselves here, as to require the intervention of the police.

As the Minister had not in his note informed the undersigned upon what proof the charge was made, against American officers, nor indicated the particular officers accused, and as the ship recently in this port had departed with all its officers, so that he had no opportunity to appeal to the officers themselves, he considered it his duty to institute an inquiry into the facts, at the place where the outrages were committed, and of the persons present on the occasion. He finds that the particulars of the disturbance are not naturally different from those related by the Minister in his note; but in regard to the persons, he ascertained that he who broke the lamp & thereby incommoded the gentleman sitting there, was not an American, but one who from his language & habiliments might have been mistaken for one; and that he is probably at this time, within the reach of the police officers of the City. Whether the other is, or is not an American he cannot precisely ascertain, but it is evident from the description of his dress that if he is an American, he is not a commissioned officer. It is a fair presumption however that as the two persons were associated in their amusement at the Coffee house they were fellow countrymen. It is due to them that I should add, that I was also informed that they freely paid the damages they had occasioned before they left the Coffee house, and made no effort to avoid the police officers. As the police officers had abundant time to interfere, it would have afforded the undersigned much satisfaction, and would have enabled him to pursue his inquiries effectually if they had taken the precaution at least to ascertain their country and their names.

The undersigned is well aware that the youth of all Countries even those ordinarily of correct deportment, are subject to occasional excesses, and while he renews the assurances of his ready cooperation with the authorities of this country in checking irregularties in his own countrymen, temporarily here, he will not refrain from expressing at the same time, his earnest desire to vindicate them from any unfounded accusations.

If the Minister should still beleive [sic] that the charges have not been misapplied to American officers, and will cause the proper proofs to be taken and communicated to the undersigned, so that the individuals may be identified he will make a prompt representation of the matter to the proper authorities. The undersigned avails himself with great pleasure, of the occasion to renew to his Excellency the Minister of State charged with the portfolio of foreign affairs the assurances of his high consideration & respect.

E. T. THROOP TO J. FORSYTH

Naples July 16. 1840. [Despatch N°. 21]

Sir,

I write you again at this time to keep you advised that nothing new of interest has occurred. The King went to Sicily, returned, went again after a few days, and is now daily expected back. We are at the season when it is the habit to transact but little business of any kind.

The King, either by accident or design, has thus managed his controversy with the British government with considerable adroitness. About the time the messenger arrived here with the mediation of France, accepted by England, he embargoed the English vessels in his ports and acceeded to the mediation, and removed the Embargo the next day. He afterwards insisted that it was unfair for the English to retain his ships, after he had so promptly restored theirs, and the differences were in the hands of a friendly power to adjust; and upon this pretence he would do nothing definitely.

The English have, at length, probably under french [sic] advice, given up the captured ships; and as the french [sic] government claims only to mediate by advice, and not to enforce its decisions, the parties are now back again in the position they stood before the English seizures were made. The policy of the King will now be, I think, to protract the negociation again, and do nothing, unless the English government reduce to a small amount their claim for damages, or relinquish them entirely.

I have been told that dispatches were received from England and communicated yesterday to the acting minister for foreign affairs, which roused him to take the advice of the council, and that the price of Stocks fell a little, in consequence of it. These symptoms are not entitled to much consideration, although the English have become impatient and probably have sent another menacing communication.

I send herewith the notice published in the government journal of the release of the Neapolitan ships.[111]

I have received no intimation of an intention on the part of this government to renew our negociation; nor is it to be expected until the difference with England take a decided character.

The information which I communicated in my last in reference to the Prince of Cassaro is at least premature; he still remains at Foggia, without any apparent change in his condition or prospects.

---

[111] This notice, published under the heading "domestic news," and dated Naples, June 17, announced that His Majesty had presided over the ordinary session of the Council of State, and gave details concerning the release of the ships.

E. T. Throop to J. Forsyth

Naples August 13, 1840. [Despatch N°. 22][112]

Sir

The dispatches which I noticed in my last, as having just arrived for this government, embraced a treaty, signed by the English and Sicilian Ministers at Paris, under the mediation of France, forwarded for the ratification of the King. It was carried by the Minister of foreign affairs to the King in Sicily, where he then was, ratified by him immediately and returned.

The terms of this treaty confirm the conjectures in my two last dispatches, that the King would not treat except upon the basis of a virtual relinquishment of the claim for damages. Whether it is by address or accident I will not pretend to say, but he has drawn himself out of the difficulty without loss; and the British have reaped only the wind from the whirlwind which they had sown. The Sulphur monopoly contract is annulled, and the King under the treaty has appointed commissioners, from among the Chamberlains of his own Court, to settle the amount of damages to be paid into the company in lieu of their contract. For the British claims, a board is to be created of five commissioners, two Neapolitan, two English and one French, who are to determine upon the damages of the English residents in Sicily, proprietors of the sulphur manufactories; but they are to award compensation for those damages only, sustained on the marketting [sic] of the sulphur actually on hand, at the time the monopoly went into operation.

The Company of Taix & Co. seem to be well satisfied with the manner of ascertaining their damages; and as the commissioners dare do nothing to displease the King, I account for it by their reliance upon the same influence which procured them their contract, as I mentioned in a former dispatch. As those who had sulphur on hand at the time the contract went into operation, could not have been so inattentive to their own interests as not to get it away, if in their power, into foreign markets where the prices would be much exaggerated by the operation of the monopoly; and as those who could not do this,

---

[112] This despatch is numbered by Mr. Throop No. 23, dated August 13, 1840. He also numbered the one sent on September 12 as No. 23. The earlier of these two despatches should be called No. 22, as there is correct sequencing, after the second one, from No. 24 onward. The correction in date (from July to August) seems to be in a different hand and pen. It appears that the correction in date was a change made in the State Department in Washington, upon receipt of the despatch on Sept. 18, and not by Mr. Throop ere it left his hand.

yet had the market open to them through the company, at prices certainly not much diminished, as the object of the monopoly was to enhance the price abroad, I conceive that the claims of the English sufferers, upon the principles of compensation established in the treaty, must be of very small amount, even trifling. I beleive [sic] that the British government intended by this stipulation to cover their retreat, from the claim of damages; and that the King so readily accepted it because he was aware that it would result in a very small amount.

To indemnify himself, however, for the four hundred thousand ducats, which he relinquishes as his profit upon the contract with Taix & Co., and for such damages as may be awarded to the English claimants, he has imposed a duty of two ducats upon each cantar of sulphur exported; which, at six hundred thousand cantars the minimum amount of demand, as estimated by the company of Taix & Co., gives a revenue of one million two hundred thousand ducats. The English government has therefore, by its menacing movements only shifted the form of the impositions, without diminishing the price of the article, which was their great object. I send herewith the King's rescript carrying into effect the treaty, by which you will see, that he still means to exercise the right of regulating the amount of sulphur to be taken from the mines, and the time and manner of its importation, and has directed a report to be made to him on that subject.

The most to be regretted effect of these unskillful measures of the british [sic] government, is the state in which the question of the commercial treaty is left. I don't think that the king has yet entirely developed his character. With a good deal of obstinacy in his nature, and a full beleif [sic] in his own capacity, and a consciousness of the unlimited extent of his regal power, he begins to make all his ministers tremblingly submissive to his will, and is indignant at any encroachment upon his prerogatives. He is just beginning to feel his power, and the manner in which he has carried through this contest and the incidents connected with it, may give a new cast to his rule & render him hereafter more impracticable. I do not think it proper to say more at present upon this topic.

The Suggestions which I made in regard to the Prince of Cassaro, on the authority of a person whose opinions had weight with me, on account of his means of information, have turned out to be entirely incorrect, and must be regarded as wishes, only in a quarter where there is not as much influence exercised as has been hitherto supposed. The last account of the Prince reported him sick with the fever which is known to prevail at Foggia, at this season of the year. His daughters and some of his brothers have supplicated the King to permit his place of confinement to be changed, which he has refused; and he is said to have replied to one of them, that if this had occurred thirty years ago, his head would have paid the forfeit. I have been recently told, however, that he is now permitted to be at large in any part of Puglia.

At all events he is ruined, and will never again be received into the King's councils; and with him has fallen his foreign policy. His enemies pursue him with bitterness, and exasperate the King, and I do not beleive [sic] that there is a single advocate of a commercial treaty left around the King's person. As soon as the King had signed the treaty with Great Britain he dismissed from the office of foreign affairs four of the chief clerks who had been in the service of Cassaro, and gave them less important employments elsewhere.

At a late court circle M^r. Kennedy volunteered to talk to me about their affairs, and suggested that it would be well for me and M^r. Temple to have an interview, and unite our efforts in pressing for a commercial treaty. I mentioned to M^r. Temple, M^r. Kennedy's suggestion, but I found from the manner he received it, that it did not spring from him. It satisfied me, however, with other things that they desired a treaty and had not much prospect of making one.

I have no suggestion to make in regard to future action on our part except to wait, at present, for further developements [sic]. If we ever succeed in treating with them, it is necessary for us to proceed with great delicacy just now. I apprehend that a part of the King's present resentment against Cassaro grows out of the treaty of indemnity with us: he is very capable of beleiving [sic] that he was bribed by our government, and utterly incapable of understanding that such a thing is impossible. It is a matter which the enemies of Cassaro have always urged against him to prejudice him with the King; and the manner in which the English here have talked of the Americans having compelled him by their fleet, to pay them an indemnity, has had it's influence upon his disposition. He thinks that advantage was taken of his youth, and that such an affair could not have happened at this time.

It might be expected of me to say something on the subject of the present interesting attitude of the European powers; but I am conscious that I cannot impart to you any valuable information, and therefore I refrain from it altogether.

E. T. Throop to J. Forsyth

Naples September 12. 1840. [Despatch N°. 23.]

Sir,

I have the honor to send herewith a copy of my dispatch N°. 3 dated December 6, 1838, which I am informed has not been received at the department. It treats on two subjects, one of which I have had occasion to allude to subsequently, and do so in a manner, I suppose, unintelligible from a beleif [sic] that the former dispatch was before you. I allude to Carusi's case, as to which the correspondence is contained in dispatch N°. 3. I have recently received a letter from M^r. Marston, expressing an anxiety to hear from the department, in relation to his exequatur, and saying that it remains in the same state, that it did when he wrote me before.

With regard to affairs here, there is no change. It is a season in which but little attention is given to public affairs, although I understand that M^r. Temple has attempted to renew his negociations in regard to the commercial treaty without success. I am credibly informed that the King says that he will have nothing more to do with them. I beleive [sic] that he keeps the Prince of Scilla in charge of the Portfolio of foreign affairs, so that there shall be no organ of communication.[113]

If my last dispatch should have been dated July 13 instead of August 13th its true date, I beg the favor to have it corrected.

---

[113] Enclosed with this letter was a clipping containing the text of the decree of Ferdinand II, dated Palermo, July 21, 1840, abolishing the contract with the Taix, Aycard Co. The decree was countersigned by Fulco Ruffo di Calabria, Prince of Scilla, Duke of S. Cristina, as minister of foreign affairs, and by the Marquis Pietracatella, as president *ad interim* of the council of ministers. On Ruffo, see note 98, p. 467.

E. T. Throop to J. Forsyth

Naples November 12. 1840. [Despatch N°. 24.]

Sir,

I have the honor to write you at this time, merely to let you know that I am at my post, where I have continued all the Summer, but that no change has occurred, since my last dispatch, interesting to communicate, or affording any opportunity to renew our negociations with this government. I find the same complaint with all the legations that there is no person in charge of foreign affairs, with whom any negociations can be had. The Prince of Scilla has still charge of the Port folio.

Until the King shall be in a better mood it will be of no use to call his attention to our relations with him. He is very much exasperated against the British, and considers the existing treaty with them an obstacle to negociation with any other nation.

I have recently received volume 2ᵈ. of the American Archives.

E. T. Throop to J. Forsyth

Naples December 9. 1840. [Despatch N°. 25.]

Sir,

As I have the means of sending by private conveyance to Paris, I avail myself of the occasion to write more freely about affairs here, than I should think prudent, if I were obliged to trust to the mails of the Kingdom.

I have heretofore said nothing of the Eastern question,[114] to which all eyes in Europe have for some time past been turned, because the government has agents at all the Courts in Europe, principally interested in the struggle, and at all the points in Asia which are the theatres of action, and because my means of obtaining correct information here has been very limited. I have therefore judged it more prudent to say nothing, than to send you accounts not well authenticated, or embarass you with valueless speculations.

Hostilities are now at an end by means of negociations conducted principally by Great Britain, which power has also been

---

[114] The Eastern question was the trouble between Turkey and Egypt, which was settled by the Convention concluded between the courts of Great Britain, Austria, Prussia and Russia, and the Sublime Ottoman Porte, for the pacification of the Levant. Signed at London, 15 July 1840. Lewis Hertslet, *Treaties and conventions between Great Britain and foreign powers*, London, 1827-1925, V, 544).

the main agent in the force employed to reduce the Pacha to his present condition, in which he has been obliged to accept such terms as were dictated to him.

The pretence of any other principle than that of acquiring power as the motive of Great Britain to act the part she has, is too absurd for a moment's consideration: her ambition has been wonderfully excited by the tempting prospects before her of extending her power, and she now aims at nothing less than to overlay with her gigantic proportions all Asia. Having enlarged her dominions and protectorship in India, possessed herself of the Keys to all the Commerce of Arabia, and flattering herself with the hope of being able to bow the pride of China with her power, she is determined to link as closely as possible her government at home with these possessions; and as she has consented to leave Mehemet Ali in possession of Egypt, it can be upon no other terms than that Egypt & Syria shall be open to her. To us this view of her strength can not be indifferent. Russia has objects to gain sufficient to make her a confederate, and together they can dictate the terms of peace.

During the period when an European war was considered an event which might happen, there were many conjectures and rumors in regard to the disposition of the King of Naples, and the part that he might take. His consent to take France as an Umpire between him and England, his apparent good terms with France, together with the intimate family alliance between them was said to have aroused the jealousy of Austria & Russia, and explanations were said to have been demanded, and coolness to have existed, and is said still to exist between him and the representatives of those Courts.

The King is so exclusively his own counsellor [sic], and so much secrecy is observed here in the several legations, that it is impossible to ascertain the exact truth of these stories. I should judge from my intercourse with these legations, that there has existed some little coolness in the quarters indicated, but I believe [sic] it to have grown out [of] some obstinacy on the part of the King in refusing to answer inquiries about facts and intentions in reference to his connexion with France, which might have been easily & satisfactorily explained.

It is however absurd to suppose that he, a despotic king, without the love of his subjects, or any feeling of nationality on their part, and determined to maintain his despotism undiminished, should think for a moment of defying the holy alliance, the protector of despotism, and of uniting himself to a constitutional government, with all the elements of reform still in agitation. In addition to this, the only power which sways his opinions is the priesthood, which is gaining entire possession of his mind. His chambers of Councillors have little influence over him, and it is beleived [sic] that all his measures are dictated by his confessor and other priests who are established about his person, and to whose suggestions, I doubt not, he is mainly indebted for that high opinion of his prerogative, which is now so fully developed in him. He has become very observant of the established religious rites, and does not avail himself of the Pope's dispensation from the observance of the prescribed fasts, but religiously excludes meats from his table twice or thrice every week.

Yesterday being the *Conception* I went to the camp to witness a new ceremony, which is to become an annual one. It was the blessing of the flags of the army, and the placing it under the protection of the Madonna of the Conception. High mass was said in an elevated pavillion in the centre of the field, and about twenty thousand troops were blessed by the Cardinal archbishop, and reviewed by the King.

Not content with the indirect power, which their influence over the King gives them, the priests by a natural impulse, have induced him to give them the means of employing it directly. He has established one commission consisting of some priests of high rank and the prefect of the police, with general authority, and a subordinate commission of two priests and an officer of the police, for each of the twelve wards of the city, to inquire into and punish immoralities, particularly negligence in attending to the ordinances of religion, and without doubt, political indiscretions also. They have the power of judgment and execution in their own hands, and whoever reflects upon the means possessed by these boards combining the priesthood and the police, through spies and confession, and secret arrests and proceedings will see the peril under which every person lives.

Things had not grown to this head in the time of the Prince of Cassaro, and but for the injudicious haste of the British and their violence, the King would have signed the treaty which had been prepared, and he would have felt himself committed to a liberal policy in his foreign relations, and perhaps would have taken a pride in it. But the opponents of that policy, among whom are to be reconed [sic] the priests in his secret councils, availed themselves of his resentments at the arrogance of the British, to induce him to expel Cassaro, and with him the foreign policy which he advocated.

The King is determined to enter into no treaty at present, from the causes mentioned, strengthened by the anger which still burns in him, against the English, and gives himself up to the exercise of his power at home and in amassing wealth. He is very fond of military displays, and one of the interesting incidents of the day of the Conception was his declaring himself Captain General of his army: an office which had been vacant for some years, but had always before been enjoyed by another.

The time may arrive when it will be proper for us to attempt a renewal of our negociations with this King, and perhaps to attempt to awaken him to a sense of the interests of his kingdom by arranging our tariff to that end in respect to the objects of merchandize between the two countries, but the present, in my opinion, is not the time. In the present condition of his pride of power, his irritated feelings, and an inflated opinion that his Kingdom has sufficient resources within itself, and is not dependant upon foreign commerce, any movement, carrying the appearance of an attempt to compel him would have an unfavorable effect.

I was made acquainted through the British Legation at Turin with the unfortunate condition of our Chargé at that court, M^r. Rogers,[115] and requested to repair to his aid. On reflection it seemed to me more proper to refer the matter to General Cass, and I accordingly wrote to him, and to the consul at Genoa.[116] I have since been informed, by both Gen. Cass and the Consul that the requisite measures have been taken.

J. FORSYTH TO E. T. THROOP

Department of State. Washington 28 Dec. 1840. [Instruction No. 7.]
[Sent by Minor K. Kellogg, Bearer of Despatches]

Sir,

By direction of the President, as soon as practicable after this despatch shall have been placed in your hands by Mr. Kellogg,[117] you will proceed to Turin, for the purpose of taking such steps

---

115 H. Gold Rogers, of Pennsylvania, commissioned Chargé d'Affaires at Turin, on June 30, 1840. He left Nov. 22, 1841.
116 The United States Consul at Genoa at this time was J. I. Bailey who was nominated on July 20, 1840. He remained in office to May 1842.
117 Minor K. Kellogg was official bearer of despatches.

as are rendered necessary by the unfortunate mental affliction of M^r. Rogers, U.S. Chargé d'Affaires to Sardinia. On arriving there you will cause the public property and archives of the Legation to be carefully separated from the private property of M^r. Rogers, which is to be deposited in the care of the U.S. Consul at Genoa. — You will make the cordial acknowledgements of the President to Baron Truxess[118], [sic] the Prussian Minister for his humane and friendly attentions to M^r. Rogers, and request him to receive and retain the archives of the Legation in his care until the recovery of M^r. Rogers or the arrival of his successor. The archives must be carefully sealed after being properly packed in boxes or cases as may be required. Should you not be able to proceed to Turin yourself you will send some confidential and trustworthy person with the like instructions.

J. FORSYTH TO M. K. KELLOGG

Department of State. Washington 28 Decr. 1840.

Sir,

By direction of the President you will proceed forthwith to Boston and embark on board of the U.S. Ship of War Preble which is shortly to sail from that port. You will leave the Preble at the nearest port at which she touches from which you can promptly reach Naples, and proceed with as little delay as possible to that city, where, you will place the accompanying despatch[119] in the hands of M^r. Throop the U.S. Chargé d'Affaires. You will be allowed your travelling expenses of which vouchers must be kept, from Washington to Naples, but it must be distinctly understood that the Department will not be responsible for any other charges on your account.

---

118 Friedrich Ludwig Graff Truchsess von Waldburg (1776-1844). In 1803, he married Princess Marie Antonie Philippine Josepha von Hohenzollern-Hechingen (1781-1831). He was at first an officer in the Prussian army, then, in 1801, he entered the diplomatic service. In 1807, he became chamberlain to King Jerome of Westphalia; in 1809, he was in the Bavarian civil service. However, in 1813, he again entered the Prussian military service, soon attaining the rank of lieutenant-general. In 1814, he accompanied Napoleon I to Elba. Subsequently, he re-entered the diplomatic service and was successively Prussian envoy to Turin (1818-1824), Naples, The Hague (1827-1831), and again to Turin (1832-1844). Little is known of his services at the Court of Turin. Yet the fact that he was married to a princess of a ruling sovereign house suggests that he was popular with the Turinese Court.

119 This was Instruction No. 7 to Mr. Throop concerning his "rendering assistance to Mr. Rogers, United States chargé d'affaires to Sardinia, also as to taking the necessary precautions to protect that Legation's records, etc." See above, p. 494.

E. T. Throop to J. Forsyth

Naples January 20ᵗʰ. 1841. [Despatch N°. 26.]

Sir,

Since the last dispatch which I had the honor to transmit, nothing has occurred here worthy of notice. We have just entered upon the carnival, and all are intent upon the customary amusements of the Season.

I have just received the following notice which I have the honor to transmit in compliance with my duty: —

"Napoli 11 Gennaio 1841.

Or che S M la Regina è di già entrata negli alti mesi di sua gravidanza, ha determinata [sic] il Re di informarsene il Corpo Diplomatico accreditato presso la sua Real persona, onde questa lieta notizia sia portata alla conoscenza delle rispettive loro corti; essendo S. M. persuasa dell'interesse che prendranno [sic] le medesime in sì fausto avvenimento, di cui il popolo delle due Sicilie e vivissimente [sic] rallegrato.

Il Sottoscritto Consigliere Ministro di Stato, Incaricato degli portafogli degli Affari Esteri adempie con infinita soddisfazione a siffatto sovrano commando, rendendone consapevole il Signor Throop Incaricato di Affari degli Stati Uniti di America, e profitta dell'occasione per aver l'onore di ripetergli i sensi della sua particolare considerazione."

Signed. "Principe di Scilla Duca di S. Cristina"

E. T. Throop to J. Forsyth

Turin March 27 1841. [Despatch N°. 27.]

Sir

I have the honor to acknowledge the receipt on the fifteenth instant of your dispatch (no. 7) dated 28 December 1840, from the hands of Mʳ. Kellogg bearer of dispatches.

In pursuance of the instructions contained therein, I made immediate preparations to visit this city, and to take charge of, and place in security the archives of the legation entrusted to Mr. Rogers Chargé d'Affaires at this Court, and who had left his post in a State of derangement of mind.

At Genoa, on my way, I sent for the present Consul at that

place, and for M^r. Crockat,[120] the present person into whose hands the affairs of that consulate fell at the death of M^r. Campbell[121] and obtained from them all the intelligence they could give me of the public property belonging to the legation. M^r. Bailey,[122] the Consul shewed [sic] me a letter received not long before from M^r. Rogers dated at Paris, in which he mentions an escritoire with an iron safety drawer which he had left at the hotel in Turin, which seemed to contain every thing he had left there except three old chairs. From M^r. Crockat I learned that there were three boxes and a trunk in the public store at Genoa, directed to the care of the Consul at Genoa for M^r. Rogers. I went to the public store and examined them, and found that one of the boxes bore the mark of the department of State upon it, and that the other two and the trunk had not that mark, although those boxes very much resembled the other. I concluded that the two boxes and trunk contained M^r. Rogers' private property, and the other box public books. I was informed that the property would be entirely safe where it was, and that it might remain there for a long time, and until it should be claimed by the owners. It appeared to me to be perfectly safe. The boxes and trunk had been forwarded from Liverpool and had never been in M^r. Roger's possession, and M^r. Bailey the Consul afterwards told me that he had the bills of lading in his possession.

On arriving at this city I inquired of the keeper of the hotel d'Europe, where M^r. Rogers remained during all the time he spent at Turin, who told me that M^r. Rogers had left in his apartment, when he went away, an escritoire and three chairs, and a large box entirely empty; and that after a month and advising with the Prussian Minister & the Minister of foreign affairs here, he had removed them from the apartment, that he might have the use of it, and had stored them away in a place of safety in his house.

I went with him to see the escritoire & found it locked safely, and so heavy with the iron safe within it, that I could not stir

---

120 Charles Crockat was American acting consul at Genoa, after Mr. Campbell's death. The United States National Archives preserves three despatches from Mr. Crockat (May 15, July 10, 1840, and Jan 10, 1841) on the subject of trade.

121 Robert Campbell was twice consul of the United States at Genoa: from 1832 to 1834 and again from 1837 to 1840. *Executive Journal of the Senate*, III, 314, 325, 354, 372, and V, 31, 42.

122 J. I. Bailey was nominated American consul for Genoa, on July 20, 1840, in place of R. Campbell, deceased. *Executive Journal of the Senate*, V, 303, 307, 309.

it. I then called upon M^r. Abercromby[123] the British Minister, & Count de Waldbourg-Truchsess the Prussian Minister, both of whom had been very kind and attentive to M^r. Rogers, the latter particularly, and from the information I could gather from them, & from the Innkeeper, and the servants who were in attendance upon the rooms of M^r. Rogers I was satisfied that every thing which remained here belonging to the Legation was in that escritoire with the iron safe, carefully locked up, and that the key was taken away by M^r. Rogers.

M^r. Abercromby showed me a letter from him dated in Paris, the latter part of January, which indicated a sound state of mind at that time, and proved that if he was not entirely recovered he had, at least, lucid intervals. I was much gratified to learn that he had sent from Paris funds to pay all the expenses he had incurred, and that everything was paid except a claim of the hotel keeper for room rent for one month after his departure, and a small balance due Mr. Crockat on his account for expenses &c.

It was the opinion of both M^r. Abercromby and the Count de Truchsess that no correspondence could have taken place between M^r. Rogers and the government here, except the accustomed compliments on his arrival, and that he had in no manner compromised the government. His symptoms of insanity manifested themselves soon after his arrival here, and his condition was such, as to be constantly observed, as well by the physicians who attended upon him, one of whom was the physician of the British Minister, as by those gentlemen who sympathized in his sufferings.

I had the honor, in obedience to your instructions to say to the Count de Truchsess, that I was commanded by the President to convey to him his cordial acknowledgements for his humane and friendly attentions to M^r. Rogers, which he received with due acknowledgements. I then stated to him that it was the

---

123 Dunfermline. Ralph Abercromby Lord, K. C. B. (1803-1868). He was attached to the mission at Frankfort in 1821; to the embassy at The Hague in Feb. 1824; and to Paris, Nov. 1824. He was secretary to the plenipotentiaries for negotiating with the United States in Dec. 1826, and précis writer in the foreign office, July 5, 1827. He was secretary to Viscount Strangford's special mission to the Brazils, Aug. 19, 1828, to Lord Ponsonby's special mission to Brussels, Dec. 2, 1830. He was appointed secretary of legation at Berlin, July 14, 1831; minister resident to the Grand Duke of Tuscany, Nov. 27, 1835; minister plenipotentiary to the Germanic Confederation, Jan. 2, 1839; envoy extraordinary and minister plenipotentiary to the King of Sardinia, March 17, 1840. He retired on a pension, Nov. 28, 1849. He was appointed envoy extraordinary and minister plenipotentiary to the King of Netherlands, on Nov. 26, 1851. He resigned Oct. 13, 1858.

President's desire that he should take charge of the archives of the legation until M[r]. Rogers, or his successor should arrive here. He cheerfully consented to do so, and I caused the escritoire, which I beleive [sic] contains all the papers of the legation, unless M[r]. Rogers has taken them with him, to be immediately carried to his house. I sent also a note to him, of which the following is a copy:

"Turin March 26, 1841.

[''] The Undersigned Chargé d'affaires of the United States of America at Naples, presents his best compliments to the Lieutenant General Comte de Waldbourg-Truchsess, Envoy extraordinary & Minister plenipotentiary of his Majesty the King of Prussia, and, referring to the conversation which he had the honor to hold with the Count this morning, in which he communicated to him the wish of the President of the United States that the undersigned should request him to take charge of the archives of the legation here until M[r]. Rogers should return to his post or his successor should arrive, begs leave now to add, that the master of the hotel d'Europe Mr. Mottura informs him that he has already carried the escritoire, which was in his possession to the house of the Count who has kindly consented to take charge of it. The escritoire seems to be safely locked, and the key of it was taken away by M[r]. Rogers when he left Turin, as the undersigned is informed. It is supposed that all the archives of the legation are locked up in this escritoire.

[''] There remains in the public store at Genoa, under the care of the Consul there, three boxes and one trunk, one of which probably contains public property and the others the private property of M[r]. Rogers, although this is only the conjecture of the undersigned from the external appearance of the boxes and trunk.

[''] The Undersigned, while he repeats to the Count the cordial acknowledgments of the President for his kind & humane attentions to Mr. Rogers, has the honor at the same time to thank him for his polite attentions to himself, and for the frank and ready manner in which he has consented to accept the temporary custody of the archives of the American legation. The Undersigned intends to leave Turin on his return to Naples early tomorrow morning, and while he bids adieu to the Count he avails himself of the occasion to renew to him the assurances of his highest consideration and regard."

Signed. "E. T. Throop."

To which I have received this morning the following reply:

"Turin 27. March 1841. Count Waldbourg Truchsess[124] begs pardon of M^r. Throop Chargé d'affaires of the United States of America, that he did not answer immediately his kind note of yesterday, but the party he had in his house hindered him from satisfying sooner to this duty.

['''] He finds himself much honored by the acknowledgment of the President of the United States, and that which M^r. Throop expressed in his gentil [sic] note, at the present occasion; and it is with the greatest pleasure that he will take care of the Scristorie [sic], the chest & three arm chairs, deposed in his house in conformity of the order of M^r. Throop till Mr. Gold Rogers's return, or his successor's arrival at Turin.

['''] The Undersigned prevails [sic] himself of the present opportunity to offer to M^r. Throop the assurances of his most distinguished consideration.

(Signed) ['''] Count Waldbourg-Truchsess."

Having called upon the Minister of foreign affairs,[125] and

---

124 See prior note 118, p. 495, and note his signature below.

125 Clemente Solaro della Margherita. (1792-1869). Count and statesman. In 1812, he graduated from the University of Turin. In 1816, he was sent as secretary of the Sardinian Legation at Naples. He was chargé d'affaires at Madrid from 1825 to 1834, after a brief mission to Rome and Naples. Having been promoted to the rank of minister plenipotentiary at Vienna, he did not proceed to his post, because on March 21, 1835, King Charles Albert appointed him minister of foreign affairs. He held this post for twelve years, always showing himself a staunch supporter of the legitimacy of the House of Savoy. A bitter enemy of Metternich, he thought that Italy would be able to solve her problems alone. He concluded several treaties of commerce with other nations, exerted every effort to abolish the rights of escheat to the crown, established new consulates, and promoted and protected Italian labor in foreign lands. In 1847, in order not to appear as though he feared the revolution, he refused to resign his position, but on October 9, 1847, he was dismissed with the title of Grande of the Crown. From 1854 to 1860, he was a member of the Chamber of Deputies, representing the electoral college of S. Quirico. In the Chamber and in numerous pamphlets, he opposed the policies of Cavour. He revealed his views in two volumes entitled *L'Uomo di stato indirizzato al governo della cosa pubblica*, published in Turin in 1863 and 1864. In 1851-1852, he had defended his work as minister in two publications entitled *Memorandum storico-politico* and *Appendice al Memorandum*. Keenly interested in historical studies, he published *Journal historique du siege de la ville et de la citadelle de Turin en 1706* (Turin, 1838) and *Traités de la Maison de Savoie depuis la paix de Cateau-Cambrésis jusqu'à nos jours*. See: C. Lovera and P. I. Rinieri, *Clemente Solaro della Margherita*. Turin, 1931, 3 volumes.

500

left my card not finding him at home, and knowing no reason why I should stay longer here, I have requested the Count de Truchsess to explain to the Minister the causes why I shall not remain to pay my respects to him personally, and I am now prepared to leave Turin immediately on my return.

I hope that I have discharged my mission here in a manner satisfactory to the government.

As nothing new has occurred since my last dispatch in the condition of affairs at Naples, worthy of being communicated, I will add nothing more and have the honor to remain

E. T. Throop to D. Webster[126]

Naples May 2. 1841. [Despatch No. 28.]
Sir

I have received within a few days past dispatch N°. 8, dated 6ᵗʰ. March last, in which you have done me the honor to notify me that you had, that day, entered upon the discharge of the duties of Secretary of State of the United States. Permit me to congratulate you on receiving this high mark of the confidence of your country, and to add to it my sincere wishes that you may find your office agreeable, and that your administration of it may shed additional lustre on your public life.

I respectfully refer you to my correspondence hitherto with the department for the State of our relations with the Neapolitan government, so far as they have been affected by the charge committed to me. I have but little now to add.

The King has recently releeved [sic] the Prince of Cassaro from exile, and he is gone to Sicily. It is by some supposed that he may be restored to the Councils of the King; but every thing, in that respect, is mere conjecture. The British government is undoubtedly mortified at the result of its late conflict with the King of the Two Sicilies; and that portion of their subjects for whose benefit they made that demonstration of their power, do not conceal their dissatisfaction. In the pride of their recent successes in other countries, it seems to me that they will endeavor to renew the dispute with this government (and a pretext is not wanting) and in the end force it into a treaty.

The encouragement which this government gives to its own navigation renders the advantages in favor of british [sic] com-

---

126 Secretary of State from March 5, 1841 to May 8, 1843.

merce, stipulated by the treaty now in force, null; and it is this circumstance which produces both the complaints of the british [sic] against the faith of the Neapolitan government and their desire to exchange their subsisting treaty for one of reciprocity. The British cannot succeed in this object without another quarrel, as the King of the Sicilies is bent upon having no further negociation with them. I think however, that he will be compelled in the end to yield; and if he should do so it is very probable that he will previously take the Prince of Cassaro again into his Council. That would be a favorable circumstance, as his policy is unrestricted trade, and he entertains no prejudice against us.

It is important for us to watch these movements that we may secure for our commerce, when the change takes place, equal advantages with those which the British may obtain.

E. T. THROOP TO D. WEBSTER

Naples June 5. 1841. [Despatch N°. 29.]

Sir,

I have the honor to transmit to you a copy of a note which I have received from the Minister charged with foreign affairs, on the evening of the 28th. May:

Napoli 28. Maggio 1841. Il Sottoscritto Consigliere Ministro di Stato Incaricato del Portofoglio degli affari esteri, si onora portare alla conoscenza del Sig^r. Throop Incaricato di affari degli Stati Uniti di America, che maturando ne' primi giorni del prossimo vegnente Giugno l'ottava delle nove rate annuali di pagamento a farsi da questo R^le. Governo agli Stati Uniti di America la Real Tesoreria Generale ha di già ammanita la somma per farsene il pagamento alla persona fornita di pieni e legali poteri per parte del Governo Americano. Potendo però tali poteri essere stati sottoscritto [sic] dal defunto Presidente dell'Unione General Harrison, il Governo di S. M. Siciliano desidera conoscere, se ostante siffatta circostanza il mentovato pagamento può farsi alla Casa Bancaria de' Sig^ri Wells, che trovasi di già munita di procura sottoscritto [sic] dal Summentovato Presidente Harrison.

Il Sottoscritto prega il Sig. Throop compiacersi chiarire su tal proposito, e le offre le proteste della sua particolare considerazione.

Signed. Principe di Scilla Duca di S. Cristina.

502

The next day I sent to the office of foreign affairs for the Minister, the following note in reply:

"Naples May 29. 1841. The Undersigned Chargé d'affaires of the United States of America hastens to reply to the official note of his Excellency the Prince of Scilla Duke of S. Cristina, Consellor Minister of State charged with the Portfolio of foreign affairs, bearing date yesterday, the receipt of which he has the honor to acknowledge. He assures the Minister that the death of the late President Harrison does not, *per se,* invalidate the power which he may have given to receive the instalment, now soon becoming due from this royal government to the government of the United States of America; and that payment to any person who may hold said authority will be good and valid, unless the government of the United States should previously notify this government that it had revoked or annulled such authority. The Undersigned with pleasure, avails himself of the occasion to renew to the Minister of the assurance of his most distinguished consideration." —

Signed "E. T. Throop."

Through the friendship of the Chevalier de Barboza the Brazilian Minister[127] here, I was informed that the Prince of Scilla said that no answer had been received from me, and that the money would not be paid. I immediately transmitted a duplicate of my note of the 29th.

On the 3rd. inst. I met the Minister of foreign affairs, and the Minister of Finance at the house of the Baron de Rothschild (who has the draft) and they both assured me that the money would be paid.

I have nothing else important in our affairs here to communicate, and I hope to receive some instructions from the department.

While I participate in the general grief which every American should feel at the loss which the country has sustained by the death of the late President, I, at the same time, rejoice that the intentions of the framers of the Constitution are so well fulfilled in this contingency by the Presidency falling upon an individual, who has so many claims upon the confidence of his Country.

[127] Paulino da Silva Barbosa. He was Brazilian chargé d'affaires in the Kingdom of the Two Sicilies in 1839.

Dispatch No. 9 communicating the death of the late President,[128] is the last which I have received.

E. T. THROOP TO D. WEBSTER

Naples July 29 1841.[129] [Despatch N°. 31.]

Sir,

Having received under cover from M^r. Markoe of the State Department, with a request that I should present it, a memorial from Daniel J. Desmond,[130] a lawyer of Philadelphia praying compensation of the King for services rendered, at the request of the Consul General of the Two Sicilies, in negotiating some change in the terms of payment of the indemnity stipulated to be paid by the treaty, I transmitted it to the Acting Secretary of State for foreign affairs, accompanied by the following note:

"Naples June 26 1841. The accompanying document marked N°. 27 has been forwarded to me with a request that I should transmit it to Your Excellency. On perusing it I find a reference to a document N°. 26 addressed to the Prince of Cassaro, which, being in my possession I have the honor to transmit to you at the same time. It is perhaps proper that I should add that document N°. 26 came to my hands in a manner which imposed no obligation to deliver it according to its direction and I have therefore retained it until this time. I beg your Excellency to accept the renewed assurances of high consideration with which I have the honor to be Your Excellency's very obedient servant, E. T. Throop. To the Prince of Scilla Duke of S. Cristina &c &c &c."

Not supposing it to be the intention of the Government to enforce this claim as a government affair, I endeavored to shape my note in a manner to preclude that idea. I had been informed that M^r. Desmond had made several previous applications for compensation to the King, which had been rejected by him, and,

---

128 William Henry Harrison died at the President's House in Washington City on April 5th, 1841. All the references to the White House, as now designated, were in the above phrase, the President's House. All the early official papers regarding its construction, furnishings, etc., used this designation.

129 Despatch No. 30, Naples, June 26, 1841; Mr. Throop transmitted to Secretary of State Webster a general statement of his account with the government.

130 Daniel J. Desmond was consul general of the Papal States at Philadelphia. See Leo Stock, *Consular Relations between the United States and the Papal States,* (Washington, 1945), 396-405.

as I received the memorial N°. 26 under cover only, without any accompanying letter or explanation, and as the King was at that time somewhat excited in regard to the American indemnity treaty which is explained in my former dispatches, I considered it discreet not to present the memorial.

Immediately on the receipt of the President's message in a pamphlet form, I sent it to the Minister of foreign affairs with the following note:

"Naples July 11. 1841. Mr. Throop chargé d'affaires of the United States presents his best compliments to His Excellency the Prince of Scilla, Duke of S. Cristina and has the honor to send him herewith, a copy of the message of the President of the United States, recently sent to the congress of the United States, at the opening of its present session. And he avails himself of the occasion to renew to him the assurance of his most distinguished consideration. E. T. Throop."

"To His Excellency the Prince of Scilla Duke of S. Cristina &c."

And I received from him the following reply:

"Il Principe di Scilla, Duca di Sta. Cristina, rende i suoi ringraziamenti al Sig^r. Throop, Incaricato di Affari degli Stati Uniti d'America, per lo esemplare in istampa del Messaggio del Presidente della Unione, rimessa col suo pregevole viglietto del dì 11 corrente.

"Lo scrivente rinnova al Sig^r. Throop le proteste della sua particolare considerazione."

[''] Napoli 14 Luglio 1841."

I received from the Minister of foreign affairs the following note:

"Napoli 15 Aprile 1841. Il Direttore del Ministero di Guerra e Marina desidera conoscere se ne' contratti fatti con gli Esteri passati a servire nelle diverse fabbriche del Regno da manufatturieri, macchinisti, ecc. vi sia stata omologazione degli Agenti Diplomatici o Consolari qui residenti.

"Il Sottoscritto Consigliere, Ministro di Stato, incaricato del Portafoglio degli Affari Esteri, si rivolge al Sig^r. Enos T. Throop Incaricato d'Affari degli Stati Uniti d'America pregandolo volergli favorire tale notizia che riguardar potesse i Sudditi Ameri-

505

cani e Le rinnova le proteste della sua particolare considerazione. (Signed) Principe di Scilla, Duca di S. Cristina.

"Al Signor Enos T. Throop, Incaricato d'Affari degli Stati Uniti d'America."

To which I returned the following reply:

"Naples June 16 1841. The Undersigned Chargé d'Affaires of the United States regrets that he has not been able to make an earlier reply to the official note of his Excellency the Prince of Scilla, Duke of S. Cristina, Counsellor, Minister of State, charged with the portfolio of foreign affairs, of the 15th. of April last, in consequence of its having been received during his absence on a visit to Turin, and mislaid.

"In regard to the inquiry made by the Director of the Ministry of War, whether contracts made by American citizens who may have been employed in the various manufactories of this Kingdom, have received the sanction of the Diplomatic or consular agents residing here, he has the honor to reply that he is not aware that any American citizen is employed in any manufactory of any kind, in this kingdom, and he believes there is none: if however there should be any, no such contract as is here spoken of, has been submitted to the consideration of the diplomatic or consular agent of the United States, and consequently has received no official sanction. The Undersigned avails himself of the occasion to renew to his Excellency the Prince of Scilla, Duke of S. Cristina, the assurances of his distinguished consideration.

E. T. Throop. To His Excellency the Prince of Scilla Duke of S. Cristina, Counsellor, Minister of State &c &c &c."

I have the honor to send herewith three Extracts (which I have cut out of the Government journal to reduce the bulk of this Dispatch):[131]

No. 1 contains the rescript of the King by which he directs that the duty on Sulphur is reduced from twenty to eight carlins, the Cantaro: to take effect after the first day January 1842.

No. 2. The Statistics of the City of Naples for the year 1840. and N°. 3. A notice of the President's message to Congress.

I have the honor to acknowledge the receipt on the 24th inst.

---

131 These are clippings from *Giornale del Regno delle Due Sicilie* for various days. The first page of the issue of July 15, is also enclosed. This issue contains extracts from President Tyler's message to the Senate and House.

of Dispatch N°. 10[132] dated 7 June ult°. in which I am informed that my recal [sic] from this station will speedily be communicated to me. I am obliged to you for this previous notice, and assure you that my successor will find on his arrival, whenever it may be, everything belonging to this Legation in order for him.

My anxiety now is to have my accounts closed, or at least to have them examined, and to be informed of the principles upon which they will be settled, what items will be allowed and what additional evidence is required. For this purpose I have made a general statement from the period of my entering upon the duties of my office to the 14th. of May last, which I am informed by my agent at London, was forwarded by the great Western on the 14th. instant. Judging from the tenor of your notice that my official connexions with the government will cease before I can have a response to my account, I shall repair immediately after I shall be discharged from my responsibilities here, to Paris, and await there the communication of the decision of the government in relation to them. If my vouchers should be deficient in any respect, it will be convenient to me at Paris to collect from London, Naples, and other parts of England and France the necessary additional proofs and save me and the department such trouble and delay in closing my accounts with the government.

I send herewith my account for contingent expenses for the last quarter directed to the fifth Auditor of the Treasury.

Nothing new has occurred here which I consider necessary to communicate.

D. WEBSTER TO E. T. THROOP

Department of State, Washington, 14th. Septr. 1841.
[Unnumbered and final Instruction.]

Sir: On the 7th. June last, a letter from this Department informed you that the President had in contemplation arrangements which would render your recall from Naples necessary. This information of the purpose of the Government was conveyed in advance of a formal recall at as early a date as was

---

[132] Instruction No. 9, Washington, April 4, 1841, sent the day of President Harrison's death, informed Mr. Throop of the death of the President. See acknowledgment in Mr. Throop's No. 29, June 5, 1841. See above, pp. 502, 504.

practicable in order to afford time to prepare for your departure with the least inconvenience to yourself. I have now the honor to announce to you that the period for the termination of your mission has arrived, and to inform you that the President by and with the advice and consent of the Senate has appointed Mr. William Boulware[133] as your successor.

It is hoped that Mr. Boulware may find you at Naples, in which event you will in person transfer to him the archives, books, and property of the Legation, and at the same time afford him such advice and aid, from your own experience, as will enable him to enter advantageously upon the duties of the Legation. If, however, your own convenience shall have impelled you to leave Naples before his arrival, the property is presumed, will be found in the hands of M^r. Hammett, the Consul or some other trustworthy American citizen, who will deliver it to Mr. Boulware.

You will find enclosed a letter addressed to the Minister of Foreign Affairs of the Two Sicilies, acquainting him with your recall. The delivery of this letter will afford you an opportunity of which you will avail yourself, of assuring His Excellency of the sentiments of friendship entertained by this Government for that of the Two Sicilies and of the continued desire of the President to strengthen the bonds of good understanding which now so happily subsist between the two countries.

The Bankers of the United States in London will be informed that your credit upon them for your salary is to cease on the day of your taking leave of the Court, of which you will inform them, as well as this Department. Your draft on account of your return quarter's allowance will take effect from the same date, and your credit upon them for the contingent expenses of the Legation will also cease on the same day.

I have the honor to inform you that your despatches to N°. 31, inclusive, have been received. In consequence of the statement you have made, I have authorized the payment of your salary to commence on 14th March instead of the 14th May, 1838. I do not feel justified in extending the time back to the date of your commission.

Your accounts are still under examination in the Treasury

---

133 With his Instruction No. 10, dated Washington, June 7, 1841, Mr. Webster informed Mr. Throop that the President was contemplating his (Throop's) recall from Naples. William Boulware, of Virginia, was commissioned chargé d'affaires on Sept. 13, 1841. He left the service on June 19, 1845. The next following chapter gives Mr. Boulware's despatches.

Department. As soon as the decision of that Department is made you will be apprized of it, and the despatch containing the information will, by your desire, be transmitted to you at Paris.

E. T. Throop to D. Webster

Paris February 23, 1842.

Sir

Your letter of the 14th. Sept. last was received by me at Naples, where I was awaiting the further orders of the government, not deeming it proper to leave the Court without instructions to that effect. Mr. Boulware arrived on the 28th. of December, and I hastened the same day to tender him my services in any way that could be useful to him to enable him to enter advantageously upon his duties; in which I am happy to know that I fulfilled the wishes of the government while I discharged an agreeable duty. I presented him with as little delay as possible to the Minister of foreign affairs, and availed myself of that opportunity to present to the Minister the letter with which I was charged, and to assure him of the continued desire of the President to cultivate and strengthen the good understanding happily existing between the two governments; to which he replied in the most friendly terms, assuring me that his Majesty reciprocated the feelings which I had expressed, and was earnestly desirous of continuing and cultivating the most friendly relations.

Having thus transferred my official duties to my successor I asked of the Minister an audience to take leave of their Majesties the King and Queen, which he fixed for the 12th of January, his Majesty's birthday, and he appointed the same day for the presentation of Mr. Boulware. I took my leave of the Court on the day appointed and left Naples for this city on the 17th. day of January and informed the Messrs. Rothschilds at London, as I was instructed that my functions as Chargé ceased on the twelfth day of January 1842.

In taking official leave of you, Sir, permit me to tender you my thanks for the kindness and liberality which I have experienced from you, and the delicacy with which you have conveyed to me the intentions and determinations of the government.

I send herewith the receipt of Mr. Boulware for all the books and other property of the government with which I was entrusted.[134]

I transmit at the same time to the fifth Auditor's office a general statement of my account in which I make a balance due me of eight hundred and sixty one dollars 25/100. In making out this balance I have recharged against the government an item of two hundred and ninety four dollars and twelve cents which was deducted in the statement of my account by the auditor up to the thirtieth of June last for gains in exchange, and it will be seen that I claim the full amount of the other drafts, which I have made for salary, without that deduction.

I do not dispute the equity of the rule in itself applied by the accounting officer; but I object to its application to my account under the circumstances of having been instructed by the government to draw quarterly for my salary, and having been told by the bankers that they were instructed to pay at the rate of 4/6. the dollar, & having settled with them the amount of my quarterly drafts, to which I have strictly conformed. Having been suffered to draw to the end of my mission, under the beleif [sic] that I was drawing only my due, I consider it a hardship and unjust to be called upon to refund as overdrawn a part, because the losses I suffered in drawing my money were not equal to the difference between the £s at 4,44. and some other sum, the amount of which I know not, but which is called I beleive [sic] the par of exchange. I have stated my views more at length to the auditor, but I repeat here that I should have been content with the treasury rule if I had been previously notified that the government would pay me the amount of my Salary at Naples; but I solemnly assure you that I had no notice, intimation or suspicion of this rule, until I received the auditor's general statement and settlement of my account to which I have above referred. I therefore think that my claim is good both in law and conscience, to retain the amount of my drafts without any deduction for what is called gains in exchange; and I trust that you will so consider it.

I find that the diplomatic corps that I have met here, maintain with unanimity, their right under the law to retain the amount of their drafts, but I consider my case sufficiently strong without taking that ground. I have not followed the example of some

---

[134] A marginal note reads: "not rec^d. by M^r. Markoe." Mr. Markoe was a clerk of the State Department. It was sent March 20, 1842. See pp. 511-517.

of them in drawing for the amount to await the issue, for the reason which has governed me throughout, to wit, an unwillingness to have money in my hands which I may be obliged to refund at a later day; I have therefore aimed to draw so as not to have over drawn by any rule which the government may apply. I am anxious to have my account finally settled, and I would ask as a favor that the auditor may give it his earliest attention.

As I did not during the continuance of my mission go out of Italy and France, it is my wish, now that I am in Europe to pass one or two years in seeing it. I am not aware of any thing which requests my immediate return, and I hope therefore that the President will indulge me in this wish, and not require my return. I will wait here until I receive a reply to this request, and the final statement of my account by the auditor. I have nothing in my possession belonging to the government except the Cypher. I don't know whether it is the same furnished to the other Ministers, but suppose it is. I can deposit it with Gen. Cass, or any other of our ministers open or sealed up as may be directed. If any signature should be required of me in a final settlement, I can give it here, or authorize some person to do it for me at Washington.

With my renewed thanks for your kindness I have the honor to be

E. T. THROOP TO D. WEBSTER

Paris March 20 1842. [Unnumbered Despatch.]

Sir

I have the honor to send you, herewith, the receipt of Mr. Boulware for the government property at Naples,[135] which ought to have accompanied my last letter.

Enclosure with Paris, Unnumbered Despatch, March 20, 1842

A Schedule of Books and other property of the United States remaining in the Legation at Naples.

Sent with Mr. Throop. (Jan. 16, 1842)[136]

1 & 2 Sessions[137] XIV Congress ...... 16 volumes (6 of them folio)		
Do XV Do ...... 23 Do		

135 For this list see following pages 511-517.

136 This date was not thus placed in the original despatch, but the list is so dated at the end. The date is here inserted at the beginning for convenience in reference use.

137 Mr. Throop and his successor Mr. Boulware list these first 12 items differently, Mr. Boulware making of them only four items. The Boulware list was

Do	XVI	Do	 33	Do
Do	XVII	Do	 32	Do
Do	XVIII	Do	 36	Do
Do	XIX	Do	 38	Do
Do	XX	Do	 30	Do
Do	XXI	Do	 20	Do
Do	XXII	Do	 26	Do
Do	XXIII	Do	 40	Do
Do	XXIV	Do	 30	Do
1st session	XXV	Do	 4	Do
Diplomatic Code[138]		 2		Do
Do Correspondence[139]		 19		Do
Commercial Regulations[140]		 3		Do
Blue Book[141]		 1		Do

that of the books as Mr. Hammett received them from Mr. Boulware. See *hic opus,,* pp. 596-597. It would also appear from an attempt to identify just what document Mr. Throop was listing in his first 12 items, and what Mr. Hammett included in his first four items, that in one or both cases there were actually a considerable number of duplicates included among these particular items. It seems clear, however, that in spite of the wording of Mr. Throop, he was not listing what are called the *Session Laws,* those separates, not yet bound up, of which Congress authorized the printing at the close of each session.

[138] Since the Hammett list, (see *hic opus,* pp. 596-597) refers only to the Elliot's *Diplomatic Code* we take it that volume is the same as referred to in Mr. Throop's list. See, *Diplomatic code of the United States, embracing a collection of treaties and conventions between the United States and foreign powers, 1778-1827, with index to principal cases decided in the courts of the United States upon points connected with their foreign relations, and official acts, papers, and useful information, for public ministers and consuls,* by Jonathan Elliott, junior, 1827. In 1834, Jonathan Elliott, republished this work with slightly altered title, additional materials, and in two volumes, the first giving treaties to 1827, the second those to 1834. Mr. Throop's use of the shorter title seems to imply that he had only the one-volume edition, as is shown also by his count of '1'. See later chapters of this work, for the full title of the latter two-volume edition of the *Code.*

[139] *Diplomatic Correspondence of the Revolution,* edited by Jared Sparks, compiled by resolution of Congress, March 27, 1818. 1st series, 12 vols.; 2nd series, 1782, 7 vols., published by Act of Congress, May 5, 1832; Boston edition, 1829-30, 12 vols.; Washington edition, 1857, 6 vols. A second series covered the years 1783-1789. It is clear from Mr. Throop's giving the count of 19 volumes, that he had been given the older 1818 edition plus the 7 volumes of the 2d series, of this latter, plus the 12 volumes of the Boston edition published between these two first mentioned editions.

[140] It is not clear, either in this list or in that of Mr. Hammett (see *hic opus,* pp. 596-597), whether here is meant to be listed the *Commercial Regulations of the Two Sicilies,* by J. Q. Adams, Jan. 30, 1824. (See Executive Papers, No. 130, p. 314, 18th Cong. 1st sess., vol. VII, the regulations adopted Aug. 11, 1823), or *Digest of Commercial Regulations* (U.S., 1831) published under Resolution of the House, Mar. 3, 1831.

[141] The *Blue Book* was the biennial *Official Register of the United States,* issued every two years by the Secretary of State, conformant to an order of Congress. It comprises a register of all officers and agents, civil, military and naval, in the service of the United States, the printers of the laws (i.e., officially contracted newspapers, so to print the laws), the printers to the Congress (who printed the public documents), also all mail contractors. See *Official Register of the United States.* The issues for 1820, 1822, 1830, 1832, 1835 [sic], 1838, 1839, 1841, 1843, 1845, and so on to date, are in the *Public Documents Series,* in the Library of the United States National Archives. As Mr. Throop left for Naples in May 1838, he probably took with him, and so included in the above list, the issue for that year, or possibly that for 1835.

American State Papers (Gales)[142] ..... 21 Do
Laws of the U. S.[143] .... 8 Do
Seybert's Statistics[144] .... 1 Do
Pitkins   Do[145] .... 1 Do

<hr />

[142] The Gales and Seaton edition of *American State Papers* are today the best known and the most readily usable of all the series that have been published. They comprise 21 volumes, grouped in several series, of which the one devoted to *Foreign Relations* includes 6 volumes in chronological sequence. Volume 6 carries the document to the year 1859, its date of publication. See: *American State Papers, Documents, Legislative and Executive, of the Congress of the United States, from the 1st to the 35th Congress inclusive, commencing Mar. 4, 1789. VI: Selected and edited under the authority of Congress.* Volumes I, II, III were edited by Walter S. Lowrie, Secretary of the Senate, and Matthew St. Clair Clark, Clerk of the House; Volume IV by Lowrie and Walter S. Franklin, Clerk of the House; V and VI volumes by Asbury Dickins, Secretary of the Senate and James C. Allen, Secretary of the House of Representatives. Washington, Gales & Seaton publishers, 1832-1859, 6 vols. folio.

[143] This is the J. Bioren and W. J. Duane, edition of the *Laws of the United States*, the first 6 volumes of which were edited by John B. Colvin; $15 a volume. This publication was authorized by Act of Congress, Apr. 18, 1814, on a plan prepared by Attorney General Richard Bush; vol. V is an index; vol. VI, printed by Peter Force, 1822, covers additional laws, 1815-1821, and has an index thereto; volume VII, also printed by Peter Force, included laws and treaties from March 3, 1821 to March 3, 1827, with index, also another index, covering all seven volumes, prepared by Samuel Birch; it is the best of the indexes; volume VIII carried the laws and treaties from 1827 to 1833; volume IX, up to 1839 (edited by Langtree & O'Sullivan); volume X, published by J. & G. S. Gideon, laws to 1845; volume XI, printed in Philadelphia, 1848, edited by George Sharswood. These later volumes, not included in the count of eight volumes in Mr. Throop's list herein above, will be found listed in the similar lists filed by the later chargés in Naples, Legation of the United States. The edition of the laws, called *United States Statutes at Large* followed this Bioren and Duane edition, and today is better known and more accessible to the general reader; it was published 1845-1873, and since has been continued as the *Revised Statutes at Large*. Up to 1873, seventeen volumes had been published. And see above, Throop Chapter, p. 400, note 45.

[144] Adam Seybert, the elder. *Statistical Annals.* Philadelphia, published by Thomas Dobson & Son, and Wm. Fry, Printer, 1818. xxviii plus 803 p., 4°. Statistics covering the years 1789-1818, on population, commerce, revenue, etc., founded on official documents, March 4, 1789 to April 28, 1818. The whole issue was purchased by Congress and is, therefore, listed as among the Public Documents Series. It is a standard reference work in all government offices. See also: *Joint Resolution relating to Statistical Annals of Adam Seybert,* April 4, 1818, State Papers, 179, 15th Cong., 1st Sess., v. II: authorizing the Secretary of State to obtain for the use and disposal of Congress, 500 copies of the edition of *Statistical Annals* printed by Adam Seybert of Philadelphia, 1 p. Also see: *Committee Report on Resolution relating to Statistical Annals,* April 10, 1818: State Papers, 185, 15th Cong. 1st Sess. vol. II. (The committee recommended a subscription for 500 copies of Adam Seybert's *Statistical Annals,* also a certain number of copies of a *Statistical View of the Commerce of the United States* by Timothy Pitkin). Also see, Resolution for distributing Seybert's *Statistical Annals,* Jan. 23, 1819.

[145] Probably *Statistical View of Commerce of the United States.* Timothy Pitkin. 1st edition, Hartford, 1816; 2d edition, 1817; 3d edition, 1835. Doubtless the third edition was the one taken over by Mr. Throop and herein listed. Pitkin, however, had also published a work entitled *Statistical View of the Population of the United States, from 1790-1830,* printed by order of the Senate of February 26, 1833, and March 31, 1834. This is sometimes referred to as the Duff Green's work, since Green printed it. The State Department took the Census in those years. The full title of Pitkin's *Statistical View of the Commerce of the*

Watterston & V^n Zandt[146]	2	Do
Journal of the Federal convention[147]	1	Do
Secret Journals of Congress[148]	4	Do
Wait's State Papers[149]	12	Do

United States adds the following information: *Commerce, its connection with agriculture and manufactures and an account of the public debt revenues and expenditures of the United States; with a brief view of the trade, agriculture and manufactures of the Colonies previous to their independence; and a table illustrative of the principles and objects of the work.*

[146] For the complete bibliographical entry of this reference work by George Watterston and Nicholas Biddle Van Zandt, see footnote 80, page 431. These two volumes are included, we believe, under the one listing in Mr. Throop's list; Mr. Hammett (see Boulware, pp. 596-597)) does not list them.

[147] *The Journal of the Federal Convention* held at Philadelphia, beginning May 14, 1787, otherwise known as the Constitutional Convention since it drafted the Federal Constitution of the United States of America, is a document, which, although printed at the time and within the next half-century in many editions, and as combined with many other public documents, and privately printed by many noted publishers and the press of the country, is nevertheless, today, a document rather elusive for the bibliographer. The title varies for the several editions: the first edition was the *Journal of the Acts and Proceedings of the Convention assembled at Philadelphia, May 14 1787, which formed the Constitution.* Boston, Thos. B. Wait, 1819. Published under the direction of the President of the United States in conformance with a Resolution of March 27, 1818. The manuscript of this edition is at the Library of Congress, with the *Madison Papers* in the Manuscript Division of the Library.

A companion volume, claiming the same authority for publication, but published in Philadelphia, has a somewhat similar title: *Journal of the Constitutional Convention.* This volume contained the credentials of the deputies to the Convention, the text of the Constitution, the ratifications by the State Conventions, etc.

Judging by the nearly contemporary dates of the publication of the various other books Mr. Throop took with him to Naples, we identify the edition of the *Journal of the Federal Convention* which he took with him, as that of the first volume of the 4-volume edition, viz., the 2d edition "published for Congress by Jonathan Elliott, Washington, 1836." The arrangement of this edition differed somewhat from the earlier 1819, or first edition, in that it gave the whole text of the *Journal,* instead of merely the index thereto. The binder's title in both cases was *Debates of the Constitutional Convention, May 14, 1787.*

This 1836 edition, the second edition, included: Volume I, *The Journal of the Federal Convention; Yates' Minutes, and Martin's Letters;* Vol. II, *Debates in Massachusetts, Connecticut, New Hampshire, New York, Pennsylvania, and Maryland;* Vol. III, *Debates in Virginia;* Vol. IV, *Debates in North Carolina, South Carolina;* the *Virginia and Kentucky Resolutions.*

For the first edition: Vol. I gave *Debates of Massachusetts and New York;* II, *Debates of Virginia;* Vol. III, *North Carolina and Pennsylvania;* Vol. IV contained the index to *Journal of Federal Convention,* index to *Secret Debates of Federal Convention,* index to *Congressional opinions on questions of confederation from 1789 to 1830, the Articles of Confederation, memoranda relative to drafts and plans in the Convention that framed the Constitution.*

[148] *Secret Journals of the Continental Congress.* Published by Way & Gideon, 1823; 4 vols. (Vol. I, *Domestic Affairs;* Volumes II, III, and IV, *Foreign Affairs.*)

[149] Wait's *State Papers* followed those similarly titled which were published

American Archives, vol. 1 of the
    fourth series[150] 1   Do

Subsequently received by him.

1 & 2 sessions of XXV Congress[151] ......39 vols /43 complete
Drawings of the Alexandria Acqueduct[152] accompanying the
    report of Capt. Trumball [sic]
A Chart of St. George's Shoal & Bank, 1838[153]

---

by Peter Force. The first 9 volumes of Wait's *State Papers* were published under
the Act of March 25, 1816; the 2nd edition, also 9 volumes; an Act approved
the 3d of March, 1817 "authorized the secretary to subscribe for the 10th volume"
(volume 10 contained confidential documents). The 3rd edition contained all
twelve volumes carrying the documentary record through 1818. See, *State Papers
and Publick documents of the United States from the accession of George Washington to the Presidency, exhibiting a complete view of our foreign relations
since that time.* Washington, Thomas B. Wait & Sons, 3d edition, 1818. *State
Papers,* individually, appeared also as pamphlets in great number of places and
from many publishers. These, however, always are to be inspected for inaccuracies of text, as they were sometimes copied from preliminary texts, never
officially authorized. All the public journals, such as *National Intelligencer,
Niles' Register,* etc., also gave space to the public documents, texts, sometimes
only in abstracts, more often in full text. The *Annals* and the *Globe,* and the
Register, of course, printed many of them. Force and the Wait family rendered
great public service by bringing these documents together in readily consultable
series; as also did Duff Green to a certain extent, though he was hampered by
the typesetters he employed. Gales and Seaton put out the most enduring set,
on larger pages, with easier read type, and much more enduring bindings; also
there was, on the whole, perhaps greater organization in the volumes, and somewhat more complete and accurate printing of the documents.

    150 *American Archives,* compiled by Peter Force and M. St. Claire Clark.
From 1774. A documentary history of the causes and accomplishments of the
American Revolution. Published by order of Congress at Washington. 9 volumes
folio: 4th series, volumes I-V, to the Declaration of Independence; 5th series,
volumes I-III, from the Declaration to the Treaty of Peace.

    151 Evidently duplicates of, or additions to, the documents in the first twelve
items of the above list.

    152 These were the huge engraved drawings contained in folios accompany-
ing Executive Document 459, 25th Cong., 2d sess., July 2, 1838. 107 pp. *Documents relating to the Potomac Aqueduct.* In relation to the survey and construction of the aqueduct. See also: Executive Document 261, 24th Cong., 1st sess.,
May 25, 1836. 12 pp. Letter of Secretary of the Treasury Levi T. Woodbury,
transmitting a *Report on the construction of the Alexandria Aqueduct.* (The
two names for this public work meant the same project).

    153 St. George's Shoal and Bank in Massachusetts Bay, off Boston Harbor,
shallowest of the routes of entrance thereto. This chart escapes identification
because it is listed with so little identification detail. St. George's Shoal and
(St.) George's Bank lie between Cape Cod and the Isle of Sables, athwart the
most difficult and shoal of the routes of ingress from the Atlantic to Boston,
Massachusetts, harbor. On Jan. 14th, 1825, this region had come to public attention: Secretary of War, J. C. Calhoun on that date addressed a letter to the
Speaker of the House of Representatives "on the condition of Boston Harbor,"
calling the attention of the House to the fact that "George's Island and Nantasket
Head . . . are in danger of being entirely swept away by the sea if not immediately secured, thus depriving the harbor of two important sites for fortifications." See, *House Documents, 18th Cong., 2d sess., Jan. 14, 1825.* But there
was a far more pacific attention paid to this location a decade later. See, *Petition of Seward Porter, Jan. 1, 1837, praying that a lighthouse may be erected on
St. George's Shoals.* Senate Document No. 143, serial No. 297, Feb. 4, 1837.
Referred to Committee on Commerce. That this petition had its weight with

Sessions of the Laws[154] of the U. S. for the years 1838, 1839,
1840, 1841.
American Archives[155] ....1 vol.

Purchased by him

Book entitled Saggio politico[156] ....1 vol.
Almanach Reale delle Due Sicilie per l'anno 1840 ....1 Do.
Leggi doganali[157] .... 2 Do.

Found by him at the Legation

A Seal[158]
The first of 7 vols. & an Index of
the Laws of the United States[159] ....8 vols.

the House may be judged from the fact that in Senate Document 223, 24th
Congress, 2d sess., on March 27, 1837, there was included in the *Statement of
all appropriations during the Second Session, — op. cit.,* p. 9, — this item: —
"To defray the expense of examining the shoal of George's Bank for the purpose
of determining upon the practicability of erecting a light house upon the same
. . . in aid of the general appropriation of the Navy . . . $5,000." From the
date (1842), when the Chart of the Shoals was listed by Mr. Nelson in his inventory, in the Legation at Naples, it would appear that he was referring to one
of the charts thought to have resulted from the survey which the above $5,000
made possible. The expenditure under the auspices of the Navy takes the matter, so far as this present work is concerned, out of its purview, which obscurely
recorded details of the preliminaries which would appear to have caused the
creation of the Chart in question, in order to reveal the documentary searching
process which must be gone through to establish documentation for the most
casual of references in diplomatic dispatches, but also to bring to notice that, if
one but search far enough, it is almost always entirely possible to clear up such
details of reference and to find the original documents concerned. In this particular instance, War and Navy old records would require to be subjected to
search, following the leads given above.

[154] *Session Laws of the United States* are those officially edited by the State
Department and grouped for publication, in paper covers, at the end of each
session of Congress. Such pamphlets contain all the laws of that particular session. Prior to these, and often repeatedly during the stages of debate before
various bills are enacted into law, the successive texts of the bills are printed
and reprinted for use by members of the Congress. These are 'slip bills.' As
soon as an act is signed, its carefully edited text is rushed into print, singly for
each such law (act) and these called 'slip laws' have the force of law in courts
throughout the land, until the *Session Laws* printed texts are available; these, in
turn, have full force of law until, after the end of the whole congress the finally
edited texts appear in the form of bound volumes, serially numbered on continuous *Public Documents Series.* Thereafter, appear in due course the annotated
volumes of the *United States Statutes at Large,* which are described in detail in
footnote 143, p. 513, together with the earlier printings of the final texts of the
laws passed by the earlier congresses.

[155] Probably another volume of the Fourth Series. See, note 150, above.

[156] It has not been possible to identify this work.

[157] Laws regulating customs duties of the Two Sicilies.

[158] The seal of the United States Legation in Naples was most carefully
guarded. The consuls had their own official seal. These were fine steel dies
used for stamping on wax covered with a 'wafer' of special paper, so as to hold
the impression and make the imprint legible, to officialize all public documents
signed at the Legation by the Minister or at his orders. The beauty of the seal
design and the quality of wax and paper used in that day, remain, on these cen-
tury-old documents, to delight the modern viewer of them.

[159] Probably the same (Bioren and Duane) edition as Mr. Throop had
brought with him.

Wait's State Papers[160] ....12 vols.
Le Droit de la Nature et des gens par Pufendorf[161] ....2 vols.

Received from E. T. Throop the property
of the United States
mentioned in the preceding schedule
together with a book of Records of
the Legation & several bundles of Papers.

(sgd) Wm. Boulware[162]

Jan᷒ 16, 1842.

---

[160] These also duplicate what Mr. Throop had brought.

[161] The 1712 edition, published in French, in Amsterdam, with the Jean Barbeyrac notations. See also, prior, Throop Chapter *hic opus*, p. 400, item 4, also note 47 thereon; also Nelson chapter, *hic opus*, p. 268, note 59. This famous work, of the "father of international law," written originally in Latin by the German Baron Pufendorff has been continually reprinted in full, translated into French, into English from the French, English from the Latin, into German from the Latin and the French, into Italian, etc. Originally published in 1694, this work remains so standard and basic that its translators and editors have retained the text intact, but each has made notable additions to the extensive annotations and case illustrations thus bringing the principles of international law successively for each nation and each era into the grasp of public men, citizens and lawyers of that period, by citing as illustrations well known and intellectually and ethically stimulative incidents well known to the audience addressed. The most recent edition of this great work on the *Law of Nations* is that published in 1916 by the Carnegie Institution for International Peace. Other works of Pufendorff's have been reprinted since the date. Probably no other single work of the seventeenth century has had so great an influence on the history of the world during the life of the United States. The author is said to have been the son of a Protestant minister. John Nelson's grasp of the great work on the *Law of Nations* and the people was in itself remarkable and well merits careful study of the arguments he laid down in his note to the Minister of Foreign Affairs of the Two Sicilies. See also Boulware Chapter, *hic opus*, p. 597, note 99.

[162] The signature and date are in Mr. Boulware's hand. The list itself is neither in his nor in Mr. Throop's hand, and was probably compiled by a clerk.

WILLIAM BOULWARE
(September 13, 1841 to June 19, 1845)

D. WEBSTER TO WM. BOULWARE

Department of State Washington, 15th. Septr. 1841. [Instruction No. 1]

Sir:

I transmit to you the following papers[1] necessary to your entrance upon the discharge of the duties of the mission to which the president by and with the advice and consent of the Senate,[2] has appointed you.

1. Your commission as Chargé d'Affaires of the United States near the Government of the Two Sicilies.

2. A special passport for yourself and suite.

3. A letter of credit on the Bankers of the United States in London, authorizing them to pay your drafts for your salary as it becomes due with the contingent expenses of the mission actually incurred which, however, are limited to the sum of five hundred dollars per annum. In availing yourself of this authority you will be careful not to exceed in the amount drawn for the sums to which you may be entitled on account with the United States at the respective dates of your drafts. You will designate in your drafts the accounts upon which they may be drawn stating particularly whether they are for salary or for contingent expenses. And if you draw for both, you will name the respective amounts which are chargeable to each account.

4. A letter of credence addressed to the Minister of Foreign Affairs of the Two Sicilies.

5. A full power.

6. A set of printed personal instructions with a supplement prescribed by the Department of State for the government of all the diplomatic representatives of the United States abroad.

7. A printed list of the Diplomatic and Consular Agents in foreign countries.

Your compensation, as fixed by law, is at the rate of four thousand five hundred dollars per annum, with an outfit equal

---

[1] None of the enclosures to this Instruction No. 1 is herewith reprinted.

[2] Emissaries such as Boulware for negotiating treaties were not then always appointed with the advice and consent of the Senate.

to a year's salary, and a quarter's salary for your return to this country. It will commence on the day of your commission, (the 13th September of the present year) provided you proceed upon your mission within one month from such date, unless you should obtain special leave for further delay. For your outfit you will draw on this Department.

Enclosed is a copy of a letter addressed to your predecessor, which you will deliver to him if he should still remain at Naples. If he should have left that city, the books, archives, and property will of course be delivered to you by the person to whose charge they may have been committed by M^r. Throop.

I transmit a letter from the President of the United States to His Majesty Ferdinand II, King of the Kingdom of the Two Sicilies in reply to a communication from His Majesty of the 28th. March of the present year, announcing the fact that Her Majesty the Queen had given birth to a Prince on whom the names of Alfonso Maria Giuseppe Alberto had been bestowed. You will seize an early occasion after the presentation of your letter of credence, to convey to His Majesty's principal Secretary for Foreign Affairs, the accompanying copy of the President's letter, and take the proper measures to deliver in person or to transmit the original in the manner most agreeable to His Majesty's wishes as they may be made known to you by his Minister.

The Instructions given to M^r. Throop under date of the 19th. May, 1838, and the documents which accompanied those instructions, all of which will be found by you among the papers of the Legation[3] will explain clearly to your mind the relations of the United States with the Two Sicilies, as well as the important objects which have long been cherished by your Government having in view to promote and improve those relations for the mutual benefit of the two countries, and they will serve as a guide for your direction. To this end, a full power to conclude a treaty of commerce and navigation with the Two Sicilies is herewith transmitted, and you will lose no time in endeavoring to renew the negotiations for this purpose which are now suspended, and to bring them to a prompt and favorable issue. At the same time, it is expressly enjoined upon you to accept no proposition nor enter into any stipulation which may vary from

---

[3] See Throop chapter, *hic opus,* p. 511. The Legation papers were left in Mr. Hammett's care when Mr. Throop left Naples.

the direct instructions given to your predecessor without previously submitting them to this Department and receive its sanction.

WM. BOULWARE TO D. WEBSTER

Naples Jan^y. [no day], 1842. [Despatch, Unnumbered]

Sir

I arrived at this place in the 24th Ult., having come by way of London and Paris. At each of these places I was detained in making preparation necessary for my residence and pursuits here. My journey through France was also retarded by the inclemency of the weather & the wretched state of the roads at this season of the year.

Upon my arrival here I found that the Christmas festivities had commenced, and I delayed making a communication to the Minister of Foreign Affairs until the 27th. Ult. On that day I addressed him a note informing him of my arrival and asking an audience for the purpose of presenting my letter of credence. On the next day I received an answer appointing the ensuing day for my reception. I was then met by him with all proper courtesy and kindness; and after presenting my letter of credence, I was able to inform him that I was charged with a letter from the Pres. of the U. S. to his Majesty, acknowledging the reception of a communication from his Majesty, giving information of the birth of a royal Prince; that I was instructed to deliver to him a copy of the letter and take his advice as to the proper mode of delivering the original to the King. He informed me that if I would send it to his Department enclosed to him, that he would deliver it to his Majesty. This I did and rec^d. from him a note acknowledging it's [sic] reception. He appointed the 12th. of the present month for my presentation to the King, that being the anniversary of his birth & a day on which the Ministers are generally rec^d.

On that occasion I attended at the palace and was presented by the Minister of Foreign Affairs to his Majesty & also to the Queen. My reception was courteous, but as it was in the midst of a large circle composed of all the Foreign Ministers & the principal nobles of his Kingdom, there was little opportunity for conversation & but little occurred.

I have not deemed it expedient to bring to the consideration of this government, the subject of a commercial treaty. I have thought it best to wait a little and make myself better acquainted with the state of things here & the subjects involved.

The treaty with England which was considered during the Administration of the Department of Foreign Affairs by Prince Cassaro, as a necessary preliminary to a treaty with us, has not yet been consummated. The fall of Cassaro & the sulphur question having arrested it just on the point of it's [sic] completion. The Sulphur question is now adjusted but I have not yet been able to inform myself what is the state of their negotiation on the subject of their commercial relations. It is obvious that it is the interest of Great Britain & that it is her wish to surrender the treaty now in force in favor of one upon reciprocal principles or at any rate upon some different principle, the advantage of ten per cent which her imports now enjoy, being shown by France & Spain & countervailed to a considerable extent by a discrimination in favor of the imports from the East & West Indies & America, in Sicilian bottoms to the amount of thirty per cent & also by other commercial arrangements of this Kingdom.

The Prince of Cassaro having been relieved from exile is now here & is rec^d. at court. Should he return to power, it would be an event very favorable to our objects, as he is known to be in principle in favor of open trade. It would be useless for me at present to hazard a conjecture as to his prospects.

At present I am able to say but little as to the chances of a successful negotiation on our part. I will reserve myself on this subject until I have more extended information.

It gives me great pleasure to say that M^r. Throop, whom I found here, rec^d. me with kindness, and I believe he has done all in his power to furnish me with information, to facilitate my intercourse & promote the objects of my mission.

Mr Hamet [sic] our Consul has also extended to me all the attentions & kindness which I could ask, and he has been to me of great service from his thorough acquaintance with Sicilian affairs.

M^r. Throop who has started on his return to the U. S. is furnished with an inventory[4] of the books papers & property of the U. S. which is now at this Legation, which he will deliver at the Department of State.

You will find enclosed my account up to the 30th. Dec. I thought it proper, as you will perceive to advance to M^r. Miller our agent in London £ 10 to meet future expenses of this Legation

---

4 See Throop chapter, pp. 511-517.

in London, not thinking it right that he should be compelled to advance his funds to pay postage, &c. &c.

I rec^{d}. the Presidents [sic] message through Galignani[5] about a week since.

WM. BOULWARE TO D. WEBSTER

Naples Mar 12. 1842 [Despatch No. 2]
Sir

After the expiration of the Carnival, I addressed a note to the Prince of Scilla requesting an interview. I did not deem it proper to do this sooner because during the festivities of this season, little attention is given to business of any kind. I did not anticipate much from this interview & the result justified my anticipation.

It took place in the last day of February. After the usual civilities, I commenced the conversation by remarking that it must be well known to him that the interests of this country as well as of the United States suffered from the want of some commercial treaty adopted to their mutual necessities. That the trade was now carried on, for the most part indirectly, through the medium of other ports, enhancing the expense and increasing the embarrassments of both parties. That there was a large demand in the U. S. for the productions of this country. That of receiving silk alone from the city of Naples, we consumed an amount equal to six hundred thousand dollars in value. That their wines would find an extensive market with us, if their ports were thrown open to us upon terms of fair reciprocity. That I had been induced to seek this interview and introduce the subject, partly from the fact that his Majesty's government had manifested a disposition in times past to enter into a convention.

He said at once that he was perfectly aware of the truth of my remarks, but that I knew the difficulties which stood in the way of a commercial treaty, alluding to the engagements with England, France & Spain. I told him, I did, but asked if something could not be done to remove those difficulties. He said, he did not know, and I thought, seemed afraid to speak on the subject and anxious to terminate the conference. It is true, he

---

5 William Galignani (1798-1882) and his brother John Anthony Galignani (1796-1873) of London. After 1821, they were editors and publishers in Paris of the newspaper, *Galignani's Messenger,* which, in 1814, had been founded by their father who was a native of Brescia, Italy.

gave no decided evidence of a wish to close the conversation, though I thought from appearances that such was the case. I then said to him that I wished to know what was the disposition of His Majesty's Government on this subject. He said, he would consult the King, and let me know. I then took my leave believing that nothing would be gained by protracting the conversation with him, for in the first place he knows but little, & in the second place, that little he is afraid to tell.

His reputation is that of a very weak, timid, ignorant man. He is not, as you know, the Minister of State for foreign affairs, but is simply designated as "Charged with the portfolio of foreign affairs," indicating a temporary arrangement. I believe that he does nothing but the merest detail except by the command of the King.

I had a conversation a short time since with M^r. Temple the British Minister, and endeavored to ascertain, whether it was his intention, to attempt a resumption of his negotiation for a commercial treaty now that the sulphur question is settled. You are aware that the difficulty which arose on this suspended a negotiation. I believe he spoke with me with perfect frankness, for he knows well that we are interested in his success as well as all other powers who wish to trade with Naples. He said that the Prince of Scilla was so utterly incompetent to conduct a negotiation, that it would be difficult to do any thing with him. That he was at some loss how to proceed. That the ten per cent abatement of the duties on their imports was worth but little to them. That they were anxious to release it, for a treaty on liberal principles of reciprocity. That the Cabinet here were divided on the subject of opening their ports to the trade of other countries, &c. &c.

This Government has heretofore acted for the most part on the principle of isolation, endeavoring to make every thing which they want & be indebted to other countries for nothing. In pursuance of this principle they have now a system of duties so high as to exclude most of the products of other countries. They have formed treaties for the purpose of commerce with none, for those which exist with England, France & Spain, and which are the only treaties that they have, were entered into many years ago as a consideration to get rid of the "free flag" which those nations had previously enjoyed in the ports of this country. At present a part of the Cabinet & a large part of the commercial men of the country are in favor of a change of sys-

523

tem. This would probably have occurred before this time, but for the difficulty with England on the subject of the sulphur monopoly. They seem anxious to get rid of the trammels of that ten per cent privilege that they may negotiate. And they have adroitly contrived by remitting thirty per cent of the duties upon the imports in their own vessels from the East & West Indies & the continent of America, and twenty per cent on those from the Baltic as also by their scale of duties to render the privilege almost valueless.

I have recently heard of a curious result of one of the facts just stated. During the present year a large cargo of crushed sugar has been sent from England to the United States to be reshipped to this port in Neapolitan vessels. For the same reason the fish brought to this country from the banks of New Foundland, which constitute one of the principal items of British imports, will probably make their way into the vessels of this nation to the injury of British commerce. And here our countrymen will have an opportunity of competing successfully in this trade, with British merchants who, in times past, drove our fish from this market by the ten per cent advantage.

During the year 1838, the number of vessels that sailed from the city of Naples, was 1215, of these 976 were Neapolitan, 81 French, 34 Tuscan, & 292 English. In 1839 the imports from Great Britain were of the value of 4,337,108 Ducats, and of this amount 1 687 979 Ducats were imported in the vessels of this country. This amount of imports and tonnage to a country productive as this, a country whose annual revenue exceeds that of the United States, being twenty eight millions of Ducats may well produce dissatisfaction among the statesmen of Britain & excite an anxiety to release their present treaty for one modelled upon different principles.

In this state of things when both parties are anxious for a change it seems probable that before long there will be a change, and the Government having rid itself of the incumbrances which now clog it's action, will adopt a different policy and form commercial treaties with other nations. In reference to this subject, the same position is occupied towards us as all other nations except the three named. Austria, although the King is indebted to her for the throne he occupies, has never been able to obtain a commercial treaty though striving for it, for the last twenty years.

My impression then is that at present, we can expect to do

nothing in the way of a treaty. But after I hear from the King & ascertain decidedly that such is the case, I intend then to make an effort to induce them to modify their tariff upon some articles in which we have an interest. Cotton from Egypt & the East Indies pays ten per cent top duty than that from America. They have some of our Sea Island cotton & it is possible and perhaps not improbable that I may induce them to equalize the duty.

I have received nothing from the Department of State since my arrival here. I should be glad at least to have transmitted to me the message of the President & the reports of the heads of Departments. I suppose however, I should have received them long since but for some difficulty or mistake on this side of the Atlantic for my newspapers have none of them arrived.

WM. BOULWARE TO D. WEBSTER

Naples April 20 1842. [Unnumbered Despatch]
Sir

I hasten to inform you of a very serious difficulty which has arisen between their Majesties of Holland & Belgium, and his Majesty of Naples.[6]

Some years ago a bank was established at this place, called the Tavoliere di Puglia, of which the greatest part of the capital was furnished by citizens of Holland & Belgium. After a few years of very successful business, this institution expired in hopeless insolvency.

A claim was then set up by the Dutch & Belgian capitalists who had thus invested their funds, that the Government of the Two Sicilies had rendered itself responsible for the maladaministration of the Bank, and that it is now bound to indemnify their losers. Their governments have espoused their cause, and they now claim at the hands of the King of the Two Sicilies the money which has been Squandered by his Subjects.

The King on his part treats the claim with contempt, denies all responsibility & refuses all arbitration.

In this state of things, it is generally believed here, and I do not doubt it that reprisals have been threatened. It is obvious

---

[6] The difficulties between Holland, Belgium, and the King of Naples were due to economic questions of minor importance which even the historians of the period seldom mention. In April 1842, the proposal was made, through diplomatic channels, to negotiate a treaty of commerce with Holland similar to the one with Sardinia. *Archivio di Stato,* Naples, *Affari Esteri,* folder 2416.

that this government anticipates them. A paper has just been sent from the Ministry to the Chamber of Commerce, advising Merchants to be on their guard, and especially those who are sending cargoes on distant voyages. It is further suggested by the ministry that it may be *expedient* for them, when it is possible, to *assume another flag* than the Neapolitan.

There are vessels now in the U. S. belonging to the Two Sicilies and these will be followed by others when this communication arrives. It would probably be well for Americans, at present, to be on their guard, and not to entrust their property to the Neapolitan flag.

I have sent you by M[r]. Payson a document which gives the details of the controversy at length.

At the request of an agent of some American Mercantile Houses, here I have written to our Chargé d'affaires at the Hague[7] & at Brussels[8] to inform them of six Neapolitan vessels now on the ocean loaded with American property, to call their attention to this subject, that if any of these vessels should be taken by the cruisers of these powers, they may at once do what is proper in reference to the case.

In my dispatch of the 12th. of March I expressed the opinion that there would be on the part of this government, a change of policy as to commercial treaties. That change seems to be nearier at hand than I anticipated. Since that period, a Minister plenipotentiary has arrived here from Great Britain, to be associated with the resident Minister, for the purpose of resuming & bringing to a close their treaty of commerce. They are now actively engaged in this business, both parties are anxious that it should be brought to a successful issue, and I believe there is a strong probability of success.

This will open the way to treaties with other powers unless France should interpose some obstacle, which they seem not to anticipate. Indeed they say, that with her, they will now have no difficulty. The Minister of Foreign Affairs told me, his great object was to get rid of the ten per cent privilege that he might negotiate with other powers.

---

[7] Virgil Maxcy (1785-1844). Lawyer, legislator, diplomat of Massachusetts. He later moved to Maryland. He was appointed solicitor of the Treasury in 1830 by President Jackson and held that office until 1837 when he was appointed American chargé d'affaires at Brussels; he served till 1842. *Dictionary American Biography*, 1933, XII, 434-435.

[8] Harmanus Bleecker of New York, chargé d'affaires in the Netherlands; he was commissioned on May 15, 1839; he left service on August 26, 1842. Official Record of the United States State Department at the National Archives.

We agreed that it would be useless for us to discuss the terms of a treaty until the negotiation was concluded with England.

I have had no communication from the Department of State since my arrival.

WM. BOULWARE TO D. WEBSTER

Legation of the U. S. Naples June 5, 1842. [Despatch No. 4]

Sir,

In my last despatch, I had the honor of informing you of a serious controversy which had arisen between the King of the Two Sicilies and the Governments of Holland & Belgium. At that time immediate reprisals were apprehended at this place, and notice was given from the Ministry to the Chamber of Commerce of the danger which was supposed to be impending. I have previously stated that it was advised by the Government, in case it should be found necessary, that the flag of the Two Sicilies should be abandoned, and some other adopted to escape pursuit.

A few days after this extraordinary counsel to the Chamber of Commerce I was much astonished to receive from the Prince of Scylla, [sic] an official note, advising me of the controversy, of the communications made to the Merchants, and containing also a suggestion, that in case of foreign property being taken in the vessels of this Kingdom, under existing circumstances, there would be no cause for reclamations. They have been so often harassed by reclamations, that the idea seems now to haunt their imaginations and fright them from their propriety. But it appears, after all their anxiety & alarm on this subject, that there was no cause or at most, but little. I have received from our Chargé d'affaires at the Hague, a letter in which he expresses the belief, that there has been no cause for the apprehension of reprisals. The interest felt here on the subject has subsided, and thus the bubble has burst. It is rumored, with what truth I know not, that both France & Austria have intervened to settle the controversy.

A short time since I received a note from the Prince of Scylla [sic] requesting to see me at the Ministry. I met there the Secretary of the Finance, who wished an interview on the subject of the payment of the last instalment of the indemnity. He seems not to be content with the authority given to our bankers at

Paris, and to fear that they were not sufficiently empowered to give a receipt in full. I examined the papers and thought the powers were ample. After some conversation and explanations, he appeared better satisfied and said the money was ready, and that it should be paid as soon as it became due. He further said that he would be pleased to have a receipt from Washington giving a full discharge of the whole claim. I told him that the authority of our bankers was plenary but that if he preferred it and would send me a draught of the sort of receipt that would be agreeable to him, I would transmit it to Washington; and I had no doubt, it would be signed. But I further expressed a hope that there would be no delay in the payment of the money. He said there should be none. I have not heard from him since, and I think it probable that upon reflection he has concurred with me that any other receipt than that which the bankers will give, would be utterly superfluous.

The British treaty is progressing. I deem it a matter of much moment to keep myself informed of the state of it's [sic] progress for the commercial interests of Great Britain conflict here as well as at most every where else with our own. Thus far, nothing has been proposed to which we can object. If we had been represented at this Court, at the time of the restoration of the Bourbons, I doubt if the three favored powers would ever have secured to themselves a renewal of the ten per cent discriminating duties. It is understood that the King, who is the Government and the whole Government, is now in favor of a change of policy. He is anxious for the success of this negotiation and wishes to favor commercial treaties with other countries as soon as the way is laid open by the conclusion of this treaty with Great Britain. In the French journals are various statements in reference to this subject, which are without any foundation. In truth, nothing has been said by them concerning this negotiation which is not false. My impression is that there is a strong disposition on the part of the Neapolitans to increase their intercourse with us. Sicilian vessels, that is the vessels of the Two Sicilies trading to America, now enjoy a remission of duties to the amount of forty per cent, that is thirty per cent over those of the three favored powers. Whenever I have an opportunity I endeavor to exhibit to them the advantages of our trade. They have various products which find a profitable market in the U. S. Their silks, wines, fruit, sulphur are imported in considerable quantities. The trade with Sicily is large and is annually increasing. According to a report just received from our Consul at Palermo, the number of our vessels, which sailed from that port & district during the last year for the U.S., was sixty seven, the tonnage 16,987. The number of Sicilian vessels for the U. S. 13, tonage 2,500. From the Consul at Messina, I have not yet obtained any report, but I doubt not that this report would add very largely to the amount.

To this place, they are now importing sugars from America in vessels of the two [sic] Sicilies. And if the present state of things continue, the British trade in this article, will be driven from this market. Cotton might also be brought here with great profit at the present prices in the U.S.

This is a country of great fertility, blessed with a climate well suited to the production of all the necessaries and most of the luxuries of life, with a soil so rich that much of it gives three crops during every year. It's [sic] culture is admirable, as far as I have seen, and its peasantry active sober & laborious.

The population is estimated at from eight to nine millions. The revenue of the King is 28,000,000 of Ducats. The tonnage of the kingdom 213,000, number of sailors, 52,514, standing army 50,000. I give these statistics because I know in the U.S. it is almost impossible to obtain any accurate information in reference to this country.

The present King has the reputation of a very rigid economist. His enemies call him parsimonious. When he ascended the throne he found the state embarrassed with debt, which is not entirely removed. He has abridged many expenses and among others those of his diplomatic corps, having diminished the number & the grade. Brazil is represented here in the same way as the U.S. without this Kingdom's having any representative at Rio Janeiro. And this is the case at a time when the most intimate relations exist between the two countries, the emperor being about to marry the King's sister, the contract having been already signed and the princess being about to depart for that Kingdom.

I transmit with this despatch a letter from M[r]. Persico.[9]. He

<hr>

9 On Luigi Persico's work in the Capitol, see: "Memorial on sculpture for the Capitol." Philadelphia, Artists Society, Feb. 1, 1837. *Executive Documents No. 159,* 24th Congress, second session, vol. IV, recommending the appointment of Persico to superintend the sculptural decoration of the Capitol. See also *hic opus,* pp. 541, 552, 556, 564. Flanking the central stairway of the eastern façades of the Capitol in Washington, D. C., on the south, is Persico's *Discovery of America;* within the portico in wall niches are his *Ceres as Peace* and *Mars as War.* The central pediment is decorated with Persico's *Genius of America.* The *Niles National*

is surprised that the instalments due him, have not been paid. He informs me that M^r. Buchannan [sic] of the Senate wrote to him, that the appropriation for the last year, was made by Congress.

I send herewith a statement also of my account for the first quarter of the present year.

I have received no communication from your department.

WM. BOULWARE TO D. WEBSTER

Legation of the U. S. Naples June 21, 1842. [Despatch No. 5]

Sir

Two days ago I received from the Prince of Scylla, a note informing me that the last instalment of the indemnity from the Government of the Two Sicilies to the United States, had been paid on the 8th. Inst. to the House of Green & Co. of Paris.

At the same time, His Excellency enclosed to me the model of a receipt which he requests shall be given by the Pres. of the U.S. as a final quittance of the debt arising under the convention of the 14th. Oct. 1832. I herewith transmit the model.

I deem it proper to say that in an interview with the Prince of Scylla, I said to him that I did not believe, there would be any objection on the part of the Pres. to give a final receipt; and that if he would render me a model that would be satisfactory I would forward it to Washington.

I have at present nothing of importance to communicate.

[Form of Receipt Requested by H. M. the King]

Enclosure with Mr. Boulware's Despatch No. 5 of June 21, 1842.

Il Governo degli Stati Uniti di America, e per esso l'attuale Presidente Sig^r. John Tyler, dichiara aver ricevuto dal Governo di S. M. il Re delle Due Sicilie, in Napoli, la somma di ducati duemilionicentoquindicimila, insieme con gl'interessi al 4. per 100. in altri ducati quattrocentoventitremila in moneta dello stesso Regno, a' termini, ed in esecuzione della Convenzione del 14. Ottobre 1832, ed inoltre dichiara, che il pagamento è avvenuto in nove rate annuali nel seguente modo, cioè:

Register, for August 15, 1840, reported that Congress in 1840, had appropriated "for payment to Luigi Persico . . . for statues to adorn the two blockings on the East front of the Capitol . . . $8,000." See also, *House Reports, No. 2*, 26th Congress, first Session, 1840; and Niles, *op. cit.*, 380, the end of column 3.

Ducati 319,600 de' quali ducati 235,000 di Capitale, e D[10].
84600 d'interessi, con polizza notata fede a' 17. Settb°. 1834 a
favore di C. M. Rothschild in estinzione di cambiale tratta da
Parigi dai Sig^rı. Welles e Compagni.

Ducati 310,200 de' quali D. 235.000 di Capitale, e D. 75,200
d'interessi, con polizza notata fede a' 6. Giugno 1835. a favore
dei Signori Welles e Comp^i. di Parigi.

Ducati 300,800 de' quali D. 235,000 di Capitale e D. 65,800
d'interessi, con polizza notata fede agli 8. Giugno 1836. a favore
dei Sig^rı Welles e Comp^i di Parigi.

Ducati 291,400 de' quali D. 235,000 di Capitale, e D. 56,400
d'interessi, con polizza notata fede a' 7. Giugno 1837. a favore
de' Sig^rı. Welles e Compagni di Parigi.

Ducati 282,000 de' quali D. 235,000 di Capitale, e D. 47,000
d'interessi, con polizza notata fede a' 23. Giugno 1838. a favore
de' Sig^rı. Welles e Comp^ı. di Parigi.

Ducati 272,600 de' quali D. 235,000 di Capitale, e D. 37,600
d'interessi, con polizza notata fede agli 8 Giug°. 1839. a favore
de' Sig^rı. Welles e Compagni di Parigi.

Ducati 263,200 de' quali D. 235,000 di Capitale e D. 28,200
d'interessi, con polizza notata fede a' 9. Giug°. 1840, a favore de'
Sig^rı. Welles e Comp^ı. di Parigi.

Ducati 253,800 de' quali D. 235,000 di capitale, e D. 18,800
d'interessi, con polizza notata fede agli 8. Giug°. 1841. a favore
de' Sig^rı Welles a Compagni di Parigi.

Ducati 244,400 de' quali D. 235,000 di Capitale, e D. 9,400 d'interessi con polizza notata fede agli 8. Giug°. 1842 a favore della
Casa Bancaria Greene e Compagni di Parigi

Atteso il pagamento anzidetto, il Governo degli Stati Uniti,
e per esso il suo attuale Presidente Sig^r. John Tyler fa col presente
atto ampia e finale quietanza a favore del Governo di S. M. il
Re delle Due Sicilie di tutto il debito, per Capitale ed interessi,
nascente dalla mentovata Convenzione de' 14. Ottobre 1832, ed
in conseguenza il Governo degli Stati Uniti non rimane altro
a conseguire dal Governo di S. M. il Re delle Due Sicilie.

_____[11]

---

[10] This is the ducat abbreviation—D.

[11] Since this document is a sample text of what the King desired the President
to sign as a receipt, there obviously was no signature to it when the text was
handed to Mr. Boulware.

Legation of the U. S. Naples July 17, 1842. [Despatch No. 6]

Sir

I write at present merely to acknowledge the receipt of your despatch[12] No. 2, which reached me a few days since. It's [sic] date is the 14th. of April and yet it did not arrive at this place until the very last of June, having been sent by some ship from Liverpool instead of coming by post.

I transmitted immediately to the Prince of Scilla, the letter which was enclosed.

It would be well if any communication should be addressed to me from your Department which requires secrecy, that the despatch agents of the Government should be instructed not to send it by any ship to this place, but by post, for letters received by the former mode are usually opened at the Quarantine ground.

The mistake which you notice was to me a source of some surprise as well as mortification. It is not probable that it would have occurred again, even if my attention had not been called to it. The necessity of numbers, had escaped me at that time, but the other omission I can not account for.

I have nothing at this time, of interest to communicate.

The Prince de Joinville[13] arrived here a few days ago with eight ships of the line, four frigates and a steamer. He was received by the Court with the most distinguished honors. A palace has been assigned him for his residence, carriages for his use, dinners given him and every variety of attention shown, which the most friendly and most intimate relations between this and the French court could alone render appropriate. The King of Bavaria was here this winter, and also the two brothers of the King of Prussia but they did not receive a tenth of the honors which have been accorded to the son of the French Monarch.

---

12 Instruction No. 2, Washington, April 14, 1842; Secretary of State Webster transmitted a communication to the Minister of Foreign Affairs of the Two Sicilies from Daniel J. Desmond. In this Instruction, also, Mr. Boulware's attention was called to the desirability that all his despatches be regularly numbered, and that in all respects he "should conform to the personal instructions given him" and to which he was "particularly referred."

13 Orléans, François Ferdinand, Philipe, Louis Marie d'. Prince de Joinville. The fourth son of King Louis Philippe. French naval officer (1818-1887?). He was appointed lieutenant in 1836; in 1838 he distinguished himself in the port of Vera Cruz. In 1843, he went to Rio de Janeiro where he married the Princess Francesca de Bragance, sister of Dom Pedro II. In 1845, he was raised to the rank of vice-admiral. From 1848 to 1861 he lived in retirement in England. He wrote Etudes sur la Marine (1859). In 1861 he came to the United States. In 1870 he rejoined the French navy. Grande Encyclopédie, no date, XXV, 581-582.

It is said that Austria is becoming a little jealous of French influence in the controversy between this government & England. His Majesty of the Two Sicilies selected the French King as Umpire. In the difficulty with Holland, report says that both powers have volunteered their friendly aid. For my own part I do not believe that either exerts any influence. It has taken the French ambassador more than two years to negotiate a petty post-office treaty.

The story is told here that the King being asked why he kept so large an Army replied to assist Austria in case of need.

I mention these things as having some interest with the diplomatic circle here, but I presume they will have none in War.

With the other members of the diplomatic corps I paid my respects in due form to the Prince de Joinville.

WM. BOULWARE TO D. WEBSTER

Legation of the U. S. Naples Aug. 20, 1842. [Despatch No. 7]

Sir

Enclosed are my accounts for the second quarter of 1842.

I regret that I am not able to give you an account of some progress in the negotiation between this government and England. My impression is that the movement is very slow. But their proceedings are conducted with great secrecy, and it is difficult to learn what is the real state of the parties at present.

One thing, however, seems well known, that the English insist that their vessels shall be placed on an equality with the Neapolitan in the ports of this Kingdom, except as to the coasting trade. This, it is believed, by the Neapolitans, would destroy all their foreign commerce, as they say, they can not compete with the English on equal terms.

In addition to this, there seems to be in the community a fear of all treaty with England. Apprehension is felt, either that she will obtain some advantage in the terms, or that she will so construe them as to make them even to her advantage and their injury. And being the strongest power, they will enforce any construction which she may choose to adopt.

On the other side, England contends that the protection now given to the commerce of this Kingdom is inconsistent with the treaty now existing with herself; in truth that it is destruction of it. It is further said, and it is by no means improbable, that in case of failure to obtain the treaty which she is now endeavoring to make, she will enforce her views of the former. If this should occur, it would equally result according to the Neapolitan view, in the destruction of their commerce; and that without any of the advantages which are now proposed to be given.

It is confidently asserted that the King wishes a new treaty and a general change of policy. If this be so, it will be done, whatever may be the sentiments of the community. The English are very anxious, and I believe, are prepared to do whatever is just and proper and even more. It would be an arrangement highly advantageous to them, and not less so to the Neapolitans, to exchange their manufactures for the wines, oil & sulphur of this country.

But I will not pursue these desultory observations. The particulars of the English negotiation can have no great interest for you.

WM. BOULWARE TO D. WEBSTER

Legation of the U. S. Naples Nov. 28, 1842. [Despatch No. 8]

Sir

I have delayed writing to you for a long time in the hope that I would be able to announce the conclusion of the British treaty with this Government. I regret to say, it is not yet definitely settled but I believe, now, there is but little doubt it will be. After a labor of about nine months, they appear finally to have agreed to adopt the principle of commercial reciprocity, each sovereign granting to the subjects of the other in his port the same advantages which are enjoyed by his own. The only difficulty, which exists at present, is the extent to which this principle shall be carried, the British Ministers, wishing to limit it to Great Britain & Ireland and their Mediterranean possessions, and the Neapolitan Commissioners, desiring to embrace all the colonies of Great Britain. They now await instructions on this point from London. But I believe and, I have the assurance of one of the British ministers to that effect, that this question will be arranged.

I incline to think that Neapolitan competition on the ocean, can be of little moment to English seamen. They never have been, and there is no probability that they will be able to compete successfully with them. To stimulate American voyages, his

Majesty of the Two Sicilies, has for some time past, given an advantage of thirty per cent to the ships of his subjects engaged in this trade. This, of course, will be annulled by the treaty or the English admitted to the same privilege. My impression is that they may grant them full liberty to trade to the Indies East & West, and so long as the principle of free and equal competition remains, the Neapolitans will be driven from the Ocean. Far apart from the fact that the capital which is invested in nearly all distant voyages from this Kingdom, is English, except in the trade of the U. S., and, of course, ceteris paribus, the capitalists would prefer English ships, these last are considered more secure, they sail considerably faster and are manned with fewer sailors. The wages of the Neapolitans are less, but that does not countervail the other advantages.

I perceive in the instruction given to my predecessor to which I am referred in those given to myself, that it is made his precise duty and one of the principal objects of his mission to secure the introduction of our tobacco into this Kingdom. In Sicily this article is already admitted; on this side of the Strait, it is a monopoly in the hands of a company & is the source of a large revenue. This company not only imports all the tobacco which is brought here, but they purchase all which is made in this country. A license is necessary to it's [sic] cultivation, it is subject to a rigid system of inspection, and even the number of plants set out by each cultivator is registered in the archives of the Government. Under all these restrictions, the ordinary retail price of tobacco is, I incline to think, not more than it is in the U. S., but the quality is inferior.

When we enter upon the subject of a treaty, this question will present a difficulty. I do not anticipate that this government can be induced to change their system. But I do not believe, it is of much consequence to us; for if the trade were thrown open and it's [sic] cultivation at the same time made free here, it is doubtful whether we should derive any great advantage. Being liberated from the shackles which now restrain it's [sic] cultivation, there would be an increased production. How far that would be resisted by the competition from without, it is not possible to say with any accuracy. But producing tobacco at the low price which they do here, upon one of the most fertile soils on the face of the earth, and at the same time, with the wages of labor reduced to the lowest point of European compensation, I do not believe that we could supply the ordinary consumption. It is only the high priced species, such as are consumed by the wealthy, that we could expect to furnish.

At present, this side of the Strait of Messina, there are consumed annually about three millions of pounds of tobacco. Of this amount, the American, brought here from intermediate ports, where it is purchased by the Regia, constitutes a little more than one fourth, taking the years 1839, 1840, & 1841 as a guide in the estimate. The price which is paid for the tobacco of the country varies from four ducats to thirteen, according to quality, for a hundred pounds. This being the state of facts, it seems to me exceedingly doubtful whether we should be much benefited by a change of system. For under any circumstances, in the event of the destruction of the monopoly, the article would be subjected to a heavy duty.

I wish that the representatives of our country could know how much our national character is affected by the repudiation of their debts on the part of some of our states.[14] None can know it's [sic] full extent except those who have been in Europe since these occurrences. Universal execration is our lot on this continent. Our reputation moral political & commercial is soiled, blackened by these lamentable events. The petty dukedoms of Italy, enjoy more credit than the U. S. A. The cause of democracy itself has rec^d. a melancholy wound. The supporters of monarchy rejoice in our misfortunes and gloat upon our disgrace. It is to them a sweet savour. They delight to hold up our people to the European world as demoralized, utterly corrupt, disregarding the ordinary obligations of justice. Americans hold down their heads with shame. I have just seen in one of the continental journals, a quotation from the Message of the Governor of the State of Illinois,[15] in which he recommends "a large reduction of

---

14 See footnote 17, p. 538.

15 The message of the Governor of Illinois concerning "the reduction of taxes" to which Mr. Boulware referred must be Governor Thomas Carlin's message to the special session of the 12th General Assembly which convened a month ahead of time on November 23, 1840. Governor Carlin called this session to take action upon the payment of interest due on January 1st, 1841, on account of the internal improvement debt, for which there were insufficient funds in the state treasury. His message was read on November 26, 1840, and a note of it appears in the Illinois Senate Journal for 1840/41 on pages 9-20, and in the Illinois House Journal for the same year on pages 10-30, both inclusive. Actually, the message was not concerned primarily with the reduction of taxes, but rather with the problem of how to prevent an immediate increase of taxes. Carlin said, (Illinois Senate Journal, page 13): — "The policy of paying the interest out of the money borrowed must ere long be abandoned, and the only alternatives which have suggested themselves to me is an increase of our banking capital, and a resort to direct taxation." Actually, however, the General Assembly did not take Carlin's advice, since it was found impossible to borrow money to meet the January interest payment without

taxes," at the same time that he announces that "at present" it will not be possible to collect revenue to pay any portion of the public debts. This is followed by the commentary of the Editor. We are regularly denounced from week to week as a nation of sharpers and the vocabulary of their languages is ransacked to find terms of vituperation sufficiently strong for their taste.

I should be very glad to receive from the Department a copy of the late tariff.

I have the honor of acknowledging the receipt of Despatch N°. 3. with a copy of our recent treaty with Great Britain.[16]

If it is consistent with the views of the Department, it would be to me very gratifying, to obtain leave of absence from this capital for two or three months. In this enervating climate, I have found myself much enfeebled and my health exceedingly deranged. I am advised by my physician that I should probably be benefited by travel. I wish to leave here about the end of March, if this Government is not then ready to enter into a negotiation with us, and if there is nothing else, which particularly requires my presence.

WM. BOULWARE TO D. WEBSTER

Legation of the U. S. Naples Jan.ʸ 20. 1843. [Despatch No. 9]
Sir

Nothing has occurred here of much interest to our Government since the date of my last despatch. The British treaty is yet unfinished. France has been consulted on the subject, for she is enjoying the same privilege of ten per cent, it is desired that the treaty with England may meet her approbation, and that one of the same kind, that is, one embracing the principle of relief from the ten per cent incumbrance may also be made with her. I have but little doubt that treaties will be made with the two governments, and this object accomplished, but the movements here are exceedingly slow.

In my last communication, when speaking on the subject of the desire of the Neapolitan government, that the principle of

giving security. Abraham Lincoln's suggestion that a special tax of 2 mills be imposed as a guarantee for the debt was passed, and this provision was made a clause in the 1848 Constitution. The editor is indebted to Mr. Edward J. Barrett, Secretary of State and State Librarian of the Illinois State Library, Springfield, Illinois, for this information.

16 For the text of the Webster-Ashburton Treaty, signed Aug. 9, 1842, see Miller, *op. cit.,* IV, 363-478.

reciprocity, in the treaty proposed with Great Britain, should extend to her colonies throughout the world, I intimated an opinion, that the English could not fear Neapolitan competition on the Ocean and I was disposed to believe that if an arrangement of this kind could be made consistently with their engagements with other powers, there would be no very strong objection. I am disposed on further investigation to have some doubt of the correctness of that opinion. I find in a pamphlet published by the English Consul at Palermo, that he states that vessels may be built and fitted out in his Kingdom from twenty five to thirty per cent below the cost in the Thames, that they sail cheaper and find insurance at Naples and Messina on lower terms than are charged at Lloyds in London. The Neapolitan and Sicilian captains are less daring but they are more careful & are often preferred.

I find also that the Neapolitan Marine has been increasing with great rapidity for some years past. In 1824, it's [sic] total capacity was about 8.000 tons: in 1828 it had reached 99.000 and in 1837, it amounted to 150.634.

For some weeks past the Journals of this continent & of England, have been busy with the President's Message.[17] They devote to it much more space than I could have anticipated. They profit by the occasion to reiterate many times that American credit has ceased to exist, that we are bankrupt in reputation, that in our "model republic" the virtues have so declined, that integrity is but little known or respected. It is with nearly all of them, a subject of complaint, that the President has not mentioned "repudiation." They say that he has not even expressed his disapprobation, and much less has he afforded any hope of the

---

[17] See, *Second Annual Message of President John Tyler* in Richardson, *op. cit.,* IV, 194. (Serial No. 3265, House Document 210). In this speech President Tyler stressed the enormous increase in bank capital and bank issues in the form of notes resulting in inflation of prices and ending in a general indebtedness on the part of states and individuals, the prostration of public and private credit, a depreciation in the market value of real and personal estate, which left large districts of the country almost entirely without any circulating medium. From 1830, to 1837, the bank note circulation increased from $61,323,898 to $149,185,890. This increase was due in part to the ease with which money could be obtained from European capitalists. The trouble started with the withdrawal of some of these notes from circulation in 1837. President Tyler declared that American credit had suffered a considerable shock in Europe from the large indebtedness of the states and the temporary inability of some of them to meet the interest on their debts; the utter and disastrous prostration of the United States Bank of Philadelphia had contributed largely to increase the sentiment of distrust by reason of the loss and ruin sustained by the holders of its stock, a large portion of whom were foreigners and many of whom were alike ignorant of our political organization and our actual responsibilities.

debts being guaranteed by the government of the U. S. The distinction between the States and the U. S., they will not take, but most obstinately persist in invariably confounding them. Cheats, sharpers, rogues are epithets often applied to us. But none are so liberal in their abuse as the English Journals. For them the tone of the message is too religious, for the Chief Magistrate of a nation of repudiators. To them, at least, to many of them it seems that the President has produced an impression inconsistent with the facts on the subject of the arrangement as to the right of search in the recent treaty. The message is also deficient in style — and there is too much boasting and glorying as to our high destiny & great resources. In truth to these gentlemen of the English press, there seems to be nothing as it should be. With the French, the example set by us as to the right of search, is worthy of all imitation. But in other respects, their criticisms are severe, though not manifesting the bitterness of the English Journalists.

The uniform and tranquil flow of life here, has been recently disturbed by the death of one of the brothers of the King, the Count di Lecce.[18] This event has suspended the balls for a fortnight, and consequently has produced a powerful impression on Neapolitan society.

On the occasion of the funeral, a correspondence took place between the Nuncio as head of the diplomatic corps and the Prince of Scilla on the subject of the place assigned the corps the day of the obsequies. He furnished me a copy that I might transmit it to Was.. I do not think it worth the postage. On all subjects of ceremonial I have deemed it proper to conform to the usages of the Diplomatic Corps resident here. At present we are in mourning for the prince, and in a few days, we shall present in a body to his Majesty, an address of condolence.

I rec^d. a few days ago, from the Prince of Scilla, a note informing me that the Queen was in the last months of her pregnancy. Believing that such information has no great interest for you or the people of the U. S., I usually pass over such communications and others of a kindred character in silence, and make no mention of them in my correspondence with your Department.

Enclosed are my accounts for the last quarter.

---

[18] Antonio of the Bourbons (1816-1843). The Count of Lecce, a brother of the King, was born on Sept. 23, 1816. He never played any important political rôle and is remembered chiefly for his dissolute life.

Since the date of my last despatch I have rec^d. nothing from Was[hington].

WM. BOULWARE TO D. WEBSTER

Legation of the U. S. Naples March 2. 1843. [Despatch No. 10]
Sir

It is now more than a month since I had the honor of addressing you a communication. I deem it my duty again to write though I have nothing of interest to communicate.

The movements of this Government are exceedingly slow and cautious, and is always suspicious of the great powers and takes no step with them, without the most profound and long continued consideration. You can well conceive then, in making the advance now proposed of opening this country to the free commerce of the world, and admitting other nations to a competition with the Neapolitan Marine on equal terms, in the ports of this Kingdom, there will be no relaxation of the usual precautions. But I have no doubt they are now decided on taking this step; and the only difficulties which exist are in the arrangement of details.

Sir Woodbine Parish,[19] the British Commissioner here, informed me a few evenings since, that the treaty with his country, was about being concluded. It will be, of course, necessary to obtain the assent of France to the principles involved, before it can go into operation. The Duke of Montebello, the French Ambassador said to me in a conversation which we held on this subject, that he believes there would be no difficulty on the part of France and that he thought the subject could be easily arranged.

The way being once cleared and the principles settled by negotiations with England and France, they will inure to the benefit of the rest of the world. I believe, I shall then have but little difficulty in making a treaty, which will be highly beneficial to our countrymen. They will be able to find here a market for

---

[19] Sir Woodbine Parish (1821-1890). British minister plenipotentiary to Sicily 1842-45. He had joint full power with Mr. Temple to negotiate a commercial treaty with Sicily Feb. 1842. Mr. Parish was already at Naples as one of the commissioners to liquidate claims under the Sicilian sulphur contract. He began commercial negotiations in June 1842, and concluded preliminary articles on June 26, 1843. With Mr. Temple he signed the commercial treaty with Sicily on April 29, 1845. He left Naples at the end of Nov. 1845. *British Diplomatic Representatives 1789-1852.* Royal Historical Society, L., 1934.

sugar, cotton, fish, rice and probably some kinds of manufactures.

It is my impression that the duties will be reduced on many articles. The doganiere[20] of the customs here has published a pamphlet, in which he advocates a large reduction of the tariff, and he offers to increase, by one third, I believe, the sum which, he pays, on condition of certain reductions. He shows that such is the extent of the smuggling, that the sugar entered for the whole Kingdom, is not as much as is consumed by the City of Naples alone. It seems to me that the discussions and investigations which are now taking place will lead inevitably to an amelioration of the tarif [sic], which must conduce much to the interests of this Kingdom, and afford a more extensive opening to our commerce when our treaty is made.

There exists here a strong disposition to promote intercourse with us. They regard us as the great commercial rivals of England, and one of the ideas thrown out by them, is, that, if they can succeed in effecting a large commerce with us, we would be disposed to sustain them against any encroachments on the part of England or any injuries she might wish to inflict — that they would be able to profit by the one great commercial power as a set-off to the other.

There is, at present, a sheme [sic] here, which it is said, will soon be carried into effect, of establishing a line of steam packets between this port and New York. Whether the design will be accomplished or not, I am unable to say. But his Majesty conversed with me on the subject, the other evening, and seemed to think it would be a profitable investment.

I am happy to inform you, that the statue which Mr. Persico[21] is preparing for the Capitol will be finished during the present month. They have been the subject of much interest here among a people devoted to the fine arts, and have excited general admiration. His Indian woman has particularly attracted the panegyrics of amateurs and connoisseurs. His Columbus also is a noble figure and personates well the beau ideal which one forms of the great discoverer.

I cherish a sanguine hope that during the present year, I shall be able to accomplish the object of my mission. No proper effort

---

20 This term is used in Italian for the collector of customs.
21 See note 9, page 529; also pp. 542, 552, 556, 564; also see Throop chapter, p. 430.

shall be omitted on my part, — no one can be more anxious to accelerate this consummation.

I have received nothing from the Department since the date of my last despatch, except another copy of the treaty with England.

D. WEBSTER TO WM. BOULWARE

Department of State, Washington, 21 April, 1843.
Instruction Unnumbered *Private.*

Dear Sir: With your despatch N°. 10, I this day received your Private note of the 4ᵗʰ. March. You have no doubt received the leave of absence communicated in my despatch of the 8ᵗʰ. February last, in time to meet your wishes.

In regard to Mr. Persico,[22] I have to inform you that the President has not the power to authorise the return of that gentleman, with the statues, in the manner you have suggested, — there being no appropriation to meet the expenses named.

WM. BOULWARE TO H. S. LEGARÉ[23]

Legation of the U. S. Naples July 20. 1843. [Despatch No. 11]
Sir

I arrived at this place two days since from a little tour in the East. My absence was protracted beyond the time intended by an unexpected quarantine and another of a duration equally unlooked for. In passing from Syria into Egypt, I was obliged to submit to the first of these imprisonments, and again in arriving at Malta, I was consigned to the Lazaretto, for the space of twenty days. It was my misfortune to be caught in the midst of the plague in Egypt, and hence the length of my last incarceration. But I am happy to say that the interests of my country have sustained no detriment by my absence.

Upon my arrival, I found here despatches from Was., from N°. 4 to N°. 8 inclusive.[24]

---

[22] See *hic opus,* pp. 529, 542, 552, 556, 564; also Throop chapter, p. 430. Also see note 9, p. 529, and note 35, p. 552.

[23] Hugh S. Legaré of South Carolina. Attorney general. He was appointed by President Tyler as Secretary of State *ad interim* on May 9, 1843; he died in office on June 20, 1843.

[24] These were the Instructions and Instruction Circulars addressed to Mr. Boulware during this period: *No. 3,* Washington, Sept. 13, 1842, Secretary Web-

Permit me to express my pleasure and to present you my congratulations on your promotion to the Department of State. But I regret to be informed that it is an appointment ad interim. It would have given me and I doubt not the great majority of my countrymen, much greater satisfaction if it had been permanent.

The President's letter to His Majesty of the Two Sicilies, on the occasion of the death of his brother the Prince of Lecce, has been delivered and met by a most cordial response on his part.

During the month passed, the younger sister[25] of the King was married to the Emperor of Brazil, and she is now on her way to that country.

In my last despatch, I gave information that the negotiation going on between England and this country was nearly concluded. It is now finished and a treaty is made but not signed. It is necessary to have the sanction of France. That this will be obtained, the parties immediately interested, seem to have no doubt. I have before said that the Duke of Montebello states to me as his opinion, that there would be but little difficulty. The negotiation on the part of France is daily progressing. As to Spain, I presume, England will obtain her consent. But if not, they seem to regard it here, as of but little consequence. In truth, she has no commerce with this country. After France then comes

---

ster transmitted confidentially a copy of the Aug. 9, 1842 (boundary, slave-trade, extradition) treaty between the United States and Great Britain; *No 4,* Washington, Feb. 8, 1843, Mr. Webster transmitted to Mr. Boulware a letter from Daniel J. Desmond to the Minister of Foreign Affairs of Sicily. Mr. Webster also informed Mr. Boulware that the President had granted permission for a leave of two or three months for reasons of health; *Circular,* Washington, March 18, 1843, requested Mr. Boulware to obtain information as to Sicilian experience with an insect which then ravaged the orange groves of Florida; *No. 5,* Washington, March 30, 1843, Mr. Webster transmitted a letter from the President to His Majesty on the death of the King's brother; *Circular,* Washington, Mar. 30, 1843, communicating copy of a House Resolution; *No. 6,* Washington, Apr. 20, 1843, informing Mr. Boulware of the appointment of Messrs. Baring Brothers & Co., as bankers of the United States in London, from and after July 1, 1843; *No. 7,* Circular, Washington, May 9, 1843, informing Mr. Boulware that the President had appointed Mr. Legaré, *ad interim* Secretary of State; *No. 8,* Washington, May 17, 1843, Mr. Legaré informed Mr. Boulware of the appointment of a public mission to China for the purpose of cultivating friendly and commercial relations with the Empire.

25 She was Teresa Cristina Maria of the Two Sicilies (1822-1889). She married D. Pedro II (Dom Pedro d'Alcantara, João, Carlos). (1825-1891), the second Emperor of Brazil. He was the son of D. Pedro I and the Empress Leopoldina. He succeeded to the throne on the abdication of his father on April 7, 1831. By an amendment of July 23, 1840, to the Imperial Constitution, Dom Pedro II attained his legal majority. He reigned until Nov. 15, 1891, when the Republic of Brazil was established. A constant and devoted friend, the Empress distinguished herself for her charitable works which won for her the title of "Mother of the Brazilians." By the revolution of 1889, Dom Pedro was expelled from Brazil with all his family.

our time. I hope that in a few months we shall be able to make a beginning.

The treaty with England has not yet been made public, and consequently I can not give details. But the general understanding is, that it is a treaty of navigation on principles of perfect reciprocity. And this is the information given me by the Ministers engaged on it. I have, as far as possible kept myself acquainted with the proceedings from their commencement to the conclusion. But I have not been able to obtain a view of the treaty itself. Since my arrival from the East, I met Sir Woodbine Parish, the principal negotiator on the part of England, and he informed me that the treaty was very similar to that between England and Portugal. The subject of duties has not been touched. It is left to subsequent negotiation. The intention is, as soon as the treaty of navigation has been disposed of to take up the tariffs of the two countries and endeavor to make some arrangement by which access may be given to the production of their industry.

In one of the despatches which I found here, it is stated that the late tariff of the U. S., which I had requested "is herewith enclosed." Unfortunately if enclosed, it did not reach this place. I should be very happy to obtain a copy of it.

Enclosed are my accounts for the first and second quarters of 1843.

WM. BOULWARE TO THE SECRETARY OF STATE

Legation of the U. S. Naples Au. 21. 1843. [Despatch No. 12]
Sir

A few days since I had the honor of receiving despatch No. 9,[26] and with it a circular giving the melancholy information of the decease of the Hon. H. S. Legaré. This lamentable occurrence must be a source of regret to all Americans, but it is peculiarly so to those who knew his reputation in Europe.

In the incomprehensible decrees of providence, [sic] he has been removed from the world, at that period of his career, when his information and position enabled him to render most service to his country. He had accumulated by many laborious years of study & observation, rich stores of varied knowledge, and now when he had just commenced to employ them on a theatre, where

---

[26] Instruction No. 9, Washington, June 22, 1843, W. S. Derrick, Acting Secretary, transmitted a letter of ceremony from the President to His Majesty concerning the birth of Princess Maria Annunziata Isabella.

they could be most available death has arrested his labors and his life.

At the same time, I received a letter from the President of the United States for His Majesty King of the Two Sicilies. I hastened to transmit it to the Prince of Scilla, and received in a few days a note, announcing it's [sic] delivery to His Majesty and containing the courteous remarks common to such occasions.

I have been making efforts to obtain a view of the treaty with England but have not yet been able to accomplish it. It has been promised as soon as it is returned to the Department of Foreign Affairs, from which it happens now to be absent.

The principle of reciprocity which has been adopted, does not embrace the Colonies of England.

As to the progress of the negotiation with France, I have nothing new to communicate.

The proceedings of the Government of the Two Sicilies are generally of so little interest to our country the subjects which occupy it, so seldom affect us, and in addition, such is the secrecy with which their deliberations are ordinarily conducted, I have rarely much to communicate to your department. Should the changes take place, which I anticipate from the Treaties now in progress, and those which are projected in reference to the tariff of the Kingdom, our commercial relations with this country, will become more extensive and important, and the subjects agitated here of more interest to us.

WM. BOULWARE TO THE SECRETARY OF STATE

Legation of the U. S. Naples Sept. 13, 1843. [Despatch No. 13]

Sir

I have this day obtained a view of the treaty with England.[27] It is substantially what I have before had the honor of representing it to you — a treaty of navigation based on the principles of perfect reciprocity. But it is limited in it's [sic] operation to the direct trade between this country and Great Britain and Ireland and the British possessions in the Mediterranean — that is the Ionian Isles, Malta & Gibraltar.

---

[27] The treaty Mr. Boulware refers to here was probably merely the text of a proposed treaty since the treaty of commerce and navigation between Great Britain and the Two Sicilies was not actually signed at Naples until April 29, 1845. For text see: Lewis Hertslet, *Treaties and conventions between Great Britain and foreign powers. 1827-1925*, VII, 970.

His Majesty of the Two Sicilies reaffirms the grant of ten per cent reduction upon British imports, but at the same time reserves to himself the right of making the same reduction upon imports from other countries. He will be, of course, excluded by this treaty, from making those discriminations in favor of imports in the ships of this country, which now exist. You are aware those commodities which are imported from America in Neapolitan bottoms enjoy a remission of thirty per cent duty. The same articles in English or French, would have an abatement of only ten per cent. Hence we have an advantage at present, over these nations of twenty per cent and thirty over the rest of the world. But this advantage extends to all America and the West Indies. And again imports from the Baltic and the Black Sea have also an abatement of twenty per cent duty, when under the Neapolitan flag. The effect, then, of this treaty when it goes into operation, will be an increase of twenty per cent upon the imports from America in Neapolitan vessels. That is, there will be instead of the remission of thirty per cent an abatement of only ten per cent — it being taken for granted that His Majesty will place his marine on the same level with the favored nations.

We cannot complain of these stipulations, but it becomes the more necessary, that we have a treaty for the purpose of raising our Marine to the same level. As soon as the King gets rid of the embarrassments of those old treaties of which I have so often spoken, I believe there will be no difficulty.

One clause in this English treaty struck me by it's [sic] novelty. It is provided that importers shall make a declaration at the custom House of the value of the mechandize entered; And the officers of the customs shall have the privilege of taking the commodities at the value named, upon payment of all expenses and ten per cent profit. This is to prevent a false valuation. Upon inquiry I find that this is the general usage in this Kingdom.

There has been, recently, some commotion here arising from the fact that various persons have been set fire to, in the streets. The utmost vigilance of the police has been unable to discover who are the culprits or the manner in which the combustions have been effected. Most of the unfortunate sufferers have been women, some of whom have lost their lives. The facts are involved in mystery. It is believed that the fire has been communicated by means of some chemical preparation cast upon the persons. But this is merely conjecture.

About the same time that the cases occurred here, similar cases are reported to have taken place at Milan and Rome. There was also in Bologna, an effort at revolution. It is the impression of the officers of the Government, that these fires are produced through the instrumentality of some secret society, whose object is revolution[28] — that their means are used for the purpose of producing disturbance, dissatisfaction & commotion. I must confess I do not comprehend how setting fire to innocent women can promote the overthrow of Government. Yet this seems to be the understanding of the police, and numerous arrests have been made. But nothing has been discovered and the affair is yet enveloped in utter darkness.

The United States ship Delaware left here two days since for Mahon. The officers and crew have left a most favorable impression in this city. It was a general remark that the crew was the most orderly ever known here.

I had the honor of presenting to his Majesty Com. Morris[29] & Capt. McCauley[30]. He rec^d. them with the greatest courtesy & amiability. The Commodore invited his Majesty to visit the ship, he graciously accepted the invitation, made his visit and was very liberal of compliment upon all that he saw. And in truth the compliments were well merited for no ship could be in better order, no crew in a higher state of discipline. Many persons of distinction visited her and all brought away the most agreeable impression.

The Commodore has left here for Mahon to obtain more certain information on the subject of the burning of the Missouri steamer

28 In the years 1842, 1843, 1844 several unfortunate attempts at revolts, instigated by Mazzini, resulted in the sentencing of many patriots to the galleys and death. Fortunately, many others were able to seek refuge in Tuscany. In the Kingdom of the Two Sicilies there were many followers of Mazzini who were in correspondence with exiles in London, Paris, and Marseilles. From 1831 to 1843 there were many attempts made at uprisings in nearly all the principal cities of the kingdom. The most important were the uprisings of Cosenza in 1843 and 1844. The revolutionists, flying the tricolor to the cry of "Long live the constitutional Italian Kingdom," fought against the Bourbon militia. Nearly all were arrested and shot on July 22, 1844. The members of the central committee in Naples were arrested. (N. Rodolico, *Sommario Storico*. Florence, Le Monnier, 1933, 3 vols. III, 187-188). The uprising in Bologna in 1843 actually occurred at Savigno. It too failed in its purpose. See, *Dizionario del Risorgimento Nazionale*, I, 973-974. For a fuller account of this uprising see D. Brasini, *Il tentativo rivoluzionario di Pasquale Muratori a Savigno (notizie e documenti.)* Bologna, 1888; E. Masi, *Cospiratori in Romagna dal 1815 al 1859*. Bologna, 1891.

29 Charles Morris (1784-1856) of Connecticut. Commander of the Brazil and Mediterranean squadrons from 1841 to 1844. He was called by Farragut "the ablest sea officer of his day." *Dictionary American Biography* XIII, 202.

30 Charles Stewart McCauley (1793-1869). Born in Philadelphia, Pa. He was Commander of the *Delaware* in the Brazil and the Mediterranean squadrons from 1841 to 1844. He was Commandant of the Washington navy yard from 1846 to 1849. *Dictionary American Biography*, 1933, XI, 572.

at Gibraltar & to render any assistance which may be necessary.

It is to be understood, that in my remarks upon the remission of duties, when I speak of an abatement of twenty per cent, ten per cent, & thirty per cent, the abatement is of this or that per cent upon the duty: that is, if the abatement be ten per cent and the duty upon the commodity be twenty, it would be reduced to eighteen.

Since the date of my last, I have received nothing from the Department and I regret that I do not yet know, with whom I have the honor of communicating.

WM. BOULWARE TO THE SECRETARY OF STATE

Legation of the U. S. Naples Oct. 18. 1843. [Despatch No. 14]

Sir

I regret that I have nothing to communicate on the advance made in the French treaty. It seems to me that the proceedings are exceedingly dilatory. I fear that for the purpose of obtaining some advantage, the French are endeavoring to produce the impression that they are indiffirent on the subject. And his Majesty's Ministers will not hasten lest it should be thought they are anxious. I conjecture also that the French have demanded a reduction of duties on certain commodities before they will accede to the proposition of releasing their exclusive privileges. This renders more complicated the negotiation. Thus, I believe, at present the business lingers.

In the last communication, I had the honor of addressing you, I spoke of the frequent combustions of individuals in the streets here, of the agitation of the public mind, and of the views & vigilance of the government on the subject. The fires have ceased, but all the efforts of the police have been unavailing to discover the incendiaries or the source of these extraordinary proceedings. The frequency of the cases and their entire similarity here and elsewhere, indicate a common origin; but what that may be, can only be, at present, the subject of conjecture. If they had taken place at night, it might be supposed that robbery was the object, but they have occurred in open day & the most public streets of the city.

It is difficult to concur in the view taken by the officers of the Government; that they originate with some secret political society. The atrocity of these proceedings, and the victims

selected, inoffensive women, seem to forbid the idea. Besides, I
I can not conceive, how such means can promote any object that
any political society may entertain.

Such was the alarm, at one time that the public promenades
were almost deserted by the ladies, and those who ventured out
did so with fear and trembling. Now they are crowded as usual
and apprehension has ceased.

The revolution in Greece[31] has excited great interest here. The
two countries are so contiguous, the moves of the one being
visible from those of the other, such an event necessarily produces
a strong impression in this Kingdom. Revolutions are contagious
and this revolution has been conducted with so much propriety,
characterized by so much moderation; it has been so just in it's
[sic] inception it's [sic] conduct and it's [sic] conclusion, it commends itself to the admiration of the world. It is a spectacle, on
which, absolute monarchs look with dismay. If doubt before
existed of the capacity of the Greeks for self government, they
have now shown that that doubt was unjust. Not one drop of
blood has disfigured their achievement, not one act of licentious-
ness or injustice has marked the period of their unrestrained
power. The King, who was placed upon the throne, pledged to
give them a constitution and a national representation, though
he had violated his pledge and become odious to the nation, was
treated with courtesy and moderation.

I was in Athens during the past winter and had some opportunity of making myself acquainted with the true state of Greece.
It was my good fortune to be honored with the attentions and
invitations of his Majesty and the diplomatic corps. It was
obvious then that affairs were rapidly approaching a crisis. The
government had failed to pay the interest on the loan guaranteed
by the three powers. Taxation was oppressive and the tariff gave
great dissatisfaction. The King was ruling as an absolute
monarch, and to him were imputed all the defects of administration. This was not the government for which the Greeks had
waded through a revolution of unexampled horrors, with the
spirit & heroism of their illustrious ancestors. They still had a
free press, and it's [sic] conductors were resolute & doing. The

---

31 On Sept. 15, 1843, a military revolt broke out in Greece which compelled
the King to dismiss the Bavarians and to accept a constitution. King Otto, son
of King Louis I of Bavaria, came to the throne in 1832, and surrounded himself
with Bavarian advisers and Bavarian troops and his rule was never popular. After
the revolt a responsible ministry, a senate nominated by the King, and a chamber
elected by universal suffrage were instituted.

state of the nation, the course of it's [sic] miseries and the character of it's [sic] govern[ment] were fully presented to the people. They were clamorous for a national representation. This, with a constitution, they believed, would remedy their evils.

The King and those by whom he was surrounded, said that the people were not yet prepared for a constitution, that in due time, when they were capable, he would redeem his pledges. That at present, there was not a sufficient diffusion of intelligence or enough of wealth in the country to justify this measure.

My association with the diplomatic corps led me to a knowledge of the singular fact that Russia and England were cooperating to effect a national representation. I asked of the English minister an explanation of so extraordinary an union, and for a purpose still more extraordinary, on the part of the Czar. He told me that Russia was convinced, that King Otho[32] could not carry on the government, upon the principles of an enlightened despotism; the experiment had been made; that he was incompetent, and hence a representation of the people was a necessity. The French minister took no active part and was believed rather to sustain the King. And we see now the "Debats" the organ of the French government sympathizing with King Otho. But with Russia & England united and France nearly neutral, or at least in a position, in which her ministers and ministry dare not take a decided part, against a revolution, whose object was constitutional government, the Greeks felt that they could, with safety, coerce their monarch to give them popular institutions.

The Journals and the politicians of the continent are now occupying themselves much with this event. Many are anticipating serious political results in the councils of the great powers. It is ordinarily taken for granted that Russia is malcontent, that Austria is exasperated and that Prussia looks on with dissatisfaction. It is said also that Mr. Guizot has but little confidence in the capacity of the Greeks for self government, that he has always preferred a national senate appointed by the King. This

---

[32] King Otto (Othon) I. Prince royal of Bavaria. He was born on June 1, 1815. He was elected by virtue of the authority transferred by the Greek nation to France, Great Britain, and Russia (allied by the preliminary convention of London of July 6, 1827) by the treaty concluded in London on May 7, 1832, and ratified by the King of Bavaria on May 27, 1832. He accepted the crown on Oct. 5, 1832 and occupied the throne of Greece on Jan. 25 (Feb. 6) 1833 as regent. He assumed control of the government on June 1, 1835. On Nov. 22, 1836, he married Queen Marie-Frédérique-Amélie, daughter of the reigning Grand Duke of Oldenbourg. (*Almanach de Gotha*, 1840, 25).

experiment of a Senate has been fully made and this body has placed itself at the head of the revolution.

I do not doubt myself, from the course taken by the protecting powers, previous to this movement, that they will now permit the Greeks to consummate their revolution, without molestation, on their part. They have a strong pecuniary interest which induces them to wish a change of policy apart from political considerations. In addition to this, the belief is now general that King Otho has but little capacity for government. And indeed the results of his administration fully justify the conclusion. Russia would prefer, without doubt, that the King should have made the concessions of his own accord, which have been now coerced. Popular outbreaks are, of course, her abhorrence. But that she will now attempt to defeat the objects of a revolution, which objects she herself sustained, is not to be believed.

The Greeks have always had a certain degree of liberty, even under Turkish rule. They have elected the officers and controlled to a considerable extent, the affairs of their municipalities. Here are the first elements of popular government, & these are familiar to them.

I presume, it is not necessary to apologize for presenting to you these considerations on the Greek revolution. I doubt not that this subject, interesting to the friends of freedom, throughout the world, is peculiarly so to you and the American people.

I received this day from our consul at Malta, a letter informing me, that Com. Malcom, a bearer of despatches from Mr. Henry Pottinger,[33] the English Commissioner at Hong Kong, had arrived there, on his way to England, and that he gave the information that the Emperor of China would not permit any minister to reside in that country, and no representation of any higher grade, than Consul or Consul General.

The Consul has thought it proper to communicate to me this fact, and I have now the honor of making it known to you, with the same definiteness and detail with which I received it.

Enclosed are my accounts for the last quarter.

I have received nothing from your Department since the date of my last despatch.

---

[33] Sir Henry Pottinger (1789-1856). Soldier and diplomat. He accepted Lord Palmerston's offer of the post of envoy and plenipotentiary in China and superintendent of British trade. He was instrumental in affecting the Treaty of Nanking, which ceded Hong Kong to England. In April 1843, he was appointed first British governor of Hong Kong.

(Enclosure with Despatch No. 14 (?) or immediately thereafter).

(Undated)[34]

I take the liberty of saying to M^r. Webster that I have received Mr. Persico's statue[35] of an Indian woman intended for our Capitol. I have heard but one expression of opinion in reference to it, that of admiration. His Columbus is not yet finished, but it will be by Sep. next. The transportation of these statues will require great care and delicacy to prevent their sustaining injury. Their location, after they arrive in the U. S. will require still more, and in addition much judgment & taste. It is natural that one who has expended so much toil on these statues, and who looks on them as monuments upon which his reputation will depend with posterity should feel much anxiety for their preservation. To watch over & preserve them & to superintendent their location, M^r. Persico would willingly accompany them to the U.S., but he can not afford to do it & pay his own expenses. Nor would it be just that he should. If the President would suggest to him the propriety of his attending them, he would gladly do so and trust to the liberality of Congress.

---

[34] This unsealed, unaddressed and undated note is properly to be considered an enclosure with Despatch No. 14. It is found in the bound volume of Despatches, between despatches No. 14 and No. 15, and both are stained by the discoloration of the pigment of the smaller letter. It is written on small size personal stationery, folded; it is of deep cream color. As found in the volume, this small sheet has been mounted upon a sheet of pale blue despatch paper of folio size. This blue sheet lies between the two pages (despatches 14 and 15) which show the shape of the stain mark from the small paper.

[35] Mr. Webster was especially interested in the whole question of the statues for the new Capitol, as will be seen, following, in various notes relating to the Persico statues. This page is one of a series of references to Mr. Persico in this group of despatches. See pages 529, 542, 552, 556, 564; also see in the section of Throop's despatches, p. 430. These tell the story of Mr. Persico's creation of the statues, their execution in the Neapolitan Kingdom, and the artist's jealous desire personally to accompany them and see to their safety on their voyage to America for erection in the portico of the Capitol. For further details, there may be consulted the Records of the Public Buildings, now in custody of the Interior Department Records Division at the United States National Archives. Mr. Persico's whole relation to this project was full of colorful detail.

WM. BOULWARE TO A. P. UPSHUR[36]

Legation of the United States Naples Nov 1. 1843. [Despatch No. 15]

Sir

A few days, since, I had the honor of receiving your despatch [!] No. 11 of the date of Sep. 1st.[37]

The communication with this Legation would be much accelerated if letters were sent by the steamers to London instead, of by the Packets to Havre. Some time since I requested my newspapers to be transmitted by this latter route, to save the expense of the English postage,[38] but it would be much more agreeable to me, that my letters should pass by London. They would reach me in a little more than half the time.

I am happy to perceive that you are now presiding over the Department of State. Permit me to congratulate you upon your advancement to this lofty position, and to express this confident hope, that it may be an occurrence fortunate for the interests of our country and of your own distinguished reputation.

---

[36] Abel P. Upshur, of Virginia. (1791-1844). He was appointed Secretary of State by President Tyler June 24, 1843, as Secretary *ad interim*, and commissioned as Secretary July 24, 1843; he died in office Feb. 28, 1844. *Dictionary American Biography*, 1936, XIX, 127.

[37] The following Instructions and Circulars were transmitted to Mr. Boulware: Circular, Washington, June 23, 1843, announcing the death of Legaré; Instruction No. 10, Washington, June 24, 1843, informing Mr. Boulware that Mr. Upshur had been appointed Secretary of State, *ad interim*; Instruction No. 11, Washington, Sept. 1, 1843, Mr. Upshur transmitted a letter of ceremony from the President to His Majesty concerning the marriage of His Majesty's sister, Donna Teresa Cristina Maria.

[38] To modern readers accustomed to international postal rates paid in United States postage stamps, this reference may seem obscure. In 1843, it was the rule that mail shipped to the continent of Europe, via England, must pay both the United States and the English postal rates. This was indeed a sore point with American business men, as they felt that this amounted to a tax upon their ordinary business intercourse with customers abroad, and with the bankers abroad who handled exchange accounts for American business firms' convenience. The matter was made the subject of petitions to Congress, and in the Post Office Department's records, and historical accounts, considerable emphasis was placed upon the desirability of getting this handicap to international commerce adjusted as soon as possible. England had instituted the 'fixes' (literal translation of the term 'affiches' still used by the French for 'postage stamps') in 1830. This caused inconvenience to American business men, for these English affixes (gummed stamps) had to be procured in advance, and local United States post masters were somewhat reluctant to put out money in advance for stamps which were such a new device at that time, making the investment in those needed to pay the British part of European mail somewhat of a dubious venture. In addition the marine postage was high and for its own mails the United States government found it necessary, soon, to issue a new (30c) stamp. This feeling expressed by Mr. Boulware, in this despatch, then was one small puff in a rising storm of objections that later arose and many years later, eventuated in what we know as the single rate international postal cabals with various maritime countries.

The letter of the President to His Majesty of the Two Sicilies, enclosed with your despatch, has been presented through the Prince of Scilla and received with the usual civilities. I do not send our copies of the notes which pass on such occasions, because they being all substantially the same and mere formal expressions of courtesy, I can not conceive that they can be of any interest to the Department of State. If there were any change in the ordinary form, any diminution in the degree of the expressions of politeness, I should then esteem them worthy of transmission. If I were to follow rigidly my instructions in this subject, I should burden your records with much that is utterly worthless.

I enclose a correspondence of a different character. I presume it needs no explanation.[39] In truth I know nothing on the subject except what is contained in the correspondence. I shall send also a copy to Com. Morris.

Permit me to call your attention to the situation of our Consuls in this Kingdom. My immediate predecessor addressed the Department on this subject, a short time after his arrival in this country and requested instructions. I can not find that he ever received them. The question remains in the same state as at the time of his request. It is explained in despatch No. 3 of my predecessor.

The news from Greece continues favorable to the friends of constitutional government and sustains the views I had the honor to present in my last communication.

In the Greek Observer, a journal published at Athens, it is stated that the representatives of the three Powers have received from their respective courts, the most satisfactory declarations relative to the "constitutional desires of Greece." I have recent private advices from Athens, informing me that a conspiracy to effect a counter revolution had been detected, in that city and the leaders banished. On this occasion the Council of State induced the King to make a public declaration of hostility to all such attempts and a cordial desire to carry out the wishes of the Greek people in the establishment of Constitutional government. Separated, as the King[40] now is, from the Bavarians who accom-

---

[39] Regarding Mr. Persico, see prior, pp. 529, 542, 552; seq., pp. 556, 564; also, Throop chapter, p. 430.

[40] A bloodless revolution in Greece resulted in the dismissal of King Otto's Bavarian ministry and the King's acceptance of a constitution, which left the King almost as absolute as before — yet this government was weak and slipshod. The wretched fiscal system and heavy taxation of the old Turkish régime were retained, while ill-managed innovations from Bavaria, such as military conscription, drove many to brigandage.

panied him to Greece and who have surrounded him and exerted a most lamentable influence up to the period of the recent revolution, it is possible he may adopt other principles than those which he learned in the absolute Court of his Royal Father. But that this adoption is the result of necessity, not of choice no one can doubt. Yet he is made to say "that after having once accepted the constitutional system, which he regards as useful and necessary for the welfare of Greece, he is desirous it should be carried into effect peacefully and orderly." That it is "his firm purpose and desire that no one deceived about the royal will, should be led astray into acts or language opposed to the new order of things."

Such language as this may be agreeable to the Greeks, as it is favorable to their object, and evinces the power of public sentiment, but it certainly can not elevate the character of their Sovereign. They can give but little confidence to the expression of convictions wrought by force and opposed to the principles of all his previous life. Such professions must be more than suspected.

To day is the meeting of their National Assembly. I hope that the course of this body may be consistent with the moderation and lofty patriotism, which have thus far distiguished their revolution. But I much fear that powerful efforts will be made to render abortive their exertions. Ferdinand the first, of this Kingdom, forced by circumstances, granted the Sicilians a constitution, and then rendered it void by the influence which he brought to bear on the elections and the Legislative Assembly.

On the subject of the French treaty, I have nothing to communicate.

Enclosed is a copy[41] of Despatch No. 9 of my predecessor in accordance with your request.

I have this moment received Despatch[42] No. 10 from Washington and also a copy of the Laws of the last session of Congress.

---

41 Not reprinted here.
42 This should have been called Instruction No. 10.

THE PRINCE OF SCILLA TO WM. BOULWARE

[Enclosure with Despatch No. 15, of Nov. 1, 1843.]

Naples Oct. 27, 1843

The Undersigned Counsellor, Minister of State, charged with the Portfolio of Foreign Affairs, has been informed by the Minister of General Police, that in transporting upon the American vessel the Delaware, when she was in this port, the statues made by the Sculptor D. Luigi Persico,[43] Neapolitan, he persisted in leaping aboard in spite of the opposition of the sanitary guard, the ship being in rigorous quarantine. And the efforts of the police with the American consul to obtain the landing of Persico, in accordance with the sanitary rules, resulted in vain, whilst a short time after the ship sailed.

It being a question of a royal subject, departed for a foreign country, without passport, the undersigned has the honor to make known all this affair to Mr. Boulware Chargé d'Affaires of the United States of America, at the same time praying him that he may be willing to make such arrangements that like abuses may not be renewed, they being able to produce serious inconveniences.

WM. BOULWARE TO THE PRINCE OF SCILLA

[Enclosure with Despatch No. 15, of Nov. 1, 1843]

Legation of the United States Oct. 29. 1843.

The Undersigned, Chargé d'Affaires of the United States, has had the honor of receiving from His Excellency, the Prince of Scilla, Duke of St. Cristina, Minister of State Charged with the Portfolio of Foreign Affairs, a communication of the date of the 27 inst., complaining that D. Luigi Persico[44] embarked on board the United States ship Delaware, when she was in this port, without passport, while the ship was in quarantine and in spite of the efforts of the sanitary guard to prevent him.

The Undersigned knew nothing of the circumstances of this

---

[43] See above, pp. 529, 542, 552; and below, pp. 556, 564; also Throop chapter, p. 430.

[44] See above, *hic.*, pp. 529, 542, 552; and below, p. 564; also Throop chapter, p. 430, note 77.

case, at the time of their occurrence, nor had he any communication with the Delaware, after Mr. Persico was received aboard.

He is also informed by the Consul of the United States at this place, that he had no information on this subject, except what he had derived from the Chancellor of the Commissariat of Police of the port, after it was too late to communicate with the ship.

It being then night, the Health Officer prevented a note written immediately by him and given to the Chancellor from being carried to the ship.

The Undersigned can not believe that there was any intention on the part of the Commander of the Delaware, to infringe or treat with any disrespect, any of the regulations or usages of this Kingdom. In addition to the obligation he must have felt, when in this port, to respect it's [sic] laws, the great courtesy and kindness with which he was received and honored here by His Majesty and the authorities of this city, induced as is well known to the Undersigned, the most friendly feelings and every disposition to give all deference to all the regulations, laws usages & wishes of the Government of this Country.

The Undersigned will transmit to his Government, a copy of the communication, which he has had the honor to receive on the subject.

He believes, there is no danger of the recurrence of any such case in future.

He profits by this occasion to renew to the Prince of Scilla the assurance of his distinguished consideration.

WM. BOULWARE TO A. P. UPSHUR

Legation of the U. S. Naples, Dec. 3, 1843. [Despatch No. 16]

Sir

Since the date of my last communication, nothing has occurred here which can be of much interest at Washington. The tranquil and monotonous current of events has been only varied by the arrival of the Duke d'Aumale.[45] Indeed the reception given to him was so extraordinary as to give rise to various conjectures among diplomats and others. The reception of royal personages

---

[45] Bourbon-Orleans, Henri, Prince d'Orleans, Duke d'Aumale (1822-1897). Fourth son of Louis Philippe. He married Caroline de Bourbon of the Two Sicilies (1822-1860), the daughter of the Prince of Salerno. See: M. H. Weil, "Le voyage du Duc d'Aumale en Italie et ses consequences (1843-1844)." *Revue des études historiques*, Paris, 1923, 18.

is, here, an ordinary occurrence and usually produces no sensation. But the French Prince was received with honors so unusual that curiosity has been much excited to discuss the cause.

The King's Major-domo was despatched by His Majesty to the frontiers to receive him; refreshments and accommodations were prepared at convenient distances on the route. His coming was telegraphed in the various cities and he was met by all the honors due to his rank. His Majesty left this city, accompanied by His Royal Highness the Prince of Salerno, his uncle to meet his guest. Upon his arrival here, a royal palace was assigned him, and he was entertained from day to day by dinners, balls, military reviews and various other amusements contrived with great care and attention to render his time agreeable and do him the highest honor offered to royalty.

I have seen many royal personages received here, but this reception far surpassed all others. The general impression seemed to be that His Majesty was anxious to marry his sister to the Prince. Others affirmed that he had been offended by advice volunteered by Austria, and that he had given offense in return, and not that he was peculiarly anxious to strengthen his relations with France. Which of these opinions is correct or whether either is, I will not venture to say, nor do I suppose it is of much interest to you to know.

In my diplomatic capacity, I waited on the Prince in company with the representatives of the other powers at this Court.

The negotiation between France and this Kingdom lingers at present, as the French Legation awaits instructions from Paris.

An observer in this country can not fail to be impressed by the contrast presented of the advantages conferred by Nature, and the injuries inflicted by Government. Here is a climate among the mildest most uniform and most healthy in the world; a soil whose fertility in many ports even surpasses the valley of the Nile, whose productiveness never ceases, which is no sooner relieved of one crop than it is succeeded by another; a land so picturesque and beautiful that painters from all over the earth have ever delighted to delineate it's [sic] scenery, and poets have sought successful inspiration amid it's [sic] enchantments and its souvenirs. But here is a government, which, almost from time immemorial, has made war on all the interests of the people, which seems to have tortured invention to find impediments for the obstruction of commerce, which has burdened agriculture to such a degree that but a mite of the products of the soil remains to the producer, which in it's [sic] stupid efforts to regulate industry and production, has only trammeled the exertions of the farmer and impeded the development of the latter, which has so extended it's [sic] harrassing interference into the minutiæ of life, that a cup of water can not be taken from the sea, nor a plant of tobacco reared in the fields without it's [sic] permission. Add to this, a church the most expensive and profligate that exists, which inculcates the principles of human obligation in such a manner that the bandit often confesses himself before proceeding on an expedition of plunder and vows to the virgin a portion of the spoils. Then, here are the fountains of justice poisoned by a Judiciary so notoriously venal, that presents to the judges form an ordinary part of almost every proceeding in the courts.

Yet such is the bounty of Nature that the population seems comfortable, cheerful and gay. In spite of all the exactions, oppression and injustice, there is but little positive suffering. In a climate so mild, the wants are few and these are easily supplied on this exuberant soil. The policy of the government seems also for a half century past to have borne with less rigour upon the people than the aristocracy. Taxation seems to have fallen with less weight on the farmer though all are heavily burdened.

The present King participating in the spirit of the age, manifests a strong disposition to change the system of his ancestors. He is engaged in the construction of railroads, in facilitating the intercourse between the different parts of his Kingdom by means of steamboats and in various other schemes of internal improvement. He had introduced a most important and useful change, after the example set in Germany, by placing his soldiers to labor on the public works. But I believe the honor is due to the present Pashaw of Egypt of first making this excellent innovation. It is in pursuance also of his principles of amelioration that he is engaged in an anxious effort to rid himself of the shackles of those old treaties with England France and Spain, which have thus far prevented the formation of liberal treaties and profitable commerce with the rest of the world. But even under existing circumstances, during his reign, commerce has increased with rapidity, and the commercial and naval marine still faster. But this augmentation is as nothing compared with what would take place if a judicious scale of duties was adopted and commerce freed from the thousand trammels which now encumber it. The peninsular form of this country, the great extent of it's [sic] coast, it's [sic] position between the Eastern and European world,

559

the excellency of its sailors, the fine timber produced by it's [sic] forests for ship-building and all the great variety of it's [sic] agricultural and mineral products are all eminently favorable to commerce.

I have remarked that throughout Italy, there is great jealousy of Austria. Since 1823, when her army overthrew the representative system in this country, and when several regiments of her troops remained quartered in this city, for several years, for the protection of the throne, there has been a deep-rooted hatred of this power here among the people. And the government, instead of cherishing feelings of gratitude, seems influenced by apprehension of his power, dislike of all interference on her part, an antipathy to her councils and no disposition to strengthen the alliance between them either by giving or receiving favors.

In the recent revolutionary movements at Bologna, which have not yet been entirely quelled, she has been anxious to send troops to the assistance of His Holiness. But her offers have been refused. In all the Lombardo-Venetian states, she is so cordially hated that her officers occupying stations there and indeed all Austrians are excluded from Italian society. And if, perchance, any Italian should receive them, he is excluded and placed on the same footing as the Austrians. But it is Austria and Austria alone who preserves the tranquillity of Italy. But for her, the present governments could not exist. It is perfectly well known that she would gladly embrace any invitation to send down her troops. There is no loyalty in Italy, except perhaps in Tuscany, — there is either indifference or aversion. Here I think it is the former, but in Sicily there is an ardent hatred. The two parts of this Kingdom are governed on totally different principles. In the Roman States there is a general agreement except among the priests, that their government is the worst in the world after that of the Grand Sultan. They would welcome any change with pleasure, believing as they do, that any movement must be upward. For their present Pontiff, my impression is, they have neither love nor hatred, but an intense aversion to the system. And well may they, when it has made almost a desert of one of the loveliest countries of the world. Rome and Constantinople are the only two cities of [sic] earth surrounded by extensive deserts. And that which renders the circumstance still more extraordinary is, that in each case, it is a desert of great fertility. Nor does the resemblance cease here, but throughout the Roman States as well as in Turkey, there are many extensive tracts of country of miles in extent, without a single habitation or a single cultivated spot to indicate the existence of man. There might be an extended parallel drawn between these two countries for there is great similarity in many points between the operations of their systems. But I forbear.

I have received nothing from Was. since the date of my last despatch.

WM. BOULWARE TO A. P. UPSHUR

Naples Legation of the U. S. Jany. 13. 1844. [Despatch No. 17]

Sir

A short time after the arrival of the Duke d'Aumale in this city, it became known, that one of His Majesty's steamers left here under mysterious circumstances. In the middle of the night, the Captain of the boat was ordered to receive the Prince Carini[46] aboard, to leave the port immediately, and be subject to his orders. He knew nothing of his destination and rumor says that the Prince himself knew no more, but that he received despatches which he was directed to open after he left the harbor.

A few weeks elapsed, the mystery was dispelled and all was known. The steamer carried an Ambassador to Spain.[47] It is known to you that since the death of the last king of that country, the Two Sicilies have never recognized the government, but have always sustained the claims of Don Carlos. In this they have followed the policy of Austria, Russia, Prussia and the Powers of Italy. They have been induced to pursue this course by a double motive. In the first place, the reigning family has an interest in the crown of Spain. It may become the heir. This chance has been diminished one half by admitting females to the throne. In the second place, the principle of legitimacy as established through a series of ages, has been violated. And there is prob-

---

[46] Antonio La Grua. Prince of Carini. Diplomat of a noble Sicilian family, he was perhaps of Catalonian origin. He was envoy extraordinary and minister plenipotentiary at Madrid in 1838. On October 10, 1851, he was appointed envoy extraordinary and minister plenipotentiary to the Kingdom of Great Britain and Ireland. On May 3, 1859, while on leave at Palermo, he was assigned to the Neapolitan mission at Berlin. On July 16, 1859, he was again appointed chargé at London, but he was later transferred with the same rank to the King of Prussia at Dresden. Finally, on Aug. 11, 1860, he was sent to Vienna where he was later replaced by P. S. Leopardi. La Grua was removed from office in Oct. 1860. He married a daughter of General Kellermann. De Cesare describes him as "a bad diplomat." *Archivio di Stato,* Naples, *Scrivania di Razione, Assienti,* vol. 1011, 44, 169; vol. 1012, 61. Bib: Raffaele De Cesare, *La fine di un regno,* etc. I, 102, 112, 113; Alfredo Zazo, *La politica estera, etc.,* 9, 102; Ruggero Moscati, *Ferdinando II,* 53, 55. *Almanach de Gotha,* 1845.

[47] The Spanish ambassador to Naples was Angel Saavedra Duc de Rivas. *Almanach de Gotha,* 1845.

ably a third, which may have had some influence. The sister of the present sovereign is married to the nephew of Don Carlos and the son of his wife. But Queen Isabella is also his niece.

Under these circumstances, great was the surprise, when it came to light, that the King had despatched an Ambassador to recognize the Queen of Spain. Austria, Russia and Prussia were utterly unprepared for it. It was a separation from them, least expected — it was a breach in the family of despots. The anguish was increased from the fact that here was a triumph of France. Louis Philip had conceived the project of giving to the Queen of Spain, a Neapolitan Prince, for her husband the brother of His Majesty. This idea was an exceedingly happy one — it was to secure Spain under the influence of France and at the same time, separate the royal family of Naples from the northern allies and attach them to the Orleans dynasty. The bait was too tempting, the King would not refuse it, and the result has been the mission to Spain. In the mean time, it is believed the Northern Powers were kept in the dark and knew scarcely any thing of the proceedings. The chagrin of their ministers is obvious.

The impression here is that England makes no opposition to this alliance. The Queen Mother Cristina, whose wishes on the subject, will doubtless have much influence, is supposed to be altogether favorable. It remains to be seen whether this is a union, which may be made agreeable to Isabella herself and the Cortes. France will have no difficulty to encounter at Madrid from [sic] the opposition of the northern powers, for having never recognized the Queen, they have of course no representatives there. That is, she will meet no open opposition, but without doubt, they will spare no efforts but will avail themselves of all the means in their power to baffle France and disappoint the King of the Two Sicilies.

Austria feels this the unkindest act of all on the part of His Majesty of Naples. But it is not on that account, perhaps, the less agreeable to the King. Probably his obligations are too weighty to be pleasant. It is said that shortly after coming to the throne, he said he was quite disposed to give his people a constitution to vex Austria.

All the arrangements for the marriage of another brother of the King with the Princess Januaria of Brazil have been concluded, and he will leave here in a few weeks for that purpose.

The negotiation for a treaty of commerce between France and the Two Sicilies is progressing, but I have no details to give upon the subject. It is said there is every prospect of a speedy conclusion, but it is impossible to speak with certainty on this subject.

I received, a few days since, the President's message[48] in Galignani, accompanied by the criticisms of all the prominent English journals. As usual, they are filled with abuse without exception. They contrast it with the speech of the King of the French both in style and sentiment and give His Majesty the advantage. They censure it not only for what it contains but for what it does not. They complain that there is no rebuke of the defaulting states and suggest that if there had been less about Providence and more about "state bonds" it would have been in better taste. I remark that the comments of the French Journals are in a different tone, except the *Debats,* which indulges in the same strain with the English. These Journals, that is the English, never speak of us but to denounce us, and the message furnished them an opportunity to pour out a torrent of their invectives. Repudiation is always the theme, whenever America is mentioned. Here is a wound they delight to tear open and expose to the light of day. And unfortunately there is no defence. Their communications are sometimes copied into the Papers of the continent, but these last never manifest the same bitterness. But we have now been so often denounced as thieves and robbers that an American citizen travelling in Europe finds need of much courage to avow his country. Unfortunately, the English Journals are nearly the only sources whence information is derived of us for the continent. But it is true, that it is generally known that the articles in them concerning us are always influenced by prejudice and passion. This is fortunate, but still they have succeeded in producing impressions most unfavorable to us; and my opinion is, that our government and the republican system never stood lower since the first French revolution than at present. The failure of the states to meet their engagements has furnished arguments against us which have produced these lamentable results

I have received this day from Mr. Persico, on board the United States ship Delaware, evidence that the charge made against him

---

[48] John Tyler's third Annual Message. Dec. 1843. See: Richardson, *op. cit.,* V, 2110. In this message Tyler referred to the boundary between Great Britain and the United States in the Oregon territory as being unsettled; the holding of American vessels on the African coast by the English; interference with our fisheries by the British on the coast of Nova Scotia; some violation on the part of Great Britain of the terms of the treaty of 1815, between Great Britain and the United States.

of entering that ship in the port against the efforts of the Sanitation guard to prevent him, is untrue. I had the honor of transmitting to you in despatch No. 15 the conversation between the Prince of Scilla and myself on this subject. I shall now hasten to communicate with the Minister and put this affair in its proper light.

Mr. Carr,[49] our Minister to Constantinople, left here for that place on the fifth.

I have received nothing from the Department, since the date of my last communication. Enclosed are my accounts for the last quarter.

WM. BOULWARE TO A. P. UPSHUR

Legation of the U. S. Feb. 15. 1844 Naples. [Despatch No. 18.]

Sir

In the last communication I had the honor of addressing you, I remarked that I had received information from Mr. Persico,[50] and I might also have added from Com. Morris, showing that the charges which had been made in the note of the Minister of Foreign Affairs, which I have transmitted to you, were unjust. On this subject, I addressed the following note to His Excellence [sic].

Legation of the U. S. Naples Jany. 18. 1844

The Undersigned, Chargé d'Affaires of the United States, immediately after the communication, which he had the honor to receive, from His Excellence, charged with the Portfolio of Foreign Affairs, of the date of the 27th. October last, on the subject of D. Luigi Persico, addressed a note to Com. Morris, in command of the Delaware, informing him of the complaint, which had been made and transmitting at the same time a copy of the correspondence. Com. Morris in answer to this note, states that the undersigned had with justice believed that he had no intention of infringing any of the laws or usages of this Kingdom, in the affair of Mr. Persico — that he thought the intention of Mr. Persico to embark with the statues was publicly known, and presumed he would do all which the laws of this country required to enable him to embark with propriety — that had he known that any thing had been omitted, which was necessary, he certainly would not have admitted Mr. Persico aboard.

---

49 Dabney S. Carr, of Maryland, was commissioned minister resident to Constantinople Oct. 6, 1843. He left the post on Oct. 20, 1849.

50 See above, pp. 529, 542, 552, 556; also Throop despatches, p. 430.

In answer to a note which he addressed to Mr. Persico, demanding an explanation, which answer has been transmitted to the Undersigned, he denies the charge of leaping aboard the ship, in spite of the efforts of the Sanitary Guard — he denies that there was any opposition made to his embarkation; and in this denial he is sustained by the Officer of the deck, whose statement has been also sent to the Undersigned. This officer writes that he was standing on the accommodation ladder from the time of the approach of the lighter containing Mr. Persico and the statues, until he came on board — that he saw Mr. Persico take leave of the Sanitary Guard, and not the slightest opposition was made to his embarkation, either at that time or any other, while the lighter remained along side of the ship — that on the contrary, there seemed to be a perfect understanding of his intentions and of their propriety. In these statements, he is supported by other officers, who witnessed the proceedings.

Mr. Persico also alleges in his answer above referred to, as an excuse for not obtaining a passport that he was so hurried in embarking the statues, that he had no time to give to any thing else, and further, that he did not deem it important, as in 1834, he left this country for the United States in the U. S. Ship of war Constellation without passport, and no complaint was ever made by this government. He also denies that he is a Neapolitan subject and affirms that he is a citizen of the United States.

Under these circumstances, the Undersigned trusts that His Excellence is convinced not only of the good disposition of the Commander of the Delaware in this affair but that no censure can with justice be imputed to him. The embarcation of Mr. Persico was made in open day, with the greatest publicity, in the presence of the authorities of the city; no opposition was seen or known to be made and the Commodore had good reason to believe that every thing had been done, which was necessary and proper.

The Undersigned avails himself of this occasion to renew to His Excellency the Prince of Scilla the assurance of his distinguished consideration.

Wm. Boulware

To His Ex. .
Prince of Scilla
Duke of St. Cristina
&c &c &c

The recognition of the Queen of Spain by His Majesty and the attempt to make a marriage with her for his brother, seem to have produced a considerable effect in the northern courts. Metternich administered so strong a rebuke to the Austrian Minister here, for his not discovering the proceeding while it was in progress, that he has given in his resignation and it has been accepted. The Minister is Count Lebzeltern, an old, and distinguished diplomatist, who has been very long resident at this Court. He is truly unfortunate for he has, in time past, rendered himself disagreeable to His Majesty here, by his excessive vigilance and the unceasing efforts which he made to pry into all the secrets of the court. Now he has offended Metternich by a neglect to exercise these qualities. He has had the singular bad fortune to be wrecked on both Scilla and Charybdis.

As to the marriage itself, the impression here, is, that no progress has thus far been made in it in Spain. The Minister who has been despatched to that country, it would seem from the Spanish Journals, was not a fortunate appointment, as he is represented to have been formerly a Carlist and to have fought in the ranks of Don Carlos.

An occurrence has however just taken place, which removes one of the obstructions in the way of this alliance. I mean the news which we have, just received of the death of the wife of Don Francesco Paolo.[51] She is represented to have been an "intrigante," a woman of talent and influence and anxious to effect an union, between her own son and the Queen. It is believed that France will use all her best exertions to promote the wishes of the King of the Two Sicilies as it involves an utter separation of this Court from the Northern Courts hostile to the French and a close friendship and union between these last and His Sicilian Majesty. It will also secure probably in Spain as great a degree of French influence as is possible to exist in that country. If the marriage should take place, it will be entirely due to Louis Philippe. Under these circumstances, there will be the strongest obligations created.

---

[51] Francesco di Paola. Count of Trapani (1827-1892). A brother of the King, usually regarded as the least influential of all the brothers. On April 10, 1850, he married Marie Isabelle of Tuscany. A propos this marriage, there appeared in *Il Nazionale* of Florence (March 6, 1850), an injurious article against the policies of Naples, accusing the Tuscan Government of having come under the influence of Naples, and of having encouraged the marriage "for political reasons." On March 21, 1850, *Il Nazionale* was obliged to correct that remark and to state that the Tuscan minister had declared that the marriage was solely the result "of views of reciprocal convenience and that it had been arranged as far back as June 1849." This reply offended Ferdinand II which resulted in a diplomatic note presented to the Tuscan government by the Marquis Riario Sforza, Neapolitan minister at Florence. See: Benedetto Croce, "Gli ultimi Borbonici." In *Atti della R. Accademia di Scienze Morali di Napoli,* 1927; Ruggero Moscati, *Austria, Napoli e gli stati* etc., 117 ff.

WM. BOULWARE TO A. P. UPSHUR

Legation of the U. S. Naples March 30 1844 [Despatch No. 19]
Sir

We have recently had an insurrection in this Kingdom, which, but for information previously obtained of the designs of the conspirators, would probably have involved this country, if not all Italy in civil war. About the middle of this month in the town of Cosenza in Calabria,[52] a considerable body of men rose in the night and paraded the streets crying "Viva la repubblica" and "Giovine Italia." They attacked the fortress, but the King's troops, who were stationed at this place, succeeded in the first rencontre, in killing the leader along with various others of the insurgents. This dispirited the party and they retired without gaining their object, though not until they had avenged themselves by the death of the Commander of the troops together with some of the soldiers.

The Government had been previously informed, it is believed, through the kindness of Louis Philippe by means of discoveries made by the Police at Paris, of what was intended, and were on their guard. But for this fortunate information, it is not improbable that all Italy would have now been in a convulsion. There is reason to believe there was a conspiracy which pervaded the whole peninsula. Some of the leaders were in Paris, being refugees from previous efforts of the same kind. Numerous arrests have taken place in this city.

The rising which occurred in Bologna some time since has not been yet quelled. It is said that considerable alarm and no small embarrassment now pervade the Papal councils. They are believed to be anxious to call down an Austrian force for their protection, and Austria herself is ready and anxious to afford it. But France puts her veto on the design and says if another soldier of His Imperial Majesty is marched into the Roman States, she will take possession of Ancona. His Holiness is thus harrassed with dangers within and without.

Italy is volcanic — the smothered fire will explode sooner or

---

[52] The five leaders of the revolt were executed on July 11, 1844; a sixth died from natural causes just before the execution. For accounts of the uprising at Cosenza on March 15, 1844, see: G. Storino, *La sommossa cosentina del 15 marzo 1844. Cronaca documentata.* Cosenza, Aprea, 1898, 126 pp.; *Dizionario del Risorgimento Nazionale,* I, 275-276. This attempt was soon followed by another led by Attilio and Emilio Bandiera, both brothers, on June 16, 1844, landed near Cotrone, for the purpose of aiding an insurrection which was to break out. However, they were betrayed by a Corsican, and the insurrection failed.

later — if not before, the first war in Europe will witness a grand eruption. Light is diffused, though not rapidly; yet it is diffused. Liberal sentiments are making their way, in spite of all the barriers which can be opposed to their progress. Peace, steam, travel are carrying the seeds of amelioration every where.

A minister from Spain[53] has recently arrived here, and now diplomatic relations are fully established between the two courts.

If I have not been misinformed, some time during the past year, a consul was appointed to supersede our former Consul at Florence. I understand he has never arrived at his post and still further that the Grand Duke will not receive consuls in that city. I believe that this may be relied on. I obtained the information from good sources in that city more than twelve months since. He made an exception in favor of M^r. Ombrosio [sic] our Consul,[54] and granted him extraordinary privileges. He permitted him to make presentation at Court, whereas at most courts, consuls themselves are not received. M^r. Ombrosio [sic] thought that this proceeded from personal kindness to himself. It may have also resulted in part from the fact that we had no representative. If the gentleman appointed, does not intend to come out and take his chance, for at best it is only a chance, I suggest under the circumstances the propriety of reappointing M^r. Ombrosio [sic]. He is a man of great respectability, a naturalized citizen of the United States and has been always exceedingly useful to our citizens visiting Florence. Under the most favorable view, it is doubtful, if any other would be admitted as the general rule is against it. It would seem the choice is between him and none. I make this suggestion without any communication with M^r. Ombrosio [sic] and without having heard any thing from him on the subject. I know that he was proud of his office and his connection with America, and I am sure he would be delighted to be replaced. The place is of no value except in the honor it confers.

The negotiation between the Two Sicilies and France is in a state of progress but I have no details to give. I most cordially hope that it may be soon concluded, for I am impatient to commence our negotiation.

I should be much obliged if my letters could be sent by the Steamers — my letters — not my newspapers.

---

[53] See note 46, p. 561.

[54] J. Ombrosi was originally nominated consul of the United States for Florence on Feb. 27, 1823, serving till 1835. The consulate remained vacant until Aug. 29, 1842, when E. Gamage, of South Carolina, was appointed. Mr. Gamage served to 1845. From 1845 to 1847 Mr. Ombrosi served as acting consul, and similarly during 1851 after Mr. Gamage left.

WM. BOULWARE TO J. NELSON[55]

Legation of the United States Naples April 30. 1844. [Despatch N°. 20]

Sir

A few days since I received the circular containing the information of the afflicting occurrence aboard the Princeton, and at the same time, the notice of your advancement to the position of Secretary of State "ad interim."[56] Permit me to felicitate you upon this distinguished mark of the President's confidence and to express a hope that you may find the post agreeable and a means of advancing still further your high reputation.

I had the honor of addressing some months since, to your department a dispatch containing a correspondence between the Prince of Scilla and myself on the subject of Mr. Luigi Persico's embarcation aboard the Delaware when she was in this port. After the lapse of six months, a few days past I received a response to the answer which I submitted to the complaint. It contains a report of the case made by the Minister of Police, which does not differ in any very important particulars from that given by Lieutenant Barosi and contained substantially in my answer. I do not deem it necessary either to reply to it or to forward it to Washington, as the subject needs no further discussion.

It appears that the revolutionary movements in Calabria have not yet been quelled. The insurgents have taken to the mountains and number, it is said, between four and five hundred. More troops have recently been despatched into that district. It is the impression here, that the insurgents will sell their lives dearly as a surrender would be useless.

There is a report now in circulation of a negotiation for a marriage between the remaining single sister of His Majesty and the Duke of Bordeaux.[57] It is impossible not to connect this

---

[55] John Nelson, of Maryland. Attorney General. He was appointed Secretary of State *ad interim* by President Tyler on Feb. 29, 1844, serving to March 31, 1844. See also note 1, p. 201.

[56] Instruction No. 12 from the Department of State, dated Feb. 29, 1844, announced the death of Mr. Upshur and the appointment of John Nelson as Secretary of State *ad interim.* See, *Book of Instructions to Ministers,* volume *Spain,* 171.

[57] Chambord, Henri Charles Ferdinand Marie Dieudonné d'Artois. Duke of Bordeaux (1820-1883). He was the "King Henry V" of the French legitimists. His father was the Duke of Berry, the elder son of the Count d'Artois (afterwards Charles X); his mother was the princess Caroline Ferdinande Louise of Naples. On Nov. 7, 1846, he married at Bruck, in Styria, the Princess Marie Thérèse Béatrice Gaëtane, Arch-Duchess of Austria-Este, the daughter of the Duke of Modena, Francis IV. He remained without issue. Of the enormous literature

report with the failure of the efforts to effect an alliance between His Majesty's brother and the Queen of Spain. You are aware that to accomplish this object, the Queen of Spain was recognized by this Government to the astonishment of all the world and in violation of all its previous policy. This was all done under the influence of Louis Philippe who was to give his assistance to secure the marriage. Here was the "quid pro quo." Now this having failed, it is well surmised that His Majesty is disposed to avenge himself, by the union of his sister with the French Pretender. I give conjecture, for nothing certain is known.

For some time, the members of our corps, were kept duly informed of the progress of the pregnancy of Her Majesty. Finally we received an invitation to "assist" at her accouchement, which was to be announced as soon as the pangs commenced by the firing of cannon from the royal forts. A few days since, the expected signal was given and we repaired forthwith to the palace. Her Majesty was already delivered. The King produced the offspring and exhibited it apparently with much pride to the members of our corps separately and collectively, at the same time giving us some of the details of the occurrence. We then attended the baptism and were afterwards regaled with dinner at the royal table, though, as usual His Majesty did not honor us with his presence. All of which were diplomatic duties, your representative had not anticipated at the time of his appointment, excepting the dinner. But they were not the less amusing for being unexpected novelties.

The French treaty is not yet concluded. The negotiation is conducted with great secrecy, but it is understood, they are now occupied with the tariff question, which is always difficult and embarrassing in all countries. The English, in their negotiation, avoided this question altogether, leaving it for subsequent arrangement. They were content, simply to settle the question of reciprocity.

I wish to return to the United States in the Spring, but I cherish the hope that all obstacles being removed, our treaty may be made by that time.

---

relating to him, see : Dubosc de Pesquidoux, *Le Comte de Chambord étudié dans ses voyages et sa correspondance*. Paris, H. Oudin, 1881, and *Henri de France* by H. de Pène. Paris, H. Oudin, 1884. *Grande Encyclopédie*, Paris, H. Lamirault et Cie, 1890, X, 315-318.

Legation of the United States Naples July 1. 1844 [Despatch N° 21]

Sir

A short absence in the north of Italy, prevented my receiving your Circular,[58] N°. 13, informing me of your appointment to the Department of State, until a few days since. Permit me to express the sincere pleasure I feel at your acceptance of this post in the present crisis of our affairs. Our country has now need, in this branch of her service, of the highest abilities among her citizens. I doubt not, my countrymen now feel assured that all which ardent patriotism and lofty talents can accomplish, will be done in any negotiations which may take place with other powers. For myself, I hope, I shall be excused for saying, it is to me a source of peculiar satisfaction that you are at the head of the Department, with which I am connected and to whom I am subject.

Upon my arrival here, I was happy to find two of our Frigates the Columbia and Cumberland in this port. They excite much interest and are visited by crowds of people. As usual with our ships in Europe, they call forth general admiration by their appearance, their equipment, their extraordinary neatness and excellent discipline. When the Delaware was here, His Majesty upon visiting the ship, among other compliments said to the Commodore, it had been his effort in his own navy to imitate us. The Corvette Plymouth has just arrived. The Columbia and Cumberland will remain here a few days more and then the first will proceed to Tangiers and the latter to the Adriatic and the Levant.

In my last despatch I spoke of an attempt at revolution in Calabria. This section of the Kingdom has since become the theatre of another attempt still more desperate.[59] A few young Italians collected in Corfu to the number of about twenty and passed over and effected a landing on the Italian shore. They

---

[58] Instruction No. 13 from the Department of State, dated April 1, 1844, announced the appointment of John C. Calhoun as Secretary of State. Mr. Calhoun was Secretary of State from March 6, 1844 to March 10, 1845. See: *Instructions to United States Ministers*, Volume *Spain*, 174.

[59] For an account of this revolt see: A. Bonafede, *Sugli avvenimenti dei fratelli Bandiera e di Michele Bello in Calabria nel 1844 e 1847.* Gerace Marina, Fabiani, 1894, 159 pp.; M. H. Weil, "Le condizioni del Regno di Napoli nell'autunno del 1843 e dopo la fucilazione dei fratelli Bandiera (Luglio-Agosto)." *Archivio storico per le Provincie Napoletane.* Naples, 1923, 365-388; R. Pierantoni, *Storia dei fratelli Bandiera e loro compagni in Calabria, con numerosi documenti inediti e 31 illustrazioni.* Milan, Cagliati, 1909, xv-546 pp.

expected to be there joined by the people of the country, but instead of meeting with this reception, they were attacked by the people, several killed and some taken prisoners. Afterwards, the rest were apprehended by the police and thus has ended another mad attempt to revolutionize Italy — an attempt without concert, without foresight, without any of the most ordinary precautions.

One of the most singular circumstances connected with this movement, is the fact that two of the sons of the Admiral Bandiera[60] of the Austrian Navy, themselves officers in the same service, deserted their ships and united in this undertaking. They are Venetians and belong to what is called "La Giovine Italia." So far as the facts are known and have come to light, nothing could be more foolish than this enterprise in all its stages.

News has just been received here, that eighty persons engaged in this and the preceding attempt have been condemned to death by a Court Martial, but it is believed that His Majesty with his usual clemency will mitigate the punishment.

Some months since rumors have been afloat of a proposition from the Duke of Bordeaux for the hand of the sister of His Majesty. The French papers gave a report that the Duke of Montebello had given notice to this Court, that if this proposition was accepted, he would suspend all intercourse with this Government. Now it is believed that a marriage between the Princess and the Duke d'Aumale is the subject of negotiation, and that the Count of Syracuse the King's brother has been sent to Paris on this mission. Should this alliance be effected, it will not only be another link of union between this country and France, but another source of discontent and estrangement between this court and the northern courts. Thus far this is the only court upon the continent of Europe where Louis Philippe has succeeded in obtaining any sympathy unless Spain be an exception.

I regret to say that I have nothing to communicate upon the progress of the French treaty. It is the understanding in the diplomatic circle, that some questions which arose in the negotiation have been referred to Paris for instructions and at present nothing is doing here.

My accounts for the last quarter are herewith transmitted.

It has been to me a source of surprise that the Journals usually sent to me from the State Department, have not arrived of late.

---

[60] On July 23, 1844, all seventeen were condemned to death. Nine of them were shot on July 25; the others had their sentence commuted to life imprisonment. The Bandiera brothers died with the cry "Viva l'Italia." It is generally admitted that the Bandiera attempt was a mad but an heroic effort to liberate Italy.

The last dates which I have received are of the first days of April.

In one of my late communications I took the liberty of recommending the appointment of a Consul at Florence. In my excursion to the north of Italy I stopped some days in that city, and I am now more assured than ever of the propriety of the remarks and the recommendation submitted on this subject. The convenience of our citizens certainly demands a Consul at this place and now we have none.

WM. BOULWARE TO J. C. CALHOUN

Legation of the United States Naples Sept. 13, 1844
[Despatch N°. 21 (22)]

Sir

Since the date of my last dispatch nothing has occurred in this Kingdom, which can be of much interest, either to the Government or the people of the United States.

The disturbances in Calabria have ceased and the sentence of the law has been carried into effect upon the unfortunate men, who were engaged in the late revolutionary movements; with the exception of those who have experienced the clemency of His Majesty.

It is said that some circumstances a little singular attended the execution of those engaged in the last effort. When they were led out to die, one of their number addressed the troops, who had been drawn up to inflict the sentence; and strange to say, this was permitted by the commanding officer. He spoke boldly, for now he had nothing to fear. He spoke of the wrongs of Italy, of his intention having been to contribute his efforts to redress them — that he was now a martyr in the cause of liberty and that he died willingly for his country. The order was now given to fire, he having been permitted to conclude, but such was the emotion of the Commander himself, his sword fell from his hand in giving the order. The condemned all shouted "La giovine Italia" — the guns were discharged and not a man was touched. The second fire concluded the tragedy.

To the surprise of the diplomatists here, the various rumors which have been in circulation, for some months, on the subject of the marriage of the Duke d'Aumale with the sister of His Majesty have been terminated by the conclusion of a marriage contract, for his union, with a daughter of Prince Leopold the Uncle of the King. It is believed that this change is a mere affair of taste on the part of the Duke, and the political effect will be the same — a closer and more cordial union between the court of Naples and that of the Tuilleries. But there is nothing on which His Majesty of the Two Sicilies more prides himself than his independence, and, so far as he can, he will cautiously guard against any foreign influence.

Some time since, one of the Journals in Paris, attributed the success of this Government in putting so speedy an end to the disturbances in the country, to the timely notice given from Paris of the machination of conspirators. A few days afterwards, there appeared in the Government Journal of this city, an indignant article, believed to be written by the Minister of Police[61] himself, repelling as a calumny, this statement and boasting that this Government needed no exterior assistance of any kind for its defense or for the good order of the Kingdom.

This was truly unkind, for there is but little doubt that His Majesty Louis Philippe is the best police officer of this Kingdom. Paris, it is well known has been the source from which have emanated nearly, if not quite all the plots against the established order of Italy. Under the present vigorous government of that city, then, conspiracies are all made known to the Police, and forthwith, information is given to the authorities of this country, upon which it is prepared to act. If I mistake not, during the past year, formal notice was given to all the Italian states that no conspiracy should be carried out in France to disturb the peace of Italy. In this respect, the present dynasty is a much more efficient supporter of old institutions and a much more vigorous opponent of progress than that which it has supplanted. But thus far, all this friendly assistance seems to have been received with but little good will, on the part of them, upon whom it has been lavished. Now good fortune seems to have dawned, at length,

---

[61] The minister secretary of state of the general police was the Marquis Francesco Saverio Del Carretto (1778-1861). A Field Marshal and Inspector-Commander of the Gendarmery, he was sent to Sicily after the Restoration. As a Colonel, he was in charge of the military command in Basilicata. He commanded the Farnese Regiment against brigandage. In 1821, he was Chief of Staff in the constitutional army of Guglielmo Pepe. In 1828, he suppressed the revolt in Cilento. From Feb. 16, 1831, to Jan. 26, 1848, he was minister of police. When Ferdinand granted the Constitution, he resigned, and went into exile, succeeding, with difficulty, to reach Montpelier. In 1856, he was made Lieutenant General. See: H. Castille, *Le Marquis Del Carretto ancien ministre du Roi de Naples.* Paris, 1856, passim; Ruggero Moscati, *Il Regno delle Due Sicilie e l'Austria.* etc., passim; F. Niccolini, *Nicola Nicolini e gli studi giuridici nella prima metà del secolo xix.* Naples, 1907; *Dizionario del Risorgimento Nazionale,* 1933, II, 885.

upon the many kind offices of His Majesty, Louis Philippe, and a cordial union appears to have taken place with the royal family of this Kingdom.

I regret to inform you that the negotiation between this country and France for a treaty of commerce, is making no progress. Such is the jealousy of England that it seems almost impossible for France to cooperate with her in any thing. I am not able to say what is the present state of the negotiation, but it is, for the present, suspended.

I have been obliged recently to enter into a correspondence with this Government on two successive occasions to obtain an entry into this country for Americans, who have arrived here and been refused. One was the case of a gentleman, who came as passenger in one of our ships of war direct from America. The ship stopped at Gibraltar and he omitted to obtain the "vise" [sic] of the Neapolitan Consul to his passport in that port. The other was the case of an individual who had the misfortune to have a name, very like one on the list of those, prohibited to enter this Kingdom. I was appealed to in each of their cases, and interested myself to obtain permission for them to land, but there were difficulties, and one of them was obliged to remain one week aboard his ship in port before he was allowed to come ashore. I deemed it proper, at length, though with some reluctance, to become responsible for these gentlemen as it seemed to be wished by this government & as they seemed well worthy of it. This course adopted on their part proceeds from no unkindness to us — far from it, but from the fact that the late commotions have alarmed the Government, and the Minister of police has deemed it necessary to exact a more rigid execution of the laws on the subject of passports and to enforce extreme vigilance throughout his department.

Some idea may be formed of the nervous apprehension, which existed in this Government, a short time since, from the fact that a proclamation was issued in the name of His Majesty, forbidding all the officers of Government to harass the people in the execution of their duties.

I received, a few days since from our Consul at Malta,[62] a communication, informing me that the English Government charges letter postage on American newspapers transmitted to His

---

62 W. W. Andrews, of Massachusetts, United States Consul at Malta, was appointed on Dec. 30, 1834. He changed his name to William Winthrop about Sept. 2, 1845. He died at his post July 3, 1869. See: Hasse, *op. cit.*, 1709.

Majesty's packets. I have the honor to make known the fact to you, that you may take whatever action if any be deemed necessary, that may be thought proper.

His Majesty of the Two Sicilies departed from this city a few days since for Trieste. He is expected to meet there the Emperor of Austria. Whether this is a mere trip of pleasure or whether political considerations induce it, is at present a subject of speculation. It has been conjectured that this meeting has some reference to the marriage of His Majesty's brother with the Queen of Spain, but in what way it does not appear.

I have received nothing from the Department since the date of my last despatch. As to American newspapers, they have ceased to come.

WM. BOULWARE TO J. C. CALHOUN

Legation of the United States Naples Sep. 30. 1844 [Despatch No. 23]

Sir

Some time during the last spring, the Secretary of State did me the honor, to transmit to me, a letter from the Hon. D. Levy,[63] requesting information, with a view to the discovery of a remedy for an insect, which, he says, is devouring the orange groves of Florida and threatening the total destruction of that branch of production.

I put this letter into the hands of the Chevalier Monticelli, President of the Academy of Sciences[64] of Naples and requested of him, as the highest authority, the best information on the subject. I have the honor to enclose the response of the Chevalier, from which it will be seen that he is of opinion, that the insect in question is known in Europe and that the best remedy is a decoction of tobacco applied to the tree with a brush.

The book which he recommends I will endeavor to obtain and transmit to Washington by the first opportunity.

---

[63] David Levy Yulee (1810-1886). Born in St. Thomas, West Indies. Railroad promoter. Senator from Florida, 1845-51 and 1855-61. Changed his name from David Levy to David Levy Yulee by special act of Florida legislature on Jan. 22, 1846. *Dictionary American Biography*, 1936, XX, 638.

[64] Chevalier Michele Monticelli, President of the Academy of Sciences of Naples, from 1840 to 1844. A relative, Teodoro Monticelli (1759-1845), well-known as a naturalist, was notable for his long studies on the minerology of the Vesuvius. *Enciclopedia Italiana*, Milan, 1934, XXIII, 773.

[Enclosure with Despatch No. 23 of Sept. 30, 1844.]

Michele Monticelli presents his respects to the Hon. Mr. Boulware and returns to him the letter which he had the kindness to give him with the following remarks on the subject, received from Cavalier Giovanni Gussone.[65]

"The worm mentioned in the letter is well known and in Europe it often attacks other plants besides oranges, especially those cultivated in green houses. The insect is also often produced by warm cloudy weather, on plants growing in the open air.

"The best means of destroying it is to wash the plant, with a brush dipped in a decoction of tobacco.

"The best work treating on the cultivation of oranges, is that of Ferrari;[66] it is not new, but is still the best as it contains facts not words: it is much preferable to the work of a certain Arrosto[67] of Messina, and to that of Gallesio[68] which is entirely philosophical."

---

[65] Giovanni Gussone (1787-1866). A botanist and physician, he was director of the Botanical Garden of Boccadifalco, near Palermo, Sicily, from 1817 to 1827; later he directed the Botanical Garden of Caserta, and finally, in 1861, he was appointed Director of the Botanical Garden of Naples, and Professor of Botany at the University of Naples. He travelled extensively in southern Italy. His principal works include: *Plantae rariores,* Naples, 1826; *Florae Siculae prodromus,* Naples, 1827-1828, 2 vols.; *Florae Siculae synopsis,* Naples, 1842-1844, 2 vols.; *Enumeratio plantarum vascularium in insula Inarime,* Naples, 1854. His herbarium, which includes 14,000 species, is found in the Botanical Institute of Naples; other collections exist at Florence and Padua. See: Fabrizio Cortesi, "Giovanni Gussone," *Enciclopedia Italiana,* Milan, 1933, XVIII, 278.

[66] By Ferrari, a Jesuit monk, only the following title was available: G. Battista Ferrari, *Hesperides sive de malorum aureorum cultura et usus Libri quattuor.* Rome, 1646.

[67] It has not been possible to identify definitely the Arrosto of Messina. Several of the experts in the United States Department of Agriculture, familiar with the botanical literature of past years in Italy, have tried to locate the man but find no traces of him. They believe his name was Arosto, and that he hailed from Messina, but they sought to identify him under either name, and completely without success. Nor was it possible to identify the "book" referred to on page 576 as transmitted to Washington. Possibly the "book" itself never was listed and that, instead, it was at once transmitted to the Honorable Senator from Florida by whom in turn it may have been sent to some citrus grower.

[68] Giorgio Gallesio (1772-1839). Botanist. He graduated from the Faculty of Law of the University of Pavia. He was auditor of the Council of State; later, in 1810, he was sub-prefect of Savona, and, in 1814, of Pontremoli. He took part, as legislative secretary of the Genoese legation, in the Congress of Vienna where he advocated the union of Liguria to Piedmont. His *Traité du Citrus,* Paris, 1811, is one of the earliest works on the subject, having been used also by Gregory Mendel and Charles Darwin. Gallesio also published *Teoria della riproduzione vegetale,* Vienna, 1813 and Pisa, 1816, and *Pomona Italiana,* Pisa, 1802-1839, an extensive treatise on fruit culture and pomology. Among his minor works are:

Legation of the United States Naples Nov. 30, 1844 [Despatch N°. 24]

Sir

I have delayed writing to the Department, a very long time in the hope of being able to transmit something definite in reference to the French treaty. When I last had the honor of writing to you, and for some months previous, the negotiation was suspended, the French Ambassador awaiting instructions from Paris. The instructions have now arrived and he has given notice to the Neapolitan Commissioners that he is ready to resume the negotiation. The contents of the instructions have not transpired.

The negotiation is one of much interest to the representatives of all the Powers at this Court, for they are all anxious for commercial treaties, and all await the action of France. England has again sent here Sir Woodbine Parish to aid M^r. Temple, the regular Minister in his efforts to bring to a conclusion the long exertions she has been making to effect a new commercial treaty. It is generally believed here that His Majesty will accede to the demands of France. Indeed one of his Commissioners has given some very decided intimations to that effect. In addition it is well known that there is nothing on which His Majesty piques himself so much, as independence, and so long as the present treaty with France continues his hands are tied.

Another and powerful reason for a change is found in the fact, that in the last year, there has been a considerable failure in the revenue arising from the Customs. The general exclamation is that something must be done for the commerce of the country. Nearly all seem convinced that their old system has been a bad one, that there must be a revision and reduction of their tariff, and that first of all they must be relieved from the obligations of those old treaties with the three Powers; then, treaties with all the world connected with the changes in their customs.

I have been and I am still exceedingly anxious to make a treaty with this government before I leave here. I still hope it may be possible. But I wish to return to my country in the Spring, unless I should be then occupied in a negotiation. I hope the President

Memorie sulla canapa, Turin, 1829; Delle uva e dei vini italiani e più specialmente della Toscana, Florence, 1839; Della teoria degli innesti e della loro classificazione, Pisa, 1839. See: B. Braschi, "Giorgio Gallesio" in Annali di Botanica, Rome, XIX; Fabrizio Cortesi, "Giorgio Gallesio," in Enciclopedia Italiana, Milan, 1932, XVI, 303-304.

will be willing to grant me the permission to retire upon these terms. I am exceedingly anxious to leave here in the first days of March. Under these circumstances, I trust you will find it convenient to respond to this request immediately, as this will probably be necessary to enable me to receive the permission in time for my object.

The mission of the United States at this Court was instituted, in accordance with a suggestion, made to M^r. Davezac, or M^r. Nelson, at the time that one or the other of them was here, occupied with the indemnity demanded for the spoliations of Murat. If I mistake not, we were invited to enter into a commercial treaty. Indeed M^r. Davezac was absolutely engaged in the negotiation, when this government must have known perfectly well, that neither we nor any other Nation would make a commercial treaty with this country, so long as the English, French and Spanish nations enjoyed the exclusive advantages which old treaty stipulations secured to them. These advantages were of course unknown to us. My impression is that their object was simply to assure our Minister and our Government, and by that means, obtain some delay in the negotiation for the indemnity. M^r. Throop my predecessor, upon his arrival, entered into various consultations with the Minister of Foreign Affairs upon the subject of a treaty and at length learned from him the obstacles which existed in the secret stipulations with the nations before named. But negotiations had then been commenced with the view of a release from these impediments, which negotiations have been continued ever since. They have been successful with England. As to France you are aware of their present state. With Spain, there will be no difficulty, I presume for there is no commerce, literally none. Under such circumstances, this mission originated and has continued, now, eight or nine years. During all this time no minister has been sent by His Majesty to Washington.[69] Is it consistent with the respect due to ourselves to continue it under such circumstances? The state of things may be changed, if I obtain a treaty before my departure. It might be then necessary to have some one here to see it carried into effect, and His Majesty might then perhaps think it worth his while to send a Minister to Washington. But if I should not, should we send another, a third [sic] representative here to attend upon His

---

69 The King of the Two Sicilies never did send a minister to the United States. The highest ranking diplomatic representative from 1846 to 1861, was a chargé d'affaires.

Majesty and wait an opportunity of effecting a treaty? Should we not rather wait for him to make the next movement? Is it not due to ourselves that the mission should cease after so long a continuance without any reciprocation?

I take the liberty of throwing out these suggestions for your consideration, but at the same time I would not have it thought that I deem a mission, at this Court, unimportant. Far from it. This is much the most important state of Italy. We have a considerable commerce with Sicily, the exports amounting to something less than a million of dollars. And under a different state of things, with such a tariff as would be adapted to the circumstances of the country, indeed with such changes as we now anticipate soon to take place, our commerce would be largely augmented. In addition this city is the resort of many of our countrymen it being the usual conclusion of the classic tour of Italy, and they often need such protection and assistance as can only be afforded by a representative of our country. Under these circumstances I consider a mission here highly important, if it can be continued consistently with our own dignity and self-respect.

In Brazil, His Majesty has only a Chargé d'Affaires[70] although the Emperor has married his sister and has here a Minister Plenipotentiary.[71] It is now a subject of complaint on the part of Brazil and it will not improbably lead to the withdrawal of the Minister. My impression is that in this case, and in our own, the reason of the King is simply parsimony. It may be also that the fact that our relations are merely commercial, and in addition that we are not connected with the political systems of Europe, take no part in these combinations, in general, and are not likely to participate in their wars; it may be and probably is true that these considerations have their influence.

There being practically no Minister of Foreign Affairs here, the incumbent being a mere cypher, we can obtain no information on such a subject, as this without addressing to him a formal note, which would be submitted to the King for an answer. This

---

[70] Gennaro Merolla was appointed Neapolitan consul general in Brazil by decree of May 28, 1837. On July 27, 1842 he was appointed chargé d'affaires at the Court of the Emperor of Brazil. On Oct. 13, 1850, he was appointed minister resident at the same court. He died on Dec. 3, 1850. (*Archivio di Stato,* Naples - *Scrivania di Razione,* Assienti, vol. 1007, 66; vol. 1009, 80).

[71] The minister plenipotentiary of Brazil in Naples on Oct. 17, 1844 was Manoel Rodrigues Gameiro Pessôa (Viscount of Itabaiana). (-1846). Diplomat. Born in Portugal. He became a subject of Brazil after the country's independence. His last diplomatic mission was to the Kingdom of the Two Sicilies. He was buried in the Church of Saint Anthony of the Portuguese in Naples.

being a question of delicacy, one of courtesy, I have been unwilling to demand explanations, or say any thing on the subject, although ever since my arrival, I have felt much in regard to it and have been anxious to learn from an authentic source the cause of this neglect. But I do not doubt that I have assigned the true causes. But if you deem it important as connected with the continuance of the mission and think it proper to ask an explanation, I will have no hesitation in making the demand.

On the 25th Ultimo, His Royal Highness the Duc d'Aumale was married to D. Maria Carolina Augusta Bourbon daughter of His Royal Highness the Prince of Salerno Uncle of His Majesty. I do not deem it necessary to say any thing of the various ceremonies festivities &c which attended the union.

I have had the honor of receiving despatch No. 15 from your Department with its enclosure.[72]

J. C. CALHOUN TO WM. BOULWARE

Department of State Washington, 3rd. February, 1845.
[Instruction No. 17.][73]

Sir: I am directed by the President to inform you, that he has yielded to your renewed solicitations to be permitted to quit your residence near the Government of Naples, and to return home. It is his wish that you should remain at your post until the arrival of your successor, that he may enjoy the advantages of entering upon the duties of the mission under your advice and experience. The President, however, does not entertain the idea that, under present circumstances, either policy or the public service will render your remaining at Naples, for this purpose, indispensably necessary; and if your private interests should make it important

---

[72] Instruction No. 14, from the Department of State, dated June 26, 1844, transmitted a letter of congratulations to the King on the birth of a daughter, Princess Maria Immaculata Clementina. Instruction No. 15, from the Department of State, dated Sept. 12, 1844, transmitted a copy of a despatch addressed to the Hon. Wilson Shannon, expressing the views of the United States on the proposed invasion of Texas by Mexico. See, Instructions to United States Ministers, Volume *Spain,* 182. Wilson Shannon, of Ohio, was commissioned envoy extraordinary and minister plenipotentiary to Mexico, April 9, 1844. Diplomatic intercourse having been suspended, he demanded his passports and left Mexico, May 14, 1845. See Hasse, *op. cit.,* 1811.

[73] Instruction No. 16, from Secretary of State Calhoun to Mr. Boulware, Dec. 7, 1844, transmitted a letter from the President in answer to an announcement of the marriage of the King's brother, the Count of Aquila, to Dona Januaria Maria, eldest sister of the Emperor of Brazil.

for you to return to the United States, you will be at liberty to embark as soon after the receipt of this despatch, as you may find it convenient; taking care to leave the archives and property of the Legation in the hands of M͏ʳ. Hammett, the Consul, or, of some other trustworthy citizen of the United States, to be carefully preserved till further orders. — You are requested to transmit a correct inventory of them to this Department.

In accepting your resignation the President directs me to convey to you his entire approbation of the manner in which you have discharged the public duties with which you have been entrusted; and I transmit, enclosed, a letter addressed to the Minister of Foreign Relations of the Two Sicilies, with an office copy of the same, informing him of your recall, which you will present in the usual form, and accompany by assurances to His Excellency of the sentiments of friendship entertained by this Government towards that of the Two Sicilies.

Of the exact date of your taking leave, you will inform this Department and the Bankers of the United States; who will be desired to settle your accounts accordingly.

Your despatches N͏ᵒˢ. 21, 23 and 24 (and one dated the 13th September last, not numbered),[74] have been received. I have to direct your attention to despatch N°. 11 from this Department, desiring you to transmit a copy of Mr. Throop's No. 9, which has not yet been received.

WM. BOULWARE TO J. C. CALHOUN

Legation of the United States Naples April 2. 1845 [Despatch N°. 25]

Sir

Since the date of my last despatch, I have had the honor of receiving despatches N͏ᵒˢ. 16 & 17. The last arrived three days since, having been nearly two months on the passage. I am under great obligations to you for the promptness, with which you have responded to my request, though my object has been partially defeated, owing to the tardiness of the passage. I am under still more for the kind terms in which you convey the approbation

---

[74] In the original volume there is no unnumbered despatch of this date, although there is one so dated that bears the number "21" corrected to "22" which the text shows to be missing as "22" and which, in that sequence, falls into the proper date sequencing, both as to sending and receiving dates, with all the other letters. The words "not numbered," therefore, are in error.

given by the President to the manner in which I have discharged the public duties, with which I have been entrusted. I have only one regret in reference to this Mission, that circumstances over which I have had no control, have prevented my making a treaty with this Government. I have even now some faint hope. It seems that the French treaty is about being concluded. I say, it *seems,* for in diplomacy, particularly in this country, where Machiavel is not yet forgotten, nothing is sure until names are signed. Notwithstanding my great anxiety to return home, having now been absent from my family more than three years, yet if I find in the course of fifteen or twenty days that the French treaty is really concluded, and the our's [sic] can probably be negotiated in a short time, I will not hesitate to delay here to accomplish the principal object of my mission. If this should occur, of which I have not much hope, knowing the numerous obstacles which impede the progress of every thing in this government, I believe the Department will not, nor will my successor esteem it any infringement of his rights that I enter on such a negotiation. If in a few days, I find that something may be done, I will immediately inform you. I naturally feel great reluctance after having prepared for this negotiation, after having awaited it for three years, now to abandon it.

The Consul General of His Majesty[75] to the United States, is now here, and he is at present engaged in urging this Government to send a Chargé d'Affaires to Washington. He represents us as dissatisfied with the neglect and appeals to the debates which took place in Congress at the time of my appointment to sustain him.[76] He has had several interviews with me on the subject. I have informed him that I have no instructions, but at the same time, I have given him my individual opinion that there was a strong dissatisfaction. He informs me that he has made the Government to understand that this neglect will not improbably

---

[75] Rocco Martuscelli. Diplomat. He was appointed Consul General of the second grade in the United States by decree of July 15, 1838. By royal edict of Nov. 13, 1843, he obtained a six months' leave of absence, beginning March 9, 1845. On June 9, 1846, he was appointed chargé d'affaires in the United States. On May 8, 1848, he took the oath to the Neapolitan Constitution. On Jan. 3, 1853, for reasons of health, he obtained a leave of absence for four months, which were later extended to Dec. 22, 1853. He died in the United States on Nov. 8, 1853. *Archivio di Stato,* Naples - Scrivania di Razione, Assienti, Vol. 1007, 51; Vol. 1009, 104; Vol. 1011, 49.

[76] William Boulware was nominated chargé d'affaires to the Two Sicilies by the President on July 16, 1841; it was referred to the Committee on Foreign Relations the same day; on July 22 it was moved that the appointment lie on the table; debated July 27; it was considered again Aug. 23, again voted to lie on the table; the appointment consented to Sept. 13, 1841. *Sen. Exec. Journal.* V.

terminate our mission at this Court, if there is not an immediate change. He was anxious that I should converse with the Prince of Scilla on the subject. I told him it was a question of delicacy, involving an act of courtesy, a question of a civility not reciprocated, and that I must decline *seeking* any conversation on this subject, but that he was at liberty to make any use he pleased of the opinions expressed by me. I hope that his exertions may be successful. They will be the more energetic from the fact that he wishes the place. I shall contribute to them in any way that I can, consistently with my duties. Indeed, I have felt it to be a part exceedingly disagreeable, ever since I have been at this Court, that we alone of all the nations of the earth were not represented and honored with a reciprocation of our mission. I feel much interest on this subject and great anxiety for the success of the Consul; that is in his inducing a Mission to our country; and on this account I am the more content to protract my stay here a little longer.

Enclosed are my accounts for the last quarter and also the despatch required.

WM. BOULWARE TO J. BUCHANAN[77]

Legation of the United States, Naples May 1. 1845. [Despatch No. 26.]

Sir

Though I have received no official notice of your appointment to the high office, which you now occupy, yet the Journals inform me of the fact and there exists no longer any doubt of it. Under these circumstances, I address with pleasure this communication to you. And in this my first act of official intercourse, permit me to felicitate you upon your promotion, and to express the sincere pleasure it has afforded me; and at the same time to assure you of my cordial wishes for your success, and that of the administration with which you are connected.

By a reference to my correspondence you will have already learned the state of things in this Legation up to the date of my last despatch. Since that time, the French treaty has been finished, and it has now been sent to Paris for the ratification. The English

[77] James Buchanan, of Pennsylvania, was commissioned Secretary of State by President Polk on Mar. 6, 1845; he retired on Mar. 4, 1849. Mr. Boulware frequently mispelled the name of the Secretary of State, writing it "Buchannan."

treat also, which was concluded some two years since but which awaited the French, has now been sent to London for the same purpose.

By these two treaties, the Government of the Two Sicilies has been relieved from those obligations, which have heretofore prevented their forming commercial conventions with other countries; a relief they have ardently and perseveringly sought ever since His present Majesty came to the throne.

And now, finding themselves free and in a condition to treat with other nations, they are anxious to profit by it. It seems their treaty with Spain, which is similar to those with England and France, will not delay their negotiation. No commerce existing with Spain, the rights conferred are of no practical value. Besides, they construe the treaty, as not excluding them from the right of giving the same privileges to other countries which is their present intention. Indeed they speak of Spain, whenever she is mentioned, as nothing. But, doubtless, they will negotiate with her. Indeed, overtures have been already made; but this will not retard their action with other Powers. They seem now disposed to adopt the reciprocity principle and throw open their ports to the commerce of the world. Today, one of the Commissioners, charged by His Majesty with the negotiation of treaties, informed me that this Government was now free and ready to enter into negotiations with us. I replied that I was prepared, at any time, he would propose, to make a beginning. He then said he would take His Majesty's orders on the subject.

In this state of things, I feel it my duty to remain here, though exceedingly anxious to leave for the United States. My anxiety to accomplish the object of this mission is still greater. Having prepared myself for this subject, having anxiously awaited it three years, knowing now the men with whom I shall have to deal and the influences and circumstances which will probably attend a negotiation, I cannot hesitate as to the course to be pursued. If my successor should arrive, before or after a commencement has been made, I will with great pleasure transfer the negotiation to his hands and convey to him whatever information I may have collected, which may assist him in bringing it to a favorable conclusion.

I trust that this course on my part will meet with the approbation of the President. If our policy on the subject of treaties of commerce and navigation were not a fixed and permanent policy, one that has been persisted in for a long series of years and that has met with the general approbation of the country, I might hesitate without receiving instructions from the new administration. But as the reverse is clearly true, I have every reason to presume the same system will continue to be pursued, and that in following my instructions given by the late administration, I shall act in accordance with the wishes of the present.

In an interview, which I had a few days since, with the Minister of Foreign Affairs, he expressed a strong desire that I should remain and conduct this negotiation. It is certainly important, in acting with such a government as this, when many casualties might entirely change the intentions of the Ministry and the Sovereign, to profit immediately by their readiness and anxiety.

Our commerce with this country is, at present, merely in an incipient state. The exports direct and indirect, I should estimate at about a million of dollars, without making any very accurate calculation. From the port of Palermo alone during the last year, the exports were about six hundred thousand dollars. The direct imports are very small, the indirect more considerable. The exports are for the most part made in American vessels, owing to the advantages enjoyed by them in our ports; the imports in Sicilian, on account of the remission of forty per cent on the duties in this country. American tobacco is brought here from London and Marseilles and Sicilian olive oil is carried to the United States from Trieste. The exports are for the most part from the island of Sicily, the imports to this city.

In my instructions, my attention is particularly directed to the subject of tobacco. I hope to obtain a reduction of duty for the island of Sicily — a large reduction, but on this side of the strait of Messina, nothing is to be hoped for, since here it is a monopoly and productive of a large revenue. Here I am perfectly sure we can effect no change; and I doubt very much, if any change would be beneficial to us. On this subject I have given my reasons in a former communication.

With a moderate duty on cotton, our merchants might send a considerable quantity of this article into this Kingdom. The price here is about fifteen cents, the pound and the duty about ten cents. I hope to succeed in obtaining a reduction of this enormous duty. At least, I shall insist on it. It seems to me these are the only two articles of peculiar interest to us, which we have any chance to importing here to any amount. Doubtless, there are other things of which we shall participate in the supply, when placed on the footing of the most favored nations.

There are fish of which we brought to this market large quantities before the English enjoyed ten percent advantage, and drove us away. We already send here sugar, coffee and some naval stores. There are many other little things also that are now sent. Perhaps we may be able to compete with the English in the supply of spun cotton.

But there is a peculiar difficulty with which we have to contend, when we ask a diminution of duties. We are always met with a reciprocal demand. To which we can make no other than a negative response. They say to us "Who asks, must give" — "Where is your quid pro quo?" They will demand of me, here, a diminution of the duties on their wines, which are in truth enormous, being more than fifty per cent ad valorum. But of course I can make no stipulations of this kind. The red wines of this country pay one hundred per cent upon the original cost, the Marsala an average of more than fifty. But on the other hand, cotton and tobacco pay much more still in this Kingdom.

His Majesty's Consul at New York called to see me the other day, and informed me, in the course of conversation, that when the subject of sending a Chargé d'Affaires to the United States was brought to the notice of His Majesty, he announced that he should send no one, until there was a commercial treaty with our country.

Since the reception, here, of the President's inaugural address and the debates in the British Parliament on the subject,[78] there has been much conversation in the diplomatic circles on the probability of war between the two countries. I hope that such a calamity is to be averted; but at the same time I hope — No, I do not hope — I have no doubt the national honor will be maintained.

[78] In his inaugural address of March 4, 1845, President Polk made no direct reference to England. However, he went out of his way to congratulate his fellow-citizens "on the entire restoration of the credit of the general government of the Union and that of many of the states . . ." See, Richardson, *op. cit.*, IV, 373.

Legation of the United States Naples June 15. 1845 [Despatch No. 27]

Sir

In my last despatch, I had the honor of informing you, that one of the Commissioners charged by His Majesty with the negotiation of treaties, had given me the information that this Government was now ready to enter into a negotiation with us. This gentleman is the Chevalier Fortunato,[79] high in the confidence of the King and the Master spirit in the negotiations with France and England. He is a Minister of State without Portfolio.

About ten days after I had received this information from him, I met him by accident and we had a long conversation on the subject of the proposed negotiation. I then told him that I was anxious to enter immediately upon the negotiation, that I had sent in my resignation of this mission, that it had been accepted, that a successor was probably named and that I was now only detained at Naples by the hope of being able in a short time to conclude a treaty. That if it were not possible to enter at once upon the subject I could not wait, but should return immediately to my country. He said that as soon as the King returned to this city, he would take his orders and that he already

---

[79] Giustino Fortunato (1777-1862). Statesman. After completing his studies at the University of Naples, he taught mathematics at the Military College. In 1799, he was appointed justice of the peace of the Republican Government. While defending the Republic at the Ponte della Maddalena, he was captured by the Sanfedisti and imprisoned in the Castello del Carmine. He succeeded in escaping and, for a while, hid himself at Moliterno at the home of General Parisi whose niece he had married the previous year. Later he returned to Naples where he practised law. In 1806, when the French returned to Naples, he was attached to the Ministry of the Police, but shortly afterwards he was appointed chief of a division in the Ministry of Justice. In 1808, he re-established the Pontaniana Academy with headquarters in his own home. The following year Joachim Murat appointed him Attorney General of the Great Criminal Court. Subsequently he held important posts on the State Council, the Supreme Court, and the Budget Ministry. On October 24, 1814, he was appointed commissioner to Chieti where he restored order after the uprising of March 1813. Following the restoration of the Bourbons, he was retained at the Budget Ministry with the title of Attorney General. In 1831, he and Minister Intonti tried to temper the absolute government in the Kingdom. In 1841, Ferdinand II appointed him minister without portfolio and, in 1847, he was named Minister of Finance. On July 9, 1848, he was a member of the Chamber of Pari. From Aug. 7. 1849, to Jan. 19, 1852, he was President of the Council of Ministers and Minister of Foreign Affairs. For reasons that are not known, Fortunato suddenly relinquished his powers. On Sept. 25, 1850, Ferdinand II bestowed upon him the title of Marquis. See: A. Musco, *Di un economista basilicatese in Ciasca Romolo. Nel primo centenario dell'elevazione di Rionero a comune autonomo.* Florence, 1912; Raffaele De Cesare, *La fine di un Regno,* I, 9, 11, 67; Ruggiero Moscati, *Ferdinand II,* etc. passim.

knew his wishes and that he was sure, we would be able to begin immediately.

His Majesty returned on the 20th., and the following day, I addressed the Chevalier Fortunato the following note, marked "private"

Excellence

When I last had the honor of a conversation with your Excellence, you informed me that as soon as His Majesty returned to this city, you would take his orders on the subject of the negotiation, of which we conversed. His Majesty having now arrived, I doubt not, you will recall the subject and acquaint yourself with His Majesty's wishes.

When we had the interview to which I have just referred, I made to you some statements as to the position I occupy. Permit me briefly to recapitulate the facts. Some months passed [sic] I gave in my resignation of the official position, which I have the honor of occupying near this Court, and requested permission of the President of the United States to return to my own country. I received from the President the permission desired, but accompanied by an instruction that he would prefer that I should remain until the appointment of a successor. The President concluded by leaving it to my own discretion to remain or not, as I may deem proper. I have thus far had no official notice of the appointment of a successor, nor have I any knowledge, when one will come to my relief.

In this state of things, I deem it my duty and it will also be my pleasure to remain and enter into a negotiation with this Government if it meet His Majesty's wishes. It would give me great satisfaction to take with me to America, a treaty, which would promote the interests of both countries, increase their intercourse and add new ties to the bonds of friendship between them. But I deem it necessary to say to your Excellence that if this negotiation is to be delayed, which I should much regret, I shall not be able to await it longer, but shall profit by the permission of the President to take my leave for my own country. This I should much lament, but such is the urgency of my private interests, that I can not delay, unless it be for an immediate negotiation.

I have thought it proper to explain thus clearly and frankly my position in this unofficial manner, believing you will not consider it ill-timed nor uncalled for.

Permit me to express in conclusion the hope that no obstacle will longer retard the commencement of our negotiation nor prevent its successful termination.

I have not thought it necessary to write your Excellence in the French language, knowing you read English with perfect facility.

May 21, 1845

To His Ex.

The Chevalier Giustino Fortunato Minister, Secretary of State &c. &c.

I was induced to send this note that I might accelerate, if possible, his movements, knowing the disposition to procrastinate, so prevalent always in the offices of this Government. Three or four days afterwards, I met him at the English Minister's and he then told me that the King was so occupied, at present, with his fleet, with the manoeuvres of which, he was engaged every day, that he would not be able to converse with him on the subject, before the 30th of the month. That is of May.

On the 7th Inst. I addressed him a note enquiring if the orders of His Majesty had been taken. He replied that they had not. Two days afterwards, I announced to him by note that I had decided to await no longer a negotiation which seemed so uncertain as to time. This was accompanied by expressions of courtesy and regret.

The course which this affair has taken, has disappointed, but not astonished me. It is only in accordance with the usual mode of proceeding in a country, where five years were required to make a postal treaty with France. But under such circumstances, it seemed utterly unnecessary for me to wait longer. I commenced forthwith my preparations for departure and I hope to be able to leave here in a very few days.

You may perhaps think it extraordinary that I did not address myself to the Prince of Scilla as he is charged with the Portfolio of Foreign Affairs. The Prince, is a cypher, though the regular medium of communication with His Majesty. But I believe it may be said with truth, that the irregular mode, through the Chevalier Fortunato or some other of the three Commissioners, is oftener pursued. Before leaving this subject, I deem it necessary to add that it is by no means improbable that they delayed to negotiate with me, wishing to receive first the ratification of the treaties with France and England. But in the commencement they told me they should not wait for this purpose.

On the 23rd. of last month Commodore Smith[80] made his appearance in this harbor with the two ships under his command. The 25th being the anniversary of the birthday of the British Queen, M^r. Temple the British Minister politely sent invitations to the commanding officers to dine with him — a distinguished courtesy on his part and very properly appreciated on theirs. They hoisted the British flag, one fired a salute in honor of the day.

On the 30th. the name day of His Majesty of the Two Sicilies, I had the honor of presenting them at court. They were fine looking fellows in person and bearing, and I had good reason to be proud of my countrymen. Their ships have been much visited and universally admired. The corvette Plymouth under the command of Capt. Henry[81] has been the subject of more compliment than any other ship I have ever known in this port. It is kept in a state of such beautiful neatness as would do honor to the saloon of a private gentleman. The very courteous bearing of the Captain and his officers give additional attractions. Nor are the officers of the Frigate at all inferior. Since they have been here, the harbor has been filled with ships of war, Neapolitan French and English — and it may be truly said that none have been compared with our's. [sic].

News received here, rendered it necessary as I believed to address to Commodore Smith the following note.

Legation of the United States Naples May 7, 1845.

To Com. . Smith

Sir

Information has been received in this city by the Malta Journals as well as by private communications, that a war has broken out in Syria between the Maronites and Druses of a most savage, and extraordinary character, even in that country. It is said that this war originating in Lebanon has been accompanied by out-

---

80 Joseph Smith (1790-1877), Naval officer. He was born in Hanover, Mass. In 1813 he was commissioned lieutenant. From 1838 to 1840, he was commander of the *Ohio* of the Mediterranean Squadron, and from 1843 to 1845, he continued to command the Squadron with the *Cumberland* as his flagship. This was his last sea duty. In 1862, he was commissioned as Rear Admiral. *Dictionary American Biography* (1935), XVII, 309-310; Hamersly, *op. cit.* 28-29.

81 Henry Henry (-1857), Naval officer. He was born in Maryland. He was appointed sailing master in the United States Navy, July 1, 1812. His third and final cruise was to the Mediterranean and the coast of Brazil in command of the U. S. S. *Plymouth*. He was in the Mediterranean, where he was actually engaged under Commodore Joseph Smith, from April 1844 to October 28, 1845. Information supplied by John B. Heffernan, Captain, United States Navy, Director, Naval Records and Library.

breaks in various other sections, all of which had for their object the destruction of the Christian population of that country. That large numbers have been killed, that some of the convents have been sacked and their inmates murdered, that many churches have been burnt and that the Turkish Government so far from repressing these disorders has encouraged them. But I am happy to say that one of the letters from Beyrut states, that thus far in the midst of the general massacre of the Christians, the American missionaries alone have been respected. It is further stated that Col[n]. Rose[82] the English Consul at Beyrut put himself at the head of a detachment of soldiers (but what soldiers I do not know) and rescued about seven hundred of the Christians from destruction.

Letters received at the British Legation here, confirm the general statements, but seem to be so far as I am able to learn destitute of specific facts.

I submit to you whether in this state of facts, it would not be judicious to despatch one or both of the ships under your command to the coast of Syria. We have some valuable citizens in that country, whose lives are not improbably in danger. This would seem to be the more necessary from reports received here that some ill feeling exists on the part of the authorities towards our Missionaries.[83] Under any circumstances, your appearance on that coast would probably have a salutary effect. An American citizen should be protected, wherever he may be; and it is well to remind the Barbarians of Syria, that we have a force in the Mediterranean and that it may reach them.

After the reception of this communication, Com. Smith ordered the Corvette to Beyrut.

June 16. This day I met with the Chevalier Fortunato — the first time since I announced to him my decision. He immediately drew

---

[82] Strathnairn, Field Marshal Rt. Hon. Hugh Henry Rose. Lord, G. C. B., G. C. S. I., LL.D. (1801-1885). He went with the British officers and detachments and took part in the military operations in Syria in 1840 and 1841. He was appointed Consul-General in Syria on Aug. 20, 1841. While there, he succeeded in rescuing the Prince of Lebanon and others from the Druses. He was appointed secretary of embassy at Constantinople, Jan. 2, 1851, and was chargé d'affaires from June 23, 1852, till April 4, 1853. He served in the Crimean War and the Indian Mutiny. He died at Paris on Oct. 16, 1885. *Dictionary of National Biography* (1921-1922), XVII, 233-240.

[83] There is very little published information on American missionary activities in Syria during this period. However, on page 5 ff of Stephen B. L. Penrose Jr.'s *That They May Have Life,* published by the Trustees of the American University of Beirut, by the Princeton University Press, 1941, there are some comments on missionary activities in Syria.

me aside and expressed surprise at the communication which I had made him. He then enquired, if His Majesty gave now the necessary orders on the subject, whether I would be disposed to enter into a negotiation. I told him that I had asked an audience of the King to take leave, that my baggage was ready and that I only awaited the reception of His Majesty to depart. He then wished to know if it was only the audience which now detained me. I answered the audiences of the King and the other members of the royal family. But said he, if before your departure, we are ready, will you consent to negotiate? I asked him if he thought the negotiation might be brought to a successful termination in a very short time. He replied, he had been examining the subject, and he thought it might. He then spoke of the treaties proposed by M^r. Davezac and M^r. Nelson and intimated that he was pleased with them. I said to him that I did not comprehend the object of those gentlemen in the treaties which they had proposed. They had been willing to stipulate for a reduction of duties on the part of our Government, that this was opposed to our uniform policy; that we did not regulate our tariff by treaty stipulations; that only one case had occurred in our history, a treaty with France now expired and not renewed, and that in that, there was merely an agreement for the reduction of the duties on limes. That a treaty made by M^r. Wheaton[84] with the Zollverein had been recently rejected by our Senate, though highly advantageous to our interests in many respects, on account of its containing some stipulations for a reduction of duties. That the assent of our Congress was necessary to any change of duties and I did not believe that could be obtained, for our Government had always been opposed to binding itself by treaty on this subject.

I then told him, I was willing still, if before I left Naples, they found themselves ready, to negotiate, but that it must be on the basis of the treaty proposed by M^r. Throop. He said he thought in eight days they might be ready; that I could go on with my preparations for departure and if they obtained the authority of His Majesty to treat even after my audience of leave, he would come and inform me with the hope of thus making yet a treaty. Thus we parted.

---

[84] Henry Wheaton, of New York, was envoy extraordinary and minister pleni-potentiary to Prussia. He was empowered on Dec. 15, 1837, to negotiate a treaty of commerce and navigation with Hanover; such a treaty was concluded June 10, 1846. For a brief account of the negotiations between Mr. Wheaton and the Zollverein, see: Henry Merritt Wriston, *Executive agents in American foreign relations*. Baltimore, Johns Hopkins Press, London, H. Milford, Oxford University Press, 1929, 647-650. See also note 8, p. 379.

It is barely possible something may yet be done. M^r. Nelson's treaty of indemnity was made the day of his departure. But I build no anticipations on it, on the moment I have gotten through my audience, if not then in the midst of a negotiation, I shall leave this city.

WM. BOULWARE TO J. BUCHANAN

Legation of the United States Naples June 24. 1845 [Despatch No. 28.]

Sir

In accordance with my intentions, announced in my last despatch, I have since been busily engaged in making preparations for my departure. On the 13 Inst. I asked an audience of his Majesty to take leave, which was granted on the 19th. I then addressed His Majesty in the following language.

En quittant la position que j'ai eu l'honneur d'occuper près de la Cour de Votre Majestè, je suis chargè du President des Etats Unis, d'assurer Votre Majestè de son amitie la plus sincere et de son desire [sic] le plus fort de garder et fortifier les rapports de l'harmonie qui existent si heureusement entre les deux pays.

Pour moi meme [sic], c'est avec une vive emotion que Je me presente aujourdhui pour prendre congé. J'ai été obligè de mes interets particuliers de demander ma demission. Qu'elle permette que Je temoigne ma reconnaissance respecteuse pour toute la bontè avec laquelle, il a plu à Votre Majestè de m'honorer. Je ne puis pas l'oublier, et Je ferais toujours mes voeux pour son bonheur et sa prosperitè.

In construing the force of the language employed, it is to be recollected that in this country, words, especially words of courtesy always convey a much more just idea than they literally signify.

To my remarks the King replied in substance, that he was very grateful for the sentiments which I had expressed — that they were entirely reciprocated by him and that it was his sincere desire to cultivate the most friendly relations with our country. That as for myself I had done my duty in the position which I had occupied. And then he expressed his regrets, as I understood him at my departure, accompanied by other complimentary expressions and by good wishes for my prosperity.

But I deem it necessary to say that His Majesty speaks with great indistinction and in a very low tone so that I could not hear clearly all which he said. Since this Audience, I have been occupied every day with taking leave of the different members of this numerous royal family, in formal audiences of a similar character with that of the King. They are all amicable and have treated me with uniform kindness. But for the most part they know very little about America and rarely speak of it. Our ships of war which come here excite their interest and they accordingly ask questions about our navy and commercial marine. In my interview with the Prince of Salerno he asked me some questions about our Steamers. When I told him we had eight hundred upon the Mississippi, he looked at me with great astonishment, and, I presume he did not believe one word of it.

Having now finished the royal audiences today, I delivered my letter of recall and took leave of the Prince of Scilla.

It is with much regret that I shall depart from Naples, without seeing my successor. I fear his position will be at first, a little embarrassing. To relieve him as much as lay in my power, I have addressed him a letter which I have left with the Consul, in which I have taken the liberty of making a free communication to him on the subject of the forms and ceremonies and various other things connected with this Court & this Legation, which it will be important to him to know and difficult to learn when there is no teacher. You are, doubtless, well aware of the inevitable embarrassments to which a representative of the United States is subjected who comes abroad for the first time in charge of a Legation. These difficulties are much enhanced in this Court by the character of the individual charged with the Portfolio of Foreign Affairs.

I have one more regret in leaving this Legation, that I have not had the honor of receiving any communication from the Department, since you have been called to preside over it. But you had reason to believe that I had left here, and since information has been received to the contrary, there has not been time. I cherish the hope that my course has met with your approbation.

My accounts are enclosed up to this date and also a list of the books left with the Consul.[85]

---

[85] This list numbered 668 volumes, large and small, their manner of counting being different from that of Mr. Throop. See enclosure with No. 28, p. 596 following.

Account of Books left in my possession[86] by W. Boulware Esqr.
Chargé d'Affaires of the United States at Naples and belonging
to the U. S.

State papers[87] ....Vols. 177.
Executive documents .... "   86.[88]
Senate documents .... " 120.
House Journals, Reports, &c. .... " 107.
Weekly Register with Index[89] .... "   52.
American Archives.[90] .... "   5.

---

[86] Another of the inventories of books, documents and other property of the
Government, always made by a departing diplomatic representative for the information both of his successor and of the State Department. As volumes were
constantly added to the reference resources of the men in posts abroad these lists
grew apace. This particular inventory seems of particular importance, for it reveals not only that the chargé was being given a far more intimate knowledge
of the acts, debates, and attitudes of the legislative and executive branches of
the United States Government, but also because it gives for the first time the
titles of several of the then most used reference books included in all the earlier
lists. The tendency to use short titles, or familiar terms of reference to well
known books of their day, makes complications for those who would study these
lists bibliographically with any degree of accuracy and understanding of what they
meant to the education of the diplomatic agents of the United States Government.
The books being published in early years of the nation's history are not as well
known today, either as to their exact titles, manner of publication or especially
as to their contents as they ought to be. Hence the added details in these present
bibliographic notes.

[87] *State Papers* were first published, much as the laws were, in 'separates' or
'slip' publication form. At considerably later dates they were combined in various
official pamphlet collections. The collections of Peter Force, of Thos. B. Wait and
Sons, and of Gales and Seaton all bore the designation *State Papers,* while other
collections, containing in whole or in part the same documents as the aggregates
bound up by these three publishers, bore less generic titles. The count of 177 here
set against *State Papers* inclines one to believe that here are several sets of the 'slip'
form, possibly of Force, or of Wait's printing, rather than the known 21 volumes
of the Gales and Seaton set, although these last named may have been included in
the count.

[88] The same apparently excessive (duplicating?) counts appear against the next
three items listed. It would seem here that these were the paper-covered 'session printings' of individual 'volumes' of the various kinds of documents published by order of Congress, later published again for the bound up 'public documents series,' which would have been much fewer, as several of the pamphlet-
groups (called at first volumes I, II, etc., of 'Executive Documents') are later
bound up together in the leather bound books of the 'Public Documents Series.'
These differences of binders' forms lead to much confusion among persons un-
familiar with the printing practices of Congress.

[89] Probably *Niles' Weekly Register* which was subscribed to for the use of all
government departments, and for each of the legations abroad. It carried regularly, and very promptly, carefully printed records of the debates and proceedings of Congress, together with much general and special news of the country.
It was published in Baltimore, Md.

[90] *American Archives. A diplomatic History of the American Revolution.*
Edited by Peter Force, who was at one time the Mayor of Washington City, and
a notable publicist. See this title also in Mr. Throop's inventory list, and note
thereto appended. See *hic opus,* p. 515, note 150.

Diplomatic Correspondence[91] .... '' 19.

Laws of the U. S. with 2 indexes
    irregular (several duplicates)[92] .... '' 16.

Congressional Debates[93] .... '' 16.

Seybert's Statistical Annals[94] .... '' 1.

Commercial Regulations[95] .... '' 3.

U. S. Biennial Register of 1838[96] .... '' 1.

Pitkin's Statistical View[97] .... '' 1.

Books of Census & Statistics of 1840[98] .... '' 4.

Puffendorf[99] .... '' 2.

Blank Books (red cover) .... '' 3.

Eliot's Diplomatic Code[100] .... '' 2.

---

[91] Jared Sparks edited the *Diplomatic Correspondence of the American Revolution*. See notes on this in Mr. Throop's list.

[92] Laws . . . with 2 indexes. The Bioren & Duane edition. See Mr. Throop's list.

[93] *The Register of Debates of Congress* (binder's title, *Congressional Debates*) *as reported for the United States Telegraph, revised and corrected by suggestions of the Speakers. 23d Congress, 1st session. Washington, Duff Green, 1834.* (Also another Duff Green edition, 1834, with slightly different contents.) A better known work, published the same year, was *Debates and Proceedings of Congress, with appendix containing State Papers and public documents and all laws of public nature. With index, vols. 1 and 2, March 3, 1789-March 3, 1791,* published 1834. Other volumes subsequently. Compiled from authentic materials by Joseph Gales. Washington, printed and published by Gales & Seaton, 1834. Large 8°. Vol. 1 in this edition, also vol. 2, contained the same general coverage of materials as the *Annals of Congress,* with certain notable variations therefrom (q.v. *Check List of Government Documents,* p. 1493). It is not clear which of these editions had been sent to Mr. Boulware, nor does the Throop list make the matter clear. See later inventories also.

[94] For *Seybert's Statistical Annals* and continuation of same, see Mr. Throop's inventory, *hic opus,* Throop chapter, p. 513.

[95] Probably three different issues of this publication, then being issued under State Department auspices.

[96] This work called by Mr. Throop, more familiarly, and as contemporaneously known then in Washington circles (as it is today) the "Blue Book." See *hic opus,* Throop chapter, inventory, p. 513 ff.

[97] Pitkin's, also listed in Mr. Throop's inventory, was a volume of commercial statistics of the United States.

[98] The Sixth Census of the United States summarized population data, etc.

[99] The 1712 edition of the Amsterdam text in French, annotated by Barbeyrac. This edition, purchased abroad by John Nelson, when chargé at Naples, had been translated into English, by Chitty, in London, and subsequently had been several times republished in America by P. H. Nicklin & T. Johnson, of Philadelphia. It is probable, therefore, that the second volume here mentioned in Boulware's list turned over to Hammett's care, is the 6th edition of the American issue of Nicklin & Johnson, which was published in 1844. Vattel's much older commentary, and full text of Puffendorf, had received American publication as early as 1796.

[100] See Throop chapter, *hic opus,* p. 512, for full note on this work of Jonathan Elliot. This work contained treaties, etc., 1787-1827 (vol. I); and 1827-1834 (vol. II); the same volumes as Mr. Throop brought over with him. See *hic opus,* Throop chapter, p. 511 ff. For interesting biographical details regarding Jonathan Elliot, the editor, and printer of this and many other government works of his era, see the *Dictionary American Biography.* 1931, VI, 92-93,

U. S. Almanack of 1845[101] .... " 1.
American D°. . . . 1842 .... " 1.
Almanack of the Two Sicilies for 1840 .... " 1.
Acts 1ˢᵗ. Sess. 28ᵗʰ. Congress[102] .... " 1.
D°. 2 D°. 27ᵗʰ D°[103] .... " 1.
Other Pamphlets unbound .... " 48.

N°. 668[104]

In all six hundred and sixty-eight large and small.

Naples 24 June 1845.

Alex. Hammett.[105]

In duplicate.

where his surname, contrary to his own signatures as printed by himself, is spelled with two "t's." Elliot was born 1784; died 1846; see also *Appleton's Cyclopedia of American Biography,* 1888, II, 331.

[101] Sometimes called *Disturnell's United States Almanac & National Register.* This work was published under various titles. In 1850, it bore the designation *United States Almanack and National Register;* from 1873-1874, it was called *United States Register or Blue Book;* from 1876-1877 it was called *American Register or Blue Book;* published by John Disturnell, compiler, Philadelphia, 1872-1876. This work was the predecessor of the *United States Register* (Biennial) called *Blue Book* from its fine dark blue morocco binding chosen for its durability under constant handling in government offices. It contained the names of principal civil officers of the federal government, the army and navy lists, political and state information, also data on the territories of the United States. Under earlier titles Disturnell published the work to 1877, including maps of great interest abroad.

[102] This and the succeeding item in this list represent the *Session Laws* edition of the acts of these Congresses, which preceded, in point of time of issuance, those found in the *Public Documents Series,* as did these latter precede the final publication in the *United States Statutes at Large.* Each edition was potent as text of the law until the succeeding edition came from the press. Fewer typographical variations and other differences today exist between these several editions of the Acts of Congress than occurred in those early days when Congress was dependent upon a number of independent printeries in order to secure the quantity of such documents as were needed for the public needs. See also note 154, Throop chapter, p. 516, *hic opus* for further notes on the issues of the laws.

[103] These 48 unbound pamphlets probably were the earlier *Session Laws,* as all other publications of the Congresses are accounted for in the high counts for the first four items on the Boulware-Hammett listing.

[104] This reduction in the total count of the Legation library contents, as compared with the Throop list, does not necessarily mean loss of part of said contents but rather that the men who listed the same did not similarly identify 'volumes' in the process of counting. In later years this was rectified, in practice, by an order from the State Department that volumes must be listed in a certain manner, uniformly, by each successive incumbent of the legation posts.

[105] Hammett received the papers and books, etc., of the United States Legation at Naples each time the departing and the incoming diplomat for that post failed to meet. Hammett was the consul at Naples, for over 44 years; occasionally he was deputed to act as chargé d'affaires *ad interim.* See *hic opus,* Hammett chapter.

WILLIAM HAWKINS POLK[1]
(March 13, 1845-August 31, 1847)

J. Buchanan to Wm. H. Polk

Department of State, Washington, 22nd. April, 1845.
[Instruction No. 1.]

Sir: I transmit to you the following papers necessary to your entrance upon the discharge of the duties of the mission to which the President, by and with the advice and consent of the Senate, has appointed you:

1. Your commission as Chargé d'Affaires of the United States near the Government of the Two Sicilies.

2. A special passport for yourself and suite.

3. A letter of credit on the Bankers of the United States in London, authorizing them to pay your drafts for your salary as it becomes due, with the contingent expenses of the mission actually incurred, which however, are limited to the sum of five hundred dollars per annum. In availing yourself of this authority, you will be careful not to exceed, in the amount drawn for, the sums to which you may be entitled in account with the United States, at the respective dates of your drafts. You will designate in your drafts the accounts upon which they may be drawn, stating particularly, whether they are for salary, or for contingent expenses. And if you draw for both, you will name the respective amount which are chargeable to each account.

4. A letter of credence addressed to the Minister of Foreign Affairs of the Two Sicilies.

5. A full power.

6. A set of printed personal instructions with a supplement, prescribed by the Department of State for the government of all

---

[1] William Hawkins Polk (1815-1862) of Tennessee, brother of James Knox Polk. William studied law at the University of Tennessee and was admitted to the bar in 1839. He practised law in Columbia, Tenn. He was a member of the state house of representatives, 1842-45. On March 13, 1845, he was commissioned chargé d'affaires at Naples, holding this office until Aug. 31, 1847, when he resigned to serve in the Mexican war. He was commissioned Major of the Third Dragoons, and served until July 20, 1848. He was elected to the 32nd Congress, 1851-53. He then returned to the practice of law. *Biographical Dictionary of American Congress,* United States Government Printing Office, 1928, p. 1420. For a brief account of Polk's mission to Naples: see, Howard R. Marraro, "William H. Polk's mission to Naples, 1845-47." *Tennessee Historical Quarterly,* Nashville, Tenn., Sept. 1945, IV, 222-231.

the Diplomatic Representatives of the United States abroad; and to these instructions your attention is specially directed.

7. A printed list of the Diplomatic and Consular Agents in Foreign countries.

Your compensation, as fixed by law, is at the rate of four thousand five hundred dollars per annum. By a general rule, the compensation of Ministers to foreign courts is made to commence on the day of their leaving their residence to prepare for their departure on their mission, and to cease on their taking leave of the Courts to which they are accredited, after having received orders or permission to return. In your case, it will commence on the 10th. instant.

I transmit, herewith, a letter from the President of the United States, to His Majesty Ferdinand II, King of the Kingdom of the Two Sicilies, &c. &c. in reply to a communication from His Majesty, of the 25th. of November last, announcing the marriage of the Princess Donna Maria Carolina Augusta, daughter of His Royal Highness the Prince of Salerno, to His Royal Highness the Duke D'Aumale, Son of His Majesty the King of the French. You will avail yourself of an early occasion, after the presentation of your letter of credence, to convey to His Majesty's Principal Secretary of State for Foreign Affairs, the accompanying copy of the President's letter, and take the proper measures to deliver in person, or to transmit the original, in the manner most agreeable to His Majesty's wishes, as they may be made known to you by his Minister.

It is more than probable that your predecessor, will have left Naples before your arrival there, having been placed at liberty to do so, as soon after a despatch to him on the subject, dated on the 3rd of February, last, and numbered 17, could reach him. He was, in that event, instructed therein, to leave the archives and property of the United States in the Legation, in the hands of M^{r}. Hammett, the U. S. Consul at Naples, or in the hands of some other trustworthy American citizen, to be carefully preserved, until further orders. A letter has been addressed by this Department to M^{r}. Hammett, upon this subject. Of this property, you will make an inventory, and forward a copy of it to this Department.

Instructions given to your predecessor, so far as they are applicable, or may remain unexecuted, are to be considered by you as a part of your own. Further instructions will be sent to you from time to time, as occasion may appear to demand.

J. BUCHANAN TO WM. H. POLK

Department of State, Washington, 24th. April, 1845
[Instruction No. 2]

Sir: The Government of the United States has given the strongest evidence of its desire to maintain the most friendly relations with his Sicilian Majesty, by still continuing their mission at Naples, although his Majesty has never accredited any Diplomatic Agent to this country. This want of mutuality in the relations between the two Governments cannot long continue. The usual courtesy observed between independent nations requires that there should be a reciprocity in their diplomatic intercourse; and you may informally communicate to His Sicilian Majesty's Government, that such is the feeling entertained by the President of the United States.

The successive Representatives of the United States at Naples have been instructed, if possible, to negotiate a commercial Treaty with His Sicilian Majesty's Government. Whilst they have pursued this object with diligence, neither of them has ever yet succeeded even in drawing from the Minister of Foreign Affairs a single note upon the subject. All that has transpired between them, and him, have been informal and unsatisfactory conversations, without any result.

That no obstacle has existed during the last quarter of a century to prevent the Sicilian Government from placing our commercial relations on the same footing with those of England, appears conclusively from the Treaty, signed at London on the 26th. September 1816, between Great Britain and the Two Sicilies. Whilst that Treaty, by its Seventh article, and by the separate and additional article, of the same date, makes a reduction of ten per cent from the amount of the duties payable upon the total of the merchandize or production of the United Kingdom of Great Britain and Ireland, her Colonies, possessions, and dependencies, imported into the States of his Said Sicilian Majesty, it expressly provides, "that nothing in this article shall be construed to prevent the King of the Two Sicilies from granting, if he shall think proper, the same reduction of duty to other foreign nations." The same reduction of duty has been granted to France and Spain; though the commerce of the latter Kingdom, with Naples, is quite insignificant. You will thus perceive that, if an American and a British vessel enter any of the port of the Two

Sicilies together, freighted with similar productions of their respective countries, whilst these American productions are subject to an impost of fifty per cent ad valorem, those of Great Britain are charged with only forty five per cent. By some strange mistake, the impression seems heretofore to have prevailed, that His Sicilian Majesty was bound by Treaty in such a manner to Great Britain, France, and Spain, as to preclude him from placing the commerce of the United States on the same level with that of these favored nations. You will be furnished with a copy of the Treaty and separate additional article, of 1816, together with the Decree of His Sicilian Majesty, to give them effect, extracted from MacGregor's Commercial Tariffs and Regulations,[2] &c., volume second.

It appears from a review of the correspondence of Mr. Boulware, your immediate predecessor, with this Department, that the Governments of Great Britain, and the Two Sicilies, have been for some years engaged in framing a new Commercial Treaty. It was to have been hoped, as well from the early portion of that correspondence as the enlightened spirit of the age, that Great Britain would no longer have insisted upon the advantage of ten per cent which she had acquired over the United States by the Treaty of 1816. It would seem, however, from M^r. Boulware's despatch of September 13th. 1843, that the Treaty agreed upon between these two Powers, but not yet ratified, still retains this ten per cent advantage in favor of British productions imported in British vessels; although, for the rest, it is a reciprocal Treaty, so far as Navigation is concerned. The final execution of this Treaty has been suspended, to await the result of negotiations still pending between the Governments of France and the Two Sicilies; as it seems to be agreed that Great Britain and France shall be placed upon the same footing; and if French diplomacy can obtain greater concessions than those embraced in the Treaty with Great Britain, these are to become common to both the favored nations. Nay, more; if we have a correct understanding on this subject, these pending Treaties, should they be concluded would affect, still more injuriously, the interests of the United States than even the Treaties now in existence. At present, although American productions, imported into the Two Sicilies in American vessels, are subject to the unjust discrimination of

---

2 John MacGregor, *Commercial tariffs and regulations of the several states of Europe and America together with the commercial treaties between England and foreign countries.* London, 1841-50, 8 vols. See note 92, p. 459.

ten per cent in favor of British and French productions, and navigation, yet a reduction of 30 per cent is now made from the common rate of duties on American productions, when imported in Sicilian vessels. This discrimination, although intended alone to encourage Sicilian Navigation, operates indirectly in favor of our productions when brought into competition with those of a similar character of Great Britain and France. Should the pending Treaties be finally ratified, it is more than probable that we shall be deprived even of this advantage.

In view of these circumstances, you are instructed, at the earliest convenient moment after your arrival in Naples, to remonstrate respectfully, but strongly, in a diplomatic note, against the grant of any privileges to British and French navigation and commerce, in which the United States shall not equally participate; and to ask that our country shall enjoy the same advantages in the ports of the Two Sicilies, whatever they may be, which shall be extended to these two nations. In a separate note, you will respectfully request that the Sicilian Government may exercise its clear right reserved under its Treaty with Great Britain; and, by a Royal Decree, grant to American commerce and navigation the same privileges which are now extended to those of Great Britain and France. In making this request, you may state that, the President is anxious to receive an answer in time to be presented to Congress at the commencement of its next session. We trust, and believe that this answer will be favorable; but should his confident expectations be disappointed, it will then be for the wisdom of that Body to decide what countervailing discriminations ought, in justice, to be made against the productions of the Two Sicilies, imported into the United States. The ardent desire of the President to cultivate the most friendly relations with the Government of the Two Sicilies, causes him earnestly to hope that, after so long a delay, no necessity may exist to resort to any such commercial retaliation.

The Government of the United States have long desired to conclude a commercial Treaty with the Two Sicilies, they have been pursuing this object for years with a steady aim, and it is now time that they should know the final decision of the Sicilian Government upon the subject. They sincerely believe that such a Treaty would be equally beneficial to both countries. The United States seek no advantages over other nations. All they desire is, a perfect reciprocity in trade. The civilized world is now rapidly advancing towards this great principle; and experience has already demonstrated that its universal prevalence in practice, so far at least as regards the direct trade, would be beneficial to all nations. This policy was adopted at any early period by the Government of the United States; and has been developed before the World by the Acts of Congress of March 3ᵈ. 1815, January 7ᵗʰ. 1824, and May 24ᵗʰ 1828.[3]

The first of these Acts offers to all nations to admit their vessels laden with their productions, into the ports of the United States on the payment of the same duties of tonnage and import exacted from our own vessels; provided similar advantages shall be extended by them to American vessels. The Act of 1828, abolishes all restrictions in regard to the origin of the productions imported. Under it, the United States offer to throw wide open their ports to the vessels of all nations, with their cargoes, no matter to what country these cargoes may owe their origin, upon payment of the same duties with our own vessels; provided such nations shall extend similar privileges in their ports, to vessels and cargoes belonging to citizens of the United States.

You are authorised to conclude a Treaty of Commerce and navigation with the Government of the Two Sicilies upon the most liberal principles of reciprocity. It is more than probable, however, that the Sicilian Government would prefer to confine this reciprocity to the direct trade between the two Countries according to the provisions of the Act of March 3ᵈ. 1815; and with such a Treaty the United States would be entirely satisfied, provided Great Britain and France should be placed in the same position.

You will find models of a reciprocal Treaty of Commerce for your guidance, in every variety of form, in Elliott's American Diplomatic code,[4] now in the Library of your Legation. This will furnish you many precedents; as we have either concluded such Treaties, or made commercial arrangements of the same

---

[3] March 3, 1815. An act for the protection of the commerce of the United States against the Algerine cruisers. *Annals of Congress,* 13th Cong., 3rd sess., XXVIII, col. 1943.

Jan. 7, 1824. An act concerning discriminating duties of tonnage and impost. *Annals of Congress,* 18th Cong., 1st sess. House, XLII, col. 3193.

May 24, 1828. An act in addition to an act, entitled "An act concerning discriminating duties of tonnage and impost" and to equalize the duties on Prussian vessels and their cargoes. *Register of Debates in Congress,* 20th Cong., 1st sess., House, IV, pt. 2, appendix p. xxviii.

[4] Jonathan Elliot. *The American diplomatic code, embracing a collection of treaties and conventions between the United States and foreign powers from 1778 to 1834.* Washington, 1834. 2 volumes.

character, through the intervention of Legislation, with almost every civilised nation.

You can urge convincing arguments to the Government of His Sicilian Majesty, that such a Treaty would be highly advantageous to his Kingdom. Under the blighting influence of existing restrictions, the direct trade between the two countries is considerably less than it was some years ago; and falls very far short of what it would soon become under a fair reciprocal Treaty. Commerce always flourishes most between the two countries whose productions are different; because then they can mutually supply each other's wants. For this very reason, if the existing restrictions were removed, the commerce between the United States and the Two Sicilies, must rapidly increase, greatly for the benefit of both nations. We should then export to that country, our dried, smoked and salted fish; our cotton, rice, tobacco, naval stores, and other articles which I might enumerate, and receive in return their silks, wines, olive oil, fruits, Leghorn hats, sulphur, and crude brimstone, with many other Sicilian commodities. It is lamentable to reflect, that, a commerce which might be so mutually beneficial, is limited to such a comparatively small amount by unwise restrictions. Herewith, you will receive an abstract of this commerce, since the year 1834; prepared at the Treasury Department.[5]

Great reliance is placed on the zeal, discretion and ability with which you will devote yourself to accomplish the important objects of your mission; and good hopes are entertained that you will prove successful.

Wm. H. Polk to J. Buchanan

Legation of the United States, Naples, July 26th. 1845. [Despatch No. 1.]

Sir —

I arrived at Naples on the 18th. Inst. having made London and Paris in my route. — I remained in London two days and in Paris three weeks, making suitable and necessary arrangements for my residence at this Court. — From Paris I took the most direct and expeditious route to this place. — On the 23rd. Inst. I addressed a note to His Excellency the Prince of Scilla &c &c charged with the Portfolio of Foreign Affairs, apprising him of

---

[5] This extract does not accompany the letter.

my appointment by the President, of Chargé d'Affaires of the United States, at the Court of Naples, and requesting that he would indicate a day and hour when I could have the opportunity of presenting my letter of credence. — The day after the dispatch of my note I received an answer appointing the same day for that purpose. — At the hour designated, I waited on him at the Department of Foreign Affairs and was received with courtesy and proper civility. — After delivering my letter of credence, I also delivered the original and copy of the letter of the President of the United States, addressed to His Majesty Ferdinand II, with which I was charged, he having informed me that the usual course of such communication was through his hands. Our conversation was chiefly of a general character. He however, took occassion [sic] to mention without any remark or observation on my part calculated to elicit it, that he had very recently succeeded in negotiating treaties with England and France, but supposed his labors were not closed, as the United States would probably insist on making a treaty. — To which, I responded that we had for a number of years urged the necessity and represented the advantages which would result to the commerce of both Countries, by the adoption of liberal commercial regulation, and I presumed the treaties with England and France having been settled, no obstacle now interposed to delay action or prevent the attainment of the object. — In answer, he expressed an entire willingness, at this time, to negotiate a treaty with the United States, and turned the conversation from the subject. — I did not deem it prudent or proper, in this our first interview, being one more of form and ceremony than otherwise, to renew the conversation or revert to the subject again, for fear of imparting too much colour to our anxiety and thereby cripple future negotiation. — It may be well here to mention that the Prince of Scilla, who has the *honor* of being charged with the Portfolio of Foreign Affairs, is reputed to be a very feeble man, and is not usually *trusted* by the government with the exclusive control of any foreign negotiation, and possibly his expression of readiness and disposition to conclude a treaty, may not correctly reflect the views of the Government. But, when taken in connection with the general tone of the Dispatches and correspondence of his immediate predecessor, [sic] which looks to the ratification of treaties with England and France as removing the main difficulty which has heretofore forbid the entertainment of any proposition to establish commercial regulation with our country,

I am inclined to beleive, [sic] he in this case, correctly shadows the policy and disposition of this King and his advisers. — This opinion is further strengthened, by information derived from our estimable and intelligent Consul M^r. Hammett who from his long residence in this country is enabled to form reasonably correct opinions, that it is the policy of this Government, having been released through the recent Treaties from the secret trammels and obligations to England and France to extend their commerce to its full scope. — I trust this is true, and if so, no time shall be lost or exertion spared to frame such a treaty as will remove present restrictions and place our commerce on a fair field of competition with that of England and France.

In case the way is cleared, and the negotiation of a treaty entered upon, I fear that some difficulty will be encountered in obtaining a fair reduction of present duties exacted on our Cotton, Tobacco &c. imported into Sicily, and our Cotton &c. finding its way into the port of Naples, the Tobacco trade at Naples being a Government Monopoly yielding an annual revenue of near a Million of dollars, no hope can be entertained of effecting any change in existing regulations. — In Sicily no such influence opprerates [sic] to forbid a reduction, but I apprehend in asking such a reduction as will justify the importation of our Cotton, Naval stores &c. into Naples and our Tobacco Cotton and various other articles into the ports of Sicily, they may expect and demand in consideration a corresponding diminution of present duties imposed in the U. S. on their Wines, Sewing Silks, oils, &c. — I make the suggestion merely to call attention to a difficulty which will probably be presented.

The Prince of Scilla &c &c informed me that His Majesty was absent in Sicily and would not return to Naples for three or four weeks which will delay my *presentation* and necessarily prevent any official intercourse for that length of time, with the Minister of Foreign Affairs.

I send you with this Dispatch a copy of the French & English treaties.[6]

---

6 This copy of treaties is not found with this letter in bound volume of original despatches.

Extracts from private letters of Wm. H. Polk[7] Chargé d'Affaires
at Naples —

From letter of 17 Sep. 1845.

"The prospect of making a treaty is encouraging, it is doubtful
what extent of reduction I will be able to secure on our cotton,
Tobacco &c if any at all, but hope to cut down present
duties to such rate as will permit the introduction of our products.
My despatch to the Department of State will explain what progress has been made in forming a treaty — The Minister of Foreign affairs by letter suggested that I would submit a detailed
or general proposition for a treaty — not being furnished by
the Government with the provisions of a treaty in detail I thought
it best to enclose the minister a copy of the treaty concluded between the United States & Austria, with additional articles providing for the reduction of duties on our products. This copy of
the treaty I merely submitted as presenting the general principles
which formed the basis of most of our treaties with other nations
and expressed a willingness to make a *similar treaty* if a proper
reduction of duties was granted. I give you the substance of the
correspondence hastily. The treaty with Austria[8] covers the
substance of my *instructions*. The treaty between this country
& England is confined to the direct trade and I will scarcely be
able to secure one possessing the feature of perfect and general
reciprocity, but must confine it to a direct trade — This my
instructions authorize me to do. I sent Mr. Buchanan a copy of
the English treaty with this country and suggested in case the
negotiation with the U. S. was commenced, that much difficulty
would be presented in securing a reduction of duties on our products imported into this Kingdom, which I hope will draw from
him some suggestions to govern me in the negotiation — Would
it do to make a treaty similar to the English without adhering
to the reduction of duties? We cannot expect them to grant us
any reductions unless we give them a corresponding reduction on
Wines, Oils, Sewing silk &c.

Extract from note of 28. Sept —

I have not as yet had an interview with the Commissioner
appointed by the King to negotiate a treaty with me, but expect

[7] These extracts are from letters that Mr. Polk wrote to the President. See
p. 614.

[8] Refers to the treaty of commerce and navigation between the United States
and Austria concluded August 27, 1829.

every day to be called on as in the note of the Minister of State giving me information of their appointment he reserved the right to name when the commission should begin. My *despatch* to the State Department sent a few days ago will give you full information. The delay is occasioned by the meeting of the scientific Congress which convened in Naples on the 15th Inst. Since then every thing has been laid aside for pleasure — it will adjourn on 5th Oct. after which I may expect to commence the negotiation. I don't think there will be much difficulty in making the treaty; I hope not at least — Excuse hasty note.

WM. H. POLK TO J. BUCHANAN

Legation of the United States Naples Sep^t. 28th. 1845

[Despatch No. 2] (*Duplicate*)[9]

Sir,

By my dispatch of the 26th. of July I had the honor to inform you of my arrival at Naples, and of the absence of the King in Sicily, which would delay all official intercourse with the Minister of Foreign Affairs until his return to this capital and the formality of my presentation to His Majesty was observed. He returned to Naples on the 17th. Augt. and on 22^d. I was by the Minister of Foreign Affairs presented. — From the declaration of the Minister of State on the occassion [sic] of the delivery of my letter of credence, that a readiness and willingness existed on the part of this Government to form commercial regulation with the United States, considered in connection with the contents of the last dispatch of my immediate predicessor, [sic] I considered the time highly favorable to solicit attention to the subject and accordingly on the 26th. addressed the following note to the Minister in charge of the Portfolio of Foreign Affairs.

Legation of the United States Naples Augt. 28th. 1845

"To His Excellency the Prince of Scilla &c &c

"The undersigned Chargé d'Affaires of the United States of America being vested by his Government with full powers to negotiate a treaty of Commerce and navigation with the Kingdom

---

9 This is the *duplicate* referred to as sent May 4, 1846 (see p. 621). Mr. Polk's Despatch No. 4. A notation on top of the page, signed by Mr. Markoe, the clerk, shows that this duplicate copy of the despatch was received in Washington on June 16, 1846.

609

of the Two Sicilies, requests the privilege of an interview with His Excellency the Prince of Scilla &c &c at such time as it may please His Excellency to designate, that he may learn the disposition of His Majesty's Government on the subject. —

"The undersigned renews the assurance of his distinguished consideration."

"William H. Polk"

I did not deem it necessary in the above note to assay any arguments in favor of the formation of a Commercial Treaty between the Two Countries, or suggest the great advantages which would flow therefrom, to both Nations, my object being merely to open the subject, and if possible either elicit an answer expressive of the views of the King, or secure an interview by which I might learn his intentions, leaving my course to be shaped by the information obtained. On the 9th Inst. I received the following note in reply: —

(Translation)

The Undersigned Minister of State, charged with the Port Folio of Foreign Affairs, having made it a duty to submit to the King his August Master the note of the 26th. of the present month of August, by which M^{r}. Polk Chargé d'Affaires of the United States of America made known that he was furnished with the full powers of his Government to negotiate a treaty of commerce and navigation with the Kingdom of the Two Sicilies. — His Majesty has received such communication with lively complaicency [sic] and His Majesty calculating all the advantages which the two Countries may derive from a convention tending to regulate and extend between the same the relations of Commerce, has authorized the Secretaries M. Cav°. D. Gustino [sic] Fortunato, and the Prince of Comitino, and also the Commendatore D. Austonio [sic] Spinilli [sic] member of the Consulate Chamber and Director General of the Archives of the Kingdom, to enter into negotiation with M^{r}. Polk Chargé d'Affaires &c &c for the object.[10] The undersigned in making this known to M^{r}. Polk &c &c reserves to let him know the day on which the

---

10 An official copy in Italian of the royal decree appointing the commission of three persons is in the Archives of the American Embassy, Rome, which now have been transferred to the custody of the United States National Archivist in Washington, D.C. The decree is signed by King Ferdinand and Fulco Ruffo di Calabria, Prince of Scilla (1773-1852). Councillor of state. Ambassador to Spain. From March 1840 to February 1848, he was Minister of Foreign Affairs of the Kingdom of Two Sicilies.

Commissioners may begin, and in the mean time he thinks it convenient to suggest should M^r. Polk Chargé d'Affaires &c &c have received from his Government any project of a Treaty or propositions in general, the negotiation might go on more expeditiously, if he would communicate them to the undersigned who in expectation of his reply profits with the pleasure of the occassion [sic] to repeat the protestation of his distinguished consideration.

(signed) Prince of Scilla, Duke of S. C^{na}.

Desiring to take advantage of every means which might tend to expedite the negotiation and not having been furnished by the Department of State with any "project" of a treaty in detail, I considered it best not to defer the negotiation until a specific proposition could be received from the Government, but to submit in answer to the suggestion contained in the note of the Prince of Scilla &c &c a copy of the existing treaty between the United States and Austria, *attatching* [sic] thereto the substance of other *Articles* providing for the reduction of present duties exacted on the produce of our Country in this Kingdom. — In submitting the Austrian Treaty I addressed the following note to the Minister of Foreign Affairs.

Legation of the U. S. Naples, Sep^t. 13th. 1845

To His Excellency the Prince of Scilla &c. &c.

The Undersigned Chargé d'Affaires of the United States in reply to the communication of His Excellency the Prince of Scilla, Minister of State, charged with the Port Folio of Foreign Affairs, of the 9th. Ins^t. has the honor herewith to transmit for the consideration of His Majesty's Plenopotentiaries [sic], a copy of the existing treaty between the United States and the Emperor of Austria together with the substance of other additional Articles. — This treaty fully presents the principles on which the Government of the United States has formed treaties with many other Nations, and on which basis it would be preferred to settle commercial regulations with the Kingdom of the Two Sicilies. The undersigned is pleased to learn that a disposition and readiness exists on the part of His Majesty to frame such liberal regulations as will encourage to more lively activity the commercial intercourse between the two countries and flatters himself that the importance of the subject will claim the early attention of His Majesty's Plenopotentiaries [sic].

The undersigned profits of the occassion [sic] to renew to His Excellency the Prince of Scilla the assurance of his very high consideration.

(signed)   William H. Polk

Although, in submitting the Austrian treaty the principle of general and perfect reciprocity in trade is presented for consideration, there is I fear scarcely a probability that it will meet with favour or in any case be adopted, it being contrairy [sic] to the policy of this Government as exhibited by the recent treaties with England, France and Russia, copies of which, I had the honor to transmit with my dispatch N°. 1. — My instructions, however, authorize me to make a treaty confining the trade to the direct intercourse between the two countries, still, I will urge the policy of general reciprocity with the same earnestness and solicitude as if I possessed no reserve power, and if it cannot be obtained I may by conceding derive strength to some other point of difference, which may arise pending the negotiation involving advantage to our Commerce. I have delayed writing until the last hour to be in time for the Steamer sailing from Liverpool on the 11ᵗʰ. October, with the hope of having an interview with the Commissioners appointed to conduct the negotiation and be able to communicate some progress; but have been disapointed [sic]. This delay I am convinced does not proceed from any indifference to the importance of the subject or indisposition to conclude a treaty, but is occassioned [sic] by the conveining [sic] of the Scientific Congress of Italy at present holding its session in this City. — The Congress will ajourn [sic] on the 10ᵗʰ. Oct. soon after which I may expect to receive the "notice" when "the Commissioners may begin" the right to give which is reserved in the communication of the Prince of Scilla of the 9ᵗʰ. Insᵗ. The fact that Treaties have been recently concluded by this government with England, France, and Russia of a liberal character when compared with the suicidal policy hereterfore [sic] pursued, gives every encouragement to beleive [sic] that a similar course will be adopted toward the United States, as it most certainly evidences an awakening knowledge to the true interests of this Country and the birth of a new spirit to encourage their Commerce and extend their intercourse with the Nations of the World.

In my dispatch N°. 1 I suggested the probability of difficulty arising in the course of the negotiation from any demand for reduction of duties imposed on the produce of the soil and industry of the United States in the ports of this Kingdom, and from all I have since learned indirectly of the views of the Government my apprehensions in this respect are strengthened. — I am induced to beleive [sic] we cannot secure such reduction unless we are prepared to give in consideration similar ones applicable to Sicilian produce in the ports of our Country. — In regard to this question my instructions from the Department of State give me no direction, and without special instructions I am withheld from proposing to plant such an Article in any Treaty I may negotiate, however convinced I may be of the beneficial effects which would result to our commerce by such an arrangement, by the fate of the Zoll-verein Treaty which was rejected by the Senate a few years ago. As at present advised weighing the general advantages we will derive from a Treaty placing our commerce on an equal footing with the most favoured Nation, without any special provision for any Article or class of Articles the production of the United States, I will feel it my duty to conclude such a Treaty, unless instructed otherwise, rather than leave our commerce to labour under the oppressive exactions which at present cripples its activity and retards its prosperity. If stipulations of this character were once in full effect my impression is that the trade between the countries would in a few years grow so rapidly in importance that this government would be readily convinced of the propriety of removing all onerous embarrassments and afford full latitude to the interchange of commodities with the United States. When it is considered that the policy of the Government in this respect is in the first hours of its existence and consequently its developement [sic] restrained by timidity and extreme caution, it cannot be expected at once to reap all the advantages that will flow, when time shall have ripened the system and experience exhibited the substantial advantages which it possesses over the narrow policy that has for so many years stifled the commercial prosperity of this people. I would be greatly obliged if instructions were furnished me, directing my course on the subject of granting and receiving a reduction of duties. —

I have received no communication from the State Department since my arrival at Naples, and regret to state that I have not received a single number of the Washington Union, or any other Journal from Washington. —

J. BUCHANAN TO WM. H. POLK

Department of State, Washington, 12th. November 1845.
[Instruction N°. 5.]¹¹

Sir: Your despatch N°. 1, was received on the 5th. September; but no other despatch from you has yet come to hand. Since its date, (the 26th. July), we have learned nothing of your progress in the negotiation of the Treaty, except what you have communicated in your private letters to the President of the 17th. and 28th. of September. From these I find that, since the date of your despatch, (No. 1), you have forwarded one or more despatches; but neither of them has as yet reached the Department.

It would certainly be desirable that you should obtain if possible a stipulation in the proposed Treaty to reduce the existing duties in the Kingdom of the Two Sicilies on cotton, tobacco, or any other articles, of the production of the United States. This, in your opinion, you will not be able to accomplish without the grant of equivalents on our part. The fate of the Zoll-verein Treaty in the Senate, as well as the embarrassments with other nations with whom we have commercial Treaties, which would result from a reduction of duties by Treaty on the productions of that country, would prevent us from granting this equivalent required. For the present, therefore, you are instructed to conclude a Treaty without insisting upon a reduction of duties in the ports of the Two Sicilies on any of our productions. It is deemed of so much importance to obtain a commercial Treaty on the terms which we have adopted with other nations, that you will not delay its conclusion by insisting on any thing further. A reciprocal reduction of duties on the productions of the two countries may hereafter be accomplished under more propitious circumstances.

You acted correctly in presenting our Treaty with Austria as a model for that with the Neapolitan Government. It is probable, however, as you suggest, that they may not be willing to conclude such a Treaty of general commercial reciprocity with the United States. Their Treaty with Great Britain, which you have for-

---

11 This Instruction No. 5 is published in Buchanan, *The Works,* etc. VI, 307-308. The following communications were also sent to Mr. Polk: Circular No. 3, Washington, July 25, 1845, respecting Mr. Polk's contingent expenses. See, *Instructions to Ministers,* vol. *Spain,* 194; Instruction No. 4, Washington, September 19, 1845, Mr. Buchanan transmitted the commission of Charles Sherwood, appointed United States Consul at Messina.

warded to the Department, is limited to the direct trade, and it is not likely that they will be willing to grant us more extensive privileges.

I would, however, call your special attention to the 11th. article of the Neapolitan Treaty with Great Britain. By this it provided that the subjects of Great Britain shall continue to enjoy a reduction of ten per cent upon the duties payable according to their Customs' Tariff upon British Merchandize and productions; but it is also stipulated that the same privilege may be granted to other nations. You will insist upon a grant of this privilege to the United States to the full extent in which it is enjoyed by Great Britain; and conclude no treaty which does not clearly embrace such a provision.

There are several Treaties, confined to the direct trade between the United States and foreign countries, to which you may refer as models. I would instance that with Portugal of the 26th. August, 1840,[12] because it is our latest Treaty of this character. I transmit you a copy.

WM. H. POLK TO J. BUCHANAN

Legation of the United States, Naples, December 1, 1845. Copy[13]

Sir:

I have the honor to transmit, herewith, for ratification by the President, by and with the advice and consent of the Senate, a treaty of commerce and navigation,[14] which I have this day concluded and signed on the part of the United States with the Kingdom of the Two Sicilies, together with the full powers granted by the King to the plenipotentiaries whose names and seals are thereunto affixed. Throughout the negotiation I have endeavored and I hope successfully, to confine myself within the limits of my instructions from the Department of State. Every effort was made to secure a treaty of general and perfect reciprocity, embracing

---

12 For the text of the treaty of commerce and navigation between the United States and Portugal, concluded on August 26, 1840 see Miller, *op. cit.,* IV, 295-324.

13 Copy of this despatch is also in the Archives of the American embassy, Rome. See note 10, p. 615. A notation at the top of this despatch gives the following information: Source: 18 Regular Confidential Documents; U. S. Senate 27th-29th, Congresses; 1841-1846. [p. 512-14] p. 18-20.

14 For text of treaty of commerce and navigation concluded on Dec. 1, 1845 between the United States and the Kingdom of the Two Sicilies, see Miller, *op. cit.,* IV, 791-812. A copy of the text of the treaty was also located in the Archives of the American Embassy, Rome. See note 10, p. 615.

the productions of the soil and industry of every nation entering the ports of the Sicilies under the American flag, but without success. The recent treaties between this Kingdom and England, France, and Russia restrict their reciprocal commercial intercourse to the direct trade, and it could not be reasonably expected that this government would change its settled policy in this respect, and extend greater advantages to the United States than to other countries.

Prior to the conventions between the Two Sicilies and England, France, and Spain, concluded in 1816 and 1817, by which these three powers secured for the production of their respective countries a reduction of *ten per cent.* on the tariff of duties in the ports of this Kingdom, the vessels of the United States frequented all its ports, laden with cargoes the produce of our country, and in return took away cargoes the production of this country. The privilege of the *ten per cent.* being now equally extended to the United States, there is every reason to believe that the trade between the two countries will revive to the same activity which existed previous to 1816. For twenty-five years or more, an American vessel has been seldom seen to arrive in the port of Naples, though Palermo and Messina have been, and still continue to be, [sic] visited by our vessels on their return from Trieste, Marseilles, Genoa, and Leghorn, but it is always without cargoes,[15] and with money or bills to purchase fruit or other produce. Now that our vessels are not subjected to other or higher duties of tonnage than national vessels, and our productions are relieved from all differential duties, it may be expected in future that they will, instead of paying money, be able to exchange commodities. No means have been spared to get reduced the duty on cotton and tobacco; but as this government has, for many years, been steadfastly pursuing the encouragement of the cultivation of these articles, all that has been practicable has been done to reduce the duty on cotton from *twenty ducats* per cantar[16] which is about one hundred and ninety pounds English weight, to *ten ducats;* and as the duty on tobacco was found to have been reduced in the last year from *twenty-eight* ducats per cantar, which it has for many years paid, to *fifteen ducats,* they could not be induced to make any further diminution. It has not

---

15 Blunt, *op. cit.,* 699, states: "American vessels rarely enter the ports of the Sicilies except in ballast."

16 Cantar here is equivalent to 190 English pounds for here it is a *cantaro* of cotton. Elsewhere, and for different kinds of materials, such as grains, tobacco, nuts, etc., the *cantaro* has various other equivalent English weights.

been possible to change their system for the article of tobacco at Naples; it being a government monopoly, yielding an annual revenue of nearly a million of dollars, they cannot be induced to alter the regulation. I do not think, however, that the consumption of American tobacco is the less on this account, for the persons or company who contract for the exclusive privilege of introducing the article into Naples import large quantities, either directly from the United States, or indirectly, as it suits best where to make their purchases. There exists, also, a differential duty on the exportation of oil[17] between national and the vessels of nations with whom they have no treaty regulations. This will now cease with regard to us, and it may be that vessels of the United States will find freights of this and other articles for the north of Europe as well as the United States. The tonnage duty heretofore exacted from American vessels of *forty grains*[18] per ton, and which, according to their manner of measurement, is equal to *forty cents,* is now reduced to *four grains.* This obstacle to many merchant vessels touching the ports of this Kingdom being now removed, is of no small importance when it is considered that from eighty to one hundred of our vessels load annually in Sicily. It may be that the tonnage of only six cents per ton on Sicilian vessels in the United States, and the extra duty of *ten per cent.* levied on the cargoes of vessels belonging to nations with whom we have no fixed commercial regulations, may serve to increase the number of their vessels in the ports of our country, but still they can never reach that of our vessels which will visit the Two Sicilies. The tariffs of each country have not been altered in else than to place each nation on a footing of national, or the most favored. They always answered to any demand for reduction of their duties, "We cannot change ours, increase yours if you think proper." When, however, they will have concluded treaties now in progress with other nations, I am assured their tariff will be revised, and such changes made as may seem advantageous to their new system of liberal commercial intercourse with the world. Being now placed on an equal

---

17 Olive oil.

18 The citation of 40 grains as equivalent to 40 United States cents is rather an approximation and is open to challenge in the light of the cambist tables of contemporary date. Moreover, there was no direct exchange between Naples and the United States of America; the exchange was only via London, Paris, Amsterdam, etc. It is possible that Mr. Polk had not as yet sufficient knowledge of the Neapolitan currency, nor of the 'money of accounts,' nor of the difference between Naples and Sicily rates of exchange, nor even that they had an exchange rate between the two parts of the Kingdom of the Two Sicilies.

footing with national vessels, or those of the most favored nations, it depends on our merchants and captains to contend in a field of fair competition, and I believe they will do it successfully, from their known intelligence and activity. You will discover by the twelfth article of the treaty that it takes effect from the day it bears date. This I was induced to adopt by the urgent solicitation of our consul at Palermo. This being the season of the year when American vessels chiefly visit the Kingdom of the Two Sicilies, it was considered desirable to give them the advantages of treaty regulations, which would relieve them from the existing burden of tonnage and other duties; of course, the old rate of duties will be exacted until the treaty shall have been ratified and exchanged by both the contracting parties, as provided by the twelfth article, subject to be refunded.

By my despatch No. 2, I had the honor to furnish you with the substance of the correspondence with the Minister for Foreign Affairs which preceded and led to the opening of the negotiation. My quarterly accounts I sent with my last despatch. I received the commission of Charles Sherwood, recently appointed United States Consul for Messina, and enclosed it to the Minister for Foreign Affairs, as directed to receive the necessary exequatur, but have not as yet received any answer.

The irregularities of the mails between Naples and Paris, at this particular season of the year, are such as to render the safe transmission of a document, the size of a treaty, very uncertain, and I have therefore deemed it my duty to carry it myself as far as Paris, from whence it can be safely sent to the United States. I will remain a few days only in Paris before returning to Naples.

Enclosures:

[The full powers to Italian negotiators, and the Treaty with Great Britain are not reproduced in this printing.]

J. BUCHANAN TO WM. H. POLK

Department of State, Washington, 14th. March, 1846.

[Instruction No. 6.][19]

Sir: I transmit, herewith copy of a letter from Messrs. Charles & Henry Borie,[20] of Philadelphia, dated on the 27th. of October last, in which it is stated, that, under a law, in favor of national vessels of the Two Sicilies, making a reduction of 30 per cent on the duties upon goods when imported in Neapolitan vessels, (in which law was reserved the right of abolishing said privilege, after six months previous notice), their firm had recently shipped to Naples sundry merchandise, which was entitled to this privilege. But the Sicilian Government having abolished it without due notice, the Messrs. Borie had been precluded therefrom, and full duties had been exacted upon the merchandise shipped by them upon the faith of that law: whereby they have suffered heavy loss. Under these circumstances they have asked the intervention of this Government for their protection.

I have, therefore, to request, that you will examine into the facts; and, should they be as stated, make the proper representation to the Sicilian Government in behalf of the parties interested. They have already been informed that you would be instructed on the subject, and have been directed, to transmit to you, all necessary information in relation to their claim.

No despatches have been received from you, at this Department, except that of the 26th of July, N°. 1, and that of the 1st December.[21] The latter was accompanied by the Treaty[22] con-

---

[19] Instruction No. 6 is published in Buchanan, *Works*, VI, 409-410.

[20] Charles and Henry Borie obtained their mercantile education in the counting room of their father's business. He was the senior member of the firm Borie, Keating & Laguerenne who were manufacturers of cotton prints. After the death of their father, Charles and Henry branched out for themselves as sugar dealers and had their offices on Front Street in Philadelphia. However, this business venture was a failure and they were reputed to have lost their entire fortune which was left to them by their father. About the time they retired a Frenchman by the name of Audrade who had a very excellent business as a note broker and banker decided to retire. Thus Charles and Henry Borie succeeded him. The firm was organized about 1857, and had offices on Walnut Street in front of the Exchange in Philadelphia. The brothers' business was not successful. They entered very heavily into the railroad financing business and for many years were intimately connected with the Reading Railroad and the Jersey Central. (The editor is indebted to R. N. Williams, 2nd, Director of the Historical Society of Pennsylvania, 1300 Locust Street, Philadelphia, Pennsylvania, for this information).

[21] No. 1, July 26, 1845, see above, p. 605; Dec. 1, 1845, see above, p. 615, this chapter.

[22] See Miller, *op. cit.*, IV, 791-812 for text of treaty concluded Dec. 1, 1845.

cluded and signed by you in the same day, — which was communicated to the Senate on the 28th. January.[23]

J. BUCHANAN TO WM. H. POLK

Department of State, Washington, 14th. April, 1846.
[Instruction No. 7.][24]

Sir: I transmit to you, with this despatch, a ratified copy of the
Treaty of Commerce and Navigation between the United States
of America and His Majesty the King of the Kingdom of the
Two Sicilies, concluded and signed by you, at Naples, on the 1st.
day of December last; which has been approved and ratified by
the President, by and with the advice and consent of the Senate.
I transmit, at the same time, a special power from the President,
authorising you to exchange the ratifications of the Treaty.

The time limited for this exchange having so nearly expired,
the President has thought it expedient to commit the Treaty to
the care of M^r. Washington Greenhow, as special Bearer of
Despatches, who will be directed to proceed without any delay to
Naples, for the purpose of placing it, and this despatch, in your
hands. Mr. Greenhow will also be instructed to take charge of the
exchange copy of the Treaty, which you will be pleased to deliver
to him for this Department.

No despatch has been received from you since that of the 1st.
of December last, (which is not numbered),[25] nor any other,
except a previous one of the 26th. of July, which is numbered 1.
You are particularly requested to transmit by Mr. Greenhow
copies of any other despatches which you may have written; and
you will be careful, in future, to number regularly all your
despatches, and to conform in all other respects to your personal
instructions.

---

[23] See *Executive Journal of the Senate* for this and succeeding dates; also the
Debates of Congress.
[24] This Instruction No. 7 was published in Buchanan, *Works*, VI, 450-451.
[25] This counts as No. 2 in the Polk series of despatches.

J. Buchanan to Washington Greenhow

Department of State, Washington, 14th. April, 1846.
[Instruction, Unnumbered]

Sir: The President has selected you as a Bearer of Despatches from this Department to M[r]. William H. Polk, the Chargé d'Affaires of the United States at Naples. These despatches are to be delivered without delay; and you, will, therefore, proceed with them in your charge to New York and embark in the packet of the 16th. instant, or, if that be not possible, in the first or quickest conveyance for the nearest and most convenient port on the route for your place of destination. It is necessary that you should reach Naples by the 1st June or earlier, if possible, as the exchange of the ratifications of the Treaty of Commerce and Navigation between the United States and the Two Sicilies, of which you are the Bearer, is, by an article of the Treaty, to be made on or before that day. On your arrival at Naples, you will immediately deliver to M[r]. Polk, or, in his absence, to M[r]. Alexander Hammett, the Consul of the U. S. at Naples, the documents committed to your care, and return to the U. S. by the first opportunity; bringing with you the exchange copy of the Treaty, and such letters and papers as shall be entrusted to you by M[r]. Polk.

Your compensation will be $6 per day from the time of your leaving this city until your return, and all your necessary travelling expenses, actually incurred, of which, you will keep a regular account, to be sustained by vouchers where they can be procured. This allowance must not be understood to include your expenses during your detention at Naples. The sum of $900 will be advanced to you on account.

Wm. H. Polk to J. Buchanan

Legation of the United States Naples May 5th. 1846 [Despatch No. 4]

Sir —

I have the honor to transmit herewith a copy[26] of my lost or missing dispatch of the 28th. of September last. I cannot account for its loss or delay, having mailed at the same time other communications of a private nature, all of which I have been advised

---

26 This "copy" will be found on page 609.

reached their destination in due time, and I still hope the dispatch has been ere this received. —

My dispatch of the 28th of Sep^t. contains all the correspondence which took place preceding the negotiation of the Treaty which I had the honor to forward to the Department of State in December last for the approbation of the President and Senate, — no question of difficulty having originated during the negotiation requiring the exchange of communications in writing. —

A few weeks ago a Sicilian Merchant Vessel returned to Naples, having entered one of the ports of the United States after the 1st. day of December, when the new rate of duties are to receive effect, as provided by the 12th. Article of the Treaty, and complained that the Vessel and Cargo were subjected to the old rate of duties. — Concerning this complaint I received no official or other communication from the Minister of State, but learned from our worthy and excellent Consul M^r. Hammett that some disatisfaction [sic] existed and fearing lest the Government might possibly participate in the discontent or had fallen into some error as to the agreed meaning of the 12th. Article of the Treaty, I took occassion [sic]) a few days after, a good opportunity occurring [sic] to allude to the circumstance when in conversation with one of the gentlemen who was engaged in the negotiation, and from him learned that the exaction of the old rate of duties was expected, until the ratifications were exchanged, when according to the clearly understood meaning of the 12th. Article all duties which had been levied and received by either Government over and above the rate settled by the Treaty, should on application in proper form, being made, be refunded — to which I assented — such being the distinct agreement when the date was fixed from which time the provisions of the Treaty should take quallified [sic] effect. — He in the course of the conversation expressed some doubt of the ratification by the Government of the United States, and intimated that His Majesty participated in his doubts, arising altogether from the fact that we had in former years so urgently represented the advantages of similar commercial regulation — that the six months alowed [sic] for the exchange of the ratification had nearly expired, and that no action had been taken on the subject. — I stated to him that all the information I had received left scarcely a doubt in my mind but that the Treaty would be ratified — that it had been by the President submitted to the Senate for its approbation and I had good reason to expect it before the six months elapsed — and further, that it could not have escaped his attention or that of His Majesty that questions connected with our Foreign relations of a deeply interesting character had claimed the attention of our Congress, and in this might probably be found reasonable cause for the delay which had given existence to his doubts. — He expressed himself satisfied, and remarked in the absence of all information it was reasonable to entertain doubt, but was pleased to learn that no good cause existed for apprehension — I hope the Treaty if approved by the Senate will arrive before the expiration of the six months, for I entertain an indefinite fear that the King may possibly be disposed to take advantage of any circumstance which relieves him from direct obligation to refuse his sanction to the Treaty. — this unsettled fear is not founded on any information received, or even rumors in circulation, but from the stated character of His Majesty, to be governed, frequently in questions of the gravest importance, by impulse, or the wayward disposition of the moment. —

I have received, from the Department of State, Dispatches[27] N°. 5 and 6 — the first communicating *instructions,* in answer to the request contained in my dispatch N°. 2, and also in my private letters to the President. — Although the instructions were received after the Treaty was concluded and signed, owing entirely to the loss or delay of my dispatch N°. 2, I was greatly gratified to learn that the course I had deemed it best to pursue in the absence of special information was in perfect accordance with the views of the Government as reflected by the instructions. — The dispatch N°. 6 containing the copy of a letter from Messrs Charles and Henry Borie of Philadelphia was only received two days ago, and shall receive prompt attention, — though from the partial information which I at present possess I am inclined to believe, that no application for their relief can be made with any chance of success. —

I have not received a number of the Washington Union[28] later than the 10th. of Feb. this may possibly be owing to their not being sent by the Havre Packets from New York. —

---

27 Instructions No. 5 and No. 6 are the officially correct form of reference here.
28 A daily newspaper published in the Capital City.

Legation of the United States Naples June 2ᵈ. 1846
[Despatch, Unnumbered]

Sir

I have the honor to acknowledge the receipt from the Department of State, by Mʳ. Washington Greenhow special bearer of dispatches of a ratified copy of the Treaty of Commerce and Navigation concluded and signed at the city of Naples on the 1ˢᵗ. day of December last, between the United States of America and His Majesty the King of the Kingdom of the Two Sicilies, together with your dispatches Nº. 7 & 8²⁹ and all the papers therein mentioned as having been transmitted to this Legation.

Mʳ. Greenhow reached Naples on the morning of 28ᵗʰ. May, three days before the expiration of the time limited for the exchange of the ratifications and on the same day I addressed a note to the Minister of Foreign Affairs informing him that I was prepared to exchange the ratifications at such time and place as he would be pleased to designate. On the following day I received his answer appointing the 1ˢᵗ. Inst. for that purpose. — At the hour designated I attended at the office of Foreign Affairs and after having carefully compared the original and copies, exchanged the ratifications, and herewith transmit the copy delivered to me with the sanction and approval of the King endorsed thereon. — When I presented to His Majesty's plenipotentiaries the special power from the President authorizing me to exchange the ratifications, they informed me that this authority was contained in the original power granted by the King to conduct and conclude the negotiation, which I forwarded to the Department with the Treaty in December last, and by reference to which will be found correct. I at the same time delivered to the Minister of State the original and copy of the President's letter to the King.

With my dispatch Nº. 4 having date 5ᵗʰ. of May I forwarded to the Department a copy of my lost or missing dispatch of the 28th of September, marked Nº. 2 which I hope has been received. I regret having failed to number my communication of 1ˢᵗ. December, and will be more particular in future.

---

²⁹ For Instruction No. 7, April 14, 1846, see above, p. 620, this chapter. Instruction No. 8, Washington, April 14, 1846, Mr. Buchanan transmitted a letter of ceremony from the President to His Majesty respecting the birth of Prince Gaetano Maria Federico.

Information was received a few hours ago, by Express of the death of Pope Gregory 16th. of Rome.[30]

WM. H. POLK TO J. BUCHANAN

Legation of the United States Naples July 15th. 1846 [Despatch No. 6]

Sir —

Since my communication accompanying a ratified copy of the Treaty of Commerce and Navigation with this Kingdom I have to acknowledge the receipt from the Department of Dispatch N°. 9[31] announcing the formal declaration of war against Mexico, and stating the ultimate and peaceful intentions of the government in prosecuting hostilities. — I noted the suggestions contained in your communication and sought an early opportunity to converse with the Minister of Foreign Affairs on the subject of the war and the causes leading to it, and also informed him of the intention of the United States to enforce a strict blockade of all the ports of Mexico both in the Atlantic and Pacific, this was necessary as some trade is carried on by this country with Mexico. Ever since the consummation of the great measure, the Annexation of Texas,[32] the European mind seems disposed and I so found the Minister of Foreign Affairs inclined, to regard any act of our Government bearing on the policy adopted toward the neighbouring republic of Mexico, as having for its ultimate object the acquisition of territory and the extension of our National limits. Our motives being prejudged it is difficult to secure a fair, liberal and unprejudiced examination of the various injuries which have lead [sic] to the present hostile variance between the two Countries or to convince that we have any

---

[30] Gregory XVI, (Mauro or Bartolomeo Alberto Cappellari (1765-1846), was elected Pope in 1831. He was a reactionary and supported the Jesuits. On his reign, see: *Storia documentata della diplomazia europea in Italia dall'anno 1814 al 1861.* (Turin, 1865-1872), Vol. III; Frederick K. Nielsen, *History of the papacy in the nineteenth century.* (London, 1875), II, 51-101; C. Sylvain, *Gregoire XVI et son pontificat* (Lille, 1889); *The Catholic Encyclopedia*, 1910, VII, 6-9; J. A. von Helfret, *Gregor XVI und Pius IX.* (October 1845-November 1846). Prague, Tiskem I. Otty, 1895, iv-189 pp.

[31] Instruction No. 9 (circular), Washington, May 14, 1846, announcing declaration of war between the United States and Mexico. See, *Instructions to Ministers,* vol. Spain, 202.

[32] On March 2, 1836, Texas declared her independence of Mexico. The following year Texas was recognized by the United States. The question of annexation aroused bitter feeling between the two countries which ended, 1846-48, in war between Mexico and the United States.

wrongs to redress save those which have originated from our own act in the annexation of Texas, or to persuade that the only object we have in view is to "conquer an honorable peace" and establish such amicable relations as will preserve the national honor and rights of each, and contribute to the prosperity of both. Taking for my guide the facts stated in the Special Message of the President calling forth the declaration of war by Congress, and the sentiments embodied in your dispatch, I have endeavoured to remove such erroneous impressions and exhibit our conduct in the justifiable light which our multiplied injuries and indignities received from Mexico furnishes, and believe that I have succeeded, at least, in cutting loose the fastenings of the mind from one exclusive point and directed attention and awakened inquiry into the many grave wrongs, scattered over the space of twenty years, so long patiently borne in the hope of peaceful redress, leading to our difficulties with that unfortunate Republic. —

The precarious situation of Gen[1]. Taylor,[33] as represented by the English and French journals, surrounded, and under the watchful eye of a vastly superior force, cut off from supplies of men and provisions, frequently formed the topic of conversation, and lead to the certain anticipation that the first act of hostility would be marked by signal defeat to our arms, but the result proving so different from general expectation, and exhibiting the gallantry and chivalry of our army in so brilliant a light, has had the effect to elevate us in the scale of consideration as a people skillful in War and courageous in the hour of battle.

From information received from our consul at Palermo, it is probable that some difficulty will arise with regard to the tonnage duty to be exacted of our vessels entering the ports of this Kingdom, partly laden with produce taken in at Leghorn, Genoa, Malta, Trieste, or Marseilles, for the purpose of completing their cargoes with the produce of this Kingdom before sailing to the United States. The consul expresses the confident opinion, that in such cases, this Government will be disposed to exact the old rate of tonnage duty, even though it should be clear and palpable that the vessel entered the port with the exclusive object of taking in additional freight, and not for purposes of trade. Most of the American vessels visiting the ports of this Kingdom

---

[33] Zachary Taylor (1784-1850), was born in Orange Co., Va. After encountering early defeats in the war, General Taylor succeeded in crossing the river on May 18, 1846, and unfurled the Stars and Stripes on Mexican territory. This was followed by other and more brilliant successes by the Americans.

are in the habit of taking in part cargoes at the various points mentioned, before coming to Naples, Messina, and Palermo, and if this Government shall adopt the construction, which it is presumed it will, our vessels will in many instances be subjected to the old rate of duties. My own opinion is, that a fair and liberal construction of the 3ᵈ. Article of the Treaty which applies directly to this question, will not justify the claim to the old rate of duty; but being uninformed what interpretation the government of the United States has placed upon similar Articles embraced in our treaties with other nations confining the reciprocity to the direct trade between the countries, I have not, as yet, called the attention of this Government to the subject, and will not do so, until I am advised by the Department what has been the construction adopted in like cases with other countries with whom we have commercial regulations confining the intercourse to the direct trade. —

I received on the 9ᵗʰ. Inst. a communication from the Minister of Foreign Affairs informing me, that His Majesty the King, had appointed Chevʳ. D. Rocco Martuscelli[34] Chargé d'Affaires of the Kingdom of the Two Sicilies near the Government of the United States.

I herewith enclose my accounts for the year ending the 10th of April 1846. The item for expenses to and from Paris, to carry the Treaty, I submit for the decision of the Department, having considered it my duty to incur the labour and expenses of the voyage, to insure its safe and speedy transmission to the United States.

WM. H. POLK TO J. BUCHANAN

Legation of the United States Naples Oct. 15ᵗʰ. 1846 [Despatch No. 7]

Sir. —

In my last dispatch I informed you that I had made some enquiry into the claim, of Messers [sic] Borie & Co. of Philadelphia against this Government, concerning which I received information from the Department of State in June last, and was under the impression from a partial investigation of the matter that no redress could be obtained. Upon a more full examination, the

---

34 Rocco Martuscelli presented his credentials on December 1, 1846. See also note 75, p. 583. For his Notes to the United States Secretary of State, see chapter Legation Notes, *hic opus.*

chances of success appeared so feeble that I have considered it best not to call the attention of the Government to the claim at all, as it could only have the effect to irritate without any fair probability of obtaining redress. — It appears that a Royal ordinance was issued, granting *thirty per cent* reduction on the duties, besides the *ten per cent,* the privilege of the flag, to vessels of the Two Sicilies for return cargoes from America, with the condition of their exporting cargoes the produce of this Kingdom, and as was understood solely with the view to encourage them to undertake distant voyages. It is true that six months notice was promised to be given to those engaged in this distant trade previous to its discontinuence [sic]; but in this respect good faith was not observed, the violation of the promise, however being more the result of inattention or omission, on the part of the Commissioners who negotiated the recent treaty with England, than any wilful or interested desire to do wrong to those who had been induced by such flattering advantages to rest capital in the trade. The Commissioners in making the English treaty failed to make provision for this case. They in consequence found themselves embarrissed [sic] as England was prepared to demand the same allowence, [sic] should it be extended to any Sicilian vessel. — Under these circumstances the Government resorted to the only available means, except[35] directly paying such losses as might be incurred, to reduce the Tarriff [sic] on many articles, sugar, for example was cut down from *sixteen Ducats* p. Cantar to *ten ducats* besides the abolition of the consumption duty, as a remuneration for the withdrawal of the thirty per cent privilege. Even this appeared to me as not being just, it seeming to be a mere subterfuge, for what became common, could no longer be an advantage to those persons who had acted on the faith of the ordinance. — To strengthen their position, and impart an appearance of justice to their course, they have, or mean to pay, from the Treasury, the *thirty per cent* allowance, on a few Articles of small importance, the duties levied on which have not been reduced, whilst they consider nothing due on Sugar, Coffee &c in consequence of the reduction. — The case of Messers. [sic] Borie & Co. does not stand alone, there being many others of a precisely similar character, in which English subjects and subjects of this Kingdom are exclusively interested. — These persons being so strongly convinced of the justice of their claim,

---

35 The word "without" is crossed out in the original, with the word "except" written over it.

on being refused by the proper officer of the Government, having control of the subject, asked and obtained an audience of the King, but all their representations produced no effect. I clearly admit, that if good faith was observed by the King to his subjects, their claim would be paid; but cannot see how foreigners who have availed themselves of the flag of the Two Sicilies to get an allowance of duties, granted by the King to his subjects, on certain conditions, can in case he violates his promise, found a strong claim for redress. It is their misfortune to have too implicitly and confidently trusted the commercial regulations of a government swayed by the will of one man, and the representations of persons interested in soliciting consignments. — I will, however, should you differ with me in the view I have taken of the subject, on being so informed, readily urge the claim against this Government, and use every means to obtain it.

Nothing has occurred at this court since my last communication, that could prove of the least interest to our government.

J. Buchanan to Wm. H. Polk

Department of State, Washington, 29th. March, 1847.
[Instruction No. 13.]36

Sir:

The President has communicated to me your request for a leave of absence from your post for a period of three months; and, under the peculiar circumstances of the case, it is granted.

If your object in returning to the United States had been merely to attend to your own private business however urgent, this would have been denied, as it has been to others, during the continuance of the Mexican war. The domestic circumstances, however, which render it a filial duty on your part to visit your country without delay, are of such a character that I cannot deny your request. Besides, Mr. Hammett, our excellent Consul at

---

36 This Instruction No. 13 is published in Buchanan, *Works,* etc. VII, 257. The following Instructions were sent to Mr. Polk during this period:

Instruction No. 10, Washington, July 14, 1846, Mr. Buchanan informed Mr. Polk that his request for permission to leave Naples was granted, but it was not to exceed one month or six weeks. See below, p. 635.

Instruction No. 11, (Circular), Washington, July 31, 1846, concerning the use of despatch bags of the Department. See, *Instructions to Ministers,* vol. Spain, 207.

Instruction No. 12, Washington, Dec. 10, 1846, Mr. Buchanan transmitted a letter of ceremony from the President to His Majesty concerning the birth of a princess.

Naples, is so competent to attend to any official business which may arise, in the mean time, that the public interest cannot materially suffer from your brief absence. Upon your departure, you will leave the archives and other property of the Legation in his custody.

WM. H. POLK TO J. BUCHANAN

Legation of the United States Naples Jan. 4th. 1847 [Despatch No. 8]

Sir —

I write in obedience to a sense of duty, without any thing of interest to communicate, making it necessary. —

The failure of the grain crop in this Kingdom the past season is beginning to be felt very severely by the poorer classes of the people, chiefly on account of the high prices demanded for food of every discription [sic]. —The Government influenced by a fear of more extensive want, and with the object of forcing holders to relax in their exorbitant prices, have published an ordinance prohibiting the exportation of every kind of food, with the hope of crippling the cupidity of holders, and forcing a reduction of prices to the scale demanded in ordinary times. — Thus far, the ordinance has produced no such effect. — The dealers in this branch of foreign trade seeming to be influenced by a proper appreciation of the high handed wrong inflicted by Government, maintain a stubborn firmness. — It cannot be said that actual starving misery exists, approaching the degree of destitution and suffering experienced in England and parts of France, but the curtailment of the usual supply is sufficiently great, to make scarcity apparent. The ordinance will effect France more directly and extensively than any other Nation — she having been in past years the main market for the excess produced in this Kingdom, owing to the ready and easy means of transportation by the Mediterranean — Though should the approaching season prove as disasterous [sic] to the agricultural interest of this Country, as the last, there will be no necessity for royal ordinances to forbid exportations. — The miserable cries of starving thousands, will by quiet or violent means prevent it — and it will in such case, devolve on the United States, not only to furnish means of human subsistence to the millions of England and France, but to the inhabitants of this sunny land of ordinarily rich and exhuberant

630

[sic] production. The sufferings, at present experienced by the "Old World," is highly calculated to awaken the deepest toned feelings of sympathy and commiseration, but out of their sufferings, is produced a good, which must be gratifying to every American — not gratifying on account of the pecuniary prosperity afforded our Country, but because it has directed more extensive inquiry and investigation into our resources as a Republic, and our growing greatness as a people, of which, the European world, as far as my observation has extended, are most offensively ignorant. —

The marriage[37] of the Queen of Spain, has very materially weakened the influence of the French King at this Court. — It being no doubt true, that the King of the Two Sicilies was induced as late as 1843, directly contrary to the wishes of Austria, to so far repudiate the salic law,[38] which has always been in force in this Kingdom, as to recognize the daughter of Ferdinand 7th. as Queen of Spain, in consideration that the influence of the French Court would be exercised at Madrid, to accomplish the marriage of Count Trapani, his brother, with the young Queen. — France, by so readily consenting, and as is well known intriguing in favor of the successful Prince, taken in connection with the Montponsier [sic][39] marriage, has it is beleived [sic] subjected herself very clearly to the charge of bad faith toward this Government. — Of these things it is difficult to obtain minute information, and indeed the measure of influence which this small Kingdom exercises in the scale of European affairs is so trifling, that its fixed, firm friendship, or open enmity is of little importance to a power like France when in the way of the accomplishment of any cherished purpose.—

I have not as yet availed myself, of the permission granted last summer to leave Naples for a few weeks, but propose doing so during the next month to make a visit to Rome, if entirely consistent with a proper observance of my official duties. —

---

[37] See below, this page, note 39.

[38] On March 29, 1830, Ferdinand VII abolished the salic law and in 1833, his daughter Isabella was recognized Queen of Spain.

[39] The Moderado Party or Castilian conservatives made their Queen (Isabella) marry, at 16, her cousin Prince Francisco de Assisi de Bourbon on the same day (Oct. 10, 1846) on which her younger sister married the Duke de Montpensier (the youngest son of Louis Philippe). These marriages suited the views of France and Louis Philippe, who almost quarrelled in consequence with Great Britain.

Department of State. Washington, 5th. May, 1847.
[Instruction No. 14.][40]

Sir:

Your despatchs [sic] to N°. 8 inclusive, have been received. Your No. 8, dated 4th. January, 1847 did not reach the Department until the 23rd. ultimo.

Until a few days ago, my attention was not directed by the appropriate clerk, to the enquiry contained in your despatch N°. 6 of the 15th. July last; nor did I until then ever know of its existence. I presume the cause of this neglect was my absence at Saratoga on the 5th. September, when it reached the Department.

Your inquiry is, whether, under the Treaty of the first of December, 1845, an American vessel, having taken part of her cargo, destined for the United States, at any foreign port not within the Kingdom of the Two Sicilies, may enter a port of that Kingdom for the purpose of completing her cargo, without being subject to a discriminating tonnage duty? This Treaty is one of direct reciprocity. It does not embrace the indirect or triangular carrying trade. According to its correct construction, vessels arriving directly from ports of the United States at Sicilian ports, are alone exempted from discriminating tonnage duties. Vessels arriving indirectly in the ports of either country, from those of a third Power, are not embraced by the Treaty; but are left to the rules and regulations of the respective Governments, in regard to tonnage duties. In this particular, they stand on the same footing, as though the Treaty had never been concluded.

But it would surely be contrary to the interest of Sicilian navigation to exact discriminating tonnage duties from American vessels in the cases to which you have referred.

Under the 2nd. Section of the Act of Congress of the 31st. May, 1830, "all Acts and parts of Acts imposing duties upon the tonnage of the ships and vessels of any foreign nation, so far as the same relate to the imposition of such duties, shall be repealed: *Provided, that the President of the United States shall be satisfied that the discriminating or countervailing duties of such foreign nation, so far as they operate to the disadvantage of the United States, have been abolished.*"

---

[40] This Instruction No. 14 was published in Buchanan's *Works,* VII, 298-301. Cf. *hic opus* and chapter, p. 635.

Under this law, all tonnage duties whatever have been abolished in the United States, except in the cases embraced by the proviso. Should the Sicilian Government levy discriminating tonnage duties on vessels of the United States arriving in their ports from those of a third Power, a similar rule will be applied to Sicilian vessels, arriving under like circumstances, in the ports of the United States. Instead of being freed altogether from tonnage duties, these vessels will then, under our laws, be obliged to pay a tonnage duty of 50 cents per ton, and, also, a duty of 50 cents per ton for "light money," amounting in the aggregate to $1.00 per ton.

I have communicated the preceding part of this despatch to the Treasury Department, which confirms the opinions I have expressed.

It is so manifestly the interest of the Two Sicilies not to levy discriminating tonnage duties on vessels of the United States arriving in their ports from other foreign ports in the Mediterranean, merely for the purpose of completing their cargoes with Sicilian productions, that it is probable they will not resort to so impolitic a measure. As I have heard nothing from our Consul at Palermo, and nothing further from yourself on the subject, in your two subsequent despatches, I have reason to hope that they have abandoned, if they ever entertained, such an intention. Should the fact be otherwise, you will immediately communicate this information to this Department.

Your despatch N°. 7, of the 15th. of October last, relative to the claim of Messrs. Borie & Company for indemnity from the Sicilian Government, never reached the Department until the 23rd. of April. So great a delay is wholly unaccountable. If I correctly understand the facts of the case in question, the claim of these gentlemen presents a fair subject for the interposition of this Government.

The Sicilian Government, to encourage their own navigation, decreed, "that any Neapolitan or Sicilian vessel, which shall export from the Kingdom a cargo of national produce for Eastern or Western America, and shall import into the country a cargo of produce, shall obtain a reduction of 30 per cent on the amount of duties;" and they reserved to themselves the right to abolish this privilege at any time after six months preventive notice.

This decree was an invitation to all American merchants to ship their goods destined for the Two Sicilies, on board of Sicilian vessels which had brought a cargo of national produce to the United States in preference to American vessels; and both as a consideration and an inducement for doing this, the faith of His Sicilian Majesty was pledged that these goods should be admitted into Sicilian ports, "at a reduction of 30 per cent on the amount of the duties on said cargo."

The case of Messrs. Borie & Company is not that of a private contract between a Foreign Government and an American citizen; in which the citizen must trust to the faith of the other party for its execution, and in the event of failure, has no right, as a general rule, to demand the interposition of his own Government. It resembles much more nearly the violation of a public Treaty, granting to American citizens a reduction of 30 per cent of the Sicilian duties, provided they would ship their merchandize on board of Sicilian vessels which had brought a cargo of national produce to the United States. It was a public law to this effect, enacted by the authority of the only Legislative power in the Kingdom.

Now, if it were possible, let us suppose that Congress should pass a law, enacting, that the cargoes, shipped in a foreign country on board of American vessels which had carried American productions abroad, should be relieved, when imported into the United States, of thirty per cent of the amount of duties under our existing Tariff, until six months notice of the repeal of this law should be given. A British or French subject, upon the faith of this enactment, makes such a shipment, but on the arrival of the vessel in the United States, he finds that Congress, from some high motive of public policy, has violated the national faith and suddenly repealed this law, without giving the notice required, would he not, under such circumstances, be clearly entitled to indemnity? Would Congress refuse for a moment to grant it to him? And if they did, would not the Government of Great Britain or France have a right to interpose and demand redress for such an outrage on national faith? It appears to me that, the claim of Messrs. Borie & Company upon the Sicilian Government, presents a case parallel to the one I have supposed.

It is no sufficient reason for this Government not to interpose for the protection of one of its citizens, that Great Britain may have submitted in silence to a similar imposition practised on British subjects. If she should persist in doing this, it will be a new leaf in her history. Neapolitan subjects, of course, have no alternative but submission. For these reasons which I might extend to a much greater length, I regret to differ from you in opinion.[41]

You will, then, carefully examine into all the facts of the case of Messrs. Borie & Company; and if you should find them to be in accordance with their statement, now in your possession, you will firmly, but respectfully, in the name of your Government, ask of the Sicilian Government, that Messrs. Borie & Company be indemnified for the losses which they have sustained in the premises.

WM. H. POLK TO J. BUCHANAN

Washington City August. 31st 1847 [Unnumbered despatch]

Sir

I have the honor to request that I may be recalled, and that my mission as Chargé d'Affaires of the United States, near His Majesty the King of the Kingdom of the Two Sicilies may cease from this date. — I am prompted to make this request, by the strong desire, I feel to participate in the War, in which my country is engaged with Mexico. — This desire I expressed when I first heard that the war existed, but I could not abandon my post, and return to my country without the permission of my government. When I asked[42] and obtained leave of absence for a short time to visit the United States, under the belief that the war would probably be of short duration, it was my intention to return to Naples in the steamer of the 1st. proximo. — I find that the prospect of a speedy termination of the war is not likely to be realized, and I therefore ask to be relieved from the duties of my mission, with the intention of participating in it. —

---

[41] The foregoing despatch, addressed to Mr. Polk, was sent to Alexander Hammett, Esqre., U. S. Consul at Naples, with a letter of instructions, dated May 6, 1847, for which, see the Consular Records. The text of this Instruction No. 14 to Mr. Polk, May 5, 1847, sent to Mr. Hammett, on May 6, will be found, *hic opus*, Polk chapter, p. 632 ff, and note 40 therein. Alexander Hammett, of Maryland, was nominated consul of the United States at Naples on June 6, 1809. He retained the post to 1860. He acted as chargé d'affaires *ad interim* from about May 11, 1847 to June 29, 1848. See *Register of State Department*, 1874, 104.

[42] See above Instruction No. 10 to Mr. Polk p. 629. No despatch from Mr. Polk making request for leave of absence can be found. The reply to the request, however, if found on pages 629-630, in Instruction No. 13.

ALEXANDER HAMMETT[1]
(May 1, 1847 - June 29, 1848)

A. HAMMETT TO J. BUCHANAN

U. S. Consulate, Naples 3ᵈ. July, 1847. [(Consular) No. 45.]

Sir,

Your communication of the 6ᵗʰ. May last,[2] ordering me to carry out the instructions contained in the dispatch [sic] to Mʳ. Polk in date of the 5th of the same, has been received.

Without loss of time I delivered to the Minister of Foreign Affairs the two Notes of which I have the honor to enclose copies. What the result may be, it is impossible for me yet to say.

For the countervailing tonnage on our vessels which may touch the ports of the Kingdom, with part cargoes laden in others out of it, merely to fill up, I doubt whether they will relinquish it. They fear they would have to grant the like to other nations with whom they have also made commercial treaties, and that such would lead to the introduction of a clandestine commerce injurious to their revenue, for vessels partly laden could not be well searched.

Our Consul at Palermo, to whom I wrote to ascertain with certainty, whether any change had been made, has replied in the negative, so that Sicilian vessels are to be treated in the U. S. accordingly, untill [sic] they find it their interest to adopt a different system.

---

[1] Hammett's signature varied. Sometimes he spelled out the given name; more often he wrote it Alex. or Alexʳ. This variation applied as well in his formal letters to the Minister of Foreign Affairs of the Two Sicilies as to those which were his despatches to the Secretary of State in Washington.

[2] In his letter to Mr. Hammett dated May 6, 1847, Secretary of State Buchanan requested him to execute the instructions enclosed for Mr. Polk in the event that the latter had already left his post. Mr. Hammett was particularly instructed to carry on from where Mr. Polk had left off in the matter of Borie & Co. See Instructions to Consuls, X, 429. A few despatches from Mr. Hammett, for the period when he acted as chargé d'affaires *ad interim,* are found in part in the diplomatic files and in part in Hammett's Consular Despatches. By his own statement, Mr. Hammett served *ad interim* from May 1, 1847, to June 22, 1848. See this chapter, p. 651. It should be realized also, that as consul, and in that proper capacity, he also handled, often for several years, the preliminary phases of these matters which eventually came up for the minister's attention. A consul's duties were wide and he was expected to serve in every possible and legitimate way all needs either of individual American citizens travelling or resident in the Sicilies or their problems and those of American shippers, and ship owners and masters and crews, arising out of commercial intercourse with the Kingdom.

The affair of M^r. [sic] Borie has been a shameful violation of public faith, for which he is entitled to redress, but you must be aware how difficult it is to get justice from such Governments. The answers to the one or both Notes, shall be remitted, as soon as I receive them.

A. HAMMETT TO THE PRINCE OF SCILLA

Enclosure with Mr. Hammett's Consular Despatch No. 45.

Consulate of the United States of America, Naples, July 1st 1847

In the absence of Mr. Polk, the Chargé d'Affaires of the United States of America, it becomes the duty of the Undersigned, to submit to H. E. the Prince of Scilla, Counsellor Minister and Secretary of State Charged with the Department [sic] of Foreign Affairs, some facts concerning the interests of the Commercial house of Borie and Co. of Philadelphia, the particulars of which will be found in the accompanying paper.[3]

These circumstances do not constitute a private contract, between a Foreign Government, and an American citizen, in which faith is to be given to the other party, for its execution and in case of failure the individual is not entitled by general rule, to require the interposition of his own Government: it on the other hand approaches more nearly in its nature, to the violation of a public treaty, granting to American Citizens a reduction of thirty per cent of Custom-house duties, on condition that they should ship their merchandize, in preference, on vessels of the Kingdom of the Two Sicilies, which should have introduced National productions into the United States. This was a public law, promulgated to that effect, by the competent authorities.

Now, if the Congress of the United States had made a law, declaring that Cargoes brought from a foreign Country, in American vessels which had exported national productions, should be exonerated from thirty per cent of the duties, to which they would be subjected on their entrance, according to the existing tariff, and that, until six months, or a year after notice of its abrogation; and if English, French or Neapolitan merchants on the faith of such law, send their cargoes, on the arrival of which in vessels of the United States, it should be found that the Congress from some motive of high policy, had violated the national

---

[3] See pp. 638-639.

faith, and annulled the said law, without the proper notice, would they not be justly entitled to indemnification, for their losses and would Congress hesitate an instant to allow it to them? and if it should, would not the Governments of those merchants, have the right to interpose and demand indemnification on account of such failure?

From these considerations it is the duty of the Undersigned, agreeably to the orders, and in the name of his Government, to call the attention of H. E. the Prince of Scilla, Minister, Counciller [sic], and Secretary of State, for the Department of foreign [sic] Affairs, to the above mentioned circumstances, with the certainty that he will direct the necessary measures to be taken, for doing justice to Messrs. Borie & Co., upon their claim as here stated. With this expectation he has the honor to repeat to H. E. the assurances of his very high consideration.

A. HAMMETT TO THE PRINCE OF SCILLA

Enclosure with Mr. Hammett's Consular Despatch No. 45.

Consulate of the United States of America, Naples July 1ˢᵗ. 1847

The Undersigned has the honor to submit to the consideration of H. E. the Prince of Scilla, Minister Counciller [sic] and Secretary of State Charged with the Department of foreign affairs [sic], some observations on the Treaty of December 1ˢᵗ. 1845.

An American vessel, which has taken in a part of a cargo, destined for the United States, may enter into another Port in the Kingdom of the Two Sicilies, in order to complete her cargo, but in that case, she becomes subject to discriminating duties of tonnage. That treaty has for its object to establish a direct reciprocity, and does not embrace the indirect, or triangular commerce. Consequently the vessels of either nation, are on the same footing with regard to indirect commerce, as if the treaty had never been made. But it would certainly be contrary to the interests of the navigation of the Kingdom, to exact the tonnage duty upon American vessels, different from that laid upon National vessels, when the former enter the Ports of the Kingdom, for the sole object of completing their cargoes, by taking in productions of the country, for transportation to the United States.

And if an American vessel be laden in the United States, for Leghorn and Naples, for example, and after having discharged the portion intended for Leghorn, she should come to Naples, with the remainder, she would be considered as coming direct; provided, she should not have taken on board, another merchandize, as is practised with regard to certain English Steam Vessels, coming from Southampton, by way of Genoa and Leghorn.

The Undersigned makes it his duty to inform H. E., that in the second section of the act of Congress of the 31st of May 1830, all acts and parts of acts imposing discriminating duties on tonnage, are abolished in cases where the President may be convinced, that the Foreign Government acts with reciprocity, and does not subject American vessels to the least disadvantage. By this law, all tonnage duties have been abolished in the United States, except in the cases embraced in the above condition.

When we reflect, that according to the regulations in force, Sicilian vessels arriving in the United States, will be, from want of reciprocity, (unless they come in ballast, or with cargoes direct according to the treaty) subjected to the payment of fifty cents per ton, besides the duty for lighthouses, which would raise the whole amount of duty, to one dollar per ton, the Undersigned flatters himself, that this Royal Government will find it advantageous to the navigation of the Kingdom, to carry into effect the measures suggested, in conformity with the views of the Government of the United States.

With the certainty of seeing this difficulty removed, in a manner favorable for both Nations, the Undersigned has the honor to repeat to H. E. the assurances of his high consideration.

THE PRINCE OF SCILLA TO A. HAMMETT

Enclosure with Mr. Hammett's Consular Despatch No. 45.

Naples August 14 1847.

The Undersigned, Counciller [sic] Minister of State, Charged with the Department of Foreign Affairs, in answer to the two notes, addressed to him on the 8 and the 30 of July[4] last, by M'. Alex. Hammett, Consul of the United States of America, hastens to inform that Gentleman, that proper orders have been given by the Secretary of State for Finances, on the 11th

---

4 See Consular Despatches, Naples, Hammett, and these dates.

instant, to the Treasurer General in Palermo, to pay to the Consul of the U. S. at that place, the sum of 723 Ducats, 9 Grani, to be transmitted to the respective owners, of the 6 American vessels, described in Mr. Hammett's first note.[5]

A. HAMMETT TO J. BUCHANAN

U. States Consulate Naples 18 August 1847. (Consular) No. 146

Sir,

I had the honor to inform you on the 3^d. of last month of the receipt of your dispatch [sic] to Mr. Polk in date of the 5th of May, and to enclose copies of Notes addressed to the Neap^n. Minister to carry out the instructions contained in it.

I repeated on the 5th inst the request to the said Minister to consider the subject of my Notes and to give a reply. I called a few days after at the Office of Foreign Affairs, and the Chief of Division assured me that as soon as he could learn the decision on his reports, both of M^r. Borie's affair and the Countervailing tonnage on our vessels, he would send me the answer. That, His Majesty, to whom they must be referred, had been absent, & much occupied, since his return, so that there was unavoidable delay.

A. HAMMETT TO J. BUCHANAN

U. States Consulate Naples 27. Septr. 1847.

[Consular Despatch No. 148]

Sir,

Having received after much delay the Minister's answer[6] to my note of the 1 July last,[7] demanding indemnity for Messrs. Borie & Co. in the case of their cargoes imported here from Philadelphia and New York in the Neap^n. vessels Nuovo Raffaele and Ferdinando, I have the honor to enclose a copy of it, as well as a Copy of my answer thereto.[8]. I do not expect they will reply again, and I apprehend that other arguments than I command will be necessary to bring them to pay what is so justly claimed.

---

[5] Compare July 1st, above, this chapter, pp. 638-639. Also see reference to Messrs. Borie & Co. in Consular No. 148, below, dated Sept. 27, 1847.

[6] For the Minister's answer dated Aug. 14, 1847, see above, p. 639.

[7] For copy of Mr. Hammett's note to Minister Scilla, see this chapter, above, pp. 637-638, as Enclosure, dated July 1, 1847, with Mr. Hammett's Consular Despatch No. 45, of July 3, 1847.

[8] For Mr. Hammett's reply of Sept. 27, 1847, to the Minister's reply of Sept. 21, 1847, see this chapter, below, pp. 643-644.

A. Hammett to J. Buchanan

U. S. Consulate Naples 20 Octr. 1847.

[Consular Despatch No. 149]

Sir,

My last communication was on the 27th. of September, enclosing copies of the Minister's letter and my answer thereto, relative to the claim of Mess: Borie & Co. —

Having had occasion yesterday to see the Director General of the Customs, he mentioned that affair to me, without my saying anything about it. I perceived from his observations that there is a disposition in this Government to come to an arrangement and I think it well to inform you, though I hold nothing certain.

The question of reducing the duty on foreign cotton, to enable their Manufacturers to compete with Foreigners, is now in discussion. The Cultivators of the article are however opposed to it, and it remains, to be seen which interest will get the better.

The Prince of Scilla to A. Hammett

Enclosure with Mr. Hammett's Consular Despatch No. 149[9]

Naples 21st. of September 1847.

In his despatch of the 1st. of July[10] of the present year, Mr. Hammett, Consul of the United States of America, addressed to the Undersigned, Counciller [sic] Minister of State, charged with the portfolio of Foreign Affairs, a memorial, by which Messrs. Borie & Co., American Merchants, claimed the premium of thirty per cent, on merchandize imported into the royal dominions, from Philadelphia, and New York, in the vessels Nuovo Raffaele, and Ferdinando, under the flag of the Two Sicilies, which entered the port of this capital, the first on the 10th. of October 1845, and the other on the 25th. of January 1846; in virtue of the Royal rescript of December 26th. 1839, whereby it was declared that whensoever the Royal Government should choose to suppress the premium of twenty per cent, on importations from the Baltic,

---

9 The reference to No. 147 seems to be in error, for it is the letter which is referred to in Mr. Hammett's letter No. 148. His No. 147, is not in the folder at all. Mr. Hammett's No. 148 mentions enclosing both the Italian letter he had received and also his English translation thereof.

10 See enclosure, July 1, 1847, with Mr. Hammett's Consular No. 45, of July 3, 1847, q.v., this chapter, pp. 637-638.

and of thirty per cent on those from the East or West Indies, allowed to vessels under the Royal flag, this should be announced to those engaged in commerce, four months previously, with regard to importations from the Baltic, and six months previously for those from the Indies.

The Undersigned having taken pains to procure information on this subject, from the Minister of the Royal Finances, he has received a communication to the effect that — when the privileges enjoyed by the Royal flag on voyages to the Baltic and in the Indies, were abolished, the King took into consideration that the suppression of the premiums, though counter-balanced by the reduction of the duties, on several foreign articles, might in some manner prove injurious to vessels, which, previous to the said promulgation, may have taken from those regions merchandize on which the duty has been reduced, where such reduction did not amount to the sum of the premiums revoked. His Majesty had designed to prescribe under date of the 26th. of August of the same year

—1— That no compensation should be given on merchandize, imported from the Baltic or the Indies, above the amount of the duties on the greater portion of which, a corresponding reduction has been made; the persons interested having obtained an advantage superior to the premium suppressed.

—2— To allow compensation on merchandize, on which no reduction of duties has been made, or if made has not been equal to the premium suppressed; such compensation to be equal to the amount of the said premium, under the conditions then required for obtaining it.

—3— A compensation to be immediately made, for importations from the Baltic, when they should have been entered before the 22nd. of November, 1845, and for those coming from the Indies, before the 22nd. of January 1846.

Applying these provisions to the case of the two vessels in question the first having imported sugar & coffee, articles on which a considerable reduction had been made in the duties, the owners have no right to compensation, having obtained a greater advantage in another way . . . and the other vessel, the Ferdinando, although she had not imported such merchandize, should be excluded from any favor of this kind, having arrived on the 25th. of January, three days after the period prescribed.

In addition to the above mentioned motive of exclusion, it is to be remarked, that the memorial of Mes^{rs}. [sic] Borie & Co.

contains no notice of the burthen of the two vessels, nor of their having arrived in a direct voyage; and that it wants the certificate, giving the fact of the exportation from the territory of the American Confederacy; the failure of which conditions, would have prevented the compensation from being given, even though it were due on other grounds.

A. Hammett to the Prince of Scilla

Enclosure with Mr. Hammett's Consular Despatch No. 147[11]

Naples September 27th. 1847.

In answer to the honored letter from H. E. the Prince of Scilla, Counciller [sic] Minister of State, charged with the portfolio of Foreign Affairs, written in answer to the note from the Undersigned, Consul of the United States of America, dated the 1st. of July, in which he asks for the premium of thirty per cent. reduction in the duty, according to the custom house tariff, then in force, on the cargoes brought into this port, by the Nuovo Raffaele & Ferdinando, under the Royal flag from Philadelphia, and New York, the first on the 10th. of October 1845, and the other on the 25th. of January 1846, a few observations are indispensable, in order to shew H. E. how untenable are the reasons, to which he has had recourse, in opposition to his just claims, advanced by express order of his Government.

The two vessels were despatched from the ports of the Kingdom laden with indigenous productions, whilst the Royal rescript was in full force. The returned cargoes, were also prepared in Philadelphia and New York, before any idea had been entertained, of abolishing the premium of thirty per cent, on the duty on such merchandize. No provision could in justice effect the cargoes of these vessels, as no warning had been given to those engaged in commerce, as promised in the rescript.

—1— To refuse any compensation on Merchandize, on which the duty has been reduced, because such reduction amounts to more than thirty per cent, and the persons interested have gained an advantage, superior to the suppressed premium, is to assert a thing, the result of which has proved its unsubstantiality. On the contrary, the reduction being made common to all, the privilege

11 This should be No. 148. See footnote 9, p. 641.

ceases; and ruin is brought in on those, who have undertaken voyages with the expectation of being named in due time.

—2— The assignment of a recompense for merchandize, on which a reduction has not been made in the duties is a sufficient proof of the existence in force, of the Royal rescript, and of the right to the premium, even on those articles on which the duties have not been reduced; any disposition to the contrary would be entirely arbitrary.

—3— To limit such compensation on articles imported from the Indies, only to those entered before the 22nd. of January 1846, is to prescribe a date *ad libitum* like that of the 26th. of August, not in harmony with the Royal rescript.

If the voyages in question have been undertaken, and almost completed before the promised warning was given, how can it in good faith, be applied, to the Nuovo Raffaele & Ferdinando?

H. E. will therefore permit the Undersigned to insist on the precise and absolute execution of the Royal rescript. That rescript, promised to those engaged in commerce a warning of one year, for merchandize imported from the Indies; and not of six months as stated: and if it had even been of six months, as this warning was not given, nor promulgated, to those engaged in commerce, the reasons of Messrs. Borie & Co. are valid, in all respects; and they justly claim the protection of the Government of the United States of America, to obtain the due observance of a public act, so sacred as a Royal rescript, whatsoever may be the posterior dispositions.

The documents from His Majesty's Consul in the United States, have proved to this Chief Custom house, the regularity and the direct importation of the said cargoes, from Philadelphia & New York; and the Undersigned, Consul regrets to see such excuses offered, in order to avoid doing justice to Messrs. Borie & Co.

He therefore flatters himself that H. E. will do justice to the strong reasons advanced in support of the demand, for indemnification; and that this Royal Government will be induced speedily to make the reparation required by that of the United States, in the name of which he addresses the present note, in obedience to orders received.

A. Hammett to J. Buchanan

U. S. Consulate, Naples 21. Oct. 1847. [Consular Despatch No. 150]

Sir,

Confirming my letter of yesterday, I have to add, that having met in the street, the Chief of division in the office of Foreign Affairs,[12] I observed from him the like symptoms of a disposition in the Government to arrange M. Borie's affair. He even added, Laissez faire, as well for this, as for the other matter contained in my different notes, copies of which I had the honor to transmit you.

A. Hammett to J. Buchanan

Consulate of the U. S. of America Naples 28. Oct. 1847.
[Consular Despatch unnumbered, filed after Consular No. 150]

Sir,

I have the honor to add at foot Copy of the Minister's answer[13] to my last note about M^r. Borie's claim. — It would seem that they are at a loss to controvert it. It may be that they will offer a compromise, and in such case, I shall refer them to the consignee of M^r. Borie's cargoes, if you be pleased to so order.

A. Hammett to J. Buchanan

U. S. Consulate Naples 28. Oct. 1847. [Consular Despatch No. 151]

Sir,

The Board of Health has lately adopted measures of rigor for arrivals from the Gulph [sic] of Mexico, having previously suspended *pratique* for those from the ports of N. America, so that the quarantine of each would be regulated according to circumstances. There is not much injury to be feared here as we have no American vessels visiting this port, but the contrary may be expected in the ports of Sicily, from whence I have already received complaints. I have not failed to make the necessary representations, but as the Boards of Health in Sicily, are independent of that at Naples, I apprehend, without any success.

---

12 This was the Prince of Scilla. See pp. 643-644.
13 See p. 646, Oct. 20, 1847.

At foot I copy the Minister's communication,[14] and have the honor to remain,

THE PRINCE OF SCILLA TO A. HAMMETT

[Enclosure with Mr. Hammett's Consular Despatch unnumbered of Oct. 28, 1847]

Naples Octob. 20 1847.

The Undersigned, Councillor [sic] of State charged with the portfolio of Foreign Affairs, hastened to submit to the Minister of Finance, the note addressed to him on the 27th. of September, by M^r. Hammett the Consul of the United States of America, respecting the refusal of the premium, on the cargoes of two vessels, admitted into the Kingdom, on account of Messrs. Borie and Co. The Undersigned has the honor to declare, to the Consul, for the present, that the said secretary of State, is engaged in collecting the information, required to enable him to answer the said note, and in the mean time, he avails himself of the occasion, to repeat to M^r. Hammett the assurances &c.

J. BUCHANAN TO A. HAMMETT

Department of State, Washington, 9th. November, 1847.
[Instruction No. 1.]

Sir: I wrote to you on the 6th. May[15] last, and placed under the same cover, a communication addressed to Mr. W. H. Polk, and dated on the 5th. of that month, containing instructions,[16] which, in the absence of the Chargé, you were requested to carry into execution. Soon after his arrival in Washington, M^r. Polk resigned, and has proceeded to join the army in Mexico, in the

---

[14] In this communication dated, Naples, Oct. 21, 1847, the Prince of Scilla informed Mr. Hammett that "in consequence of the appearance of the yellow fever in various ports of New Orleans, the Supreme Magistrate of Health" had decided that vessels and cargoes arriving from that place would be "provisionally refused admittance into the royal dominions" and that with regard to articles coming from New Orleans by way of England, Gibraltar, France, and the Austrian ports in vessels from those places, the same measure would be observed, as with regard to those from Vera Cruz and Havana. The original Italian and the English translation are in the National Archives.

[15] Secretary of State Buchanan's Instruction to Mr. Hammett of May 6, 1847, is not in Buchanan's *Works*.

[16] See *hic opus,* Polk Chapter, p. 632, and note 40 thereon, re: Instruction No. 14.

capacity of Major of Dragoons. You will, therefore, continue to discharge the indispensable duties of the mission, until further orders, or during the period that may elapse before a successor shall be appointed by the President.

On the 4th. August last, I received your despatch, N°. 45, of the 3rd. of the preceding month, with copies of notes addressed by you to the Minister of Foreign Affairs, in conformity to the instructions of N°. 14; and on the 8th. instant, that of the 27th. September, No. 148, containing copy of your further correspondence with the Minister, respecting the claim of Messrs. Borie & Co. This subject will receive my consideration as soon as the papers, which are in Italian, shall have been translated.

I transmit, herewith, a letter from the President of the United States to His Sicilian Majesty, in reply to a communication received from him on the 12th. August last, announcing the fact that, Her Royal Highness, the Countess of Aquila had given birth to a Prince, who had received in baptism, the names of Filippo Luigi Maria.

You will take an early occasion to deliver the letter of the President, and the open copy which is also sent, herewith, to the Minister for Foreign Affairs, and to request him to cause the original to be placed in the hands of His Majesty.

A. HAMMETT TO J. BUCHANAN

U. S. Consulate Naples 20 Nov. 1847. [Consular Despatch N°. 152]

Sir,

It is a painful duty to be obliged to inform you, that a M^{r}. Huertas,[17] private secretary of M^{r}. Polk, after the departure of the latter, gave out that he was Chargé d'Affaires, and that on the arrival of Count Bresson,[18] the new Ambassador of France,

---

17 See below, Rowan chapter, p. 654—concerning the obligation to discharge his debts.

18 Bresson, Charles. Count de. (1798-1847). French diplomat. He entered the diplomatic service while still very young, rapidly attaining important positions. He was minister in the United States, ambassador at Brussels and Berlin. His most significant negotiation was that of the Spanish marriages. While ambassador at Madrid, he arranged the marriage of the Infante Isabelle with the Duke of Cadiz, her cousin, and of his sister with the Duke of Montpensier, the son of King Louis Philippe. In 1847, Count de Bresson was appointed ambassador at Naples, but distressed by domestic difficulties, he committed suicide before he reached his post. See François Pierre Guillaume Guizot, *Mémoires*, Paris, Michel Lévy frères, 1858-1867, 8 vols.; Joseph D'Haussonville, *La politique extérieure du gouvernment français*. Paris, 1850, 2 vols.; *Grande Encyclopédie*, no date, VII, 1132.

he actually dressed himself in uniform and visited him in such character.

Applied to by creditors for his debts, which reflect upon the Legation, I cannot refrain from stating the facts, because it's [sic] honor is thereby compromised, complaints in this sense being continually made to me on the matter.

I have to observe that the Books of the Legation have been for most of the time there has been a Legation here, in my keeping, and that this has caused me some expense and inconvenience. As the Books are never revised, it seems to me, that the trouble and expense, except for the laws, were totally unnecessary, & might have been well spared. I am also burthened [sic] with additional postages.[19]

Though I have not the honor of being personally known to you, yet if length of service and zeal can form a title to your consideration for me, I flatter myself, that I ought justly to expect something better than the post I have so long held.

Since my dispatch of the 28th. of October N°. 151 I have received no further communication for Mr. Borie's affair. Should I not soon receive one, as promised, I will again call their attention to it.

A. HAMMETT TO J. BUCHANAN

U. S. Consulate Naples 31 December 1847 [Consular N° 153]

Sir,

I have the honor to enclose the Consular Statement[20] of fees for the last six months, with account of postages for same time, and the half year previous, besides $2. to Mr Haines a distressed seaman, amo'tg. together to $14..89. which be pleased to order to be paid to Messrs. Hicks & Co. of N. York for my acct. It takes always a year to get back these disbursements, and at a loss of, 5 or 6 pr Cent.

I had repeated my demand for Mr. Borie's affair a short time previous to the receipt of your dispatch [sic] of the 9 Novr., N°. 1.[21] The enclosure by it for His Majesty was put by me into

---

[19] See p. 654.

[20] Not copied. See the original letter in "State Department: Consular Despatches, Naples, III, Hammett, 1839-50."

[21] See *hic opus,* Polk chapter, p. 632 and note 40 re: Instruction No. 14 to Mr. Polk; for the Instruction No. 1 to Mr. Hammett, next day, see Consular Despatches, Naples, III, Hammett 1839-50." Also cf. text of No. 1, *hic opus,* Hammett chapter, p. 646, repeating Instruction to carry out Mr. Polk's No. 14.

the Ministers [sic] hands. I took the opportunity of soliciting his attention to the claims of my Government, observing that I should be rejoiced if he would authorize me to state to you that they would be complied with. He answered that it was not his affair, but he would do all he can to succeed.

A. HAMMETT TO J. BUCHANAN

U. S. Consulate, Naples, 13 Jany. 1848 [Consular No. 1][22]

Sir,

It is with much displeasure I have to inform you of the death of M^r. Sherwood, our consul at Messina, which took place on the 2^d. inst.

Mr. Marston, our Consul in Palermo, charged M^r. Francis S. Blake of Boston, to proceed there giving him the character of Acting Consul. As it solely entered in his attributions to name a Cons^r. Agent, for whose acts he is responsible, upon receipt of their joint letters, I immediately asked from the Minister the necessary exequatur in such character, untill [sic] the President's pleasure be known as to a Successor.

Mr. Blake writes me that his sole motive in going to Messina was to assist the family of M^r. Sherwood to return to the U. S. an act worthy of the highest praise.

A. HAMMETT TO J. BUCHANAN

U. S. Consulate, Naples, 31 Jany. 1848. [Consular Despatch No. 2]

Sir,

The disturbed state of the Kingdom since some time, has prevented me from further pressing the matter contained in your dispatch of the 6th. of May last. An entire change of ministry has just been made here. I have the honor to enclose copies of the communications of the new Minister of Foreign Affairs, and

---

[22] Consular despatches were, as a rule, more numerous than those from Ministers and, therefore, were often numbered beginning anew with No. 1, with each year. This is another reason why it is so necessary to define clearly the volume and the series in citing references to documents in the National Archives of the United States. In the early volumes the despatches of each consulate were filed in separate volumes, but the instructions sent to all the consuls were filed together seriatim and chronologically.

my replies to him.[23] His Majesty has promised a Constitution to his subjects, so that the dawn of brighter days appears to open for them.[24] A reaction is however threatening from the Lazzaroni who want to plunder, and consequences may be expected to result, from the change here, to all Italy. —

It will require sometime before things get settled, but I always keep in view my instructions.

A. HAMMETT TO J. BUCHANAN

U. States Consulate Naples 10 March 1848.[25]

[Consular Despatch, Unnumbered]

Sir,

Having performed the duties of the Mission to Naples according to your despatches of the 6th. of May, and the 9th. of November 1847, it is but just that I be paid as Chargé during the time of my services for the same. I do not expect however, that the Executive can pay me without an appropriation, and that my claim will have to be laid before Congress.[26] I have accordingly directed my friends Messrs. Hicks Co. of N. York to do it, for I learn, that the President has been pleased to appoint

---

[23] In a communication dated Naples, Jan. 27, 1848, the Duke of Serracapriola informed Mr. Hammett that His Majesty had just appointed him (the Duke) Minister Secretary of State for Foreign Affairs. Mr. Hammett acknowledged the receipt of the Duke's communication on Jan. 29, 1848. Copies of both communications are in the National Archives.

[24] King Ferdinand II, following the outbreak of revolts in many cities of his Kingdom, made haste to proclaim, on January 29, 1848, a popular Constitution. An extract from the *Giornale Uffiziale* of Jan. 29, 1848, was sent to the State Department by Mr. Hammett. This issue contained the Italian text of the royal decree signed Naples, Jan. 29, 1848, by King Ferdinand, in which he announced that he had asked his new minister of state to submit, within ten days, a bill to be approved by the King, providing: 1) That the legislative power be vested in two houses—the Pari and the Chamber of Deputies. 2) That the Catholic religion be the only dominant religion and that other religions will not be tolerated. 3) That the person of the King will always be sacred, inviolable, and not subject to any responsibility. 4) That the ministers will always be responsible for all acts of the government. 5) That the armed forces of land and sea will be dependent on the King. 6) That the press is free, etc. etc. However, soon, on May 15, 1848, the Neapolitan Parliament was dissolved and within a little less than a year (May 13, 1849) Ferdinand regained control of the kingdom, resuming his tyrannical rule.

[25] On Feb. 28, 1848, Mr. Hammett sent to the Duke of Serracapriola a letter from Mr. Marston, consul at Palermo, "preparatory to possible claim." See Rowan chapter pp. 656-657.

[26] See House Report 566, 25th Congress, 2nd session, "to accompany H. R. Bill No. 556." Also see: House Document 342, 26th Congress, 1st session, Apr. 4, 1840 "to accompany Bill No. 318." For fate of these bills, see *House Journal*. See also below, p. 651, and note 28.

another Chargé to Naples,[27] and observe on a N. York paper of the 5ᵗʰ. of february, that amongst other objects a Bill had been reported for his outfit &c. My object, therefore is to get the action of the present session of Congress on my claim, and not to wait another year, though I have received no order to discontinue to discharge the duties of the mission. —

I flatter myself, Sir, that you will be pleased to lend your kind protection to the claim, as precedents are not wanting to justify it.

A. HAMMETT TO J. BUCHANAN

United States Consulate, Naples 30 June 1848. [Consular No. 3]

Sir,

I have the honor to enclose Consular Statement of fees for the last six months. Also the account of Storage & Keeping of the Books of the Legation, &c. which Mr. Rowan told me you would pay. If so, as I hope, be pleased to pass the amount for my account to Messʳˢ. Hicks & Co. of New York. I flatter myself besides, that you may have been pleased to insert in the appropriation Bill,[28] my claim for having discharged the duties of the Legation, from the first of May 1847, when Mʳ. Polk left, to the 22ᵈ. of June 1848, when Mʳ. Rowan arrived at Naples.

---

[27] In his Instruction No. 2, dated Washington, Feb. 16, 1848, Secretary of State Buchanan notified Mr. Hammett that the President had appointed Mr. John Rowan, of Kentucky, to be chargé d'affaires at Naples and that Mr. Rowan was about to proceed upon his mission. On Mr. Rowan's arrival at Naples, Mr. Hammett was instructed to deliver over to him the books, archives, and papers of the Legation.

[28] See above, this chapter, p. 650, note 26. For application to Congress for a law enabling the compensation of Alexander Hammett for his long service as Consul, and specifically for the period during which he was Chargé d'affaires in Naples *ad interim,* for more than a year, see Livingston to Nelson, Instruction No. 3, Feb. 25, 1832. Instructions to Ministers, XIII, 276-277. Mr. Morris commends Mr. Hammett's services during 44 years in Naples as Consul; see Morris' chapter, *hic opus.* See also, report on the Petition of Alex. Hammett. House Foreign Affairs Committee, Feb. 17, 1838. Reports of Committees, No. 566, 25th Cong., 2nd ses., 2 pp. 8°. It "Recommended that he be allowed for expenses incurred as United States Consul at Naples. BILL REPORTED." Also see Report on Petition of Alexander Hammett. By Repr. N. Clifford, Apr. 4, 1840. House Reports, No. 342, 26th Cong., 1st sess., II. "The Petitioner acted for many years as Consul of the United States at Naples, and rendered valuable service to citizens of the United States in attending to claims arising out of the seizures and confiscations of American property, in doing which he incurred expenses which he prays may be refunded." "Reported, with recommendation he be paid $2000 in full."

JOHN ROWAN[1]

(January 3, 1848 to January 1, 1850)

J. BUCHANAN TO J. ROWAN

Department of State, Washington, 16th. February, 1848
[Instruction No. 1.]

Sir:

The President, by and with the advice and consent of the Senate, having appointed you Chargé d'Affaires of the United States, I transmit, herewith, the following papers.

1. Your commission, as Chargé d'Affaires.

2. A letter of Credence addressed to the Minister of Foreign Affairs of The Two Sicilies, and an office copy of the same.

3. A Special Passport for yourself and suite.

4. A Letter of credit on the Bankers of the United States in London, authorising them to pay your drafts for your salary as this shall become due, and, also, those for the contingent expenses of the Legation. The latter credit is to be used only for expenses actually incurred, and these are not to exceed the sum of $500 per annum. In availing yourself of this authority you will be careful to conform strictly to the rules laid down in the printed "Personal Instructions," referred to below, and in the printed letter giving directions on the subject of drafts drawn by Diplomatic Agents of the United States.

5. A printed copy of "Personal Instructions to the Diplomatic Agents of the United States in foreign countries," with the "Supplement" thereto; to both which your attention is specially directed. Also, [marked A and B] two printed Circulars[2] the ones giving certain directions to be observed by the Diplomatic Agents of the United States in drawing bills on public account;

---

[1] John Rowan, of Kentucky, commissioned Chargé d'Affaires January 3, 1848. He left about Jan. 1, 1850. *Appleton's Cyclopedia of American Biography,* V, 337, confuses this John Rowan with his distinguished father, John Rowan (1773-1843), who was judge of the Court of Appeals of Kentucky 1819-1821; he was elected to the U. S. Senate, 1825-1831. John Rowan, the second, was born Feb. 9, 1807; he died Aug. 14, 1855. An article by Howard R. Marraro on "John Rowan's mission to the Two Sicilies (1848-1850)" was published in *The Register of the Kentucky State Historical Society,* Frankfort, Ky., July 1945, XLIII, 263-271.

[2] Not reproduced in this printing.

the other, establishing a rule respecting the salaries of those Agents, when absent from their posts on leave.

6. A printed list of the Diplomatic and Consular Agents of the United States in foreign countries.

Your salary, as fixed by law, is at the rate of $4.500 per annum, with an outfit equal to a year's salary and an amount equal to one quarter's salary for your return to this country. By a general rule the salary of Ministers to Foreign Courts commences on the day of their leaving their residence to prepare for their departure on their mission, and ceases on their taking leave of the Courts to which they are accredited, after having received orders or permission to return home. In your case it will commence on the 28ᵗʰ. of January.

When your predecessor left Naples, on leave of absence to visit the United States, the property and archives of the Legation were left by him in the custody of Mʳ. Hammett,[3] who has long resided at Naples, in the capacity of American Consul. Mʳ. Polk subsequently resigned, and Mʳ. Hammett was desired by me to execute certain instructions which had been transmitted to the former; since which period he has been acting as Chargé d'Affaires *ad interim*.

Mr. Hammett is well acquainted with the relations subsisting between the two countries, and has had much experience in the business of the Legation; and his advice and assistance — which would, no doubt, be cheerfully afforded, will be found useful to you on entering upon the duties of your mission. He will deliver to you the archives and property of the Legation; and you are requested to take an early occasion to transmit an exact inventory[4] of the same to this Department.

Instructions given to your predecessor, and to Mʳ. Hammett, as far as they are applicable, or may remain unexecuted, are to be considered as a part of your own. Further instructions will be sent from time to time as occasion may require.

---

[3] See Hammett chapter, *hic opus.*
[4] Transmitted July 10, 1848, with Mr. Rowan's Despatch No. 2, q.v., *hic opus* and chapter, p. 656.

J. BUCHANAN TO J. ROWAN

Department of State, Washington, 12ᵗʰ. May, 1848.
[Instruction No. 3.]⁵

Sir:

I transmit, herewith, a letter from the President of the United States, to His Sicilian Majesty, in reply to a communication received from him dated on the 4ᵗʰ. March last, announcing the fact that Her Majesty the Queen, had given birth to a Prince, who had received in baptism the names of Giuseppe Maria Luigi.

You will take an early occasion to deliver the letter of the President, and the open copy which is also sent, herewith, to the Minister for Foreign Affairs, and to request him to cause the original to be delivered to His Majesty.

Mʳ. Hammett's despatches of the 27ᵗʰ. September, 20ᵗʰ. 21ˢᵗ. and 28ᵗʰ. October and 20ᵗʰ. November last; and those of the 31ˢᵗ. January and 10ᵗʰ. March of the present year, have been received.

In his letter of 20ᵗʰ. November last, Mʳ. Hammett makes complaint against a Mʳ. Huerta.⁶ His misconduct is to be regretted; but, at the same time, there exists no obligation, whatever, on the part of the Government to discharge the debts contracted by that individual, who is represented to have acted as Private Secretary of Mʳ. Polk, but was certainly never recognized in any official capacity by this Department.

In regard to the archives, and to the extra postage, you will inform Mʳ. Hammett, that the necessary expense of the Storage of the former, in case of, and during the absence of the Diplomatic Representative, will be allowed;⁷ and that any charges for postage on account of the Legation, to which he may have been subjected, will be paid upon his rendering a proper account therefor.

---

⁵ In Instruction No. 2, Washington, March 27, 1848, Secretary of State Buchanan transmitted the commission of Mr. F. W. Behn, of Kentucky, who had been appointed United States Consul at Messina, instructing Mr. Rowan to apply for the exequatur for Mr. Behn. See also note 36, page 666.

⁶ See Hammett chapter, p. 647. Consular Despatch, Naples, No. 152, Nov. 20, 1847.

⁷ See note 6, above.

J. ROWAN TO J. BUCHANAN

Legation of the U. States Naples 1 July 1848 [Despatch N°. 1]

Sir

I arrived here on the 21st. June, and without loss of time informed the Prince of Cariate,[8] [sic] Minister of F. Affairs of that fact. As he was unwell, several days elapsed before I could present him my letters of credence. This took place on the 27th. and on the 29th. following, I was presented[9] by him to the King. My reception by both was very flattering, and kind. — I assured them in return of the President's sincere desire to cultivate the most friendly understanding with His Majesty's Government, as well as to extend to both countries, the relations of Commerce, which would redound to mutual advantage.

After repeated delays the Representative Chamber will be opened here this day.[10] The King does not go in person, but will be represented by a Delegate. He appears apprehensive for his personal safety. It is understood that he will concede every thing that has been demanded by his Subjects.

It will require time before things get settled. Sicily is *de facto* a separate state except the Citadel of Messina, and the Calabrias are in a state of anarchy and confusion. It is expected however that the insurgents of the latter will ultimately be put down, as that Sicily will be able to maintain her independence.

In their actual relations any agency here on my part, would avail nothing for American interests in Sicily, all communications having ceased between them. The steamer leaves this morning & this dispatch merely serves to announce the commencement of my official duties, successive ones will instruct you more fully with passing events.

---

[8]Gennaro Spinelli Barile. Prince of Cariati. (1780-1815). Field marshal. During the constitutional period, he was charged with a diplomatic mission to Vienna. After the restoration he went into exile, but was permitted to return to the kingdom on Nov. 20, 1825. From Mar. 6, to Apr. 3, 1848, he held the post of minister of foreign affairs; finally, from May 16, 1848, to Aug. 7, 1849, he was president of the council of ministers and minister of foreign affairs. Ruggiero Moscati, *Il Regno delle Due Sicilie e l'Austria,* 378.

[9] In the original the word 'introduced' was first written, then crossed out, and the word 'presented' written above it.

[10] On July 1, 1848 the Neapolitan Parliament was inaugurated with only 33 out of 78 members of the Pari and 71 out of 164 Deputies present. The Duke of Serracapriola, who was charged by the King to address the opening session, said that the Sovereign had been greviously afflicted by the delay in the meeting of the assembly which was due to the deplorable events that had occurred. The Duke of Serracapriola made clear that the liberal institutions, promised and sworn to by the King, would be vain unless laws were passed to carry them out. The Duke urged Parliament to direct its attention to public finances which were in a deplorable condition. *Almanach de Gotha,* 1850, 649.

J. ROWAN TO J. BUCHANAN

Legation of the United States, Naples, 10th July, 1848.

[Despatch No. 2]

Sir,

I have the honor to enclose a list of the Books[11] belonging to the U. S. transferred to me by Mr. Hammett, the American Consul, on my arrival here; also, two papers relative to property of American Citizens, exposed during the late disturbances in Messina, on which a loss of $17,716 67/100 is pretended.

Mr. Hammett informs me, that on the 28th of Feb. last, he transmitted to the Duke of Serra Capriola, then Minister of Foreign Affairs, a letter from Mr. Marston,[12] our Consul in Palermo, requesting him to take note of it, as preparatory to any claims for Indemnity, which might be made by Americans; and that he has not since heard from him.

It appears to me doubtful, if there has been loss, on any American property, whether such loss was occasioned by the Neapolitans, or by the Sicilians themselves.

I have conversed with Cap. Engle,[13] of the U. S. steamer Princeton, who was there at the time, and it is his opinion, as well as the opinion of all the officers that there exists no claim whatever on this Government. They doubt if any loss of American property occurred at all, but if there was loss, it was occasioned by the Sicilians themselves. I have thought it better, before talking

---

11 The list included 678 "volumes" but in this total Mr. Hammett counted as one volume, the locked trunk of the Legation's correspondence, also one missing volume. Mr. Rowan later corrected his total count, in his certification of the Legation's books etc. See, Enclosure with Despatch No. 2 of Mr. Rowan, July 10, 1848. This enclosure is not herein reproduced, but is filed with the despatches of Mr. Rowan in custody of the United States National Archivist. Mr. Rowan altered the total to 677. This list, compared with earlier ones, has several notable additions to the Legation's library resources, including works published more recently. This list, however, is less specific as to titles than some of the earlier ones.

12 See United States Legation, Naples, post papers, Consular: Mr. Hammett's Despatches. Only Mr. Hammett's despatches while acting *ad interim* as Chargé d'affaires are printed *hic opus*. See Mr. Hammett's chapter but note that these commercial claims of all kinds usually went through Mr. Hammett's hands as Consul in their preliminary stages; when he felt he had exhausted all his powers to get action on the claims he referred them, as other consuls would also do, to the United States chargé d'affaires or the incumbent United States minister.

13 Frederick Engle (1799-1868) was born in Pennsylvania. He was admitted to the navy as a midshipman in 1814; Lieutenant, 1825; Commander, 1841; Captain, 1855. His rank was not that of a Captain in 1848, but he may have acted as captain of the vessel.

or taking any steps in this matter here, to submit the papers[14] to you, before whom proofs can be furnished by the owners, who are now in the U. S., of the losses, if suffered. If the claims be just, the claimants will loose [sic] nothing by the delay occasioned by this course, as this Government, in its present distracted condition, is unable to pay.

The two houses of Parliament were opened on the first of July by commission, but were unable to form a quorum until the 8th inst.

The city is at present quiet, and the official papers state that the insurrection in Calabria has been quelled, but the Government continues to send large bodies of troops, almost daily.

MARIANO COSTARELLI TO F. S. BLAKE[15]

[Enclosure with M[r]. Rowan's Despatch of 10 July 1848]

Messina, 25th January 1848

Sir

Upon your request of this date I give you a note[16] with the value of the property I hold, consisting of sundry Articles it belonging, and are for account of the American citizens, also the names of American vessels now lying in this port, and consigned to me.

"Bark "Pico" John Leckey Master —

"Bark "Prompt" Francis O. Wellman Jr.

Be so kind advise me reception of the present and Remain with due respect,

Your Most Ob[t]. Serv[t].

Mariano Costarelli[17]

---

14 See the letter (claim) of Mr. Mariano Costarelli, Messina, Jan. 25, 1848, to Mr. F. S. Blake, acting consul of the United States at Messina, regarding the barks *Pico* and *Prompt,* q.v., this chapter, below, p. 658, the inventory of same.

15 F. S. Blake was Acting Consul of the United States at Messina, serving from the recall of C. Sherwood of N. Y. in 1847, to the appointment of Mr. Behn on March 9, 1848.

16 See Inventory, p. 658.

17 Costarelli was consignee for many American firms. For some of these, see, July 29, 1850, Legation to Fortunato, Minister of Foreign Affairs, the Two Sicilies showing Costarelli the consignee of Beecher & Draper, and an earlier claim placed by Costarelli for the *Spartan,* October 1849, for Draper and Payson of Boston. Costarelli served for some time as United States vice-consul at Messina.

[Reverse of letter signed "Mariano Costarelli dated 25 Jan. 1848, "from F. S. Blake, Acting Consul of U. S. at Messina," and enclosed with Mr. Rowan's Despatch No. 3, of 17th Jy. 1848]

Note Of Merchandize existing for account of American Citizens this day, in the following Warehouses—Viz

Store Sta. Catharina Street [sic] (N$^\circ$. 39)
property
of Mr. Francis Alecsi [sic]

130 Bags	130 Cant^{rs}.	Canary Seed .....at Oz.	1.15	C^r.	Oz.	195.—.—
36 D.	36.50 D$^\circ$.	Shelled Almonds .."	8.—	"	"	292.—.—
30 Cases	32.—D$^\circ$.	Sicily Licorice Paste "	6.10	"	"	202.20.—
30 "	50. Salms [sic]	Filberts ...."	4.20	s^m.	"	233.10.—
" "	230 Boxes	Dryed [sic] prunes "	".29	B^x.	"	153.10.—
" "	51 Salms [sic]	Walnuts ...."	3.15	s^m.	"	178.15.—
128 Cases	1278 Cant^{rs}.	Maccheroni [sic] .."	4.26	C^r.	"	253. 2.—
426 Bales	1278 Cant^{rs}.	Rags [sic] ...."	2.20	d$^\circ$.	"	3408.—.—
400 Bags	380 d$^\circ$.	Sumac ...."	1.6	d$^\circ$.	"	456.—.—

Store Sta. Catharina Street (N$^\circ$. 11)
property
of Mr. Francis Russo

" "	400 Cant^{rs}.	Loose Brimstone .."	16 Taris, Cant^r.	"	213.10.—

Under the house of my abitation [sic]
Strada Ferdinanda (N. Jenro)
and now Pio IX.

" "	6000 lbs	Oil of Bergamot ..."	18	T. p^r. lb.	"	3600.—.—
" "	4000 "	" of Orange ....."	8	"	"	1066.20.—
" "	2500 "	" of Lemon ......"	12	"	"	1000.—.—

Store in the "Teatro Marittimmo" [sic]
(N$^\circ$. —) property of M^r. Gius^e. Sciva

" "	8000 Boxes	Oranges ...."	15	^{ts}. p^r Bx	"	4000.—.—
	2000 d$^\circ$.	Lemons ...."	15	"	"	1000.—.—

Store in the "teatro Marittimo"
property of M^r. Letterio Vadalà

" "	10,000 Boxes	Lemons ...."	15	^{ts}. p^r Bx.	"	5000.—.—

Messina 25th January 1848   E.E.   [oz]21251.27.—[18]

[18] The oncie of Sicily reckoned in gold at 30 carlini, but accounts were kept in oncie of 30 tari (gold), worth but one-half that at Naples. Blunt, *op. cit.,* gives Sicilian oncie as equal to $2.485 (U. S.).

J. ROWAN TO J. BUCHANAN

Legation of the U. S. A. Naples 17 July 1848. [Despatch No. 3]

Sir

I have this moment received the documents which I hasten to enclose to you.[19] As the steamer (the only one that leaves within this month) is on the eve of starting, I have not time to say more.

THE PRINCE OF CARIATI TO J. ROWAN

[Enclosure with Mr. Rowan's Despatch No. 3 sent without waiting to translate]

Napoli 16. Luglio 1848

Il sedicente Governo provvisorio di Palermo, con deliberazione degli 11. del Corrente, à chiamato al Trono di Sicilia S. A. R^{le}. Duca di Genova,[20] figlio secondo genito di S. M. il Re di Sardegna. Il Real Governo non dubita che S. M. Sarda, pel rispetto e la religiosa fede dovuta da ogni Principe a solenni trattati approvati, sottoscritti e sanzionati da tutti i Sovrani di Europa, e pel desiderio di serbare illese le relazioni di amicizia e di buon'armonia felicemente esistenti tra i due Stati, non permetterà al suo figlio di accettare una Corona offertagli da turbolenta fazione.

Pur nondimeno in vista di provvedere alle future eventualità, il Re ed il suo Consiglio giudicano opportuno emanare una nuova protesta, con lo scopo di serbare illesa la unità e la integrità della Monarchia delle Due Sicilie, non che i sacri diritti della Persona del Re e della sua Dinastia.

Il Sottoscritto Ministro Segretario di Stato degli Affari Esteri, Presidente del Consiglio de' Ministri, si affretta rimetterne copia al Signor Rowan, Incaricato di Affari degli Stati Uniti di America, pregandola di portarla alla cognizione del suo Governo,

---

19 This was a letter to Mr. Rowan from the Prince of Cariati dated July 16, 1848, informing him that on July 11, 1848, the General Parliament of Sicily issued a decree offering the throne of Sicily to the Duke of Genoa, second son of the King of Sardinia. See below. Enclosure with No. 3 was sent without being translated. On July 15, a Sicilian extraordinary ambassador had arrived at Genoa to announce the news that the Sicilians had nominated the Duke of Genoa as their constitutional King. King Ferdinand II of the Two Sicilies protested against the Sicilian decree.

20 The Duke of Genoa was Ferdinand of Savoy, a son of Charles Albert, King of Sardinia. The progress of the revolution and the rapidly changing political scene made it impossible for the Duke of Genoa to accept the crown of Sicily.

sicuro che lo stesso, occorrendo vorrà appoggiare co' suoi buoni uffizi presso il Gabinetto di Torino, i reclami di quello di Napoli, con tutti quegli argomenti che logicamente e lucidissimamente si presenteranno alla mente di ogni uomo di Stato senza esser necessario qui lungamente riferire.

Si limiterà soltanto il Sottoscritto a far rilevare, come nelle presenti circostanze dell'Europa in generale, e dell'Italia in particolare, per le nuove circoscrizioni territoriali, che probabilmente avran luogo, diviene indispensabile la integrità, unità e forza del Regno delle Due Sicilie, onde serbare l'equilibrio e la indipendenza della Penisola.

Nè può il Real Governo supporre che si vorrà lasciare al Re di Sardegna, il diritto di decidere di moto proprio una così grave quistione, nella quale sarebbe ad un tempo giudice e parte. E che sarebbe della indipendenza e della stabilità delle Monarchie, pietra angolare del diritto internazionale, e del sistema politico del mondo incivilito, qualora si concedesse ad una fazione o ad una parte di una Nazione la facoltà di sottrarsi al dominio del proprio Sovrano, e distaccarsi dalla Potenza di cui fa parte, grande o piccola che sia, per isceglersi a suo capriccio un nuovo Sovrano ed accrescere la forza di altro Stato, specialmente quando questo fosse già potente e ben costituito?

In attesa di favorevole riscontro che il Sottoscritto prega il Signor Incaricato di Affari di sollecitare dal suo Governo, egli profitta di siffatta occasione per rinnovarle le proteste di sua particolare considerazione

P.° di Cariati.

J. BUCHANAN TO J. ROWAN

Department of State, Washington, 31st. August, 1848.
[Instruction No. 4.]

Sir: I have the honor to acknowledge the receipt of your despatches of the 1st., 10th. and 17th. ultimo, the first and last numbered 1 and 3, whilst that of the 10th. July was not numbered.

The agitations of Italy, and the precarious position of several of its States, give a special value to the communications from our Diplomatic Representatives in that part of the world. In the difficult position in which you may be placed, I would refer you as a guide for your conduct, to my despatch to Mr. Rush of the 31st. March last, of which I transmit you a copy, containing an exposition of the policy of this Government in regard to the recognition of foreign Governments, and to our non-interference in the domestic concerns of foreign nations.[21]

The Department has not yet received intelligence of the arrival of M^r. Martin[22] at Rome.

J. ROWAN TO J. BUCHANAN

Legation of the United States Naples, 2nd September 1848.

[Despatch No. 4]

Sir,

It is my painful duty to announce to you the death of Mr. Martin,[23] the United States Chargé d'Affaires at Rome. This melancholy intelligence came to me this morning, in a letter from our Vice-Consul at Rome.[24] None of the particulars of his illness are given, save that he was ill but a short time, and had good medical attendants. He died on the 26th of August, and was buried with distinguished honors on the 28th. I had received a letter from him, dated a few days before his death: he was then in fine health and spirits. By this sad event, our Country has lost a most accomplished gentleman and an able representative. I have written to the Vice-Consul to take charge of whatever Mr. Martin may have left belonging to the Government, as also his private papers and property, until they shall be called for by his successor; and through him, to Mr. Martin's family.

---

[21] For Secretary of State Buchanan's despatch to Mr. Rush, see Buchanan *Works* VIII, 32-37. Richard Rush (1780-1859) was minister of the United States to France 1847-51. Mr. Rush arrived in France in the closing days of the July monarchy, witnessing the February revolution. Mr. Buchanan's letter to Mr. Rush, dated March 31, 1848, contained an exposition of the policy of the United States respecting the recognition of foreign governments and interference in their domestic affairs. For American reaction, see Marraro, *American opinion*, etc., 32, 69, 72.

[22] Jacob L. Martin, of North Carolina, was commissioned chargé d'affaires to the States of the Church on April 7, 1848. He had been nominated Apr. 7, 1848, instead of Joshua L. Martin. (Hasse, *op. cit.*, 1820). Jacob died at his post on August 26, 1848. See: Leo F. Stock, *United States Ministers to the Papal States* (Washington, D. C., 1933). Despatches to and from Mr. Martin, 1-16. On Mr. Martin's mission to Rome, see: Howard R. Marraro, "American Travellers in Rome, 1848-1850." *The Catholic Historical Review*, Jan. 1944, XXIX, 488-496; Sister Loretta Clare Feiertag, *American public opinion on the diplomatic relations*, etc. 36-42. Martin's death was notified to the State Department by Mr. Rowan's Despatch No. 4, of Sept. 2, 1848, p.v.

[23] See above, note 22.

[24] Antoine Ardisson was United States vice-consul at Rome at that time. For an account of his consulship, see: Stock, *Consular Relations United States and Papal States*, 97-104; 106-107, 110-120, 123-129, etc. His despatches on the death of Martin are given, *ibid*, 124-128.

On yesterday, the Neapolitan fleet, with a large army, sailed for the invasion of Sicily. But little doubt is entertained of its success in retaking that portion of the Kingdom.[25] The English and French have both large fleets here; but they made no effort to prevent the departure of the Neapolitan fleet. It was British influence that caused the Sicilians to offer the Crown to the Duke of Genoa and if he had accepted it, they would not have allowed the Invasion. They are now anxious that a son of the King of Naples shall have the crown. A majority of the Sicilians themselves prefer to return to the old order of things; and there is little doubt but such will be the case.

I ought, before this, to have mentioned to you the many obligations I have been under to our excellent Consul here, Mr. Hammett. His familiarity with the language of the country, and perfect knowledge of the business of the Legation, with his very obliging disposition, has made me feel much less embarrassed than I otherwise would. Will not the Government allow him the pay of a Chargé during the time he has been acting as such? I feel that he deserves it, and I *know* that he is *poor.*

Will you have the kindness to have the Editors of the Union[26] directed to send my paper by the steamers: other american [sic] papers that come by them, are twenty days in advance of the Union.

J. ROWAN TO J. BUCHANAN

Legation of the United States Naples Nov. 26th 1848 [Despatch No. 5]

Sir:

On the 6th. October I addressed the following Note to the Prince of Cariati. A desire to have furnished you with his answer and a rather severe attack of fever must be my apology for so long a silence.

"The undersigned, Chargé d'Affaires of the United States of America, has the honor to call the attention of his Excellency, the Prince of Cariati, Minister Secretary of State for Foreign Affairs, and President of the Council of Ministers, to the subject

---

[25] The Neapolitan troops landed near Messina on Sept. 2, 1848. The fighting between the government troops and the insurgents began on Sept. 3, and the bombardment of the city continued to Sept. 7 when, after brave resistance, Messina was taken by the Neapolitan army, which occupied all the forts including the lighthouse. *Almanach de Gotha,* 1850, 26.

[26] The *Washington Daily Union,* a non-official newspaper.

of two notes addressed to his Excellency the Prince of Scilla then charged with the Portfolio of Foreign Affairs by M^r. Hammett, Consul of the United States of America, then also charged with the affairs of this Legation.[27] One of said notes was dated on the first of July 1847, and the other on the 27th of Septr. following, in answer to the reply of His Excellency, dated the 21st. Septr. a few days before, for claims of the House of Messrs Boire [sic] & Co. of Philadelphia, on cargoes of Brigs Nuovo Raffael, [sic] and Ferdinando. The Prince of Scilla stated in his note of the 27th. of Septr. that copies of the same as stated, had been passed to his Excellency, the Minister of Finance, who was actually collecting information on the subject. In consequence of the disturbed state of the Kingdom, the Consul did not see fit to press the claim further at the time, and the Undersigned, since his arrival, has from like motives also forborne to do it. But when it is considered what serious injury redounds to the interests of Messrs Boire [sic] & Co. he cannot longer abstain from carrying out the Orders of his Government; and he feels conscious, that by fixing again the attention of His Majesty's Government on the Affair in question, it will be brought to a speedy and Equitable adjustment. In this conviction the undersigned has the honor to repeat to his Excellency, the assurances of his high consideration."

I have not as yet received an answer to my note. I have however, this day called his attention to it, and have requested an early answer. I have also received, and presented for adjustment the following claims of American citizens upon this Government, for injuries done to their property in the late difficulties with Sicily. — A claim by William P. Wheeler Master of the Ship Panama at Trepani [sic], for damages received by his Ship, from the Bombardment of that place by the Neapolitan troops, for which he claims of this Government the sum of two hundred and fifty dollars. Also a claim by Marston & Co. for the taking and destroying, by the Neapolitan troops before their evacuation of Palermo, a large quantity of filberts, and walnuts valued at thirty three hundred Ducats. Likewise a claim of the American Consul at Palermo, of one hundred and ninety eight ducats; the amount he states it cost him to remove the Archives, and Effects

---

[27] As a matter of fact in a letter dated Washington, May 5, 1847, Mr. Buchanan had instructed Mr. Polk to examine carefully all the facts of the case of Messrs. Borie & Co., and that if Mr. Polk found them to be in accordance with their statement, he [Mr. Polk] was firmly, but respectfully, in the name of his government, to ask of the Sicilian Government that Messrs. Borie & Co. be indemnified for the losses which they had sustained in the premises. See above. J. Buchanan, *Works,* VII, 298-301. See also Hammett chapter, pp. 637 ff.

of the Consulate to the American Ship European and Barque Ohio, and for storage of the same. These claims are all properly authenticated, and I presume will be paid.

There has been no alteration in the Sicilian matter since the interference, of the French and English. — They are all anxiously waiting the arrival of Mʳ. Temple,[28] the British Minister. He will be here today or tomorrow, and as Lord Napier[29] has promised to keep me advised of the progress of the negociations I will be enabled in a few days to give you certain information upon this very vexed, and intricate subject. In the meantime the King of Naples has been very active in increasing the fortifications of this City, as well as enlarging his Army which now numbers 80,000 men. Parliament was to have met on the last day of this month, but it has been postponed by the King until February next. The most startling incident that has occurred in Europe for a long time, and one of course that engrosses all attention, is the revolution in Rome.[30] The assassination of the Prime Minister, and the flight of the Pope.[31] The particulars that

---

[28] The Sicilians knew that England was keenly interested in their affairs. Lord Palmerston, who had vainly offered British mediation to Ferdinand, openly defended the uncompromising attitude of the Sicilies. Cf. Marraro, *American Opinion*, 29, 112, 115, 117, 118, 202, 203.

[29] Francis Napier (Baron Ettrick) (1819-1898). He was appointed Secretary of the British Legation at Naples on May 27, 1846, and was chargé d'affaires in 1848-49. He favored the liberals, aiding Luigi Settembrini, their leader, to escape on an English frigate. His efforts to effect a reconciliation between the Sicilians and the Neapolitan Government proved fruitless.

[30] On the pontificate of Pius IX and the political disturbances of this period in Rome, see: Carlo Tesi-Passerini, *Pio Nono e il suo tempo.* (Florence, 1877); Alfred O. Legge, *Pius IX, the story of his life to the restoration in 1850.* (London, 1875); A. de Saint-Albin, *Histoire de Pie IX.* (Paris, 1870); G. Mollat, *La question romaine de Pie VI à Pie IX.* (Paris, 1932); R. Giovagnoli, *Pellegrino Rossi e la rivoluzione romana.* (Rome, 1898-1911, 3 volumes); R. de Cesare, *The last days of papal Rome, 1850-1870.* (Abridged and translated by Helen Zimmern) (London, 1909); Giuseppe Spada, *Storia della rivoluzione di Roma e della restaurazione del governo pontificio, 1846-1849.* (Florence, 1868-1869); Giovanni Conti, *La Repubblica Romana del 1849: studio storico politico.* (Rome, Libreria Politica Moderna, 1920); Luigi C. Farini, *The Roman State from 1815 to 1850.* Translated by W. E. Gladstone, London, 1851-1854; Giuseppe Leti, *Roma e lo stato pontificio dal 1849 al 1870.* Ascoli Piceno, G. Cesari, 1911; A. Ballendier, *Histoire de la Révolution de Rome* (1846-1850). Geneva, 1851, 2 volumes; R. M. Johnston, *The Roman Theocracy and the Republic, 1846-1849.* London, Murray, 1901; F. Torre, *Memorie storiche sull'intervento francese in Roma nel 1849.* (Turin, 1851-1853); Ferdinand De Lesseps, *La mia missione a Roma.* (Florence, 1849); Ferdinand De Lesseps, *Recollections of forty years.* (New York, 1888); René Bittard des Portes, *L'expédition française de Rome sous la deuxième République.* (Paris, 1905); W. J. Stillman, *Autobiography of a journalist.* (Boston and New York, 1901).

[31] Pope Pius IX left Rome at 5 p.m. on Nov. 24, 1848, arriving at Gaeta on the following day. *Almanach de Gotha,* 1850, 48.

664

led to all this have not transpired; but that He made his escape in the disguise of a footman to the Bavarian Minister,[32] & that He is now at Gaeta, a very strongly fortified city of this Kingdom, there is no doubt. All the Royal family have gone to welcome His Holiness, and are now with Him. The following is the account given of His Escape by the Government paper here and is doubtless correct.

"Pio the Ninth is safe! The Angel of the Lord covered with His shield the supreme pastor of all Christendom, and He passed unobserved in the midst of his Guardians in arms, and came in safety to our territory. The prayers of Believers were heard; and now to the Humble prayer succeeds the Hymn of thanks to the Most High. — No, the holy name of Pio could no longer be profaned amidst the orgies of men who to the magnanimity of His Heart now correspond with the blackest ingratitude. He the Supreme head of a religion of Peace, Pardon, & Love, opened the doors of their prisons, and they, as in compensation, changed His Palace to a Prison, and in his name cast amongst the People the most subversive, and anarchical Ideas. — The news which we have received about the departure of the Pontiff from Rome, places us in a state to satisfy the just anxiety of our readers, for an event of such grave importance and consequences which will benefit all.

["] Late in the evening of the 24th. the Ambassador of Bavaria, Count Spaur, presented himself at the palace of the Pope, and demanded to see Him; at first objections were started, but He resolutely said, that it was indispensable to see him; from whoom [sic] it was necessary to receive a dispensation which was earnestly demanded by his Government. A Servant followed him with a bundle of papers, and thus gained admittance to the Rooms of the Pope without difficulty. Shortly after, arrived the French Minister,[33] who remained in the antechamber waiting until the Bavarian Minister should come out. In the meantime the Pope put on the livery of the Bavarian Minister, in which He came out, whilst the servant went out of the room by another door. The Count Spaur, followed by the Pope thus disguised,

---

32 The Bavarian minister was Count Charles Spaur (1794-1854). A very vivid account of the Pope's flight is that given by an "eye-witness" in the *Metropolitan* (Balto.), I, 49-62.

33 He was Duke François Eugene d'Harcourt. (1786-1865). In 1831 he was French Ambassador in Spain. In 1848 he was ambassador at Rome. See: *Dizionario del Risorgimento Nazionale,* III, 226. The fullest account of French participation in Roman affairs that year is given by René Bittard des Portes, *L'expédition Française* etc.

entered the room where the French Minister was and manifested to him the desire of the Pope to speak with him. The Minister of France entered immediately into the rooms inhabited by the Pope, and remained for an hour and a half, whilst the Pope accompanied by the Bavarian Minister in a traveling carriage, took the road to the fronters [sic]. When the French Minister came out he said to those on guard that the Pope wanted to take some rest and that they should not disturb him.[34] The Pope was safe! He arrived at Gaeta in the night of Saturday — Hardly had the King received the letter by which the Pope announced his arrival, than he immediately set out with the Queen and all the Royal family for Gaeta where they remain. A Battallion of the Royal Guards, with one of the line, by Royal Order have marched to Gaeta to show the due honor to the Vicar of Christ. It is hoped that the Pope will come to Naples, and already, appartements [sic] are preparing for Him. The Ministers of France, Spain, & Bavaria have arrived. The whole Diplomatic corps are expected."

I have given you this very literal translation from the Government paper that you might see who were the prominent actors in this strange affair, and it is also, the best exponent of the feelings of these people upon this subject. The paper omits to mention the important fact that his Holiness left a letter addressed to the new and objectionable Ministry declaring that they were not to be blamed for the step He was about to take, and urging them to exert themselves, to preserve order and to prevent bloodshed. Mr. Holt,[35] a distinguished American gentleman, who was there at the time, informs me that there was no apparent necessity for the Pope's leaving, as the city was then and is now quiet —

Mr. Behn[36] the Consul to Messina passed through this city on

---

34 For an account of the attitude of the foreign ministers towards the Pope and his flight, see Luigi Carlo Farini, *Storia dello Stato Romano dall'anno 1815 al 1850.* (Florence, 1853) III, ch. 2.; and Alfred O. Legge, *Pius IX, the Story of his Life,* ch. 3. For the part played by the United States minister, see: H. R. Marraro, "Unpublished American documents on the Roman Republic of 1849." *The Catholic Historical Review,* Washington, D. C. Jan. 1943, XXVIII, 459-490.

35 This was Joseph Holt (1807-1894) who was born in Kentucky. He became a judge and secretary of war (1861). He had arrived in Rome on Oct. 23, 1848, from Leghorn. See: H. R. Marraro, "American Travellers in Rome, 1848-1850" in *Catholic Historical Review,* Jan. 1944, XXIX, 470-509. See also *Dictionary American Biography,* 1932, IX, 181-183.

36 F. W. Behn, of Kentucky, was nominated consul of the United States at Messina on March 9, 1848. He was recalled late in 1849, but was reappointed to the same post on Jan. 11, 1854, remaining this time to 1859. On Feb. 21, 1861, he was appointed a third time to the same consulate. See note, in Owen chapter, *hic opus,* concerning political cause of Mr. Behn's recall. Also see above p. 654, this (Rowan's) chapter.

his way to that place about a month since. I enclose my accounts of incidental expences [sic] for the Quarter ending with September. They would have been sent earlier, but that I did not receive them from London.

J. ROWAN TO J. BUCHANAN

Legation of the U. S. of America Naples, March 3ʳᵈ. 1849
[Despatch No. 8][37]

Sir,

I have the honor to inform you that the good offices of the cabinets of Paris & London having been accepted by His Sicilian Majesty for the settlement of the differences existing between His Majesty and His Sicilian Subjects, there is an immediate probability of the matter being adjusted: You will recollect that the terms proposed by the King through the agency of Earl Minto[38] had been rejected by the Provisional Government of Palermo, and that the latter having declared the Independence of the Island, proceeded to elect the Duke of Genoa, second son of the King of Sardinia as their Sovereign. It will likewise be in your remembrance, that no definitive answer had, or has been given by the Duke of Genoa, and that the King of Naples in the prosecution of his sovereign rights, fitted out an expedition, and reduced the cities of Messina and Melazzo [sic] to obedience.[39] I have further to remind you that the operations of the Royalist troops were then suspended by the interference of the English & French Admirals who declared that they would oppose them by force, and that an armistice was concluded by the agency

---

[37] Despatches No. 6 and No. 7 are missing from volume of despatches. They probably were not received by the Department. Cf. Enclosure dated Jan. 30, 1849, written to Mr. Rowan. For Instruction No. 7, to Mr. Morris, see Morris chapter, *hic opus.*

[38] Gilbert Elliott, second Earl of Minto (1782-1859), was ambassador to Berlin (1832-1834), first lord of the admiralty (1835-1841), and lord privy seal from 1846 to 1852. In 1847, the Earl of Minto was sent on a diplomatic mission to Italy, to ingratiate Sardinia and Tuscany, to assist in carrying out the liberal reforms of Pius IX on his accession to the papacy, and then to report to his home government on Italian affairs generally. The mission was a failure, excepting that he induced the King of Naples to grant the Sicilians a separate parliament. Malmesbury, *Memoirs,* London, Longmans, Green & Co., (1885), 127. *Dictionary of National Biography* (1921), VI, 675-676.

[39] The Bourbon army, moving from Messina, on Apr. 2, 1849, was soon able to reoccupy the entire island. See, *Dizionario del Risorgimento Nazionale,* 1931, I, 657. For an account of the revolution in Sicily, see: V. Finocchiaro, *La rivoluzione siciliana del 1848-49, e la spedizione del generale Filangieri.* Catania, Battiati, 1906, xvi-462 pp.

of the Senior officers of both squadrons at Messina, under which no renewal of hostilities has taken place. Since that period the Ministers of England and France[40] at this Court have repeatedly pressed the acceptance of their mediation on the Government of the King, but His Majesty, seemingly determined to admit no interference with his prerogative, has as constantly, refused it. Latterly however the mediation being converted into the less objectionable form "friendly offices" the King alarmed by the events in Tuscany, and in the Roman States and anxious for the safety of his continental dominions has listened to that advice, and after several interviews and much discussion between the Ministers of France and Great Britain and Prince Satriano[41] Commander in chief of the army of operation at Messina, and after a personal appeal by the Ministers & Admirals of both nations to the King, an Agreement has been come to, so far as the two powers and His Majesty are concerned. By that agreement the terms proposed many months ago by the Earl of Minto to the Sicilians are again adopted. The Constitution known as the Constitution of 1812, with a seperate [sic] Parliament and seperate [sic] administration are secured to the Sicilians, whilst on the other hand Sicily is declared as permanently attached to the Neapolitan Crown, and the King is to have the right of Military occupation of the Island with a certain part of it's [sic] revenues for the maintenance of an armed force and conjoint Diplomatic Corps. It is still uncertain whether the Provisional Government of Palermo will accept these terms, or whether they will, supported, or rather coerced by the Ultra radical party in the Island, prefer to take the chance of war, and resist by force the progress of the Neapolitan army. The two Admirals propose immediately to go to Palermo for the purpose of explaining to the Provisional Gov^t., the true state of their position, recommending them to submit to their lawful sovereign, and declaring, that

---

[40] The French minister at Naples was Gérard de Rayneval, Louis Alphonse Maximilien (1813-1858). The British minister was the Hon. William Temple. De Rayneval had a brilliant diplomatic career, serving as ambassador at Naples (1851) and at St. Petersburg (1857). *Grande Encyclopédie*, XVIII, 831. For an excellent account of the revolution in Sicily and its relation with foreign governments, see: G. La Farina, *Istoria documentata della rivoluzione siciliana e delle sue relazioni coi governi italiani e stranieri* (1848-49). Capolago, 1850-51, 2 volumes.

[41] Carlo Filangieri, Prince of Satriano and Duke of Taormina (1784-1867). From 1848 to 1852, he was governor of Sicily; and from June 7, 1859 to March 16, 1860, president of the council of ministers at Naples. His *Autobiography*, (manuscript), is preserved in Società Napoletana di Storia Patria (xxix, A. 14); see also the biography by his daughter: Filangieri Fieschi-Ravaschieri, *Il Generale Carlo Filangieri*. Milan, 1902.

if they should refuse to do so, then, the Admirals would withdraw their ships from the waters of Sicily, and leave the matter to be settled by force of arms. It is hoped that as the terms now offered are liberal in the extreme, and give as much constitutional freedom as is consistent with the union of the Island and the Crown of the Two Sicilies, that the Provisional Government will submit, but in case it should not, the British and French squadrons will be withdrawn from Palermo, and the Prince Satriano, whose army at Messina is now receiving considerable reinforcements from this, will march at once upon the Capital of the Island, and decide the question by force of arms. The proclamation of the King to his rebellious [sic] Sicilian subjects,[42] and the terms he is willing to offer, are now being proposed, and as soon as they shall have been promulged [sic], I shall have the honor to transmit them to you. My opinion is, that the advice and remonstrances of the two Admirals will prevail at Palermo, and that if it should not, the Provisional Government has not the means of successfully resisting the Royal troops.

His Holiness the Pope still remains at Gaeta. It was said four days since that a Congress of the Catholic powers was to be held at Naples, for the purpose of concerting the best means of restoring the holy Pontiff to the Quirinal, but nothing has been done, and I have reason to beleive [sic] that the Pope has addressed himself specifically to the Emperor of Austria, and that the Emperor has promised immediate support.[43]

The restoration of the Pope to his dominions has in my opinion been materially advanced by the late events in Tuscany. You are aware that the Grand Duke, unwilling to become a party to the Roman Constituente, lately embarked on board a British man of war steamer at San [sic] Stefano, and is now at Molo [sic] di Gaeta.[44] The effect of that step has been to leave the throne va-

---

42 For a resumé of the King's ultimatum of Feb. 28, 1849 to the Sicilians see *Almanach de Gotha*, 1850, 73-74.

43 Meanwhile, it will be remembered that in Rome, Giuseppe Mazzini, Aurelio Saffi, and Carlo Armellini formed a triumvirate to exercise executive power over the Republic which had been declared by the Constitutional Assembly, Feb. 5, 1849. Mazzini was in reality the autocrat of the Republic. Concerning the various acts of the Republic, see: Giovanni Conti, *La Repubblica Romana del 1849, studio storico politico.* (Rome, 1920).

44 On Feb. 18, 1849, the Popular Club and the People's Assembly proclaimed the Republic at Florence. After the flight of Grand Duke Leopold a provisional government was set up in Tuscany under a Triumvirate comprising Guerrazzi, Mazzoni, and Montanelli. For an account of the disturbances in Tuscany, see: Antonio Zobi, *Storia civile della Toscana dal 1737 al 1848*, etc.; Giovanni Baldasseroni, *Leopoldo II granduca di Toscana*, etc.; L. G. Cambray-Digny, *Ricordi sulla*

cant, and in the letters Patent by which the father of the Grand Duke was invested, declare that in case the throne of the Grand Duchy should become vacant, Tuscany should revert to Austria, and the same provision was renewed in the investiture of the present Grand Duke. This fact alters the Italian question altogether, and as heretofore the Austrians declined to cross the Po, except in concert with the French, they have now the abstract right to do so, and I understand they have determined in the course of a few days to march on Florence. The inevitable consequence of this will be the end of the Provisional Government at Florence, and I do not doubt that the Provisional Government at Rome, seeing itself deprived of the aid of Tuscany will likewise abandon the position it now occupies, and that the restoration of the Pope to the Quirinal must be the natural consequence of their flight.

The Italian people, unable to comprehend the principle which binds our Country, in a union of peace, power & prosperity seem unsuited to the reception of Democratic Institutions.

In every place where a republic has been established, it has been preceded by acts of violence and crime, & however repugnant to our ideas of freedom, the march of Austrian troops into Italy, may be, the friends of good order, see no other means of being protected from the plunder of Ephemeral bodies assuming the reins of Government. I cannot help feeling with the deep regret that must be experienced by a citizen of the U. States, that a better developement [sic] of the noble principle of Democracy has not taken place, and I am inclined to beleive [sic] that to adapt republican institutions to minds trained under monarchical and despotic governments must fail from the very nature of the soil on which they are implanted.

Nevertheless, tho' I am not sanguine enough to expect that Republican ideas will for the present be received in Italy, I have every reason to hope & to beleive [sic], that an improved spirit of Government is abroad, that constitutional forms, suited to the character of the people, will take place in every part of the Peninsula.

I have little to add on the subject of Naples itself. The chambers are sitting, but no progress is under way or made in any measure

commissione governativa toscana del 1849. Florence, Galileiana, 1853, 200, 176 pp.; G. Montanelli, *Schiarimenti nel processo politico contro il ministero democratico toscano.* Florence, Le Monnier, 1853, 72 pp.; F. Russo, *Lettere inedite di G. Mazzoni, ex-triumiviro del governo provvisorio toscano ad Atto Vannucci.* Turin, Lattes, 1905, 171 pp.; C. Scavone, *Il movimento unitario repubblicano in Toscana nel '48-'49.* Catania, Monachini, 1918, 140 pp.

beneficial to the Country. A change of ministers is at hand, Gen'. Filangieri being destined by the King to form it and immediately after the present Chamber will be dissolved, and a new one called, the pecuniary qualifications of the Deputies being raised. At present the City is entirely quiet.

J. ROWAN TO THE SECRETARY OF STATE

Legation of the U. S. of America Naples 23ᵈ. March 1849.
[Despatch No. 9]

Sir

I have just been informed by this Government of their intention to blockade[45] Palermo from the first of next month, and establish cruisers around the island of Sicily to prevent arms and supplies from being landed; and that they would not be responsible for any injury or damage done to American citizens in consequence.

Hostilities are to recommence also by the army at Messina, if the British and French Ministers, who are now at Palermo, should not succeed in persuading them to submit it to the terms offered; I have protested against any violation of the usages established in cases of blockade, as we have vessels going there continually to load with fruit and other produce. Since my last, nothing else of importance has occurred here.

J. ROWAN TO THE SECRETARY OF STATE

Legation of the U. States Naples April 9ᵗʰ. 1849. [Despatch No. 12][46]

Sir,

I forward the regulations of the bloccade [sic] of Sicily.[47] I have however but little doubt that the bloccade [sic] will never be carried into effect, as the success of the Kings [sic] troops,

---

45 See Regolamento concernente Il Blocco della Sicilia, q.v., note 47, this chapter, below.

46 Despatches No. 10 and No. 11 are missing at the National Archives. They were not received by the State Department.

47 A printed copy of the regulation, in Italian, concerning the blockade of Sicily, dated Naples, April 1, 1849. The regulation, ten pages long, contained 18 articles. The copy is bound in with No. 12 Despatch. See, *Regolamento concernente il blocco della Sicilia*. Napoli, Stamperia Reale, 1849.

is already such, (having taken Catania[48] and Syracuse) as to leave it quite certain, that the whole island, will in a few days be again under the control of His Majesty.

J. Rowan to J. M. Clayton[49]

Legation of the U. States of America, Naples 31 May 1849.

[Despatch Nº. 13.]

Sir,

I had the honor to receive but lately your despatch of the 8th. of March, and beg to congratulate you on your appointment to the office of the Department of State.

I enclose my accounts of contingent expenses of the Legation for the quarters ending the 31st. of December 1848, and the 31st. of March this year, the first amot[g]. to $46, and the second to $113,,84. together $159,,84. This would have been done earlier but for want of the accounts from London.

Copy of the answer of the Neapolitan Government on the claim of Mess[rs]. Borie & Co. of Philadelphia with that of my reply thereto, which from their continual postponements I have thought proper to make this strong, are here enclosed. I do not expect they will ever adjust it, unless recourse be had to decided measures.

Sicily has returned to obedience, and it is said that her people will have most of the institutions that they have been contending for. There are various speculations about the manner in which they have succeeded to obtain them. The Provinces this side the Straits of Messina, are also quiet, but the prisons are filled with political and other offenders. Robbers, brought out by the misery of the times, render travelling insecure.

The Pope remains still at Gaeta. The time of his return to Rome is uncertain. It seems that the Powers which apparently undertook to reinstate him, are not now agreed about the manner of doing it.[50]

---

[48] Catania was occupied on April 6 by the Neapolitans commanded by Filangieri; Syracuse, Augusta, and Nola surrendered between April 2 and April 23.

[49] John Middleton Clayton (1796-1856) was Secretary of State from 1849-1850, replacing Mr. Buchanan. For a brief biographical sketch and bibliography, see, *Dictionary American Biography*, 1930, IV, 185-186.

[50] Another good account of French participation in Roman affairs at that time is entitled *Précis Historique et militaire de l'expédition française en Italie*, by "Un officier d'Etat Major." See Giovanni Conti, *La repubblica romana del 1849*. etc. 113.

All the liberal institutions in the world cannot now better the condition of the Italians, so corrupt are they.

This Government has again adopted their former flag used before the Constitution.

THE PRINCE OF CARIATI TO J. ROWAN

[Enclosure with Mr. Rowan's Despatch No. 13, May 31, 1849.]

Naples May 3rd. 1849.

The Undersigned, Minister Secretary for Foreign Affairs, President of the Council of Ministers, in addition to his previous communication of the 18th. of April last, relative to the claim for indemnification, advanced by Messrs. Borie & Co. of Philadelphia, has the pleasure of transmitting to Mr. Rowan, the Chargé d'Affaires of the United States, a copy of the note addressed to him on that subject, by the Minister of Finance, which will make known to him, the state of that affair, and he avails himself of this opportunity, to repeat to that gentleman, the assurances of his special consideration.

F. P. RUGGIERO[51] TO THE PRINCE OF CARIATI

[Enclosure with Mr. Rowan's Despatch No. 13, May 31, 1849.]

Naples April 30th. 1849.

I have now the honor of replying to Y. E.'s note No. 229, of the 10th. inst, relative to the claim of the Merchants Borie & Co., for the premium of 30 per cent, on goods imported by them from New York.

The premium of 30 per cent on the amount of the duties was allowed by Royal decrees of 1837 and 1839, on all the importations which might be made from the Baltic and the Indies, under the flag of the Kingdom.

Although in the decree of the 16th. of December 1839, it was

---

[51] Francesco Paolo Ruggiero (1798-1881) was Minister Secretary of State for Finance. See: *Dizionario del Risorgimento Nazionale,* IV, 147-148; Cfr. S. Iannuzzi, *Commemorazione di Francesco Paolo Ruggiero letta all'Accademia Pontaniana nella tornata del 2 luglio 1882.* Naples, 1883; G. Paladino, *Il quindici maggio del 1848 in Napoli.* Rome 1921; M. Schipa, *Miscellanea per nozze Scherillo-Negri.*

said, that notice would be given to merchants, of the future abrogation of that allowance, neither the manner, nor the form of that notice, was stated. By another decree of the 26th. of December 1839, the period between the notice and the abolition of the allowance was shortened.

In 1845, two important events took place, one was the abolition of the above mentioned allowance which was ordered in the council of State, on the 20th. of July; the other was the diminution of duties on Colonial goods and on dry and salt fish, which formed exactly the articles of import, from the Baltic, and the Indies, and are the very merchandize shipped by Messrs. Borie & Co. This diminution of duties was ordered by decree of August 29th., and as the last decree of 26th. December 1839, which was then communicated in due time, to the Directors General of indirect taxes of Naples and Sicily, fixed at four months after the notice, the termination of the allowance in favor of imports from the Baltic, and at six months, the cessation of the allowance on those from the Indies, it is evident that merchandize imported from the Baltic, after the 20th of November, 1845, and from the Indies after the 20th. of January 1846, could not have availed themselves of the bounty.

It is also to be considered, that the general reduction of the duties on the merchandize introduced from those parts of the world, into the Kingdom, was so great, as to render inefficient the concessions already granted, and to make a direct notice of the abolition useless. The grant could however not be regarded in any other light, than as an incouragement [sic] to the Mercantile Marine of the Kingdom; it did not in any way flow from treaties, or other international transactions, which might lead to the belief, that it was the result of a contract made with foreign producers.

It was necessary openly to abrogate and revoke it, because it was no longer of any value; but it might be abrogated, not only by proclamation, but also in virtue of a fact, which by terminating the reasons for its adoption, would render the law itself useless, on the grounds of the old legal aphorism, that on the cessasion [sic] of the motive for a law the law itself ceases; which if it be true with regard to any law, is most true and evident, respecting privileges which are from their nature special and temporary laws. Hence the important fact, involving the abrogation of the privilege itself, was really that of the reduction of the duties, which were in force at the time of the allowance of the bounty.

The promise to publish the abrogation of the privilege did not involve the obligation not to grant to others the same or a greater privilege; nor did it involve the prohibition to contest the privilege into a law, that is to say the special advantage into a general advantage. These two considerations presented two probable cases of loss, against which the Messrs. Borie & Co. should have provided, as incident to the commerce in which they engage.

Finally if the bounty was granted upon the duties as they stood at the time of the allowance, the reduction was then such as to leave the duty at 70 per cent that is to say to the payment of 70 instead of a hundred. If by any posterior law this *hundred* should be reduced to *sixty-five* the allowance is not made less, but rather thirty five per cent is granted, not only to the persons enjoying the privilege, but to all producers.

The case was therefore not one respecting the abrogation of an advantage allowed, but respecting the increase or extension of the same advantage.

These reasons are presented by the commission of Presidents charged by me, with the examination of the question. All the other reasons forbidding the admission of the claim of Messrs. Borie & Co. have been communicated to you with my note of September 1st. 1847, (No. 3957) and I hope that you will be pleased to communicate both of them to the persons interested, in order to show that the said merchants have no right to indemnification for the bounty above claimed.

J. ROWAN TO THE PRINCE OF CARIATI

[Enclosure with Mr. Rowan's Despatch No. 13, May 31, 1849.]

Legation of the U. States of America Naples 10th. May 1849. Copy

Your Excellency's communication of the 3^{d}. inst. accompanying a report of His Excellency the Minister of the Royal Finances on the claim of Messrs. Borie & Co. of Philad^{a}. grounded on reasons represented by a Commission of Presidents appointed by him to examine the question, has been received.

I have to observe that such reasons are only specious. The Consul of the U. S. by his letter of the 27 Septr. 1847 to His Excell^{y}. the Prince of Scilla, placed it in it's [sic] true light. It is not necessary to enter with His Excellency into the history of what has been done. If the Directors general of the Customs were opportunely advised not to grant but four months from the Baltic, and six from the Indies, after the advice, they kept it to themselves. The nonfulfilment of solemn engagements to the Public, whether native, or foreign, strengthens the obligation of the allowance promised. This Government was well aware that the owners of Neapolitan vessels with few exceptions had not the Capital to load their vessels in America, and that they were dependent on foreigners. Are these then to be the victims of measures so repugnant to good faith. The Minister's aphorism may suit his views of morality, but I deny that the abolition of a law cancels the engagements promised by it, or those of royal rescripts general, or special, when the promises held out, have not been maintained. —

The abrogation ought to have been as public as the rescripts themselves, and in the same way. When it is said by the Minister of Finance, "neither the mode or form of the advice was indicated" it shews such a double dealing, which I can never believe, that your Excellency or His Majesty will ever approve. Then to say again, that Messrs. Borie & Co. should have foreseen the probable result. This aggravates still more the injustice. What, by relying on His Majesty's rescript, they ought to have expected to be deceived! I beg your Excellency to reflect to what consequences such principles lead. They will not be received in the U. States. —

The privilege, as soon as made common, became no longer such, but those, who relied upon it's [sic] promises, are entitled to indemnity, as soon as the faith of the Government has not been kept. If it suited their policy to annul the royal rescripts, whether by secretly curtailing the time, or reducing the then existing Tariff, during the voyages of the Brigs Nuovo Raffaele and Ferdinando; I say in plain terms that it does not alter the case, and that Messrs. Borie & Co. have right to the indemnity demanded. I think that I do not risk too much in assuring your Excellency that my Government will find it to be their duty to afford them the proper protection to obtain justice. —

J. M. CLAYTON TO J. ROWAN

Department of State, Washington, 5ᵗʰ. June, 1849.

[Instruction No. 7.]⁵²

Sir: The President, having determined to make a change in the U. S. mission at Naples, I am directed by him to inform you, that he has appointed Mʳ. Thᵒˢ. W. Chinn,⁵³ of Louisiana, to succeed you in the capacity of Chargé d'Affaires of the U. S., near the Government of the Two Sicilies. I take the earliest occasion to acquaint you with this change in order to afford you as much time as practicable, to enable you to make all necessary preparations for leaving Naples. Mʳ. Chinn will proceed upon his mission, on or about the 1ˢᵗ. proxᵒ. a duplicate of this letter will be placed in his hands to be delivered to you upon his arrival. It is presumed that Mʳ. Chinn will find you at your post, in which event you will deliver to him the archives, books and property of the U. S. in your possession, & at the same time, afford him such advice & aid, from your own experience, as will enable him to enter advantageously upon the duties of the Legation. Of the books and property in the Legation you are requested to make an inventory and transmit it to this Department, giving to your successor at the same time a copy of it, for which he will deliver a proper receipt.

Of the exact date of your taking leave of the Neapolitan Government, which, it is supposed, will be the same on which Mʳ. Chinn will receive his audience of reception, you will inform the Department, and the Bankers of the U. S. at London, who will be desired to settle your accounts accordingly.

---

⁵² Instruction No. 5 is missing. Instruction No. 6 (March 8, 1849) informed Mr. Rowan of Mr. John M. Clayton's appointment as Secretary of State.

⁵³ Thomas Withers Chinn, a Louisiana sugar planter, judge, congressman, was born in Vermont on November 20, 1791. After arriving in Louisiana, he married Elizabeth Johnson (daughter of Isaac Johnson and Mary Routh). In 1826, Mr. Chinn was judge of the Feliciana district. He moved to East Baton Rouge parish in 1829, when he purchased Cypress Grove plantation, where he died on May 22, 1852. He went to Washington as a member of the 26th Congress and was appointed chargé d'affaires to Naples by President Zachary Taylor, according to family accounts. The *Biographical Directory of American Congress* 1774-1927, Washington, United States Government Printing Office, 1928, states that he was appointed "Minister to the Two Sicilies" and served from June 5, 1849 to October of the same year," and also states that he was born in Kentucky. Judge Chinn who was a second cousin to Sir Walter Scott, according to family tradition, left numerous descendants mostly through married daughters. The editor is indebted for this information to Mr. Stanley C. Arthur, Executive Director of the Louisiana State Museum, New Orleans, Louisiana.

J. M. CLAYTON TO J. ROWAN

Department of State, Washington, 26th September, 1849.
[Instruction No. 9.][54]

Sir: We have just learned, that M[r]. T. W. Chinn, who was selected by the President to succeed you as the Representative, of the U. S., near the Government of the Two Sicilies, became so ill, at Paris, on his way to Naples, that he has been compelled to relinquish all thought of proceeding further, and that he will, as soon as he is able, return to the U. S. Under these circumstances it is the President's wish that you would continue in charge of the Legation, until the arrival of the person who may be appointed in Mr. Chinn's place, of which you will be duly informed.

A despatch was addressed by this Department to M[r]. Chinn, on the 1st. ult. This you will be pleased to open, make the application to the Sicilian Government for the Exequatur for M[r]. Clements,[55] as Consul of the U. S. for the Port of Messina, respecting which Mr. Chinn was therein instructed.

If it should not suit your personal convenience to remain at Naples after the receipt of this despatch, you will be at liberty, to return, whenever you shall think proper, leaving the archives and business of the Legation in charge of M[r]. Hammett, the Consul, in whom the Department has entire confidence, as well as in yourself.

Enclosed is a letter addressed to the Minister of foreign affairs of Naples (with an office copy) informing him of your recall, which you will present in the usual form, & accompany by assurances to His Excellency of the sentiments of friendship entertained by this Government towards that of the Two Sicilies. It is left to your discretion to present it at once, or to await a successor.

I transmit a copy of my instructions N°. 1, to M[r]. Chinn,[56] & of the enclosure which was addressed to yourself.

Of the exact date of your taking leave you will inform this Department and the Bankers of the United States at London, who will be instructed to settle your accounts accordingly.

---

[54] Instruction No. 8, June 15, 1849, refers to a claim by a Mr. Angelo Conci against Mr. Polk for money alleged by Mr. Conci to be due to him.

[55] Alexander H. Clements, of the District of Columbia, was nominated consul of United States for Messina, Sicily, on Jan. 4, 1850. He was recalled in Jan. 1854.

[56] Mr. Chinn never served. See following p. 679 and footnote 57 thereon; also see p. 681, footnote 62 this chapter. Only three despatches are on file from Mr. Chinn, q.v., *hic opus,* Chinn and Powers chapter.

J. M. CLAYTON TO A. HAMMETT

Department of State, Washington, October 10. 1849.
[Consular Instruction, Unnumbered]

Sir: I wrote to Mr. Rowan on the 26th. ult°. & to you on the following day. By these despatches you will see that in the failure of Judge Chinn, through ill health, to reach Naples, Mr. Rowan was desired to continue in charge of the Legation, until the arrival of a successor, but to place it in your charge, if it was not convenient for him to meet the President's wishes in this respect.[57]

I now transmit a copy of a letter from Messrs. Chas. & Henry Borie, of Phila., of the 6th inst., & of an enclosure, being a copy of a letter addressed by those gentlemen to Mr. Chinn, on the 22nd. ult°. respecting their claim upon the Neapolitan Government. It is presumed that the letter to Mr. Chinn & its enclosures have reached Naples, & that you, or Mr. Rowan have presented the claim anew to the Government of Naples.[58]

Whatever decision may be made in their case you will be pleased to communicate to them in full & announce the same to this department.[59] They are desired to correspond directly with the Legation.

J. M. CLAYTON TO J. ROWAN

Department of State, Washington, 22nd. October, 1850 [1849?]
[Instruction No. 10.]

Sir: I have the honor to transmit, herewith, a letter from the President of the United States, to His Majesty, Ferdinand II, King of the Two Sicilies, &c. &c. in reply to a communication from His Majesty, of the 3rd. August, last, announcing the fact, that Her Majesty the Queen had given birth to a Princess, on whom the names of Maria delle Grazie, Pia, had been bestowed.

---

[57] In an Instruction dated Washington, Sept. 27, 1849, Mr. Clayton instructed Mr. Hammett to assume charge of the Legation, until further notice, if Mr. Rowan had already left Naples, and to communicate Mr. Rowan's lettter of recall to the minister of foreign affairs.

[58] See Instructions to Ministers, No. 9 q.v., this chapter, p. 678.

[59] See Mr. Rowan's chapter, *hic opus*, "favourable result conceded," but see later, *hic opus*, Mr. Morris' chapter, "this claim not yet paid."

You will avail yourself of an early opportunity to convey to His Majesty's principal Secretary for foreign affairs, the accompanying copy of the President's letter, and take the proper measures, to deliver in person, or to transmit, the Original in the manner most agreeable to His Majesty's wishes, as they may be made known to you by his Ministers.

I transmit, herewith, an extract of a letter from Judge Chinn, dated at Louisville, Ky., on the 12th. inst., by which you will perceive, that while in London he ordered stationary [sic] to be forwarded to Naples for the use of the Legation, to which purpose it will be applied, and charged to the proper account.

Your despatch of the 6th. ultimate, announcing the death of Capt. Gwynn, has been received.[60]

I have to request, that you will forward to this Department, a copy of instructions N°. 5, of the 6th. of November last, which is missing from our files, & has not been recorded.

J. ROWAN TO J. M. CLAYTON

Legation of the U. States Naples Novr. 9th. 1849. [Despatch No. 15]

Sir

Your dispatch dated 26th. Septr. found me in Naples where I have been, and I fear will be detained for some time, by the serious indisposition of Mrs. Rowan. In accordance with the wish of the President I will attend to the duties of this Legation until I am enabled to leave, or the arrival of the new agent of our Government.

Mr. Chinn had remitted to me from Paris the patent of Mr. Alexander H. Clements as Consul for Messina, and without delay I passed it to the Minister of Foreign Affairs to obtain the Royal Exequatur. After a lapse of some days, I repeated the request,

---

[60] Mr. Rowan, in a despatch dated Naples, Sept. 6, 1849, had notified Mr. Clayton of the death of Captain John Gwinn, United States Navy, at Palermo, Sept. 4, 1849. This despatch is not found in the Despatch volume. John Gwinn, (-1849), naval officer, was born in Maryland. He was appointed Midshipman on May 18, 1809. In 1848, he was ordered to command the U. S. S. *Constitution*, Mediterranean Squadron. He died on Sept. 4, 1849, at Palermo, Sicily, while in command of that vessel. The cause of death was chronic gastritis with severe cerebral complication. He was buried in the Protestant burial ground near the Lazaretto at Palermo. The body was brought to the United States in 1850, and buried in Philadelphia. In 1931, the remains were brought to Washington and re-interred in Arlington Cemetery with military honors. Information supplied by John B. Heffernan, Captain, United States Navy, Director, Naval Records and Library.

but up to the present moment I have not received it. M^r. Clements however after stopping a few days in Naples continued his journey to Messina, prior to his departure and in answer to enquiries made upon the subject the Government remarked that he must have patience, that he could proceed to Messina, and that it would be sent to him. It seems that upon the subject of admitting any one to Sicily they are excedingly sensative [sic].

I have much pleasure in announcing to you the favorable result of the claim of Mess. Borie & Co. His Majesty has been pleased to concede the allowance of 30 p^c. for their cargoes, per Briggs [sic][61] Nuovo Raffaele, and Ferdinando, on the basis of the reduced duty which amounts to D. 8.301.91 viz D. 5643,,35 [sic] for the first, and for the second D. 2658,,58 [sic]. The Royal resolution has been communicated as stated to the Director General of the Indirect Duties for the liquidation and payment, to whom of right they may belong.

Herein are enclosed accounts of two quarters of the contingent expenses of this Legation, one for $90.67 & the other $69.67 together $160,34 with Mr. Miller's bill of postages.

J. M. CLAYTON TO J. ROWAN

Department of State, Washington, 17th. January, 1850.
[Instruction N°. 11.]

Sir: I have the honor to inform you, that the President, by & with the advice and consent of the Senate, has appointed M^r. Edward Joy Morris,[62] of Philadelphia, as Chargé d'Affaires of the U. S., to reside near the Government of the Two Sicilies, & that this Gentleman intends to embark from New York for Liverpool, on the 23rd prox°., on his way to Naples. I have to request that you will render him your best services on entering upon his official duties.

---

61 Inventories called these ships "barks."

62 After the resignation of Judge Chinn, the President appointed James M. Power, of Pennsylvania, who was commissioned on Nov. 1, 1849, but declined. Then on January 10, 1850, Edward Joy Morris, of Pennsylvania, was commissioned Chargé d'Affaires. Mr. Morris left his post on August 26, 1853. See above pp. 678, 679 and footnotes on same. Morris (1815-1881) was a lawyer, diplomat, author. He was elected as a Whig representative to the 28th Congress for one term 1843-1845. On June 8, 1861, President Lincoln appointed him minister to Turkey; he took leave there on Oct. 25, 1870.

Your letter of recall has already been transmitted, in my despatch N°. 9, of the 26ᵗʰ. September, last.[63] This you will deliver immediately upon the arrival of Mʳ. Morris, if it has not already been delivered, giving the proper notice to the Bankers and to this Department, of the day on which you take leave of the Neapolitan Government.

Your despatches, as received at this Department, are as follows:

Despatches

No. 1.	1 July	1848.
	11 July	1848
No. 3	17 July	"
No. 4	2 September	"
No. 5	26 September	"
No. 8	3rd March	1849
No. 9.	5th March	"
No. 9	23rd March	"
No. 12	9th April	"
No. 13.	31st May	"
	6th September	"
No. 15.	9th November	"

From the above you will perceive, that some of your despatches are not numbered, as required by the instructions; two are numbered 9; — & several appear to be missing altogether. This deficiency you will be pleased to supply.

THOMAS W. CHINN

(June 5, 1849 to October 1849.)

Thomas W. Chinn, of Louisiana was commissioned chargé d'affaires June 5, 1849. Due to ill health he never reached Naples, and his resignation was accepted in October 1849. There are three instructions from Secretary of State Clayton to Judge Chinn regarding his appointment, his instructions, and the appointment of Alexander H. Clements as Consul of the U. S. for the port of Messina. There is also one letter from Judge Chinn to Secretary Clayton accepting the appointment as chargé d'affaires.

---

[63] Cf. Mr. Clayton to Mr. Rowan, Instruction No. 9, Sept. 26, 1849. q.v., Rowan Chapter, *hic opus,* p. 678.

JAMES M. POWER

(Commissioned November 1, 1849 but never served.)

James M. Power, of Pennsylvania, was commissioned chargé d'affaires Nov. 1, 1849 to succeed Judge Chinn (who never served). He accepted the appointment on Dec. 10, 1849 in a letter to Secretary of State Clayton; in this same letter he made inquiry as to his instructions and salary. He apparently asked for salary in advance because Mr. Clayton, in his reply, stated that this was unusual and could not be done. There are only two instructions, one informing Mr. Power of his appointment, and the other replying to Mr. Power's acceptance. Mr. Power, however, later declined.